In memory of

Professor Sir Robert Y. Jennings
1913-2004

President of the Eritrea-Yemen Arbitral Tribunal

Keith Highet
1933-2000

Member of the Eritrea-Yemen Arbitral Tribunal

In memoriam

Professor Sir Robert Y. Jennings
1913-2004

président du Tribunal arbitral Erythrée-Yémen

Keith Highet
1933-2000

membre du Tribunal arbitral Erythrée-Yémen

PERMANENT COURT OF ARBITRATION AWARD SERIES

The Eritrea-Yemen Arbitration Awards 1998 and 1999

With an Introduction by Professor Jean-Pierre Queneudec

L'Arbitrage Erithree-Yemen Sentences 1998 et 1999

Avec une Introduction de Professeur Jean-Pierre Queneudec

Series Editor

BETTE SHIFMAN

Deputy Secretary-General
of the Permanent Court of Arbitration

T·M·C·ASSER PRESS

Published by T·M·C·ASSER PRESS
P.O.Box 16163, 2500 BD The Hague, The Netherlands
<www.asserpress.nl>

ISBN 978-90-6704-992-4

Softcover reprint of the Hardcover 1st edition 2005
The Permanent Court of Arbitration (PCA) is an intergovernmental organization, founded at the first Hague Peace Conference in 1899, and based in the Peace Palace in The Hague. It provides a wide range of dispute resolution mechanisms – including arbitration, conciliation and fact finding – in disputes involving various combinations of states, private parties and intergovernmental organizations. The PCA is committed to meeting the rapidly evolving dispute resolution needs of its member states and the international community.

International Bureau
Permanent Court of Arbitration
Peace Palace
Carnegieplein 2
2517 KJ The Hague
The Netherlands
Telephone: +31 70 302 4165
Facsimile: +31 70 302 4167
Email: bureau@pca-cpa.org
Website: www.pca-cpa.org

SUMMARY OF CONTENTS
SOMMAIRE DES MATIÈRES

FOREWORD

In 1997, the arbitral tribunal established to resolve a dispute between Eritrea and Yemen invited the Permanent Court of Arbitration (PCA) to act as its Registry. This first major international arbitration to be administered by the PCA in decades marked a watershed in the process of revitalizing the nearly century-old organization. A mere eight years later, the PCA has a full and varied docket, not limited to disputes between sovereign States, involving parties of many different nationalities. These include a dispute between the Swiss-based Bank for International Settlements and its private shareholders, two tribunals established under the OSPAR and UNCLOS Conventions in a dispute between Ireland and the United Kingdom, an investment dispute involving a subsidiary of a major Japanese concern and the Czech Republic, and the Boundary and Claims Commissions established by the peace treaty between Eritrea and Ethiopia.

By the time the second Eritrea-Yemen award was delivered in December 1999, the PCA had celebrated its centenary and effectively transformed itself from "the sleeping beauty of the Peace Palace" into a dynamic institution for the resolution of all types of inter-governmental and international disputes, with an expanded staff representing over ten different nationalities.

The importance of the Eritrea-Yemen Arbitration, however, extends far beyond its contribution to the "comeback" of the PCA. As Professor Queneudec writes in his insightful introduction to this volume, the Eritrea-Yemen Arbitration "is one of the most significant international arbitrations of the end of the 20th century", in large part because it "solved the thorny problem of ownership of the southern islands of the Red Sea . . . the solution of which had been awaited since the end of the First World War." Much of this is attributable to the quality of the tribunal itself, composed of Judges Rosalyn Higgins and Stephen M. Schwebel, Dr. Ahmed El-Kosheri and the late Keith Highet, and presided over by the late Sir Robert Jennings.

Despite an increasingly debilitating illness, Keith Highet worked tirelessly throughout the proceedings, his characteristic meticulousness and incisiveness never faltering. He was particularly committed to seeing the case through to completion of the second-stage award. It was, unfortunately, to be the last major case of his unparalleled international legal career, and he will be sorely missed, particularly here in his second home, the Hague Peace Palace. It is especially fitting that this edition of the Eritrea-Yemen awards dedicated to his memory is *bilingual.* Not only was Keith remarkably proficient in the French language, he also had a particular affection and affinity for it.

The international legal community has yet to recover from the loss, in August 2004, of Sir Robert Jennings. There are but few of its members who do not claim him as an inspiration and – in the case of those most fortunate – a mentor. Sir Robert's unparalleled curriculum vitae as an educator, academic, practitioner, and member and president of the International Court of Justice is well known, and needs no further elaboration here. Perhaps less well known is the pivotal role he played in the revitalization of the PCA in the 1990s. He was the first in decades to entrust important international arbitrations, including the Eritrea-Yemen case, to PCA administration, thereby laying the groundwork for subsequent developments. Robbie – as he usually insisted on being called, despite his impressive titles – will long be remembered by the staff of the PCA as a staunch supporter and trusted sounding board.

The decision to translate the two Eritrea-Yemen awards into French for publication in this bilingual edition was prompted, inter alia, by France's pivotal role in the negotiations leading up to the agreement between the governments of Eritrea and Yemen to submit their territorial dispute to arbitration. The sole purpose of the translations is to make the text of the awards more easily accessible to the francophone community worldwide; they in no way constitute an official French version of the awards.

The awards as reproduced here contain one official amendment and a handful of minor editorial rectifications. In November 1998, the arbitral tribunal agreed to a modification of paragraph 198 of the first-stage award. The new text is printed in italics and accompanied by a footnote. Minor typographical errors and mistakes in certain page and date references have been indicated in footnotes as "editorial corrections" and do not form part of the official text of the award. To the extent that cross-references refer to pages rather than paragraphs, these have been adapted to the pagination of this volume and are indicated in italics. Internal inconsistencies in capitalization and punctuation have been corrected without further indication. Some effort has been made to apply a consistent citation style in footnotes, while endeavoring insofar as possible to retain the integrity of the original texts. In addition, the lists of appearances on the caption pages of the two awards have been supplemented to include counsel; the originals referred only to the agents and co-agents of the parties.

The PCA would like to express its immense gratitude to Jean-Pierre Queneudec, Professor emeritus at the University of Paris I, for agreeing to provide a substantive introduction to this volume. It is difficult to imagine an international legal scholar more capable of synthesizing and distilling the essence of the awards and their contribution to international legal discourse.

Special mention must also be made of the two Deputy Secretaries-General of the PCA who served successively as Secretary to the arbitral tribunal: Ms. Bette E. Shifman in the first stage, and Ms. Phyllis Hamilton in the second. The challenging task of translating the awards into French fell to Ms. Nicole Perlstein and Mr. Jean-Roch Dartis, while Ms. Sarah Adams provided the excellent English translation of Professor Queneudec's introduction.

The Hague, October 2004

Tjaco T. van den Hout
Secretary-General, Permanent Court of Arbitration

AVANT-PROPOS

Le tribunal arbitral mis en place pour résoudre un différend entre l'Erythrée et le Yémen a demandé en 1997 à la Cour Permanente d'Arbitrage (CPA) de servir en tant que greffe. Ce fut, depuis des décennies, le premier grand arbitrage international rendu sous les auspices de la CPA. Il a en effet marqué une étape décisive dans le processus de revitalisation de cette institution qui était à l'époque presque centenaire. Huit ans à peine, après le prononcé de la sentence de cet arbitrage, force est de constater qu'un grand nombre d'affaires variées sont désormais inscrites au rôle de la CPA. Celles-ci ne concernent pas uniquement les différends interétatiques mais impliquent aussi des parties de différentes nationalités. Parmi ces arbitrages figurent un différend entre la Banque suisse pour les règlements internationaux et ses actionnaires privés, deux tribunaux établis en vertu des Conventions OSPAR et UNCLOS pour un litige entre l'Irlande et le Royaume-Uni, et un différend entre une filiale d'une grande entreprise japonaise et la République tchèque. Il convient également de mentionner les deux commissions relatives à la délimitation et à la démarcation de la frontière et des réclamations en nombre établies en vertu du traité de paix entre l'Erythrée et l'Ethiopie

Au moment où la deuxième sentence Erythrée-Yémen a été rendue en décembre 1999, la CPA a célébré son 100ème anniversaire. Cette "Belle au bois dormant" s'est métamorphosée en une institution dynamique pour la résolution de tout différend de nature intergouvernementale et de manière générale tout litige d'ordre international. Cette métamorphose a été accompagnée par une expansion du personnel. Plus de dix nationalités différentes sont actuellement représentées.

Toutefois l'importance de l'arbitrage Erythrée-Yémen va au-delà de son rôle de catalyseur. Comme l'a écrit le professeur Queneudec dans l'introduction éclairée de ce volume, l'arbitrage Erythrée-Yémen est l'un des arbitrages les plus importants de la fin du 20^{éme} siècle, parce que dans une large mesure, il "restera surtout dans l'histoire comme l'arbitrage par lequel a été réglé l'épineux problème de l'appartenance des îles du sud de la mer Rouge".

Ceci s'explique en grande partie par l'excellence des membres du tribunal composé des juges Rosalyn Higgins et Stephen M. Schwebel, du Dr Ahmed El-Kosheri et du regretté Keith Highet enfin du Président, le regretté Sir Robert Jennings.

Malgré sa longue maladie, Keith Highet a travaillé sans relâche tout au long de la procédure. Sa méticulosité et sa perspicacité ne lui ont jamais fait défaut. Il voulait mener l'affaire jusqu'au terme de sa deuxième étape. Ce fut malheureusement la dernière affaire importante de sa carrière inégalée de juriste international. Il nous manquera, particulièrement ici, dans sa deuxième maison, le Palais de la Paix. Non seulement il maîtrisait remarquablement bien la langue française, mais également il lui vouait une affection particulière. C'est ainsi naturellement que nous lui dédions cette édition *bilingue*.

La communauté juridique internationale ne s'est pas encore remise de la perte, en août 2004, de Sir Robert Jennings. Ce dernier a inspiré presque tous ses membres et a été le mentor de quelques privilégiés. La feuille de route incomparable de Sir Robert en qualité d'éducateur, d'universitaire, de praticien et de membre et président de la Cour internationale de Justice est bien connue ; nul n'est besoin d'en faire ici davantage état. Le rôle clef qu'il a joué dans la revitalisation de la CPA au cours des années 1990 est peut-être moins connu. Il fut le premier, après plusieurs décennies, à confier d'importants arbitrages internationaux, notamment l'affaire Erythrée-Yémen, à l'administration de la CPA, posant ainsi les fondations de l'évolution qui allait suivre. Le personnel de la CPA se remémorera longtemps Robbie, comme il insistait habituellement pour qu'on l'appela malgré ses titres impressionnants, en tant qu'ardent défenseur et personne de confiance à qui soumettre des idées.

La décision de traduire les deux sentences arbitrales Erythrée-Yémen en français a été motivée par le rôle clef que la France a joué dans les négociations qui ont abouti à l'accord entre les gouvernements de l'Erythrée et du Yémen de soumettre leur différend territorial à l'arbitrage. L'unique objectif de cette traduction est de rendre le texte des sentences plus accessible à la communauté francophone. Toutefois, cette traduction ne peut être assimilée à la version officielle des sentences.

Les sentences reproduites contiennent un amendement officiel et quelques corrections éditoriales mineures. En novembre 1998, le tribunal arbitral a modifié le paragraphe 198 de la première étape de la sentence. Le nouveau texte est imprimé en italique et accompagné d'une note de bas de page. Les erreurs typographiques, les fautes à certaines pages et les dates référencées ont été indiquées en notes de bas de page comme corrections éditoriales. Elles ne constituent pas une partie du texte officiel de la sentence. Tous les renvois aux pages au lieu des numéros des paragraphes, ont été adaptés à la pagination courante et sont indiqués en italiques. Les fautes relatives aux majuscules et à la ponctuation ont été corrigées automatiquement. Les éditeurs se sont efforcés d'adopter un style uniforme dans les citations figurant dans les notes de bas de page, toutefois sans porter atteinte aux textes originaux des sentences. De surcroît, le terme "conseil" a été ajouté, sur la page de garde, aux listes des personnes habilitées à comparaître tandis que les originaux faisaient simplement référence aux agents ou co-agents des parties.

La CPA exprime sa profonde gratitude au Professeur Jean-Pierre Queneudec, professeur émérite à l'Université de Paris I, pour son introduction o combien passionnante. Il est difficile d'imaginer un juriste international capable à la fois de synthétiser, d'analyser les sentences et d'évaluer leur impact sur le débat juridique international.

Enfin, il convient de mentionner les deux Secrétaires Générales adjoints de la CPA qui ont servi successivement comme Secrétaire du tribunal arbitral : Mme Bette E. Shifman dans la première étape de la procédure et Mme Phyllis Hamilton dans la seconde.

Le défi de traduire les sentences en français revient d'une part à M. Jean-Roch Dartis et à Mme Nicole Perlstein d'autre part. Mme Sarah Adams a fait une excellente traduction en anglais de l'introduction du professeur Queneudec.

La Haye, octobre 2004

Tjaco T. van den Hout
Secrétaire Général, Cour Permanente d'Arbitrage

THE ERITREA–YEMEN ARBITRATION

Its Contribution to International Law

by

Jean-Pierre QUENEUDEC*

The two awards of 9 October 1998 and 17 December 1999 between the State of Eritrea and the Republic of Yemen were rendered in English in accordance with Article 9 of the Arbitration Agreement signed in Paris on 3 October 1996. French-speaking jurists are therefore grateful to the International Bureau of the Permanent Court of Arbitration for the initiative it has taken to ensure the translation and publication in French of these Awards, as this is one of the most significant international arbitrations of the end of the 20th century.

Its significance is due firstly to the quality of the persons who comprised the Arbitral Tribunal. Indeed, among the five members who made up the Tribunal, there were notably two current judges and one former judge of the International Court of Justice, including the President in office and one former President of the Court. The latter, moreover, also assumed the presidency of the Tribunal. There is no doubt that the presidency of Sir Robert Jennings served to strengthen the prestige of the decisions rendered. In addition, the fact that each of the two awards was the result of unanimous finding by the five arbitrators further increases their authority.

The significance of this arbitration is also due to the result obtained through it. It has certainly brought a definite end to the conflict which broke out in 1995 between Eritrea and Yemen; on 18 April 2001 in Asmara the two States signed a co-operation agreement in which, in addition to various specific undertakings, they formally reproduced the conclusions of the Arbitral Tribunal. However, this arbitration has also much wider consequences extending beyond the limits of this particular case. It also opened the way to a peaceful solution to other conflicts in the Horn of Africa region, notably between Eritrea and Ethiopia.[1]

---

* Professor emeritus at the University of Paris I (Panthéon – Sorbonne); President of the *Société française pour le droit international.*

[1] The text of the Eritrea-Ethiopia Agreement of 12 December 2000 is available on the website of the Permanent Court of Arbitration (http://www.pca-cpa.org, under Recent and Pending Cases). For a commentary, see Emmanuelle Jouannet, *Le règlement de paix entre l'Ethiopie et l'Erythrée: un succès majeur pour l'ensemble d'Afrique?*, 105(4) REVUE GÉNÉRALE DE DROIT INTERNATIONAL PUBLIC 849-896 (2001).

It will especially stand out in history as the arbitration that solved the thorny problem of ownership of the southern islands of the Red Sea, and in particular of the Hanish Islands. Situated in the middle of one of the most frequently used waterways of the world, these islands of no apparent specific attraction, were the subject of a long-standing controversy, the solution of which had been awaited since the end of the First World War. In this regard, it is perhaps to be regretted that no specific name was given to the case submitted for arbitration and that it was not officially designated as, for example, the "Red Sea Islands Case."

The Eritrea-Yemen arbitration is also significant for a further reason, which lies with the method retained by the Parties and the procedure followed by the arbitrators in the handling of the dispute.

In the Arbitration Agreement, Eritrea and Yemen requested the Tribunal to provide rulings in two stages; the first concerning the territorial sovereignty and the definition of the scope of the dispute, the second concerning exclusively the delimitation of the maritime boundaries.[2] This manner of proceeding provided the advantage of taking the problems one by one. It was not only logical but also efficient, as the delimitation of the maritime boundaries between the two States depended in part on the answers provided beforehand to the questions of sovereignty over the islands under dispute. Once the first Award was made, the Parties were able to move forward with full knowledge of the facts as to their claims and arguments regarding the maritime delimitation, without concerning themselves with any need to present alternative positions and without basing themselves on pure surmise.

From this point of view, the procedure adopted for the Eritrea-Yemen arbitration was certainly preferable to that followed in the quite similar case of the *Maritime Delimitation and Territorial Questions between Qatar and Bahrain* which was pending at the time before the International Court of Justice. Indeed, in this case, the undertaking by both States to submit the whole dispute to the Court in the framework of one and the same instance[3] had as consequence to place each Party in the

---

[2] The Agreement on Principles of 21 May 1996, signed by the two States in Paris after mediation by the French Government, initially provided that the Tribunal would in a first stage rule on the definition of the scope of the dispute and in a second stage on the one hand on the questions of territorial sovereignty and on the other hand on the questions of delimitation of the maritime boundaries. The text of this Agreement on Principles and the text of the Arbitration Agreement are published in 100(4) REVUE GÉNÉRALE DE DROIT INTERNATIONAL PUBLIC, 1119-1137 (1996); the Arbitration Agreement is also reproduced as Annex 1 to the second stage award; p. 219 in this volume. On the circumstances surrounding the recourse to arbitration, see the remarks by the Deputy Director of Legal Affairs of the French Ministry of Foreign Affairs, Monsieur Jean-François Dobelle, who presided over the meetings between the representatives of Ethiopia and Yemen, in 42 ANNUAIRE FRANÇAIS DE DROIT INTERNATIONAL 477-481 (1996).

[3] See Judgments of 1 July 1994, 1994 I.C.J. 112, and of 15 February 1995, 1995 I.C.J. 6, on jurisdiction and admissibility.

uncomfortable position of being obliged to indicate the maritime boundary it was defending, without knowing how the Court would dispose of its territorial claims and thereby acting as if the Court had already decided in its favor on the questions of territorial sovereignty.[4] On this point, it is therefore to be hoped that the Eritrea-Yemen arbitration will serve as a model for the future.

In the observations that follow, I would like first to examine some of the characteristics that stand out in the decisions made and which marked the procedure followed and the role played by the Tribunal. Afterwards, it will be seen that a considerable amount of originality is contained in the reasons underpinning the Award on the territorial sovereignty, whereas the Award concerning the problem of the maritime delimitation applies rules and methods which are now well-established and fit perfectly into the framework of international case law which has progressively asserted itself in this field.[5] An in-depth analysis or detailed commentary of these decisions shall

---

4 The absence of two separate stages obviously did not cause the same inconvenience to the Court. In its Judgment of 16 March 2001, 2001 I.C.J. 40, it logically ruled first on the territorial questions before giving its decision on the maritime delimitation; and while it settled the problem of sovereignty over a tiny islet (Qit'at Jaradah) and a low-tide elevation (Fasht ad Dibal) whilst examining the question of the maritime delimitation, this is because the two aspects were very closely linked here, due to the specific characteristics of these maritime features (see paras. 191 to 209 of the Judgment).

5 Each of the two Awards has been the subject of a number of commentaries in various reviews. See in particular Nuno Sérgio Marques Antunes, *The Eritrea-Yemen Arbitration: First Stage – the Law of Title to Territory Re-averred,* 48(2) INTERNATIONAL AND COMPARATIVE LAW QUARTERLY 362-386 (1999), and *The 1999 Eritrea-Yemen Maritime Delimitation Award and the Development of International Law*, 50(2) INTERNATIONAL AND COMPARATIVE LAW QUARTERLY 299-344 (2001); Gilles Despeux, *Das Schiedsurteil Jemen gegen Eritrea II vom 17. Dezember 1999: Entschiedung über die Seeabgrenzung*, 60(2) ZEITSCHRIFT FÜR AUSLÄNDISCHES ÖFFENTLICHES RECHT UND VÖLKERRECHT 447-487 (2000); Jean-François Dobelle & Jean-Michel Faure, *Le différend entre l'Érythrée et le Yémen: la sentence arbitrale du 9 octobre 1998 sur le champ du différend et la souveraineté territoriale*, 44 ANNUAIRE FRANÇAIS DE DROIT INTERNATIONAL 337-355 (1998), and *Le différend entre l'Erythrée et le Yémen: la sentence arbitrale du 17 décembre 1999 sur la délimitation des frontières maritimes*, 45 ANNUAIRE FRANÇAIS DE DROIT INTERNATIONAL 554-565 (1999); Giovanni Distefano, *La sentence arbitrale du 9 octobre 1998 dans l'affaire du différend insulaire entre le Yemen et l'Erythrée*, 103(4) REVUE GÉNÉRALE DE DROIT INTERNATIONAL PUBLIC 851-890 (1999), and *La sentence arbitrale du 17 décembre 1999 sur la délimitation des frontières maritimes entre l'Erythrée et le Yemen: quelques observations complémentaires*, 46 ANNUAIRE FRANÇAIS DE DROIT INTERNATIONAL 255-284 (2000); Barbara Kwiatkowska, *Red Sea: Award of the Arbitral Tribunal in the First Stage of the Eritrea/Yemen Proceedings*, 14(1) INTERNATIONAL JOURNAL OF MARINE AND COASTAL LAW 125-136 (1999), and *The Eritrea-Yemen Arbitration: Landmark Progress in the Acquisition of Territorial Sovereignty and Equitable Maritime Boundary Delimitation,* 32(1) OCEAN DEVELOPMENT AND INTERNATIONAL LAW 1-25 (2001); W. Michael Reisman, *The Government of the State of Eritrea and the Government of the Republic of Yemen: Award of the Arbitral Tribunal in the First Stage of the Proceedings (Territorial Sovereignty and Scope of the Dispute)*, 93(3) AMERICAN JOURNAL OF INTERNATIONAL LAW 668-682 (1999), and *Eritrea-Yemen Arbitration (Award, Phase II: Maritime Delimitation)*, 94(4) AMERICAN JOURNAL OF INTERNATIONAL LAW 721-735 (2000).

obviously not be entered into here; the following are merely a few introductory remarks.

I

(1) The first characteristic concerns the manner in which the Tribunal rendered its decision relating to the definition of the geographical scope of the dispute.

The Arbitration Agreement provided that the first stage of the arbitration would result in an award on both the territorial sovereignty and the definition of the scope of the dispute. With regard to this last question, it moreover stipulated that "the Tribunal shall decide on the definition of the scope of the dispute on the basis of the respective positions of the two Parties" (Article 2, paragraph 2).

However, the decision the Tribunal reached on this point is not mentioned in the *dispositif* of the Award on territorial sovereignty, i.e., in the part of the Award which in principle is the only part invested with *res judicata*. It is included in the conclusion to Chapter II which presents the positions of the Parties regarding the scope of the dispute, i.e., it is in reality included in the grounds for decision of the Award. Indeed, the Tribunal indicated there that it "prefer[red] the view of Eritrea" and that it would accordingly make "an Award on sovereignty in respect of all the islands and islets with respect to which the Parties have put forward conflicting claims."[6] However, there is no formal mention that it "ruled" on this point. The arbitrators were no doubt able to reasonably assess that it was unnecessary to expressly restate the decision they reached on this matter in the main body of the *dispositif*, as this decision could be seen to result implicitly from the other decisions which were mentioned there.

All the same, what appears surprising is that the Tribunal omitted to indicate whether its decision on this matter was unanimous or by majority. This seems even more surprising in that on the various other points decided in its Award on territorial sovereignty, the Tribunal did not withhold from providing such information. That the Tribunal decided unanimously on these other points is indeed not indicated solely in the *dispositif* of the Award, as is usually the case. It is also indicated in a chapter of the grounds for decision entitled "Conclusions," having regard to each of the groups of islands about which the Tribunal gave a decision.[7]

(2) A further characteristic which should be mentioned came to light during the actual proceedings.

---

6 Eritrea-Yemen Arbitration, Award of 1998, para. 90.

7 See Eritrea-Yemen Arbitration, Award of 1998, paras. 475, 482, 484, 508 and 524, in which the expression used is either: "the Tribunal unanimously finds . . .", or: "are therefore unanimously determined by the Tribunal . . . ."

During the first stage of the arbitration, neither of the two Parties raised or even mentioned the petroleum contracts and concessions that one or other of them had concluded concerning the Red Sea and the islands under dispute. Each was apparently waiting to raise this issue during the second stage on the maritime delimitation. The Tribunal obliged them to discuss this matter already during the first stage by asking questions at the end of the oral proceedings. However, finding the replies of the Parties to be insufficient, the Tribunal was led not only to ask them for further written comments but also to organize further oral proceedings, this time concentrating exclusively on the petroleum agreements and activities.

Although the Arbitration Agreement did indeed authorize the Tribunal, even after the close of the oral proceedings, to "request from the Parties their written views on any issues necessary for the elucidation of any aspect of the matters" (Article 8, paragraph 3.3), it did not, however, contain any indication as to the authority of the Tribunal to provoke any reopening of the debate. In the absence of any disposition to the contrary in the Arbitration Agreement, it is nevertheless to be considered that this authority is inherent to any international jurisdiction,[8] the understanding being that reopening of the debate serves only to allow the Parties to put forward oral comments strictly limited to the issue that the Tribunal wishes to elucidate.

This obligation to handle the offshore petroleum contracts in the first stage of the arbitration was obliged to result in a paradox: although the conclusions likely to be drawn in the case in point were not of a kind that would influence the decision on territorial sovereignty, taking account of these contracts, however, could indeed play a role in the definition of the maritime boundary. The Tribunal effectively found, in its first Award, that these contracts neither allowed for the determination nor the strengthening in any significant manner of the claims of either State to sovereignty over the islands under dispute, but these contracts "lend a measure of support to a median line between the opposite coasts of Eritrea and Yemen."[9] By basing itself on this aspect of the case, the Tribunal was then led, in its second Award, to adopt as basic principle for the maritime delimitation the idea that the method of the median line should be applied between opposite coastlines.[10]

(3) Finally, one cannot forget that, in international arbitration proceedings, the concern of the arbitrators is not only to "state the law" and to settle the dispute before them by strict application of the legal rules. It is also to ease the tensions and encourage

---

[8] In this regard, see in particular DURWARD V. SANDIFER, EVIDENCE BEFORE INTERNATIONAL TRIBUNALS 299 (1939). Article 72 of the Rules of Court of the International Court of Justice expressly provides for the possibility of reopening the oral proceedings, but it would appear that this has never in fact occurred before the Court. See GENEVIÈVE GUYOMAR, COMMENTAIRE DU RÈGLEMENT DE LA COUR INTERNATIONALE DE JUSTICE. INTERPRÉTATION ET PRATIQUE 467 (1983).

[9] Eritrea-Yemen Arbitration, Award of 1998, para. 438.

[10] Eritrea-Yemen Arbitration, Award of 1999, para. 83.

the re-building and development of lasting co-operation between the two disputing States.[11] To this end, there would appear to be no doubt that an arbitral tribunal has the authority to make recommendations to the Parties during the arbitral proceedings, as was notably recalled by the Award rendered in the *Rainbow Warrior* case between New Zealand and France: "The power of an arbitral tribunal to address recommendations to the parties to a dispute, in addition to the formal finding and obligatory decisions contained in the award, has been recognized in previous arbitral decisions."[12]

The Eritrea-Yemen Arbitral Tribunal made use of this authority on two occasions, setting the exercise of this authority, however, within the particular context of the neighborly relations between the local populations.

By basing itself on the fact that "Western ideas of territorial sovereignty are strange to peoples brought up in the Islamic tradition" and invoking the need to respect the "regional legal traditions," it thus recommended the maintenance and perpetuation of the traditional fishing regime which had long existed around the disputed islands for the benefit of the fishermen from both shores of the Red Sea.[13] However, this was more than a mere recommendation, as the manner in which it is worded makes it almost an obligation and it is moreover expressly incorporated in the *dispositif* of the Award on territorial sovereignty.

In addition, in the Award on the maritime delimitation, the Tribunal was anxious to provide a certain amount of detail regarding the nature and extent of this traditional fishing regime. As it is neither an entitlement in common to the resources, nor a shared right in them, this regime authorizes the fishermen from both States to freely practice traditional fishing throughout the waters surrounding the islands attributed to Yemen, independently of the international boundary. Moreover, they include the enjoyment of connected rights and privileges such as free access to the islands and the right to put ashore and sell catches without discrimination in the ports of the other State. They also imply sustainment of the traditional system for the settlement of disputes between local traditional fishermen.[14]

---

11 The Arbitral Award rendered on 22 January 1926, in the case of the *Cayuga Indians* (Great Britain v. United States), emphasized that "something more than the strict law must be used in the grounds of decision of arbitral tribunals in certain cases," VI UNITED NATIONS REPORTS OF INTERNATIONAL ARBITRAL AWARDS 173, at 180. Quite a remarkable illustration was given in the second decision rendered on 19 February 1968 in the case concerning the Indo-Pakistan Western Boundary (Rann of Kutch) (India/Pakistan), in which the Tribunal took particular consideration of stability and peace in the region. XVII UNITED NATIONS REPORTS OF INTERNATIONAL ARBITRAL AWARDS 1.

12 Rainbow Warrior (New Zealand/France), Arbitral Award of 30 April 1990, para. 128, XX UNITED NATIONS REPORTS OF INTERNATIONAL ARBITRAL AWARDS 217, at 274. For the French text, see 94(3) REVUE GÉNÉRALE DE DROIT INTERNATIONAL PUBLIC 838 (1990).

13 Eritrea-Yemen Arbitration, Award of 1998, para. 526.

14 Eritrea-Yemen Arbitration, Award of 1999, paras. 103-107.

In this way, the Tribunal aimed to determine the existence of a special legal order which is non-territorial in nature; a transnational order of inter-individual dimensions encompassing exclusively the traditional fishing activities; a kind of *lex pescatoria*, the perpetuity of which is now guaranteed by international law through application of the decisions of the Arbitral Tribunal.

In the same way, but in a much less original manner, with regard to liquid or gas petroleum deposits which may be discovered in the future and which may be situated across the maritime boundary or in its immediate vicinity, the Tribunal could only recommend to the two States that they commit to common or joint exploitation of these resources. It did this not only by basing itself on the normal practices by States in the field of exploitation of marine resources located across maritime boundaries, but by consideration also here of local issues. According to the Tribunal, this recommendation was especially justified by the historical links existing between the peoples concerned and having regard to the renewed amicable relations between the two States since the pronouncement of the Award on sovereignty.[15]

II

By requesting the arbitrators to rule "on" the question of the territorial sovereignty, the Arbitration Agreement set the task of the Tribunal in terms it considered to be "different."[16] Indeed, this disposition, which it even qualified as "unusual,"[17] offered the Tribunal a range of possibilities since such a form of words, although effectively allowing the Tribunal to attribute sovereignty to one or other State, also authorized it at the same time to declare joint sovereignty, or to declare itself in favor of any other form of shared sovereignty over the islands. Contrary to the *Palmas* case, in which the arbitrator had to choose between two inchoate titles, one following from the start of occupation, the other derived from the discovery of the land, the Eritrea-Yemen Arbitral Tribunal was neither bound to rule on the grounds of the relative value of the titles invoked by each Party, nor to decide in terms of a marginal difference between the elements of proof put forward.[18]

In addition, the Tribunal had to decide more particularly on the grounds of historic titles liable to be invoked on both sides. Given the volume of documentation in its possession, it was thus brought to indicate on this occasion that if the expression "ancient title" generally designated "a title that has so long been established by

---

15 Eritrea-Yemen Arbitration, Award of 1999, para. 86.

16 Eritrea-Yemen Arbitration, Award of 1998, para. 455.

17 Eritrea-Yemen Arbitration, Award of 1998, para. 102.

18 Eritrea-Yemen Arbitration, Award of 1998, para. 454. For the text of the Award by Max Huber of 4 April 1928, see II United Nations Reports of International Arbitral Awards 829. French text also available in 39 Revue générale de droit international public 156-202 (1935).

common repute that this common knowledge is itself a sufficient title," the notion of historic title had the more precise meaning in international law of "title that has been created, or consolidated, by a process of prescription, or acquiescence, or by possession so long continued as to have become accepted by the law as a title."[19] In either case, the demand for consideration of continuity and passing of time was obviously an essential part of the deliberations. However, the titles adduced by the Parties could not satisfy this dual demand by reason of the specific legal situation of the islands of the Red Sea. According to the Tribunal, after the Treaty of Lausanne with Turkey in 1923, these islands had become "international waifs."[20]

Indeed, Article 16 of the Treaty of Lausanne stated: "Turkey hereby renounces all rights and title whatsoever over or respecting the territories situated outside the frontiers laid down in the present Treaty and the islands other than those over which her sovereignty is recognized by the said Treaty, the future of these territories and islands being settled or to be settled by the parties concerned."[21] Applicable as it was to the islands of the Red Sea, this provision was of dual consequence for them.

On the one hand, by renouncing its sovereignty over these islands, Turkey relinquished the territorial title it had held until then. This renunciation necessarily implied that there could be no other territorial title over the islands in question and, more particularly, that any title which had existed before Ottoman sovereignty began could not re-emerge. This was a logical consequence which the Tribunal summarized by declaring: "the relinquishment by the Ottoman Empire of its sovereignty . . . logically and legally adversely affects any pre-existing title."[22] The result was therefore that there could be no question of accepting the idea of any reversion of an ancient title, as claimed by Yemen. This was because to admit that an ancient title had remained in force during the Ottoman period would amount to rejecting the legality of the Ottoman title to full sovereignty, whereas under the principle of intertemporal law, this sovereignty was legitimate and included the right to dispose of the islands in question.[23]

On the other hand, the abandonment of Turkish sovereignty did not have the effect of transforming the islands of the Red Sea into *res nullius* and rendering them open to appropriation by way of acquisitive prescription. The goal of the Allied Powers at the time of the disruption of the Ottoman Empire was to conserve freedom of navigation in a region which had become important for the international community since the

---

[19] Eritrea-Yemen Arbitration, Award of 1998, para. 106.

[20] Eritrea-Yemen Arbitration, Award of 1998, para. 192.

[21] Treaty of Lausanne (Treaty of Peace with Turkey, signed at Lausanne 24 July 1923, 2 THE TREATIES OF PEACE (1919-1923) 959, at 966 (1924). For the text in French, see LOUIS LE FUR & GEORGES CHKLAVER, RECUEIL DE TEXTES DE DROIT INTERNATIONAL PUBLIC 752 (2d ed. 1934).

[22] Eritrea-Yemen Arbitration, Award of 1998, para. 124.

[23] Eritrea-Yemen Arbitration, Award of 1998, para. 444.

opening of the Suez Canal. To this end, they devised a safeguard consisting in subjecting any acquisition of sovereignty over the islands to proof of capacity to fully assume the international responsibilities attached to them, having particular regard to the maintenance of the lighthouses on the islands. This is the reason why the Treaty of Lausanne led to a halt in the territorial claims over the islands of the Red Sea and created "an objective legal status of indeterminacy pending a further decision of the interested parties"[24] for them.

Later, the international agreement concerning the management of certain lighthouses in the Red Sea was adopted by a conference of the States which were the principal users of the Suez Canal and opened for signature in London on 20 February 1962. After recalling in its Preamble that no agreement on the future of these islands had been concluded between the States concerned, it further stated in its Article 8: "Nothing in the present Agreement shall be regarded as constituting a settlement of the future of the Islands or territories referred to in Article 16 of the Treaty of Lausanne or as prejudicing the conclusion of any such settlement in the future."[25] In the eyes of the Allied Powers concerned, the undefined legal situation of the islands had therefore remained unaltered since the entry into force of the Treaty of Lausanne in 1926. It remained so, even after the retreat of the British from the region in 1967, until the termination of the London Agreement on 31 March 1990. Consequently, throughout this period it had not been possible to acquire any territorial title over the islands in question, whether directly by effective occupation or indirectly by succession as was claimed by Eritrea.

The islands were only ultimately opened for territorial acquisition after the end of the regime established by the 1923 Treaty and more precisely after termination of the international agreement on the management of the lighthouses, when the States using the maritime route released themselves from obligation. The "interested parties" then became the States bordering on the Red Sea which substituted themselves for those using the route in the international responsibilities concerning navigation in this area. This is indeed included in the preambles of the Agreement on Principles and the Arbitration Agreement itself: Eritrea and Yemen declared themselves to be "[c]onscious of their responsibilities toward the international community as regards . . . the safeguard of the freedom of navigation in a particularly sensitive region of the world."

---

[24] Eritrea-Yemen Arbitration, Award of 1998, para. 445.

[25] International Agreement for the Maintenance of Certain Lights in the Red Sea, done at London 20 February 1962, TIAS 6150, 17 UST 2145. Text also in NAGENDRA SINGH, I INTERNATIONAL MARITIME LAW CONVENTIONS 90 (1983). Apart from the original signatories (Federal Republic of Germany, Denmark, United States of America, Greece, Italy, Liberia, Norway, Pakistan, Panama, the Netherlands, United Arab Republic, United Kingdom, Sweden, USSR), this Agreement was later accepted by the Peoples Republic of China and Portugal, but Ethiopia and Yemen were never Parties. See John M. Gardner, *The Red Sea Lights Agreement: Another Instance of International Cost-Sharing*, 69(1) AMERICAN JOURNAL OF INTERNATIONAL LAW 129-134 (1975).

Examination of the attitude of the successive Red Sea coastal States led the Tribunal to determine that neither Great Britain nor Italy, nor subsequently Yemen, Ethiopia or then Eritrea had demonstrated a real *animus occupandi*, that is "an intentional display of power and authority over the territory, by the exercise of jurisdiction and state functions, on a continuous and peaceful basis."[26] In addition, drawing inspiration from the jurisprudence of the International Court of Justice, which had considered in 1953 that the activities connected with the lighting and buoying of islands or islets could not be regarded "as sufficient evidence of the intention . . . to act as sovereign,"[27] the Tribunal was mindful to emphasize that "the operation or maintenance of lighthouses and navigational aids is normally connected to the preservation of safe navigation, and not normally taken as a test of sovereignty."[28] From then on, it was not possible to find convincing arguments among all those put forward by Eritrea and Yemen concerning the display of functions of state on the islands under dispute.

Under these circumstances, the matter of territorial sovereignty over these islands, as brought before the Tribunal, could neither be settled on the basis of a legal claim, that is a clearly established right, neither according to obviously determinative "*effectivités*." This represented a relatively unprecedented situation in territorial disputes submitted to arbitration or judicial settlement at that time. Indeed, in the international case law which developed over the years preceding the Eritrea-Yemen arbitration, when recourse to the legal title was unlikely to provide the basis for the settlement of the territorial conflict, the "*effectivités*" were called upon to establish a kind of supplementary or residual title.[29] This is what was particularly visible in the decisions of the International Court of Justice in the cases of the *Frontier Dispute (Burkina Faso/Republic of Mali)*[30] and the *Land, Island and Maritime Frontier Dispute (El Salvador/Honduras: Nicaragua Intervening)*.[31]

The Tribunal was therefore obliged to rely on presumption of fact and to base itself on probabilities which could reasonably cause it to favor one or other of the Parties. By taking into consideration "the geographical situation that the majority of the islands and

---

26 Eritrea-Yemen Arbitration, Award of 1998, para. 239.

27 Minquiers and Ecrehos (Fr./U.K.), Judgment of 17 November 1953, 1953 I.C.J. 71.

28 Eritrea-Yemen Arbitration, Award of 1998, para. 328. In the case of the Maritime Delimitation and Territorial Questions between Qatar and Bahrain, the I.C.J. however moderated its earlier case law and admitted that, among the activities purporting to demonstrate intention to act according to sovereign title, "[t]he construction of navigational aids . . . can be legally relevant in the case of very small islands." Judgment of 16 March 2001, 2001 I.C.J. 197.

29 See Giovanni Distefano, *La notion de titre juridique et les différends territoriaux dans l'ordre international*, 99(2) REVUE GÉNÉRALE DE DROIT INTERNATIONAL PUBLIC 335-366 (1995), and PHILIPPE WECKEL (DIR.), LE JUGE INTERNATIONAL ET L'AMÉNAGEMENT DE L'ESPACE: LA SPÉCIFICITÉ DU CONTENTIEUX TERRITORIAL (1998).

30 Judgment of 22 December 1986, 1986 I.C.J. 554.

31 Judgment of 11 September 1992, 1992 I.C.J. 351.

islets and rocks in issue" form an archipelago extending across a stretch of sea between the Eritrean and Yemeni coasts, the Tribunal had perceived of a decisive element, in the absence of any conviction on its part that there existed any other possible source of sovereign title. It then made the presumption that "any islands off one of the coasts may be thought to belong by appurtenance to that coast unless the state on the opposite coast has been able to demonstrate a clearly better title."[32] With specific regard to the Mohabbakah islands off the Eritrean coast, it moreover invoked the "principle of the territorial sea" by virtue of which the islands situated in the territorial sea of a State necessarily belong to that State. The Tribunal stated, however, that although this principle generated strong presumption, this was only *juris tantum* as demonstrated in particular by the example of the Channel Islands.[33]

The reference to the notion of geographical proximity and the recourse to the presumption that the islands form part of the nearest land mass did not, however, constitute real innovation. The idea of contiguity had already been introduced at least on two occasions in the past as representing a projection of the principle of effective occupation and thus enabling the creation of an inchoate title. Indeed, this idea had been used as grounds on the one hand for the Award rendered by the Queen of Spain on 30 June 1865 in the *Aves* case between the Netherlands and Venezuela and, on the other hand for the Award by the President of the United States of America dated 21 April 1870 in the *Bulama* case between Great Britain and Portugal.[34] Everything indicates that the influence of the President of the Tribunal was determinant here in making the notion of proximity or contiguity a substitute of sorts to effective occupation. It may be recalled that he had not long since affirmed to this effect in a leading book on the subject: "Contiguity is no more than evidence raising some sort of presumption of effective occupation."[35]

The Tribunal found itself strengthened in this approach by the fact that the proximity factor on which it based itself had exerted an influence in the legal history of the islands. Indeed, at the time of the Ottoman domination, "when even under the common sovereignty of the whole region it was found convenient to divide the jurisdiction between the two coastal local authorities,"[36] some of the islands fell under the jurisdiction of the Egyptian *khedive* on behalf of the Ottoman Empire until 1882, while others were part of the Ottoman *vilayet* of Yemen until the disbandment of the Empire

---

32 Eritrea-Yemen Arbitration, Award of 1998, para. 458. See also para. 480, in which the Tribunal applied the same concept: "the geographical arguments of proximity to the . . . coast remain persuasive and accord with the general opinion that islands off a coast will belong to the coastal state, unless another, superior title can be established."

33 Eritrea-Yemen Arbitration, Award of 1998, paras. 472 and 474.

34 Albert De Lapradelle & Nicolas Politis, eds., II Recueil des arbitrages internationaux, at 413 and 613 (1905-1954).

35 Robert Y. Jennings, The Acquisition of Territory in International Law 75 (1963).

36 Eritrea-Yemen Arbitration, Award of 1998, para. 458.

at the end of the First World War.[37] The reference thus made to the legal history of the islands was however fully superfluous in the reasoning of the arbitrators, as the Tribunal had considered elsewhere that this history was not in itself conclusive.

This is the reason why, in order to settle the issue of sovereignty over the group of islands known as the Hanish Islands, the Tribunal was ultimately led to take into consideration especially very recent elements, and its decision was "based to an important extent upon what seems to have been the position . . . in the last decade or so leading up to the present arbitration."[38] This is without doubt not the least of the paradoxes revealed by this case. Required to rule on the grounds of historic titles and having been placed in possession of a voluminous historical file by the Parties, the Tribunal was led to set aside the ancient titles invoked and to disregard the events of a distant past. It gave its decision by finally basing itself on elements descended from the most recent part of history. It also emphasized this point itself by making a comparison with the attitude of the International Court of Justice in a similar case: "as indeed was so in the *Minquiers and Ecrehos* case where there had also been much argument about claims to very ancient titles, it is the relatively recent history of use and possession that ultimately proved to be a main basis of the Tribunal decisions."[39] It could furthermore be suspected that this is a persistent tendency of international case law in questions of territorial sovereignty.[40]

III

The Arbitration Agreement defined the role of the Tribunal with regard to the maritime delimitation by requiring it to carry out this delimitation "in a technically precise manner" and by indicating that it should take into account not only its earlier decision on the issue of territorial sovereignty – which went without saying for obvious reasons – but also the United Nations Convention on the Law of the Sea, together with "any other pertinent factor" (Article 2, paragraph 3).

The reference to the 1982 Convention was all the more remarkable in that this Treaty was not in force between the two disputing States; Yemen being the only one of the two which was a party. Consequently, by accepting inclusion of this reference in the Arbitration Agreement, Eritrea also accepted application by the Tribunal of those provisions of the Convention on the Law of the Sea which it deemed relevant to the delimitation issue at hand.

---

37 Eritrea-Yemen Arbitration, Award of 1998, para. 134.

38 Eritrea-Yemen Arbitration, Award of 1998, para. 503.

39 Eritrea-Yemen Arbitration, Award of 1998, para. 450.

40 See Marcelo G. Kohen, *L'influence du temps sur les règlements territoriaux*, *in* SOCIÉTÉ FRANÇAISE POUR LE DROIT INTERNATIONAL (COLLOQUE DE PARIS), LE DROIT INTERNATIONAL ET LE TEMPS 131-160 (2001).

Apart from the rules concerning the delimitation of territorial waters between neighboring States, it is well known that the provisions of the Convention concerning the delimitation of other national maritime areas are especially characterized by their vagueness of expression and uncertainty as to their precise content. This was also noted by the Tribunal in its use of a euphemism when it remarked, with regard to Articles 74 (economic zones) and 83 (continental shelves) of the Convention, that "in any event there has to be room for differences of opinion about the interpretation of articles which, in a last minute endeavour . . . to get agreement on a very controversial matter, were consciously designed to decide as little as possible."[41]

The rules applicable in the field are essentially rules of custom. However, the Arbitration Agreement made no mention of customary law. The Tribunal nevertheless considered that this lack of reference to customary law of the sea was balanced by the fact that the 1982 Convention included a number of relevant customary elements.[42] This was a gratuitous assertion and represented a bizarre pirouette on the part of the Tribunal which it could well have done without. It would have sufficed here to recall that the Arbitration Agreement had requested it "to provide rulings in accordance with international law, in two stages" (Article 2, paragraph 1) and that these general terms also authorised it, in the second stage, to apply the customary rules of the law of the sea.

As to the mention of "any other pertinent factor" in the text of the Arbitration Agreement, this was not abundantly clear. It would seem that the Tribunal felt ill at ease when it attempted to ascertain the meaning and the extent of this expression. In some respects, it arrived at a synonymous expression for "pertinent circumstances" but used the term "factor" to designate them, in the same way the Arbitral Tribunal had done in the case of the *Guinea/Guinea-Bissau Maritime Delimitation* in its Award of 14 February 1985.[43] It is without doubt to be regretted that it did not grasp this opportunity to attempt to bring a little more order and structure into the use of terms or expressions which still remain influenced by the quite primitive and sometimes succinct character of the law applicable to delimitation of maritime boundaries. The Tribunal contented itself with noting that the expression concerned "is a broad concept, and doubtless includes various factors that are generally recognised as being relevant to the process of delimitation such as proportionality, non-encroachment, the presence of islands, and any other factors that might affect the equities of the particular

[41] Eritrea-Yemen Arbitration, Award of 1999, para. 116.

[42] Eritrea-Yemen Arbitration, Award of 1999, para. 130.

[43] Affaire de la délimitation de la frontière maritime entre la Guinée-Bissau et le Sénégal, Decision of 31 July 1989, XX UNITED NATIONS REPORTS OF INTERNATIONAL ARBITRAL AWARDS 121. See in particular para. 89 of the Award. French text also in 89(2) REVUE GÉNÉRALE DE DROIT INTERNATIONAL PUBLIC 484-537 (1985).

situation."[44] In so doing, the Tribunal gave the impression that the notion at hand was a sort of hold-all.

If one is thus able to express a certain amount of regret regarding some aspects of the Award on the maritime delimitation, this is to a large extent because the Tribunal could have made better use of the fact that its task was easier here than in the first stage. It fulfilled its role by strictly adhering to the prescriptions of the Arbitration Agreement. However, credit must be given for the explanations it provided here and there which represent a non-negligible contribution to the development of the law of maritime delimitation.

Thus, the Tribunal emphasized that as it had been asked to determine the "maritime boundaries," the word "boundary" should be taken by its normal and ordinary meaning of international boundary between the two States taking part in the arbitration proceedings. It grasped at exactly the right moment this opportunity to fully distinguish the difference between a maritime boundary understood in this way and what is usually referred to as a maritime "limit," an expression by which is usually designated the external limit of a national maritime area, such as the external limit of territorial waters. It was also moreover mindful to recall that if the external limit of a national maritime area was able to coincide with the international maritime boundary, it could also find itself modified by the establishment of that boundary.[45]

The value of the explanation thus provided becomes clear if it is set against a number of declarations made by the International Court of Justice concerning the expressions "*frontière maritime*" and "maritime boundary." It suffices to recall that in the case of the *Delimitation of the Maritime Boundary in the Gulf of Maine Area*, the Court noted that the term "maritime boundary" could appear inadapted to the case at hand, in so far as it "might suggest, incorrectly, the idea of a real *frontière* (boundary) between two sovereign States," while what was exclusively at issue was a delimitation between the areas subject to different forms of partial jurisdiction.[46] More recently, in the case of the *Maritime Delimitation and Territorial Questions between Qatar and Bahrain*, the Court persistently used the expression "*limite maritime unique*" in the official French text of its Judgment where the expression "single maritime boundary" was used in the English version. In addition, by emphasizing that "the concept of 'single maritime boundary' may encompass a number of functions," it considered in the matter at hand that "the single maritime boundary will be the result of the delimitation of various jurisdictions."[47]

---

44 Eritrea-Yemen Arbitration, Award of 1999, para. 130.

45 Eritrea-Yemen Arbitration, Award of 1999, para. 129.

46 Judgment of 12 October 1984, 1984 I.C.J. 265, para. 19.

47 Judgment of 16 March 2001, 2001 I.C.J. 169. The Eritrea-Yemen Arbitration Award applies this same concept and also indicates that "the international boundary shall be a single all-purpose boundary." See Eritrea– Yemen Award of 1999, para. 132.

Furthermore, the Tribunal retained and applied the most established principles and precepts in the field of maritime delimitation. These are:

- the fundamental norm of the equitable result, to which any operation of delimitation is subjected;[48]

- the principle according to which "between coasts that are opposite to each other the median or equidistance line normally provides an equitable boundary . . . ";[49]

- the rule by virtue of which "[this median line] should, as far as practicable, be a median line between the opposite mainland coastlines";[50]

- the rule according to which the coast to be retained as a reference for the construction of the median line is that which is determined by the low-water mark which figures on the nautical charts officially recognized by the disputing States;[51]

- the necessity to determine whether and to what extent an effect can or must be attributed to the islands located within the area to be delimited, having regard to their size, their significance and other aspects of the general geographical context;[52]

- the principle of non-encroachment which aims at preventing the exercise, in the immediate vicinity of the coast of one of the States, of rights which would compromise the security of that State;[53]

- the obligation to determine the maritime boundary so as to avoid areas to which a third State would be able to assert a claim;[54]

- the demand for simplicity in the determination of the international boundary in the immediate vicinity of a major maritime route;[55]

---

48 Eritrea-Yemen Arbitration, Award of 1999, paras. 116-117.

49 Eritrea-Yemen Arbitration, Award of 1999, para. 131.

50 Eritrea-Yemen Arbitration, Award of 1999, para. 132.

51 Eritrea-Yemen Arbitration, Award of 1999, paras. 133 and 135.

52 Eritrea-Yemen Arbitration, Award of 1999, paras. 117 and 147. Considering the relatively large number of islands and islets in the region, it is significant that the Tribunal felt it necessary to stipulate that "an island, however small, and even rocks provided they are indeed islands proud of the water at high-tide, are capable of generating a territorial sea of up to 12 miles . . ." (para. 155).

53 Eritrea–Yemen Arbitration, Award of 1999, para. 157.

54 Eritrea-Yemen Arbitration, Award of 1999, paras. 136 and 164.

55 Eritrea–Yemen Arbitration, Award of 1999, para. 128.

– the principle of proportionality as a "test of the equitableness of a delimitation" such that any disproportion is avoided in the ratio between the lengths of the coastlines of both States and the extent of the maritime areas attributed to each.[56]

On these various points, the Tribunal positioned itself in line with case law which is now well-established, even if some shadowy areas still exist which occasionally detract from the foreseeability of the equitable solution expected by the States from the judge or international arbitrator.

*

On the whole, the task accomplished by the Tribunal between Eritrea and Yemen was quite remarkable, not only for the reasons given above, but also because, as shown by the two Arbitral Awards reproduced hereafter, the Tribunal endeavored to fulfil a pedagogical role towards the two States while taking great care to scrupulously analyze the arguments put forward by each and to readily reveal the grounds on which it deemed it had to retain or, on the contrary, reject them. The solicitude it demonstrated in providing as much explanation as possible has without doubt been crowned with success.

---

[56] Eritrea-Yemen Arbitration, Award of 1999, paras. 165-168.

IN THE MATTER OF AN ARBITRATION
PURSUANT TO AN AGREEMENT TO ARBITRATE
DATED 3 OCTOBER 1996

B E T W E E N :

THE GOVERNMENT OF THE STATE OF ERITREA

-and-

THE GOVERNMENT OF THE REPUBLIC OF YEMEN

AWARD OF THE ARBITRAL TRIBUNAL IN THE FIRST STAGE OF THE PROCEEDINGS (TERRITORIAL SOVEREIGNTY AND SCOPE OF THE DISPUTE)

The Arbitral Tribunal:

Professor Sir Robert Y. Jennings, President
Judge Stephen M. Schwebel
Dr. Ahmed Sadek El-Kosheri
Mr. Keith Highet
Judge Rosalyn Higgins

Representatives of the Government of the State of Eritrea:

His Excellency Mr. Haile Weldensae, Agent
Professor Lea Brilmayer and Mr. Gary B. Born, Co-Agents
Professor Gregory Fox, Mr. John Trenor and Ms. Chiara Georgetti, Counsel

Representatives of the Government of the Republic of Yemen:

His Excellency Dr. Abdulkarim Al-Eryani, Agent
His Excellency Mr. Abdullah Ahmad Ghanim, Mr. Hussein Al-Hubaishi, Mr. Abdulwahid Al-Zandani and Mr. Rodman R. Bundy, Co-Agents
Mr. Ian Brownlie, Q.C., Mr. B. Donovan Picard, Ms. Loretta Malintoppi and Mr. Paul Luther, Counsel

AWARD

TABLE OF CONTENTS

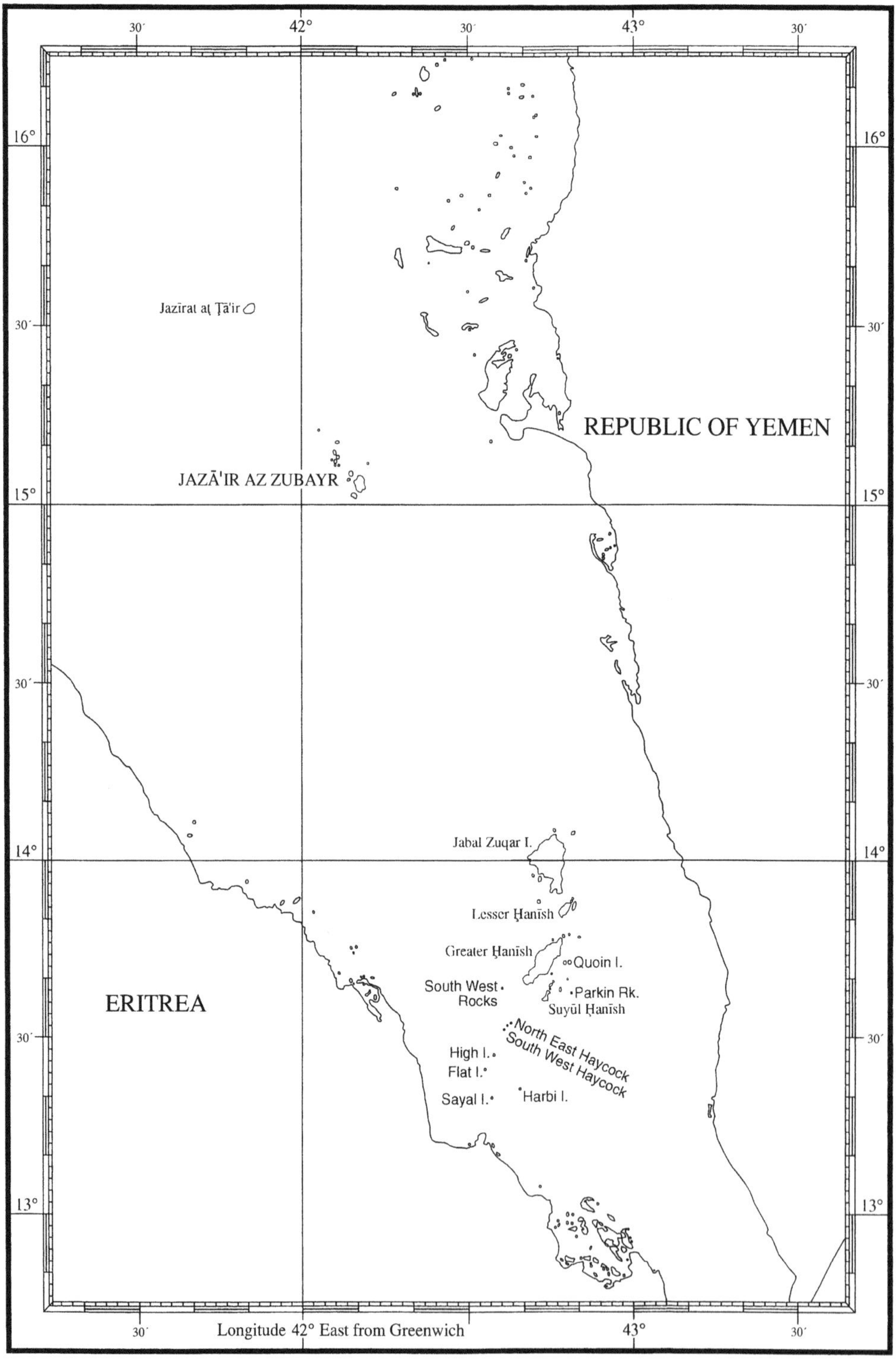

30′
42°
30′
43°
30′
16°
16°
30′
30′
15°
15°
30′
30′
14°
14°
30′
30′
13°
13°
Jazīrat aṭ Ṭā'ir
REPUBLIC OF YEMEN
JAZĀ'IR AZ ZUBAYR
Jabal Zuqar I.
Lesser Ḥanīsh
Greater Ḥanīsh
Quoin I.
South West Rocks
Parkin Rk.
Suyūl Ḥanīsh
ERITREA
North East Haycock
South West Haycock
High I.
Flat I.
Sayal I.
Harbi I.
30′
Longitude 42° East from Greenwich
43°
30′

IN THE MATTER OF AN ARBITRATION
PURSUANT TO AN AGREEMENT TO ARBITRATE
DATED 3 OCTOBER 1996

B E T W E E N :

THE GOVERNMENT OF THE STATE OF ERITREA

-and-

THE GOVERNMENT OF THE REPUBLIC OF YEMEN

AWARD OF THE ARBITRAL TRIBUNAL IN THE FIRST STAGE OF THE PROCEEDINGS (TERRITORIAL SOVEREIGNTY AND SCOPE OF THE DISPUTE)

CHAPTER I – The Setting up of the Arbitration and the Arguments of the Parties

Introduction

1. This Award is rendered pursuant to an Arbitration Agreement dated 3 October 1996 (the "Arbitration Agreement"), between the Government of the State of Eritrea ("Eritrea") and the Government of the Republic of Yemen ("Yemen") (hereinafter "the Parties").

2. The Arbitration Agreement was preceded by an "Agreement on Principles" done at Paris on 21 May 1996, which was signed by Eritrea and Yemen and witnessed by the Governments of the French Republic, the Federal Democratic Republic of Ethiopia, and the Arab Republic of Egypt. The Parties renounced recourse to force against each other, and undertook to "settle their dispute on questions of territorial sovereignty and of delimitation of maritime boundaries peacefully." They agreed, to that end, to establish an agreement instituting an arbitral tribunal. The Agreement on Principles further provided that

> . . . concerning questions of territorial sovereignty, the Tribunal shall decide in accordance with the principles, rules and practices of international law applicable to the matter, and on the basis, in particular, of historic titles.

3. Concurrently with the Agreement on Principles, the Parties issued a brief Joint Statement, emphasizing their desire to settle the dispute, and "to allow the re-establishment and development of a trustful and lasting cooperation between the two countries", contributing to the stability and peace of the region.

4. In conformity with Article 1.1 of the Arbitration Agreement, Eritrea appointed as arbitrators Judge Stephen M. Schwebel and Judge Rosalyn Higgins, and Yemen appointed Dr. Ahmed Sadek El-Kosheri and Mr. Keith Highet. By an exchange of letters dated 30 and 31 December 1996, the Parties agreed to recommend the appointment of Professor Sir Robert Y. Jennings as President of the Arbitral Tribunal (hereinafter the "Tribunal"). The four arbitrators met in London on 14 January 1997, and appointed Sir Robert Y. Jennings President of the Tribunal.

5. Having been duly constituted, the Tribunal held its first meeting on 14 January 1997, at Essex Court Chambers, 24 Lincoln's Inn Fields, London WC1, UK. The Tribunal took note of the meeting of the four arbitrators, and ratified and approved the actions authorized and undertaken thereat. Pursuant to Article 7.2 of the Arbitration Agreement, the Tribunal appointed as Registrar Mr. P.J.H. Jonkman, Secretary-General of the Permanent Court of Arbitration (the "PCA") at The Hague and, as Secretary to the Tribunal, Ms. Bette E. Shifman, First Secretary of the PCA, and fixed the location of the Tribunal's registry at the International Bureau of the PCA.

6. The Tribunal then held a meeting with Mr. Gary Born, Co-Agent of Eritrea, and Mr. Rodman Bundy, Co-Agent of Yemen, at which it notified them of the formation of the Tribunal and discussed with them certain practical matters relating to the arbitration proceedings.

7. Article 2 of the Arbitration Agreement provides that:

> 1. The Tribunal is requested to provide rulings in accordance with international law, in two stages.
>
> 2. The first stage shall result in an award on territorial sovereignty and on the definition of the scope of the dispute between Eritrea and Yemen. The Tribunal shall decide territorial sovereignty in accordance with the principles, rules and practices of international law applicable to the matter, and on the basis, in particular, of historic titles. The Tribunal shall decide on the definition of the scope of the dispute on the basis of the respective positions of the two Parties.
>
> 3. The second stage shall result in an award delimiting maritime boundaries. The Tribunal shall decide taking into account the opinion that it will have formed on

questions of territorial sovereignty, the United Nations Convention on the Law of the Sea, and any other pertinent factor.

8. Pursuant to the time table set forth in the Arbitration Agreement for the various stages of the arbitration, the Parties submitted their written Memorials concerning territorial sovereignty and the scope of the dispute simultaneously on 1 September 1997 and their Counter-Memorials on 1 December 1997. In accordance with the requirement of Article 7.1 of the Arbitration Agreement that "the Tribunal shall sit in London", the oral proceedings in the first stage of the arbitration were held in London, in the Durbar Conference Room of the Foreign and Commonwealth Office, from 26 January through 6 February 1998, within the time limits for oral proceedings set forth in the Arbitration Agreement. The order of the Parties' presentations was determined by drawing lots, with Eritrea beginning the oral proceedings.

9. At the end of its session of 6 February 1998, the Tribunal, in accordance with Article 8.3 of the Arbitration Agreement, closed the oral phase of the first stage of the arbitration proceedings between Eritrea and Yemen. The closing of the oral proceedings was subject to the undertaking of both Parties to answer in writing, by 23 February 1998, certain questions put to them by the Tribunal at the end of the hearings, including a question concerning the existence of agreements for petroleum exploration and exploitation. It was also subject to the proviso in Article 8.3 of the Arbitration Agreement authorizing the Tribunal to request the Parties' written views on the elucidation of any aspect of the matters before the Tribunal.

10. In its Communication and Order No. 3 of 10 May 1998, the Tribunal invoked this provision, requesting the Parties to provide, by 8 June 1998, written observations on the legal considerations raised by their responses to the Tribunal's earlier questions concerning concessions for petroleum exploration and exploitation and, in particular, on how the petroleum agreements and activities authorized by them might be relevant to the award on territorial sovereignty. The Tribunal further invited the Parties to agree to hold a short oral hearing for the elucidation of these issues.

11. Following the exchange of the Parties' written observations, the Tribunal held oral hearings on this matter at the Foreign and Commonwealth Office in London on 6, 7 and 8 July 1998. By agreement of the Parties, Yemen presented its arguments first. In the course of these hearings, the Tribunal posed a series of questions concerning the interpretation of concession evidence, and the Parties were requested to respond thereto in writing within seven days of the end of the oral hearings. On 17 July 1998, both Parties submitted their written responses to the Tribunal's questions. Eritrea indicated at that time that it anticipated a brief delay in submission of the documentary appendix accompanying its submission; this documentary appendix was received by the International Bureau of the PCA

on 22 July 1998. On 30 July 1998, the International Bureau received from Yemen a submission entitled "Yemen's Comments on the Documents Introduced by Eritrea after the Final Oral Argument." Eritrea objected to this late filing by Yemen.

12. In the course of the supplementary hearings in July 1998, the Tribunal informed the Parties of its intention to contact the Secretary-General of the Arab League, in order to ascertain the existence, and obtain copies, of any official Arab League reports of visits to any of the islands in dispute, particularly in the 1970s. A letter on behalf of the Tribunal was sent by fax to the Secretary-General of the Arab League on 20 July. His response, dated 28 July, was transmitted by the registry to the Co-Agents and the Members of the Tribunal.

* - *

Arguments of the Parties on Territorial Sovereignty

13. Eritrea bases its claim to territorial sovereignty over these "Red Sea Islands" (hereinafter the "Islands")[1] on a chain of title extending over more than 100 years, and on international law principles of "effective occupation." Eritrea asserts that it inherited title to the Islands in 1993, when the State of Eritrea became legally independent from the State of Ethiopia. Ethiopia had in turn inherited its title from Italy, despite a period of British military occupation of Eritrea as a whole during the Second World War. The Italian title is claimed then to have vested in the State of Ethiopia in 1952-1953, as a consequence of Eritrea's federation with, and subsequent annexation by, Ethiopia.

14. Eritrea traces this chain of title through the relevant historical periods, beginning with the Italian colonization of the Eritrean mainland in the latter part of the 19th century. The Parties do not dispute that, prior to Italian colonization, the Ottoman Empire was the unchallenged sovereign over both coasts of the Red Sea and over the Islands. Bypassing the Ottomans and dealing directly with local rulers, Italy established outposts in furtherance of its maritime, colonial and commercial interests. Despite Ottoman objections, it proclaimed the Italian colony of Eritrea in 1890. Eritrea contends that in 1892 Great Britain recognized Italian title to the Mohabbakah islands, a group of islands proximate to the Eritrean coast.

15. Eritrea asserts that, without challenging Ottoman sovereignty, Italy also maintained an active presence in other southern Red Sea islands at that time.

---

[1] The identification of the specific islands or island groups in dispute between the Parties has been entrusted to the Tribunal by Article 2 of the Arbitration Agreement (see para. 7, above), and is dealt with in the part of this Award dealing with the scope of the dispute. References to "the Islands" in this Award are to those Islands that the Tribunal finds are subject to conflicting claims by the Parties. The geographic area in which these islands are found is indicated on the map on page 20.

Italian naval vessels patrolled the surrounding waters in search of pirates, slave traders and arms smugglers, and the colonial administration allegedly issued concessions for commercial exploitation on the Islands. According to Eritrea, there was no Yemeni claim to or presence on or around the Islands during this time. The Imam Yahya, who ultimately founded modern Yemen, occupied a highland region known as the *Gebel*, and, according to Eritrea, openly acknowledged his lack of sovereignty over the coastal lowlands known as the *Tihama*. This territorial arrangement was confirmed by the 1911 "Treaty of Da'an," an understanding between the Imam and the Ottoman Empire.

16. Eritrea asserts that the weakening of the Ottoman Empire in the years immediately preceding the First World War fuelled Italian plans to occupy an island group known as the "Zuqar-Hanish Islands." These plans were preempted by a brief period of British military occupation in 1915, which was short-lived and, according to Eritrea, without legal consequences. At the end of the War, Italy purportedly renewed and expanded its commercial and regulatory activities with respect to what Eritrea refers to as the "Zuqar-Hanish and lighthouse islands." These activities are cited by Eritrea as evidence of Italy's intent to acquire sovereignty over the Islands.

17. The question of sovereignty over the Islands formed part of the post-First World War peace process that culminated in the signature of the Treaty of Lausanne in 1923. While certain former territory of the defeated Ottoman Empire was divided among local rulers who had supported the victorious Allies, Eritrea contends that none of the Arabian Peninsula leaders who had supported the Allies was in sufficient geographical proximity to the Islands to be considered a plausible recipient. The Imam of Sanaa was not a plausible recipient of the Islands, both because of his alliance with the Ottoman Turks, and because his sovereignty did not extend to the Red Sea coast. Eritrea cites Great Britain's rejection of claims made by the Imam in 1917-1918 to parts of the Tihama, and relies on the Imam's characterization of these territories as having been "under the sway of his predecessors" as acknowledging that the Imam indeed lacked possession and control at that time.

18. Eritrea traces Great Britain's failure to persuade the remaining Allies to transfer the Islands to Arab rulers selected by Great Britain, or to Great Britain itself, through the unratified 1920 Treaty of Sèvres and the negotiations leading up to the conclusion of the Treaty of Lausanne in 1923. Eritrea relies on Articles 6 and 16 of the Treaty of Lausanne as having left the Islands open for Italian occupation. Article 6 established the general rule that, in terms of the Treaty, "islands and islets lying within three miles of the coast are included within the frontier of the coastal State." Eritrea interprets this provision, and subsequent state practice under the Treaty of Lausanne, as withholding the islands in question from *any* Arabian peninsula leader, because none of the Islands are within three miles of the Arabian coast. Eritrea further argues that the Imam

could not have been given the disputed islands pursuant to Article 6, because his realm was neither a "state" nor "coastal" at the time the Treaty of Lausanne was signed.

19. Article 16 of the Treaty of Lausanne contained an express Turkish renunciation of all rights and title to former Ottoman territories and islands, and provided that their future was to be "settled by the parties concerned." Eritrea argues that because Article 16 did not transfer the Islands to any particular state, and did not specify any particular procedure for conveying ownership of the Islands, their ultimate disposition was left to general international law standards for territorial acquisition – conquest, effective occupation, and location within the territorial sea. Eritrea claims to find further support for this in subsequent state practice interpreting Article 16.

20. Eritrea asserts that by the end of the 1920s, Italy had acquired sovereignty over the disputed islands by effective occupation, and that neither the 1927 conversations between Great Britain and Italy, which came to be known as the "Rome Conversations," nor the aborted 1929 Lighthouse Convention were contra-indications. This effective occupation consisted, inter alia, of the construction in 1929 of a lighthouse on South West Haycock Island, which Eritrea claims led Great Britain to repeat acknowledgments of Italian sovereignty over the Mohabbakahs, previously made in 1892 and 1917. Eritrea finds further support for effective Italian occupation during this period in the dispatch of an expedition to the Zuqar-Hanish Islands and their subsequent occupation by Italian troops. Eritrea asserts that in the period 1930-1940 Italy exercised sovereign rights over the Islands through the colonial government in Eritrea. Eritrea cites, inter alia, the granting of fishing licenses with respect to the surrounding waters, the granting of a license for the construction of a fish processing plant on Greater Hanish, and the reconstruction and maintenance of an abandoned British lighthouse on Centre Peak Island. These satisfy, in Eritrea's view, the *corpus occupandi* requirement of effective occupation and, accompanied as they were by the requisite sovereign intent (*animus occupandi*), constitute the acquisition of sovereignty by effective occupation.

21. Eritrea further asserts that Yemen did not protest or question Italy's activities on the Islands during this time. Great Britain, however, sought assurances that Italian activities did not constitute a claim of sovereignty. Eritrea characterizes Italy's responses that the question of sovereignty was "in abeyance" or "in reserve" as a refusal to give such assurances. According to Eritrea, this formula was understood by both Italy and Great Britain as preserving Italy's legal rights while allowing Great Britain to withhold diplomatic recognition of those rights. Tensions between the two states on this and other matters led to conclusion of the 1938 Anglo-Italian Agreement, which Eritrea claims is probative of Italian and British views at that time. It is said to reflect, among other things, the parties' understanding that the Islands were not appurtenant to the Arabian Peninsula, and

that Italy and Great Britain were the only two powers with a cognizable interest in them.

22. The 1938 Anglo-Italian Agreement also contained an express undertaking on the part of both Italy and Great Britain with respect to the former Ottoman Red Sea islands, that neither would "establish its sovereignty" or "erect fortifications or defences." This constituted, in Eritrea's view, not a relinquishment of existing rights, but simply a covenant regarding future conduct. Eritrea argues that, at the time of the Anglo-Italian Agreement, Italy's sovereignty over the Islands had already been established as a matter of law, and it remained unaffected by the agreement. Eritrea further asserts that in December of 1938, Italy formally confirmed its existing territorial sovereignty over the Islands by promulgating decree number 1446 of 1938, specifically confirming that the Islands had been, and continued to be, part of the territory of the Eritrean *Commissariato* of Dankalia.

23. Eritrea characterizes the eleven-year British occupation of Eritrea that commenced in 1941 in the wake of the Second World War as congruent with the law of belligerent occupation. Eritrea's territorial boundaries remained unchanged, and the territory of "all Italian colonies and dependencies" surrendered to the Allies in the 1943 Armistice "indisputably included," in Eritrea's view, the Islands. The 1947 Treaty of Peace provided for disposition of Italy's African territories by the Allied Powers, which was accomplished in 1952 by the transfer to Ethiopia, with which Eritrea was then federated, of "all former Italian territorial possessions in Eritrea." This marked, in Eritrea's view, the passing to Ethiopia of sovereign title to the Islands.

24. Eritrea claims that the drafting history of the 1952 Eritrean Constitution confirms the inclusion of the disputed islands within the definition of Eritrean territory. This is, according to Eritrea, the only plausible interpretation of the phrase "Eritrea, including the islands" in the definition of the territory of Eritrea, and it is said to be supported by advice given to Ethiopia at the time by its legal adviser, John Spencer. Eritrea claims that this was further reinforced by similar language in subsequent constitutional and legislative provisions, in particular, the 1952 Imperial Decree federating Eritrea into the Ethiopian Empire, and the 1955 Ethiopian Constitution.

25. Another basis for Ethiopian sovereignty put forward by Eritrea is the inclusion of the Islands within Ethiopia's territorial sea. Eritrea relies on the rule of international customary and conventional law that every island is entitled to its own territorial sea, measured in accordance with the same principles as those applicable to the mainland. In Eritrea's view, a chain of islands linked to the mainland with gaps no wider than twelve miles falls entirely within the coastal state's territorial sea and therefore under its territorial sovereignty. Thus, measuring from the Mohabbakah islands, which Eritrea asserts were indisputably

Ethiopian, Ethiopia's 1953 declaration of a 12-mile territorial sea encompassed the Zuqar-Hanish islands.

26. The 35-year period between 1953 and Eritrean independence in 1991 is characterized by Eritrea as one of extensive exercise of Ethiopian sovereignty over the Islands. This allegedly included continuous, unchallenged naval patrols, which became increasingly systematic as the Eritrean Liberation Movement gathered strength. In addition, following transfer of the administration of the lighthouses to Asmara by the British Board of Trade in 1967, Ethiopia is said to have further consolidated its sovereignty by requiring foreign workers on the lighthouse islands to carry passports and similar documents, overseeing and regulating the dispatch of all provisions to the lighthouse islands, being involved in all employment decisions affecting lighthouse workers, approving all inspection and repair visits to the lighthouse islands, and tightly controlling radio transmissions to and from the lighthouse islands. Other alleged acts of Ethiopian sovereignty put forward by Eritrea include the exercise of criminal jurisdiction over acts committed on the Islands, regulation of oil exploration activities on and around the Islands, and an inspection by then President Mengistu and a group of high-ranking Ethiopian military and naval personnel during the late 1980s, for which Eritrea has submitted videotape evidence.

27. Eritrea claims that throughout the 1970s the two Yemeni states and their regional allies acknowledged Ethiopian control over the Islands by their statements and actions. It alleges that, until the early 1970s, neither North Yemen nor South Yemen had displayed any interest in the Islands. Regional interest in the Islands is said to have been sparked by false reports of an Israeli presence there in 1973. According to Eritrea, the presumption on the part of Yemen, its neighbouring states and the Arab media that Ethiopia had leased the Islands to Israel constituted an acknowledgment of Ethiopian sovereignty. In support, Eritrea claims that the Arab states not only condemned Ethiopia for having made Ethiopian islands available to Israel, but also looked ultimately to Ethiopia for permission to visit the Islands in order to investigate the allegations of Israeli military activity.

28. Eritrea contends that the final years before Eritrean independence were marked by aerial surveillance and continuous naval patrols by Ethiopian forces.

29. Eritrea claims that, after winning its independence in 1991, it acquired sovereign title to the Islands and exercised sovereign authority over them. Eritrea asserts that, as they have been throughout recent history, Eritrean fishermen are dependent upon the Islands for their livelihood. Eritrean administrative regulations are said strictly to control fishing around the Islands, prescribing licensing and other requirements for fishing in the surrounding waters. Eritrea further contends that its vessels police foreign fishing vessels in Eritrean territorial waters, and routinely patrol the waters around the Islands in order to

enforce fishing regulations, seizing vessels that fail to comply. It asserts that Yemen did not maintain any official presence in the Islands, and that it was only in 1995 that Eritrean naval patrols discovered a small Yemeni military and civilian contingent purportedly engaged in work on a tourist resort on Greater Hanish Island. This led, in December 1995, to hostilities that ended with Eritrean forces occupying Greater Hanish Island, and Yemeni forces occupying Zuqar.

30. With respect to territorial sovereignty, Eritrea seeks from the Tribunal an award declaring that Eritrea possesses territorial sovereignty over each of the islands, rocks and low-tide elevations specified by Eritrea in its written pleadings, "as to which Yemen claims sovereignty."

* - *

31. Yemen, in turn, bases its claim to the Islands on "original, historic, or traditional Yemeni title." Yemen puts particular emphasis on the stipulation in Article 2.2 of the Arbitration Agreement, that "[t]he Tribunal shall decide territorial sovereignty in accordance with the principles, rules and practices of international law applicable to the matter, and on the basis, in particular, of historic titles." This title can, according to Yemen, be traced to the *Bilad el-Yemen*, or realm of Yemen, which is said to have existed as early as the 6th century A.D. Yemen advances, in support of this claim, map evidence,[2] declarations by the Imam of Yemen, and what it refers to as "the attitude of third States over a long period."

32. Yemen contends that its incorporation into the Ottoman Empire, from 1538 to *circa* 1635, and again from 1872 to the Ottoman defeat in 1918, did not deprive it of historic title to its territory. Yemen asserts that the creation of the Ottoman *vilayet* of Yemen as a separate territorial and administrative unit constituted Ottoman recognition of Yemen's separate identity. It relies on the work of 17th, 18th and 19th century cartographers who allegedly depicted Yemen as a separate, identifiable territorial entity. Further map evidence is adduced in support of Yemen's contention that the Islands form part of that territory.

33. In further support of its assertions that Yemen maintained historic title to the Islands, Yemen retraces the drafting history of its 1934 Treaty with Great Britain, citing several exchanges of correspondence in which the Imam insisted, in one form or another, on his rights to the "Islands of the Yemen." Yemen cites Great Britain's rejection of the Imam's proposal to attach to the Treaty a secret appendix concerning the Islands, on the grounds that the Islands, as former

---

[2] Although Eritrea has also submitted cartographic evidence showing the Islands to be Ethiopian, Eritrean or, in any event, not Yemeni, it places relatively little weight on this type of evidence. Eritrea takes the position that maps do not constitute direct evidence of sovereignty or of a chain of title, thereby relegating them to a limited role in resolving these types of disputes.

Ottoman possessions, were to be dealt with pursuant to Article 16 of the Treaty of Lausanne.

34. Yemen argues that this did not constitute a denial of traditional Yemeni title, and puts forward documents that it claims support the characterization of British official opinion in the period 1933 to 1937 as being reluctant to challenge Yemeni title. Yemen further contends that the Treaty of Lausanne had no effect on Yemeni title, because Yemen was not a party to the Treaty, and because Turkey's renunciation of rights could not prejudice the interests of third parties. Yemen takes the view that the effect of Article 16 was not to make the Islands *terra nullius*, but rather, territory "the title to which was undetermined." Yemen argues in addition that Article 16 has, in any event, ceased to have effect between "the parties concerned," because of their own conduct, and that of third states, in recognizing, or failing to make reservations concerning, Yemen's sovereignty in respect of the Islands.

35. Another ground put forward in support of Yemen's claim that its original title extends to the Islands is "the principle of natural or geographical unity." Yemen argues that this doctrine is a corollary of the concept of traditional title, and that it operates in conjunction with evidence of the exercise of acts of jurisdiction or manifestations of state sovereignty. Yemen cites case law of the International Court of Justice and arbitral decisions in support of the premise that once the sovereignty of an entity or natural unity as a whole has been shown to exist, it may be deemed, in the absence of any evidence to the contrary, to extend to all parts of that entity or unity. According to Yemen, there is a "concordance of expert opinion evidence on the character of the islands as an entity or natural unity," including British admiralty charts, the *Red Sea and Gulf of Aden Pilot*, produced by the United Kingdom Hydrographic Office, and the *Encyclopedia Britannica*.

36. Yemen relies on various categories of evidence of sovereignty, which it asserts may serve to confirm and supplement the evidence of traditional or historic title, as well as constituting independent sources of title. These include economic and social links between the Islands and the Yemeni mainland, the exercise of sovereignty in the form of acts of jurisdiction, recognition of Yemen's title by third states, and confirmation of Yemeni title by expert opinion evidence.

37. Yemen cites case law and commentary in support of its contention that, within the appropriate geographical context, the private activities of individual persons constitute relevant evidence of historic title to territory. Yemen's analysis of these facts and activities begins with the names "Hanish" and "Zuqar," which, it asserts, have Arabic roots. Yemen also notes the presence on the Yemeni coast of inhabitants with names derived from the word "Hanish," and a family history, as fishermen, intertwined with that of the Islands. Yemen points out that, during the disturbances of 1995, two members of such a family were taken prisoner by

Eritrean forces while fishing near Greater Hanish Island. Yemen also alleges the existence of anchorages and settlements on the Islands bearing distinctly Yemeni Arabic names. Yemen claims that, for generations, Yemeni fishermen have enjoyed virtually exclusive use of the Islands, even establishing, in contrast to Eritrean fishermen, permanent and semi-permanent residence there.

38. Yemen further asserts that the Islands are home to a number of Yemeni holy sites and shrines, including the tombs of several venerated holy men. It points to a shrine used primarily by fishermen, who have developed a tradition of leaving unused provisions in the tomb to sustain their fellow fishermen.

39. In addition, Yemen points out that the Islands fall within the jurisdiction of a traditional system of resolving disputes between fishermen, in which a kind of arbitrator may "ride the circuit" along the coast and among the Islands, in order to insure access to justice for those fishermen who are unable to travel.

40. Yemen emphasizes the economic links between the Islands and the Yemeni fishermen who rely for their livelihood on them and their surrounding waters, and who sell their catch almost exclusively on the Yemeni mainland. Yemen contrasts this with the situation of the Eritrean fishermen, pointing out that, because of the difficulty of hygienic transport of fish to the interior of Eritrea (including the capital of Asmara), Eritrea lacks a fish-eating tradition. According to Yemen, most Eritrean fishermen find a better market for their wares on the Yemeni coast. Yemen asserts that for centuries, the long-standing, intensive and virtually exclusive use of the Islands by Yemeni fishermen did not meet with interference from other states.

41. Yemen provides an historical review of alleged Yemeni acts of administration and control, which are said to supplement and confirm Yemen's historic title to the Islands, as well as forming independent, mutually reinforcing sources of that title. The earliest of these acts, a mission sent to Jabal Zuqar by the King of Yemen in 1429 to investigate smuggling, predates Ottoman rule. In the Ottoman period, Yemen asserts that the Islands were considered part of the *vilayet* of Yemen, and that the Ottoman administration handled, inter alia, tax, security, and maritime matters relating to the Islands. Yemen cites an 1881 lighthouse concession by the Ottoman authorities to a private French company, for the construction of lighthouses throughout the empire, which included some of the islands in the *vilayet* of Yemen. Yemen also cites 19th century Ottoman maps and annual reports, which place the Islands within the *vilayet* of Yemen.

42. Yemen emphasizes that the post-Ottoman British presence on the Islands was intermittent, and that Great Britain never claimed sovereignty over them. Following establishment of the Yemen Arab Republic in 1962, its Government allegedly asserted legislative jurisdiction over the Islands on at least two occasions. Yemen claims that its navy conducted exercises on and around the

Islands, and that its armed forces played a key role in confirming the absence of Israeli troops on the Islands in 1973. In Yemen's rendition of the events surrounding the 1973 incident, the Islands are consistently characterized as Yemeni, rather than Ethiopian.

43. Yemen cites a number of examples of the issuance of licenses to foreign entities wishing to engage in scientific, tourist and commercial activities in and around the Islands, and of the granting of permits for anchorage. Yemen presents evidence concerning the authorization given to a German company by the Yemeni Ministry of Culture and Tourism and the Yemen General Investment Authority in 1995 for the construction of a luxury hotel and diving centre on Greater Hanish Island. Yemen further asserts that it exercised jurisdiction over the Islands in respect of fishing, environmental protection, the installation and maintenance of geodetic stations, and the construction and administration of lighthouses, including the publication of relevant Notices to Mariners. Yemen has placed in evidence elaborate chronological surveys, covering a variety of time periods, of alleged Yemeni activities "in and around the Hanish Group."

44. Yemen contends that from 1887 to 1989, at least six states confirmed, by their conduct or otherwise, Yemen's title to the Islands. Yemen points out that upon conclusion of the Anglo-Italian Agreement of 1938, which Eritrea characterizes as being limited to future conduct, the Italian Government informed the Imam of Yemen that, pursuant to the agreement, Italy had undertaken not to extend its sovereignty on or to fortify the "Hanish Island group," and that it had, in the negotiations, "kept in mind . . . above all Yemen's interests." Yemen claims to find further acknowledgment of Yemeni rights in British practice and "internal thinking," as reflected in Foreign Office and Colonial Office documents of the 1930s and 1940s. French recognition of Yemeni title is said to include a request for permission to conduct military manoeuvres in the Southern Red Sea in 1975, and for a French oceanographic vessel to conduct activities near the Islands in 1976.

45. Yemen attributes similar evidentiary value to German conduct and publications, and to official maps published by the United States Army and Central Intelligence Agency, as recently as 1993. Yemen offers evidence of what it terms "revealing changes in Ethiopian cartography" in support of its contention that Ethiopia did not claim title to the Islands. It relies particularly on Ethiopian maps from 1978, 1982, 1984 and 1985, on which all or some of the Islands appear, by their colouring, to be allocated to Yemen.

46. Yemen also puts forward cartographic evidence on which it relies as official and unofficial expert evidence of Yemeni title to the Islands. Such evidence serves, according to Yemen, as proof of geographical facts and the state of geographical knowledge at a particular period. Yemen supplements this cartographic evidence with the published works of historians and other professionals.

47. Yemen gives an historical review of this evidence, beginning with 17th and 18th century maps depicting the independent *Bilad el-Yemen*. Yemen asserts that while some 18th century maps fail to depict the Islands accurately, the more accurate of these attribute them to Yemen. Yemen places great emphasis on writings and maps reflecting the first-hand impressions of Carsten Niebuhr, a Danish scientist and explorer who visited the Red Sea coast from 1761-1764. Niebuhr's works suggest political affiliation and other links between the Islands and the Yemeni mainland.

48. Yemen further submits in evidence a large number of 19th and 20th century maps, of varied origin, the colouring of which appears to attribute all or some of the Islands to Yemen. At the same time, it did not deny that certain Yemeni maps attribute the Islands to Ethiopia or Eritrea; or at least not to Yemen.

49. In addition to proffering cartographic and other evidence in support of its assertions of historic title to the Islands, Yemen argues that, until the events of December 1995, Ethiopian and Eritrean conduct was consistent with Yemeni sovereignty. Yemen alleges that as recently as November 1995, Eritrea acknowledged in an official communique to the President of Yemen that the Islands had ". . . been ignored and abandoned for many years since colonial times, including the eras of Haile Selassie and Mengistu, and during the long war of liberation."

50. Yemen insists that, during the Ottoman period, the Islands were consistently administered as part of the *vilayet* of Yemen, and that title never passed to Italy during the period of Italian colonization of the Eritrean mainland. Yemen cites several occasions on which, in its view, Italy had declined to claim sovereignty. These include exchanges between the British and Italian Governments in the late 1920s and 1930s and culminated in the 1938 Anglo-Italian Agreement which amounts, in Yemen's view, to a definitive agreement by both parties not to establish sovereignty over islands with respect to which Turkey had renounced sovereignty by Article 16 of the Treaty of Lausanne. Yemen interprets Italian decree number 1446 of 20 December 1938 not as a confirmation of existing territorial sovereignty but rather as a mere "internal decree providing for the administration of the islands to be undertaken from the Assab department of Eritrea."

51. Yemen argues further that the phrase "the territory of Eritrea including the islands" in the 1952 UN-drafted Eritrean Constitution does not refer to the disputed islands, because the official Report of the United Nations Commission for Eritrea, prepared in 1950, indicates Yemeni title to the Islands, by depicting them in the same colour as the Yemeni mainland on UN maps accompanying the Report. Yemen contests all Eritrean allegations of Ethiopian acts of sovereignty or administration, and asserts that Ethiopian conduct, particularly its publication

of official maps on which the Islands were the same colour as the Yemeni mainland, constituted recognition of Yemeni sovereignty over the Islands.

52. According to Yemen, while Yemeni fishermen historically fished around the Islands and used them for temporary residence, Yemen exercised a wide array of state activities on and around them. These activities are alleged to have included, during the 1970s, the consideration of requests by foreign nationals to carry out marine and scientific research on the Islands, periodic visits of Yemeni military officials to Greater Hanish and Jabal Zuqar, and related patrols on and around these Islands. Yemen also claims to have protested the conduct of low-level military flights by France over the Hanish islands, as well as Ethiopia's arrest of Yemeni fishermen in the vicinity of the Islands, and further asserts that it investigated a number of lost or damaged foreign vessels around Greater Hanish and Jabal Zuqar.

53. With respect to the 1980s and 1990s, Yemen alleges that various Yemeni air force and naval reconnaissance missions were conducted over and around the Islands. Yemen also asserts that it granted licenses allowing nationals of third states to visit the certain islands for scientific purposes and tourism, and that some of these visitors were accompanied by Yemeni officials. In 1988, Yemen is said to have embarked on a project to upgrade and build a series of lighthouses, accompanied by Notices to Mariners, on Centre Peak Island, Jabal al-Tayr, Lesser Hanish Island, Abu Ali, Jabal Zuqar and Greater Hanish Island. Yemen also claims to have erected geodetic stations on Greater Hanish and Jabal Zuqar and authorized construction of a landing strip on Greater Hanish, which was used frequently in the early 1990s. Yemen also contends that, during this period, it continued its patrols of the Islands, arresting foreign fishermen and confiscating vessels found operating in waters around the Islands without a Yemeni license.

54. With respect to territorial sovereignty, Yemen seeks from the Tribunal an award declaring "that the Republic of Yemen possesses territorial sovereignty over all of the islands comprising the Hanish Group of islands . . . as defined in chapters 2 and 5 of Yemen's Memorial."

* - *

Arguments of the Parties on the Relevance of Petroleum Agreements and Activities

55. In response to specific questions from the Tribunal, which were dealt with in supplemental written pleadings, at resumed oral hearings in July 1998, and in post-hearing written submissions, both Parties have presented evidence of offshore concession activity in the Red Sea. Yemen contends that its record of granting offshore concessions over the last fifty years reinforces and complements a consistent pattern of evidence indicating Yemeni title to the

Islands. As the granting of oil concessions serves to confirm and maintain an existing Yemeni title, rather than furnishing evidence of effective occupation, it need not, in Yemen's view, be supported by evidence of express claims. This is said to be congruent with Yemen's assertions of historic title.

56. In evidence of what it terms "longstanding and peaceful administration of its petroleum resources" on and around the Islands, Yemen has submitted agreements and maps concerning concession blocks granted or offered since 1974. One of these concession blocks (Tomen) encompasses some of the Islands, in this case, the "Hanish Group," while another (Adair) is bounded by a line that cuts through Greater Hanish. Yemen further relies on a 1991 hydrocarbon study of the Red Sea and Gulf of Eden regions carried out by the United Nations Development Programme (UNDP) and the World Bank. As this study enjoyed the participation of the governments concerned, particularly Ethiopia and successive Yemeni governments, Yemen relies on it as a useful overview of petroleum activities undertaken by the two states from the early 1950s.

57. Yemen relies on both case law (in particular the *Eastern Greenland* case[3]) and scholarly writing in support of its assertion that the granting of exploration permits and concessions constitutes evidence of title, addressing such evidentiary categories as: the attitude of the grantor state, its grant and regulation of the operation of the concession, ancillary government-approved operations, and the attitude of the concessionaire and of international agencies. In addition, Yemen derives from the absence of protests evidence of Ethiopian and Eritrean acquiescence.

58. Yemen invokes the presumption that a state granting an oil concession does so in respect of areas over which it has title or sovereign rights. The activity of offering and granting concessions with respect to blocks that encompass or approach the Islands constitutes, in Yemen's view, a clear manifestation of Yemeni sovereignty over the Islands. Yemen cites, in addition, express reservations, in the relevant agreements, of Yemeni title to the concession areas. In addition to demonstrating Yemen's attitude regarding title, the granting of these economic concessions to private companies is said to constitute evidence of the exercise of sovereignty in respect of the territory concerned. Yemen finds additional evidence of the exercise of sovereignty in Yemen's monitoring and regulation of the operations undertaken by the various concessionaires and the granting of permits for ancillary operations such as seismic reconnaissance.

59. Yemen further argues that a company will not enter into a concession with a state for the development of petroleum resources unless it is persuaded that the area covered by the concession, and the underlying resources, in fact belong to that

---

[3] Legal Status of Eastern Greenland (Den. v. Nor.), 1933 P.C.I.J. (Ser. A/B) No. 53.

state. Furthermore, the reservations of Yemeni title in the concession agreements submitted by Yemen are said to constitute express recognition by the concessionaires of Yemeni title to the blocks concerned. The UNDP/World Bank study constitutes, in Yemen's view, recognition of Yemeni title by these international agencies, as well as expert evidence to the same effect.

60. Yemen also proffers the UNDP/World Bank study as evidence of Ethiopian acquiescence. Because the study was prepared in collaboration with, and ultimately distributed to, all concerned governments, Ethiopia can, in Yemen's view, be held to have had notice of the existence and scope of Yemeni concessions implicating the Islands, without issuing any protests. Yemen relies further on other maps and reports published in the professional petroleum literature, of which it asserts Ethiopia and Eritrea should have been aware.

61. Finally, Yemen asserts that Ethiopian and Eritrean petroleum activities did not encompass or touch upon the Islands, and therefore provide no support for a claim of sovereignty. Despite this, Yemen alleges that it consistently made timely protests with respect to those Ethiopian concessions that, in Yemen's view, encroached in any manner upon its territorial sea, continental shelf and exclusive economic zone.

62. Eritrea, in turn, proffers evidence of offshore petroleum activities, conducted primarily by Ethiopia, at a time at which, it alleges, "Ethiopia's title was already established." Eritrea cites oil-exploration related activities "on the islands" as confirming Ethiopia's pre-existing claim to sovereignty, which could not, in its view, be divested by Yemen's unilateral grants of offshore mineral concessions. Eritrea also argues that, in the absence of any physical manifestation of control either on islands or in their territorial waters, the mere granting of concessions by Yemen would not suffice to establish title through effective occupation, "even if the islands had been previously unowned."

63. According to Eritrea, the concession evidence put forward by Yemen is irrelevant, because it represents unilateral attempts by Yemen to establish permanent rights to the seabed, in violation of customary international law and the United Nations Convention on the Law of the Sea (the "Law of the Sea Convention"). Yemen's concession agreements are further said to be irrelevant because they were entered into only after the present dispute arose, were not accompanied by Yemeni government activities, and did not pertain to the territory in dispute. Eritrea also questions the factual accuracy of Yemen's allegations concerning concession agreements, pointing to Yemen's failure to submit in evidence copies of certain of these agreements.

64. Eritrea argues that, under both the Law of the Sea Convention and customary international law, mineral rights to the seabed can neither be acquired nor lost through the unilateral appropriation of one competing claimant. Pending

agreement with the opposite coastal state, Yemen was, in Eritrea's view, entitled only to issue concessions on a provisional basis. If the alleged concessions could not effectively confer the very mineral rights with which they purported to deal, they could not indirectly settle the question of sovereignty over the Islands. According to Eritrea, petroleum concessions are relevant only where they demonstrate the existence of a mutually recognized de facto boundary line. There had, in this case, been no attempt by Yemen to reach mutual agreement with Ethiopia or Eritrea.

65. Eritrea contends that the provisional character of any concessions issued by Yemen is derived not only from Article 87(3)* of the Law of the Sea Convention, which permits the provisional granting of concessions, provided this does not prejudice a final delimitation, but also from Yemen's own continental shelf legislation, adopted in 1977, which provides that "pending agreement on the demarcation of the marine boundaries, the limits of territorial sea, the contiguous zone, the exclusive economic zone . . . shall not be extended to more than the median or equidistance line."

66. Eritrea further asserts that Yemen's offshore concessions were issued after 1973, with full knowledge of Ethiopia's sovereignty claims to the Islands. This is claimed not only to have implications for the delimitation of the surrounding seabed, but to limit as well the evidentiary value of Yemen's concession evidence in resolving the question of sovereignty.

67. Thus Eritrea argues that the post-1973 grant of concessions by Yemen reflects attempts to manufacture contacts with the disputed islands. This is further supported, in Eritrea's view, by the lack of any related Yemeni state activity pertaining specifically to the territory in dispute. According to Eritrea, concessions can be brought to bear on the question of territorial acquisition in two ways. The first is exemplified by the deep sea fishing concession granted by Italy to the *Cannata* company in the 1930s, which led inter alia to construction of a commercial fishing station on Greater Hanish Island. According to Eritrea, the *Cannata* concession was accompanied by the direct involvement of state officials, including Italian troops stationed on the island.

68. Another way in which concessions may be relevant to territorial acquisition is that reflected in the *Eastern Greenland* case. *Eastern Greenland* does not, in Eritrea's reading, necessarily require the physical presence of a particular state official, but rather activities by individuals who, while not themselves employees of the state, act under colour of state law. Eritrea cites doctrine in support of its position that the concession activity of private individuals is relevant only when it involves some kind of real assertion of authority, since "the exercise or display

* *Editorial correction: the correct reference is to Article 83(3) of the Law of the Sea Convention.*

must be genuine and not a mere paper claim dressed up as an act of sovereignty." Eritrea argues that the scope of Yemeni and private activity with respect to petroleum concessions "does not approach the quality and significance of Ethiopia's long-standing pattern of governmental activities on and around the disputed islands." Eritrea further asserts that the few concession agreements actually placed in evidence by Yemen ultimately bear little or no relationship to the islands in dispute.

69. In addition, Eritrea characterizes much of Yemen's petroleum activity as pertaining to "marine scientific research," rather than economic exploitation. Article 241 of the Law of the Sea Convention expressly precludes marine scientific research activities from constituting the legal basis for any claim to any part of the marine environment or its resources.

70. Eritrea argues that its failure to protest Yemeni concessions does not amount to acquiescence, particularly in light of military and political upheaval in Ethiopia during the relevant period. Eritrea has submitted evidence aimed at demonstrating that the 1991 UNDP/World Bank report relied on by Yemen as evidence of notice to Ethiopia may never have been received by Ethiopia, embroiled as it then was in the fall of the Mengistu regime and the end of the civil war. And even if it had been ultimately received, Eritrea posits that in 1991, knowing it would soon lose its entire coastline to the soon-to-be independent Eritrea, Ethiopia would have had no reason to protest Yemeni concessions.

71. Even if it had had actual notice of some or all of Yemen's concessions, Eritrea contends that it was entitled to rely on their being provisional under Article 87(3)[*] of the Law of the Sea Convention and under Yemen's own 1977 continental shelf legislation.

72. Finally, at the oral hearings in London in July 1998, Eritrea produced evidence of a 1989 Ethiopian concession agreement which, in its view, included at least some of the Islands, notably Greater Hanish, on which Eritrea relies as evidence of related activities which are said to have taken place on Greater Hanish Island, including the placement of beacons. Moreover, it has introduced evidence of publication in 1985 of a series of maps, one of which is entitled "Petroleum Potential of Ethiopia" and purports to encompass a block of the Red Sea that includes the Hanish islands.

* - * - *

[*] *Editorial correction: the correct reference is to Article 83(3) of the Law of the Sea Convention.*

CHAPTER II – The Scope of the Dispute

73. The Arbitration Agreement seeks from the Tribunal an award "on the definition of the scope of the dispute between Eritrea and Yemen." It further instructs the Tribunal to decide on the definition of the scope of the dispute "on the basis of the respective positions of the two Parties."

74. The Parties agree that this provision was included in the Arbitration Agreement as a result of the Parties' inability to reach agreement on the definition of the scope of the dispute. According to Eritrea, at the time of the military confrontation in late 1995, which resulted in an Eritrean military occupation of Greater Hanish and some of the small surrounding islands and the Republic of Yemen's military occupation of Zuqar Island, Eritrea wished to seek a determination of all respective Eritrean and Yemeni claims, either by international arbitration or adjudication. Yemen would not agree to such a submission, insisting instead, as Eritrea relates it, on limiting the scope of the dispute to Eritrea's alleged illegal occupation of Hanish Island. Because neither Party wanted this disagreement on scope to prevent the conclusion of the Agreement on Principles and subsequent Arbitration Agreement, they agreed to leave the determination of scope to the Tribunal.

75. In Eritrea's interpretation of the phrase "the respective positions of the Parties," both Parties are free to put forth and elaborate on their positions concerning the scope of the dispute at any point in the proceedings. Eritrea purports to have done so by including in its Memorial, submitted on 1 September 1997, a non-exhaustive list of "islands, rocks and low-tide elevations" with respect to which it asserts territorial sovereignty, and requesting the Tribunal to rule that the scope of the dispute includes each of these specified "islands, rocks and low-tide elevations." Eritrea insists that as its position with regard to scope has not altered over time, the time at which it was determined is irrelevant. While indicating that it had not expected Yemen to claim the Mohabbakah Islands, Eritrea has expressed willingness to defend its claim to the Mohabbakahs: i.e., to consider them encompassed by the scope of the dispute. Eritrea further asserts that Yemen was, in fact, aware of Eritrean claims to Jabal al-Tayr and the Zubayr group.

76. Yemen, however, puts forward the view that "the respective positions of the Parties" are to be determined at the date of the Agreement on Principles (21 May 1996). Yemen submits that "the task of the Tribunal is to determine the extent to which there was a dispute between the Parties over certain islands in the Red Sea and their maritime limitation as of that date." According to Yemen, the respective positions of the Parties at that date reflected their mutual understanding that Jabal al-Tayr and the Zubayr group of islands were not considered to fall within the scope of the dispute. Yemen characterizes the scope of the dispute as involving "the Hanish Group of Islands," comprising – in its view – Abu Ali Island, Jabal Zuqar, Greater and Lesser Hanish, Suyul Hanish, the various small islets and

rocks that surround them, the South West Rocks, the Haycocks and the Mohabbakahs. It asserts that the "Northern Islands" of Jabal al-Tayr and the Zubayr group were never in dispute between the Parties, and were not reflected in Eritrea's "position" until 1 September 1997, the date of filing of the Parties' Memorials, and thus fell outside the scope of the dispute.

77. The Parties' divergent positions on the substance of the dispute are reflected in a document dated 29 February 1996, entitled "French Memorandum for Yemen and Eritrea." In the aftermath of the December 1995 hostilities, Eritrea and Yemen had, on advice from the UN Secretary-General, invited the French Government to "contribute to the seeking of a peaceful settlement of the dispute between them in the Red Sea." This memorandum was the result of three diplomatic missions to the region, consisting of in-depth talks with the representatives of the two Governments, and it led to the subsequent conclusion between the Parties of the Agreement on Principles, in May 1996, and the Arbitration Agreement, in October 1997.

78. As described in the French memorandum, "[t]he problem raised is as follows. According to Eritrea the dispute concerns at present not only the island of Great Hanish which underwent the events we know about in autumn 1995, but also all of the Hanish-Zucur archipelagoes, particularly the island of Djebel Zucur, since Yemen has stationed troops there whereas these archipelagoes come under Eritrean sovereignty." With respect to the Yemeni position, the French memorandum continues: "According to Yemen this dispute concerns the island of Greater Hanish, where Eritrea has sent troops, but cannot concern the Hanish-Zucur archipelagoes in their totality, particularly the island of Djebel Zucur, since they come under Yemeni sovereignty."

79. The French mediator therefore proposed that the arbitral tribunal be asked "to provide rulings on the questions of territorial sovereignty, as well as delimitation of maritime boundaries, in a zone defined for example by geographical coordinates." This definition would, according to a French Draft Agreement on Principles dated 29 February 1996, take into account "the undisputed sovereignty of either Party on islands and rocks, such as, for example, the Dahlak Islands for Eritrea, or the Zubair Islands for Yemen." This proposal was rejected by the Parties, in favour of leaving the determination of the scope of the dispute to the arbitral tribunal.

80. Article 1 of the Agreement on Principles of 21 May 1996 provides:

> [. . .]
>
> 1.2 They shall request the Tribunal to provide rulings in accordance with international law in two stages:

a) in the first stage, on the definition of the scope of the dispute between Eritrea and Yemen, on the basis of the respective positions of the two parties;
b) in the second stage, and after having decided on the point mentioned in letter a) above, on:
 i) questions of territorial sovereignty,
 ii) questions of delimitation of maritime boundaries.

2. They commit themselves to abide by the decision of the Tribunal.

81. Article 2 of the Arbitration Agreement, however, provides as follows:

1. The Tribunal is requested to provide rulings in accordance with international law, in two stages.
2. The first stage shall result in an award on territorial sovereignty and on the definition of the scope of the dispute between Eritrea and Yemen. The Tribunal shall decide territorial sovereignty in accordance with the principles, rules and practices of international law applicable to the matter, and on the basis, in particular, of historic titles. The Tribunal shall decide on the definition of the scope of the dispute on the basis of the respective positions of the two Parties.
3. The second stage shall result in an award delimiting maritime boundaries. The Tribunal shall decide taking into account the opinion that it will have formed on questions of territorial sovereignty, the United Nations Convention on the Law of the Sea, and any other pertinent factor.

82. Article 15 of the same Arbitration Agreement also provides:

1. Nothing in this Arbitration Agreement can be interpreted as being detrimental to the legal positions or to the rights of each Party with respect to the questions submitted to the Tribunal, nor can affect or prejudice the decision of the Arbitral Tribunal or the considerations and grounds on which those decisions are based.
2. In the event of any inconsistency between the Agreement on Principles and this Arbitration Agreement implementing the procedural aspects of that Agreement on Principles, this Arbitration Agreement shall control. Except with respect to such inconsistency, the Agreement on Principles shall continue in force.

83. Since there is indeed in this respect an inconsistency between the Agreement on Principles and the Arbitration Agreement, under Article 15.2 of the Arbitration Agreement the provisions of the latter prevail to the extent of the inconsistency. The Tribunal must therefore decide the question of scope, as well as the resulting questions of sovereignty, in the present first stage of the proceedings.

84. This decision on scope has to be made "on the basis of the respective positions of the two Parties," and on this point the provisions of the two agreements are identical. It is apparent, however, from the submissions of the Parties in their written pleadings and in their oral presentations for the first stage that the positions of the two Parties differ with respect to the scope of the arbitration. Eritrea's position is that the scope includes all the islands of the Zuqar-Hanish

chain, the Haycocks and the Mohabbakahs, and also the northern islands of Jabal al-Tayr and the Zubayr group. Yemen, however, though claiming all the islands of the Zuqar-Hanish chain, including, in their view, the Haycocks and the Mohabbakahs, does not concede that the northern islands are in dispute in this arbitration.

85. The contention of Yemen, as mentioned above, is that the respective positions of the two Parties at the time of the Agreement on Principles (21 May 1996) were different from what they became at the time of the subsequent Arbitration Agreement (3 October 1996). According to Yemen, at the time of the Agreement on Principles, Eritrea was apparently not seeking to claim the northern islands or to bring them within the scope of the arbitration, although it may be noted that there was already an existing dispute over the northern islands.[4] It seems clear, moreover, that Yemen, at the time of the Agreement on Principles, was not claiming the Mohabbakahs.

86. But, according to Yemen, the date of the Agreement on Principles is "the critical date" for the determination by the Tribunal of the "respective positions of the two Parties" on which the scope of the Arbitration is to be decided, because it was the date of the definitive agreement of the Parties to submit the matter to this Arbitration. From this proposition Yemen concludes that the northern islands do not come within the scope of the present arbitration.

87. This somewhat technical "critical date" argument, fails, in the opinion of the Tribunal, to take sufficient account of the crucial change brought about in the Arbitration Agreement in the specification of the first stage of the Arbitration as being that in which this question of scope was to be determined by the Tribunal. Whereas, in the Agreement on Principles, the decision on scope was to be the whole matter of the first stage, the later Arbitration Agreement joined within that stage both the award on sovereignty and the decision on scope. This now meant that the Tribunal was to decide the issue of scope "on the basis of the respective positions of the two Parties" only after having heard the entire substantive contentions of both Parties on the question of sovereignty. This later provision must throw doubt upon the proposition that the Parties nevertheless intended the earlier date of the Agreement on Principles still to be the critical date for the determination of scope.

88. In addition, the later Arbitration Agreement did not, in its Article 2.2, qualify in any way its use of the phrase "on the basis of the respective positions of the two

---

[4] In a letter dated 4 January 1996, Yemen formally protested an Eritrean oil concession to the Andarko Company which, according to Yemen, constituted "a blatant violation of Yemeni sovereignty over its territorial waters in so far as it extends to the exclusive territorial waters of the Yemeni Jabal al-Tayr and al-Zubayr islands, in addition to the violation of the rights of the Republic of Yemen in the Exclusive Economic Zone."

Parties." If not qualified, the ordinary meaning of that phrase in its context, and in the light of the object and purpose of the Arbitration Agreement, would seem to be that it is "the respective position of the two Parties" as at the date of the Arbitration Agreement, and not at some unspecified date, that should form the basis for the determination by the Tribunal of the scope of the dispute under the Arbitration Agreement.

89. Moreover, and by implication consistent with this analysis, Yemen, although taking some care in various ways to reserve its position on scope, has in fact provided a full argument in support of its claim to sovereignty over Jabal al-Tayr and the Zubayr group, and in the July 1998 supplementary hearings on petroleum agreements, considerably elaborated on that argument.

90. The Tribunal therefore, on the question of the scope of the dispute, prefers the view of Eritrea and accordingly makes an Award on sovereignty in respect of all the islands and islets with respect to which the Parties have put forward conflicting claims, which include Jabal al-Tayr and the Zubayr group, as well as the Haycocks and the Mohabbakahs.

* - * - *

CHAPTER III – Some Particular Features of This Case

In General

91. It is convenient at the outset to call attention to some features of this case. There is one striking difference between the Parties themselves. Yemen traces its existence back to medieval times and even before the establishment of the Ottoman Empire; Eritrea on the other hand became a fully independent state, separate from Ethiopia, in the early 1990s. Nevertheless, Eritrea traces what it regards as its own title to the disputed islands through an historical succession from the Italian colonial period as well as through the post-Second World War period of its federation as part of the ancient country of Ethiopia. Accordingly the Tribunal has been presented by both Parties with great quantities of material put forward as evidence of the establishment of a legal title through the accumulated examples of claims, possession or use or, in the case of Yemen, through consolidation, continuity and confirmation of an "ancient title." All these materials of quite varying character and weight have had to be sifted, analysed and assessed by the Tribunal.

92. Since much of these materials relates to the actions and reactions or conduct of the Parties or of their predecessors, it is well to have in mind that both have experienced periods in which they were preoccupied by civil wars on either side of the Red Sea: Yemen from 1962-1970, and Ethiopia with the severe and bloody conflict with Eritrean rebels which resulted in the independence of Eritrea in 1993.

93. The disputed islands and islets range from small to tiny, are uniformly unattractive, waterless, and habitable only with great difficulty. And yet it is also the fact that they straddle what has been, since the opening of the Suez Canal in 1869, one of the most important and busiest seaways in the world. These contradictory aspects of the disputed islands are reflected in the materials presented to the Tribunal. During the earlier periods the Islands seem often hardly to have been noticed by coastal countries other than by local traditional fishermen who used them for shelter and their waters for anchorage; but did receive considerable attention, amounting even to temporary occupation, from rival colonial powers, notably Great Britain and Italy. This was no doubt because, after the opening of the Canal, this sea, narrowing in its southern part where the Islands are situated, was the principal route from Europe to India, the East Indies and the Far East.

94. The former interest in these Islands of Great Britain, Italy and to a lesser extent of France and the Netherlands, is an important element of the historical materials

presented to the Court* by the Parties, not least because they have had access to the archives of the time, and especially to early papers of the British Governments of the time. Much of this material is interesting and helpful. One general caveat needs, however, to be made. Some of this material is in the form of internal memoranda, from within the archives of the British Foreign Office, as it then was, and also sometimes of the Italian Foreign Office. The Tribunal has been mindful that these internal memoranda do not necessarily represent the view or policy of any government, and may be no more than the personal view that one civil servant felt moved to express to another particular civil servant at that moment: it is not always easy to disentangle the personality elements from what were, after all, internal, private and confidential memoranda at the time they were made.

Critical Date

95. Faced with such a mass of legal and political history, the Tribunal has felt it right to consider whether the notion of the "critical date" or "critical period" might assist in the organisation or the interpretation of this voluminous material. It has noted, however, that the Parties themselves have spoken of a critical date only in relation to the question discussed above: whether, in deciding on the scope of the Arbitration, the critical date is that of the Agreement on Principles or the Agreement on Arbitration. Neither of them has sought to employ a critical date argument in relation to any of the questions involving the substance of the dispute. In this situation the Tribunal has thought it best to follow the example of the1966 award in the arbitration between Argentina and Chile presided over by Lord McNair, and has accordingly "examined all the evidence submitted to it, irrespective of the date of the acts to which such evidence relates."[5]

Uti Possidetis

96. Yemen in its Counter Memorial introduced the doctrine of *uti possidetis* to explain what it holds to have been the legal position of these islands after the dissolution of the Ottoman Empire following the end of the First World War. The position is said to have been, in the words used by Yemen, that "[o]n the dismemberment of an empire like the Ottoman Empire, there is a presumption, both legal and political in character, that the boundaries of the independent states which replace the Empire will correspond to the boundaries of the administrative units of which the dismembered Empire was constituted." The principle of *uti possidetis* presumably provides the legal aspect of this presumption on which Yemen relies. Eritrea strongly contests this.

---

* *Editorial correction: substitute "Tribunal" for "Court."*

[5] Argentina v. Chile (9 Dec. 1966), 16 R.I.A.A. 111, 115; 38 I.L.R. 16, 20 (1969).

97. There is, however, a prior problem regarding the facts on which a legal presumption of *uti possidetis* would purport to be based. For such a legal presumption to operate it is necessary to know what were indeed "the boundaries of the administrative units of which the dismembered Empire was constituted." It is known that by *firmans* issued in 1841, 1866 and 1873, the Sublime Porte granted to the Khedive of Egypt the right to exercise jurisdiction over the African coast of the Red Sea. Presumably this right of jurisdiction over the African coast might naturally have extended to the islands which were in the neighbourhood of the coast and geographically at least seemed to belong to that coast. But how far this jurisdiction extended over the archipelago which is the principal element in the present dispute is to some extent a matter for conjecture. It seems that, unsurprisingly, the *firman* did not mention the archipelago. The sources provided by the Parties in relation to this question are primarily British Foreign Office internal papers and memoranda. And the answers there given were, it is made quite clear, based upon informed speculation. It is known that there were from time to time small Ottoman garrisons upon Zuqar and upon Hanish, and there are suggestions that they came from the Arabian side, and probably had their supplies from that coast.

98. There is particularly the September 1880 memorandum of Sir Edward Hertslet (author of the celebrated and influential *Map of Africa by Treaty*, and Librarian of the Foreign Office) compiled in the Foreign Office for the use of the Board of Trade, which was responsible for lighthouses in the Red Sea and which had sought Foreign Office help with the question of jurisdiction over lighthouse islands. In this memorandum Hertslet carefully distinguished between sovereignty, which the Ottoman Empire possessed over all these possessions, and a right of jurisdiction over the African side, which had been conferred on the Khedive. He drew up three long lists of the islands in the Red Sea. The first list was of the islands which in his opinion could be said to be "in close proximity" to the African coast, and the second list was of those in close proximity to the Arabian coast. The first list includes the Mohabbakahs and the Haycocks; the second list contains the islands in the "Jabel Zukar Group," those in the "Little Harnish Group," and those in the "Great Harnish Group." This memorandum appears to have been accepted as a working paper by both the Foreign Office and the Board of Trade, notwithstanding the fact that the perception of the second group as being "in close proximity" to the Arabian coast might be regarded as questionable in terms of physical geography. The third list was a relatively short one of islands near "the Centre of the Red Sea" including Jabal al-Tayr and the Zubayr group, the jurisdiction over which was thought by Hertslet to be "doubtful," although the sovereignty remained Ottoman.

99. It is doubtful how far it would be right to base a legal presumption of the *uti possidetis* kind upon these speculations of a concerned but not disinterested third-government department; and this quite apart from the legal difficulties of creating a presumption which would be plainly at odds with the specific provision made

for at least some of these islands by Article 16 of the Treaty of Lausanne of 1923.[6] Yemen of course pleads that this was *res inter alios acta.* But Turkey having been in a position to refuse to accept the Treaty of Sèvres, the sovereignty over these islands must have remained with Turkey until the Treaty of Lausanne was signed, and presumably until 1926 when it was ratified. Added to these difficulties is the question of the intertemporal law and the question whether this doctrine of *uti possidetis*, at that time thought of as being essentially one applicable to Latin America, could properly be applied to interpret a juridical question arising in the Middle East shortly after the close of the First World War.

100. Nevertheless, all this material about the position of the Islands during and shortly after the period of the Ottoman Empire remains an instructive element of the legal history of the dispute. It is especially interesting that even when the whole region was under Ottoman rule it was assumed that the powers of jurisdiction and administration over the Islands should be divided between the two opposite coasts.

Article 15, Paragraph 1 of the Arbitration Agreement

101. This paragraph provides as follows:

> Nothing in this Arbitration Agreement can be interpreted as being detrimental to the legal positions or to the rights of each Party with respect to the questions submitted to the Tribunal, nor can affect or prejudice the decision of the Arbitral Tribunal or the considerations and grounds on which those decisions are based.

The Tribunal finds this provision less than perspicuous. A question to the Parties about it evoked different answers; both were to the general effect that this clause was meant as a "without prejudice" clause concerning the arguments and points of view they might wish to present to the Tribunal. As both Parties have fully argued their cases without either of them having occasion to invoke this provision, it seems to the Tribunal best to leave the matter there.

The Task of the Tribunal in the First Stage

102. The Agreement for Arbitration provides in the second paragraph of its Article 2:

> 2. The first stage shall result in an award on territorial sovereignty and on the definition of the scope of the dispute between Eritrea and Yemen. The Tribunal shall decide territorial sovereignty in accordance with the principles, rules and practices of international law applicable to the matter, and on the basis, in

---

[6] Throughout this Award, the date used for the Treaty of Lausanne is its date of signature, in 1923, rather than that of its entry into force (1926). *[Editorial correction: the correct year of entry into force of the Treaty of Lausanne is 1924.]*

particular, of historic titles. The Tribunal shall decide on the definition of the scope of the dispute on the basis of the respective positions of the two Parties.

Several of the clauses of this paragraph call for consideration. First there is the requirement that this stage shall "result in an award on territorial sovereignty." Thus, the Agreement does not require the Tribunal, as is often the case in agreements for arbitration, to make an allocation of territorial sovereignty to the one Party or the other. The result furthermore is to be an award "on" territorial sovereignty not an award "of" territorial sovereignty. The Tribunal would therefore be within its competence to find a common or a divided sovereignty. This follows from the language of the clause freely chosen by the Parties. It seems right that to call attention to the broader possibilities admitted by this unusual arbitration clause. The Tribunal has indeed considered all possibilities.

103. Further consideration must be given to the clause that requires the Tribunal to "decide territorial sovereignty in accordance with the principles, rules and practices of international law applicable in the matter, and on the basis, in particular, of historic titles."

104. As already mentioned, both Parties rely on various elements of evidence of possession and use as creative of title, and this is itself an appeal to what is a familiar kind of historic claim. As Judge Huber said in the *Palmas* case, "[i]t is quite natural that the establishment of sovereignty may be the outcome of a slow evolution, of a progressive intensification of State control."[7]

105. But Yemen also relies primarily upon what it calls specifically an "historic title." This calls for reflection upon the meaning of "title." It refers not to a developing claim but to a clearly established right, or to quote Pollock, "the absolutely or relatively best right to a thing which may be in dispute."[8] It is a matter of law, not of possession, though it would normally indicate a right in law to have possession even if the factual possession is elsewhere.

106. The notion of an historic title is well-known in international law, not least in respect of "historic bays," which are governed by rules exceptional to the normal rules about bays. Historic bays again rely upon a kind of "ancient title": a title that has so long been established by common repute that this common knowledge is itself a sufficient title. But an historic title has also another and different meaning in international law as a title that has been created, or consolidated, by

---

7 Island of Palmas (Neth. v. U.S.) 2 R.I.A.A. 829 at 867 (Apr. 4, 1928). Professor Max Huber, at the time President of the Permanent Court of International Justice, acted as sole arbitrator in proceedings conducted under the auspices of the Permanent Court of Arbitration, pursuant to the 1907 Convention for the Pacific Settlement of International Disputes.

8 Sir Frederick Pollock, A First Book of Jurisprudence 177 (6th ed., 1929).

a process of prescription, or acquiescence, or by possession so long continued as to have become accepted by the law as a title. These titles too are historic in the sense that continuity and the lapse of a period of time is of the essence. Eritrea pleads various forms of this kind of title, and so also does Yemen, which relies upon this latter kind of title as "confirmation" of its "ancient title."

107. The injunction to have regard to historic title "in particular" can hardly be intended to mean that historic title is to be given some priority it might not otherwise possess; for if there is indeed an established title – the best right to possession – then it is by definition a prior right. So perhaps the phrase "in particular" is put in out of abundant caution, lest the Tribunal, faced with a welter of other interests and uses, were to forget that there can be a separate category of title that does not depend upon use and possession, but is itself a right to possession whether or not possession is enjoyed in fact. At any rate, as will appear below, the Tribunal has not failed to examine historic titles of all kinds in its consideration of this case.

108. There have been different points of view between the Parties about the effects of this twofold division of a first stage award on territorial sovereignty and a second stage award on maritime boundaries. It was in the course of the supplementary proceedings on the Parties' petroleum agreements that Yemen became strenuously exercised over the possibility that the Tribunal might be tempted to "prefigure" (a nicely chosen expression) an eventual stage two maritime solution as an element of its thinking about stage one. Thus paragraph 20 of Yemen's written pleadings in the supplementary petroleum agreements phase states as follows:

> This last element [prefiguring] is of particular concern to the Government of Yemen. It is always attractive to seek to discover a basis for dividing a group of islands, not least in an arbitration. The attraction must be the greater when the task of the Tribunal extends to the process of maritime delimitation, and no doubt caution will be needed to avoid a prefiguring of equitable principles and concepts, which are in law only relevant in the second phase of these proceedings.

This paragraph was repeated word for word in Yemen's oral argument in the July 1998 supplementary hearings.

109. A novel feature of Yemen's arguments, introduced at a late stage of the proceedings but clearly and strongly felt, concerned an apparently unacceptable supposition that an equitable solution was being contemplated for the first stage. This was curious, if only because it seems to have been the first and only reference to equity or equitable principles by either Party in [the]* course of the

---

* *Editorial correction: insert the word in brackets.*

pleadings. Furthermore, no member of the Tribunal had mentioned equity or equitable principles.

110. This matter arose again in a somewhat different form in Yemen's answers to four questions put to both Parties at the close of Yemen's oral argument in the supplementary proceedings, and which questions both Parties answered later in writing. The purpose of these questions was simply to ask both Parties how it was that some of their petroleum agreements, particularly those of Yemen, appeared to be drawn to extend to some sort of coastal median line. In response, Yemen felt obliged to "express the strongest possible reservation against the 'prefiguring' of a median line."

111. Eritrea replied, in the Tribunal's view rightly, that Article 2.2 of the Arbitration Agreement requires the Tribunal to "decide territorial sovereignty in accordance with the principles, rules and practices of international law applicable to the matter, and on the basis, in particular, or* historic titles." That formula must include any principles, rules or practices of international law that are found to be applicable to these matters of sovereignty, even if those principles, rules or practices are part of maritime law. Certainly the Tribunal is not in this first stage to delimit any maritime boundaries or to prefigure any such delimitation. But that is an entirely different matter from applying all international law that may [be]** relevant for the purpose of determining sovereignty, which is the province of this first stage.

112. In general, the Tribunal is unable to accept the proposition that the international law governing land territory and the international law governing maritime boundaries are not only different but also discrete, and bear no juridical relevance to each other. Such a theory is indeed disproved by Yemen's own request to the British Government to be allowed to attend the 1989 Lighthouses Conference on the ground that the northern islands were within Yemen's Exclusive Economic Zone.

113. It is well to have the considered view of the Tribunal on these questions stated at the outset of this Award. At the same time, it may be said that the Tribunal has no difficulty in agreeing with Yemen, and indeed also with Eritrea, that there can be no question of even "prefiguring," much less drawing, any maritime boundary line, whether median or indeed a line based on equitable principles, in this first stage of the arbitration.

* - * - *

* *Editorial correction: insert the word in brackets.*

** *Editorial correction: substitute "of" for "or".*

CHAPTER IV – Historic Title and Other Historical Considerations

114. Article 2 of the Agreement for Arbitration enjoins the Tribunal to decide territorial sovereignty in accordance with applicable international law "and on the basis, in particular, of historic title." The Tribunal has thus paid particular attention both to the arguments relating to ancient titles and reversion thereof proposed by Yemen and arguments relating to longstanding attribution of the Mohabbakahs to the colony of Eritrea and to early establishment of titles by Italy pronounced by Eritrea. An important element of Yemen's case is that of an asserted "historic title" to the Islands, and this is indeed reflected in the very language of both the Agreement on Principles and the Arbitration Agreement. Thus the Tribunal fully recognises that the intention of Article 2 is that, among all the relevant international law, particular attention should be accorded to such elements. Notwithstanding its analysis of how the principles, rules and practices of international law generally bear on its decision on territorial sovereignty, the Tribunal has had the most careful regard to historic titles as they bear on this case.

115. For its part, Eritrea makes no argument for sovereignty based on ancient title, in spite of the undeniable antiquity of Ethiopia. Rather, Eritrea in part asserts an historic consolidation of title on the part of Italy during the inter-war period that resulted in a title to the Islands that became effectively transferred to Ethiopia as a result of the territorial dispositions after the defeat of Italy in the Second World War. This argument will naturally fall to be dealt with in the chapters below dealing with the inter-war periods and the armistice and related proceedings at the end of the Second World War.

116. Yemen has asserted an historic or "ancient title" running back in time to the middle ages, under which the Islands are asserted to have formed part of the *Bilad el-Yemen*. This ancient title predated the several occupations by the Ottoman Empire, asserts Yemen, and reverted to modern Yemen after the collapse of the Ottoman Empire at the end of the First World War.

117. It is thus only Yemen that has raised substantial questions of an "historic" or "ancient" title that existed before the second Ottoman occupation of the 19th century; it is therefore to an appreciation of the historical background necessary for an understanding of that claim to an early title that the Tribunal now turns. This chapter will consider the ways in which the overall history of the Arabian peninsula must be understood in then contemporary legal terms, as a preface to the Tribunal's ultimate conclusion on the legal questions concerning "historic titles." In addition, this chapter will address Yemen's theory of "reversion," which is critical to any decision as to the legal effect of an "historic title."

118. Yemen's arguments on historic and ancient title touch upon several important historical considerations. One relates to the identity of historic Yemen and

whether it comprised the islands in dispute. A second questions the existence of a doctrine of reversion recognized in international law, and a third relates to the place of continuity within a concept of reversion of ancient title. Those claims advanced by Eritrea that are based on both history and international law are addressed elsewhere. This chapter further addresses such important historical matters as the tradition of joint use of the Islands' waters by fishermen from both sides of the Red Sea, and the Ottoman allocation of administrative jurisdiction between the two coasts.

119. Yemen's claim is based essentially on an "ancient" or "historical" title pursuant to which the Imam's inherent and inalienable sovereignty extended over the entirety of what historically has been known as *Bilad el-Yemen*, which existed for several centuries and is alleged by Yemen to have included the southern Red Sea islands. This sovereignty is further characterized by Yemen as having remained unaffected by and having survived the Ottoman annexation of Yemen, in spite of the Sublime Porte's having declared Yemen to be one of the *vilayets* falling under Ottoman rule.

120. The arguments advanced by Yemen in this respect must be evaluated within the historical and legal context that prevailed during the relevant period, extending from the end of the 19th century until the dissolution of the Ottoman Empire.

121. The particularity of the relationship between the Ottoman Empire and Yemen should be taken into account as an important historical factor. In spite of the Treaty of Da'an, concluded in 1911, which granted the Imam of Yemen a greater degree of internal autonomy, he remained a suzerain acting within Ottoman sovereignty until the total disintegration of the Ottoman Empire and the loss of all its Arabian possessions, including the *vilayet* of Yemen.[9] It was only in 1923, by virtue of Article 16 of the Treaty of Lausanne, that the Ottoman Empire not only recognized the renunciation of all its sovereignty rights over Yemen, but explicitly renounced its sovereign title over the islands that had previously fallen under the jurisdiction of the Ottoman *wali* in Hodeidah.

122. The territorial extent of Imamic Yemen as an autonomous entity must be distinguished from that of the Ottoman *vilayet* of Yemen. During the entire period from the second half of the 19th century until 1925, the Imam of Yemen had neither sovereignty nor jurisdiction over the Tihama and the Red Sea coasts. Under his agreements with the Ottoman sultan, the Imam administered an exclusively land-locked territory, limited to the high mountains. The Ottoman *wali* exercised exclusive jurisdiction over the coasts until 1917. Thereafter, the

---

[9] See, in particular, JOHN BALDRY, *One Hundred Years of Yemeni History: 1849-1948*, in L'ARABIE DU SUD VOL. II at 85 (J. CHELHOD ET AL., EDS.,1984); ROGER JOINT DAGUENET, HISTOIRE DE LA MER ROUGE: DE LESSEPS À NOS JOURS 113-116, 186-190, 240-241 (1997).

coasts came under the control of the Idrisi, a local tribal ruler supported first by the Italians, and later by the British Government. The coast came under the Imam's rule only in 1926. As will be seen later, this fact has negative legal implications for the "reversion" argument advanced by Yemen, as well as for the application of certain other rules of international law, including the concept of ancient "historic title" in its full classical sense.

123. There can be no doubt that the concept of historic title has special resonance in situations that may exist even in the contemporary world, such as determining the sovereignty over nomadic lands occupied during time immemorial by given tribes who owed their allegiance to the ruler who extended his socio-political power over that geographic area. A different situation exists with regard to uninhabited islands which are not claimed to be falling within the limits of historic waters.

124. In the present case, neither Party has formulated any claim to the effect that the disputed islands are located within historic waters. Moreover, none of the Islands is inhabited on other than a seasonal or temporary basis, or even has the natural and physical conditions that would permit sustaining continual human presence. Whatever may have been the links between the coastal lands and the islands in question, the relinquishment by the Ottoman Empire of its sovereignty over the Islands by virtue of Article 16 of the 1923 Treaty of Lausanne (discussed in greater detail in Chapter V) logically and legally adversely affects any pre-existing title.

125. It was recognized in the course of the oral hearings that, by the law in force at the time, Ottoman sovereignty over the regions in question was lawful. The fact that Yemen was not a party to the Treaty of Lausanne, and that it perceived both the British and the Italians as having been usurpers in the Red Sea, does not negate that legal consequence. It has not been established in these proceedings to the satisfaction of the Tribunal that the doctrine of reversion is part of international law. In any event, the Tribunal concludes that on the facts of this case it has no application. No "reversion" could possibly operate, since the chain of titles was necessarily interrupted and whatever previous merits may have existed to sustain such claim could hardly be invoked. During several decades, the predominant role was exercised by the western naval powers in the Red Sea after its opening to international maritime traffic through the Suez Canal, as well as through the colonization of the southern part of the Red Sea on both coasts. An important result of that hegemony was the maintenance of the status quo imposed after the First World War, in particular that the sovereignty over the islands covered by Article 16 of the Lausanne Treaty of 1923 remained indeterminate at least as long as the interested western powers were still in the region. As long as that colonial situation prevailed, neither Ethiopia nor Yemen was in a position to demonstrate any kind of historic title that could serve as a sufficient basis to confirm sovereignty over any of the disputed islands. Only after the departure of the

colonial powers did the possibility of a change in the status quo arise. A change in the status quo does not, however, necessarily imply a reversion.

126. This should not, however, be construed as depriving historical considerations of all legal significance. In the first place, the conditions that prevailed during many centuries with regard to the traditional openness of southern Red Sea marine resources for fishing, its role as means for unrestricted traffic from one side to the other, together with the common use of the Islands by the populations of both coasts, are all important elements capable of creating certain "historic rights" which accrued in favour of both Parties through a process of historical consolidation as a sort of "*servitude internationale*" falling short of territorial sovereignty.[10] Such historic rights provide a sufficient legal basis for maintaining certain aspects of a *res communis* that has existed for centuries for the benefit of the populations on both sides of the Red Sea. In the second place, the distinction in terms of jurisdiction which existed under the Ottoman Empire between those islands administered from the African coast and the other islands administered from the Arabian coast constitutes a historic fact to be taken into consideration.

127. According to the most reliable historical and geographical sources, both ancient and modern, the reported data clearly indicate that the population living around the southern part of the Red Sea on the two opposite coasts have always been inter-linked culturally and engaged in the same type of socio-economic activities. Since times immemorial, they were not only conducting exchanges of a human and commercial nature, but they were freely fishing and navigating throughout the maritime space using the existing islands as way stations (*des îles relais*) and occasionally as refuge from the strong northern winds. These activities were carried out for centuries without any need to obtain any authorizations from the rulers on either the Asian or the African side of the Red Sea and in the absence of restrictions or regulations exercised by public authorities.

128. This traditionally prevailing situation reflected deeply rooted cultural patterns leading to the existence of what could be characterized from a juridical point of view as *res communis* permitting the African as well as the Yemeni fishermen to operate with no limitation throughout the entire area and to sell their catch at the local markets on either side of the Red Sea. Equally, the persons sailing for fishing or trading purposes from one coast to the other used to take temporary refuge from the strong winds on any of the uninhabited islands scattered in that

---

[10] See in this respect, Yehuda Z. Blum, *Historic Rights*, in 7 ENCYCLOPEDIA OF PUBLIC INTERNATIONAL LAW 120 *et seq.*; and YEHUDA Z. BLUM, HISTORIC TITLES IN INTERNATIONAL LAW 126-129 (1965).

maritime zone without encountering difficulties of a political or administrative nature.[11]

129. These historical facts are witnessed through a variety of sources submitted in evidence during the arbitral proceedings. A comprehensive evaluation of the evidence submitted by both Parties reveals the presence of deeply-rooted common patterns of behaviour as well as the continuation, even in recent years, of cross-relationships which are marked by eventual recourse to professional fishermen's arbitrators (*aq'il*) in charge of settling disputes in accordance with the local customary law. Such understanding finds support in the statements attributed to fishermen from both coasts of the Red Sea, taken as a whole, which have been submitted by both Parties.

130. The socio-economic and cultural patterns described above were perfectly in harmony with classical Islamic law concepts, which practically ignored the principle of "territorial sovereignty" as it developed among the European powers and became a basic feature of 19th century western international law.[12]

131. However, it must be noted that the Ottoman Empire, which directly or through its suzerains governed the quasi-totality of the countries around the Red Sea during the first half of the 19th Century including *Bilad El-Yemen* and what became known thereafter as Eritrea, started after the end of the Crimean War in 1856 to abandon the communal aspects of the Islamic system of international law and to adopt the modern rules prevailing among the European concert of nations to which the Sublime Porte became a fully-integrated party during the Berlin Congress of 1875. According to this new modern international law, the legal concept of "territorial sovereignty" became a cornerstone for most of the state powers, and the situation in the Red Sea could no longer escape the juridical consequences of that new reality.

132. Hence, it is understandable that both Parties are in agreement that the islands in dispute initially all fell under the territorial sovereignty of the Ottoman Empire. Within the exercise of the Ottoman's sovereignty over these islands, it has to be noted that the Sublime Porte granted to the Khedive of Egypt the right to administer the Ottoman possessions (*vilayet*) on the African Coast which at

---

[11] See in particular, CHARLES FORSTER, THE HISTORICAL GEOGRAPHY OF ARABIA, VOL. I at 113, VOL. II at 337 (1984) (first published in 1844); JOSEPH CHELHOD ET AL., L'ARABIE DU SUD – HISTOIRE ET CIVILISATION, VOL. I, at 63, 67-69, 252-255 (1984); ROGER JOINT DAGUENET, HISTOIRE DE LA MER ROUGE: DE MOÏSE A BONAPARTE 20-24, 86-87 (1995); and YVES THORAVAL ET AL., LE YEMEN ET LA MER ROUGE 14-16, 17-20, 35-37, 43-47, 51-54 (1995).

[12] See in particular, A. SANHOURY, LE CALIFAT 22, 37, 119, 163, 273, 320-321 (1926); Majid Kadouri, *Islamic Law*, in 6 ENCYCLOPEDIA OF PUBLIC INTERNATIONAL LAW 227 *et seq.*; and Ahmed S. El Kosheri, *History of Islamic Law*, in 7 ENCYCLOPEDIA OF PUBLIC INTERNATIONAL LAW 222 *et seq.*

present form "the State of Eritrea," and this delegation of power included jurisdiction over islands off the African Coast, including the Dahlaks and eventually the Mohabbakahs.

133. The sovereignty of the Ottoman Empire over both coasts of the Red Sea is undisputed up to 1880 and this remained the case with regard to the eastern, or Arabian, coast until the First World War. Among the various documents introduced in support of this historical fact, Eritrea has submitted the French-language version of a memorandum dated 6 December 1881, issued by the Egyptian Khedival Ministry of Foreign Affairs, which indicates that in May 1871, Italy recognised that the Ottoman flag had been flying since 1862 over the African Coast at a point going beyond the south of Assab. The Egyptian memorandum added that until 1880 the Egyptian Government believed the affirmation of the Italian Government that the Italian presence had been essentially of private and commercial character. Consequently, the entire African coast and the islands off that coast remained until then under the Khedive's jurisdiction. At the same time, all other islands were, and continued to be, under the jurisdiction of the Ottoman *wali* stationed in Hodeidah and appointed by the Sublime Porte.

134. Hence, a clear distinction has to be made between the Red Sea islands which were under jurisdiction of the Khedive of Egypt acting on behalf of the Ottoman Empire until 1882 and the other Red Sea islands which remained under the Ottoman *vilayet* of Yemen until the dissolution of the Empire after the First World War.

135. A British Foreign Office Memorandum dated 10 June 1930, relying expressly on the Hertslet memorandum of 1880, indicates that the Khedive of Egypt exercised jurisdiction off the African coast over the "Mohabakah Islands, Harbi and Sayal." With regard to the other category, the British Memorandum describes "the Great Hanish group as being off the Arabic Coast and consequently under the sovereignty and within the exclusive jurisdiction of the Sultan."

Paragraph 16 of the same Memorandum emphasised that:

> Great Hanish, Suyal Hanish, Little Hanish, Jebal Zukur, Abu Ail, being nearer to the Arabian Coast, appear before the war to have been considered as under both the jurisdiction and sovereignty of Turkey.

136. Furthermore, Eritrea has submitted Italian Colonial Ministry documents, including a note dated 11 October 1916, entitled "The Red Sea Islands," reflecting the findings of an inquiry conducted on the Islands themselves. After devoting Part I to "Farsan" and Part II to "Kameran," Part III of the note deals with "the other islands," which included what is referred to as "Gebel Zucur." This heading included not only the "group of 12 sizeable rocks," but also "the

two great and small Hanish islands." With regard to these islands, it was noted that "[t]he Ottoman authorities kept a small garrison of 40 there under the command of a Mulazim to monitor the movement of importation vessels to the Yemen Coast from Gibut," and further that, "faced with the difficulties of supplying water and victuals on account of a shortage of resources, the Ottoman authorities withdrew the garrison." After the bombardment of Midi by Italian warships, the Ottoman authorities are said to have "restored the garrison in 1909 and increased the number of askaris to 100."

137. These Italian colonial documents, which confirm Ottoman sovereignty over the Hanish-Zuqar Islands and assert that they continued in 1916 to be administered by the *vilayet* of Yemen, are consistent with the views expressed in a telegram addressed by the Governor of the Eritrean Colony to the Italian Minister of the Colonies and transmitted on 18 October 1916 to the Italian Minister of Foreign Affairs. A Foreign Ministry note entitled: "The Red Sea Islands," dating back to 31 July 1901, is attached thereto as "Appendix II." The 1901 Note bases the division of the Islands into three groups:

> The most northerly islands, which are of little or almost no relation to the Colony of Eritrea on account of the distance, those facing Massaua and the most southerly islands which are opposite the Eritrean Coasts of Beilul and Assab. Almost all are found on the eastern coast of the Red Sea, except the Dahalac islands, which are under our rule, and a few others of much less importance.

With regard to the second group, the Italian note indicates:

> Leaving aside the archipelago of the Dahalac islands – which is under the sovereignty of Italy and which include the biggest islands in the Red Sea – Cotuma, Diebel Tair and Camaran are notable in this second group of the archipelago; all of which under Turkish rule.

The note explicitly characterizes as "Turkish": "Cotuma," "Djebel . . . called Gebel Sebair" and "Camaran."

Turning to the third group, the 1901 Italian note refers to a:

> . . . group of islands known as Hanish or Harnish (Turkish). It comprises the island of Gebel Zucar, large and small Hanish islands and the other minor islands of Abu-ail, Syul-Hanish, Haycoc and Mohabbach, and a few islets amounting to large rocks.

138. Contemporary British documents also reflect the view that the islands in question, with the exception of [the]* Mohabbakahs, formed part of the *vilayet* of

---

* *Editorial correction: insert the word in brackets.*

Yemen, and appear to link their future disposition to this historical attachment to the Arabian Coast.

139. A Foreign Office Memorandum dated 15 January 1917 and entitled "Italy and the Partition of the Turkish Empire" provides in paragraph 38:

> Lastly, everyone seems to be agreed that the islands in the Red Sea which were previously under Turkish sovereignty pass naturally to the Arab State, though some special regime will be necessary in Kamaran Island in view of the pilgrim traffic.

140. Lord Balfour, in a 13 March 1919 letter to Lord Curzon, indicated that the solution envisaged for "Abu Ail, Zabayir and Jebel Teir" as well as "Kamaran, Zukur and the Hanish Islands (Great Hanish, Little Hanish and Suyul Hanish group)" was either "to annex them" to the British Empire or "to claim that they should be handed over to some independent Arab rulers on the mainland other than the Imam of Sanaa or the Idrisi."

141. Lord Curzon's letter addressed to Lord Balfour on 27 May 1919 linked the subject of any handover to Arab rulers with the essentially political question of the area's future, "the whole question of the future of the Red Sea Islands" was to be considered "ultimately bound with that of the future status of Arabia." Therefore, Lord Curzon indicated that:

> [t]he policy of his Majesty's Government should in the first place be directed towards the recognition by the High Contracting Parties of the fact that the islands form a part of the mainland and will accordingly become the property of the Arabian rulers concerned; and that these rulers are to be in special relation with His Majesty's Government.

142. As will be expanded upon later, the allocation of administrative powers over the Red Sea islands, whether by the Ottoman Empire acting as sovereign power on both coasts or only as exercising jurisdiction from the Arabian Coast alone, represents an historic fact that should be taken into consideration and given a certain legal weight.

143. Before leaving this study of the historical considerations, it is necessary to recall the question of ancient or historic Yemeni title, to which Yemen gave such crucial importance in the presentation of its case. It has been explained in this chapter that there are certain historical problems about this argument. First, there is the historical fact that medieval Yemen was mainly a mountain entity with little sway over the coastal areas, which were essentially dedicated to serving the flow of maritime trade between, on the one hand, India and the East Indies, and on the other, Egypt and the other Mediterranean ports. Second, the concept of territorial sovereignty was entirely strange to an entity such as medieval Yemen. Indeed, the concept of territorial sovereignty in the terms of modern international

law came late (not until the 19th century) to the Ottoman Empire, which claimed, and was recognized as having, territorial sovereignty over the entire region.

144. But there are other problems with the Yemeni claim to an ancient title, in particular the effect of Article 16 of the Treaty of Lausanne and the necessity of establishing some doctrine of continuity of ancient title and of reversion at the end of the Ottoman Empire. This subject is explored in detail in the following chapter, and the final view of the Tribunal on this question of ancient title is expressed in Chapter X.

* - * - *

CHAPTER V – The Legal History and Principal Treaties and Other Legal Instruments Involved; Questions of State Succession

145. The series of major instruments engaging, in various combinations, the maritime users of the Red Sea form an important backdrop to the legal claims of the Parties in this arbitration. Their binding nature or otherwise, their status as directly legally significant or as *res inter alios acta*, and the meaning of their terms, have all engaged the attention of the Parties.

146. The so-called Treaty of Da'an of 1911 was in fact an internal instrument by which the Imam of Yemen obtained for himself greater internal powers of autonomy within the Ottoman Empire. However, sovereignty over all the Ottoman possessions, including the islands in dispute, remained vested in the Empire itself until it was legally divested of its Arabian possessions after the First World War.

147. The Principal Allied Powers (the British Empire, France, Italy and Japan) agreed at Mudros an armistice with Turkey on 30 October 1918. The 1918 Armistice of Mudros was a vehicle for ending hostilities and indeed for permitting belligerent occupation. It was not an instrument for the transfer of territory. It is not disputed that immediately before the signing of the Armistice of Mudros title to all the islands was Ottoman. It was further agreed in these proceedings that Ottoman title had been secured by military occupation, which was lawful by reference to the international law of the day. An essential component of sovereign title is the right to alienate. Just as the Ottoman Empire would have been free to cede title to the islands to a third state at any time during the period 1872 to 1918, so it still had the legal right itself to determine where title should go after 1918. Its freedom in this regard was curtailed not by the operation of a doctrine of reversion which would spring into operation upon any divesting of title by Turkey, but by the realities of power at the end of the War.

148. It cannot be the case therefore that title passed in 1918 to the Imam. Accordingly the Tribunal is not able to accept that sovereignty over the islands in dispute reverted to Yemen.

149. It was intended that a treaty of peace, containing the future settlement of Turkish territory in Europe and elsewhere, should follow the 1918 Armistice of Mudros. To that end, the Principal Allied Powers (forming together with Armenia, Belgium, Greece, the Hedjaz, Poland, Portugal, Roumania, the Serb-Croat-Slovene State and Czechoslovakia the "Allied Powers") on the one hand, and Turkey on the other, signed a Treaty of Peace at Sèvres on 10 August 1920. The long and detailed provisions contained but a single clause that might have had

application to the islands in the Red Sea in dispute in the present case. Article 132 provided:

> Outside her frontiers as fixed by the present Treaty Turkey hereby renounces in favour of the Principal Allied Powers all rights and title which she could claim on any ground over or concerning any territories outside Europe which are not otherwise disposed of by the present Treaty.
>
> Turkey undertakes to recognize and conform to the measures which may be taken now or in the future by the Principal Allied Powers, in agreement where necessary with third Powers, in order to carry the above stipulation into effect.

150. In the event, the Treaty of Sèvres was not ratified by Turkey and did not enter into effect. Accordingly, title to the Red Sea islands in dispute must thus have remained with Turkey – even though it knew that it would in due course be required to divest itself of such title. Indeed, Great Britain had been occupying certain islands since 1915 to forestall Italian activity, and had been displaying the flag but without claiming title.

151. The initial position of Great Britain at the peace talks at Sèvres was that the islands lying east of the South West Rocks off Greater Hanish Island should be placed under the sovereignty of the independent chiefs of the Arabian mainland. The British appreciated that reasons of history and geography would make the Arab mainland rulers strong claimants when Turkey finally relinquished title and future sovereignty had to be determined, and indeed that their desire to exclude any European Power from establishing themselves on the east coast would make the passing of title to a "friendly Arab ruler" a desirable outcome.[13] But that is a different matter from title passing automatically by reversion from Turkey to Yemen. In the event, a different proposal was agreed in Article 132 of the Treaty of Sèvres.

152. Much has been made by Yemen of the fact that throughout the years that ensued, the Imam protested to Great Britain that "the islands" had not been returned. These "islands" were not specified. While this may indeed support allegations of the existence of a Yemeni claim, there is no evidence that it was either intended, or interpreted, to include the islands in dispute in the present case. Furthermore, a state's protests about the refusal of others to allow it to exercise effective control over what it maintains in[*] its own territory have little legal significance if

---

13 Compare the policy objective that was explored by the Foreign Office for the islands of Sheikh Saal, Kamaran, and Farsan, and for Hodeidah, namely occupation. In the event, a 1915 telegram from the Viceroy of India indicates that the British flag had been hoisted on Jabal Zuqar and the Hanish Islands. These events were characterized, in a message to the Foreign Office from the British Resident in Aden as a "temporary annexation." By 1926 Britain did not regard itself as holding sovereign title.

* *Editorial correction: substitute "is" for "in."*

the protesting state does not, in fact, have title. More relevant is the fact that Turkey undoubtedly had title in 1918 and failed to divest itself in 1920. The instrument by which it did finally divest itself was the Treaty of Lausanne in 1923.

153. The Imam was not a party to the Treaty of Lausanne and in that technical sense the Treaty was *res inter alios acta* as to Yemen. If title had lain with Yemen at that time, the parties to the Treaty of Lausanne could not have transferred title elsewhere without the consent of Yemen. But, as indicated above, title still remained with Turkey. Boundary and territorial treaties made between two parties are *res inter alios acta* vis-à-vis third parties. But this special category of treaties also represents a legal reality which necessarily impinges upon third states, because they have effect *erga omnes*. If State A has title to territory and passes it to State B, then it is legally without purpose for State C to invoke the principle of *res inter alios acta*, unless its title is better than that of A (rather than of B). In the absence of such better title, a claim of *res inter alios acta* is without legal import.

154. These are the legal realities with which an analysis of the Treaty of Lausanne must be approached. Two further realities are, as stated just above, that the Imam had asserted claims during this period though without specificity as to which particular islands his claims attached, and that Italy, by its conduct, had also revealed its aspirations for the islands. The formulation of the Treaty of Lausanne was undoubtedly agreed upon in full knowledge both of the position of the Imam and the ambitions of Italy.

155. Great Britain (which had briefly in 1915 sent troops to Jabal Zuqar and the Hanish Islands) had been interested at one stage in an amendment to Article 132 of the Treaty of Sèvres which would have added to the rather general Turkish renunciation of all "rights and title" a specific clause which referred to "any islands in the Red Sea." As the first paragraph of this proposal referred to rights and title in the Arabian peninsula, it may be assumed that Great Britain thought the islands were not encompassed in that reference, but that some particular provision was needed if they too were to pass out of Turkish title. The Treaty of Lausanne, signed in 1923, did make reference to islands as well as to territories though by now the earlier proposal that underlay the abortive Treaty of Sèvres (that Turkish title should pass to the Allied Powers,[14] whether as a condominium or otherwise) was dropped.

---

[14] The Treaty of Lausanne, entered into five years after the end of hostilities, in fact uses the term "High Contracting Parties" rather than Allied Powers. Those High Contracting Parties were the British Empire, France, Italy, Japan, Greece, Roumania and the Serb-Croat-Slovene State on the one hand, and Turkey on the other.

156. Article 6 provided that, in the absence of provisions to the contrary, islands and islets lying within three miles of the coast are included within the frontier of the coastal state. While some of the Dahlaks and some of the Assab islands would have fallen outside the three-mile limit, they were generally regarded as appurtenant to the African littoral and thus belonging to Italy. The Mohabbakahs (the nearest being almost six miles away) and the Haycocks did not fall within the provisions, though, as will be shown below, Italian *jurisdiction* over them had been acknowledged. Whether or not the Mohabbakahs are islets rather than islands, and notwithstanding that Article 6 refers to islets, whereas Article 16 did not, the Mohabbakahs were not islets transferred to Italian title by virtue of Article 6.

157. Article 15 provided for the renunciation, in favour of Italy, of certain specified and named islands in the Aegean. Article 16 provided as follows:

> Turkey hereby renounces all rights and title whatsoever over or respecting the territories situated outside the frontiers laid down in the present Treaty and the islands other than those over which her sovereignty is recognized by the said Treaty, the future of those territories and islands being settled or to be settled by the parties concerned . . . .

158. Although "territories" and "islands" are separately mentioned, their treatment under Article 16 is identical. These phrases presumably covered also those islets not transferred by operation of Article 6. What was intended by "the parties concerned" is not wholly clear, but, given the knowledge of the claims of the Imam, as well as the hopes of Italy, and given further that the phrase used elsewhere in the Treaty is "The High Contracting Parties," it is not unreasonable to conclude that what was envisaged was a settlement of the matter in the future by all those having legal claims or high political interest in the islands, whether Treaty of Lausanne High Contracting Parties or not. A 1923 British Foreign Office document acknowledges, for example, the likelihood of France, Italy and Yemen being "interested parties." This interpretation accords with the assurances that Italy gave the Imam, at the time of the signature of the 1938 Anglo-Italian Agreement, that Yemen's "interests" had been "kept in mind," and with the working assumptions of the British Board of Trade with respect to the 1923 Treaty of Lausanne, that the "local Arab rulers on the mainland might put in their claim to be 'interested' parties."

159. It is not certain whether in 1923 either Great Britain or Italy would have regarded the reference to islands in the Red Sea over which Turkey had title as including the Haycocks. This was because Italian jurisdiction in those islands had already been acknowledged. Until the very end of the 19th century the Ottomans treated those living in Eritrea as being of Turkish nationality and subject to Ottoman jurisdiction. But certain accommodations were being reached. Italy had in 1883, 1887 and 1888 entered into a series of agreements with local Eritrean leaders.

The Treaty of 1883 with the King of Shoa provided that "Italy will protect on the sea coast the safety of the Danakil littoral" (Art. VIII) and that "Italy will watch over the security of the sea and the Colony" (Art. IX). By Article V, the Sultan Mohamed Hanfari ceded to Italy "the use of the territory of Ablis." In 1887 a further treaty, which seems to have no special relevance for the matters at issue, was signed. In 1888 a Treaty of Friendship and Commerce between Italy and the Head of the Danakils provided that Italy would guarantee the security of the Danakil coast. Further "The Sultan Mohamed Anfari recognises the whole of the Danakil coast from Afila to Ras Dumeira as an Italian possession" (Article 111). As a British Foreign Office Memorandum in 1930 was later to put it ". . . the Italian rights of surveillance drifted into what was tantamount to territorial rights to the littoral" and Great Britain, having made no protest, "could not now fall back upon the terms of the Agreement of May, 1887."

160. Exploring the possibility of a new shipping route on the African side of the Red Sea, and the need to light it, the British government wrote to the Italian government in 1892 referring to the proposed sites: North East Quoin (or alternatively Rahamet, on the coast), South West Rocks, "one of the Haycocks" and Harbi – and suggested that under Article 111 of the 1888 Treaty they appeared to be within the jurisdiction of Italy (though doubt was expressed internally about South West Rocks). It seems likely that this reading of Article 111 of the 1888 Treaty – which is not on its face self-evident – was influenced by the Hertslet memorandum of 1880 and its attached list. That memorandum spoke of the western coast of the Red Sea as being under the jurisdiction of the Khedive of Egypt and the east coast as under the jurisdiction of the Sultan. Hertslet suggested that "the various islands and reefs in close proximity to the coast, and which are enumerated in List 1, would appear to be under" the Khedive's jurisdiction. List 1 includes "Harbi," White Quoin Hill, and "Mah-hab-bakah." The "Jibbel Zukur," "Little Harnish" and "Great Harnish" groups are attributed to the Eastern coast. "Haycock" appears twice within the list of islands appurtenant and in proximity to the east coast. As to the islands "near the centre" (listed by Hertslet as "Jibbel Teer" and the "Zebayar Group"), including a further Haycock, Hertslet in 1880 thought that "jurisdiction over the islands . . . would appear to be doubtful; but the sovereignty over them no doubt belongs to the Sultan."

161. It must also be noted that others within the British diplomatic service placed less weight on proximity.[15] Italy was asked whether it did indeed claim jurisdiction. Italy confirmed that "the places mentioned" were subject to its own jurisdiction. British recognition of Italian jurisdiction over the Haycocks (and presumably *a fortiori* of the Mohabbakahs) occurred in 1892. In 1930, internal British memoranda speak of Italian sovereignty over South West Haycock (or

[15] See Reilly, ADEN AND YEMEN, Colonial Office 1960, 69-70.

sometimes, simply "the Haycocks") as having occurred in June 1892. But it was added "[e]xcept *as against ourselves*, the Italian claim to sovereignty over these islands does not appear to be very strong" (emphasis added).

162. Later evidence indicates that Great Britain regarded the issue of sovereignty as unsettled, even if Italian jurisdiction was acknowledged. Both the Mohabbakahs and the Haycocks would thus in 1923 be regarded by the Lausanne Treaty parties as Turkish territory falling, as to sovereignty, within the reach of Article 16, notwithstanding intermittent acceptance that they were under the jurisdiction of Italy.

163. The situation is clearer as regards Abu Ali, Jabal al-Tayr and the Zubayr group. They were envisaged at the time as having belonged to the Ottomans (but as never having previously been claimed by the Imam). These three islands fell under the terms of Article 16 of the Treaty of Lausanne.

164. There are three key points at issue in respect of Article 16. The first is the legal implications of it being *res inter alios acta* in respect of Yemen. The second is what islands in fact fell under this provision, i.e., were still under Ottoman sovereignty up to the date of the Treaty. The Tribunal has addressed these points above (see paras. 153-159). And the third is whether Article 16 either permitted acquisitive prescription by a single state of some or all of these islands and, if not, whether such acquisitive prescription could and did nonetheless occur (even if in violation of a treaty obligation).

165. The correct analysis of Article 16 is, in the Tribunal's view, the following: in 1923 Turkey renounced title to those islands over which it had sovereignty until then. They did not become *res nullius* – that is to say, open to acquisitive prescription – by any state, including any of the High Contracting Parties (including Italy). Nor did they automatically revert (insofar as they had ever belonged) to the Imam. Sovereign title over them remained indeterminate *pro tempore*. Great Britain certainly regarded it as likely that some undefined islands which "pertained to the Yemen" were covered by Article 16. Indeterminacy could be resolved by "the parties concerned" at some stage in the future – which must mean by present (or future) claimants *inter se*. That phrase is incompatible with the possibility that a single party could unilaterally resolve the matter by means of acquisitive prescription.

166. Given the Great Power politics in the region, the application of these legal principles was inevitably sometimes less than clear. Great Britain in fact secured jurisdiction over Kamaran island in this fashion; the records show that British civil servants and ministers over the years continued to entertain notions of appropriation of particular islands; but Great Britain was at pains to ensure the continued efficacy of Article 16 so far as Italian acts were concerned, through frequent enquiries to the Italian Government.

167. The islands to which the Article 16 proviso applied at the outset were therefore the Mohabbakahs, the Haycocks, South West Rocks, and certainly the Zuqar-Hanish group, Abu Ali, Jabal al-Tayr and the Zubayr group.

168. Far from the Treaty of Lausanne "paving the way" for Italian sovereignty, as has been suggested by Eritrea, it presented a formidable obstacle. It is arguable that acquisitive prescription might nonetheless have been effected by Italy in the face of its obligations should the other parties to the Treaty of Lausanne have so allowed. Italy would have tried to secure the most favourable position, both on the ground and in diplomacy, for that day in the future when title would be determined. In terms of political aspiration, *animus occupandi* undoubtedly existed. But whether claims to sovereignty were made and acknowledged, so that certain islands would be effectively *au dehors* the reach of Article 16 of the Treaty of Lausanne, must be doubtful. Still less plausible is the contention that the High Contracting Parties (and Great Britain in particular) would have allowed, or acquiesced in, an incremental assumption of sovereignty by Italy.

The 1927 Rome Conversations

169. This conclusion is confirmed by the history following the Treaty of Lausanne. In 1927, conversations took place in Rome between the Italian Government and the British Government relating to British and Italian interests in Southern Arabia and the Red Sea ("the Rome Conversations"). In the signed record they agreed to cooperate in seeking to secure the pacification of Ibn Saud, the Imam Yahya and the Idrisi of Asir; and noted that Great Britain regarded it as "a vital imperial interest that no European Power should establish itself on the Arabian shore of the Red Sea, and more particularly on Kamaran or the Farsan islands, and that neither . . . shall fall into the hands of an unfriendly Arab Ruler." This proviso was repeated, *pari passu,* in respect of the west coast and Kamaran and the Farsan Islands.

170. No such specific reference was made to the other islands now in dispute. Whereas Articles 4 and 6 apply to Kamaran and Farsan, Article 5 must, in the view of the Tribunal, be taken to apply to the other islands in dispute. Article 5 provided:

> That there should be economic and commercial freedom on the Arabian coast and the islands of the Red Sea for citizens and subjects of the two countries and that the protection which such citizens and subjects may legitimately expect from their respective governments should not assume a political character or complexion.

171. This article can only be understood to mean that acts which might otherwise be construed as providing an incremental acquisition of sovereignty were by the agreement of the parties not to be so construed. To seek to identify acts "having a sovereign character" thus became without legal purpose.

172. Eritrea has argued that no legal weight is to be given to these provisions, in the first place because this record was not registered under Article 18 of the Covenant of the League of Nations and in the second place because it cannot be invoked by Yemen, either for that reason or because it was *res inter alios acta*. That this was not registered was undoubtedly because it was not regarded as a treaty between states. But it was nonetheless an accurate account of what both parties had agreed and was signed by them as such. It is simply evidence of the thinking of the time – this time by both parties – in much the same way as the Tribunal has been presented with a myriad of other evidence in non-treaty form. Insofar as Yemen wishes to draw it to the attention of the Tribunal, it is not relying on a treaty that is *res inter alios acta*, nor indeed resting its own claim on it. It is diplomatic evidence, like any other, but of an undoubted interest because it reflects what was recorded by both parties as that which they had agreed to.

173. The provisions of Article 5 of the Rome Conversations were, of course, fully consistent with Article 16 of the Treaty of Lausanne, and indeed reinforced it. The former did not replace the latter but rather provided a further mechanism for assuring that fishing, commercial and navigation-related activities could continue without the indeterminate status of the islands being jeopardised.

174. Italy and Great Britain each now sought to ensure that sovereignty was indeed reserved. When Great Britain proposed to France certain arrangements concerning the management of the old Ottoman lighthouses at Abu Ali, Jabal al-Tayr, Centre Peak and Mocha, Italy asked for acknowledgment that the last belonged to Yemen and that sovereignty was reserved as to the first three islands. Great Britain was able to provide this. And when it was learned in London that Italy was preparing to build a lighthouse on South West Haycock (which it thought of as part of the Mohabbakahs) Great Britain sought assurance that the Haycocks as well as the Hanish Islands were indeed viewed by Italy as falling under Article 5 of the Rome Conversations. Italy in 1930 informed Great Britain that it had sovereignty over South West Haycock, regarding which it made a specific reservation, that it lay in the Mohabbakahs, that it was prepared for South West Haycocks and the rest of the Hanish Islands to be treated in accordance with Article 5 of the Rome Conversations. The British reaction was not to take up the offer of talks from Italy, lest Italy should seek to have its sovereignty over South West Haycock "settled" within Article 16 of the Treaty of Lausanne, but rather tacit acceptance that everything should be treated under the framework of Article 5 of the Rome Conversations.

175. In 1931, further assurances were received from Italy over its establishment of armed posts on Greater Hanish and Jabal Zuqar. Italy assured Great Britain that these posts were for the protection of concessionaires and that sovereignty over the Hanish islands remained in abeyance. The juridical status of these islands was said to be the same as that of Farsan and Kamaran in the Rome Conversations of 1927. Further, Italy recalled that it had in 1926, during the negotiation of the

abortive Lighthouse Convention of 1930, confirmed that sovereignty over Abu Ali, Zubayr and Jabal al-Tayr was equally to remain in abeyance, falling also under Article 5 of the Rome Conversations.

176. These assurances were also to be sufficient for the British authorities in the face of a 1933 incident in which *HMS Penzance* visited Jabal Zuqar and Hanish, noting, inter alia, the presence of Italian soldiers and the flying of the Italian flag. Great Britain, in the meantime, was providing comparable assurances regarding Kamaran.

177. The Italian Royal Legislative Decree No. 1019 of 1 June 1936 made arrangements for the administration of Italian East Africa. It provided, inter alia, in its Article 4, that the territory of Dankalia was constituted by reference to a line from the lowlands to the east of Lake Ascianghi at the southern limit of Aussa and was part of Eritrea. Although no islands were named in terms, the specifying of the lines which constituted these administrative boundaries brought the Hanish-Zuqar group within the commissaryship of Dankalia. None of the line-drawing provided for by Decree 1019 covered Abu Ali, Zubayr or Jabal al-Tayr.

178. This was affirmed in terms by General Government Decree No. 446 of 20 December 1938: "the Hanisc-Sucur Islands are deemed to be included within the bounds of the Commissaryship of the Government of Dancalia and Aussa (Assab)." In the view of the Tribunal these administrative arrangements cannot, in the light of the Rome Conversations and subsequent assurances, be regarded as international claims to sovereignty, rather than as to jurisdiction. Nor would they have been regarded as such by Great Britain. And only eight months beforehand Italy had assured the Imam that it had undertaken with Great Britain not to extend its sovereignty to the Hanish islands (and that it had been able to secure the dispatch of an Italian doctor to Kamaran on that basis).

179. At the same time, Italy unsuccessfully asked Great Britain to revoke its own Decree regarding Kamaran, which Italy regarded as upsetting the status quo agreement reached in 1927. At the same time, Great Britain did continue to regard the sovereignty over Kamaran as reserved.

180. Italy, which had recognised independent Yemen in 1926, entered into a treaty of Amity and Economic Relations with that country in September 1937. While Italy confirmed unconditionally its "recognition of the full and absolute independence, without restrictions" of the King of Yemen and his Kingdom, the Tribunal cannot view this as illuminating the current problems.

181. Developments in Yemen and Saudi Arabia, including their relations with each other, made Italy and the United Kingdom believe that matters should be clarified further. After several months of negotiation there was signed on 16 April 1938 an Agreement and Protocols which entered into effect on 16 November 1938. Annex

3 of the agreement included detailed dispositions of relevance to the Red Sea islands:

> *Article 1*
> Neither Party will conclude any agreement or take any action which might in any way impair the independence or integrity of Saudi Arabia or of the Yemen.
>
> *Article 2*
> Neither Party will obtain or seek to obtain a privileged position of a political character in any territory which at present belongs to Saudi Arabia or to the Yemen or in any territory which either of those States may hereafter acquire.
>
> *Article 3*
> The two Parties recognise that, in addition to the obligations incumbent on each of them in virtue of Articles 1 and 2 hereof, it is in the common interest of both of them that no other Power should acquire or seek to acquire sovereignty or any privileged position of a political character in any territory which at present belongs to Saudi Arabia or to the Yemen or which either of those States may hereafter acquire, including any islands in the Red Sea belonging to either of those States, or in any other islands in the Red Sea to which Turkey renounced her rights by Article 16 of the Treaty of Peace signed at Lausanne on the 24th July 1923. In particular they regard it as an essential interest of each of them that no other Power should acquire sovereignty or any privileged position on any part of the coast of the Red Sea which at present belongs to Saudi Arabia or to the Yemen or in any of the aforesaid islands.
>
> *Article 4*
> (1) As regards those islands in the Red Sea to which Turkey renounced her rights by Article 16 of the Treaty of Peace signed at Lausanne on the 24th July, 1923, and which are not comprised in the territory of Saudi Arabia or of the Yemen, neither Party will, in or in regard to any such island:
> (a) Establish its sovereignty, or
> (b) Erect fortifications or defences.
> (2) It is agreed that neither Party will object to:
> (a) The presence of British officials at Kamaran for the purpose of securing the sanitary service of the pilgrimage to Mecca in accordance with the provisions of the Agreement concluded at Paris on the 19th June, 1926, between the Governments of Great Britain and Northern Ireland and of India, on the one part, and the Government of the Netherlands, on the other part; it is also understood that the Italian Government may appoint an Italian Medical Officer to be stationed there on the same conditions as the Netherlands Medical Officer under the said Agreement;
> (b) The presence of Italian officials at Great Hanish, Little Hanish and Jebel Zukur for the purpose of protecting the fishermen who resort to those islands;
> (c) The presence at Abu Ail, Centre Peak and Jebel Teir of such persons as are required for the maintenance of the lights on those islands.

182. The Ministry of Foreign Affairs of Italy had, in an internal Note of 31 March, made clear that the formula being negotiated would confirm that the Red Sea islands formerly under Turkish sovereignty "belong neither to Great Britain, Italy

or the two Arab States, but remain of reserved sovereignty." An accompanying list of islands "of reserved sovereignty" indicated that Kamaran, Abu Ali and Jabal al-Tayr were at the time under British occupation, and described as occupied by Italy: Greater Hanish, Jabal Zuqar, Centre Peak, and Lesser Hanish. South West Haycock is not listed in the Italian Foreign Ministry Note as coming within this arrangement, notwithstanding the assurances on this point given to Great Britain in 1930 regarding understandings reached during the 1927 Rome Conversations. In the Treaty of 1938 itself, however, the islands agreed to fall within its provisions are not specified. Nor is there any reflection of an internal British proposal that the termination of the 1927 Rome Conversations be made clear.

183. It would seem that the 1938 Treaty is to be seen not as replacing but as supplementing and expanding the 1927 undertakings (always less than a formal treaty), the "political character and complex formula of the latter having been found unsatisfactory." The Rome Treaty was never registered with the League of Nations and by virtue of Article 18 of the Covenant could not be invoked by either party against the other. More relevant to Yemen is the fact that it is a third party to the Treaty. There is no evidence, however, that either Italy or the United Kingdom failed to proceed with registration for any reason other than the approaching war clouds. The text of the Treaty still has significance, which the Tribunal may properly take account of, as to the understanding of the parties in the autumn of 1938 regarding the current position of the islands and their intention at that moment as to how they should continue to be treated. No change is to be discerned from the essential thrust of what had gone before: claims were to remain inactive. The islands were not *res nullius* to be acquired by Italy or Great Britain.

184. The wording of Article 3 is not without its ambiguities. What it does show is that, on the one hand, there *were* some islands in the Red Sea regarded in 1938 as belonging to Saudi Arabia and to Yemen. It also shows, on the other hand, that there were other Red Sea islands regarded as belonging to neither, and whose title was still indeterminate.

185. As Article 4 clearly and specifically refers to Kamaran, Greater Hanish, Little Hanish, Jabal Zuqar, Abu Ali, Centre Peak and Jabal al-Tayr as not being under the sovereignty of Saudi Arabia or Yemen, it is uncertain what islands were regarded as "at present belong[ing] to Yemen." In any event, Italy and the United Kingdom did not in 1938 regard title to any of the named islands as belonging to Yemen or as having been settled within the terms of Article 16 of the Treaty of Lausanne; and they each undertook not to establish sovereignty thereon. There is nothing in the record to show that the term "establish" in Article 4 was intended to mean other than "acquire" or "seek to acquire" sovereignty, as used in Article 3, through the various acts referred to in the Treaty, especially fortifications. It may be concluded that the 1938 Treaty evidences no recognition by Italy or Great

Britain of any Yemeni title to the disputed islands. But at the same time the Treaty expressly excluded any Italian claims of sovereignty thereto.

186. The consequence of this series of international instruments and engagements was that from 1923 to 1938 Italy could make no claim that it already had a title that must be recognised. The only clear claim to sovereign title was to South West Haycock – but even that claim to an existing title was to be treated, at Italy's own suggestion, as "in abeyance" until title to the islands generally should later be settled by the parties concerned under Article 16 of the Treaty of Lausanne.

* - *

187. As for Yemen, it in turn made sporadic claims to Red Sea islands during this period, in general and unspecified terms. While Great Britain had assured Yemen that Italy's lighthouse activities did not prejudice Yemen's position, neither it nor Italy regarded the islands as being within Yemen's ownership up to 1938. As the Treaty of Lausanne provisions had been the mechanism by which the Ottoman Empire divested itself of ownership of these islands, that fact is not wholly without significance for Yemen, which, even putting the argument in its own terms, has to show not only a right of reversion but also that such a right overrode the decision that the previous sovereign had been obliged to make as to the future of the Islands.

188. In 1933 Great Britain was in fact negotiating a treaty with the Imam. The view was expressed within the Foreign Office that Yemen had legally been part of the Ottoman Empire and "any islands pertaining to it" were "fully covered by Article 16 of the Treaty of Lausanne and the disposal was therefore a matter for international agreement." Contrary to the submissions of Yemen, this does not clearly assume Yemeni title – it assumes that what had been sovereign had now become indeterminate, until title was attributed by the "interested Parties."

189. The islands claimed by the Imam during the negotiation with the United Kingdom for the Treaty of Friendship and Mutual Cooperation of Sanaa of 1934 were without specific identification, but they were clearly later understood by the British to have meant Kamaran and the various unoccupied islands, the largest of which are Zuqar and Greater Hanish. The assertion of that claim was acknowledged although it was not reflected in the text of the Treaty and the refusal of the British Government to do more was made clear to the Imam.

* - *

190. As neither Italy nor Yemen held sovereign title at the outbreak of the Second World War, all the islands (save perhaps South West Haycock and the Mohabbakahs) may be assumed to have fallen within the relinquishment

provisions that Italy was obliged to accept. This conclusion is also supported by an examination of the documents relating to the years 1941-1950.

191. The 1941 Proclamation of British Military Jurisdiction brought under the command of Lieutenant-General Platt "[a]ll territories in Eritrea and Ethiopia." This wording seems to the Tribunal neither "broad" nor indeed "narrow," but merely general and uninformative geographically and legally. The Armistice did speak of the "[i]mmediate surrender of Corsica and of all the Italian territory, both islands and mainland, to the Allies . . ." (para. 6). But what islands are there referred to is wholly uncertain; the explanation in Article 41 of the "Additional Conditions of Armistice" with Italy that "the term 'Italian Territory' includes all Italian colonies and dependencies . . . (but without prejudice to the question of sovereignty) . . ." carries things no further. The phrase remains question-begging and in addition carries a specific caveat. Armistice agreements are instruments directed to stopping or containing hostilities and not to acknowledging or denying sovereign title.

192. In 1944 the British Colonial Office conducted an internal assessment on the status of Kamaran, the Great Hanish group, the Little Hanish group, the Jabal Zuqar group (including Abu Ali), the Zubayr group (including Centre Peak), and Jabal al-Tayr. In correspondence the history was briefly recounted, and it was recalled that under Article 16 of the Treaty of Lausanne "their future was to be settled by the 'parties concerned'. It never has been. They are in fact international waifs." The letter continued: "Once upon a time the Italians were interested in all these islands." It was thought that the Dutch now had some interest.[16] "Apart from the British, however, the most serious claimant seems to be the Yemen, off whose coast all the islands lie." The claims of the Imam in 1934 were recalled.

193. The author of the letter (a civil servant within the Colonial Office) suggested that matters could be left as they were; or tidied up "in the same way"; or the UK could annex the islands.

194. Leaving aside the assessment of all the islands as "off Yemen's coast" or the assumption, without legal analysis, that they were free for annexation, the letter evidences what seemed to be a widely-held view within the British Government that sovereignty over these islands remained unsettled within the terms of Article 16 of the Treaty of Lausanne.

195. By 1947 the question of title had, of course, to be faced in the Treaty of Peace with Italy. Under Article 23 Italy renounced "all right and title to the Italian

---

[16] The Dutch had not been signatories to the 1923 Treaty of Lausanne and had in fact remained neutral in the First World War.

territorial possessions in Africa, i.e., Libya, Eritrea and Italian Somaliland." The third paragraph of that provision then provided:

> The final disposition of these possessions shall be determined jointly by the Governments of the Soviet Union, of the United Kingdom, of the United States of America, and of France within one year from the coming into force of the present Treaty . . . .

That this did not refer to the islands here in issue is made fully clear by Article 43, which provides:

> Italy hereby renounces any rights and interests she may possess by virtue of Article 16 of the Treaty of Lausanne signed on July 24, 1923.

Both the placement of this article (at a point distant from Article 2) and the very need for such a provision made it clear that the disputed Red Sea islands did not fall to be disposed of under Article 23(3). This provision was not meant to operate as a revision or renunciation, by parties other than Italy, of Article 16 of the Treaty of Lausanne.

196. Instead, Article 16 of the Treaty of Lausanne remained intact. Italy was now obliged to renounce "any rights and interests" under it. This refers not merely, as has been submitted by Yemen, to Italy's right to protest at a purported acquisition by another or to be party eventually to a settlement of title. It refers also to a renunciation of any claims Italy might have made and any legal interests she might have asserted regarding the islands.

197. A United Nations working paper drawn up in December 1949 in connection with the preparation of the draft Eritrean Constitution supports the view that the Hanish, Zuqar and more northerly islands were not among those to be settled (and eventually affirmed as passing to independent Eritrea). The section on the Geography and History of Eritrea says that the Italian colony "includes the Dahlak archipelago off Massawa, and the islands further south off the coast of the Danakil country." This would seem to refer to those Mohabbakahs in proximity to Assab. The section that recalls the "attempts to colonize the highlands of Eritrea" makes no reference to any colonization of the islands.

198. The Ministry of Foreign Affairs of Ethiopia did protest when it commented on the draft constitution. It pointed out that the language used in Article 2 of the draft Constitution "would impliedly exclude all archipelagoes and islands off the coast. Surely, this exclusion was not intended." *The constitution in its finally accepted form stated that "the territory of Eritrea, including the islands, is that of the former colony of Eritrea." That formulation does not indicate whether the*

islands referred to were other than those of the Dahlak archipelago and the Mohabbakahs.[*]

199. The Italian Government had also been invited to express its opinions on the future of Eritrea to the UN Commission on Eritrea. Italy urged independence for Eritrea, emphasising that its renunciation of all title did not make Eritrea a *res nullius*. It spoke of the regions that had been occupied by Italy to establish Eritrea. In that context, reference was made to the Dahlak Islands. In urging the continued unity of Eritrea no mention was made of any other islands. None of the rapidly ensuing instruments – the British Military Authority (BMA) Termination of Powers Proclamation of 1952, or the revised Constitution of Eritrea of 1955, changed matters.

* - * - *

[*] The text in italics represents a corrigendum agreed upon by the Arbitral Tribunal in November, 1998, following the delivery of the Award to the Parties.

CHAPTER VI – Red Sea Lighthouses

200. The Red Sea lights bear on this arbitration in three main ways. First, each of the parties has at various moments suggested that its establishment or maintenance of lighthouses on the various islands constitute acts of sovereignty. Second, the diplomatic correspondence relating to the lighthouses might throw some light on the underlying claims to the islands where they are located, not least because the lighthouse islands were necessarily named. So much of the other material relates to islands without specification. Third, the relationship between the several lighthouse conventions and the provisions of Article 16 of the Treaty of Lausanne might have some legal significance.

201. From the late 19th century the Red Sea lights have had an historical importance in this region, although this is now somewhat reduced with the advent of radar. But radar may not be available to many of those fishing in the Zuqar-Hanish islands. The Ottoman authorities, and later the various coastal states, along with the major shipping users, have all played a role in the story of the Red Sea lights. In 1930, a proposed treaty regime for the lights was drawn up, but never came into force. From 1962 until 1989, a treaty regime did indeed govern the lights.

202. In 1881, the Ottoman Empire granted a forty-year concession to the *Société des Phares de l'Empire Ottoman*, owned by Messieurs Michel and Collas, to build a series of lighthouses in the Red Sea and the Persian Gulf. Almost endless disputes were to arise regarding the concession for the Red Sea lighthouses.

203. The British Government had proposed to the Sublime Porte that four lights should be erected at Jabal al-Tayr, Abu Ali, Jabal Zubayr and at Mocha, to assist navigation. Anxious at the difficulties encountered with the concessionaires, it began in 1891 to revive an earlier idea to explore the possibility of a western navigation route through the Red Sea. As the envisaged route was to be "abreast of the Italian possessions at Assab," Italy was asked to facilitate the technical mission and to allow supplies to be taken on at Assab – a request to which Italy readily agreed.

204. Once a western route was recommended by the Board of Trade, the British Government had to concern itself with questions of title. The so-called "Western Hanish" route would have entailed lights on North East Quoin (or at Rakmat), South West Rocks, one of the Haycock islets and Harbi islet. In 1891 the Board of Trade, relying on the Hertslet Memorandum of 1880, suggested that North East Quoin and Harbi were within Egyptian jurisdiction and South West Rocks and the Haycocks within Ottoman jurisdiction – with the Sublime Porte claiming sovereignty to all four islands. The Marquis of Salisbury, in writing to the British Ambassador to Rome in January 1892, stated "The islands and rocks recommended by the Board of Trade . . . , with the exception of South-west Rocks, seems [sic] to be in effect within the jurisdiction of Italy. That over the

South-west Rocks would appear to be doubtful." From 1881 to 1892 there was an extended international correspondence on this subject.

205. A Note of 3 February 1892 was addressed to the Italian government to seek clarification. The Note included the statement that "according to Article 3 of the Treaty between Italy and Sultan Ahfari of Aussa of the 9th December 1888," the jurisdiction over the new sites, "with the exception perhaps of South-West Rocks, appears to belong to Italy." Italy was asked whether it claimed jurisdiction over these sites, and if so whether it would itself be prepared to erect lights there, or alternatively if it would be willing for Great Britain to do so.

206. The Italian Government replied in June of that year that "the King's Government consider these points as a maritime appendage of the territory over which they exercise their sovereignty" but urged the British Government to erect and maintain the lighthouses and to fix the method of reimbursement.

207. In the event, the western route was not proceeded with and the Ottomans arranged for the building of four lighthouses at Mocha on the Arabian coast, and on Jabal al-Tayr, on Abu Ali and in the Zubayr group (on Centre Peak). This was maintained by the French concessionaires for the Ottomans until 1915. Great Britain occupied the three lighthouse islands in 1915.

208. When the Ottoman Empire was required to renounce its possessions, sovereignty over the lighthouse islands fell, under Article 16 of the Treaty of Lausanne, "to be settled by the parties concerned." The light at Mocha was recognised by Great Britain as being within the territory succeeded to by the Imam. Great Britain had on occasion contemplated trying to acquire sovereignty over the islands it occupied but on balance thought they did not have enough strategic value. It is significant that Great Britain did not regard itself as precluded from attempting to acquire sovereignty by the terms of Article 16 of the Treaty of Lausanne. It was not until 1927 that Great Britain formally stated (to France) that it had definitely renounced this idea. And in certain quarters the idea of annexing Hanish and Zuqar, as well as Jabal al-Tayr and Abu Ali, was not totally dead even in 1944.

209. It is also striking that, throughout the series of enquiries that Great Britain was to make after 1923 to Italy about the status of certain other islands, it never once put to Italy that a claim would be contrary to the terms of Article 16 of the Treaty of Lausanne. Rather, Great Britain was content to satisfy itself that Italy's position was consistent with the bilateral understandings of the Rome Conversations of 1927.

210. Notwithstanding this, the Tribunal has already indicated that in its view the history, text and purpose of Article 16 argues against the unilateral acquisition of title over the islands whose status was left undetermined in 1923. Nor is it necessary to consider whether Italy was seeking to establish title contrary to the

agreement in hand and entered into in the Treaty of Lausanne, because Italy's posture was in fact much more cautious.

211. In 1927 Great Britain negotiated an agreement with France for the maintenance of all four lighthouses by the French company and approached the main users of the route – Germany, the Netherlands, Japan and Italy – to regulate the matter by a convention. Italy, expressing the wish that it had been consulted earlier, made two points. First, Mocha was claimed by the Imam and he should be a party. Second, Italy wished to know whether sovereignty of the islands was to be attributed to the neighbourhood coast or whether the point would be reserved. No Italian claim to any of the islands was presented. The British Government conceded that Mocha was under the rule of the Imam and affirmed that the status of the islands was to be reserved. These reassurances led to the conclusion of the Convention concerning the Maintenance of Certain Lights of 1930.

212. Although this Convention did not enter into force, and thus cannot be said to bind the parties as a treaty, it is useful evidence of their thinking at that date. The preamble and the annex refer to the renunciation by Turkey of both the islands and of Mocha, the occupation of the islands by Great Britain, and the provision in Article 16 of the Treaty of Lausanne that "the future of these islands, and of that territory [is] a matter for settlement by the Parties concerned." The annex continued: "(e) . . . no agreement on this subject has been come to among the parties concerned and it is desirable in the interests of shipping to ensure that the lighthouses on the said islands shall be maintained." It then proceeded to determine that a lighthouse company should take possession of and manage the lighthouses on Abu Ali, Zubayr and Jabal al-Tayr. Italy was prepared to put its signature to this and to Article 13, which clearly affirmed the continued operation of Article 16 of the Treaty of Lausanne:

> Art. 13. In the event of the arrangement contemplated in article 16 of the Treaty of Lausanne being concluded between the parties concerned, the High Contracting Parties will meet in conference in order to decide whether it is desirable to terminate the present Convention, or to modify its terms with a view to making it conform to the aforesaid arrangement.

213. Although the 1930 Convention was ratified by Italy and the Netherlands, it did not come into force, because the French Government was locked in disagreement with the British Government as to whether the lighthouse company, Michel et Collas, should be paid on the basis of gold. France refused to ratify.

214. In the meantime, in the very same year, Italy was preparing to erect a lighthouse on South West Haycock. The Haycocks had not been specifically mentioned in the 1927 Rome Conversations and the British were anxious to establish that Article 5 thereof should nonetheless apply, the more so as "the erection of a lighthouse . . . may be regarded as implying some definite claim to sovereignty."

Great Britain was concerned as to whether indeed South West Haycock did fall within the Rome Conversations – there were internal divisions on the question of title – and it noted that the islet was only 20 miles from the "Italian" coast. It was decided to seek assurances. These were sought in an aide-memoire of 18 February 1930, in which Italy was reminded of the earlier exchanges in 1927. In that document Great Britain referred to South West Haycock as being "in the Hanish group of Islands."

215. In its Pro-Memoria of 11 April 1930, Italy observed that the lighthouse was being built for navigational reasons. It asserted that South West Haycock was not part of the Hanish Islands, but rather belonged to the Mohabbakah archipelago over which it alleged that the Ottomans had never claimed sovereignty.[17] Italy therefore made "a special reserve regarding Italian sovereignty over this island" and then consented to "the question being considered on the same lines as that of the sovereignty of all the islands of the Hanish group, in accordance with the spirit of the conversations of Rome of 1927."

216. The Pro-Memoria can only be read as a claim to sovereignty over South West Haycock by Italy (while at the same time agreeing that the erection of the lighthouse was to be treated as a commercial rather than a sovereign act) and a failure to advance a comparable claim to title over the Hanish group. The internal evidence shows that this was an assessment that Great Britain was at the time inclined to accept, and with which it was satisfied; although in other documents Great Britain treats South West Haycock as part of the Hanish group, and as having been Ottoman. In the event, all fell to be treated as provided by Article 16 of the Treaty of Lausanne, which was reinforced by the understandings reached in the Rome Conversations.

217. The South West Haycock lighthouse was extinguished in 1940. It was abandoned after 1945. When the 1930 Convention failed to come into effect the British authorities were left with the sole financial burden of the existing lights. It [was][*] decided to abandon the Centre Peak light (in the Zubayr group) from September 1932 and Italy (which had been notified, along with France) reactivated the Centre Peak light in 1933. The decision was taken in Italy to inform the "interested powers" that this was being done for reasons of navigational necessity, and that the Imam "who lays claim to rights over the islands" should be "informed of the provisional nature of the occupation and the usefulness to himself in having the lighthouse reactivated." It was apparently originally intended to ask for contributions, but in the event this was not done.

---

[17] The Tribunal notes, however, that prior to Italian occupation, the islands off the African coast were administered by the Khedive of Egypt on behalf of the Ottoman Empire.

[*] *Editorial correction: insert the word in brackets.*

218. The British authorities were notified by Note Verbale on 4 October 1933 of the anxieties of the Captain of the Port at Massawa as to safety on the Massawa-Hodeidah route, in the absence of the Centre Peak light, and of Italy's decision to take over the lighthouse. The Note Verbale expressly stated:

> . . . the Royal Ministry for Foreign Affairs need hardly add that the presence of an Italian staff on the Island of Zebair (Centre Peak), which will ensure the operation of the light, implies no modification of the international judicial status of the island itself, which, together with the islands of Abu Ail and Gebel Taiz [sic], was considered by the Italian and British governments in 1928 during the negotiations for the Red Sea Lights Convention, when the conclusion was reached that the question of sovereignty of those islands should remain in suspense.

219. Thus in the northern islands, too, Italy had established a navigational interest but affirmed that it had no implications for sovereignty. The British decided this was a sufficient comfort not to have to pursue this matter further with the Italians.

220. The situation remained essentially unchanged by the 1938 Agreement. Article 4(2) of Annex 3 again affirmed that neither Great Britain nor Italy would establish sovereignty over the renounced islands, following Article 16 of the Treaty of Lausanne, and that no objections would be raised to lighthouse personnel.

221. By the outbreak of the Second World War it may be said that the maintenance of the lights is seen as a non-sovereign act and there is agreement that the underlying title to the islands concerned was left in abeyance – though Italy had asserted title (even if choosing not to press it) to South West Haycock. But this turned upon a perception of South West Haycock as being part of the Mohabbakahs, rather than upon any suggestion that the erection of a lighthouse thereon itself had a role in establishing sovereignty. In the course of the Second World War, the South West Haycock and the Centre Peak lights were extinguished.

222. In June 1948 the British Military Authority (BMA) in Eritrea sought legal advice as to whether it was liable under any international conventions for the re-establishment of various lights previously operated by the Government of Italy. These included those at South West Haycock and at Centre Peak. The advice (which eventually came from the Ministry of Transport) was that there was no obligation under any convention.

223. The decision by the BMA that it had no responsibility for the lights at South West Haycock and Centre Peak was not because it thought those islands were not Italian. No particular attention seems to have been given to that aspect. Rather, it was decided that as long as the Abu Ali light was maintained there was no real danger to shipping. Further, the Admiralty advised that a state was under no

obligation to light its coasts. Thus even if South West Haycock and Centre Peak had been Italian (and neither was addressed in the 1948 correspondence nor is there any evidence that Zubayr was ever regarded by the British as Italian), no obligation was passed to the BMA as the occupying power.

224. After the Second World War, the British did continue to take responsibility for the lighthouses at Abu Ali and Jabal al-Tayr, and from 1945 received financial contribution from the Netherlands. These arrangements were in 1962 brought within an agreement made between Denmark, Federal Republic of Germany, Italy, the Netherlands, Norway, Sweden, the United Kingdom and the United States, and formally accepted also by Pakistan, the Soviet Union and the United Arab Republic. Yemen was not a party. Nor was Ethiopia. The criterion for invitation was clearly that of navigational importance and not of title to the coast or islands. The opening recitals to the 1962 Agreement rehearse the history of the Abu Ali and Jabal al-Tayr lights, recall the abortive 1930 Convention, refer to Article 16 of the Treaty of Lausanne, and add: "No agreement on the subject of the future of the above-mentioned islands has been come to among the Parties concerned."

225. Further, Article 8 was to make crystal clear that nothing in the text following was to be regarded either as a settlement of the future of the islands referred to in Article 16 of the Treaty of Lausanne, "or as prejudicing the conclusion of any such settlement." This Article reproduces the provisions of Article 15A of the 1930 Lighthouses Convention. The United Kingdom was affirmed as the "Managing Government" for these two lights and was entitled to appoint an agent for this purpose (Article 2). Article 6 provided for discontinuance of this role upon notice to the other parties, and indicated the procedures to be followed in that eventuality.

226. As in 1930, the managerial role of the United Kingdom had nothing to do with the issue of title to the islands; nor did management even place the United Kingdom in a favourable position for when the title issue came to be resolved. This clearly followed the pattern of the Rome Understandings (as they bear on the management of lights) and of the abortive 1930 Convention – even though the 1962 Convention concerned two lights only.

227. The United Kingdom managed the lighthouses at Jabal al-Tayr and Abu Ali from Aden, but realised that arrangements would have to be made when the British would leave Aden upon the independence of the People's Democratic Republic of Yemen in 1967. The Savon and Ries Company was accordingly appointed agent under Article 2 of the 1962 Agreement, for management duties. It so happened that Savon and Ries were operating out of Massawa, and the staff engaged in lighthouse functions at the Board's request came increasingly from Ethiopia, but in the view of the Tribunal this was simply a matter of practical convenience. The various Ethiopian authorizations for inspection and repair visits

to the islands and the control exercised over radio transmissions were immaterial as to sovereignty. Everything remained as it had been so far as title to the islands was concerned – that is to say, Article 8 of the 1962 Convention continued to govern.

228. In 1971 the British Government decided to replace the lights by automatic lights, dispensing with the services of lighthouse-keepers. The United Kingdom notified Yemen of this intention, assured that Government that "the action of the Board of Trade in accordance with [the 1962 Convention] does not infringe upon rights of sovereignty" and asked whether Yemen had any objection. The fact that the communication was addressed to Yemen, a non-signatory of the 1962 Convention, would seem to indicate that, while the islands remained unattributed in accordance with the terms of the 1962 Treaty, Yemen was regarded by the United Kingdom as a "party concerned" within the terms of Article 16 of the Treaty of Lausanne and as having claims to Abu Ali and Jabal al-Tayr that should not be prejudiced. It may also be noted that by this time Italy had lost its possessions on the Red Sea coast and was not, therefore, any longer a "party concerned" within the meaning of Article 16 of the Treaty of Lausanne.[18]

229. Although at an earlier era the legal advice within the British Government was that Abu Ali and Jabal al-Tayr (as well as Centre Peak) were islands that were *res nullius* and various candidates had been suggested at different moments of time as "parties concerned," it would seem that by the early 1970s Yemen was regarded as the leading "party concerned" for purposes of Article 16 of the Treaty of Lausanne, at least so far as Abu Ali and Jabal al-Tayr were concerned.

230. In 1975 the management of these two lights was transferred from Savon and Ries' offices in Ethiopia to its offices in Djibouti. Five years later, the agency for management was passed by the British authorities to a new company it had formed, the Red Sea Lights Company.

231. In 1987 Yemen relit the lighthouse on Centre Peak, issued pertinent Notices to Mariners and, in 1988, upgraded it. This appears to have occasioned no protest by Ethiopia, which could not have assumed that such acts were rendered without significance by virtue of Article 16 of the Treaty of Lausanne (to which Yemen was not a party), or by the various bilateral Italian-UK agreements, or by the 1962 Lighthouse Convention – none of which were opposable to Yemen.

---

[18] Nor has Italy or, for that matter, any state asserted that it considers itself to be "a party concerned" for this purpose. The Tribunal therefore concludes that, with respect to the islands in dispute, the only present-day "parties concerned" are the Parties to this arbitration.

232. On 20 June 1989, Yemen contacted the United Kingdom regarding "the matter of the Lighthouses installed on Abu Ali (Ail) and Jabal al Tair Islands which is to be discussed on Tuesday 20 June 1989." Yemen formally stated that:

> 1. The two Islands mentioned above lie within the exclusive economic zone of the Yemen Arab Republic.
> 2. In the light of this fact the Yemen Arab Republic is willing to take the responsibility of managing and operating the said two lighthouses for the benefit of National and International Navigation. As you may be aware, the Ports and Marine Affairs Corporation in the Yemen Arab Republic is already running and operating several lighthouses some of which lie within the area of these two Islands.

233. Unless positive action was taken to extend the 1962 Convention, it would expire in March 1990. In 1988 and 1989 it became clear that many parties had denounced the 1962 Treaty or indicated their intention to do so. The United Kingdom, the managing authority of the lights, was among these. Egypt offered to take over that role, but it was clear that there were not sufficient votes for extending the Convention beyond 1990.

234. A meeting of the parties was held in London in June 1989. Having established its credentials and interest, Yemen was invited as an observer to the 1989 Conference on the future of the two northern lights, notwithstanding the fact that (like Ethiopia) it had not been a party to the 1962 Agreement. The Report to the Government of Yemen of the Yemeni technicians attending the 1989 meeting refers to the fact that the British had confirmed the installation and operation by Yemen of new lighthouses on Jabal Zubayr and Jabal Zuqar. Manifested interest and professional competence appear to be the motivating factors for Yemen's presence. Ethiopia was not invited to attend and had not requested this.

235. Yemen supported the Egyptian proposal that Yemen would manage the lighthouses on Jabal al-Tayr and Abu Ali and did so without reserve as to title. The minutes show that they also indicated their willingness to operate lights on the two islands at their own expense with almost immediate effect should the agreement lapse. The minutes contain no reference by Yemen to the islands being in its Exclusive Economic Zone – though that point had been included in the pre-meeting exchanges with the United Kingdom.

236. The reference to Yemen's Exclusive Economic Zone rather than to title to the islands themselves does not appear to have been casual. It is mentioned twice again in the internal report sent after the 1989 conference from the Yemeni Director-General of the Ports and Maritime Affairs to the Government of Yemen. Yemen's offer – which was accepted – was in language other than claim of a right of sovereign title. Yemen did not say that it had title to Abu Ali or Jabal al-Tayr, nor to the nearby islands, and thus it would be for it alone to provide any

lights. The 1961* Agreement had no chance of survival and Egypt's offer to become managing authority could not provide the answer. The international treaty regime for the Red Sea lights was coming to an end.

237. The erection and maintenance of lights, outside of any treaty arrangements and for the indefinite future, had certain implications. The acceptance of Yemen's offer did not constitute recognition of Yemen sovereignty over islands. But it did accept the reality that Yemen was best placed, and was willing, to take on the role of providing and managing lights in that part of the Red Sea; and that when the time came finally to determine the status of those islands Yemen would certainly be a "party concerned." (Yemen, of course, was not bound by Article 8 of the 1962 Convention and indeed appears not to have known at the time of the arrangements made under it.)

238. Eritrea has contended that there was no need for Ethiopia to have protested the relighting by Yemen of lights on Abu Ali and Jabal al-Tayr, as its "activities were merely a continuation of the historic activities of Great Britain on Jabal A'Tair and Abu Ali." But Yemen was not in the same legal relationship with Ethiopia over the matter of lights as had been Great Britain and, if such was the reasoning for a failure to reserve claimed Ethiopian sovereignty, it was misplaced.

* - * - *

---

* *Editorial correction: the correct year is "1962."*

CHAPTER VII – Evidences of the Display of Functions of State and Governmental Authority

Analysis of the Evidence

239. The factual evidence of "*effectivités*" presented to the Tribunal by both Parties is voluminous in quantity but is sparse in useful content. This is doubtless owing to the inhospitability of the Islands themselves and the relative meagreness of their human history. The modern international law of the acquisition (or attribution) of territory generally requires that there be: an intentional display of power and authority over the territory, by the exercise of jurisdiction and state functions, on a continuous and peaceful basis. The latter two criteria are tempered to suit the nature of the territory and the size of its population, if any. The facts alleged by Eritrea and Yemen in the present case must be measured against these tests, with the following qualification. Not only were these islands for long uninhabited and ungoverned or, if at all, governed in the most attenuated sense, but the facts on which Eritrea relies were acts by its predecessor, Ethiopia, which were not "peaceful," unless that term may here be understood to include acts in prosecution of a civil war. Nevertheless, the Tribunal cannot discount these facts, given the singular circumstances of this case.

240. The Tribunal has found it useful to classify the wide variety of factual evidence advanced by the Parties in relation to this subject, and will now examine these categories of evidence in turn.

Assertion of Intention to Claim the Islands

241. Evidence of intention to claim the Islands *à titre de souverain* is an essential element of the process of consolidation of title. That intention can be evidenced by showing a public claim of right or assertion of sovereignty to the Islands as well as legislative acts openly seeking to regulate activity on the Islands. The Tribunal notes that the evidence submitted by both Parties is replete with assertions of sovereignty and jurisdiction that fail to mention any islands whatsoever, and with general references to "the islands" with no further specificity.

Public Claims to Sovereignty over the Islands

242. Eritrea's claim that these islands were included as part of "the former Italian colony of Eritrea" by the Italian Military Armistice of 1943, the 1947 Treaty of Peace, and the 1952 Constitution is barely supported by evidence. It is true that Italy wished to claim the islands and indeed established a presence on some of them; but these facts were always subject to repeated assurances that the islands' legal position was indeterminate in accordance with Article 16 of the Treaty of Lausanne and with the Rome Conversations (see Chapter V, above). The 1952 Eritrean Constitution defined the extent of Eritrean territory as "including the

islands," but failed to specify which islands were intended. The same uncertainty existed in the language of Article 2 of the United Nations Resolution approving the 1952 Constitution, the 1955 Ethiopian Constitution, the 1987 revision of the Ethiopian Constitution, and the 1997 Constitution of the newly-independent State of Eritrea.

243. The scant evidence of Ethiopian legislation before the Tribunal suffers from the same uncertainty as do the constitutional provisions. The 1953 Ethiopian Federal Crimes Proclamation and a 1953 Maritime Order put in evidence by Eritrea were not explicit about the Islands. The former was content merely to specify "any island which may be considered as appertaining to Ethiopia," and the latter simply republished the phrase "including the islands." A Maritime Proclamation of 1953 referred merely to "the coasts of the Ethiopian islands."

244. Seventeen years later, in 1970, Ethiopia promulgated an order for a state of emergency. This Order did not specify the Islands; nor did the implementing regulations promulgated by the Minister of National Defence. Three 1971 operations orders are cited by Eritrea to demonstrate that "the islands in dispute here fell within the ambit of Ethiopia's concern." They identify Greater Hanish and Jabal Zuqar as being "areas" to be visited or as reference points for patrol routes. In 1987, the Ethiopian Ministry of National Defence was given responsibility "for the defence of the country's territorial waters and islands" but, again, those "islands" remained unidentified.

245. In 1973, the Ministry of Foreign Affairs of the Yemen Arab Republic (YAR) informed the Imperial Ethiopian Embassy in Sanaa of the YAR's plans to conduct a full aerial survey of its territory that would cover certain "Yemeni islands." These were identified as: "Great Hanish," "Little Hanish," "Jabal Zuqur," "Jabal al Zair," "Jabal Zal Tair," and "Humar." The reason given for the notification was that the photographs, which were to be taken from a height of 30,000 feet, might show "parts of the Ethiopian coasts." Ethiopia responded that "some of the islands listed in the afore-mentioned note could not be identified under the nomenclature used, while others are Ethiopian islands." This exchange of correspondence is cited in a January 1977 "Top Secret" memorandum of the Ministry of Foreign Affairs of The Provisional Military Government of Socialist Ethiopia, which details the measures Ethiopia considered taking to protect its interests. The memorandum refers to islands in the southern part of the Red Sea that "have had no recognized owner," with respect to which Ethiopia "claims jurisdiction"[19] and "both North and South Yemen have started to make claims." It names the Hanish islands, Jabal Zuqar, Jabal al-Tayr and Jabal Zubayr, and points out that the 1973 response to the YAR had deliberately been left vague,

[19] Eritrea has submitted two translations of this document, one of which refers to "jurisdiction" and the other to "sovereignty."

because there was insufficient time to collect evidence in support of Ethiopia's "claim over the islands" and for fear of provoking a military response from Yemen and its Arab allies, particularly in the wake of false reports, in 1973, of an Israeli presence on certain Red Sea islands. The memorandum urges that "Ethiopia . . . take a clear stand in this respect in order to protect its ownership."

246. Yemen relies on a claim of historic title, asserted to stem from time immemorial. It was allegedly most early evidenced in 1429, when King al-Zahir of Yemen sent a mission to Jabal Zuqar to investigate two vessels engaged in smuggling that had run aground on the island. The relevance of this happening is vigorously contested by Eritrea on various grounds which were not responded to in substance by Yemen. It appears to be unique, and isolated. The Tribunal does not consider it important in relation to the determination of title to Zuqar. Its only significance (which has been substantially weakened by Eritrea's rebuttal of its relevance, not replied to by Yemen) might be that it could support an interpretation of the Imam's aspirations so as to include at least Jabal Zuqar, but that in turn fails since there is no evidence that when he advanced his claim of historic rights in 1918, the Imam knew of the 1429 expedition. Moreover, the source for that information was only published in 1976, long after the claim of historic rights had allegedly been advanced by the Imam.

247. In his reply to a British proposal for a treaty of friendship, the Imam is recorded as having requested, inter alia, "(2) Establishment of his rule and independence over all the Yemen, i.e., over that part which was once under the sway of his predecessors . . . ." This claim could not have been more general. Indeed, the word "that part," being expressed in the singular, would not seem naturally applicable to islands. This generalized claim was apparently manifested on several occasions in bilateral diplomatic conversations during the inter-War period, but no constitutional or legislative act of Yemen or of the Imam claimed any of the Islands specifically or described them specifically as Yemeni territory.

248. Yemen asserted in the oral hearings that in 1933, ". . . certain British representatives expressed puzzlement as to why the Imam was so adamant about his claim to the islands of Al-Yemen, including the islands of the Hanish Group." The Yemeni Foreign Minister allegedly "made the Imam's claim to the Hanish Islands well known to German officials in 1930, France in 1936 and, of course, England, in connection with the 1934 treaty and on many other occasions." Yemen added that "the Imam stated and restated his historic claims to the British, to the French and to the Italians whenever this was practically possible," and this appears to be borne out by contemporaneous evidence from 1930 to 1936.

249. Other evidence of communications between the Imam and British diplomats, including the records of the Clayton mission of 1926, and Colonel Reilly's communications to the Foreign Office are too vague to serve as evidence of a specific claim by the Imam to the Islands at that time.

250. Although Yemen asserted in the oral hearings that Yemen's response to the granting of an oil concession by the United Kingdom in the area of Kamaran Island in 1956 "restated the claim to the Red Sea Islands," the language actually used in the official statement merely stated that "[t]he Yemeni Government considers Kamaran island and the other Yemeni islands to be a inseparable part of Yemen." It also added that "[t]he Yemeni Government continues to insist upon its rights to the Yemeni islands and their liberation." A likely inference to be drawn from this is that the "islands" referred to could not have been the islands now in question since those were not islands that required "liberation."

251. In 1973 there were press reports that Israel had occupied Jabal Zuqar with the permission of Ethiopia. Substantial effort was devoted by both sides in the proceedings to seeking to demonstrate that the respective reactions to the matter were relevant to sovereignty over the Islands. A 1973 press statement issued by the Embassy of the Yemen Arab Republic in Mogadishu reported that Yemeni investigations had found "Lesser Hanash, Greater Hanash, Zukar, Alzubair, Alswabe and several other islands at the Yemeni coast," to be free of foreign infiltration, and further stated that:

> [. . .]
>
> The Y.A.R. always controls and maintains its sovereignty over its islands at the Red Sea, with the exception of the islands of Gabal Abu Ali and Gabal Attair which were given to Ethiopia by Britain when the latter left Aden and surrendered power in our Southern Yemen.

This supports an inference that the phrase "its islands in the Red Sea" included the disputed Islands; moreover, the press statement emphasized that the Yemen Arab Republic maintained its claim of sovereignty over those islands "given by Britain to Ethiopia," and urged Ethiopia to surrender those islands.

252. Yemen's "historic claim" was initially expressed in vague and general terms following the end of World War I, and reiterated in bilateral diplomatic contexts in the inter-War period. After World War II it was reasserted in 1956, even though largely in doubtful and indirect terms. In 1973, however, it was expressly revived in a public statement (which, although it said that Jabal al-Tayr and the Zubayr group had been "given to Ethiopia," also reasserted Yemen's "rights and possession" to them and was specific about the other, "mentioned," islands). The statement therefore left little room for doubt that Yemen had sustained or renewed its claim over all of the larger islands, including the northern islands – or, at any rate, as of 1973. There is no evidence that Yemen subsequently abandoned or relinquished this claim. The evidence does, however, also suggest that Yemen had no presence on and little knowledge about Jabal al-Tayr and the Zubayr group at that time, and supposed that they were in the possession of

Ethiopia. The fact was that, for many years, the northern lighthouses were administered from Ethiopia by employees of the lighthouse company.

-

Legislative Acts Seeking to Regulate Activity on the Islands

253. There is no evidence of post-war Ethiopian legislation seeking expressly to regulate activity on the Islands. As discussed above, no Ethiopian legislation between 1953 and 1992 specifically purported to exercise jurisdiction and state functions over the Islands. From 1992 to the inception of the dispute in 1995, no Eritrean legislation explicitly treated the Islands as being subject to the jurisdiction and control of Eritrea.

254. The Ethiopian Federal Crimes Proclamation and the 1953 Maritime Order put in evidence by Eritrea were not explicit. They applied to "any island which may be considered as appertaining to Ethiopia" and "the islands." A related Maritime Proclamation of 1953 referred merely to "the coasts of the Ethiopian islands." These instruments would of course have applied to the Dahlak group and to the islands in the Bay of Assab; but those islands are not disputed.

255. As to Yemen, the evidence of administrative and legislative decrees advanced to support a claim of the exercise of state functions follows substantially the same pattern as the evidence introduced by Ethiopia:* there is silence as to whether the Islands are intended to be included in the ambit of the decrees. There is no evidence of Yemeni legislation openly seeking to regulate activity on the Islands. From 1923 to the inception of the dispute in 1995, no Yemeni legislation specifically treated the Islands as being subject to the jurisdiction and control of Yemen.

256. In 1967, two decrees were issued by the President of the Yemen Arab Republic concerning territorial waters and continental shelf. However these did not mention the Islands by name. Yemen contends that the subsequent Yemeni licensing in 1987 of a research program in waters off the Islands by the German research vessel, the *F.S. Meteor*, demonstrated their applicability to the Islands. While that is unclear, it is arguable that this incident can be viewed as crystallizing Yemeni intent as to the scope of the 1967 legislation.

257. In conclusion, the evidence on behalf of both Parties shows legislative and constitutional acts without any specific reference to the Islands by name. It should be borne in mind that during most of these years both Ethiopia and Yemen were distracted by civil war or strife, and serious internal instability. Yemen did

---

* *Editorial correction: substitute "Eritrea" for "Ethiopia."*

not resile from the broad and loose claims made before World War II – which might or might not have embraced the islands in dispute – but did not pursue or articulate them until 1973.

* - *

Activities Relating to the Water

Licensing of Activities in the Waters Off the Islands

258. There is much evidence that Ethiopian naval units had for many years conducted surveillance in the Red Sea and in particular around the Zuqar-Hanish archipelago. As pointed out below, it is not clear whether those actions were evidence of fisheries control and administration or whether they primarily related to security measures, or both, particularly in light of the fierce struggle by the Eritrean freedom fighters in the two decades prior to Eritrean independence. In any event, there is little evidence that the Ethiopian activity was based on fisheries regulations or laws as such.

259. As to Eritrea, the evidence only dates from early 1992. In January of that year the Eritrean provisional government issued a notice prohibiting in general terms unlicenced fishing activity in "Eritrean territorial waters." Eritrea has asserted that its Ministry of Marine Resources "has regulated fishing in Eritrean waters since shortly after Eritrean independence." On 1 April 1995, the Ministry of Marine Resources issued a "Manual and Guidelines for the Administration of Foreing [sic] Vessel Licensing and Operations."

260. In September 1995, Trawler Regulation I was issued by the Ministry of Marine Resources. The statement is made by Eritrea that the handout appended to Trawler Regulation I "includes the Zuqar-Hanish islands within Areas No. 11 and 12 (Beilul and Bera'isole)."[20] The areas are separated laterally by dotted lines. These lines do not however extend to, or surround, the Zuqar-Hanish archipelago. (Comparison with Maps 1 and 2 shows, in the case of Map 2's depiction of the Dahlak ("Dehalak") archipelago, a carefully-drawn lateral boundary around the Dahlaks.)

261. As far as Yemen is concerned, there is no evidence of any regulation or order as such regulating fisheries as such in Yemeni waters. The evidentiary record is devoid of any assertion of a formal legal basis for fisheries jurisdiction assumed by the Yemeni Government over the waters surrounding the Zuqar-Hanish archipelago. A witness statement cited in support of the proposition that Yemeni

[20] Map 3 (dated November 1993) shows Area 10 ("Bera'isole") and Area 11 ("Beilul"), but Area 12 is actually "Assab-Dumeira."

Government "launches are vigilant in controlling illegal fishing" merely details that the witness (a Navy Captain) "was assigned by [his] . . . command to arrest foreign fishermen pirates . . . who were looting our maritime wealth in a random and illegal manner," but indicates no further detail.[21]

262. Yet Yemen has asserted that it has "tightly regulated fishing activities on and around the Hanish Islands" and that "the Government has actively controlled illegal fishing." There is a substantial record of fishing vessel arrests by Yemeni authorities between 1987 and 1990. It should be noted however that they are recent in time, and appear to have been primarily directed in recent years against large Egyptian industrial fishing vessels.

263. In conclusion, the Tribunal is of the view that the activities of the Parties in relation to the regulation of fishing allows no clear legal conclusion to be drawn. The record of these activities under Ethiopian administration is, as will be seen below, open to conjecture. Since Eritrean independence, the record is less than clear. Since 1987, Yemen appears to have been engaged in some regulation of fishing, primarily directed toward larger vessels. The balance of this evidence does not appear to tilt in one direction or another.

Fishing Vessel Arrests

264. Although there is evidence before the Tribunal that a substantial number of arrests of fishing vessels for violation of the respective fishing regulations and orders have occurred, the period of time comprised in that evidence is brief. It is difficult therefore to characterize those actions as the "continuous and peaceful display of state authority."

265. The evidence before the Tribunal concerning Ethiopian regulation of fishing or fishing violation arrests is almost wholly derived from former Ethiopian naval officers. There are many detailed witness statements that recount service in the Ethiopian patrolling forces during the Eritrean war of independence. In most instances the whereabouts of particular incidents are rendered in general terms, albeit with frequent reference in particular to islands of the Zuqar-Hanish archipelago. Although there are few dates given for the various vessel arrests referred to in the witness statements, the majority of activities reported appear to have taken place during the two decades preceding Eritrean independence in 1991.

[21] The samples of fishing and boat licenses supplied by Yemen are not helpful; when they specify fishing areas, they only state "Red Sea."

266. A fair reading of the witness statements shows that by far the principal concern of the Ethiopian military during this period was to combat the EPLF* activities on and around the Islands and to deny the use of the Islands to rebel forces either as a staging area for strikes on to the Eritrean coast of Ethiopia or as supply depots and strategic bases. The Ethiopian naval officers concerned did also exercise police powers when they would stop and check fishing boats.

267. The primary purpose of such an exercise was suppression of the insurgency. In most of these cases the witnesses stated that part of their duties was to stop all fishing boats and check their papers and cargo. Thus, "[t]he Dankali fishermen were suspected of cooperating with the rebels in smuggling arms, ammunition and other supplies across the Red Sea." However the duties of these naval patrols also extended to keeping foreign fishermen out of what Ethiopia considered to be her territorial waters. Vessels that were not licensed to fish in the waters or that were of non-Ethiopian registration were arrested or requested to leave.

268. The Eritrean pleadings state that the evidence shows "the inspection of fishing and/or commercial vessels as a primary function of their routine patrols around the islands." Having regard to the fierce fighting that was going on over the years in question in and around the area in question, it is not clear that enforcing fishing regulations was the primary purpose of these Ethiopian naval patrols.

269. At the same time, the Tribunal is not disposed to discount the evidence introduced by Eritrea on the grounds that the acts were not "peaceful." Military action taken in a civil war is in any event not normally regarded as a belligerent act that would have no legal relevance for the question of title. Accordingly, even though the Tribunal does not accept Eritrea's contention that most activity was directed at fishing regulation, the Tribunal finds nonetheless that they are not without legal significance.

270. In 1976, an Ethiopian naval patrol boat arrested three Yemeni fishermen on Greater Hanish Island. Yemen protested to the United Nations Security Council this "flagrant act of aggression and . . . distinct violation of the sovereignty of the Yemen Arab Republic." Ethiopia responded, in a formal letter from its UN Permanent Representative to the President of the Security Council, that "[t]he Ethiopian patrol boats were carrying out their responsibilities within Ethiopian jurisdiction."

271. Following independence, the record shows that much attention became devoted to control of Eritrean fisheries affairs, entailing inter alia a number of vessel arrests, some of which involved Yemeni fishermen. Although a substantial number of witness statements speak of supervisory authority and activity by

---

* *Editorial correction: "EPLF" stands for "Eritrean People's Liberation Front."*

Ministry of Marine Resources authorities in conjunction with the Eritrean Navy, the evidence dates from the time of Eritrean independence and in almost all instances relates to matters occurring after 1995. Without precise fixing of coordinates and distances, it is unfortunately difficult to see whether the activities and vessel arrests in question actually occurred with respect to the waters around the Zuqar-Hanish archipelago or Jabal al-Tayr and the Zubayr group. Many witness statements and reports are not clear as to how close to the contested islands the incidents were.

272. As to Yemen, a number of incidents between 1987 and 1995 are also in evidence. There is documentary evidence of an arrest in 1989 of an Egyptian trawler "next to Zuqar island . . . in the territorial waters of Yemen." There is also testimony from a Navy Captain that in May 1995 he was assigned "to arrest foreign fishermen pirates" and that he arrested "several launches" of "Gulf ownership" with Egyptian crews after a gun battle "in Yemeni territorial waters," "in an area between al-Jah and Zuqar." Although Yemen asserted that in 1990 four Egyptian fishing vessels were arrested "in the area of the Hanish Group," and the owners required to pay an indemnity to Yemen and undertake not to repeat their actions, the supporting document does not specify the location of the arrests.

273. However, a 1990 report addressed to the Yemeni Defence Ministry describes twenty separate incidents between 1987 and 1990 in which a total of more than sixty vessels are reported to have been arrested, accosted, "escorted to" a naval base, or "warned to leave" – a good number of these incidents appear to have related to Egyptian commercial fishing vessels. While some of these are described as having been in the vicinity of the Zuqar-Hanish archipelago or Jabal al-Tayr, Zubayr and Abu Ali, the report refers to the "area of" a named island or islands; one exception is a report of unlicensed fishing by two Egyptian trawlers "at Zuqar." In most instances, when vessels were ordered to leave, the report states that the warnings specified that they should depart "from territorial waters" or "from Yemeni waters."

Other Licensing Activity

274. Apart from fishing, there have been no attempts on the part of Eritrea to demonstrate any licensing activities in respect of the waters off the Islands. For its part, Yemen asserts the official approval in 1993 of plans for a tourist boat operation between al-Khawkha and Greater Hanish. There was also a license granted by Yemen to a German company for the building of a diving centre on the north end of Greater Hanish in 1995. As will be discussed below, between 1972 and 1993 the Yemeni Government recorded eight instances of requests for approval for activities relating to the use of the waters around the Islands, and in several cases approval was given for research and diving expeditions and the like.

* - *

Granting of Permission to Cruise Around or to Land on the Islands

275. As discussed, there is an abundance of evidence before the Tribunal relating to the manifold activities of the Ethiopian Navy in the 20-year period before Eritrean independence. That evidence largely indicates that the Ethiopian naval patrols operated intensive patrolling in and around the Islands during the Ethiopian war against the Eritrean insurgents. In that role, the naval vessels stopped ships, boats and dhows in those waters, requested identification and inspected equipment and cargo. Tourist vessels anchored near the Zuqar-Hanish islands were arrested and brought into Ethiopian ports for investigation and the film from their cameras was destroyed.

276. There is evidence that informal requests from third parties for permission to cruise around, anchor at or land on the Islands were sometimes made to naval patrols. For example, one witness statement indicates that radio requests made to Ethiopian patrol craft to anchor "at the north western cove off Hanish," received from "large foreign commercial vessels" (including ones of Greek, Japanese, Yugoslavian and Italian nationality), were granted for reasons such as "repairs, shelter or rest."

277. As to Yemen, there is evidence that in 1978 three Kuwaiti fishing trawlers requested and received shelter from a storm at Jabal Zuqar, and that on two occasions in 1991 foreign flag vessels sought and received permission to anchor at Zuqar and Hanish for repairs.

278. In addition, between 1972 and 1995 Yemen received at least eight formal requests from third parties, including one from a foreign government, for permission to cruise around, anchor at, or land on the Islands: A request from an Italian organization to conduct research on Jabal Zuqar was declined by the Government of the Yemen Arab Republic in 1972; the French Government in 1975 requested permission to conduct naval exercises in the vicinity of the Hanish Islands; in 1983 a request from a French organization to film submarine life was approved; in 1987, a German request for scientific research studies to be conducted by the *F.S. Meteor* around the Hanish Islands was approved by an official governmental decree and the project was completed without incident; for indeed the *Meteor* seemingly carefully avoided the territorial waters of both Ethiopia and Yemen. In 1992 approval was given for a diving trip by a British yacht, the *Lady Jenny V*, around the Islands; in 1993 the Yemen Government approved a research expedition to the Zuqar-Hanish archipelago to be conducted with the Royal Geographical Society; in 1993, the Government approved the French research expedition of the Ardoukoba Society to Greater Hanish, and also approved a German diving expedition on the yacht *Cormoran*. There is also an unsupported statement that a Polish request for diving in the area was rejected in late 1995.

279. It should be noted however that there is no specification of the islands in the application or report of the cruise of the *Meteor* though the Report mentions the Hanish Islands and states that "maximum values were noted at the Hanish Islands . . . ." Moreover, the terms of the license specified that the "research operation must be conducted in waters at a depth of 100 meters or more," thus excluding research in any close proximity to the Islands.

280. What can be concluded is that there was somewhat greater Yemeni activity than Ethiopian/Eritrean activity in the granting of permission relating to the Islands in the periods stated.

Publication of Notices to Mariners or Pilotage Instructions Relating to the Waters of the Islands

281. Other than Eritrea's fishing regulations, Eritrea has produced no evidence of publication, by Ethiopia or by Eritrea, of general information concerning pilotage or maritime safety.

282. In the five years between 1987 and 1991 Yemen published six Notices to Mariners in connection with its installation of new lighthouses in the Islands. These were: Centre Peak (1987 and 1988); and Jabal Zuqar (1989). Following the 1989 London Conference on Red Sea Lights, Yemen issued a Notice to Mariners concerning a new solar lighthouse on Jabal al-Tayr, and one concerning a new system on Abu Ali. In 1991 the Yemen Ports Authority constructed a new lighthouse on Low Island, and an official telex notification was sent to the Hydrographer of the Royal Navy in Taunton (referring to it as "Hanish as Saghir" Island). In 1992 a similar telex was sent indicating a "beaconpipe" at "Jabal-at-Tair," a lighthouse at "Sawabey" (al-Zubayr), a lighthouse at Abu Ali, a beacon at Zuqar, and beacons at Hanish Sashir and Hanish Kabir.

283. The Tribunal notes that such notices form a natural adjunct to the operation and maintenance of lighthouses, but that latter function, in the particular circumstances of the Red Sea, does not generally have legal significance. The issuance of such notices, while not dispositive of the title, nevertheless supposes a presence and knowledge of location. Moreover, it is to be noted that in relation to these indications, accuracy in identifying the navigational aid and its location is of the prime importance, rather than the provenance of the information.

Search and Rescue Operations

284. Eritrea has produced evidence maintaining that in 1974, the M.V. *Star of Shaddia* was stranded off Zubayr. There is no evidence as to her nationality. *HMS Ethiopia* attempted a rescue, but was unable to approach the ship because of severe weather and mechanical difficulties, and departed without being able to assist.

285. In 1990, the Yemeni Ports Authority rescued an Iraqi vessel, the *Basra Sun*, from the rocky coast of Jabal Zuqar after it had requested assistance.

286. Since there is under the law of the sea a generalized duty incumbent on any person or vessel in a position to render assistance to vessels in distress, no legal conclusions can be drawn from these events.

The Maintenance of Naval and Coast Guard Patrols in the Waters Around the Islands

287. Eritrea has produced a large amount of evidence relating to naval patrolling activity in and around the Islands. The activities alleged are for the most part not referred to in documentary evidence, but rather in affidavits prepared in connection with these proceedings. However, the Tribunal takes note of statements by Eritrea that a large amount of Ethiopian naval records were destroyed in the course of hostilities.

288. **1953-1973:** For the first twenty-year period (1953-1973), Eritrea has introduced two types of evidence: naval logbooks from 1959-1967 and naval operations reports primarily from the 1970s.

289. **Naval logbooks:** The Eritrean Memorial states that "there are numerous records that the Islands were 'visited and/or observed,'"[*] implying that most of the logs indicate this. It also states that they "demonstrate in painstaking detail the continuous Ethiopian presence in the disputed islands" and characterizes them as "record[ing] visits" to the Islands.

290. However, the logs themselves – in contrast with the operations reports – relating to the years 1959, 1961, 1962, 1963, and 1967, do not use the word "visit." Moreover, it is not clear to the Tribunal what that term entailed. The "observations" are largely contained in Column (13) of the standard printed logbook form, labelled "Soundings Fixes Bearings Observations," and a study of the entries in that column shows that they are almost uniformly position "fixes" of azimuth bearings on land points and islands, sometimes from as far as fifteen miles offshore.[22] The Tribunal cannot therefore draw many useful conclusions about Ethiopian exercise of governmental functions with respect to the Islands on the basis of these logs alone.

---

[*] *Editorial correction: Page reference to Eritrean Memorial deleted.*

[22] In one example, it appears that the officer of the watch has helpfully added estimated radar ranges of distance, e.g.: "Ø Jabal at Tair Isl. 045° 6.0 by radar," and "Ø Haycock Isl. 106° 15 by radar," showing that the vessel (H.I.M.S. PC-12) was far offshore on both occasions.

291. **Operations reports and orders:** Eritrea has placed in evidence three operations reports – two cruises in April 1970 and one in July 1971. However, the language in which the missions are recorded in the operations reports is too vague to be relied upon as establishing state functions with respect to the Islands in this case, e.g., patrolling the "area south" of Greater Hanish and the Haycocks, sailing "to Grand Hanish and back," and investigating vessels "south of Zuqar" and "vicinity Jebel Attair." The only relevant precision accorded by this evidence is in the operation report of *HMS Ethiopia* for 20/21 and 25/26 July, where she "[a]nchored Zuqar" overnight in order to remedy mechanical difficulties. Episodes of that nature can hardly give rise to a legal claim of occupation and control.

292. Furthermore, although the Eritrean Memorial captions its description of the reports with a statement that they demonstrate the "continuous Ethiopian naval presence around the disputed islands," for the twenty years in question they cover only two cruises in April 1970 and one cruise in July 1971. In consequence, these documents hardly support the assertion that the Ethiopian Navy maintained a "continuous presence" around the Islands for the entire period of 1953-1973.

293. There are also in evidence four operations orders of the Ethiopian Navy, from January, July, September and October of 1971. They instructed the preparation of "a Schedule for visiting the different areas," including "Kebir Hanish" and "Zukar," and patrols "around Hanish I[s]lands," "within the route: Dumeira is – Fatmah Lt. – Rs Darma – Kabir Hanish – Zuqar – Edd and Ras Darma," and another with a similar routing. They cover less than one year out of twenty, though this may be explained by the asserted destruction of Ethiopian naval records during the civil war. In warfare continuing over several decades, it does not seem likely that Ethiopian activity in controlling insurgency would be limited to a single year.

294. **1974-1980:** Eritrea has also put forward documentary evidence of a similar nature relating to activities from 1974 up until the end of 1980, but this is just as sparse as that for the preceding twenty years. Again, it takes the form of logbooks and orders which, being contemporaneous, have a special interest, as well as correspondence. The logbook entries, for 1974, 1977 and 1980 reveal the same kind of imprecision as the earlier logbook records, one of which, for example, while purporting to "record . . . [a] visit . . . to Hanish (on August 16) [1977]," merely shows "Hanish" in the Column (13) of the Log under "Soundings Fixes Bearings Observations" as having been sighted by P-203 at 0400 on 16 August, at a bearing of 325° and at a *distance of 20 n.m.* This is not evidence of a "visit," nor of passage through the territorial sea of that island.

295. Additional evidence has been presented describing the Ethiopian/Eritrean sea battle off the island of Zuqar after the capture of the merchant ship *Salvatore* by

the ELF* on the way to Assab in June 1979, but it is not clear what evidentiary relevance can be ascribed to this incident. Finally, P-203's logbook in May 1980 records warning shots at a Canadian and a West German boat; the precise location is not indicated in the log but the incident is noted in an entry which begins "slipped out for patrolling Hanish to Zuqar." The 1980 capture of five wooden boats referred to in the pleadings is not particularized further than occurring "near the islands of Lesser Hanish." In April 1980 some Yemeni fishermen were captured "near Zuqar Island," and others were also captured "in the vicinity of the Zuqar/Hanish islands." This incident was in fact protested by North Yemen.

296. Eritrea states that the "most critical Ethiopian naval event of 1980" was "Operation Julia"; and that it "resulted in twenty four hour surveillance and a blockade of the entire area for the entire three month period of the operation." When the map submitted in evidence is consulted, it shows what appear to be four areas of patrolling off the Ethiopian/Eritrean coast: two close on shore, one half-way to Greater Hanish from the coast, and one lying approximately 3-4 n.m. west of Near Island and Shark Island on the west side of Jabal Zuqar, and running south across Tongue Island to just north of Marescaux Rock. The context of Operation Julia shows quite clearly that this was a series of grave incidents at sea between the Ethiopian naval forces and the rebel forces, and that the Ethiopian naval forces patrolled their own coastlines, and the sea mainly west of the Islands facing the Eritrean coast; a main purpose of the operation having been to stop rebels "infiltrating into Assab District."

297. **1973-1993:** For the second twenty-year period, Eritrea has also placed substantial evidence before the Tribunal, largely in the form of seven witness statements specially obtained from seven former Ethiopian navy officers and two witness statements obtained from two former EPLF naval fighters. With one exception, the testimony relates only to activities from 1968 on. The testimony, summarized in the written pleadings, largely concerns activities at sea extending over substantial periods between 1964 and 1991.

298. It is however possible only to rely on this testimony for the most general of indications. In ten out of the thirty incidents described by Eritrea the identity of the Ethiopian or Eritrean vessel is not given. The dates of the incidents are given in only nine cases. Their locations are specified in only three, but in those three instances the time frame extends over indeterminate periods of eight months, five years, and one month respectively. There is therefore no evidence of an arrest or stopping by Ethiopian or Eritrean naval forces with *both* a precise location *and* a precise date, for the entire period from 1970-1995.

---

* *Editorial correction: "ELF" stands for "Eritrean Liberation Front."*

299. In a close reading of the witness statements provided by Eritrea, three other interesting points emerge with clarity which should assist in evaluating the context and scope of this evidence. These points have not been controverted in the proceedings.

300. The first point is that out of the seven witness statements of former Ethiopian naval officers, three record no landings on the Islands. The remaining four are imprecise with respect to either date or location. There are two witness statements that mention more than isolated landings during the entire period from 1973-1993.

301. The second point relates to the nature of the patrols which, as well as being fast, appear to have taken place at night, and sometimes in conditions of darken ship. These factors bear upon the absence of protest by Yemen.

302. Third, although some of the evidence does recite that the "purpose of these patrols was primarily to apprehend vessels carrying contraband and to keep foreign fishermen, who were generally from Yemen, out of our territorial waters," it is not clear that a major twenty-year military operation increasing in intensity can be viewed as primarily related to fishing. There is certainly some validity to the argument that checking fishing boats on a regular basis was an essential part of checking for insurgents and contraband weapons. Just as checking ELF dhows for small arms and ammunition was essential to defeating the rebels ("[t]he dhows could carry hundreds of sheep and goats, so they would hide the supplies underneath the livestock where it was impossible or* us to search") so was checking fishermen (". . . we would often see Dankali fishermen further east, in the area of the islands . . . . We would check the identification papers for the boat, captain and crew and look for contraband and armaments.") However, normal fisheries surveillance does not require checking for "contraband and armaments."

303. There also appears to be, in this evidence, a discrepancy in Eritrean witness statements as to the presence of Yemeni fishermen. While some witnesses state that "Yemeni fishermen were almost never reported to be in the area of Zuqar and Hanish at this time" (the late 1980s) and "I never encountered a Yemeni fishermen [*sic*] in the waters around Zuqar and Hanish," others state: "[w]e patrolled east of the Dahlaks as well as the Hanish islands" and "[s]ometimes, our patrols would find Yemeni fishermen fishing in Ethiopian waters, including around Zuqar/Hanish."

304. **1983-1991:** These witness statements were also intended to supplement the documentary evidence put in by Eritrea as to activities from 1983 through 1991

---

* *Editorial correction: substitute "for" for "or."*

but this evidence is imprecise. Speaking almost consistently in terms such as "around Hanish and Zuqar," "the environs of Hanish," "in the vicinity of Jabal A'Tair," these operations and reports and sailing orders are sparse chronologically: May 1983, October 1984, September 1984, May 1986, July 1984, and August 1987. Even if this evidence were precise as to location and relevance to the Islands, it could still hardly provide a demonstration of a "continuous Ethiopian naval presence around the disputed islands" as it covers only six months out of ninety-six and leaves out four years entirely of that continuous naval presence.

305. Nevertheless, the extent of this evidence and its homogeneity do suggest the conclusion that the Ethiopian Navy, during the period in question, did in fact conduct widespread surveillance and military reconnaissance activities in the waters around the Islands. It is uncontroverted that these patrols were frequent and, in the course of the Ethiopian war against the ELF and the EPLF, of steadily increasing intensity. Elements of the Ethiopian Navy anchored frequently off the Islands, sent details ashore for reconnaissance missions, and even bombarded suspected rebel facilities on the Islands.

306. With the exception of the 1976 incident discussed above (which was protested to the Security Council of the United Nations), North Yemen (and, later, the Republic of Yemen) did not protest any of these Ethiopian naval activities. Although such a lack of protest would normally appear to suggest a degree of acquiescence, four elements need to be weighed by the Tribunal in considering the evidence: the location of the Islands, the fact that they were not settled, and the fact that there was no normal line of communication from persons on or near the Islands to the mainland; the fact that many of the Ethiopian patrols appear to have been conducted at night under conditions of darken ship; the fact that many of those patrols were conducted at high speed; and the fact that civil hostilities were in progress.

307. At the same time, the failure of Yemen to protest the considerable presence of Ethiopian naval forces around and sporadically on the Islands over a period of years is capable of other interpretations. If Yemen did not know of that presence, that belies Yemeni claims that there were Yemeni settlements of fishermen on the Islands and that Yemen patrolled the waters of the Islands and indeed maintained garrisons on them. If Yemen did know of this Ethiopian presence, and if, as the record shows, did not protest it, that could be interpreted as an indication that Yemen did not regard itself as having sovereignty over the Islands, or, at any rate, as an acknowledgment by Yemen that it lacked effective control over them.

308. Yemen could take the view that belligerent acts by Ethiopia against insurgents using the Islands were not elements of continuous and peaceful occupation by Ethiopia, or that Ethiopian regulation of Yemeni fishing vessels found within the waters of the Islands was incidental to Ethiopian belligerency. But such acts,

belligerent or otherwise, could not normally be reconciled with Yemeni sovereignty over the Islands. Thus, if Ethiopia's naval presence in the Islands over the years does not establish Ethiopia's (and hence Eritrea's) title, it may nonetheless be seen as throwing into question the title of Yemen.

309. The Tribunal has found it necessary to address at some length the Eritrean evidence relating to naval patrolling over a substantial period of time. At the same time it must be noted that Yemen has not suggested to the Tribunal that it conducted more than a very few activities during this entire period of naval operations by Ethiopia. Yemen has not explained its lack of protest.

310. Essentially Yemen relies on two witness statements. In one statement, Yemen asserts that patrols of the Islands were "carried out on a regular basis" – weekly in the summer and "once every month or two" in the winter but the dates are unspecified. A specific date, but a very recent one, is given by this statement for an assignment "to arrest foreign fishermen pirates" (May 1995). This statement also tells of intercepting foreign warships (American, French and Russian) "in these islands" and requesting them to leave, but no dates are supplied except for an incident with a Russian merchant vessel "on the western side of Zuqar off of Shaykh Ghuthayyan about 1977-78." Interception of an ELF dhow between Zuqar and al-Jah was recorded "about 1974-75."

311. In the other statement, evidence is given that "during the years of 1965 to 1977" the Yemeni naval forces carried out regular patrols around the Islands, saying that "[t]hey always anchored at the anchorages of these islands and patrolled around them" (specifying the anchorages by name), and that "[o]ur soldiers and officers would land onto their shores." The statement adds, without specifying dates, that "[m]any times our officers and naval enlisted personnel would land on the shores of those islands (Zuqar, Greater Hanish, Lesser Hanish, and al-Zubayr) on dismounted reconnaissance missions (on foot), as well as to swim and relax." The period is not specified other than generally from 1965 to 1977.

Environmental Protection

312. Yemen reports having investigated an oil spill reported by a Russian freighter about 10 miles from Lesser Hanish in 1990.

Fishing Activities by Private Persons

313. There was substantial debate between the Parties as to whose fishing community was more important, and as to how important a part fishing and fish played in the economic life of each state. The Tribunal does not find these arguments pertinent, since in any event it may be expected that population, and economic realities, will change inevitably over time. What may be very important today in terms of fishing may be unimportant tomorrow, and the reverse is also true.

314. For Eritrea, the evidence before the Tribunal includes the statement that "[t]here are more than 2,500 Eritrean fishermen, many of whom are artisanal fishermen engaged in small-scale fishing using traditional methods and equipment" and that "[t]he waters around the Zuqar-Hanish islands supply a significant portion of Eritrea's annual catch." For Yemen, the statement has been made that: "[f]ishing communities along the Yemeni Red Sea coast have historically depended on the neighbouring islands of the Hanish Group for their economic livelihood."

315. Numerous witness statements were submitted by both sides as to the longevity and importance of their respective fishing practices and the significance of fishing in the lives of their people. Yet, although substantial evidence of individual fishing practices in the record may be taken as a different form of "*effectivité*" – i.e., one expressive of the generally effective attitude and practice of individual citizens of Eritrea or of Yemen – it is not indicative as such of state activity supporting a claim for administration and control of the Islands. This varied and interesting evidence, on both sides, speaks eloquently concerning the apparent long attachment of the populations of each coast to the fisheries in and around the Islands, and in particular that around the Zuqar-Hanish Islands. However it does not constitute evidence of *effectivités* for the simple reason that none of these functions are acts *à titre de souverain*. For state activity capable of establishing a claim for sovereignty, the Tribunal must look to the state licensing and enforcement activities concerning fishing described above.

316. Yemen has put into evidence a substantial number of arrests of commercial fishing vessels in the past few years in the waters around the Islands. These arrests have been accompanied by legal proceedings, expulsion of the vessels from the waters, and substantial fines. The arrested vessels appear to have borne foreign registries other than Ethiopian or Eritrean and in most cases seem to have been Egyptian. No protests of these activities have been recorded from Ethiopia or Eritrea. Eritrea also produced a witness who related that "between 1992 and 1993" while a commercial captain in the Zuqar-Hanish waters he reported about 20 Egyptian trawlers. "Some of these trawlers were confiscated . . . ." He further stated that in his job at the Department of Marine Transport it is his current responsibility "to determine what should be done with them."

Other Jurisdictional Acts Concerning Incidents at Sea

317. A lost dhow was searched for off the Islands, and an investigation conducted by Yemeni authorities in 1976; a drowning at sea at Greater Hanish was investigated by Yemeni authorities in 1992.

-

Activities on the Islands

318. In order to examine the performance of jurisdictional acts on the Islands, the Tribunal must consider evidence of activities on the land territory of the Islands as well as acts in the water surrounding the Islands. This evidence includes: landing parties on the Islands; the establishment of military posts on the Islands; the construction and maintenance of facilities on the Islands; the licensing of activities on the land of the Islands; the exercise of criminal or civil jurisdiction in respect of happenings on the Islands; the construction or maintenance of lighthouses; the granting of oil concessions; and limited life and settlement on the Islands.

Landing Parties on the Islands

319. The direct evidence presented shows little or no landing activities on the Islands by either side.

320. Eritrea's evidence shows that during the twenty years of the emergency there was substantial activity onshore and off the Islands by elements of the Ethiopian navy engaged in suppressing the secessionist movements. The record indicates clearly that the Islands were used heavily by rebel forces in connection with their war of independence. As discussed above, in the context of naval operations around the Islands, two substantial patrols and a number of unspecified landing parties by Ethiopian military forces are in evidence for the period between 1970 and 1988.

321. On the part of Yemen, there was an official visit to Jabal Zuqar and the Abu Ali Islands in 1973 following the publicity about possible Israeli presence on those islands. In response to the Tribunal's request for specific information, the Secretary-General [of the Arab League]* wrote to the President of the Tribunal on 28 July 1998, informing him that there had never been "any visit to any of the islands in the red sea by any official delegation of the League of Arab States headed by the secretary general." The letter reported a 1973 meeting between the Secretary-General of the Arab League and the Ethiopian foreign minister, to discuss Arab concern about reports of Israeli use of the Dahlak islands and other islands in the bay of Assab. The Ethiopians invited an Arab League delegation to visit the islands in order to confirm that there was no Israeli presence, "but no such visit was ever made." Finally, the Arab League letter states that "in 1971 and 1973, members of the League of Arab States' military committee, including yemeni officers, visited the islands of the hanish group including zuqar as well as the zubair islands with the sole cooperation and assistance of the Governments of the People's Republic of Yemen and the Yemen Arab Republic." According to

* *Editorial correction: insert phrase in brackets.*

the Secretary-General, no report of these visits had been found in the League's archives.

322. Other Yemeni assertions of military presence on the Islands rely heavily on one witness statement describing unspecified landings over a period of time with unspecified dates, other than generally from 1965 to 1977.

323. Yemen has also placed into evidence information concerning field trips by faculty and students of the Staff and Command College in 1987 and 1990. It does not appear that the trips were for more than a very brief period of time, or left any lasting effects.

Establishment of Military Posts on the Islands

324. The evidence presented shows no permanent military posts on the Islands before 1995. Although Eritrea's statements include the mention of landing parties, it was explained that no garrison had been established and the relevance of such garrisons was denied. Rather, Eritrea emphasized that what was legally relevant were sovereign acts tailored to the character of the territory in question, namely military surveillance and fishing regulation.

325. As to Yemen, although the written pleadings state that "a temporary military garrison" was "established . . . on Jabal Zuqar at the time of" the 1973 visit, and that "[d]uring the 1970s, the Government placed guard posts on other islands in the Group, including on Greater Hanish," no evidence was submitted to substantiate that statement. Photographs introduced into the record of groups of military personnel standing on the Island do not give the impression of permanence. It is also to be noted that no structure or building is shown in the photographs; one would have expected that, had there been any structure or building available, it would have been captured on film.

326. The Tribunal concludes that it cannot accept that a permanent garrison or military post was established on the Islands until following the outbreak of the dispute in 1995.

Construction and Maintenance of Facilities on the Islands

327. There is no evidence of the construction or maintenance of any type of facilities on the Islands by Eritrea. Eritrea nevertheless claims, as an indication of Ethiopia's "consolidation of sovereign control over the disputed islands," that following the hand-over of Aden in 1967 the lighthouses on Abu Ali and Jabal al-Tayr were managed by a private company then based on Asmara, and that Ethiopian regulations applied to transactions by that company in connection with its management and maintenance of those lighthouses. The Tribunal does not consider this to be persuasive.

328. Yemen has however constructed some lighthouses and has maintained others. The operation or maintenance of lighthouses and navigational aids is normally connected to the preservation of safe navigation, and not normally taken as a test of sovereignty. Maintenance on these islands of lighthouses by British and Italian companies and authorities gave rise to no sovereign claims or conclusions. The relevance of these activities and of Yemen's presence at the 1989 Red Sea Lights Conference are examined in Chapter VI.

329. Yemen also points to the siting and installation of two geodetic stations by French companies in 1992 on behalf of the Yemeni Government on Jabal Zuqar and Greater Hanish as examples of state action. Eritrea's response is that these markers were placed secretly and are in any event modest. The Tribunal cannot give too much weight to such small monuments of this nature, and yet must also note that in fact the markers were installed before the exchange of correspondence between the two heads of state in 1995; that they do exist; and that they are reflected on a map of geodetic stations in the Yemen.

330. The maintenance of shrines and holy places that was also presented in Yemen's materials appears to be of a private nature; no governmental activity is suggested. There is unsubstantiated testimony before the Tribunal that "[o]ur government built an airfield between al-Shura and al-Habal [on Greater Hanish] for helicopters." The airstrip constructed by Total on Greater Hanish with Yemen's authorization in relation to the 1985 Total concession and subsequently dedicated to rest and recreational visits by Total employees is discussed in Chapter IX.

331. Although evidence concerning the intentions in May 1995 of the Yemeni General Investment Authority is recent, and although such indications are only of state action without specific object, it nevertheless demonstrates that on a high governmental level the Yemeni authorities were seriously considering that investment should be encouraged for tourism on Greater Hanish, Lesser Hanish, Abu Ali, Jabal al-Tayr and al-Zubayr; thus official government policy implicitly relied on Yemeni sovereignty over these Islands at that time.

Licensing of Activities on the Land of the Islands

332. Eritrea has suggested that the fact that authorization was required for the private firm Savon and Ries to ship radio transmitters to Abu Ali and Jabal al-Tayr, the islands on which that firm maintained lighthouses, was indicative of the exercise of state control. However the regulation of electronic equipment used by a private firm whose personnel were operating in a zone in which military activities were conducted cannot be viewed as an exercise of sovereign authority with respect to the land territory of the islands concerned.

333. Eritrea has produced evidence of the grant of a licence for the operation of a radio transmitting station on Greater Hanish in connection with petroleum activities to be conducted in the vicinity.

334. As to Yemen, discussion follows concerning its construction and maintenance of lighthouses on the Islands. To the extent that most of the useful economic activity and interest in the Islands is generated by their position in the Red Sea and by their relationship to their surrounding waters (whether for purposes of smuggling, fishing, or tourism), most of the licensing activities that have taken place have all been water-related. One brief but not insignificant use of the land resources on the Islands that was also water-related was the recent amphibious scientific research expedition of the Ardoukoba Society to Greater Hanish, authorized by Yemen.

Exercise of Criminal or Civil Jurisdiction in Respect of Happenings on the Islands

335. In 1976, a military court of the Ethiopian Government conducted a trial of employees of Savon & Ries, the lighthouse maintenance company servicing the lights on Abu Ali and Jabal al-Tayr, on accusations of leading and training a subversive group on those islands. The resulting execution of the finance officer and expulsion or imprisonment of a head lighthouse keeper and others caused the company to move its offices from Asmara to Djibouti.

336. The examples of contemporary exercises of criminal jurisdiction over matters occurring in the Islands by Yemeni authorities include a 1976 investigation of a missing dhow and, in 1992, the investigation of the loss at sea of a fisherman off Greater Hanish.

337. In addition, Yemen asserts that for many years the local fishermen have used their own customary law system of arbitration of local disputes under the authority of an *aq'il* – "a person known for wisdom and intelligence." There is a senior "*Aq'il* of the Sea" the most noted of whom is said to have "resided part of the year on the Yemeni mainland and part of the year at his settlement ('Izbat al-Sayyid'Ali) on Greater Hanish." The final authority above village *aq'ils* or the *Aq'il* of the Sea is the "*Aq'il* of the Fishermen," who is a dignitary officially recognized by the Government of Yemen.

338. The *aq'ils* apply what is asserted by Yemen to be a "well-established Yemeni body of customary law, known as the *urf*," to resolve the fishermen's disputes. There is evidence before the Tribunal that the judgments or decisions of *aq'ils* are

binding.[23] Indeed, in the man overboard case just referred to, the evidence before the Tribunal is that "[t]he owner and crew members both informed the local official, who is known as the *Aq'il* Sheikh of the Fishermen, and the Department was notified by the *Aq'il*."

339. The existence of this customary law system of arbitration of small disputes does not appear to be contested by Eritrea. There is evidence that the *urf* and the *aq'il* system appear to be applicable to Yemenis and non-Yemenis within Yemeni territory, and to be regularly applied to problems occurring on the Islands.

340. In the Tribunal's understanding, the rules applied in the *aq'il* system do not find their origin in Yemeni law, but are elements of private justice derived from and applicable to the conduct of the trade of fishing. They are a *lex pescatoria* maintained on a regional basis by those participating in fishing. This reflects the reality also that the principal market for fish is in Hodeidah, on the Yemeni side, and that the fishing activities in the area of the Islands have long been conducted indiscriminately by fishermen on each side of the Red Sea on a regional basis. The fact that this system is recognized or supported by Yemen does not alter its essentially private character.

Construction or Maintenance of Lighthouses

341. The question of lighthouses has already been discussed above in Chapter VI. The present section examines this material only for the purposes of the present chapter on *effectivités*. The lighthouses as Abu Ali and Jabal al-Tayr were administered by the lighthouse management company, Savon & Ries. This company maintained its operation in Asmara until 1976, when it moved its office to Somalia because of prosecution of its staff by the Ethiopian Government for allegedly subversive operations (see para. 335, above). There is however no legal basis for concluding that the location within a state of the office of a private firm, operating under a management agreement for the maintenance of lighthouse facilities on islands, constitutes an intentional display of power and authority by that state.

342. As to Yemen, starting in 1987 a program of installation of new lighthouses in the Islands was undertaken, beginning with Centre Peak in 1987 and 1988, and Jabal Zuqar in 1989.

343. Following the 1989 London Conference on Red Sea Lights, Yemen installed new solar lighthouses on Jabal al-Tayr and Quoin (Abu Ali Islands). In 1991, a new

---

[23] According to a witness statement submitted by Yemen, ". . . any disputant who seeks to avoid an unfavorable decision of the Council may find himself subject to action by the State, including, under certain circumstances, prison."

lighthouse was constructed on Low Island. Finally, a lighthouse was erected on Greater Hanish in 1991.

344. Yemeni Governmental authorities communicated the construction and identification of each of these lighthouses to the public by means of public notices or Notices to Mariners, as described more fully in paragraph 282 above.

345. The legal effect to be given to the construction and maintenance of lighthouses in this particular case has been dealt with in Chapter VI, above.

Granting of Oil Concessions

346. Because of the significant attention devoted to the legal implications of petroleum agreements and activities in supplemental written and oral pleadings, this topic is treated separately in Chapter IX.

Limited Life on the Islands

347. There is also evidence that some of the Yemeni fishermen have maintained "dwellings" on Greater Hanish, Lesser Hanish, and Zuqar, and have traditionally maintained those structures for a long time; or have "settled" on Greater Hanish for the summer, or on Addar Ail Islets or Lesser Hanish for the summer.

348. Eritrea has advanced some evidence that Eritrean fishermen would stay for brief periods on the Islands during the fishing season, but the assertions of "settlements" do not appear to be as prominent in the evidentiary record as those made on behalf of Yemen. There is evidence by one fisherman however that "the longest that I know of anyone staying on the islands is 7 to 8 months."

349. In the pleadings Yemen states that "some Yemeni fishing families have for generations maintained a permanent presence in the Hanish Group," and refers to "fishing families resident in the Hanish Group" in the same context as its discussion of "temporary dwellings" and other temporary residence by fishermen. No specific evidence has been produced about families living on the Islands.

350. One Yemeni witness statement records that naval landing parties "would meet many Yemeni fishermen . . . who were settled on some of these islands, salting and drying fish, and staying there for several months."

351. During the fishing seasons the fishermen from each side could be expected to spend days and nights on end fishing in and around the Islands, since returning to port – whether in Ethiopia/Eritrea or in Yemen – would cost a full day's sailing even if the winds were right. Eritrean evidence is that the Yemeni fishermen "would stay around the islands for only three or four days and then go home." Another old Eritrean fisherman recounts that "[w]e would go to the islands twice

a year for three months at a time. Some of us preferred to sleep on the islands, and others would sleep on the boats. Since the islands were not inhabited, no one told us we could not sleep there."

352. A Yemeni witness declared in his statement that "[a]t Greater Hanish I would settle at the al-Shura anchorage . . . . There were trees there under which we would seek the shade. We would not have to make dwellings." The statement continues to describe the anchorages on Greater Hanish, saying that "[n]ear the Jafir anchorage is the dwelling of Capt. Ibrahim Salim and his crew . . . . At the other end of the island many others have settled, such as the anchorage where I am at al-Shura, then the al-Habal dwelling, and beyond is the Ibn'Alwan anchorage. In the summer many people settle at the Ibn'Alwan anchorage. From al-Qataba alone there are over 40 *huris* [small boats]."

353. The first conclusion must be that settled life on the Islands does not exist, but that episodic or seasonal habitation occurs, and that it appears to have taken place for many years. Eritrea asserts that its fishermen have been predominant, and Yemen asserts the reverse. There is no evident manner in which the Tribunal can, on the basis of the sparse and conflicting evidence before it, decide the matter one way or another. The likelihood is not that one nationality prevailed and the other was absent, but that both were present on the Islands in varying numbers and at various times – and that any precise calculation of relative use would, over time, reveal what may be perceived as a genuinely common use of the waters and their resources.

354. The second conclusion appears to be that the manner of living on the Islands is equally indiscriminate: some fishermen stay on their boats; others sleep on the beach; some construct small shelters; other use larger shelters; some consider their structures "settlements." The one thing that is clear from the record is that there is no significant and permanent dwelling structure, or in fact any significant and permanent structure of any other kind, that has been built and that has been used to live in.

355. The third conclusion is that it is not clear from the evidence, in spite of occasional references to "families" staying on the Islands, whether any family life is in fact present on the Islands. Inasmuch as the use of the Islands is necessarily seasonal, this would seem to be *a priori* inconsistent with family life in the sense of family units migrating to a location where normal community activities continue, as for example with nomadic herdsmen.

356. The final conclusion must be that life on the Islands, such as it is, is limited to the seasonal and temporary shelter for fishermen. The evidence shows that many of them, of both Eritrean and Yemen nationality, appear to stay on the islands during the fishing season and in order to dry and salt their catch, but that residence, although seasonal and regular, is also temporary and impermanent.

357. For the time being however it would appear that there is little question but that this type of activity on the part of nationals of both Yemen and of Eritrea (and Ethiopia) is activity which, in the words of the Court in the *Anglo-Norwegian Fisheries Jurisdiction* case of 1951, represents a "consideration not to be overlooked, the scope of which extends beyond purely geographical factors: that of certain economic interests peculiar to a region, the reality and importance of which are clearly evidenced by a long usage."[24]

General Activities

358. Finally, evidence of more general activities has been presented to the Tribunal by the Parties. This evidence includes assertions of conduct relating to overflight and miscellaneous activities.

Overflight

359. The act of overflying a substantially deserted group of islands is not one that would appear to constitute with any cogency an intentional display of power and authority over them. However it may be noted that in its Attachment 2 to the response given by Yemen to Question 18 ("Chronology of Selected Yemeni Acts Manifesting Sovereignty . . .") a number of overflights are recorded, commencing in April 1982 and proceeding through 1988. Doubtless they were important incidents of watching the unfolding of the Eritrean liberation struggle during that decade, but in any event the Tribunal can accord no substantial weight to these activities.

Miscellaneous Activities

360. Yemen has listed a broad variety of actions and acts in a sixteen-page attachment to its response to the Tribunal's Question 18. A variety of actions of many different categories have been advanced as supporting the respective contentions for consolidation of title over the Islands. The Tribunal has noted the most legally significant acts and positions in its earlier analysis.

361. Considerable emphasis, however, has been placed by Eritrea on an inspection tour conducted by President Mengistu and his staff in 1988. A videocassette of this tour around the Islands was also provided to the Tribunal. The Tribunal is unable to draw any conclusions from this episode, however, as the presidential party passed the Islands at speed and at some distance offshore, and did not stop or go ashore. No question of an intentional display of power and authority over a territory would seem to be raised by such a passage.

* - * - *

[24] Fisheries Jurisdiction Case (U.K. v. Nor.) 1951 I.C.J. 116 (Dec. 18) at 133.

CHAPTER VIII – Maps

362. Finally, maps must be considered. It appears to the Tribunal that maps are used by the Parties at different times for different purposes, and that they have relevance to the dispute in several different ways.

Use of Maps by the Parties

363. Older maps, from the eighteenth and early nineteenth centuries, are adduced by Yemen in support of its thesis that the Islands once belonged to Yemen and that Yemen therefore possesses an ancient title which should cause sovereignty in the Islands to revert to it following termination of the Article 16 suspension under the Treaty of Lausanne. Similarly, maps subsequent to 1872 and earlier than 1918 are adduced by Yemen to show that the Islands fell under Ottoman sovereignty during the period in question and fell within the *vilayet* of Yemen. Eritrea then asserts that maps from the early twentieth century through the late 1930s show that Italy claimed to be, or was received as being, the sovereign over the Islands.

364. Both Eritrea and Yemen have introduced maps produced by third parties in order to demonstrate that informed opinion recognized the Islands as respectively forming part of Ethiopia, or of Yemen, during the period from the early 1950s to the early 1990s.

365. Yemen has introduced maps from the period of the early 1950s to demonstrate that the United Nations considered the Islands not to be part of the Province of Eritrea (within Ethiopia). Both Parties have introduced maps from the period of the 1960s onwards, from a variety of sources, respectively indicating that Yemen treated the Islands as non-Yemeni and that Ethiopia treated them as non-Ethiopian – and that third parties and authoritative sources considered them respectively to be one or the other.

366. Finally, Yemen has introduced evidence showing that Ethiopia, the Eritrean liberation movement before independence, and the Eritrean Government after independence have not considered the Islands to be Ethiopian or Eritrean – but rather Yemeni. Eritrea has introduced evidence to show that Yemen has attributed the Islands to Ethiopia or to Eritrea. Each side has also accused the other of waging a deliberate "maps" campaign – from the early 1970s on the part of Yemen to the early 1990s on the part of Eritrea – to alter the designations, labels, and colours on maps so as to "claim" the Islands as a part of the other's territory.

367. In general however the positions of the Parties emerged as quite different overall in the usefulness they attributed to maps. Even whilst seeking to make the points just enumerated, Eritrea's essential position was that map evidence in general (and the evidence in this case in particular) was contradictory and unreliable and could not be used to establish serious legal positions.

368. Yemen's position was diametrically different; it sought to justify its use of maps in the case for at least four reasons: as "important evidence of general opinion or repute" (in the words of Sir Gerald Fitzmaurice, cited in the oral hearings); as evidence of the attitudes of governments; to reveal the intention of the Parties in respect of state actions; and as evidence of acquiescence or admissions against interest.

The Purposes Claimed to be Served by Maps in the Case

Pre-1872

369. Older maps, from the eighteenth and early nineteenth centuries, are adduced by Yemen in support of its thesis of an ancient or historic title. Most of the maps clearly show the Zuqar-Hanish group and the northern islands as identifiable with the Arabian rather than with the African side of the Red Sea. The Tribunal is not able to judge the extent of the precise territory of the Kingdom of Yemen (*Bilad el-Yemen*). Moreover, in these older maps there is no attribution of the territory of the Islands to Yemen, as such.

370. It appears not unreasonable to infer from the map evidence that rulers (including in particular the Imam of Yemen) of Southern Arabia before the 1872 Ottoman conquest probably did perceive that the Islands fell within their territorial claim as part of Yemen or of the Arabian coast. However this impression must be qualified by the fact that it is not possible to evaluate the *colour* of maps produced during periods when hand-colouring had to be applied to maps at a second stage. These factors are therefore not determinative with regard to the issue of reversionary historic title. Moreover, there is no evidence that Southern Arabian rulers themselves ever saw or authorized these maps. Conclusions based on this material would be tenuous at best.

1872-1918 Period

371. Similarly, maps subsequent to 1872 and earlier than 1918 are adduced by Yemen to show that the Islands fell under Ottoman sovereignty during the period in question and fell within the *vilayet* of Yemen and were administered as part of that *vilayet*. The map evidence appears to confirm the fact that the Ottoman Empire was sovereign over the Islands, upon which fact the Parties are in agreement.

Period Between 1924 and 1939

372. Yemen has introduced a number of maps that appear to prove that Italy in the inter-war period did not officially consider itself as sovereign over the Islands. These maps were produced by the Ministry of Colonies in 1933, 1935, and 1937 and by the Ministry of Italian Africa in 1939, and they show that the Italian colonial authorities did not consider at the time that the Islands formed part of the

Italian Colony of Eritrea. Yemen has also submitted other official Italian maps from the Ministry of Colonies (c. 1925 and 1933) and the Ministry of Italian Africa (1939) of which the first two attribute the Islands clearly to *Yemen* as opposed to the Province of Eritrea, and the third merely omits them from territory of Italian East Africa.

373. Eritrea has introduced an official Italian map of the 1920s to a contrary purpose. It is however hard to discern and appears to be done by hand. Weighed against the evidence submitted by Yemen in terms of official Italian maps of the period, it is not as clear as the Ministry of Colonies' 1933 and 1935 Maps. Nor is its date specified.

374. To the extent that these may be viewed as admissions against interest from official Italian sources, which are not controverted by Eritrean evidence, they have relevance to the Eritrean claim that Italy considered herself sovereign over the Islands at the outbreak of the Second World War. The best interpretation of this evidence appears to be that official Italian cartography did not wish formally to portray the Islands as being under Italian sovereignty in the inter-war period – and even went so far as to assign the Islands to Yemen. On balance, the evidence seems to establish that Italy, in the interbellum period, did not consider the Islands to be under Italian sovereignty or at least does not establish that Italy in that period did consider the Islands to be under Italian sovereignty.

375. However, since the Tribunal has arrived at its legal conclusions about the status of the Islands on the basis of the diplomatic record and agreements entered into between 1923 and 1939, the map evidence – whilst supportive of and consistent with the conclusions reached – is not itself determinative. Were there no other evidence in the record concerning the attitude or intentions of Italy, this evidence would be of greater importance.

United Nations Treatment in 1950

376. Yemen has introduced maps from the period of the early 1950s to demonstrate that the United Nations considered the Islands not to be part of the Province of Eritrea (within Ethiopia). The key evidence here is a United Nations Map of 1950. Eritrea has vigorously contested the accuracy of this map, its provenance, authenticity and effect, saying that "[n]o official map was adopted by the United Nations."

377. It is well accepted that, in the United Nations practice, its publication of a map does not constitute a recognition of sovereign title to territory by the United Nations.

378. Whether the map was attached to the report of the United Nations Commission for Eritrea as an official commission map, or as a compromise – or even as a

merely illustrative map – seems to be beside the point. What it bears witness to is that it was used and circulated – and received no objection. No protest was recorded in 1950 or at any later time, and Ethiopia itself voted in favour of the report with full knowledge of the map.

379. The map however cannot affirmatively prove that the Islands were Yemeni, even if they bear the same colour as Yemen. In this instance, the United Nations was not concerned with Yemen. The map did not in fact concern Yemen as such. What it shows is that the United Nations when it acted on the future of Ethiopia and Eritrea did *not* consider the Islands to be Ethiopian or Eritrean. As already mentioned in connection with the Italian map evidence of the 1920s and 1930s, since the Tribunal has reached the conclusion that Italy had not acquired sovereignty over the Islands by 1940, it could not then reach the conclusion that Ethiopia (and thus Eritrea by derivation) could have acquired title ten years later by inheritance from Italy.

Informed Opinion

380. Both Eritrea and Yemen have introduced a number of maps produced by third parties (such as independent or commercial cartographic sources, or the intelligence, mapping and navigational authorities of third states) in order to demonstrate that informed opinion recognized the Islands as respectively forming part of Ethiopia, or of Yemen, during the period from the early 1950s to the early 1990s.

381. Although the Tribunal must be wary of this evidence in the sense that it cannot be used as indicative of legal title, it is nonetheless "important evidence of general opinion or repute" in the sense advanced by Yemen. But while a considerable number of the maps submitted appear in general to confirm an impression that the Islands, from and after 1952 to the present day, are mainly attributed to Yemen, and not to Ethiopia or Eritrea, there are noteworthy exceptions.

382. Although Eritrea, on its part, has introduced some respectable independent cartographic evidence, this evidence appears to be somewhat outweighed by the contrary evidence from the other side. In some instances the Tribunal cannot agree with the characterization of the maps sought by the Party introducing it. Moreover, the Tribunal is unwilling, without specific direction from the map itself, to attribute meaning to dotted lines rather than to colouration or to labelling. The conclusions on this basis urged by Eritrea in relation to a number of its maps are not accepted.

383. There are also Central Intelligence Agency maps introduced by Yemen and the corroborative labelling in the U.S. Defence Department Mapping Agency charts of 1994.

Admissions Against Interest

384. In 1967, the United States Department of State distributed a press package on the occasion of a state visit by Emperor Haile Selassie to Washington together with "Background Notes" that included a map that very clearly showed the Islands as not being Ethiopian. They are clearly shown in black, just as are Kamaran and the Farasan islands; the Dahlaks are also clearly shown in white, as part of Ethiopia.

385. Yemen has introduced evidence showing that Ethiopia, the Eritrean liberation movement before independence, and the Eritrean Government after independence have not considered the Islands to be Ethiopian or Eritrean – but rather Yemeni. Eritrea has also introduced evidence to show that Yemen has itself attributed the Islands to Ethiopia or to Eritrea. The Tribunal is of the view that most of this evidence tends to cancel itself out, except possibly for the Eritrean maps published after 1992.

386. Yemen further contended that a particular map, asserted by Eritrea to have been produced for the Eritrean Ministry of Tourism by a private firm and to contain a number of inaccuracies, had in fact been distributed to foreign missions, including those of Yemen and the United States, and that it also "hung in Eritrean Government offices in Asmara." This statement was not controverted. The Tribunal notes that an early map produced by Eritrea after it became independent did not attribute to Eritrea all of the islands that it now claims.

387. On its part, Eritrea asserts as well that Yemen has authorized the production of maps that can be interpreted against its interest, including a map published in 1975 which clearly appears to ascribe the Islands to Ethiopia.

Conclusions as to Maps

388. On balance, the Tribunal has reached the following conclusions:

As to the period prior to 1872

Although Yemen has shown in general that most ancient and nineteenth-century maps attributed the Islands to the Arabian sphere of influence rather than to the African coast, the precise attribution of the Islands to "Yemen" has not been demonstrated.

For the period from 1872-1918

The maps produced by each side demonstrate without difficulty that the Islands were under Ottoman domination during the last years of the Empire's existence. There is no evidence in the record, nor was there any discussion in the case, about the effect of this widespread recognition on the validity *vel non* of the asserted Yemeni claim to a reversionary interest.

For the period between the Wars

The map evidence is to some extent contradictory, but by and large the official Italian maps of the time demonstrate that even if Italy harboured a desire to annex the Islands after the Treaty of Lausanne, it certainly did not accompany this desire with any outward manifestation of state authority in its official cartography.

For the post-war period

It is not possible to conclude from the history of the 1950 United Nations maps that Ethiopia acquired the Islands after the Second World War, from Italy or otherwise.

For the period between 1950 and 1992

The evidence for this period is beset with contradictions and uncertainties. Each Party has demonstrated inconsistency in its official maps. The general trend is, however, that Yemeni map evidence is superior in scope and volume to that of Eritrea. However, such weight as can be attached to map evidence in favour of one Party is balanced by the fact that each Party has published maps that appear to run counter to its assertions in these proceedings.

For the period from 1992 to 1995

Finally, evidence is in the record showing broadly-publicized official and semi-official Eritrean cartography shortly after independence which shows the Islands as non-Eritrean if not Yemeni. The evidence is, as in all cases of maps, to be handled with great delicacy.

--*

CHAPTER IX – Petroleum Agreements and Activities

389. It is a singular fact of the proceedings that neither party on its own motion pleaded, described, or relied upon oil contracts and concessions relating to the Red Sea and the disputed Islands. The pleadings of the parties in respect of oil contracts and concessions came in response to questions posed by a Member of the Tribunal at the close of its hearings in February 1998; in the absence of those questions, it appears that those pleadings would not have been made in this phase of the proceedings.

390. Nevertheless, in response to questions put to them, both parties submitted considerable data and argument. In the view of the Tribunal, that data and argument left some questions unanswered. It accordingly called for renewed hearings to be devoted solely to Red Sea petroleum contracts and concessions. Those hearings took place in London from July 6-8, with the benefit of substantial further written pleadings as well as oral argument, in the course of which, and after which, still further material data was introduced. In those hearings, Eritrea largely maintained that these contracts and concessions were probative of little that was relevant to the issues before the Tribunal, whereas Yemen maintained that they were of major significance in support of its position. Yemen contended that the pattern of Yemen's offshore concessions, unprotested by Ethiopia and Eritrea, taken together with the pattern of Ethiopian concessions, confirmed Yemen's sovereign claims to the disputed Islands, acceptance of and investment on the basis of that sovereignty by oil companies, and acquiescence by Ethiopia and Eritrea. Yemen stated that lack of time had been the reason for its not having pleaded the contracts and concessions on its own initiative.

The Provisions of the Pertinent Contracts and Concessions

391. Both Yemen and Eritrea have concluded contracts and concession agreements for oil exploration, development, production, and sale of commercial quantities of petroleum that might be found under the Red Sea. While in the event no such quantities have so far been found, those contracts and concessions merit the Tribunal's consideration for what they show and do not show. Of particular significance for the issues before the Tribunal may be any *effectivités* arising out of or associated with those contracts and concessions.

Contracts and concessions entered into by Yemen

392. Yemen has submitted information on Red Sea contracts and concession agreements as follows.

Shell Seismic Survey, 1972

393. Yemen states that, in 1972, its predecessor, the Yemen Arab Republic, entered into a contract with Shell International Petroleum Company for "a major geophysical scouting survey in the Red Sea." It maintains that the survey, carried out on Shell's behalf by Western Geophysical Company of America in March 1972, involved the shooting of seismic reconnaissance lines in the area of the Red Sea that encompassed the islands of the Zuqar-Hanish group, the Zubayr group and Jabal al-Tayr, and from that fact argues that the survey is supportive of Yemeni sovereignty over those Islands. It states that, as a result of the survey, Shell decided that the southern third of the area surveyed, a substantial zone that encompassed the Zuqar-Hanish group, was not promising, but that it would take up a concession contract for a more northerly block which included Zubayr Island.

394. Yemen has not been in a position to provide a text of the survey contract, whose existence Eritrea questions. It does provide a report of Shell International Petroleum Maatschappij N.V. of January 1977, which refers to an offshore scouting survey whose results were used to select the area of the agreement discussed below. It introduced as well in the course of the hearings on 7 July 1998 the *Final Operations Report, Marine Seismic Survey, Offshore Yemen (Red Sea)* by Western Geophysical Company of March 1972. That report states that the objective of the survey was to provide a preliminary seismic coverage of "the concession area" (though at that stage there was no concession), and notes that the field office and base of operations for the seismic survey were in Massawa, Ethiopia. The report attaches a map of the "approximate area covered by seismic program" (Plate I), which extends right up to the Ethiopian coast.

395. That map indicates that the survey area is irrelevant to questions of title; Yemen hardly is claiming jurisdiction over the territorial waters of Eritrea, and could not have meant to do so by the authorization or performance of the seismic survey in question. The fact that the survey area embraced Islands in dispute accordingly is not probative.

Shell Petroleum Agreement, 1974

396. The Yemen Arab Republic and Deutsche Shell Aktiengesellschaft concluded a Petroleum Agreement on 16 January 1974. The contract area was defined as meaning the specified area and its subsoil and seabed "under the jurisdiction of the Yemen Arab Republic." It comprised a Red Sea block north of the Zuqar and Hanish islands, which islands it names but does not encompass. It does not encompass Jabal al-Tayr, which is to the west of the contract area, nor does it name it. It names none of the islands it does encompass. It includes the Zubayr group among the unnamed islands within the contract area.

397. A reconnaissance survey was contracted for by Shell that entailed seismic, gravity and magnetic data acquisition in the contract area; the survey report does not state that the survey was carried out within the territorial waters of the Zubayr group. A well was drilled by Shell at a point far from the islands in dispute; oil was not found in commercial quantities; and the agreement was terminated.

398. In a *Final Report on the Exploration Venture of Yemen Shell Explorations GMBH Yemen Arab Republic* of May 1981, it is stated that: "The concession area granted to Deutsche Shell . . . under the terms of the Petroleum Agreement of 16 January 1974 extended from . . . the Yemen mainland in the east to approximately the median line of the Red Sea in the west."

399. In view of that statement and the fact that the concession contract speaks not of an area and its subsoil and seabed under the sovereignty but under the jurisdiction of Yemen, the Tribunal concludes that the 1974 Shell concession was granted and implemented in exercise not of Yemen's claims to sovereignty over the islands and their waters within the contract area but in exercise of its rights to the continental shelf as they then were. It further is of the view, in the light of the foregoing factors, that, since the contract does not name the Zubayr group and since Shell conducted no activities on the islands of the Zubayr group or within their territorial waters, the 1974 Shell Petroleum Agreement was entered into without particular regard to the Zubayr group. Those islands appear to have been included within the contract area because the Zubayr group fell on the Yemeni side of the median line, on a continental shelf over which Yemen could exercise jurisdiction.

400. At the same time, the Petroleum Agreement between Yemen and Shell was known to the industry, was published, and its existence and, with sufficient diligence, its terms, could have been known to Ethiopia had it followed the pertinent publications (such as Barrow's *Basic Oil Laws and Concession Contracts*). Ethiopia may be argued to have had notice, at any rate, constructive notice, of its existence and provisions. It made no protest about the agreement, despite its contract area including the Zubayr group to which Eritrea now lays claim. Eritrea maintains that Ethiopia in fact was unaware of the terms of the agreement; that, as a poor country locked in civil war, Ethiopia cannot be charged with gaining knowledge of it, and that, in any event, since conclusion and publication of a concession contract is not a title-generating act, there was nothing to protest in the absence of concrete and visible activities of Shell or the Yemeni Government on the Zubayr group. Yemen, for its part, attaches significance to the failure of Ethiopia to protest. Such absence of protest by Ethiopia, and later Eritrea, characterizes all the concessions granted by Yemen in the Red Sea, and will be evaluated below.

401. The area of the 1974 Petroleum Agreement between Yemen and Shell is further reproduced in a map dated December 1976. That map was prepared by Shell, and

is found in a Shell Report of January 1977 marked "Confidential." It is not contended that it has been published or could or should have been known to Ethiopia. It shows the area of the agreement and the areas of detailed survey within it (which are not near the Zubayr group). To the west of the area of the agreement, there runs a line which is described as the "Approximate tentative international boundary." That boundary runs west of the Zubayr group and west of Zuqar and the Hanish islands as well. No evidence was offered about the considerations that in the view of the drawer of the line gave rise to it, nor did Eritrea specifically comment upon it. In *Yemen's Comments on the Documents introduced by Eritrea after the Final Oral Argument, 29 July 1998*, maps 5 and 6 prepared by Yemen are described as reproducing the line.

402. It appears to the Tribunal that the author of the Shell map was of the view that the "approximate tentative international boundary" was to be drawn on the basis of Yemeni sovereignty over most of the disputed islands and all of the larger ones. That impression is supported not only by the fact that the "approximate tentative international boundary" runs west of those islands. It is strengthened by the author's having accorded the major disputed islands, including Zuqar and the Hanish islands, an influence on the course of the boundary as drawn.

Tomen-Santa Fe Seismic Permit, 1974

403. A Seismic Permit Agreement was concluded between the Yemen Arab Republic and Toyo Menka Kaisha Ltd. ("Tomen") in 1974, which was extended to include Santa Fe International Corp. The agreement was initially characterized by Yemen in these proceedings as a "concession," which was contested by Eritrea; when its text was later introduced, it was found to be entitled, "Seismic Permit," and to provide for Tomen's conducting a marine seismic survey in the contract area. The contract area is specified by the contract to be outlined in "Exhibit A"; however, Yemen has not placed "Exhibit A" in evidence and has not offered an explanation for its absence from the text of a contract otherwise provided in full. The contract itself gives the coordinates of the contract area and Yemen has placed in evidence maps which it states were prepared for these proceedings on the basis of those coordinates.

404. Yemen affirms on the basis of those coordinates and maps that the contract area embraced the whole of Zuqar and the Hanish islands. However, in an "Exploration History Map" prepared by the United Nations Development Programme (UNDP) and the World Bank, undated but apparently prepared late in 1991, on whose probative force Yemen repeatedly has relied, the western line differs. The western line appears to run through, rather than to the west of, the southern extremity of Greater Hanish Island (the explanatory block on the map reads, "Tomen & Santa Fe, started 1974, ended 1975, seismic, 2150 km."). It may be that the line on the UNDP map runs through Greater Hanish along a median

line, as two other concessions, one concluded by Yemen and another by Eritrea, appear to do.

405. The Tomen-Santa Fe Seismic Permit Agreement recites that Yemen has "exclusive authority to mine for Petroleum in and throughout" the contract area, and that the contract area "means the offshore area within the statutory mining territory of Yemen" described in the permit. The term of the contract is six months (and appears to have been extended to a year). The contract specifies that, "The execution of the work program shall not conflict with obligations imposed on the Government of Yemen by International Law." It provides that the contractor shall have the right of ingress to and egress from the contract area and adjacent areas. It further provides that Tomen shall, within the contract term, have the right to apply for a Petroleum License for all or part of the contract area for the exploration, development and production of petroleum, the terms of which are to be agreed upon guided by the terms of similar licenses in OPEC countries.

406. The Seismic Permit Agreement, while not a concession agreement, accordingly is a petroleum-related contract that looks towards the conclusion of such an agreement in certain circumstances. Its assertion of an exclusive authority of Yemen to mine for petroleum within the contract area, and its reference to the statutory mining territory of Yemen, is consistent with conclusion of a contract for exercise of Yemen's rights on its continental shelf. Decree No. 16 concerning the Continental Shelf of the Yemen Arab Republic of 30 April 1967, in proclaiming Yemeni sovereign rights over the seabed and subsoil of its continental shelf and the continental shelf of its islands, asserts the exclusive right to prospect for natural mineral resources of the shelf. The contractual reference to obligations imposed upon Yemen by international law is also of interest, and may be a reference to limited continental shelf rights. In the view of the Tribunal, the Seismic Permit Agreement of itself does not constitute a claim by Yemen to sovereignty over the islands within its contract area, nor does Eritrea's failure to protest the agreement indicate acquiescence in any such claim. However to some extent it presupposes some measure of title to any islands contained within the contract area. The contract area included the land territory and territorial waters of the islands within its extent; this would have included the land territory and also the territorial waters of some or all of Greater Hanish and all of Zuqar and Lesser Hanish.

407. Eritrea argues that in any event seismic surveys are not indicative of sovereign claims. It relies on the Law of the Sea Convention, Part XIII on "Marine Scientific Research." Article 241 provides: "Marine scientific research shall not constitute the legal basis for any claim to any part of the marine environment and its resources." Article 246 provides for the regulation by coastal states of marine scientific research in the exclusive economic zone and on the continental shelf; research which shall be conducted with the consent of the coastal state. States shall in normal circumstances grant their consent for marine scientific research

projects by other states or competent international organizations "in order to increase scientific knowledge of the marine environment for the benefit of mankind." In the view of the Tribunal, these provisions do not relate to the seismic and other explorations for petroleum for commercial purposes carried out by licensees of the Parties in the circumstances of these proceedings.

408. Accordingly, activities undertaken in pursuance of the Tomen-Santa Fe Seismic Permit and other like authorizations by licensees of the Parties have a certain importance, and must be weighed by the Tribunal. In the period between 23 July 1974, when the vessel *Western Geophysical I* departed from Hodeidah, and the completion of its voyage on 9 September1974, a period of some six weeks, "Of the originally scheduled 1500 miles of program, only 1336 miles were recorded due to . . . dangerous shoaling in the offshore islands area." That suggests that there were difficulties in working close to the islands; there are a number of references in the report to the Zuqar and Hanish islands, but no indication is given that suggests any activity on the islands. It is not easy to deduce from the text and maps provided whether seismic work was performed within the territorial waters of the islands. One, for example, speaks of an aerial survey 2 square miles in extent "East of Little Hanish Island." But how far east – and whether within or without the territorial waters of Little Hanish Island – is not shown, nor was the question precisely pursued by counsel for Yemen, who confined himself to stating that operations were conducted "very close" to the islands. Figure 1 of the Santa Fe Report, "Location map & geophysical map," indicates that the areas of detailed survey avoided the immediate waters of the islands, but the map of itself does not show at what proximity to the islands seismic work was conducted. However, if, for example, the geographic position stated "West side Zuqar Island; southwest intersection Lines 50 and 8" is matched against the survey grid found in Figure 1 – each of the bigger blocks being 10 square kilometres – it appears that seismic activities did extend well into Zuqar's territorial waters. As far as can be determined from a review of the report, it is uncertain whether the same can be said for the waters of the Hanish islands.

409. The Santa Fe Report continues: "During the seismic survey, the Zuqar and Hanish islands were observed from aboard ship by the writer, appearing to be made entirely of volcanic rocks . . . . Later, Mr. Hazem Baker, a geologist with the Yemeni government, went ashore on Zuqar Island and collected samples . . . all basaltic." It seems reasonable to presume that he believed that he was landing on an island at least under Yemeni jurisdiction.

Hunt Oil Company Offshore Production Sharing Agreement, 1984

410. Yemen and Offshore Yemen Hunt Oil Company on March 10, 1984 concluded an Offshore Area Production Sharing Agreement. It recites, "Whereas, all Petroleum in its natural habitat in strata lying within the boundaries of YEMEN is

the property of the STATE; and Whereas the STATE wishes to promote the development of potential oil resources in the Area and the CONTRACTOR wishes to join and assist the State in the exploration, development and production of the potential Petroleum resources in the Area . . ." Hunt is appointed Contractor "exclusively to conduct Petroleum Operations in the Area described . . . the STATE shall in its name retain title to the area covered . . . ." The agreement provides that Yemeni laws shall apply to the Contractor provided that they are consistent with the agreement, and that the rights and obligations of the parties shall be governed by the agreement and can be altered only with their mutual agreement. The agreement was approved by Government Decree. The coordinates of the area covered by the agreement are set out in Annex A, to which is attached a map at Annex B showing those coordinates but not naming or showing any of the disputed islands. Yemen has prepared and submitted a map to the Tribunal which shows the Hunt concession as running in the west very close to the edge of, but not including, Jabal al-Tayr, and, at the southern end of the contract boundary, just including the Zubayr group.

411. In fulfilment of its exploration obligations under the agreement, Hunt contracted with Western Geophysical to conduct a seismic survey of the concession area. It did so in 1985, "infilling" Shell data collected a decade earlier. That operation included the area of the Zubayr islands and, it is claimed, Jabal al-Tayr even though the latter did not fall within the concession area. Seismic soundings were taken "around the Zubayr islands and Jabal al-Tayr" but it is not claimed or shown that seismic activities were conducted within their territorial waters. No activities on the Islands are alleged or shown. Aeromagnetic surveys in the contract area were conducted by an aircraft flying from Yemen, and consequently permission to fly through Yemeni airspace was sought and accorded; that fact neither supports nor detracts from Yemen's claims about the status of the contract area. Equally neutral is the fact that, in connection with well drilling, permission was sought "to enter YAR territorial waters and conduct offshore drilling operations," which were nowhere near the Islands. Two wells were drilled far from the Islands; neither produced oil in commercial quantities, and the concession was relinquished.

412. The Production Sharing Agreement does not in terms state a claim of sovereignty of Yemen over the concession area, and, as noted, it takes no notice of the Islands within it, verbally or in the annexed map. It could be interpreted as a concession issued within the area demarcated by a median line in implementation of Yemen's rights on its continental shelf, a concession which includes the Zubayr group but stops just short of including Jabal al-Tayr. It may be said that if it was the intention of Yemen in issuing the concession to assert sovereignty over the disputed islands, the concession would have included Jabal al-Tayr. What seems likelier is that this concession, as others, was issued with commercial considerations in mind and without particular regard to the existence of the Islands. The fact that title to the contract area is stated to remain in the State of

Yemen is not determinative; Yemen holds title to resources on and under its continental shelf; but since the agreement specifies that Yemen retains title "to the area covered" that may be read as a reservation of sovereign title. The reference to the "boundaries of Yemen" is also suggestive of a claim of sovereignty, though "boundaries" does not exclude continental shelf boundaries. The Hunt Production Sharing Agreement was reported in the petroleum literature and gave rise to no protest on the part of Eritrea.

BP Production Sharing Agreement, 1990

413. Yemen and British Petroleum concluded a Production Sharing Agreement on October 20, 1990, whose terms are very similar and in pertinent respects identical to the foregoing Hunt Agreement. It covers the same Antufash Block offshore Yemen that Hunt operated in earlier, and thus embraces the Zubayr islands but not Jabal al-Tayr. However, and this may reflect the policy of Yemen in respect of potential petroleum blocks offered by it in the 1990s, the BP Agreement's description of the block is more specific than that found in the Hunt Agreement, providing: "Whereas, the State wishes to promote the development of potential Petroleum Resources in the Agreement Area block 8, As-Sakir, Shabwa Province, ROY . . ." The text of the agreement was published in *Barrow's*. It elicited no protest from Eritrea.

414. BP conducted extensive aeromagnetic surveys of the agreement area. Low-level flights, conducted with the permission of the Government of Yemen, covered the Area, including the Zubayr islands, and Jabal al-Tayr though it was outside the Area. A Yemeni military officer accompanied the aircraft during its survey. Survey results were unpromising and BP relinquished its rights in the Area in 1993.

415. The Tribunal does not attach much importance to overflights by either of the parties of the islands in dispute. In the circumstances of the case, it is not clear that overflights of these uninhabited islands are tantamount to a claim of jurisdiction, still less sovereignty, over the Islands. However the agreement's characterization of the Antufash block as comprising or being within a province of the Republic of Yemen is a factor of significance in favour of Yemen; it indicates a sovereign rather than a jurisdictional claim. At the same time, the fact that the agreement was entered into in 1990 and published about that time is noteworthy. Ethiopia was then locked in its final struggle with the Eritrean liberation movement, the Mengistu regime was close to collapse, and to suggest that Eritrea today should be taxed with Ethiopia's failure during that period to find and protest the terms of the agreement may be unreasonable.

Total Production Sharing Agreement, 1985

416. Yemen and Total-Compagnie Française des Pétroles concluded a Production Sharing Agreement in 1985, to which Texaco later became party. Its terms appear close to those of the Hunt Agreement concluded the year before, summarized in pertinent passages above. It however recites, "Whereas, all Petroleum in its natural habitat in strata lying within the boundaries of Yemen and in the seabed subject to its jurisdiction is the property of the State; . . ." Since the area of the agreement is onshore as well as offshore, this could be read as an indication of an offshore claim only to jurisdiction and not sovereignty, and could be taken as an indication of such a Yemeni assumption in other petroleum agreements. The Area is stated to be described in Annex A and shown on the map labelled Annex B, but neither Annex is attached to the text submitted by Yemen to the Tribunal. However, it is common ground between the parties that the Total Agreement's western line runs to the east of Zuqar and the Hanish islands. There is no ground for concluding that this fact suggests a lack of entitlement of Yemen to enter into agreements embracing the disputed islands. It rather again suggests that the petroleum agreements entered into by Yemen were concluded without regard to the Islands.

417. Since the agreement area does not include any of the islands in dispute, it is of limited interest for these proceedings, except in the following respects. Total commissioned seismic studies, which were concentrated between the agreement's western line (which fell short of the Hanish islands) and the coastline of Yemen. The single well drilled – which proved unproductive and led to the agreement's termination in 1989 – was distant from the Hanish islands and towards the coast. However, less detailed seismic surveys were conducted to the west of the Hanish islands, outside the contract Area, which entered territorial waters of those islands. Yemen acted as if it were entitled to authorize, and Total's agent acted as if it were entitled to conduct, those surveys in Hanish territorial waters.

418. Having come to know the Hanish islands through its offshore concession, Total in 1993 decided to become a sponsor of the French Ardoukoba scientific mission to the islands to study marine life in the reefs. Total requested and received Yemeni Government permission to establish a landing strip on Greater Hanish so that a Total aeroplane could transport equipment to it. It is also claimed that Total sought and received permission to establish a radio station on Greater Hanish and to permit visiting scientists to use its frequency; evidence in support of this claim has not been provided. Evidence has been provided showing that access to the Hanish islands, described by Total as uninhabited, was subject to authorization delivered by the "Central Operation of the Army." After the conclusion of the Ardoukoba mission, Total produced a report that referred to "les îles Hanish en république du Yemen." Thereafter it sought and received governmental authorization to improve the landing strip and fly Total personnel to Greater

Hanish for rest and recreation. For a time, a Total aircraft flew frequently to Greater Hanish, carrying passengers for these purposes.

419. Incidental as it may have been to Total's Petroleum Agreement, the building and use of an airstrip on Greater Hanish is in the view of the Tribunal a material *effectivité*. It demonstrates the exercise by Yemen of jurisdiction over Greater Hanish, a recognition of that jurisdiction by Total, and the conduct of visible indicia of that jurisdiction – an airstrip in active use – over a period of time. Eritrea appears to have been unaware of it and in any event made no protest. However, Eritrea has introduced evidence showing that a report of activities of a French company in the waters around Greater Hanish was received in May 1986, the period when Total was operating in that area; that an Ethiopian patrol vessel was dispatched to the area to investigate, and that nothing was found. This evidence suggests that, in the perspective of Eritrea, sovereignty over Greater Hanish lay with it.

Adair International Production Sharing Agreement, 1993

420. Yemen and Adair International entered into a Production Sharing Agreement in 1993. The text of the agreement has not been offered in evidence and accordingly the Tribunal is not in a position to analyse it. The agreement was not ratified by Yemen and did not come into force. Yemen has, however, provided maps of the agreement area which show it as falling within Block 24 or the Al Kathib block in which the Tomen-Santa Fe area fell. It maintains that Yemen had on offer an offshore block that included the whole of the Hanish islands, and that Adair chose to take a contract area slightly less than the total block on offer. The maps of the Adair area provided by Yemen show the western line to cut through the southern portion of Greater Hanish Island, leaving the larger part, but not all, of Greater Hanish within the area of the agreement. It explains that Adair drew that western line for commercial reasons. As far as the Tribunal can judge, the Adair Agreement's western line roughly runs along a median line between the coasts of Yemen and Eritrea, drawn without regard to the islands in dispute.

Blocks Offered by Yemen

421. Beginning in 1990, Yemen no longer responded to proposals by prospective concessionaires for rights in areas drawn by them, but began offering concession blocks, dividing most of Yemen and its offshore into blocks. It states that the blocks include the Zubayr islands and the Hanish islands – it offers no explanation for not including Jabal al-Tayr – and maintains that this is further evidence of Yemen holding itself out as the sovereign of disputed islands.

422. Such weight as the Tribunal might be disposed to give to that contention may be qualified by the evidence about the western lines of the offshore blocks provided by Yemen. Yemen has submitted not only its depiction of the blocks. It has also

submitted and relied upon, as "expert opinion evidence confirming Yemen's exercise of State authority over the Hanish islands and other islands," a number of maps prepared by Petroconsultants S.A. of Geneva, illustrations of Petroconsultants' series, "Foreign Scouting Service, Current Status." The maps are dated from 1989 until November 1997. Three of these maps show a western line of Yemen's relevant block running not to the west of Greater Hanish Island but through it, as the Adair Area line does. The map for 1994 is linked to the Adair Agreement but the maps for 1996 and 1997 are not.

Petroleum Agreements and Activities of Ethiopia and Eritrea

423. Ethiopia in the 1970s entered into a number of offshore concession agreements, which stop short of the deep trough that runs through the middle of the Red Sea. At that time, oil technology was unable to support drilling in so deep a trough. While Yemen maintains that these agreements – which it rather than Eritrea introduced in these proceedings – showed a recognition by Ethiopia and the companies concerned that Ethiopia was not entitled to issue concessions embracing the disputed islands, in the view of the Tribunal these agreements simply reflect technological and commercial realities and carry no implication for the rights of the parties at issue in these proceedings. It is reinforced in this conclusion by the fact that Ethiopian concessions typically contain a formula such as the following (as, *mutatis mutandis*, do maps attached to Yemeni concessions): "The description of the eastern boundary of the contract area does NOT necessarily conform to the international boundaries of Ethiopia and accordingly nothing said herein above is to be deemed to affect or prejudice in any way whatsoever the rights of the Government in respect of its sovereign rights over any of the islands or the seabed and subsoil of the submarine area beneath the high seas contiguous to its territorial waters or areas within its economic zone." The Tribunal also finds unenlightening two Red Sea offshore petroleum contracts concluded by Eritrea as late as 1995 and 1996, which were promptly protested by Yemen as overlapping its waters. But Ethiopia's contract with International Petroleum/Amoco is important.

International Petroleum/Amoco Production Sharing Agreement, 1988

424. Ethiopia concluded a Production Sharing Agreement with International Petroleum Ltd. of Bermuda on May 28, 1988. The concession covered "the onshore-offshore area known as the Danakil Concession in the PDRE" (People's Democratic Republic of Ethiopia). It recites that, "WHEREAS, the title to all Petroleum existing in its natural condition on, or under the Territory of Ethiopia is vested in the State and people of Ethiopia . . . and the Government wishes to promote the exploration, development and production on, in or under the Contract Area . . . ," the Government grants to the Contractor "the sole right to explore, develop and produce Petroleum in the Contract Area . . . ." On November 1, 1989, 60% of the contract was assigned to Amoco Ethiopia

Petroleum Company. Amoco assumed operative responsibility under the assignment.

425. The map attached to the 1988 Production Sharing Agreement shows "Ethiopia-Red Sea Acreage," onshore and offshore, the latter's eastern line running through the southwest extremity of Greater Hanish Island. The description of the Contract Area runs "To the Offshore point 13 at the intersection of LAT 14 DEG 30 with the international median line between North Yemen and Ethiopia, then along the Offshore median line." The agreement contained a force majeure clause, including wars, insurrections, rebellions and terrorist acts, during which the life of the contract would be prolonged. Apparently in view of the fighting between Ethiopian and Eritrean units, force majeure was declared on 9 February 1990 and as of June 1992 was stated to be still in effect.

426. However there is ambiguity about the extent of the Contract Area, at any rate in depictions of it on maps. Amoco Ethiopia Petroleum Company filed four Annual Reports with the People's Democratic Republic of Ethiopia which are in point.

427. The Annual Report for 1989 recounts that geologic activities were undertaken in 1989, that Delft Geophysical Company was awarded a contract to acquire marine seismic, gravity and magnetic data, and that a scout trip by Delft was completed in December. Preliminary seismic interpretation and mapping was initiated. The map attached to the 1989 Report shows virtually all of Greater and Lesser Hanish within the area of the contract, i.e., considerably more than does the map attached to the Production Sharing Agreement.

428. The Annual Report for 1990 observes that activities were suspended with the advent of force majeure on February 9, 1990; as of the end of 1990, the security situation within the Danakil area was considered to remain unsafe for normal seismic operations. It reports on considerable geologic and geophysical activity before that time, and lists some $2,000,000 in expenditures under the agreement. While the description of the Contract Area matches that in the 1989 report, two maps are attached to the 1990 Annual Report. The first map of the Danakil Contract Area shows the eastern line as running not through but rather west of the Hanish islands. The second map of that Contract Area shows virtually all of Greater and Lesser Hanish within the Contract Area, duplicating the map attached to the 1989 Annual Report.

429. The 1991 Annual Report notes that force majeure has effectively extended the initial period of the contract. While normal seismic operations were unsafe in 1991, substantial technical evaluation of existing data continued. The map of the Contract Area in the 1991 Annual Report shows virtually all of the Hanish islands within the Contract Area, duplicating the maps to that effect in the 1989 and 1990 Reports.

430. The 1992 Annual Report reports limited reprocessing work. It states that Amoco and International Petroleum representatives met with officials of newly independent Eritrea in Asmara on June 24, 1993,* when assurances were received that the Danakil Production Sharing Agreement would be recognized by Eritrea. It attaches a contract summary entitled, "Eritrea Danakil Block" and gives an expiration date of February 9, 1997, "to be delayed because of force majeure." The governing law is now described as Eritrean. The Danakil Block map attached to the 1993 Annual Report shows virtually all of the Hanish islands within the Contract Area, as does a "composite magnetic map of the Danakil concession."

431. A map prepared by Petroconsultants, on whose maps Yemen has repeatedly relied, also shows the Amoco Contract Area as embracing the greater part of Greater Hanish.

432. Yemen, while not denying that it never protested the terms or geographical extent of the International Petroleum-Amoco Production Sharing Agreement, argues that it could not be charged with doing so. It observes that an article in the *Petroleum Economist* of October 1991 presents a map which shows an Amoco concession that does not include the Hanish islands. (The UNDP map, which is an "Exploration History Map," does not name the Amoco concession.) Yemen also maintains that the Amoco contract lasted only some three months and that, by the time it might have come to its attention, force majeure prevailed, which might have induced Yemen to take no action.

433. The Tribunal does not find Yemen's position entirely persuasive. As the Annual Reports summarized above demonstrate, the IPC/Amoco contract was extended well beyond three months and into the days of Eritrean independence; its life compares with that of the contracts on which Yemen relies. If Yemen had secured and read Amoco's Annual Reports – annual reports of American oil companies are generally publicly available for the asking – and if Yemen had evinced the alertness it did in respect of Eritrea's contracts of 1995 and 1996, it would have seen that Ethiopia claimed the right to contract for the exploration, development and production of oil in an area claimed as its territory that included some or virtually all of Greater Hanish islands. Amoco is a major player on the international petroleum scene, and in the immediate area; indeed, one of the maps introduced into evidence by Yemen, shows Amoco together with BP in the Antufash block and shows the Danakil Amoco concession angling into the Adair area in the Al Kathib block.

434. Yemen in its argument has made a great deal about what it alleges is the failure of Ethiopia or Eritrea to grant any concession contract that included disputed islands, and their failure to protest grants of Yemen that did include those islands.

---

* *Editorial correction: the correct year is "1992."*

But it has been demonstrated that, in the lately pleaded International Petroleum/Amoco Production Sharing Agreement, Ethiopia did grant a concession including much or virtually all of the Hanish islands, and that Yemen failed to protest that agreement. It is of further interest that the map attached to the Production Sharing Agreement speaks of drawing the boundary along the international median line between Yemen and Ethiopia.

435. Eritrea also claims certain pertinent *effectivités*. It has submitted a copy of an Ethiopian radio transmitting license granted circa 1988-89 (the earlier date on the contract is apparently of the Ethiopian calendar) to Delft Geophysical Co. for the establishment of a station on Greater Hanish Island, presumably in connection with the seismic work which Amoco had contracted with Delft to perform. It has provided the text of a detailed order to the most senior military commanders to provide protection to a petroleum exploration expedition of the Ethiopian Ministry of Mines and Energy to be deployed to areas "including Greater Hanish Island." It has provided an Ethiopian memorandum on oil exploration in the Red Sea carrying the Ethiopian date of April 13, 1982 (which is circa 1989 A.D.), stating that Amoco-Ethiopia Petroleum Company "has installed navigation beacons to enable it to conduct seismic study . . . including on Greater Hanish Island." The memorandum continues: "An Amoco professional team of contractors will be available starting 3rd week of December to select areas for the installation as follows:

> For two weeks installation of navigation beacons on the 8 selected locations; At the end of the two-week period, conduct 6 week-long seismic tests . . ."

and it calls for ensuring the protection of the contractors and their equipment during beacon installation and for the protection of the installed beacons. It further requests protection for the Delft Geophysical ship while it is conducting seismic tests. Another memorandum states that an Amoco contracting team will conduct helicopter patrols to select locations for the installation of navigation beacons, including locations "on Greater Hanish." It is not entirely clear whether these activities were in fact completed, although the Amoco Annual Report for 1989 does corroborate that Delft Geophysical did conduct a scout trip in December of 1989 (see para. 427, above).

* - *

436. In the light of this complex concession history, the Tribunal has reached the following conclusions:

437. The offshore petroleum contracts entered into by Yemen, and by Ethiopia and Eritrea, fail to establish or significantly strengthen the claims of either party to sovereignty over the disputed islands.

438. Those contracts however lend a measure of support to a median line between the opposite coasts of Eritrea and Yemen, drawn without regard to the islands, dividing the respective jurisdiction of the parties.

439. In the course of the implementation of the petroleum contracts, significant acts occurred under state authority which require further weighing and evaluation by the Tribunal.

* - * - *

CHAPTER X – Conclusions

440. Having examined and analysed in great detail the extensive materials and evidence presented by the Parties,[25] the Tribunal may now draw the appropriate conclusions.

Ancient Title

441. First there is the question of an "ancient title" to which Yemen attaches great importance; moreover the Agreement for Arbitration requires the Tribunal to decide the question of sovereignty "on the basis in particular of historic titles." Yemen contends that it enjoys an ancient title to "the islands," which title existed before the hegemony of the Ottoman Empire and indeed emanates from medieval Yemen. It contends, moreover, that this title still subsisted in international law at the time when the Turks were defeated at the end of the First World War, and that therefore, when the Ottoman Empire renounced their generally acknowledged sway over the islands by the Treaty of Lausanne in 1923, the right to enjoy that title in possession "reverted" to Yemen.

442. This is an interesting argument and one that raises a number of questions concerning the international law governing territorial sovereignty. No one doubts that during the period of the Ottoman Empire – certainly in the second Ottoman period 1872-1918 – the Ottomans enjoyed possession of, and full sovereignty over, all the islands now in dispute, and thus not only factual possession but also a sovereign title to possession. When this regime ceased in 1923, was there a "reversion" to an even older title to fill a resulting vacuum?

443. It is doubted by Eritrea whether there is such a doctrine of reversion in international law. This doubt seems justified in view of the fact that very little support for such a doctrine was cited by Yemen, nor is the Tribunal aware of any basis for maintaining that reversion is an accepted principle or rule of general international law. Moreover, even if the doctrine were valid, it could not apply in this case. That is because there is a lack of continuity. It has been argued by Yemen that in the case of historic title no continuity need be shown, but the Tribunal finds no support for this argument.

444. Yemen's argument is difficult to reconcile with centuries of Ottoman rule over the entire area, ending only with the Treaty of Lausanne (see Chapter V, above).

---

[25] The Tribunal wishes to note the sheer volume of written pleadings and evidence received from the Parties in this first phase of the arbitral proceedings. Each Party submitted over twenty volumes of documentary annexes, as well as extensive map atlases. In addition, the Tribunal has carefully reviewed the verbatim transcripts of the oral hearings, which together far exceed 1,000 pages. The Tribunal further notes that the majority of documents were submitted in their original language, and the Tribunal has relied on translations provided by the Parties.

This is the more so because, under the principle of intertemporal law, the Ottoman sovereignty was lawful and carried with it the entitlement to dispose of the territory. Accepting Yemen's argument that an ancient title could have remained in effect over an extended period of another sovereignty would be tantamount to a rejection of the legality of Ottoman title to full sovereignty.

445. The Treaty of Lausanne did not expressly provide, as the Treaty of Sèvres would have done, that Turkey renounced her territorial titles in favour of the Allied Powers; which provision would certainly have excluded any possibility of the operation of a doctrine of reversion. Yemen was not a party to the Treaty of Lausanne, which was therefore *res inter alios acta.* Nevertheless, none of the authorities doubts that the formerly Turkish islands were in 1923 at the disposal of the parties to the Lausanne Treaty, just as they had formerly been wholly at the disposal of the Ottoman Empire, which was indeed party to the treaty and in it renounced its sovereignty over them. Article 16 of the Treaty created for the islands an objective legal status of indeterminacy pending a further decision of the interested parties; and this legal position was generally recognised, as the considerable documentation presented by the Parties to the Tribunal amply demonstrates. So, it is difficult so see what could have been left of such a title after the interventions of the Ottoman sovereignty which was generally regarded as unqualified; and its replacement by the Article 16 regime which put the islands completely at the disposal of the "interested parties."

446. There is a further difficulty. Yemen certainly existed before the region came to be under the domination of the Ottomans. But there must be some question whether the Imam, who at that period dwelt in and governed a mountain fortress, had had sway over "the islands." Further, there is the problem of the sheer anachronism of attempting to attribute to such a tribal, mountain and Muslim medieval society the modern Western concept of a sovereignty title, particularly with respect to uninhabited and barren islands used only occasionally by local, traditional fishermen.

447. In keeping with the dictates of the Arbitration Agreement, both Parties, and Yemen especially, have placed "particular" emphasis on historic titles as a source of territorial sovereignty. They have, however, failed to persuade the Tribunal of the actual existence of such titles, particularly in regard to these islands.

448. Eritrea's claims too, insofar as they are said to be derived by succession from Italy through Ethiopia, if hardly based upon an "ancient" title, are clearly based upon the assertion of an historic title. There is no doubt, as has been shown in Chapters V, VI and VII above, that Italy in the inter-war period did entertain serious territorial ambitions in respect of the Red Sea islands; and did seek to further these ambitions by actual possession of some of them at various periods. Major difficulties for the Eritrean claims through succession are, as has been shown above in some detail, first the effect of Article 16 of the Treaty of

Lausanne of 1923, and later the effects of the provisions of the Italian Peace Treaty of 1947. But there is also the fact that the Italian Government, in the inter-war period, constantly and consistently gave specific assurances to the British Government that Italy fully accepted and recognized the indeterminate legal position of these islands as established by treaty in 1923. No doubt Italy was hoping that the effect of her active expansionist policies might eventually be that "the parties concerned" would be persuaded to acquiesce in a *fait accompli*. But that never happened.

449. So there are considerable problems for both Parties with these versions of historic title. But the Tribunal has made great efforts to investigate both claims to historic titles. The difficulties, however, arise largely from the facts revealed in that history. In the end neither Party has been able to persuade the Tribunal that the history of the matter reveals the juridical existence of an historic title, or of historic titles, of such long-established, continuous and definitive lineage to these particular islands, islets and rocks as would be a sufficient basis for the Tribunal's decision. And it must be said that, given the waterless and uninhabitable nature of these islands and islets and rocks, and the intermittent and kaleidoscopically changing political situations and interests, this conclusion is hardly surprising.

450. Both Parties, however, also rely upon what is a form of historic claim but of a rather different kind; namely, upon the demonstration of use, presence, display of governmental authority, and other ways of showing a possession which may gradually consolidate into a title; a process well illustrated in the *Eastern Greenland* case, the *Palmas* case, and very many other well-known cases. Besides historic titles strictly so-called the Tribunal is required by the Agreement for Arbitration to apply the "principles, rules and practices of international law"; which rubric clearly covers this kind of argument very familiar in territorial disputes. The Parties clearly anticipated the possible need to resort to this kind of basis of decision – though it should be said that Yemen expressly introduces this kind of claim in confirmation of its ancient title, and Eritrea introduces this kind of claim in confirmation of an existing title acquired by succession – and the great quantity of materials and evidences of use and of possession provided by both Parties have been set out and analysed in Chapter VII above, together with Chapter VIII on maps and Chapter IX on the history of the petroleum agreements. It may be said at once that one result of the analysis of the constantly changing situation of all these different aspects of governmental activities is that, as indeed was so in the *Minquiers and Ecrehos*[26] case where there had also been much argument about claims to very ancient titles, it is the relatively recent history of use and possession that ultimately proved to be a main basis of the Tribunal

[26] Minquiers and Ecrehos (U.K. v. Fr.), 1953 I.C.J. 47.

decisions. And to the consideration of these materials and arguments this Award now turns.

Evidences of the Display of Functions of State and Governmental Authority

451. These materials have been put before the Tribunal by the Parties with the intention of showing the establishment of territorial sovereignty over the islands, in Judge Huber's words in the *Palmas* case,[27] "by the continuous and peaceful display of the functions of state within a given region." But the kind of actions that may be deployed for this purpose has inevitably expanded in the endeavour to show what Charles de Visscher named a gradual "consolidation" of title. Accordingly, the Tribunal is faced in this case with an assortment of factors and events from many different periods, intended to show not only physical activity and conduct, but also repute, and the opinions and attitudes of other governments (the different classes of materials are set out above in Chapter VII).

452. It is well known that the standard of the requirements of such activity may have to be modified when one is dealing, as in the present case, with difficult or inhospitable territory. As the Permanent Court of International Justice said in the *Legal Status of Eastern Greenland* case, "[I]t is impossible to read the records of the decisions in cases as to territorial sovereignty without observing that in many cases the tribunal has been satisfied with very little in the way of the actual exercise of sovereign rights, provided that the other state could not make a superior claim."[28]

453. This raises, however, a further important question of principle. The problem involved is the establishment of territorial sovereignty, and this is no light matter. One might suppose that for so important a question there must be some absolute minimum requirement for the acquisition of such a right, and that in principle it ought not normally to be merely a relative question.

454. It may be recalled that this question of principle did arise in the *Palmas* case, but there Huber was able to meet it by appealing to the particular terms of the *compromis*, which, said Huber, "presupposes for the present case that the Island of Palmas (or Miangas) can belong only to the United States or to the Netherlands and must form in its entirety part of the territory either of the one or of the other of these two Powers, parties to the dispute," and "[t]he possibility for the arbitrator to found his decision on the relative strength of the titles invoked on either side must have been envisaged by the parties to the Special Agreement."

---

[27] Island of Palmas (U.S. v. Neth.), 2 R.I.A.A. 829 (1929).

[28] Legal Status of Eastern Greenland (Den. v. Nor.), 1933 P.C.I.J. (Ser. A/B) No. 53.

455. The Arbitration Agreement in the present case, however, is in different and even unusual terms. The Tribunal is required only to make "an award on territorial sovereignty" and "to decide the sovereignty." The compromissory provision which led Huber to the possibility of deciding only on the basis of a marginal difference in weight of evidence cannot be said to apply in the present case.

456. There is certainly no lack of materials, evidence, or of arguments in the present case. The materials, on the contrary, are voluminous and the result of skilled research by the teams of both Parties, and of the excellent presentations by their counsel. But what these materials have in fact revealed is a chequered and frequently changing situation in which the fortunes and interests of the Parties constantly ebb and flow with the passage of the years. Moreover, it has to be remembered that neither Ethiopia nor Yemen had much opportunity of actively and openly demonstrating ambitions to sovereignty over the islands, or of displaying governmental activities upon them, until after 1967, when the British left the region. For, as shown above, the British were constantly vigilant to maintain the position effected by the Treaty of Lausanne that the legal position of "the islands" was indeterminate.

457. In these circumstances where for all the reasons just described the activities relied upon by the parties, though many, sometimes speak with an uncertain voice, it is surely right for the Tribunal to consider whether there are in the instant case other factors which might help to resolve some of these uncertainties. There is no virtue in relying upon "very little" when looking at other possible factors might strengthen the basis of decision.

458. An obvious such factor in the present case is the geographical situation that the majority of the islands and islets and rocks in issue form an archipelago extending across a relatively narrow sea between the two opposite coasts of the sea. So there is some presumption that any islands off one of the coasts may be thought to belong by appurtenance to that coast unless the state on the opposite coast has been able to demonstrate a clearly better title. This possible further factor looks even more attractive when it is realised that its influence can be seen very much at work in the legal history of these islands; beginning indeed with the days of Ottoman rule when even under the common sovereignty of the whole region it was found convenient to divide the jurisdiction between the two coastal local authorities (see paras. 132-136, above). Moreover, in the present case, the examination of the activities material itself shows very clearly that there was no common legal history for the whole of this Zuqar-Hanish archipelago; some of the evidence not surprisingly refers to particular islands or to sub-groups of islands.

459. Thus the Tribunal has found it necessary, in order to decide the question of sovereignty, to consider the several subgroups of the islands separately, if only for the reason that the different subgroups have, at least to an important extent,

separate legal histories; which is only to be expected in islands that span the area between two opposite coasts. This may seem only a natural or even manifest truth, but Yemen in particular has emphasised the importance it attaches to what it calls a principle of natural unity of the islands, and some comment on this theory is therefore required.

Natural and Physical Unity

460. Yemen's pleadings insist strongly on what it calls "the principle of natural or geophysical unity" in relation to the Hanish group of islands; Yemen uses the name of the "Hanish Group" both in its texts and in its illustrative maps to encompass the entire island chain, including the Haycocks and the Mohabbakahs (the present comments do not refer of course to the northern islands of Jabal al-Tayr and the Zubayr group, which will be considered separately later on).

461. This "principle" is described in Chapter 5 of the Yemen Memorial, where impressive authority is cited in support of it, including Fitzmaurice, Waldock and Charles de Visscher. That there is indeed some such concept cannot be doubted. But it is not an absolute principle. All these authorities speak of it in terms of raising a presumption. And Fitzmaurice is, in the passage cited, clearly dealing with the presumption that may be raised by proximity where a state is exercising or displaying sovereignty over a parcel of territory and there is some question whether this is presumed to extend also to outlying territory over which there is little or no factual impact of its authority. The Tribunal has no difficulty in accepting these statements of high authority; but what they are saying is in fact rather more than a simple principle of unity. It will be useful to cite Fitzmaurice again:

> *The question of 'entity' or 'natural unity'*
> This question can have far-reaching consequences. Not only may it powerfully affect the play of probabilities and presumptions, but also, if it can be shown that the disputed areas (whether by reason of actual contiguity or of proximity) are part of an entity or unity over which as a whole the claimant State has sovereignty, this may (under certain conditions and within certain limits) render it unnecessary – or modify the extent to which it will be necessary – to adduce specific evidence of State activity in relation to the disputed areas as such – provided that such activity, amounting to effective occupation and possession, can be shown in the principle established by the Island of Palmas case that 'sovereignty cannot be exercised in fact at every moment on every point of a territory'.[29]

462. Thus, the authorities speak of "entity" or "natural unity" in terms of a presumption or of probability and moreover couple it with proximity, contiguity, continuity, and such notions, well known in international law as not in themselves creative of title, but rather of a possibility or presumption for

[29] 32 B.Y.I.L. (1955-56) 73-74.

extending to the area in question an existing title already established in another, but proximate or contiguous, part of the same "unity."

463. These ideas, however, have a twofold possible application in the present case. They may indeed, as Yemen would have it, be applied to cause governmental display on one island of a group to extend in its juridical effect to another island or islands in the same group. But by the same rationale a complementary question also arises of how far the sway established on one of the mainland coasts should be considered to continue to some islands or islets off that coast which are naturally "proximate" to the coast or "appurtenant" to it. This idea was so well established during the last century that it was given the name of the "portico doctrine" and recognised "as a means of attributing sovereignty over off-shore features which fell within the attraction of the mainland."[30] The relevance of these notions of international law to the legal history of the present case is not far to seek.

464. Thus the principle of natural and physical unity is a two-edged sword, for if it is indeed to be applied then the question arises whether the unity is to be seen as originating from the one coast or the other. Moreover, as the cases and authorities cited by Yemen clearly show, these notions of unity and the like are never in themselves roots of title, but rather may in certain circumstances raise a presumption about the extent and scope of a title otherwise established.

465. In spite of unity theories, the fact is that both Parties have tacitly conceded that, for the purposes at any rate of the exposition of their pleadings, it may be accepted that there can be sub-groups within the main group. The nomenclature within common use indicates at least three of the sub-groups: the Mohabbakahs; the Haycocks; and what it will be convenient at least for the moment to call the Zuqar-Hanish group and its many satellite islands, islets, and rocks. These names will all be found in the *British Pilot and Sailing Directions for the Southern Red Sea* (Yemen has cited this publication as authority for regarding all these islands as one group, but of course if one is concerned with them as sailing hazards or landmarks when traversing the Red Sea there is really no other way to do it). There are also the two northern islands: Jabal al-Tayr, and the group of which the biggest island is Jabal Zubayr. The Tribunal will now consider its conclusions in respect of each of the three subgroups and then, finally, the northern islands.

466. Thus, in order to make decisions on territorial sovereignty, the Tribunal has hardly surprisingly found no alternative but to depart from the terms in which both Parties have pleaded their cases, namely by each of them presenting a claim to every one of the islands involved in the case. The legal history simply does not

---

[30] D. O'CONNELL, THE INTERNATIONAL LAW OF THE SEA 185 (1982).

support either such claim.[31] For, as has been explained above, much of the material is found on examination to apply either to a particular island or to a sub-group of islands. The Tribunal has accordingly had to reach a conclusion which neither Party was willing to contemplate, namely that the islands might have to be divided; not indeed by the Tribunal but by the weight of the evidence and argument presented by the Parties, which does not fall evenly over the whole of the islands but leads to different results for certain sub-groups, and for certain islands.

The Mohabbakahs

467. The Mohabbakah Islands are four rocky islets which amount to little more than navigational hazards. They are Sayal Islet, which is no more than 6 nautical miles from the nearest point on the Eritrean mainland coast, Harbi Islet and Flat Islet; all three of these are within twelve nautical miles of the mainland coast. Finally, there is High Islet, which is less than one nautical mile outside the twelve-mile limit from the mainland coast, and about five nautical miles from the nearest Haycock island, namely South West Haycock.

468. Eritrea has sought to show that Italy obtained title to the Mohabbakahs along with the various local agreements Italy made with local rulers (see para. 159, above), which led to its securing title over the Danakil coast; this was not protested by Turkey and came to be recognized by Great Britain. The diplomatic history has some interest for this case, especially in highlighting the question of whether South West Haycock is a Mohabbakah island, or part of a separate group of Haycocks, or part of a larger "Zuqar-Hanish group" (see para. 215, above, for the 1930 Italian claim to sovereignty over South West Haycock).

469. Eritrea thus contends that the Mohabbakahs were comprised within what was passed to Ethiopia and so to Eritrea after the Second World War and that this is affirmed by the reference in Article 2 of the 1947 Peace Treaty to the islands "off the coast" and by the constitutional arrangements.

---

[31] In this connection it is interesting to see the statements made in the 1977 "Top Secret" memorandum of the Ministry of Foreign Affairs of The Provisional Military Government of Socialist Ethiopia, discussed above in para. 245. This memorandum refers to islands in the southern part of the Red Sea that "have had no recognized owner," with respect to which Ethiopia "claims jurisdiction" and "both North and South Yemen have started to make claims." South Yemen's position is that the islands were illegally handed over to Ethiopia by the British when Britain was giving up its rights in the protectorate of Aden. It adds "the North Yemen government has now raised the question of jurisdiction over the islands." It goes on to recommend bilateral negotiations which seem in fact to have been entered into before the time of this memorandum for it goes on to say that "[b]oth states . . . have informally mentioned the possibility of dividing the islands between the two of them. The proposal is to use the median line, which divides the Red Sea equally from both countries' coastal borders, as the dividing line . . . . Ethiopia rejected this proposal as disadvantageous."

470. Yemen claims that the only islands Ethiopia secured jurisdiction over through local rulers were the islands in Assab Bay; and that, because formerly both coasts of the Red Sea fell under Ottoman rule; and because after the end of the First World War Yemen reverted to its "historic title"; and also because the Mohabbakahs are properly to be perceived as a unity with the Haycocks and the Zuqar-Hanish group, title to all these islands lies with Yemen. The Tribunal rejects this argument.

471. The Tribunal has already noted that there is no evidence that the Mohabbakah islands were part of an original historic title held by Yemen, even were such a title to have existed and to have reverted to Yemen after the First World War. And, even if it were the case that only the Assab Bay islands passed to Eritrea by Italy in 1947, no serious claims to the Mohabbakahs have been advanced by Yemen since that time, until the events leading up to the present arbitration.

472. The Tribunal need not, however, decide whether Italian title to the Mohabbakahs survived the Treaty of Lausanne, and passed thereafter to Ethiopia and then to Eritrea. It is sufficient for the Tribunal to note that all the Mohabbakahs, other than High Islet, lie within twelve miles of the Eritrean coast. Whatever the history, in the absence of any clear title to them being shown by Yemen, the Mohabbakahs must for that reason today be regarded as Eritrean.[32] No such convincing alternative title has been shown by Yemen. It will be remembered indeed that Article 6 of the 1923 Treaty of Lausanne already enshrined this principle of the territorial sea by providing expressly that islands within the territorial sea of a state were to belong to that state. In those days the territorial sea was generally limited by international law and custom to three nautical miles, but it has now long been twelve, and the Ethiopian territorial sea was extended to twelve miles in a 1953 decree.

473. At this point it will be convenient to look at the ingenious theory enunciated by Eritrea, based on the undoubted rule that the territorial sea extends to twelve miles not just from the coast but may also extend from a baseline drawn to include any territorial islands within a twelve-mile belt of territorial sea. Thus the baseline can lawfully be extended to include an entire chain, or group of islands, where there is no gap between the islands of more than twelve miles; the so-called leapfrogging method of determining the baseline of the territorial sea. As already mentioned, the entire chain or group of these islands consists of islands, islets, or rocks proud of the sea and therefore technically islands, with no gap

[32] See D. BOWETT, THE LEGAL REGIME OF ISLANDS IN INTERNATIONAL LAW 48 (1978), where he says of islands lying within the territorial sea of a state, "Here the presumption is that the island is under the same sovereignty as the mainland nearby"; and he also interestingly quotes LINDLEY, THE ACQUISITION AND GOVERNMENT OF BACKWARD TERRITORY IN INTERNATIONAL LAW 7 (1926), writing, it may be noted, in the mid-1920s that "An uninhabited island within territorial waters is under the dominion of the Sovereign of the adjoining mainland."

between them of more than twelve miles. The only such gap is the one between the easternmost island (the Abu Ali islands) and the Yemen mainland coast.

474. The difficulty with leapfrogging in the instant case is that it begs the very question at issue before this Tribunal: to which coastal state do these islands belong? There is a strong presumption that islands within the twelve-mile coastal belt will belong to the coastal state, unless there is a fully-established case to the contrary (as, for example, in the case of the Channel Islands). But there is no like presumption outside the coastal belt, where the ownership of the islands is plainly at issue. The ownership over adjacent islands undoubtedly generates a right to a corresponding territorial sea, but merely extending the territorial sea beyond the permitted coastal belt, cannot of itself generate sovereignty over islands so encompassed. And even if there were a presumption of coastal-state sovereignty over islands falling within the twelve-mile territorial sea of a coastal-belt island, it would be no more than a presumption, capable of being rebutted by evidence of a superior title.

--*-*

475. Therefore, after examination of all relevant historical, factual and legal considerations, the Tribunal unanimously finds in the present case that the islands, islet, rocks, and low-tide elevations forming the Mohabbakah islands, including but not limited to Sayal Islet, Harbi Islet, Flat Islet and High Islet are subject to the territorial sovereignty of Eritrea. It is true that High Islet is a small but prominent rocky islet barely more than twelve miles (12.72 n.m.) from the territorial sea baseline. But here the unity theory might find a modest and suitable place, for the Mohabbakahs have always been considered as one group, sharing the same legal destiny. High Islet is certainly also appurtenant to the African coast.

The Haycocks

476. The Haycocks are three small islands situated along a roughly southwest-to-northeast line. They are, from south to north, South West Haycock, Middle Haycock and Northeast Haycock. South West Haycock is some 6 nautical miles from the nearest point of Suyul Hanish, though there is the very small Three Foot Rock about midway between them.

477. As already mentioned above, the Haycocks do have a peculiar legal history and it is for this reason mainly that they need to be discussed separately here. That legal history is very much bound up with the story of the Red Sea lighthouses. But one might begin the salient points of this legal history by recalling the 1841, 1866 and 1873 *firmans* of the Ottoman Sultan (see para. 97, above), by which the African coast of the Red Sea and the islands off it were placed under the jurisdiction and administration of Egypt, though of course the whole of this part

of the world was then under the sovereignty of the Ottoman Empire. There seems little doubt that this African-coast administration would have extended to the Mohabbakahs and the Haycocks. At this time the territorial sea was limited to three miles, and there were still grave doubts about the nature and extent of the territorial waters regime. Nevertheless there was a feeling, based upon considerations of security as well as of convenience, that islands off a particular coast would, failing a clearly established title to contrary, be under the jurisdiction of the nearest coastal authority. As mentioned above, this was sometimes called the "portico doctrine."

478. Another stage in this legal history is at the end of the nineteenth century, when the British Government was interested in the possibility of establishing an alternative western shipping channel through the Red Sea, which needed lighting if it was to be used at night. Various islands were considered as sites for a light (see paras. 203, 204, above), including South West Haycock, which is in the end proved to be the successful candidate. This involved inquiries about the "jurisdiction" under which the island would come, and the British Board of Trade satisfied itself that South West Haycock was subject to Italian jurisdiction and at any rate probably not Ottoman.

479. In 1930, when the Italians were constructing a lighthouse on South West Haycock, there was an instructive correspondence between the Italian and British Governments. An internal Foreign Office memorandum reveals the opinion that "the establishment of the Italian colony of Eritrea makes it difficult, therefore, to resist the claim that the islands off the coast of Eritrea are to be considered as an appendage of that colony.[33]" This was the official reaction to a letter from the Royal Italian Government of 11 April, claiming South West Haycock, inter alia for reasons of its "immediate vicinity" to the Eritrean Red Sea coast.

480. Eritrea employs these arguments to support its claim to the Haycocks, but puts it in the form of a succession derived from the Italian colony of Eritrea, and by way of the subsequent federation of Ethiopia and Eritrea, through to Eritrean independence in 1993. There are difficult juridical problems with this theory of succession, not least the terms of the Italian armistice of 1943 and the peace treaty of 1947, whereby Italy surrendered her colonial territories for disposition by the Allies and in default of agreement amongst them, to disposition by the United Nations, which of course is what actually happened to Eritrea. However this may be, the geographical arguments of proximity to the Eritrean coast remain persuasive and accord with the general opinion that islands off a coast will belong to the coastal state, unless another, superior title can be established. Yemen has failed, in this case, to establish any such superior claim.

---

[33] Foreign Office Memorandum dated 10 June 1930, prepared by Mr. Orchard.

481. The Eritrean claim to the Haycocks also finds some support in the material provided by both Parties for the supplementary hearing on the implications of petroleum agreements. None of the Yemen agreements extends as far to the southwest as the Haycocks; the 1974 Tomen-Santa Fe agreement appears to encompass the Hanish group, but stops short of the Haycocks. On the other hand, the fully documented agreements of the Eritrean Government and Shell, Amoco and BP do cover the areas of the Haycocks, and of course the Mohabbakahs. There was no protest from Yemen, though Yemen did protest when an agreement with Shell appeared to it to trespass upon its claim to the northern islands.

482. Therefore, after examination of all relevant historical, factual and legal considerations, the Tribunal unanimously finds in the present case that the islands, islet, rocks, and low-tide elevations forming the Haycock Islands, including, but not limited to, North East Haycock, Middle Haycock, and South West Haycock, are subject to the territorial sovereignty of Eritrea. It follows that the like decision will, apart from other good reasons noted above, apply to High Islet, the one island of the Mohabbakah sub-group that is outside the Eritrean territorial sea.

483. There remains a question whether the South West Rocks should for these purposes be regarded as going along with the Haycocks. No doubt South West Rocks are so called because they lie southwest of Greater Hanish and there is no other feature between them and that island. There is some evidence that South West Rocks were, at various times, considered to form the easternmost limit of African-coast jurisdiction. While the British Foreign Office documentation relied on by both Parties reflects divergent views (referring in at least one case to Italian jurisdiction over South West Rocks as "doubtful"), the Parties agree that in the early 1890s, Italy responded to direct British inquiries concerning potential lighthouse sites with assertions of jurisdiction over all of the proposed sites, including South West Rocks. Furthermore, Italy did not object to the subsequent British suggestion that the Sublime Porte be informed of the Italian position. This thinking surfaced again in 1914, in Great Britain's initial proposal for a post-war distribution of relinquished Ottoman territory, which would have placed everything east of South West Rocks under the sovereignty of "the independent chiefs of the Arabian mainland."

484. In light of this, it seems reasonable that South West Rocks should be treated in the same manner as the other islands administered from the African coast: the Mohabbakahs and the Haycocks. South West Rocks are therefore unanimously determined by the Tribunal to be subject to the territorial sovereignty of Eritrea.

The Zuqar – Hanish Group

485. There remains to be determined the sovereignty over Zuqar and over the Hanish islands, and their respective satellite islets and rocks, including the island of Abu

Ali, to the east of the northern end of Zuqar, which was for long a principal site for a lighthouse.

486. This has not been an easy group of islands to decide on, one reason for this being that, positioned as they are in the central part of the Red Sea, the appurtenance factor is bound to be relatively less helpful. A coastal median line would in fact divide the island of Greater Hanish, the slightly greater part of the island being on the Eritrean side of the line. Zuqar would be well on the Yemen side of a coastal median line.

487. The Parties have put before the Tribunal many aspects of the local legal history which are said to point the decision one way or the other. These have all been examined in detail in the chapters above. It is however already apparent from that examination that any expectation of a clear and definite answer from that earlier legal history is bound to be disappointed. The Yemeni idea of a reversionary ancient title has been discussed earlier in this chapter and found unhelpful in regard to these islands. More helpful perhaps is the material which suggests that, when the Ottomans decided in the later nineteenth century to grant to Egypt the jurisdiction over the African coast, this possibly included islands appurtenant to that coast, and according to some respectable authorities this did not include this central group of islands, both Zuqar and Hanish being regarded as still within the jurisdiction of the *vilayet* of Yemen. If this was so, though that position can hardly have been carried over to the present time in spite of Article 16 of the Treaty of Lausanne, it would constitute an impressive historical precedent. Hertslet's opinion about the proper distribution of jurisdiction over the islands of the Red Sea clearly impressed the British Foreign Office, but it seems to be Hertslet's view of what should be done about all the islands in the Red Sea rather than evidence of existing titles.

488. There are some echoes of the idea of Yemeni title to be found in the earlier part of the present century in for example the record of the negotiations between the Imam and a British envoy, Colonel Reilly, in which talk the Imam is said to have referred to the need to return to him certain Yemeni islands. But there is no doubt that the main grievance the Imam had in mind was the island of Kamaran and its surrounding islets, which was then occupied by the British. There was also a claim which an internal Foreign Office memorandum referred to as the Imam's claim to "unspecified islands." The British civil servants were quite prepared themselves to speculate that these islands might have included Zuqar and Hanish, which had been temporarily occupied by the British in 1915. But it is in the end difficult to attach decisive importance to a claim which could not be specified with any certainty.

489. Eritrea seeks to derive an historical title by succession, through Ethiopia, from Italy. There is no doubt that Italy had serious ambitions in respect of these central islands in the nineteen thirties and did establish a presence there. But as has been

seen above that position was constantly neutralised by assurances to the British Government that Italy fully accepted that the legal status of the islands was still governed by Article 16 of the Treaty of Lausanne. And then there is also the difficulty of deriving a title from Italy in view of the provisions of the Italian Peace Treaty of 1947.

490. Then of course there are the maps. These islands are large enough to find a place quite often – though by no means always – on even relatively small-scale maps of the region. It is fair to assert that, thanks to the efforts of counsel and especially those of Yemen, the Tribunal will have seen more maps of every conceivable period and provenance than probably have ever been seen before, and certainly a very much larger collection than will have been seen at any time by any of the principal actors in the Red Sea scene. In fact, the difficulty is not so much the interpretation of a plethora of maps of every kind and provenance, as it is the absence of any kind of evidence that these actors took very much notice of, or attached very much importance to, any of them. The Tribunal is of the opinion that in quite general terms Yemen has a marginally better case in terms of favourable maps discovered, and looked at in their totality the maps do suggest a certain widespread repute that these islands appertain to Yemen.

491. As to the other aspects of the legal history of this central group, it does inevitably reflect the ebb and flow of the interest, or the neglect, as the case may be, of both sides, varying from time to time, and qualified always by the unattractive nature of these islands, relieved from time to time by occasional usefulness, as for siting navigational lights, or by their sometimes perceived or imagined strategic importance; for they have never been considered "remote" in the sense of Greenland or the Island of Palmas. Accordingly, in the Tribunal's opinion, although some of this older historical material is important and generally helpful and indeed essential to an understanding of the claims of both Parties, neither of them has been able on the basis of the historical materials alone to make out a case that actually compels a decision one way or the other. Accordingly the Tribunal has looked at events in the last decade or so before the Agreement of Arbitration for additional materials and factors which might complete the picture of both Parties' cases and enable the Tribunal to make a firm decision about these two islands and their satellite rocks and islets. The Tribunal is confirmed in this approach by the fact that both Parties have anticipated the need for such material by providing supplementary data in connection with the hearings held in July 1998. It should be added, however, that the more recent legal history of these islands shows in some respects differences between Zuqar and Hanish. Because this is so, the islands should be, and will be, considered separately. It would be wrong to assume that they must together go to one Party or the other. In this extent the Tribunal rejects the Yemen theory that all the islands in the group must in principle share a common destiny of sovereignty.

492. Of the recent events perhaps the first heading to look at is that of the Red Sea lighthouses which have featured in the arguments of both Parties. It is evident from the lighthouse history, again dealt with in detail in Chapter VI above, that the undertaking by a government of the maintenance of one of these lights has generally been regarded as neutral for the purpose of the acquisition of territorial sovereignty, although it should also be remembered that, when Great Britain wished in 1892 to secure the building of a light for the proposed western shipping channel, the British Government was anxious to know which government had "jurisdiction" over the chosen site on South West Haycock, and Italy not only made a claim but had its claim to jurisdiction recognised by the British Government. Four lights have been constructed by and appear to be maintained by Yemen in the area now being dealt with (though it should be added that such lights are of course no longer manned). These are sited as follows: on the island of Abu Ali, which is some 3 nautical miles west of the northern tip of Zuqar, on the south-eastern tip of Zuqar itself; on Low Island which is off the north-eastern tip of Lesser Hanish; and on the north-eastern tip of Greater Hanish. The latter was constructed in July 1991 by Yemen and there is in evidence a picture of it with an inscription giving the name of the Republic of Yemen. It can hardly be denied that these lights, clearly intended to be permanent installations, are cogent evidence of some form of Yemen presence in all these islands.

493. Of relatively recent events, Eritrea attaches much importance to the history of Ethiopian naval patrols and the logbooks which evidence their occurrence, and which involved in particular the islands of Zuqar and Hanish; and this is indeed a possible factor where the islands must be taken as a group; for these were patrols in these waters generally rather than voyages to particular islands. There is no doubt that these patrols occurred on a large scale, and they are fully examined in Chapter VII and it is well known that these islands were used by the rebels, probably mainly as staging posts and relatively safe anchorages for vessels attempting to convey supplies to the rebel armies fighting on the mainland of Ethiopia, some of them possibly from Yemen, which is known to have sympathised with the rebel cause.

494. A strange aspect of these naval patrols possibly over a matter of several years – though the actual evidence Eritrea has been able to provide leaves a number of blank periods – is the lack of protest from Yemen. If Ethiopia had been patrolling the islands on the assumption that it was merely patrolling its own territory, then the lack of Yemen protest is all the more remarkable and calls for some explanation which Yemen has not altogether provided. Yemen was of course preoccupied with its own civil war between 1962 and 1970; and a good deal of this naval patrolling must have been on the high seas rather than in the territorial seas of the islands. Eritrea claims that the Ethiopian naval patrols were also enforcing fishing regulations. This seems credible for it would have provided cover for inspecting the papers of vessels even on the high seas and the rebels

would hardly have confined their supply operations to ships flying the Ethiopian flag.

495. And yet these logbooks of naval patrols give relatively little evidence of activity on or even near to the islands. It is interesting to consider in this context the press statement issued by the Yemen Embassy in Mogadishu on 3 July 1973 stating "the Y.A.R. always maintains its sovereignty over its islands in the Red Sea, with the exception of the islands of Gabal Abu Ali and Gabal Attair which were given to Ethiopia by Britain when the latter left Aden and surrendered power in our Southern Yemen." This surmise was of course mistaken. But it does amount to a statement that Yemen at this time had no presence in either of these two mentioned islands and had little idea what was happening there. This, however, was the time of the Arab press rumours of Ethiopia having allowed Israel the use of certain Red Sea islands. This same press release stated that Yemen had, accompanied by journalists and press correspondents, investigated the position on "Lesser Hanish, Greater Hanish, Zuqar, Alzubair' Alswabe', and several other islands at the Yemeni coast." These were found to be "free from any foreign infiltration whatsoever." Presumably this was also the inspection by the military committee of the Arab League (see para. 321, above). This statement has the ring of truth. It most probably was the position that these islands, including Zuqar and both Hanish islands, were then normally empty of people or activity other than that of small coastal fishermen plying their traditional way of life and calling at the islands when their work took them there. But it is significant that Yemen could apparently take the above inspection party without any repercussions from Ethiopia.

496. There is much that is ambiguous and unexplained on both sides in this evidence of naval patrols. On balance the episode appears to the Tribunal to lend some weight to the Eritrean case. But again it is a matter of relative weight. There is no compelling case here for either Party. And again it is very difficult on the basis of this material to give it great weight in claims to land territory.

497. The petroleum agreements made by Yemen and by Ethiopia (and then by Eritrea) from 1972 onwards do surprisingly little to resolve the problem, for these agreements, in so far as they extended to offshore areas, were not really concerned with the islands at all, but with either the outer boundary formed by the extent of the then exploitable depths of seabed, or by the coastal median line, which was the temporary boundary actually contemplated for such agreements by the 1977 Yemeni continental shelf legislation. As was reflected by the questions put to the Parties in the closing moments of the July 1998 hearings, the agreements seemed almost to ignore the islands; not surprisingly, considering that the volcanic geological nature of the islands meant that they were totally uninteresting to the oil companies.

498. As already stated above, the Tribunal attaches little importance to the agreements by both Parties with Shell for geological investigations. The area covered by the contract activities likely traversed these islands. But the Tribunal has little doubt that Shell was operating with the permission of both Parties, and was getting information primarily for its own use, in order to decide about which areas of the continental shelf it might be worth making production agreements.

499. When it comes to actual agreements for exploitation, whether in the form of full petroleum production-sharing agreements or less than that, two of the agreements made by Yemen encompassed the Zuqar-Hanish Islands totally (one with Adair, which was very short-lived and never went into effect, and one with Tomen-Santa Fe), while the agreements made by Ethiopia (Ethiopia/Shell) avoided extending to these islands or, in the instance of the Ethiopia-IPC/Amoco agreement of 1989, cuts across Greater Hanish, the division apparently depending on precisely how one plots the coastal median line.

500. After the careful examination of the contract areas of the oil agreements of both Parties, the conclusions to be drawn from this material seem to be reasonably clear. Eritrea can and does point to the IPC/Amoco agreement with Ethiopia which cuts the Island of Hanish. There are various versions. In some versions of the attempts to draw the contract area on a map, only the tip of Hanish is within the Eritrean side of the line; in others the line appears to portray most of the island as Eritrean, leaving only a relatively small portion of it to Yemen. It is surely apparent that the contract area was defined simply in terms appropriate for the essentially maritime interests of the contracting party, and that this, in conformity with normal practice where there is no agreed and settled maritime boundary, was made the coastal median line, ignoring the possible effect of islands. It seems in effect to have been agreed and drawn on the illustrative map of the contract simply ignoring the islands. If Ethiopia had had it in mind to use the agreement for the purpose of illustrating a claim to the island of Hanish, Ethiopia would surely not have given itself only two-thirds of the island; it would have had the line make an excursion round and embrace the whole island. As it is, it seems to the Tribunal that the Ethiopian and Eritrean agreements are in effect neutral as far as the present task of the Tribunal is concerned; as indeed Eritrea argued. This does not mean that the Eritrean claim to these islands is unfounded; but it does mean that the oil agreements do little to assist that claim, except in so far as the IPC/Amoco Agreement tends to neutralize the Yemeni argument that petroleum agreements as such provide confirmation of sovereignty.

501. Yemen, besides the unconvincing suggestion that the Shell Company's seismic investigation of a large area right across the southern Red Sea somehow confirms the Yemeni claims to the Zuqar and Hanish islands, has in the Tomen-Santa Fe seismic agreement of 1974-75 referred to an agreement in which the contract does apparently embrace both Zuqar and Hanish, or most of Greater Hanish Island. This also resulted in certain activities by the company, including a

collection of samples from Zuqar (see para. 409, above). This again does not establish that Yemen has validated its claim to both these islands. But as concluded above, the agreements produced by both parties fail to establish evidence of sovereignty. Perhaps it helps to see these petroleum agreements of the seventies in perspective to remember that in 1973 there was a Yemeni inspection of the islands, with journalists and representatives of the Arab League military committee, that found all these islands empty.

502. It was later that there was more activity; notably the construction in 1993 by the Total Oil Company of an air landing strip on Hanish, for the recreational visits of their employees, and as a by-product of their concession agreement with Yemen. That agreement did not encompass either Zuqar or Hanish. Nevertheless, the fact that there were regular excursion flights constitutes evidence of governmental authority and the exercise of it. Nor did it apparently attract any kind of protest from Eritrea; though of course by this time the civil war was over and Eritrea was established as an independent state.

503. As neither Party has in the opinion of the Tribunal made a convincing case to these islands on the basis of an ancient title in the case of Yemen, or, of a succession title in the case of Eritrea, the Tribunal's decision on sovereignty must be based to an important extent upon what seems to have been the position in Zuqar and Hanish and their adjoining islets and rocks in the last decade or so leading up to the present arbitration. Anything approaching what might be called a settlement, or the continuous display of governmental authority and presence, of the kind found in some of the classical cases even for inhospitable territory, is hardly to be expected. For very few people would wish to visit these waterless, volcanic islands except for a special reason and probably a temporary one. Nevertheless, it is clear from the documents mentioned earlier in this Award that both Yemen and Ethiopia had formulated claims to both islands at least by the late eighties and had indeed it would seem held secret negotiations on the claims; which negotiations, at least according to the Eritrean "Top Secret" internal report, had at first promised a compromise solution on the basis of a median line which would presumably have given Zuqar and Little Hanish to Yemen and Greater Hanish to Ethiopia. But this came to nothing. So now one must look at the *effectivités* for the solution.

504. Yemen has been able to present the Tribunal with a list of some forty-eight alleged Yemeni happenings or incidents in respect of "the islands," which occurred in the period between early 1989 and mid-1991. This list is not confined to the central group, for there is included for example the decisions of the 1989 London Conference on the lighthouses, and the building of a lighthouse on al Tayr in July 1989. It is evident though that Zuqar features very prominently in the list. It is also evident that Eritrea has relatively very little to show in respect of Zuqar. The Tribunal has no doubt that the island of Zuqar is under the sovereignty of Yemen.

505. In respect of Hanish the matter is not so clear cut. The Eritrean claim is well established as a claim and is clearly of great importance to that very newly-independent country. The refusal to agree to a Yemeni aerial survey of the Islands and Ethiopia's responsive claim of title to some of them is significant. So also is its arrest of Yemeni fishermen on Greater Hanish and its assertion, in response to Yemen's protest to the Security Council, that the area was within Ethiopian jurisdiction.

506. There was some emphasis by Eritrea on a scheme to put beacons on Hanish to assist Amoco's seismic testing; there is no clear evidence that they were actually installed. Any such installation of beacons covered several locations, of which Greater Hanish Island was only one, and would have been short-lived: the evidence provided by Eritrea mentions two weeks, and provides for removal of the beacons on completion of the seismic work. Moreover, the beacons were placed by the oil company, Amoco, with only a limited role for the Ethiopian government in protecting the oil company personnel and the temporary beacons from the attentions of "random individuals." Finally, there is evidence of the issuance, in 1980, of an Ethiopian radio transmitting licence to Delft Geophysical Company, which provided for a station to be located at "Greater Hanish Island, Port of Assab vicinity."

507. Yemen has more to show by way of presence and display of authority. Putting aside the lighthouse in the north of the island, there was the Ardoukoba expedition and campsite which was made under the aegis of the Yemeni Government. There is the air landing site, as well as the production of what appears to be evidence of frequent scheduled flights, no doubt mainly for the off-days of Total employees; and there is the May 1995 license to a Yemeni company (seemingly with certain German nationals associated in a joint venture scheme) to develop a tourist project (recreational diving is apparently the possible attraction to tourism) on Greater Hanish.

--*-*

508. Therefore, after examination of all relevant historical, factual and legal considerations, the Tribunal finds in the present case that, on balance, and with the greatest respect for the sincerity and foundations of the claims of both Parties, the weight of the evidence supports Yemen's assertions of the exercise of the functions of state authority with respect to the Zuqar-Hanish group. The Tribunal is further fortified in finding in favour of Yemen by the evidence that these islands fell under the jurisdiction of the Arabian coast during the Ottoman Empire; and that there was later a persistent expectation reflected in the British Foreign Office papers submitted in evidence by the Parties that these islands would ultimately return to Arab rule. The Tribunal therefore unanimously finds that the islands, islet, rocks, and low-tide elevations of the Zuqar-Hanish group, including, but not limited to, Three Foot Rock, Parkin Rock, Rocky Islets, Pin

Rock, Suyul Hanish, Mid Islet, Double Peak Island, Round Island, North Round Island, Quoin Island (13°43'N, 42°48'E), Chor Rock, Greater Hanish, Peaky Islet, Mushajirah, Addar Ail Islets, Haycock Island (13°47'N, 42°47'E; not to be confused with the Haycock Islands to the southwest of Greater Hanish), Low Island (13°52'N, 42°49'E) including the unnamed islets and rocks close north, east and south, Lesser Hanish including the unnamed islets and rocks close north east, Tongue Island and the unnamed islet close south, Near Island and the unnamed islet close south east, Shark Island, Jabal Zuqar Island, High Island, and the Abu Ali Islands (including Quoin Island (14°05'N, 42°49'E) and Pile Island) are subject to the territorial sovereignty of Yemen.

Jabal al-Tayr and the Zubayr Group of Islands

509. Both the lone island of Jabal al-Tayr, and the Zubayr group of islands and islets, call for separate treatment, as they are a considerable distance from the other islands as well as from each other. They are not only relatively isolated, but also are both well out to sea, and so not proximate to either coast, though they are slightly nearer to the Yemeni coastal islands than they are to the coast and coastal islands of Eritrea. Both are well eastward of a coastal median line. Here again, the Tribunal has had to weigh the relative merits of the Parties' evidence, which has been sparse on both sides, of the exercise of functions of state and governmental authority.

510. The traditional importance of both groups has been that they have been lighthouse islands (the Zubayr light was on Centre Peak, the southernmost islet of the group). It will be clear from the history of the Red Sea lighthouses (see Chapter VI, above) that, although, or perhaps even because, lighthouses were so important for nineteenth and early twentieth century navigation, a government could be asked to take responsibility or even volunteer to be responsible for them, without necessarily either seeming to claim sovereignty over the site or acquiring it. The practical question was not one of ownership, but rather of which government was willing, or might be persuaded, to take on the responsibility, and sometimes the cost, if not permanently then at least for a season.

511. It will be recollected that Centre Peak in the Zubayr group was an island in which Italy, in its 1930s period of colonial expansion, had taken a great interest; the Centre Peak light was abandoned by the British in 1932, but reactivated by Italy the following year. The British sought and obtained the usual assurances about the Treaty of Lausanne status of the island (see paras. 216-218 above). So for a time at least this group fell under the jurisdiction of the authority on the African coast.

512. Yet during the Second World War and the subsequent British occupation of Eritrea, it was decided that Great Britain was under no obligation to maintain the Centre Point light or indeed the Haycock light.

513. An important turning point in the history of the northern islands of Jabal al-Tayr and the Zubayr group was the 1989 London conference about lighthouses. This was rather different from previous conferences. This conference was to be the last of its kind, because its main purpose was to liquidate the former international arrangements for administration of the lights and the sharing of costs. The final arrangements made for the lights (which were then still of the greatest importance for navigation) were therefore intended to be permanent. No further conference was envisaged.

514. It will be remembered that Yemen was invited to the conference as an observer on the plea to the British Government that the two lighthouse islands of Abu Ali and Jabal al-Tayr, "lie within the exclusive economic zone of the Yemen Arab Republic," and that because of this Yemen was willing to take on the responsibility of managing and operating the lights. It was also the fact that Yemen had already installed new lights on both of these sites. The offer from Yemen was gratefully accepted by the conference. There had been hopes that Egypt might take on the work but Egypt was not willing to do so.

515. The matter of sovereignty was not on the agenda of the conference, nor was it discussed. Yemen's own request to be invited to the conference had wisely avoided raising the matter. Moreover, there were at the conference the usual references to the Treaty of Lausanne formula concerning indeterminate sovereignty.

516. Nevertheless, the decision of the conference to accept the Yemeni offer over the lights does reflect a confidence and expectation of the member governments of the conference of a continued Yemeni presence on these lighthouse islands for, at any rate, the foreseeable future. Repute is also an important ingredient for the consolidation of title.

517. There is also another matter where Yemen is able to show what amounts to important support for its case over these northern islands, and that is the substantially new information on petroleum agreements that was made available to the Tribunal at the supplementary hearings held for this purpose in July 1998. There are two such agreements which appear to be relevant for the islands presently under discussion.

518. First, there is the agreement made by the Yemeni Government with the Shell company on 20 November 1973. The western boundary of the contract area in this agreement is drawn so as to include within it the Zubayr group. It does not include Jabal al-Tayr, but passes at a distance which might encompass the territorial sea of that island, depending on the breadth of the territorial sea allowed to it for the purposes of a maritime delimitation.

519. The second is the Hunt Oil production sharing agreement ratified on 10 March 1985. The western contract area boundary of this agreement again includes the Zubayr group, but also appears from the illustrative map to brush the island of Jabal al-Tayr, and of course plainly includes a part of its territorial sea.

520. These agreements were not protested by Ethiopia (though it should be remembered that the Hunt agreement was made at a time when the Ethiopian civil war was still raging).

521. Neither Ethiopia nor Eritrea has made any petroleum agreements encompassing these islands. Eritrea did, however, make agreements in 1995 and 1997 with the Anadarko Oil Company, which extended in the direction of these islands and towards what appears to be an approximate median line between coasts. Yemen protested this line on 4 January 1997* as a "blatant" violation of the territorial waters of both groups and of her economic rights "in the region." This was, of course, some time after the signature of the Agreement on Principles and indeed the Arbitration Agreement initiating these proceedings.

522. The legal history of these northern and isolated islands has been mixed and varied. It has been seen that even as late as 1989 it was assumed that their sovereign status was still indeterminate in accordance with the status impressed upon them, until it should be changed in a lawful way, by the Treaty of Lausanne. Nevertheless, by 1995 it was doubtful whether any dispute over Yemen's claim to them would be agreed to be submitted to this Tribunal. Even Eritrea at one point made a proposal for an agreement in which these islands were not mentioned.

523. The Tribunal has not found this particular question an easy one. There is little evidence on either side of actual or persistent activities on and around these islands. But in view of their isolated location and inhospitable character, probably little evidence will suffice.

524. Therefore, after examination of all relevant historical, factual and legal considerations, the Tribunal unanimously finds in the present case that, on the basis of the foregoing, the weight of the evidence supports the conclusion that the island of Jabal al-Tayr, and the islands, islets, rocks and low-tide elevations forming the Zubayr group, including, but not limited to, Quoin Island (15°12'N, 42°03'E), Haycock Island (15°10'N, 42°07'E; not to be confused with the Haycock Islands to the southwest of Greater Hanish), Rugged Island, Table Peak Island, Saddle Island and the unnamed islet close north west, Low Island (15°06'N, 42°06'E) and the unnamed rock close east, Middle Reef, Saba Island,

* *Editorial correction: the correct year is "1996."*

Connected Island, East Rocks, Shoe Rock, Jabal Zubayr Island, and Centre Peak Island are subject to the territorial sovereignty of Yemen.

The Traditional Fishing Regime

525. In making this award on sovereignty, the Tribunal has been aware that Western ideas of territorial sovereignty are strange to peoples brought up in the Islamic tradition and familiar with notions of territory very different from those recognized in contemporary international law. Moreover, appreciation of regional legal traditions is necessary to render an Award which, in the words of the Joint Statement signed by the Parties on 21 May 1996, will "allow the re-establishment and the development of a trustful and lasting cooperation between the two countries."

526. In finding that the Parties each have sovereignty over various of the Islands the Tribunal stresses to them that such sovereignty is not inimical to, but rather entails, the perpetuation of the traditional fishing regime in the region. This existing regime has operated, as the evidence presented to the Tribunal amply testifies, around the Hanish and Zuqar islands and the islands of Jabal al-Tayr and the Zubayr group. In the exercise of its sovereignty over these islands, Yemen shall ensure that the traditional fishing regime of free access and enjoyment for the fishermen of both Eritrea and Yemen shall be preserved for the benefit of the lives and livelihoods of this poor and industrious order of men.

* - * - *

CHAPTER XI – Dispositif

527. Accordingly, **THE TRIBUNAL,**

taking into account the foregoing considerations and reasons,

UNANIMOUSLY FINDS IN THE PRESENT CASE THAT

i. the islands, islet, rocks, and low-tide elevations forming the Mohabbakah islands, including but not limited to Sayal Islet, Harbi Islet, Flat Islet and High Islet are subject to the territorial sovereignty of Eritrea;

ii. the islands, islet, rocks, and low-tide elevations forming the Haycock Islands, including, but not limited to, North East Haycock, Middle Haycock, and South West Haycock, are subject to the territorial sovereignty of Eritrea;

iii. the South West Rocks are subject to the territorial sovereignty of Eritrea;

iv. the islands, islet, rocks, and low-tide elevations of the Zuqar-Hanish group, including, but not limited to, Three Foot Rock, Parkin Rock, Rocky Islets, Pin Rock, Suyul Hanish, Mid Islet, Double Peak Island, Round Island, North Round Island, Quoin Island (13°43'N, 42°48'E), Chor Rock, Greater Hanish, Peaky Islet, Mushajirah, Addar Ail Islets, Haycock Island (13°47'N, 42°47'E; not to be confused with the Haycock Islands to the southwest of Greater Hanish), Low Island (13°52'N, 42°49'E) including the unnamed islets and rocks close north, east and south, Lesser Hanish including the unnamed islets and rocks close north east, Tongue Island and the unnamed islet close south, Near Island and the unnamed islet close south east, Shark Island, Jabal Zuqar Island, High Island, and the Abu Ali Islands (including Quoin Island (14°05'N, 42°49'E) and Pile Island) are subject to the territorial sovereignty of Yemen;

v. the island of Jabal al-Tayr, and the islands, islets, rocks and low-tide elevations forming the Zubayr group, including, but not limited to, Quoin Island (15°12'N, 42°03'E), Haycock Island (15°10'N, 42°07'E; not to be confused with the Haycock Islands to the southwest of Greater Hanish), Rugged Island, Table Peak Island, Saddle Island and the unnamed islet close north west, Low Island (15°06'N, 42°06'E) and the unnamed rock close east, Middle Reef, Saba Island, Connected Island, East Rocks, Shoe Rock, Jabal Zubayr Island, and Centre Peak Island are subject to the territorial sovereignty of Yemen; and

vi. the sovereignty found to lie with Yemen entails the perpetuation of the traditional fishing regime in the region, including free access and enjoyment for the fishermen of both Eritrea and Yemen.

528. Further, whereas Article 12.1(b) of the Arbitration Agreement provides that the Awards shall include the time period for their execution, the Tribunal directs that this Award should be executed within ninety days from the date hereunder.

--*-*

Done at London this 9th day of October, 1998

The President of the Tribunal

/s/ Professor Sir Robert Y. Jennings

The Registrar

/s/ P.J.H. Jonkman

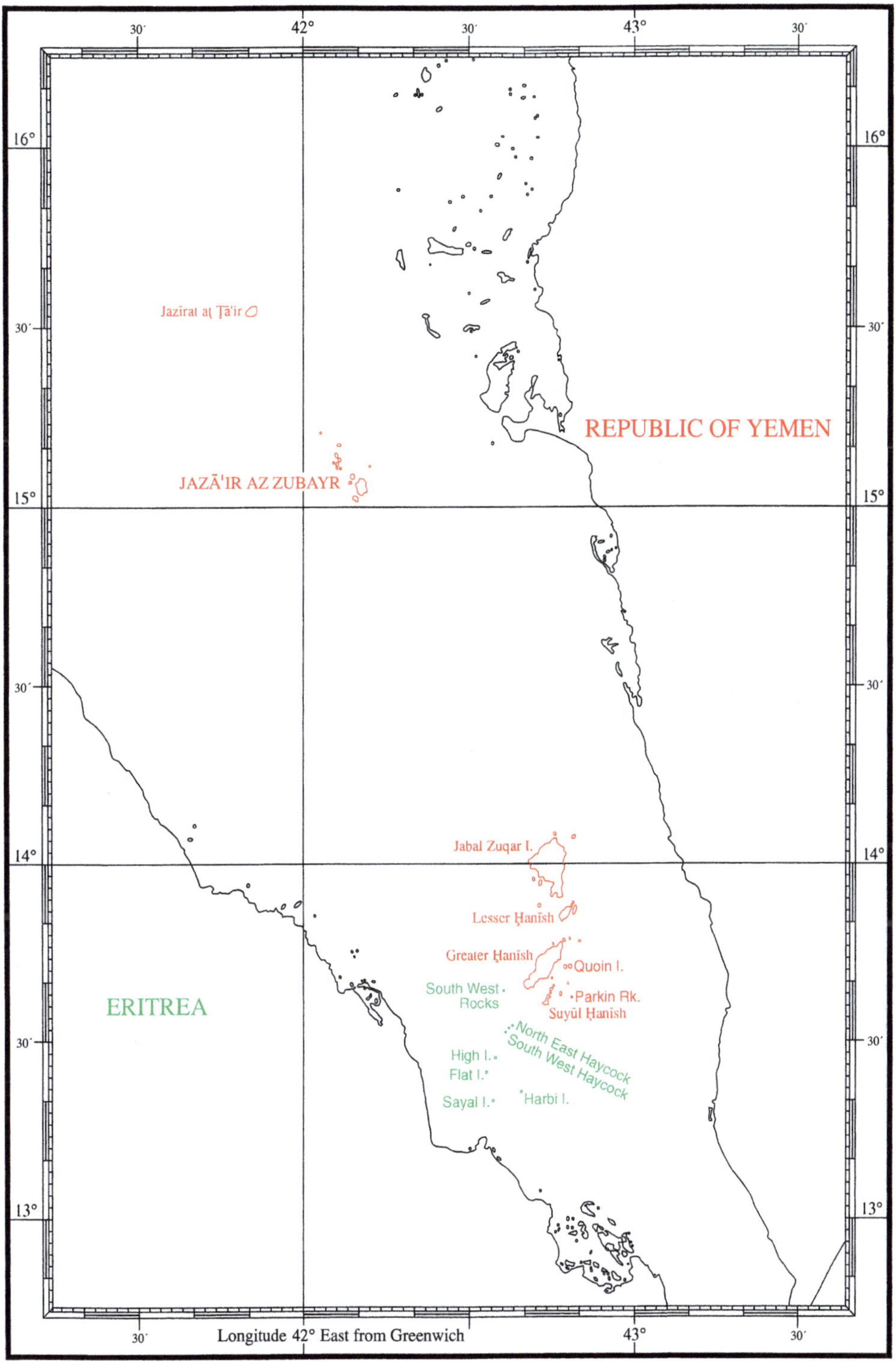

30´
42°
30´
43°
30´
16°
30´
15°
30´
14°
30´
13°
Jazīrat aṭ Ṭā'ir
REPUBLIC OF YEMEN
JAZĀ'IR AZ ZUBAYR
Jabal Zuqar I.
Lesser Ḥanīsh
Greater Ḥanīsh
Quoin I.
South West Rocks
Parkin Rk.
Suyūl Ḥanīsh
ERITREA
North East Haycock
South West Haycock
High I.
Flat I.
Sayal I.
Harbi I.
Longitude 42° East from Greenwich

IN THE MATTER OF AN ARBITRATION
PURSUANT TO AN AGREEMENT TO ARBITRATE
DATED 3 OCTOBER 1996

B E T W E E N :

THE GOVERNMENT OF THE STATE OF ERITREA

-and-

THE GOVERNMENT OF THE REPUBLIC OF YEMEN

AWARD OF THE ARBITRAL TRIBUNAL IN THE SECOND STAGE OF THE PROCEEDINGS (MARITIME DELIMITATION)

The Arbitral Tribunal:

Professor Sir Robert Y. Jennings, President
Judge Stephen M. Schwebel
Dr. Ahmed Sadek El-Kosheri
Mr. Keith Highet
Judge Rosalyn Higgins

Representatives of the Government of the State of Eritrea:

His Excellency, Haile Weldensae, Agent
His Excellency, Haile Saleh Meky
Professor Lea Brilmayer and Mr. Jan Paulsson, Co-Agents
Mr. Robert Volterra and Ms. Natalie Klein, Counsel

Representatives of the Government of the Republic of Yemen:

His Excellency, Dr. Abdulkarim Al-Eryani, Agent
His Excellency, Mr. Abdullah Ahmad Ghanim, Mr. Hussein Al-Hubaishi,
Mr. Abdulwahid Al-Zandani and Mr. Rodman R. Bundy, Co-Agents
Mr. Ian Brownlie, Q.C., Mr. B. Donovan Picard, Ms. Loretta Malintoppi and
Mr. Paul Luther, Counsel

AWARD

TABLE OF CONTENTS

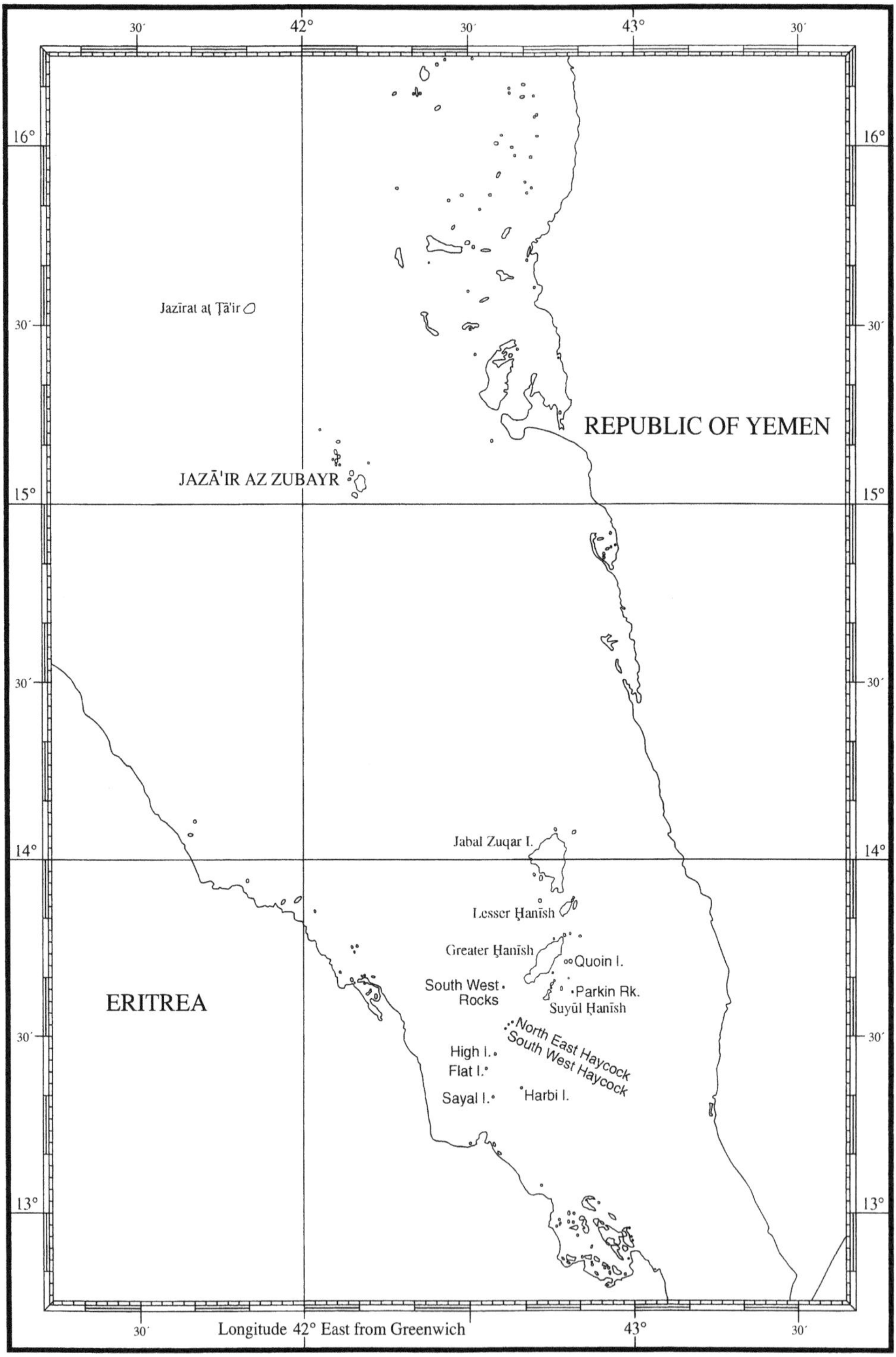
30´
42°
30´
43°
30´
16°
16°
Jazīrat aţ Ţā'ir
30´
30´
REPUBLIC OF YEMEN
JAZĀ'IR AZ ZUBAYR
15°
15°
30´
30´
Jabal Zuqar I.
14°
14°
Lesser Ḩanīsh
Greater Ḩanīsh
Quoin I.
South West Rocks
Parkin Rk.
ERITREA
Suyūl Ḩanīsh
30´
30´
North East Haycock
South West Haycock
High I.
Flat I.
Sayal I.
Harbi I.
13°
13°
30´
Longitude 42° East from Greenwich
43°
30´

INTRODUCTION – Proceedings in the Delimitation Stage of the Arbitration

1. This Award in the Second Stage of the Arbitration is rendered pursuant to an Arbitration Agreement dated 3 October 1996 (the "Arbitration Agreement"), between the Government of the State of Eritrea ("Eritrea") and the Government of the Republic of Yemen ("Yemen") (hereinafter "the Parties").

2. The Arbitration Agreement, which appears as Annex 1 on page *219*, was preceded by an "Agreement on Principles" done at Paris on 21 May 1996, which was signed by Eritrea and Yemen and witnessed by the Governments of the French Republic, the Federal Democratic Republic of Ethiopia and the Arab Republic of Egypt. The Agreement on Principles provided that the Tribunal should decide questions of territorial sovereignty and to that end the Tribunal rendered an Award in the First Stage finding the sovereignty of the disputed islands in the Red Sea to belong either to Eritrea or to Yemen. (See Award in the First Stage, Chapter XI – Dispositif, paragraphs 527-528.)

3. In a correspondence concerning the Written Pleadings for the Second Stage, and including requests for an extension of the time allowed, a question was raised by Eritrea relating to the Traditional Fishing Regime and how it might be pleaded and argued in the Second Stage of the Arbitration. The President's reply was: "the Tribunal is of the view that it is for Eritrea itself to determine the contents of its written pleadings for that stage." This is referred to in Chapter IV below.

4. Pursuant to the time table set forth in the Arbitration Agreement, the Parties filed written Memorials in the Second Stage on 9 March 1999 and Counter-Memorials on 9 June 1999. On 25 May 1999, Mr. Tjaco van den Hout, Secretary-General of the Permanent Court of Arbitration, succeeded as Registrar Mr. Hans Jonkman, who had retired. Pursuant to Article 7(2) of the Arbitration Agreement, Ms. Phyllis Pieper Hamilton, First Secretary of the Permanent Court of Arbitration, served as Secretary to the Tribunal.

5. Prior to the Hearings in the Second Stage of the Arbitration, after consultation with the Parties, the Tribunal as contemplated by Article 7(4) of the Arbitration Agreement sought assistance with the calculations of the maritime boundaries and the technical preparation of the corresponding chart. On 8 July 1999, pursuant to Article 7(4) the Tribunal communicated an Order to the Parties designating Ms. Ieltje Anna Elema, geodetic engineer, Head of the Geodesy and Tides Department of the Hydrographic Service of the Royal Netherlands Navy, as its expert in geodesy.

6. Article 2 of the Arbitration Agreement provides that:

> 1. The Tribunal is requested to provide rulings in accordance with international law, in two stages.
>
> 2. The first stage shall result in an award on territorial sovereignty and on the definition of the scope of the dispute between Eritrea and Yemen . . . .
>
> 3. The second stage shall result in an award delimiting maritime boundaries. The Tribunal shall decide taking into account the opinion that it will have formed on questions of territorial sovereignty, the United Nations Convention on the Law of the Sea, and any other pertinent factor.

7. Pursuant to the time table set forth in the Arbitration Agreement for the various stages of the Arbitration, and with the consent of the Parties regarding the venue, the Oral Proceedings in the second stage of the Arbitration were held 5-16 July 1999 in the Great Hall of Justice in the Peace Palace in The Hague. By agreement between the Parties, Yemen began the Oral Proceedings.

8. The Tribunal's task was greatly facilitated by the excellence of the oral presentations on both sides.

9. During the Oral Arguments, pursuant to Article 8(3) of the Arbitration Agreement authorizing the Tribunal to request the Parties' written views on the elucidation of any aspect of the matters before the Tribunal, counsel were asked to respond to various questions. On 13 August 1999 the Parties submitted written responses to questions put to them by the Tribunal on 13 and 16 July. The Tribunal's questions and the answers provided by the Parties are set out in Annex 2 on page *229*.

CHAPTER I – The Arguments of the Parties

Introduction

10. The purpose of the present Chapter is to summarise what the Tribunal understands to have been the main arguments of the Parties. For the Tribunal's reasons for acceptance or rejection or modification of those arguments, it may be necessary to turn to later Chapters. In this Chapter describing the arguments of the Parties, it will be convenient in general to follow the order agreed by them for the Oral Presentations and so put first the arguments of Yemen followed by the arguments of Eritrea.

11. It may be said at once that both Parties claimed a form of median international boundary line, although their respective claimed median lines follow very different courses and do not coincide. They do, however, follow similar courses in the narrow waters of the southernmost portion of the line. Eritrea's median line is equidistant between the mainland coasts, but its historic median line takes into account Eritrea's islands (but not the Yemen mid-sea islands); the Yemen line is equidistant between the Eritrean coast (including certain selected points on the Dahlak islands) and the coasts of all the Yemen islands. The Yemen line was plotted with WGS 84 coordinates of the turning points; the Eritrean line was not, although, in answer to a question from the Tribunal, the coordinates of the base points were provided. The rival claimed lines are reproduced on the Charts (Eritrea's Maps 3 and 7 and Yemen's Map 12.1) to be found in the map section at the back.

Yemen's Proposed Boundary Line

12. The Yemen claimed line was described in three sectors divided by lines of latitude: 16°N; 14°25'N; and 13°20'N. So there was (i) a northern sector between the Yemen islands of Jabal al-Tayr and the Jabal al-Zubayr group on the one hand, and the Eritrean Dahlak islands on the other; (ii) a central sector between the Zuqar-Hanish group of Yemen and the opposite mainland coast of Eritrea together with the Mohabbakahs, the Haycocks and South West Rocks; and (iii) a southern sector between the respective mainland coasts of Yemen and Eritrea south of the Zuqar-Hanish group. These sectors were fixed by the latitude of the controlling base points of the Yemen line. Thus, for instance, 14°25'N was the point on the line where the controlling base points changed from the points on the islet Centre Peak in the Zubayr group to the base points on the coast of Zuqar.

13. Yemen began its argument with the general understanding, as endorsed by the International Court of Justice in the *North Sea Continental Shelf* cases,[1] that a

[1] I.C.J. Reports 1969, p. 36, para. 57.

median line normally produces an equitable result when applied between opposite coasts. Therefore, argued Yemen, a major preliminary task for the Tribunal was to decide which were the coasts to be used as baselines.

14. In the northern sector, the proposed Yemen line assumed that the Dahlak islands, a closely knit group of some 350 islands and islets, the largest of them having a considerable population, should be recognised as being part of the Eritrean mainland coast and the waters within them as internal waters. It followed that the easternmost islets of that group might be used as base points of the median line. Yemen used the high water line as baseline on these islands.

15. Yemen proposed that the eastern base points of the line should be found on the low-water line of the western coast of the lone mid-sea island of Jabal al-Tayr and on the western coasts of the mid-sea group of Jabal al-Zubayr. Yemen argued that these islands should be used as base points because they were as important, or even more important, than the very small uninhabited outer islets of the Dahlak group. In this way, said Yemen, there would be a "balance" in the treatment of island base points on the west and the east coasts, arguing that in this northern area "each Party possesses islands of a comparable size, producing similar coastal facades lying at similar distances from their respective mainlands."

16. In the central sector the Yemen claimed line proceeded through the narrow waters between the Hanish group of islands and the Eritrean mainland coast. (This part of the boundary line area was called the "central" one by Yemen but sometimes called the "southern" one by Eritrea.) The Yemen line was a line of equidistance between the high-water line on the Eritrean mainland coast and the low-water line on the westernmost coasts of Yemen's Hanish Island group.

17. Yemen suggested that the "small Eritrean islets in between" the Eritrean mainland coast and the larger Yemen islands were inappropriate for a delimitation role. Thus, the computing and the drawing of Yemen's boundary line ignored both the South West Rocks and the three Haycocks (which had been found in the Award on Sovereignty to belong to Eritrea) as being no more than small rocks whose only importance was that they were navigational hazards. The Eritrean sovereignty over these islets was, however, recognised by placing them in limited enclaves.

18. In Yemen's "southern sector," the line entered a narrow sea which had few islets and was relatively free from complicating mid-sea islands or islets, and the line became a simple median between the opposite mainland coasts. By using the islands of Fatuma, Derchos and Ras Mukwar as base points it did, however, recognise that the Bay of Assab was an area of Eritrean internal waters. Yemen added the comment that:

> This method of delimitation has been selected in order to accord the islands in the Southern Sector the same treatment as the islands in the Northern Islands Sector.

19. Summing up the three sectors, Yemen observed that, in accordance with the applicable legal principles, the appropriate delimitation would be achieved by a median line between the relevant coasts. There was no justification for any adjustment of this line on the basis of equitable principles. This median line delimitation between the relevant coasts was the only equitable solution compatible with the purpose of this arbitration.

20. Yemen also addressed other relevant factors. There was the factor of proportionality and this, together with Eritrea's argument under the same heading, is dealt with below. There was also discussion of certain "non-geographical relevant circumstances," the first one being "dependency of the fishing communities in Yemen upon Red Sea fishing." This is a matter upon which both Parties held strong and differing views, which are described and considered in Chapter II below.

21. The other of these relevant circumstances maintained by Yemen was "the element of security of the coastal State." This, according to Yemen, "connotes nothing more exciting than non-encroachment." It was chiefly in the narrow waters between the Hanish group of islands and the Eritrean coast that the question of security or non-encroachment arose. According to Yemen, this concern is automatically addressed by the application of the principle of equidistance which was intended to effect equality of treatment.

Eritrea's Proposed Boundary Line

22. Eritrea asserted that there was a legal flaw in the Yemen argument for its claimed line. This criticism illuminated some of the basic ideas underlying Eritrea's own claimed line.

23. Eritrea pointed with some insistence to what it regarded as a fundamental contradiction in the Yemen argument. In the northern part of the line, where the question of the influence upon it of the northern mid-sea islands arose, the maritime boundary was between the respective continental shelves and exclusive economic zones (hereinafter "EEZ"). These two boundaries, of continental shelf and of EEZ, are governed by Articles 74 and 83 of the United Nations Convention on the Law of the Sea. In neither of these two articles is there even a mention of equidistance; there is, however, a clear requirement that a delimitation of these areas should "achieve an equitable solution." Nevertheless, for these very areas, Yemen insisted upon an equidistance line having included as base points for it the coasts of its small northern mid-sea islets.

24. In contrast, Eritrea contended in oral argument that, in the narrow seas between the Hanish group of islands and the Eritrean mainland coast, there was an area

involving distances less than 24 miles[2] and which was therefore all territorial sea to which Article 15 of the Convention "is going to be most directly applicable in the more southern reaches of the delimitation area in question, the area round the Zuqar and Hanish Islands. The reason for that, of course, is that the distances there are smaller. What that means is that in the area around the Zuqar and Hanish islands there is a basic rule of equidistance."

25. This would favour a median line that takes full account of South West Rocks and the Haycocks, which in the Award on Sovereignty were found to belong to Eritrea. Applying Article 15, moreover, there could be no question of enclaves of these islands.

26. Eritrea also objected that Yemen's proposed enclaves would in practice mean that there was no access corridor for Eritrea through the surrounding Yemen territorial sea. Thus, both the Eritrean South West Rocks and the Haycocks would be "completely isolated." Eritrea objected to the enclave solution because Eritrea claimed this would have put the western main shipping channel, "between the Haycock Island and South West Rocks," into Yemen territorial waters while the eastern main channel, which goes east of Zuqar, was already in undisputed Yemen territorial waters. Thus, Yemen's proposal would result in "inclusion of both of the main shipping channels within what would be Yemen's territorial waters if Yemen's proposed delimitation were accepted."

27. Eritrea's own proposed solution of the delimitation problem was in two parts. There was the proposed international boundary, and there was the proposal for certain delimited "boxes" of the mid-sea islands, the purpose of which was to delimit the areas which Eritrea claimed to be "joint resource areas." This delimitation of "the shared maritime zones around the islands" was distinguished from recognition of "the exclusive waters of Yemen, to the east, and the exclusive waters of Eritrea, to the west." These ideas represented Eritrea's understanding of what in its view was meant by the reservation in the Award on Sovereignty of the traditional fishing regime, and what was needed to ensure the fulfilment of that regime. Of this Eritrea said, "if this regime is to be perpetuated, the Parties must know what it is and where it holds sway in a technically precise manner."

28. It is to be noted that the "exclusive" Eritrean waters on the west included not merely the territorial sea but also all the waters west of the mid-sea islands and west of the historic median line. These two Eritrean proposals – the two versions of the median line and the joint resource area boxes – belonged together because they were both essential parts of the Eritrean proposal as a whole. Thus, Eritrea's "historic median line" was – although with some variations to be noted later – one drawn as a median between the mainland coasts and ignoring the existence of the

---

2 Throughout this Award the use of "miles" refers to nautical miles.

mid-sea islands of Yemen, but taking into account the islands of Eritrea. (There are precedents for this kind of boundary line in the petroleum agreements discussed in Chapter III.) Eritrea's "resource box system" provided the essential elements of a complex solution for the problem of these islands. The boxes were offered in a variety of shapes and sizes (see Eritrea's Maps 4 and 7). These "joint resource boxes" seem to have been advanced by Eritrea as a flexible set of suggestions. Its main concern was the reasonable one that it wanted to be able to tell its fishermen precisely where they might fish.

29. The coupling in the Eritrean pleadings of the two questions – the nature of the traditional fishing regime and the delimitation of the international boundary – is in contradistinction to Yemen's arguments. Yemen had expressed the view that "the traditional fishing regime should not have any impact on the delimitation of the maritime boundaries between the two Parties in the Second Stage." Yemen, in answer to a question from the Tribunal, also expressed the view that "Article 13, paragraph 3 of the Arbitration Agreement (see Annex 1) and the framework created by the 1994 and 1998 Agreements obviated any need further to take into account the traditional fishing regime in the delimitation of the maritime boundary." (The two Agreements of 1994 and 1998 are reproduced in Annex 3 to this Award.)

30. Eritrea replied to this letter from Yemen on 24 August saying that:

> Yemen's submission conveys the impression that the two States have conducted discussions since October 1998 which have resulted in arrangements for the implementation of Eritrea's traditional rights. No such discussions have taken place on this subject and no arrangements have been made to protect or preserve Eritrea's traditional rights in the waters around the mid-sea islands.

Arguments about Historic Rights and Sovereignty

31. Sovereignty over the disputed islands was the subject of the First Stage of this Arbitration. The Arbitration Agreement enjoins the Tribunal in this Second Stage to take into account "the opinion it will have formed on questions of territorial sovereignty." It is not surprising, therefore, that both Parties raised some interesting questions in this Second Stage about the nature of sovereignty and its relation to the question of delimitation and, not least, to the question of the traditional fishing regime.

32. Eritrea was moved to return to the history of the formerly disputed islands and especially to the period of Italian influence and presence. From these and some other considerations was precipitated the view urged upon the Tribunal that Yemen's "recently acquired" sovereignty over islands made them of less importance as factors to be taken into consideration for the purposes of the delimitation. This approach was expressed in these words:

> Eritrea also considers that the [mid-sea] islands come within the category of small uninhabited islands of recently acquired sovereignty and near the median line that should be recognised by the Tribunal to possess diminished maritime zones.

33. The Eritrean Prayer for Relief took this idea even further when it said in Article 4 that:

> The outer borders of the maritime zones of the islands in which these shared rights exist shall be defined as extending:
> A. on the western side of the Red Sea, to the median line drawn between the two coasts, which shall include the islands historically owned by either State prior to the decade preceding commencement of this arbitration in accordance with Article 121 of the United Nations Convention on the Law of the Sea; and
> B. on the eastern side of the Red Sea, as far as the twelve mile limit of Yemen's territorial sea.

34. Continuing the same theme Article 5 of the Prayer for Relief provided:

> 5. The waters beyond the shared area of the mid-sea islands shall be divided in accordance with a median line drawn between the two coasts, which shall include the islands historically owned by either State prior to the decade preceding commencement of this Arbitration in accordance with Article 121 of the United Nations Convention on the Law of the Sea.

35. Eritrea felt, therefore, able to urge that "Eritrea possesses historic title to all waters to the west of the historic median line, drawn by reference to the historically owned islands." This idea, it will be noted, yielded a rather different historic median line from the one drawn between the mainland coasts.

36. Yemen's reply was that Yemen's title to the formerly disputed islands was not created by the adjudication in the Award on Sovereignty, but that the adjudication was rather a confirmation of an already existing title; and, that "in arbitrations the issue of title is determined both prospectively and retroactively." These considerations led to some discussion of the effect of a critical date.

37. Yemen was also concerned that Eritrea's proposed joint resource zones were founded upon a supposition that the sovereignty awarded to Yemen in the First Stage was a sovereignty "only limited or conditional." This seems to be partly a war of words. All sovereignty is "limited" by international law. Eritrea can hardly be suggesting that Yemen's sovereignty over the islands is "conditional" in the legal sense according to which failure to observe the condition might act as a cesser of the sovereignty.

38. Eritrea, however, responded by pointing to paragraph 126 of the Award on Sovereignty which speaks of the traditional fishing regime as having, by historical consolidation, established rights for both Parties "as a sort of '*servitude*

internationale' falling short of territorial sovereignty." Other aspects of these arguments are discussed in Chapter IV below.

Proportionality

39. This factor was argued strenuously and ingeniously by both Parties. Both relied upon the statement in the *North Sea* cases that a delimitation should take into account "a reasonable degree of proportionality, which a delimitation carried out in accordance with equitable principles ought to bring about between the extent of the continental shelf areas appertaining to the coastal State and the length of its coast measured in the general direction of the coastline."[3] Both were in agreement with the warning in the *Anglo-French Arbitration* case[4] that this is a test of equitableness and not a method of delimitation, and that what had to be avoided was a manifest disproportionality resulting from the line selected. So there was little between the Parties as to principle but there was strong disagreement about the measurement of the length of their respective coasts and the significance of that measurement when it was made. The measurement is a matter on which several views are possible when Eritrea's coast extends also to be opposite to Yemen's neighbouring State, the Kingdom of Saudi Arabia; with which the maritime boundary remains undelimited.

40. The Yemen position was that proportionality is a factor to be taken into account in testing the equitableness of a delimitation already effected by other means. In relation in particular to the line to be drawn in the central sector, Yemen suggested that the relative lengths of the coasts overall were not significant because (i) in the restricted seas between the Yemen islands and the Eritrean coast any modifications of the median line would involve the principle of non-encroachment; (ii) further, in the central sector, given the general configuration of the coasts, equal division alone guarantees an equitable result; (iii) equal division is reinforced by the principle of non-encroachment; (iv) the relevant coasts for this delimitation are the Eritrean coast and the Yemen islands; (v) State practice supported the median line; and (vi) proportionality cannot be applied in the context of overlapping territorial sea.

41. The Eritrean reply to this was to question whether the Yemen claimed line in the central sector really was the median line envisaged in Article 15 of the Convention; and Eritrea suggested that it was not so, because it ignored the low-water line base points of the Eritrean islands of South West Rocks and the Haycocks.

---

3 I.C.J. Reports 1969, p. 57, para. 101.

4 18 ILM 60; 54 ILR 6.

42. It is not possible here to describe the many variations to be found in the pleadings on the theme of the method of measurements to be employed, or the discussions of the ambiguities of "oppositeness," although the Tribunal has examined them all. Suffice it to say that whereas Yemen calculated that its own claimed line neatly divided the sea areas into almost equal areas, which according to Yemen's measurements of the length of the coasts was the correct proportion, Eritrea found, in a final choice of one of its several different methods of calculation, that its own historic median line between the mainland coasts would produce respective areas favouring Eritrea by a proportion of 3 to 2, which again was said to reflect accurately the proportion of the lengths of coast according to Eritrea's method of measuring them.

43. It should be mentioned that Eritrea was particularly concerned that, in calculating the areas resulting from the delimitation, account should not be taken of the internal waters within the Dahlaks or the bays along its coast, including the Bay of Assab.

The Northern and Southern Extremities of the Boundary Line

44. There also arose a question about where to stop the boundary at its northern and southern ends, considering that in these areas it might prejudice other boundary disputes with neighbouring countries. The Kingdom of Saudi Arabia indeed had written to the Registrar of the Tribunal on 31 August 1997 pointing out that its boundaries with Yemen were disputed, reserving its position, and suggesting that the Tribunal should restrict its decisions to areas "that do not extend north of the latitude of the most northern point on Jabal al-Tayr island." Yemen for its part wished the determination to extend to the latitude of 16°N, which is the limit of its so-called northern sector. Eritrea on the other hand stated that it had "no objection" to the Saudi Arabian proposal.

45. At the southern end, the third States concerned have not made representations to the Tribunal, but the matter will nevertheless have to be determined. Eritrea was most concerned here about the arrow with which Yemen terminated its claimed line, as this arrow, according to Eritrea, pointed in such a direction as to "slash" the main shipping channel and cause it to be in Yemen territorial waters. Yemen had also used an arrow to terminate the northern end of its line and there was some discussion and debate from both sides about the propriety or otherwise of these arrows.

46. At the southern end of the line, as it approaches the Bab-al-Mandab, there is the complication of the possible effect upon the course of the boundary line of the Island of Perim. This question might clearly involve the views of Djibouti. It follows that the Tribunal's line should stop short of the place where any influence upon it of Perim Island would begin to take effect. The Tribunal has taken into

consideration these positions variously expressed and has reached its own conclusions, as more fully detailed in Chapter V below.

* – * – *

The submissions of Yemen and the Prayer for Relief of Eritrea appear below.

Submissions of Yemen

On the basis of the facts and legal considerations presented in Yemen's pleadings; and
Rejecting all contrary submissions presented in Eritrea's "Prayer for Relief," and
In view of the provisions of Article 2(3) of the Arbitration Agreement;

The Republic of Yemen, respectfully requests the Tribunal to adjudge and declare:

1. That the maritime boundary between the Parties is a median line, every point of which is equidistant from the relevant base points on the coasts of the Parties as identified in Chapters 8 through 10 of Yemen's Memorial, appropriate account being taken to the islets and rocks comprising South West Rocks, the Haycocks and the Mohabbakahs;

2. That the course of the delimitation, including the coordinates of the turning points on the boundary line established on the basis of the World Geodetic System 1984 (WGS 84), are those that appear in Chapter 12 to Yemen's Memorial.

Eritrea's Prayer for Relief

(Paragraph 274, Memorial of the State of Eritrea)

Article 2, paragraph 3, of the Arbitration Agreement requires the Tribunal to issue an award delimiting the maritime boundaries between the Parties in a technically precise manner. In order that such precision shall be achieved, the State of Eritrea respectfully requests the Tribunal to render an award providing as follows:

1. The Eritrean people's historic use of resources in the mid-sea islands includes fishing, trading, shell and pearl diving, guano and mineral extraction, and all associated activities on land including drying fish, drawing water, religious and burial practices, and building and occupying shelters for sleep and refuge;

2. The right to such usage, to be shared with the Republic of Yemen, extends to all of the land areas and maritime zones of the mid-sea islands;

3. The right to such usage shall be preserved intact in perpetuity, as it has existed in the past, without interference through the imposition of new regulations, burdens, curtailments or any other infringements or limitations of any kind whatsoever, except those agreed upon by Eritrea and Yemen as expressed in a written agreement between them;

4. The outer borders of the maritime zones of the islands in which these shared rights exist shall be defined as extending:

   A. on the western side of the Red Sea, to the median line drawn between the two coasts, which shall include the islands historically owned by either State prior to the decade preceding commencement of this arbitration in accordance with Article 121 of the United Nations Convention on the Law of the Sea; and

B. on the eastern side of the Red Sea, as far as the twelve mile limit of Yemen's territorial sea.

5. The waters beyond the shared area of the mid-sea islands shall be divided in accordance with a median line drawn between two coasts, which shall include the islands historically owned by either State prior to the decade preceding commencement of this Arbitration in accordance with Article 121 of the United Nations Convention on the Law of the Sea;

6. The two Parties are directed to negotiate the modalities for shared usage of the mid-sea islands and their waters in accordance with the following terms:

   A. Immediately following the Tribunal's rendering of an award in the second Phase, the Parties shall commence negotiations, in good faith, with a view toward concluding an agreement describing the ways in which nationals of both Parties may use the resources of the mid-sea islands and their maritime zones, as those zones are described in the Award of the Tribunal, and detailing a mechanism of binding dispute resolution to settle any and all disputes arising out of the interpretation or application of the agreement;

   B. The Parties shall submit this agreement to the Tribunal for its review and approval no later than six months after the date the Tribunal renders its award in the second Phase;

   C. The Tribunal shall determine whether the agreement is in accord with its award in the second Phase, and in particular whether it faithfully preserves the traditional rights of the two Parties to usage of the resources of the mid-sea islands;

   D. If the Tribunal determines that the agreement is not satisfactory according to the criteria described in the preceding paragraph, or if the Parties fail to submit an agreement, the Tribunal shall issue an award that either describes such modalities or else appoints the water between the two Parties equally. The Tribunal may request submissions from the Parties on this point.

   E. If the Tribunal finds that the agreement (or a revised agreement) is satisfactory, according to the criteria set forth above, it shall communicate its approval to the Parties, endorse the agreement as its own award and further direct the Parties to execute the agreement in the form of a binding treaty to be deposited with the Secretary-General of the United Nations;

7. The Tribunal shall remain seized of the dispute between the Parties until such time as the agreement regarding shared usage of the mid-sea islands has been received for deposit by the Secretary-General of the United Nations.

CHAPTER II – The General Question of Fishing in the Red Sea

47. This chapter will first deal with the evidence and arguments advanced by the Parties concerning the general question of fishing in the Red Sea. It will then set forth the Tribunal's conclusions on these arguments and evidence.

The Evidence and Arguments of the Parties

48. Each Party made much of fishing, including both the past history and the present situation, and as related not only to its own nationals but also the practices of the nationals of the other Party. The evidence advanced by the Parties and the arguments made by them can essentially be broken down into five subjects. These are: (1) fishing in general; (2) the location of fishing areas; (3) the economic dependency of the Parties on fishing; (4) consumption of fish by the populations of the Parties; and (5) the effect of fishing practices on the lines of delimitation proposed by the Parties.

49. The arguments of each Party were advanced essentially in order to demonstrate that the delimitation line proposed by that Party would not alter the existing situation and historical practices, that it would not have a catastrophic effect on local fishermen or on the local or national economy of the other Party or a negative effect on the regional diet of the population of the other Party and, conversely, that the delimitation line proposed by the other Party would indeed alter the existing situation and historical practice, would have a catastrophic or at least a severely adverse effect on the local fishermen or on the first Party's regional economy, and would also have a negative effect on the diet of the population of the first Party.

50. These elements were introduced directly and indirectly by each side against the general background of the "catastrophic" and "long usage" tests originated in the *Anglo-Norwegian Fisheries Case* of 1951 – and as brought forward in the provisions *inter alia* of Article 7, paragraph 5 of the 1982 United Nations Convention on the Law of the Sea.

51. They also found an echo in the "equitable solution" called for by paragraph 1 of Articles 74 and 83 of the Convention, it being assumed that no "solution" could be equitable which would be inconsistent with long usage, which would present a clear and present danger of a catastrophic result on the local economy of one of the Parties, or which would fail to take into account the need to minimise detrimental effects on fishing communities, and the economic dislocation, of States whose nationals have habitually fished in the relevant area.

Fishing in General

52. The position taken by Eritrea was as follows. The historical record demonstrated that the Eritrean fishing industry was substantial before the civil war in Ethiopia and had been, second only to Egypt, the most important regional fishing economy. Since the end of the civil war and independence, serious efforts were underway to reestablish the Eritrean fishing economy. It was, therefore, a mistake to consider that the Eritrean fisheries were – as Yemen argued – to a large extent dependent on Eritrean freshwater fisheries; in fact these have had no importance. On the other hand, the Yemen fishing industry was substantially based on its Indian Ocean fisheries and did not rely significantly on the Red Sea. Although Yemen's fishing industry in the Red Sea is much less significant than Yemen has claimed, it is nonetheless well established and in no event dependent for protection on the particular delimitation line proposed by Yemen.

53. Yemen argued that Yemeni nationals have long dominated fishing activities in the Red Sea; the Yemen traditional fishing activities – conducted in small boats, whether *sambouks* or *houris* – had been of much greater significance in the past than those of Eritrea, whose fishing activities had largely been concentrated on fishing close inshore along the Eritrean coastline and in and among the Dahlaks. Moreover, Hodeidah in Yemen was the most active market for fisheries production from Eritrean and Yemeni fishermen alike.

Economic Dependency on Fishing

54. The position of Eritrea was that considerable efforts had been made since the close of the war to reorganise and build up the Eritrean fishing industry – including efforts sponsored by the UNDP and FAO – and that the prospects for significant future development of the Eritrean fisheries were both promising and important. Although Eritrea did not claim present economic dependency on fishing, it did make the point that the existing fisheries practices of its nationals should not be restricted or curtailed by the delimitation to be decided by the Tribunal. As to Yemen, Eritrea asserted not only that the Yemen's Red Sea fisheries presence was far less important than Yemen had claimed, but also that most fish landed in Hodeidah were brought there by Eritrean fishermen.

55. On the other hand, Yemen argued that its fishermen have always depended on the Red Sea fisheries as their fishing grounds and that this fishing activity had long constituted an important part of Yemen's overall national economy and been a dominant part of the regional economy of the Tihama region along the Red Sea coast. Yemen claimed that Eritrea had no basis for arguing that it possessed any substantial dependency on fishing, fisheries, fish, or fish consumption, and that most of Eritrea's concerns as manifested by documentary evidence submitted to the Tribunal in both Stages of the Arbitration had concerned proposals and

projects for the development of future fishing activity and fisheries resources of Eritrea that did not now exist or were not now utilised.

Location of Fishing Areas

56. The arguments of Eritrea were to the following effect: at present, fishing in the Red Sea was by and large dominated by Eritrean artisanal fishermen who caught their fish around the Dahlaks, along the Eritrean coast, around the Mohabbakahs, the Haycocks, and South West Rocks, and in the waters around the Zuqar-Hanish group of "mid-sea islands." (As noted above, Eritrea denied that any part of its fish catch depended on inland Eritrean fisheries such as in lakes and reservoirs.) As to Yemen, Eritrea claimed that Yemeni fishermen had hardly, if at all, relied on the deep-water fishing grounds to the west of the mid-sea islands and around the Mohabbakahs, the Haycocks, and South West Rocks; there was little evidence of any Yemeni nationals' activity west of the Zuqar-Hanish group; and Yemen had failed to prove that a single gram of fish consumed in Yemen was taken from those waters.

57. For its part, Yemen argued that its artisanal and traditional fishermen had long fished in the waters around Jabal al-Tayr and the Zubayr group, in the waters around the Zuqar-Hanish group, and in the deep waters west of Greater Hanish and around the Mohabbakahs, the Haycocks, and South West Rocks. Supporting these assertions was evidence produced in the form of witness statements in the First Stage of the Arbitration in which individual Yemeni fishermen indicated that they had fished in the waters in question for a long time. As to the other Party, Yemen again asserted that Eritrea's fishing activities were confined to waters of the Dahlak archipelago and the inshore waters along the Eritrean coast and did not to any substantial extent impinge on waters surrounding the islands at issue in the First Stage of the Arbitration – including the deep waters west of Greater Hanish and around the Mohabbakahs, the Haycocks, and South West Rocks.

Consumption of Fish by the Population

58. Eritrea argued that the Eritrean coastal population consumed far more fish than Yemen claimed and that, in addition, efforts were taking place to increase the popularity and availability of fresh fish for human consumption by its general population. It further asserted that the Yemeni population's dependence on fresh fish from the Red Sea as a food source had been greatly exaggerated by Yemen's pleadings, and that the Yemeni population of the Tihama – and *a fortiori* the population of Yemen as a whole – did not rely to any significant extent on fresh fish as a food. For its part, Yemen maintained that its population, particularly in the coastal areas such as the Tihama, consumed substantial quantities of fish and that – by contrast – Eritrean fish consumption was negligible.

Effect on Lines of Delimitation Proposed by the Parties

59. The Eritrean position was that the Tribunal's indication of a line of delimitation such as the "historic median line" suggested by Eritrea would respect the historic practice of the Parties, would not displace or adversely affect Yemen's fishing activity, and would be an equitable result for both Parties. In Eritrea's view, however, the Yemen proposed "median line" would deprive Eritrean fishermen of valuable fishery areas east of the mid-sea islands, and would award to Yemen areas to the west of the mid-sea islands and around the Mohabbakahs, the Haycocks, and South West Rocks – where Eritrean fishermen had long been plying their trade and where Yemeni nationals had never engaged in substantial fisheries activity. To that extent Eritrea argued that the proposed Yemen delimitation line would be inequitable and would deprive Eritrean fishermen of an important resource.

60. On the other side, Yemen maintained that the median line proposed by it would correctly reflect historical practices, would not give Yemen anything it did not have before, would respect existing rights, would not "penalise" existing or past Eritrean fishing activity, and would constitute an equitable result. As far as the Eritrean proposed "historic median line" was concerned, it would encroach on Yemen's traditional fishing grounds without justification, would deprive Yemeni fishermen of deep water fisheries west of the mid-sea islands, and would give a corresponding windfall to Eritrea.

* – * – *

The Tribunal's Conclusions on the Evidence

61. The purposes of the arguments and evidence of the Parties were several, but were essentially directed to establishing that the delimitation advanced by each Party would respect existing historical practices, would not have a catastrophic effect on local fishermen or population, would not have a generally negative effect on the economy (or future plans) of the other Party, and would not have a deleterious effect on the diet and health of the population of the other Party. By the same token, each Party asserted or implied that the line of delimitation advanced by the other would have precisely the converse effect. The evidence advanced by the Parties has to a very large extent been contradictory and confusing.

On the basis of the arguments and evidence advanced before it the Tribunal reaches the following conclusions.

As to Fishing in General

62. Fishing in general is an important activity for both sides of the Red Sea coast. This was recognised in the Award on Sovereignty of the Tribunal. It is not necessary and probably misleading to seek to determine the precise extent of its importance at any particular time, but the plain fact appears to be that – as the Tribunal stated in paragraph 526 of its Award on Sovereignty – "the traditional fishing regime in the region . . . has operated, as the evidence presented to the Tribunal amply testifies, around the Hanish and Zuqar Islands and the islands of Jabal al-Tayr and the Zubayr group."

63. Moreover, the whole point of the Tribunal's holding in paragraph vi of its Dispositif in the Award on Sovereignty – that this traditional fishing regime shall be perpetuated so as to include "free access and enjoyment for the fishermen of both Eritrea and Yemen" – is that such traditional fishing activity has already been adjudged by the Tribunal to be important to each Party and to their nationals on both sides of the Red Sea. It thus suffices to say that fishing, fishermen, and fisheries are, and remain, of importance to each Party in the present case. Precisely because of this significance of paragraph 526 of the Award on Sovereignty and paragraph vi of its Dispositif, the fishing practices of the Parties from time to time are not germane to the task of arriving at a line of delimitation.

As to Economic Dependency on Fishing

64. It is not possible or necessary for the Tribunal to reach a conclusion that either Eritrea or Yemen is economically dependent on fishing to such an extent as to suggest any particular line of delimitation. The evidence before the Tribunal suggests that fishing activity and income appear to form an important part of Yemen's economic activity – particularly of the Tihama region – and that revitalisation and development of the Eritrean fishing industry is a priority objective of the Government of Eritrea and has received significant attention since Eritrean independence.

As to Location of Fishing Areas

65. The evidence advanced in both Stages of the Arbitration included evidence that many fishermen from Eritrea tended largely to fish in and around the Dahlak archipelago and on inshore waters along the Eritrean coastline, but it also appears that some Eritrean fishermen used the waters in and around the Hanish and Zuqar Islands as well as the deep waters to the west of the mid-sea islands and around the Mohabbakahs, the Haycocks, and South West Rocks. This conclusion was adumbrated by the Tribunal's concern for maintenance of the traditional fishing regime "in the region" as a whole, "including free access and enjoyment for the fishermen of both Eritrea and Yemen" (Award on Sovereignty, Dispositif, paragraph 527, subparagraph vi).

66. There is abundant historical data indicating that fishermen from both the eastern and western coasts of the Red Sea freely undertook activities, including fishing and selling their catch on the local markets, regardless of their national political affiliation or their place of habitual domicile.[5]

67. This information concerning the social and economic conditions affecting the lives of the people on both sides of the Red Sea also reflects deeply-rooted and common social and legal traditions that had prevailed for centuries among these populations, each of which was under the direct or indirect rule of the Ottoman Empire until the latter part of the 19th Century.

68. The evidence before the Tribunal further appears to establish that over the years Yemeni fishermen have operated as far north as the Dahlak archipelago and Jabal al-Tayr and the Zubayr group, and as far west as the Mohabbakahs, the Haycocks, and South West Rocks. Again, this conclusion is implicit in the Tribunal's concern for maintenance of the traditional fishing regime "in the *region*" as a whole.

69. On a subject not unrelated to fishing areas, it should be noted that the evidence is quite clear that Eritrean fishermen as well as Yemeni also appear to have enjoyed free and open access to the major fish market at Hodeidah on the Yemen side of the Red Sea without impediment by reason of their nationality. (This element was again taken into account by the Tribunal in its Award on Sovereignty, Dispositif, paragraph 527, subparagraph vi.)

As to Consumption of Fish by the Population

70. The evidence concerning fish consumption advanced by each Party was presumably aimed at establishing that the Tribunal's adoption of the line of delimitation proposed by the other Party would constitute a serious dietary or health threat to the population of the first Party. However, the evidence on this matter is conflicting and uncertain. It is difficult if not impossible to draw any generalised conclusions from the welter of alleged facts advanced by the Parties in this connection.

71. The Tribunal can readily conclude, without having to weigh intangible and elusive points of proof or without having to indulge in nice calculations of nutritional theory, that fish as a present and future potential resource is important for the general and local populations of each Party on each side of the Red Sea. The Tribunal can also conclude, as a matter of common sense and judicial notice, that interest in and development of fish as a food source is an important and meritorious objective. Based on these two conclusions, however, the Tribunal can find no significant reason on these grounds for accepting – or rejecting – the

5 See footnotes 9 and 11 to paragraphs 121 and 128 respectively of the Award on Sovereignty.

arguments of either Party as to the *line of delimitation* proposed by itself or by the other Party.

Concerning the Effect on Lines of Delimitation Proposed by the Parties

72. Based on the foregoing, the Tribunal finds no significant reason on any other grounds concerning fishing – whether related to the historical practice of fishing in general, to matters of asserted economic dependency on fishing, to the location of fishing grounds, or to the patterns of fish consumption by the populations – for accepting, or rejecting, the arguments of either Party on the line of delimitation proposed by itself or by the other Party. Neither Party has succeeded in demonstrating that the line of delimitation proposed by the other would produce a catastrophic or inequitable effect on the fishing activity of its nationals or detrimental effects on fishing communities and economic dislocation of its nationals.[6]

73. For these reasons, it is not possible for the Tribunal to accept or reject the line of delimitation proposed by either Party on fisheries grounds. Nor can the Tribunal find any relevant effect on the legal reasons supporting its own selection of a delimitation line arising from its consideration of the general past fishing practice of either Party or the potential deprivation of fishing areas or access to fishing resources, or arising from nutritional or other grounds.

* – * – *

74. For the above reasons, the evidence and arguments advanced by the Parties in the matter of fishing and fisheries could have no significant effect on the Tribunal's determination of the delimitation that would be appropriate under international law in order to produce an equitable solution between the Parties.

---

[6] *Cf.* Article 70, paragraph 5 of the United Nations Convention on the Law of the Sea: "Developed geographically disadvantaged States shall, under the provisions of this article, be entitled to participate in the exploitation of living resources only in the exclusive economic zones of developed coastal States of the same sub-region or region having regard to the extent to which the coastal State, in giving access to other States to the living resources of its exclusive economic zone, has taken into account the need to minimize detrimental effects on fishing communities and economic dislocation in States whose nationals have habitually fished in the zone."

CHAPTER III – Petroleum Agreements and Median Lines

75. In the matter of the pertinence and probative force for this Stage of the proceedings of petroleum contracts and concessions entered into by Yemen and by Ethiopia or Eritrea, the Parties exhibited a reversal of roles.

76. In the First Stage, Yemen laid great weight on oil contracts and concessions concluded by it. It introduced into evidence a number of such oil agreements and maps illustrating them, many of which were prepared by Petroconsultants S.A. of Geneva. Since some of these arrangements embodied western boundaries to the east of which lay some of the islands in dispute, Yemen argued that these arrangements demonstrated that both Yemen and the contracting oil companies were of the view that Yemen enjoyed sovereignty over those disputed islands. It contended that, where a State enters into a concession covering a specified area, it holds itself out as having sovereignty over that area; and that, where a foreign oil company enters into that concession, and expends resources in pursuance of it, it does so because it accepts and acts in reliance upon the sovereignty of that State. Yemen emphasised that not only were some of its petroleum contracts of a geographical extent that encompassed the disputed islands; it was also significant, it claimed, that none of the oil contracts and concessions concluded by Ethiopia or Eritrea did so. As the Award on Sovereignty summarised: "Yemen contended that the pattern of Yemen's offshore concessions, unprotested by Ethiopia and Eritrea, taken together with the pattern of Ethiopian concessions, confirmed Yemen's sovereign claims to the disputed Islands, acceptance of and investment on the basis of that sovereignty by oil companies, and acquiescence by Ethiopia and Eritrea." (paragraph 390.)

77. In the First Stage, Eritrea in contrast argued that conclusion by a State of an oil contract or concession with a foreign oil company was not evidence of title but, at most, a mere claim. Such arrangements lacked probative force unless activities in pursuance of them took place. Nevertheless Eritrea countered Yemen's argument by introducing evidence of a concession concluded by Ethiopia which covered part or all of Greater and Lesser Hanish Islands. Neither Eritrea nor Yemen attached importance to the fact that a number of the petroleum arrangements concluded by Yemen and Ethiopia or Eritrea extended to a median line between their respective coastlines.

78. In its Award on Sovereignty, the Tribunal concluded:

> 437. The offshore petroleum contracts entered into by Yemen, and by Ethiopia and Eritrea, fail to establish or significantly strengthen the claims of either party to sovereignty over the disputed islands.
>
> 438. Those contracts however lend a measure of support to a median line between the opposite coasts of Eritrea and Yemen, drawn without regard to the islands, dividing the respective jurisdiction of the Parties.

79. In the Second Stage of these Proceedings, Eritrea placed great emphasis upon paragraph 438, and other passages of the Award, that found that various petroleum arrangements indicate limits drawn along a median line, and contended that the Tribunal's Award provided support for the "historic median line" which it now advanced as the maritime boundary line between Eritrea and Yemen. Eritrea stressed that, in several petroleum contracts concluded by Yemen, the contractual area extended from the mainland coast of Yemen in the east to the median line of the Red Sea, drawn without regard to base points on the disputed islands. It observed that a contract concluded by it, and another concluded by Yemen, ran through Greater Hanish along a median line. It pointed out that one of Yemen's concession contracts contains a median line, marked "Ethiopia" to the west and "Yemen" to the east. It maintained that maps prepared by Petroconsultants, introduced and relied upon by Yemen in the First Stage, and showing concession boundaries running along a median line between the coasts of Yemen and Eritrea, cannot now be discounted by Yemen because it introduced them for another purpose. Eritrea acknowledged that the contracts and conduct of Yemen and of Ethiopia and Eritrea are not tantamount to mutual acceptance of a median maritime boundary or even of a *modus vivendi* line. But it contended that they nevertheless provide a persuasive basis for taking an "historic median line" to divide the waters of the Red Sea, to be drawn without according the "mid-sea" disputed islands influence on the course of that line.

80. Yemen for its part contended that, while it introduced the Petroconsultants maps as evidence of Yemen's sovereignty over the disputed islands, it did so not to show maritime boundaries; that the Petroconsultants maps contain "mistakes"; and that these and other maps introduced in the First Stage contain disclaimers about lines affecting or prejudicing the contracting government's sovereign rights. Yemen emphasised the Tribunal's holding that the concessions were "issued with commercial considerations in mind and without particular regard to the existence of the Islands." (Award on Sovereignty, paragraph 412.)

81. It should be noted that, in the course of making its holdings on sovereignty over the disputed islands, the Tribunal held that the petroleum contracts do "lend a measure of support to a median line between the opposite coasts of Eritrea and Yemen, drawn without regard to the islands, dividing the respective jurisdiction of the Parties."

82. At this juncture, however, the Tribunal acts in the light of the dispositive provisions of paragraph 527 of its Award. Which islands are subject to the territorial sovereignty of Eritrea, and which are subject to the territorial sovereignty of Yemen, has been determined. In delimiting the maritime boundaries of the Parties, the Tribunal is required in this Second Stage of the proceedings to take into account, *inter alia*, the opinion that it formed on the question of territorial sovereignty.

83. As is set out in other passages of this Award, the Tribunal has taken as its starting point, as its fundamental point of departure, that, as between opposite coasts, a median line obtains. The Award on Sovereignty's examination of petroleum arrangements does show, as just indicated, repeated reference to a median line between the coasts of Yemen and Eritrea. To that extent, Eritrea's position in this Stage of the proceedings is sustained by those references. But that is not the same as saying that the maritime boundary now to be drawn should be drawn throughout its length entirely without regard to the islands whose sovereignty has been determined; nor is it to say that that boundary should track Eritrea's claimed "historic median line." The concession lines were drawn without regard to uninhabited, volcanic islands when their sovereignty was indeterminate. Those lines can hardly be taken as governing once that sovereignty has been determined. While initial weight is to be given to the mainland coasts and their island fringes, some weight is to be or may be accorded to the islands, certainly in respect of their territorial waters. What weight, and why and how, are questions addressed below.

84. In respect of petroleum arrangements and a maritime boundary between the Parties in the Red Sea, the Tribunal recalls the conclusion of the International Court of Justice in its Judgment in the *North Sea Continental Shelf* cases,[7] that delimitation of States' areas of continental shelf may lead to "an overlapping of the areas appertaining to them. The Court considers that such a situation must be accepted as a given fact and resolved either by an agreed, or failing that by an equal division of the overlapping areas, or by agreements for joint exploitation, the latter solution appearing particularly appropriate when it is a question of preserving the unity of a deposit." Judge Jessup in his separate opinion in that case referred to a seminal article by William T. Onorato[8] and cited examples of such cooperation; and in the last thirty years there has grown up a significant body of cooperative State practice in the exploitation of resources that straddle maritime boundaries. The papers in a volume published by The British Institute of International and Comparative Law summarise and analyse this practice,[9] as does a more recent study by Masahiro Miyoshi, *The Joint Development of Offshore Oil and Gas in Relation to the Maritime Boundary Delimitations*, International Boundaries Research Unit, 1999.[10]

---

7 I.C.J. Reports 1969, p. 52.

8 *Apportionment of an International Petroleum Deposit*, 17 ICLQ 85 (1958).

9 Edited by Hazel Fox, *Joint Development of Offshore Oil and Gas* (1990) by R.R. Churchill, Kamal Hossein, Isa Huneidi, Masahiro Miyoshi, Ian Townsend-Gault, Anastasia Strati, H. Burmester, Clive R. Symmons, Thomas H. Walde, Brenda Barrett, P. Birnie and A.D. Read.

10 See also, I.F.I. Shihata and W.T. Onorato, *Joint Development of International Petroleum Resources in Undefined and Disputed Areas*, International Conference of the LAWASIA Energy Centre, Kuala Lumpur, 1992.

85. That practice has particular pertinence in the current case. The Red Sea is not to be compared to the great oceans. Yemen and Eritrea face one another across a relatively narrow compass. Their peoples have had a long and largely beneficent history of intermingling, a history not limited to the free movement of fishermen but embracing a wider trade, and a common rule as well as a common religion. These relations long antedate the relatively modern, European-derived, concepts of exclusionary sovereignty. While oil and gas in commercial quantities have not to date been found beneath the waters of the Red Sea that lie between Eritrea and Yemen, it is possible that either or both may be.

86. In paragraph 1 of its Prayer for Relief, Eritrea requests the Tribunal to determine that "The Eritrean people's historic use of resources in the mid-sea islands includes . . . mineral extraction." For reasons explained in paragraph 104 of this Award, the Tribunal is not in a position to accede to this request. However, it is of the view that, having regard to the maritime boundary established by this Award, the Parties are bound to inform one another and to consult one another on any oil and gas and other mineral resources that may be discovered that straddle the single maritime boundary between them or that lie in its immediate vicinity. Moreover, the historical connections between the peoples concerned, and the friendly relations of the Parties that have been restored since the Tribunal's rendering of its Award on Sovereignty, together with the body of State practice in the exploitation of resources that straddle maritime boundaries, import that Eritrea and Yemen should give every consideration to the shared or joint or unitised exploitation of any such resources.

CHAPTER IV – The Traditional Fishing Regime

87. In paragraph 526 of its Award on Territorial Sovereignty and Scope of the Dispute the Tribunal found:

> In finding that the Parties each have sovereignty over various of the Islands the Tribunal stresses to them that such sovereignty is not inimical to, but rather entails, the perpetuation of the traditional fishing regime in the region. This existing regime has operated, as the evidence presented to the Tribunal amply testifies, around the Hanish and Zuqar Islands and the islands of Jabal al-Tayr and the Zubayr group. In the exercise of its sovereignty over these islands, Yemen shall ensure that the traditional fishing regime of free access and enjoyment for the fishermen of both Eritrea and Yemen shall be preserved for the benefit of the lives and livelihoods of this poor and industrious order of men.

88. Immediately after, in paragraph vi of its Dispositif, The Tribunal determined that:

> the sovereignty found to lie within Yemen entails the perpetuation of the traditional fishing regime in the region, including free access and enjoyment for the fishermen of both Eritrea and Yemen.

89. Eritrea has taken the view that these findings entail the establishment of joint resource zones, which the Tribunal should delimit in its Award in the Second Stage. Eritrea, in its Prayer for Relief, also urged the Tribunal to direct the Parties to negotiate so as to achieve certain results it regards as required by paragraph 527(vi) of the Dispositif in the Award on Sovereignty, and to take certain other powers in relation thereto. To fail to do so, contended Eritrea, would be *infra petita*. Eritrea further contended that the final paragraph of the letter of 9 November 1998 from the President of the Tribunal to the counsel and co-agent for Eritrea left Eritrea full liberty so to submit during this Stage of the Arbitration. Some of the elements contained in Eritrea's Prayer for Relief were not pursued in oral argument; there the main plea was that the Court* specify with precision what was entailed by its finding as to the traditional fishing regime and where that regime lay within the Red Sea. However, the Prayer for Relief, unamended, was said by Eritrea to represent its final submissions.

90. Yemen took the view that it was clear from paragraph 526 of the Award on Sovereignty that it was for it, Yemen, in the exercise of its sovereignty, to ensure the preservation of the traditional fishing regime; that, while the 1994 and 1998 Agreements might prove to be useful vehicles for that exercise in sovereignty, there was no question of Yemen's sovereignty having been made conditional and thus no agreement with Eritrea was necessary for the administrative measures that might relate to this regime; that the Tribunal had not made any finding that there

---

* *Editorial correction: substitute "Tribunal" for "Court."*

should be joint or common resource zones; that the Tribunal's finding that Yemen's sovereignty entailed the perpetuation of the traditional fishing regime was a finding in favour of the fishermen of Eritrea and Yemen, not of the State of Eritrea; that Article 3(1) of the Agreement on Principles and Article 2(3) of the Arbitration Agreement meant that it would be *ultra vires* for the Tribunal to respond favourably to Eritrea's Prayer for Relief; and that the President's letter of 9 November 1998 indeed showed that the Prayer for Relief was irregular. Further, Yemen contended that there had traditionally been no significant Eritrean fishing in the vicinity of the islands.

91. The details of the positions taken by Eritrea and Yemen is recalled above at paragraphs 48-60.

92. The Tribunal recalls that it based this aspect of its Award on Sovereignty on a respect for regional legal traditions. The abundant literature on the historical realities which characterised the lives of the populations on both the eastern and western coasts was noted in the award of the Arbitral Tribunal in the First Stage of the Proceedings, paragraph 121, footnote 9 and paragraph 128, footnote 11. This well-established factual situation reflected deeply rooted common legal traditions which prevailed during several centuries among the populations of both coasts of the Red Sea, which were until the latter part of the nineteenth century under the direct or indirect rule of the Ottoman Empire. The basic Islamic concept by virtue of which all humans are "stewards of God" on earth, with an inherent right to sustain their nutritional needs through fishing from coast to coast with free access to fish on either side and to trade the surplus, remained vivid in the collective mind of Dankhalis and Yemenites alike.

93. Although the immediate beneficiaries of this legal concept were and are the fishermen themselves, it applies equally to States in their mutual relations. As a leading scholar has observed: "Islam is not merely a religion but also a political community (*umma*) endowed with a system of law designed both to protect the collective interest of its subjects and to regulate their relations with the outside world."[11]

94. The sovereignty that the Tribunal has awarded to Yemen over Jabal al-Tayr, the Zubayr group and the Zuqar-Hanish group is not of course a "conditional" sovereignty, but a sovereignty nevertheless that respects and embraces and is subject to the Islamic legal concepts of the region. As it has been aptly put, "in today's world, it remains true that the fundamental moralistic general principles of the *Quran* and the *Sunna* may validly be invoked for the consolidation and support of positive international law rules in their progressive development

[11] Khadduri, *Encyclopedia of Public International Law*, volume 6, page 227.

towards the goal of achieving justice and promoting the human dignity of all mankind."[12]

95. The Tribunal's Award on Sovereignty was not based on any assessment of volume, absolute or relative, of Yemeni or Eritrean fishing in the region of the islands. What was relevant was that fishermen from both of these nations had, from time immemorial, used these islands for fishing and activities related thereto. Further, the finding on the traditional fishing regime was made in the context of the Award on Sovereignty precisely because classical western territorial sovereignty would have been understood as allowing the power in the sovereign state to exclude fishermen of a different nationality from its waters. Title over Jabal al-Tayr and the Zubayr group and over the Zuqar-Hanish group was found by the Tribunal to be indeterminate until recently. Moreover, these islands lay at some distance from the mainland coasts of the Parties. Their location meant that they were put to a special use by the fishermen as way stations and as places of shelter, and not just, or perhaps even mainly, as fishing grounds. These special factors constituted a local tradition entitled to the respect and protection of the law.

96. It is clear that the Arbitration Agreement does not authorise the Tribunal to respond affirmatively to paragraphs 6 and 7 of Eritrea's Prayer for Relief. Nor, indeed, would it have been able so to do even if the arbitration had been conducted within the framework of a single stage or phase, as originally envisaged by Article 3(1) of the Agreement on Principles.

97. However, Eritrea is entitled to submit to the Tribunal that its finding as to the traditional fishing regime has implications for the delimiting of maritime boundaries in the Second Stage; and the Tribunal is at liberty to respond to such submissions.

98. Indeed, it is bound to do so, because it is not otherwise in a position to respond to the submissions made by Yemen as well as by Eritrea in this Second Stage. It cannot be the case that the division of the Arbitration into two stages meant that the Parties may continue to debate whether the substantive content of the Tribunal's findings on the traditional fishing regime has any relevance to the task of delimitation, but that the Tribunal must remain silent. Such formalism was never the objective of the agreement of both Parties to divide the Arbitration into two Stages.

99. Of course, in making its Award on Sovereignty the Tribunal did not "prefigure" or anticipate the maritime delimitation that it is now called upon to make in the Second Stage, after full pleadings by the Parties. Beyond that the Tribunal is not

---

[12] *Encyclopedia of Public International Law*, volume 7, page 229.

to be artificially constrained in what it may respond to by the procedural structures agreed for the Arbitration. The two-stage mechanism is not to be read either as forbidding Parties to make the arguments they wish, when they wish; nor as limiting their entitlement to seek to protect what they perceive as their substantive rights.

100. Article 15 of the Arbitration Agreement (the meaning of which is otherwise not readily intelligible) lends support to this view. Paragraph 2 speaks of the Arbitration Agreement as "implementing the procedural aspects" of the Agreement on Principles. And Paragraph 1 provides that:

> Nothing in this Arbitration Agreement can be interpreted as being detrimental to the legal positions or to the rights of each Party with respect to the questions submitted to the Tribunal, nor can affect or prejudice the decision of the Arbitral Tribunal or the considerations and grounds on which those decisions are based.

101. As the Tribunal has indicated in its Award on Sovereignty, the traditional fishing regime around the Hanish and Zuqar Islands and the islands of Jabal al-Tayr and the Zubayr group is one of free access and enjoyment for the fishermen of both Eritrea and Yemen. It is to be preserved for their benefit. This does not mean, however, that Eritrea may not act on behalf of its nationals, whether through diplomatic contacts with Yemen or through submissions to this Tribunal. There is no reason to import into the Red Sea the western legal fiction – which is in any event losing its importance – whereby all legal rights, even those in reality held by individuals, were deemed to be those of the State. That legal fiction served the purpose of allowing diplomatic representation (where the representing State so chose) in a world in which individuals had no opportunities to advance their own rights. It was never meant to be the case however that, were a right to be held by an individual, neither the individual nor his State should have access to international redress.

102. The Tribunal accordingly now responds to the diverse submissions advanced in this Stage by the Parties, both as to the substantive content of the traditional fishing regime referred to in paragraphs 526 and 527(vi) of its Award on Sovereignty and as to any implications for its task in this stage of the Arbitration. The correct answer is indeed to be gleaned from the pages of that Award itself. Attention may in particular be drawn to paragraphs 102, 126-128, 340, 353-357 and 526.

103. The traditional fishing regime is not an entitlement in common to resources nor is it a shared right in them. Rather, it entitles both Eritrean and Yemeni fishermen to engage in artisanal fishing around the islands which, in its Award on Sovereignty, the Tribunal attributed to Yemen. This is to be understood as including diving, carried out by artisanal means, for shells and pearls. Equally, these fishermen remain entitled freely to use these islands for those purposes

traditionally associated with such artisanal fishing – the use of the islands for drying fish, for way stations, for the provision of temporary shelter, and for the effecting of repairs.

104. In paragraph 1 of the Prayer for Relief, Eritrea asks the Tribunal to determine that "The Eritrean people's historic use of resources in the mid-sea islands includes guano and mineral extraction . . .." In the pleadings before the Tribunal Eritrea referred specifically in this context to guano extraction which had been licensed by Italy. Guano extraction is not to be assimilated to mineral extraction more generally. Further, as the Award on Sovereignty made clear, Eritrea's rights today are not derived from a claimed continuity from rights once held by Italy. The traditional fishing regime covers those entitlements that all the fishermen have exercised continuously through the ages. The Tribunal has received no evidence that the extraction of guano, or mineral extraction more generally, forms part of the traditional fishing regime that has existed and continues to exist today.

105. The FAO Fisheries Infrastructure Development Project Report of 1995 was a report on fishing in Eritrean waters. However, its findings on artisanal fishing would be of general application in this region. The 1995 Report makes clear that both the artisanal vessels and their gear are simple. The vessels are usually canoes fitted with small outboard engines, slightly larger vessels (9-12 m) fitted with 40-75 hp engines, or fishing *sambuks* with inboard engines. Dugout canoes and small rafts (*ramas*) are also in use.[13] Hand lines, gill nets and long lines are used. In its Report on Fishing in Eritrean waters, the FAO study states that this artisanal fishing gear, which varies according to the boat and the fish, is "simple and efficient."[14]

106. However, the term "artisanal" is not to be understood as applying in the future only to a certain type of fishing exactly as it is practised today. "Artisanal fishing" is used in contrast to "industrial fishing." It does not exclude improvements in powering the small boats, in the techniques of navigation, communication or in the techniques of fishing; but the traditional regime of fishing does not extend to large-scale commercial or industrial fishing nor to fishing by nationals of third States in the Red Sea, whether small-scale or industrial.

107. In order that the entitlements be real and not merely theoretical, the traditional regime has also recognised certain associated rights. There must be free access to and from the islands concerned – including unimpeded passage through waters in which, by virtue of its sovereignty over the islands, Yemen is entitled to exclude all third Parties or subject their presence to licence, just as it may do in respect of Eritrean industrial fishing. This free passage for artisanal fishermen has

---

[13] FAO 24/95 ADB-ERI.4, 27 February 1995, at paragraphs 2.19 and 3.44.

[14] *Ibid.*, paragraph 2.20.

traditionally existed not only between Eritrea and the islands, but also between the islands and the Yemen coast. The entitlement to enter the relevant ports, and to sell and market the fish there, is an integral element of the traditional regime. The 1994 Memorandum of Understanding between the State of Eritrea and the Republic of Yemen for Cooperation in the Areas of Maritime Fishing, Trade, Investment, and Transportation usefully identifies the centres of fish marketing on each coast. Eritrean artisanal fisherman fishing around the islands awarded to Yemen have had free access to Maydi, Khoba, Hodeidah, Khokha and Mocha on the Yemen coast, just as Yemeni artisanal fishermen fishing around the islands have had an entitlement to unimpeded transit to and access to Assab, Tio, Dahlak and Massawa on the Eritrean coast. Nationals of the one country have an entitlement to sell on equal terms and without any discrimination in the ports of the other. Within the fishing markets themselves, the traditional non-discriminatory treatment – so far as cleaning, storing and marketing is concerned – is to be continued. The traditional recourse by artisanal fisherman to the *acquil* system to resolve their disputes *inter se* is to be also maintained and preserved.

108. Yemen and Eritrea are, of course, free to make mutually agreed regulations for the protection of this traditional fishing regime. Insofar as environmental considerations may in the future require regulation, any administrative measures impacting upon these traditional rights shall be taken by Yemen only with the agreement of Eritrea and, so far as access through Eritrean waters to Eritrean ports is concerned, vice versa.

109. The traditional fishing regime is not limited to the territorial waters of specified islands; nor are its limits to be drawn by reference to claimed past patterns of fishing. It is, as Yemen itself observes in its Answers to the Tribunal's Questions, Annex 2, page *231* a "regime that has existed for the benefit of the fishermen of both countries throughout the region." By its very nature it is not qualified by the maritime zones specified under the United Nations Convention on the Law of the Sea, the law chosen by the Parties to be applicable to this task in this Second Stage of the Arbitration. The traditional fishing regime operates throughout those waters beyond the territorial waters of each of the Parties, and also in their territorial waters and ports, to the extent and in the manner specified in paragraph 107 above.

110. Accordingly, it does not depend, either for its existence or for its protection, upon the drawing of an international boundary by this Tribunal. This much was indeed acknowledged by Yemen in its Answers to the Tribunal's Questions, when it observed that "the holdings of the Tribunal in the first Award with respect to the traditional fishing regime constitute *res judicata* without prejudice to the maritime boundary that the Tribunal decides on in the second stage of the proceedings" (Annex 2, page *231*). Yemen informed the Tribunal that it was "fully committed to apply and implement the Award in all its aspects, including with respect to the perpetuation of the traditional fishing regime for the fishermen of both Eritrea and

Yemen." Nor is the drawing of the maritime boundary conditioned by the findings, in the Award on Sovereignty, of such a regime.

111. As the Tribunal has explained above, no further joint agreement is legally necessary for the perpetuation of a regime based on mutual freedoms and an absence of unilaterally imposed conditions. However, should Eritrea and Yemen decide that the intended cooperation exemplified by the 1994 Memorandum of Understanding and the 1998 Agreement can usefully underpin the traditional regime, they may choose to use some of the possibilities within these instruments. The subject matter of the 1994 instrument has a particular pertinence. (Moreover, it is the understanding of the Tribunal that the Parties did not jointly intend to deprive fishermen of their rights under this traditional regime if they failed to submit a fishing licence to the other Party within three months from the date of the signing of the Memorandum of Understanding.)

112. The Tribunal has responded to the pleadings that both Parties have made, as they were entitled to do, in this phase of the proceedings. Its answer indicates how its Award on Sovereignty is to be understood in relation to the matters that the Parties have now raised before it.

CHAPTER V – The Delimitation of the International Boundary

The Tribunal's Comments on the Arguments of the Parties

113. Since, as it will appear below, the international maritime boundary line decided upon by the Tribunal differs in some respects from both the one claimed by Yemen and the one, or the ones, claimed by Eritrea, it is right first to explain briefly where and why the boundaries claimed by the Parties have not been endorsed in this Award. This will now be done taking generally first the Yemen claim and then the Eritrean claim, as this was the order in which the Parties agreed to argue in the Oral Proceedings of this Second Stage of this Arbitration.

114. Yemen claimed one single international boundary line for all purposes. The single line it claimed was described as a "median line," because Yemen treated the westward-facing coasts of all of its islands as relevant coasts for purposes of the delimitation. For the Eritrean coast, Yemen used base points on the mainland coast of Eritrea and thus ignored the Eritrean mid-sea islands for the purpose of delimitation of the boundary. Yemen also claimed that its line can properly be described as a coastal median line. For Yemen the relevant coasts included not only the islands over which it has been awarded sovereignty, but also of certain among the Dahlak islands; thus Yemen, like Eritrea, was prepared to treat the Dahlaks as being part of the Eritrean coast, and so used base points on the islets forming the outer fringe of the group. When on the other hand Eritrea spoke of what it called "the coastal median line," it meant the median line between what in the Eritrean view represented the *mainland* coasts of both Parties. At the same time Eritrea claimed a historic median line using only its own islands as base points, and thus ignoring those of Yemen. These variations produced different claimed median lines. See Eritrea's Maps 3 and 7, and Yemen's Map 12.1. See also Charts 1 and 2 showing the base points as provided by Eritrea.

115. It is in what Yemen called the northern sector of the boundary line where this difference caused the greatest divergence, actually of several nautical miles, between the lines claimed by the Parties because of the question of how much "effect" on the line should be given to the Yemen northern islands, namely the small sole mid-sea island of Jabal al-Tayr and the mid-sea groups of islands and islets called Zubayr. Yemen allowed them full effect on the line; Eritrea's line allowed them none.

116. In considering this marked divergence of view it is well to recollect that the boundary line in its northern stretch – including indeed both the opposing claimed lines – are boundaries between the Yemen and the Eritrean continental shelves and EEZ; and are therefore governed by Articles 74 and 83 of the 1982 Convention. In any event there has to be room for differences of opinion about the interpretation of articles which, in a last minute endeavour at the Third United Nations Conference on the Law of the Sea to get agreement on a very

controversial matter, were consciously designed to decide as little as possible. It is clear, however, that both Articles envisage an equitable result.

117. This requirement of an equitable result directly raises the question of the effect to be allowed to mid-sea islands which, by virtue of their mid-sea position, and if allowed full effect, can obviously produce a disproportionate effect – or indeed a reasonable and proportionate effect – all depending on their size, importance and like considerations in the general geographical context.

118. Yemen understood this problem very clearly. Its argument was that, although these mid-sea islands and islets are small and uninhabitable (these questions figured prominently in the First Stage of this Arbitration), those considerations were nicely matched, or "balanced," by the complementary smallness and lack of importance of the outer islets of the Dahlak group which were the base points on the Eritrean side of the boundary. However, the situation of these Dahlak islets is very different from that of the mid-sea islands. The Dahlak outer islets are part of a much larger group of islands which both Parties were agreed are an integral part of the Eritrean mainland coast. Consequently, between these islets and the mainland, the sea is Eritrean internal waters. The Tribunal had therefore, as will be seen below, no difficulty in rejecting this "balancing" argument of Yemen, as it does not compare like with like.

119. In its assessment of the equities of the "effect" to be given to these northern islands and islets, the Tribunal decided not to accept the Yemen plea that they be allowed a full, or at least some, effect on the median line. This decision was confirmed by the result that, in any event, these mid-sea islands would enjoy an entire territorial sea of the normal 12 miles – even on their western side.

120. One practical result of the Yemen balancing argument regarding the northern mid-sea islands is that Yemen did not argue in the alternative about possible base points on the islands fringing the Yemen *mainland* coast – which islands could much more cogently be said to balance the Dahlaks.

121. The Eritrean argument concerning this northern stretch of the line was relatively simple: it argued strongly against the Yemen balancing suggestions, and here asked for the mainland coastal median line. At first, it was not clear what were the base points used by Eritrea. However, in answer to a question from the Tribunal, Eritrea did produce two complete sets of base points for the Eritrean coast and also a set for the Yemen coast. (See Charts 1 and 2.)

122. The latitude of 14°25'N – where the Yemen northern sector becomes the Yemen central sector – results from another factor on which the Parties differ. This line of latitude is not chosen at random by Yemen. It is the point at which the Yemen median line is no longer controlled by Zubayr as a base point but enters under the control of the north-western point of the island of Zuqar. The Eritrean lines, for

indeed there are two of them, continue southwards, ignoring the possible effect of the Zuqar-Hanish group. The "historic" median line (Map 3) cuts through Zuqar, and the coastal median line cuts through the island of Greater Hanish (Map 7).

123. The Tribunal did not find it easy to resolve this divergence of method, but finally the Tribunal decided to continue its line as a mainland coastal line until the presence of Yemen's Zuqar-Hanish group compels a diversion westwards. (The Tribunal's line, as will appear below, is neither the Yemen line nor yet the Eritrean line.)

124. In support of its enclave solution for certain of the Eritrean islands, Yemen entered upon an assessment of the relative size and importance of the Eritrean islands generally, as if they were islands whose influence on the boundary line falls to be assessed, not as being possibly in an area of overlapping territorial sea, but as if they were to be assessed solely by reference to Articles 74 and 83 of the Convention. This approach enabled Yemen to argue that these Eritrean "navigational hazards" were insignificant even when compared with the Yemen Zuqar-Hanish group; and that accordingly the South West Rocks and the Haycocks ought to be enclaved and the boundary line taken onto the Eritrean side of them, thus leaving the two enclaves isolated on the Yemen side of the boundary line.

125. The Tribunal, as will appear below, has had little difficulty in preferring the Eritrean argument, which brings into play Article 15. This solution also has the advantage of avoiding the need for awkward enclaves in the vicinity of a major international shipping route.

126. The Yemen "southern sector" began at the line of latitude 13°20'N. Again, this is not an arbitrary choice. It was the point at which Yemen's median line, which had hitherto been controlled by Suyul Hanish, first came under the control of the nearest point on the mainland coast of Yemen. The Yemen line then continued throughout the southern sector as a coastal median line.

127. In the main part of this southern sector, therefore, there were only differences of detail between the Yemen and Eritrean lines because there were no mid-sea islands to complicate the problem. There was indeed the large complication of the Bay of Assab and of its off-lying islands, but here Yemen rightly assumed that this bay is integral to the Eritrean coast and its internal waters, and that the controlling base points would therefore be on the low-water line of the outer coastal islands.

128. In the course of its passage from the overlapping territorial seas areas to the relatively simple stretch between parallel coasts of the southern sector, the Yemen line was again a median line controlled by the Yemen islands as well as by the Eritrean mainland coast. However, the line preferred by the Tribunal, mindful of the simplicity desirable in the neighbourhood of a main shipping lane, is one that

would mark this passage directly and independently of the Yemen and Eritrean islands. It is not easy to trace the Eritrean median line in this area because of the complication of its box system for the traditional fishing areas. Indeed, this review of the Parties' arguments and the Tribunal's view of them does somewhat scant justice to the complicated and carefully researched Eritrean scheme for delimitation of the traditional fishing areas, but this matter has been dealt with in Chapter IV.

This chapter will now turn to describe the boundary line determined by the Tribunal.

* – * – *

The Boundary Line Determined by the Tribunal

129. The task of the Tribunal in the present Stage of this Arbitration is defined by Article 2 of the Arbitration Agreement, and is to "result in an award delimiting the maritime boundaries." The term "boundaries" is here used, it is reasonable to assume, in its normal and ordinary meaning of denoting an international maritime boundary between the two State Parties to the Arbitration; and not in the sense of what is usually called a maritime "limit," such as the outer limit of a territorial sea or a contiguous zone; although there might be places where these limits happen to coincide with or be modified by the international boundary.

130. Article 2 also provides that, in determining the maritime boundaries, the Tribunal is to take "into account the opinion it will have formed on questions of territorial sovereignty, the United Nations Convention on the Law of the Sea, and any other pertinent factor." The reasons for taking account of the Award on Sovereignty are clear enough and both Parties have agreed in their pleadings that, in the Second Stage, there can be no question of attempting to reopen the decisions made in the First Award. The requirement to take into account the United Nations Convention on the Law of the Sea of 1982 is important because Eritrea has not become a party to that Convention but has in the Arbitration Agreement thus accepted the application of provisions of the Convention that are found to be relevant to the present stage. There is no reference in the Arbitration Agreement to the customary law of the sea, but many of the relevant elements of customary law are incorporated in the provisions of the Convention. "Any other pertinent factors" is a broad concept, and doubtless includes various factors that are generally recognised as being relevant to the process of delimitation such as proportionality, non-encroachment, the presence of islands, and any other factors that might affect the equities of the particular situation.

131. It is a generally accepted view, as is evidenced in both the writings of commentators and in the jurisprudence, that between coasts that are opposite to each other the median or equidistance line normally provides an equitable

boundary in accordance with the requirements of the Convention, and in particular those of its Articles 74 and 83 which respectively provide for the equitable delimitation of the EEZ and of the continental shelf between States with opposite or adjacent coasts. Indeed both Parties to the present case have claimed a boundary constructed on the equidistance method, although based on different points of departure and resulting in very different lines.

132. The Tribunal has decided, after careful consideration of all the cogent and skilful arguments put before them by both Parties, that the international boundary shall be a single all-purpose boundary which is a median line and that it should, as far as practicable, be a median line between the opposite mainland coastlines. This solution is not only in accord with practice and precedent in the like situations but is also one that is already familiar to both Parties. As the Tribunal had occasion to observe in its Award on Sovereignty (paragraph 438), the offshore petroleum contracts entered into by Yemen, and by Ethiopia and by Eritrea, "lend a measure of support to a median line between the opposite coasts of Eritrea and Yemen, drawn without regard to the islands, dividing the respective jurisdiction of the Parties." In the present stage the Tribunal has to determine a boundary not merely for the purposes of petroleum concessions and agreements, but a single international boundary for all purposes. For such a boundary the presence of islands requires careful consideration of their possible effect upon the boundary line; and this is done in the explanation which follows. Even so it will be found that the final solution is that the international maritime boundary line remains for the greater part a median line between the mainland coasts of the Parties.

133. The median line is in any event some sort of coastal line by its very definition, for it is defined as a line "every point of which is equidistant from the nearest points on the baselines from which the breadth of the territorial seas of the two States is measured" (Article 15 of the Convention), although the same definition will be found in many maritime boundary treaties and also in expert writings. The "normal" baseline of the territorial sea as stated in Article 5 of the Convention – and this again accords with long practice and with the well established customary rule of the law of the sea – is "the low-water line along the coast as marked on large scale charts officially recognised by the coastal State." There do arise some questions about what is to be regarded as the "coast" for these purposes, especially where islands are involved; and these questions, on which the Parties differ markedly, require decisions by the Tribunal.

134. First, it is necessary to deal with a complication that arises in the present case concerning this general rule of measuring from the low-water line. The domestic legislative definition of the territorial sea of Eritrea is still the 1953 enactment by Ethiopia which fixed Ethiopia's territorial waters as "extending from the extremity of the seaboard at maximum annual high tide." This was done even though an Ethiopian customs enactment of 1952 had provided for a customs zone measured from the "the mean low-water mark at neap tides." The Yemen claim was that, in

view of this 1953 legislation, the Tribunal should measure the median line boundary from the high-water line instead of the low-water line along the Eritrean coast (and indeed Yemen's median line does).

135. In this matter the Tribunal prefers the Eritrean argument that the use of the low-water line is laid down by a general international rule in the Convention's Article 5, and that both Parties have agreed that the Tribunal is to take into account the provisions of the Convention in deciding the present case. The median line boundary will, therefore, be measured from the low-water line, shown on the officially recognised charts for both Eritrea and Yemen, in accordance with the provision in Article 5 of the Convention. The officially recognised charts used by the Tribunal are BA (British Admiralty) Charts; those Charts use as a Chart Datum approximately the level of the Lowest Astronomical Tide. These Charts were among those relied on by the Parties in the present Stage of the Proceedings.

Northern and Southern Extremities of the Boundary Line

136. There is also a problem relating to both the northern and the southern extremities of the international boundary line. The Tribunal has the competence and the authority according to the Arbitration Agreement to decide the maritime boundary between the two Parties. But it has neither competence nor authority to decide on any of the boundaries between either of the two Parties and neighbouring States. It will therefore be necessary to terminate either end of the boundary line in such a way as to avoid trespassing upon an area where other claims might fall to be considered. It is, however, clearly necessary to consider the choices of the base points controlling the median line first, and then to look at the cautionary termination matter when the line to be thus terminated at its northern and southern ends has been produced.

137. The construction of the international single boundary decided upon by the Tribunal, working generally from the north to the south, will now be described.

The Northernmost Stretch of the Boundary Line

138. In this stretch, where the two lines claimed respectively by Eritrea and Yemen differed so markedly in their courses, there were three main problems: what to do about the Dahlak islands on the Eritrean side; what to do about the lone mid-sea island of Jabal al-Tayr and the mid-sea island group of Jabal al-Zubayr; and what to do about the cluster of islands and rocks off the northern coast of Yemen. These three questions will now be considered in that order.

The Dahlaks

139. This tightly knit group of islands and islets, or "carpet" of islands and islets as Eritrea preferred to call it, of which the larger islands have a considerable

population, is a typical example of a group of islands that forms an integral part of the general coastal configuration. It seems in practice always to have been treated as such. It follows that the waters inside the island system will be internal or national waters and that the baseline of the territorial sea will be found somewhere at the external fringe of the island system.

140. A problem that arises here, however, is that the Dahlak fringe of coastal islands is also suitable for the application not of the "normal baseline" of the territorial sea, but of the "straight baselines" described in Article 7 of the Convention (as there distinguished from the "normal" baseline described in Article 5). The straight baseline system is there described as "the method of straight baselines joining appropriate points." Yemen appears to have little difficulty in agreeing that the Dahlaks form an appropriate situation for the establishment of a straight baseline system.

141. Eritrea for its part claimed that it has such a system already established. In answer to a question from the Tribunal, Eritrea did give the coordinates for the base points on the Eritrea side for both versions of its claimed "median line." But these base points in the region of the Dahlaks appear to have been located on a line touching two or perhaps three of the outer islands and the Negileh Rock (for which see below paragraphs *143-144*) and then continuing in a more or less straight line out to sea in a south-easterly direction. This scheme is probably part of the "quadrilateral" straight baseline system to which Eritrea referred in argument.

142. The reality or validity or definition of this somewhat unusual straight baseline system said to be existing for the Dahlaks is hardly a matter that the Tribunal is called upon to decide. The Tribunal does however have to decide on the base points which are to control the course of the international boundary line. In plotting its own claimed median line boundary, Yemen has employed as its western base points the high-water line of the small outer islets of Segala, Dahret Segala, Zauber and Aucan. These islets could reasonably be included in a straight baseline system of the ordinary and familiar kind.

143. Eritrea, however, has in particular suggested a feature called the "Negileh Rock" which lies further out than these larger but still small and uninhabited islets. Yemen objected to the use of this feature by reason of the fact that on the BA Chart 171 this feature is shown to be a reef and moreover one which appears not to be above water at any state of the tide. A reef that is not also a low-tide elevation appears to be out of the question as a base point, because Article 6 of the Convention (which is headed "Reefs") provides:

> In the case of islands situated on atolls or of islands having fringing reefs, the baseline for measuring the breadth of the territorial sea is the seaward low-water line of the reef, as shown by the appropriate symbol on charts officially recognized by the coastal State.

144. This difficulty about the Negileh Rock is reinforced if there is indeed a straight baseline system in existence for the Dahlaks, for paragraph 4 of Article 7 provides:

> 4. Straight baselines shall not be drawn to and from low-tide elevations, unless lighthouses of similar installations which are permanently above sea level have been built on them or in instances where the drawing of straight baselines to and from such elevations has received general international recognition.

145. Although Eritrea is not a party to the Convention; nevertheless it has agreed to its application in the present case; and since Eritrea claims the existence of a straight baseline system, that claim seems to foreclose any right to employ a reef that is not proud of the water at low-tide as a baseline of the territorial sea.

146. As will appear more particularly below, the Tribunal has decided that the western base points to be employed on this part of the Eritrean coast shall be on the low-water line of certain of the outer Dahlak islets, Mojeidi and an unnamed islet east of Dahret Segala.

* – * – *

Next, it is necessary to decide on the treatment of the mid-sea islands of al-Tayr and Zubayr, for on this decision depends the question of whether it will be necessary to consider base points on the coast of Yemen.

Jabal al-Tayr and the Zubayr Group

147. Yemen employed both the small single island of al-Tayr and the group of islands called al-Zubayr as controlling base points, so that the Yemen-claimed median line boundary is "median" only in the area of sea west of these islands. These islands do not constitute a part of Yemen's mainland coast. Moreover, their barren and inhospitable nature and their position well out to sea, which have already been described in the Award on Sovereignty, mean that they should not be taken into consideration in computing the boundary line between Yemen and Eritrea.

148. For these reasons, the Tribunal has decided that both the single island of al-Tayr and the island group of al-Zubayr should have no effect upon the median line international boundary.

* – * – *

Base Points on the Coast of Yemen

149. Since Jabal al-Tayr and the Zubayr group are not to influence the drawing of the median line boundary, it is necessary to decide upon the base points to be used for this part of the coast of Yemen. For here again there is, if not a carpet, at least a considerable scattering of islands and islets which are the beginning of a large area of coastal islands and reefs which, extending northward, ultimately form part of a large island cluster or system off the coast of Saudi Arabia.

150. There is also the relatively large, inhabited and important island of Kamaran off this part of the Yemen coast. This island, together with the large promontory of the mainland to the south of it, forms an important bay and there can be no doubt that these features are integral to the coast of Yemen and part of it and should therefore control the median line. One significant controlling base point is therefore on the westernmost extremity of Kamaran. It seems reasonable also to use as base points the very small islands immediately south of Kamaran and west of the promontory headland mentioned above.

151. The question remains as to the islands to the north of Kamaran. The relatively large islet of Tiqfash, and the smaller islands of Kutama and Uqban further west, all appear to be part of an intricate system of islands, islets and reefs which guard this part of the coast. This is indeed, in the view of the Tribunal, a "fringe system" of the kind contemplated by Article 7 of the Convention, even though Yemen does not appear to have claimed it as such. Indeed the Tribunal does not have the advantage of any views of Yemen about this part of its coast because it chose to deploy its arguments differently. It is however the view of the Tribunal that it is right to use as median line base points not only Kamaran and its satellite islets which appear in the Yemen Map 12.1, but also the islets to the northwest named Uqban and Kutama.

152. The above decisions having been made, it is now possible to compute and plot the northern stretch of the boundary line between turning points 1 and 13 (the list of the coordinates of the turning points is given below; see also the illustrative Charts 3 and 4). For this entire part of the line, the boundary should be a mainland-coastal median, or equidistance, line.

153. At turning point number 13, however, a simple mainland/coastal median line approaches the area of possible influence of the islands of the Zuqar-Hanish group, and clearly some decisions have to be made as to how to deal with this situation.

The Middle Stretch of the Boundary Line

154. It will be convenient for obvious reasons if the Tribunal first decides the question of the boundary in the narrow seas between the south-west extremity of the Hanish

group on the one hand and the Eritrean islands of the Mohabbakahs, High Island, the Haycocks and the South West Rocks on the other. In this part of the boundary there is added to the boundary problem of delimiting continental shelves and EEZ the question of delimiting an area of overlapping territorial seas. This comes about because Zuqar and Hanish, attributed to the sovereignty of Yemen, both generate territorial seas which overlap with those generated by the Haycocks and South West Rocks, attributed to the sovereignty of Eritrea. It would appear from Yemen Map 12.1 that Yemen assumed that Eritrea is entitled only to a strictly 12 mile territorial sea extending from the Eritrean base points chosen by Yemen along the high-water line on the Eritrean coast; the outcome would be, according to Yemen, that the Haycocks and South West Rocks are thus left isolated outside and beyond the Eritrean territorial sea proper.

155. This proposition is questionable, quite apart from the obvious impracticality of establishing limited enclaves around islands and navigational hazards in the immediate neighbourhood of a main international shipping lane. There is no doubt that an island, however small, and even rocks provided they are indeed islands proud of the water at high-tide, are capable of generating a territorial sea of up to 12 miles (Article 121.2 of the Convention). It follows that a chain of islands which are less than 24 miles apart can generate a continuous band of territorial sea. This is the situation of the Eritrean islands out to, and including, the South West Rocks.

156. The point that the Yemen suggestion omits to take into account is that the effect of what has been referred to as "leap-frogging" the Eritrean islands and islets in this area is to extend the mainland coast territorial sea beyond the limit of 12 miles from the mainland coast. According to Article 3 of the Convention, the territorial sea extends "up to a limit not exceeding 12 nautical miles, measured from the baselines determined in accordance with this Convention." This is permissible because each island, however small or unimportant of itself, creates a further low-water baseline from which the coastal territorial sea is to be measured. This "leap-frogging" point was invoked strongly in support of Eritrea's claims to sovereignty. This reasoning was not accepted by the Tribunal in its Award on Sovereignty, it nonetheless has relevance in the present context.

157. If any further reason were needed to reject the Yemen suggestion of enclaving the Eritrean islands in this area beyond a limit of 12 miles from the high-water line of the mainland coast, it may be found in the principle of non-encroachment which was described by Judge Lachs in the *Guinea/Guinea-Bissau* Award[15] in the following terms:

> As stated in the award, our principal concern has been to avoid, by one means or another, one of the Parties finding itself faced with the exercise of rights, opposite to

[15] 25 ILM 251.

and in the immediate vicinity of its coast, which might interfere with its right to development or put its security at risk.

158. It will be seen that the international boundary line must therefore lie somewhere in a belt of sea no more than four or five miles wide. Once it is established that there is an area of Eritrean mainland coast territorial sea, potentially extending beyond the South West Rocks and the Haycock group of islands on the one hand and overlapping the territorial sea generated by the Yemen islands of the Hanish group on the other, the situation suggests a median line boundary. Under Article 15 of the Convention the normal methods for drawing an equidistant median line could be varied if reason of historic title or other special circumstance were to indicate otherwise. However, the Tribunal has considered these reasons and circumstances and finds no variance necessary.

159. Further bearing in mind its overall task of delimitation, the Tribunal also finds this line to be an entirely equitable one. The decision of the Tribunal is therefore that the median line is the international boundary line where it cuts through the area of overlap of the respective territorial seas of the Parties.

* – * – *

There remains, however, the part of the boundary line which is to connect the mainland coastal median line and the line delimiting the overlapping territorial seas. To the description of this line the Award now turns.

The Boundary Line Which Connects Turning Point 13 and Turning Point 15

160. If the mainland coastal median were continued south of turning point 13, it would cut first the territorial sea of Zuqar and then the territorial sea of Hanish, and then cut through the land territory of the island of Hanish. It must therefore divert to the west round the Zuqar-Hanish group, also respecting the territorial seas of these islands if they are to be regarded as generating a territorial sea. That they ought *to*[*] be regarded as having a territorial sea seems reasonable.

161. Various possibilities were considered by the Tribunal. If therefore the international boundary is, after turning point 13 where it meets a 12 mile territorial sea extending from the island of Zuqar, to be diverted in order to respect that area of territorial sea, it could trace the sinuosities of the Zuqar territorial sea boundary until it has to turn southward again in order to join the Article 15 boundary. The Tribunal has decided, however, that it would be better that the line here should be a geodetic line joining point 13 with point 14, making the necessary south-westwards excursion to join the territorial sea median line described above.

---

[*] *Editorial correction: insert word in italics.*

Moreover, the Tribunal's task is, as mentioned above, to determine the maritime boundary; this does not include setting the limits of the territorial seas.

162. From turning point 14, again with a simple line in view, the southward excursion of the international boundary is a geodetic line joining points 14 and 15 where it becomes the Article 15 median. This boundary decided upon by the Tribunal between turning points14 and 15 is also very near to the putative boundary of a Yemen territorial sea in this area, but makes for a neater and more convenient international boundary.

The Southern Part of the International Boundary Line

163. From turning point 20, which is the southernmost turning point on the overlapping territorial seas median line, the boundary needs to turn generally south-eastwards to rejoin the mainland coast median line. This it does through a geodetic line which connects turning point 20 and point 21, the latter being the intersection of the extended overlapping territorial seas median line and the coastal median line. Thence the international boundary line resumes as a median line controlled by the two mainland coasts. The Bay of Assab is internal waters, so the controlling base points of the boundary line are seaward of this bay.

The Northern and Southern End Points of the Boundary Line

164. Reference has been made above to the need not to extend the boundary to areas that might involve third parties. The points where the decision of the Tribunal halts the progress of the boundary line are, for the northern end, turning point 1 and, for the southern end, point 29. The effect can, of course, also be seen on the illustrative Charts 3 and 4 in the map section of the Award. The Tribunal believes that these terminal points are well short of where the boundary line might be disputed by any third State.

* – * – *

The Test of Proportionality

165. The principle of proportionality was described by the International Court of Justice in the *North Sea Continental Shelf* cases as "the element of a reasonable degree of proportionality, which a delimitation in accordance with equitable principles ought to bring about between the extent of the continental shelf areas appertaining to the coastal State and the length of the coast measured in the general direction of the coastline, account being taken for this purpose of the effects, actual or prospective, of any other continental shelf delimitations between adjacent States in the same region." This was also described as one of the

"factors" to be taken into account in delimitation.* It is not an independent mode or principle of delimitation, but rather a test of the equitableness of a delimitation arrived at by some other means.** So, as the Award stated in the *Anglo-French Channel* case, "it is disproportion rather than any general principle of proportionality which is the relevant criterion or factor."[16]

166. The Parties in the present case have disagreed strongly in their arguments of this matter, not so much about the meaning of "proportionality" as over the respective lengths of their coasts for the purposes of this calculation. There is in the Tribunal's view no doubt that the "general direction" of the coast means that the calculation of the Eritrean coastal length should follow the outer circumference of the Dahlak group of islands, although Eritrea was more inclined to have it follow the line of the mainland coast.

167. A much debated point was: how far north the Eritrean coast should go. Eritrea wished to include in the proportionality calculation the whole of its mainland coast up to the latitudinal line of 16°N; and, indeed, this line was used by Yemen to define what it called its northern sector of the area in question. The Tribunal however doubts the appropriateness of employing a horizontal line of latitude to divide, for the purposes of the proportionality test, waters of the Red Sea which lie at an angle of roughly 45°. The Tribunal has therefore considered the relevant proportion of the Eritrean coast, which can be said to be "opposite" that of Yemen, as ceasing where the general direction of that coast meets a line drawn from what seems to be the northern terminus of the Yemen land frontier at right angles with the general direction of the Yemen coast. In the same way the Tribunal determined the southern end point to be considered for the computation of the length of the Yemen coast.

168. The Tribunal through its expert in geodesy has calculated the ratio of the lengths of the coasts concerned, measured by reference to their general direction, and the ratio between the water areas it has attributed to the Parties. The first ratio, of coastal lengths, Yemen : Eritrea, is 387026 metres to 507110 metres, or *1 : 1.31*. The second ratio of water areas, including the territorial seas, Yemen : Eritrea, is 25535 kilometres^2 to 27944 kilometres^2, or *1 : 1.09*. The Tribunal believes that the line of delimitation it has decided upon results in no disproportion.

---

* I.C.J. Reports 1969, p. 54.

** See I.C.J. Reports 1981, p. 58, the *Libya/Malta* case. *[Editorial correction: the correct reference to the Libya/Malta case is "I.C.J. Reports 1985, para. 58."]*

16 18 ILM 60.

CHAPTER VI – Dispositif

169. Accordingly, **THE TRIBUNAL,**
taking into account the foregoing considerations and reasons,

UNANIMOUSLY FINDS IN THE PRESENT CASE THAT

The International Maritime Boundary between Eritrea and Yemen is a series of geodetic lines joining, in the order specified, the following points. The points are defined in degrees, minutes and seconds of the geographic latitude and longitude, based on the World Geodetic System 1984 (WGS 84). The line and the numbers of the turning points are shown for purpose of illustration only in Charts 3 and 4 in the map section of this Award.

Turning Point	Latitude	Longitude
1	15° 43' 10" N	41° 34' 06" E
2	15° 38' 58" N	41° 34' 05" E
3	15° 15' 10" N	41° 37' 31" E
4	15° 04' 00" N	41° 46' 43" E
5	15° 00' 12" N	41° 50' 42" E
6	14° 46' 06" N	41° 58' 47" E
7	14° 43' 30" N	42° 00' 42" E
8	14° 36' 05" N	42° 10' 02" E
9	14° 35' 14" N	42° 11' 35" E
10	14° 27' 16" N	42° 16' 54" E
11	14° 21' 11" N	42° 22' 04" E
12	14° 15' 23" N	42° 26' 09" E
13	14° 08' 39" N	42° 31' 33" E
14	14° 03' 39" N	42° 28' 39" E
15	13° 39' 30" N	42° 37' 39" E
16	13° 36' 13" N	42° 38' 30" E
17	13° 35' 51" N	42° 38' 14" E
18	13° 33' 38" N	42° 39' 37" E

19	13° 27' 28" N	42° 43' 25" E
20	13° 26' 39" N	42° 48' 21" E
21	13° 24' 01" N	42° 52' 47" E
22	13° 14' 23" N	42° 59' 47" E
23	13° 10' 54" N	43° 03' 03" E
24	13° 06' 57" N	43° 05' 21" E
25	13° 06' 08" N	43° 06' 06" E
26	13° 04' 05" N	43° 08' 42" E
27	13° 00' 27" N	43° 10' 54" E
28	12° 58' 10" N	43° 12' 45" E
29	12° 54' 23" N	43° 13' 58" E

Done at London this 17th day of December 1999

The President of the Tribunal

/s/ Professor Sir Robert Y. Jennings

The Registrar

/s/ Tjaco van den Hout

ANNEX 1
The Arbitration Agreement

The Government of the Republic of Yemen and the Government of the State of Eritrea (hereinafter "the Parties");

Prompted by the desire to re-establish their peaceful relations in the spirit of the traditional friendship between their two peoples,

Conscious of their responsibilities toward the international community as regards the maintenance of international peace and security as well as the safeguard of the freedom of navigation in a particularly sensitive region of the world,

Considering the "Agreement on Principles" between Yemen and Eritrea signed at Paris the twenty-first day of May, 1996 (hereinafter "the Agreement on Principles");

Have agreed as follows:

Article 1

1. On or before 31 December 1996, the Parties will provide the names and addresses of their appointed arbitrators to one another and to France. The four arbitrators thus named shall meet within two weeks to consider the choice of the President of the Tribunal.

2. Within two weeks thereafter the four arbitrators will narrow their consideration to a list of five names which they will then circulate to the Parties.

3. The Parties will have two weeks from the date of circulation of the list during which they may present their views concerning the list.

4. The four arbitrators shall then attempt to reach agreement on the choice of the President. On reaching agreement, they will inform the Parties that the Tribunal has been formed.

5. If no agreement has been reached by 15 March 1997, they shall so inform the President of the International Court of Justice and, pursuant to the Agreement on Principles, they shall request him to choose the President of the Tribunal. In transmitting this request, the four arbitrators shall make known any views that the Parties have expressed on the choice of the President of the Tribunal. The President of the International Court of Justice shall choose within two weeks and after consultation with the Party-appointed arbitrators. By 31 March 1997 at the latest, he shall notify the Parties, the four arbitrators and France that the Tribunal has been formed and of the name of the President of the Tribunal.

6. The Tribunal shall meet on or before 11 April 1997.

7. All the members of the Tribunal commit themselves to exercise their powers impartially and conscientiously.

8. France shall transmit a certified copy of the Agreement on Principles and of this Arbitration Agreement to the members of the Tribunal as soon as they are chosen.

Article 2

1. The Tribunal is requested to provide rulings in accordance with international law, in two stages.

2. The first stage shall result in an award on territorial sovereignty and on the definition of the scope of the dispute between Eritrea and Yemen. The Tribunal shall decide territorial sovereignty in accordance with the principles, rules and practices of international law applicable to the matter, and on the basis, in particular, of historic titles. The Tribunal shall decide on the definition of the scope of the dispute on the basis of the respective positions of the two Parties.

3. The second stage shall result in an award delimiting maritime boundaries. The Tribunal shall decide taking into account the opinion that it will have formed on questions of territorial sovereignty, the United Nations Convention on the Law of the Sea, and any other pertinent factor.

a) The Tribunal shall describe the course of the delimitation in a technically precise manner. To this end, the geometric nature of all elements of the delimitation shall be indicated and the position of all the points mentioned shall be given by reference to their coordinates in the World Geodetic System 1984 (W.G.S. 84).

The Tribunal shall also indicate for illustrative purposes only the course of delimitation on an appropriate chart.

b) After consultation with the Parties, the Tribunal shall designate a technical expert to assist it in carrying out the duties specified in letter a) above.

Article 3

1. The participation of all Tribunal members shall be required for the awards. The presence of all members shall also be required for all proceedings and decisions other than the awards except that the President may determine that the absence of not more than a single member from any proceeding or decision other than the awards is justified for good cause.

2. a) If a member of the Tribunal chosen by a Party is unable or unwilling to act and to continue to perform his functions, this Party shall name a replacement within a period of one month from the date on which the Tribunal declares the existence of the vacancy.

b) If the President of the Tribunal is unable or unwilling to act and to continue to perform his functions, a replacement shall be chosen by the Party-appointed members of the Tribunal within a maximum period of two months from the date on which the Tribunal declares the existence of the vacancy. If they cannot agree within this period, the President of the Tribunal shall be chosen by the President of the International Court of Justice.

c) Where a vacancy has been filled after the proceedings have begun, the proceedings shall continue from the point they had reached at the time the vacancy had occurred.

3. All members of the Tribunal shall be deemed to be present for the purposes of the provisions of paragraph 1 of this Article and notwithstanding the existence of vacancies where the only matter for consideration is the declaration of vacancies for the purposes of paragraph 2 of this Article or where either Party has neglected to fill a vacancy as provided by paragraph 2, letter a) of this Article.

Article 4

1. Subject to paragraph 2 of this Article, the decisions of the Tribunal concerning questions of substance or questions of procedure, including questions related to the competence of the Tribunal or the interpretation of this Arbitration Agreement shall be made by a majority of its members if those decisions cannot be made unanimously.

2. In the case of an even division of the votes in the circumstances referred to in paragraph 3 of Article 3 above, the vote of the President shall be decisive.

Article 5

Subject to the provisions of this Arbitration Agreement, the Tribunal shall decide on its rules of procedure and on all questions relating to the conduct of the arbitration.

Article 6

1. Each Party, within thirty days of the signature of this Arbitration Agreement, shall designate an Agent, who will represent it and act on its behalf for the purposes of the arbitration, and shall communicate the name and address of its Agent to the other Party and, upon its formation, to the Tribunal.

2. Each Agent so designated shall be entitled to name one Co-Agent or more to act for him where necessary. The name and the address of the Co-Agent(s) so named shall be communicated to the other Party and, upon its formation, to the Tribunal.

Article 7

1. The Tribunal shall sit in London.

2. The Tribunal shall appoint a Registrar after consultation with the Agents, as soon as possible and in any event no later than its first meeting. The Registrar shall perform his functions impartially and conscientiously.

3. After consultations with the Agents the Tribunal may engage such staff and secure such services and equipment as it deems necessary.

4. The Tribunal may consult any experts of its choice after notice to the Parties. Such experts shall perform their functions impartially and conscientiously.

5. a) At any time during the arbitral proceedings the Tribunal may call upon either Party to produce documents or other evidence relevant to the question within such a period of time as the Tribunal shall determine. Any documents or other evidence so produced shall also be provided to the other Party.

b) If either Party fails to respond to a request for the production of documents or evidence under paragraph a), the Tribunal may draw from this failure any appropriate evidentiary inference and may make an award based upon the evidence before it.

c) At any time during the arbitral proceedings the Tribunal may request if necessary that a nonparty to this Arbitration Agreement provide to it documents or other evidence relevant to the question. Any documents or other evidence so provided shall be transmitted simultaneously to both Parties.

Article 8

1. The proceedings before the Tribunal shall be adversarial.

2. Without prejudice to any question relating to the burden of proof, the proceedings before the Tribunal shall include two stages as follows.

3. The first stage concerning questions of territorial sovereignty and the definition of the scope of the dispute mentioned in Article 2, paragraph 2 of this Arbitration Agreement shall include two phases, one written and the other oral.

3.1 The written pleadings shall consist of:

a) A memorial to be submitted by each Party to the Tribunal and to the other Party not later than 31 August 1997;

b) A counter-memorial to be submitted by each Party to the Tribunal and to the other Party not later than three months after submission of the memorials;

c) Any other pleading that the Tribunal deems necessary, such pleading to be submitted not later than two months after submission of the counter-memorials.

3.2 An oral phase shall follow the written phase.

a) It shall be held at the seat of the Tribunal, at the place and on the dates determined by the Tribunal after consultation with the Agents. The oral phase shall start in so far as possible not later than three months after the submission of the last written pleadings of the Parties under Article 8, paragraph 3.1 above.

b) Each Party shall be represented in the oral phase of the proceedings by its Agent or, as appropriate, by its Co-Agent, and by such counsel, advisers and experts as it may designate.

3.3 At the conclusion of the oral phase, the Tribunal shall declare the end of the proceedings in the first stage. Notwithstanding such declaration, the Tribunal may request from the Parties their written views on any issues necessary for the elucidation of any aspect of the matters before the Tribunal until the award on questions of territorial sovereignty and the definition of the scope of the dispute is rendered.

3.4 The Tribunal shall render its award, which shall be binding, on questions of territorial sovereignty and the definition of the scope of the dispute in so far as possible not later than three months from the end of the proceedings as declared under Article 8, paragraph 3.3 above.

3.5 The Tribunal shall communicate this award to the Agents on the day of its rendering. The Tribunal and the Parties may make public this award as of the day of its rendering.

4. The second stage concerning questions of delimitation of maritime boundaries mentioned in Article 2, paragraph 3 of this Arbitration Agreement shall begin immediately upon the rendering of the award which concludes the first stage. It shall include two phases, one written and the other oral.

4.1 The written pleadings shall consist of:

a) A memorial to be submitted by each Party to the Tribunal and to the other Party not later than four months after the rendering of the award on questions of territorial sovereignty and the definition of the scope of the dispute;

b) A counter-memorial to be submitted by each Party to the Tribunal and to the other Party not later than two months after submission of the memorials;

c) Any other pleading that the Tribunal deems necessary, such pleading to be submitted not later than two months after submission of the counter-memorials.

4.2 The oral phase shall follow the written phase.

a) It shall be held at the seat of the Tribunal, at the place and on the dates determined by the Tribunal after consultation with the Agents. The oral phase shall start in so far as possible not later than three months as of the submission of the last written pleadings of the Parties under Article 8, paragraph 4.1 above;

b) Each Party shall be represented in the oral phase of the proceedings by its Agent or, as appropriate, by its Co-Agent, and by such counsel, advisers and experts as it may designate.

4.3 At the conclusion of the oral phase, the Tribunal shall declare the end of the proceedings in the second stage. Notwithstanding such declaration, the Tribunal may request from the Parties their written views on any issues necessary for the elucidation of any aspect of the matters before the Tribunal until the award on questions of delimitation of maritime boundaries is rendered.

4.4 The Tribunal shall render its award on questions of delimitation of maritime boundaries in so far as possible not later than three months after the end of the proceedings before it as declared under Article 8, paragraph 4.3 above.

5. The Tribunal shall be empowered for good cause only to extend the time periods established in this Article on its own or at the request of either Party. The total cumulative extension of the time periods granted by the Tribunal at the request of either Party during the proceedings under the provisions of this sub-paragraph cannot exceed two months for each Party for each stage.

6. The Registrar shall provide the Parties with an address for the filing of their written pleadings and of any other document. The Registrar shall transmit to the Parties simultaneously copies of all written pleadings and documents upon receipt thereof.

7. If, within the period of time fixed by this Arbitration Agreement or by the Tribunal, either Party fails to make a scheduled appearance or file a written pleading, the Tribunal

shall continue the proceedings nonetheless and shall make an award based upon the pleadings before it.

Article 9

1. The written and oral pleadings before the Tribunal shall be in English. Decisions of the Tribunal shall be in English.

The Tribunal shall keep a verbatim transcript of all hearings.

Verbatim transcripts of the oral proceedings shall be communicated to the Agents as soon as possible.

2. All documentary evidence shall be filed in their original languages by the Parties. The Parties shall arrange for any translation that they deem necessary for their own preparation of the case.

The Tribunal may avail itself of translation services where it deems appropriate.

Any translations thus generated shall be provided to the Parties.

3. All written pleadings and verbatim transcripts of the oral proceedings and all the deliberations of the Tribunal shall be confidential.

4. Members of the public shall not be admitted to the oral proceedings.

Article 10

1. The remuneration of the members of the Tribunal and of the Registrar shall be borne equally by the Parties.

2. The general expenses of the arbitration shall be borne equally by the Parties. The Registrar shall keep a record and render a final account of the expenses.

3. Each Party shall bear all the expenses incurred by it in the preparation and conduct of its case.

Article 11

1. Without prejudice to the provisions of the Agreement on Principles, the Tribunal, either on its own or after examining the request of one of the two Parties, may prescribe any provisional measures which it considers appropriate under the circumstances to prevent irreparable harm or damage to the natural resources of the area or to preserve the *status quo* as of 21 May 1996. The Parties shall apply such measures within the time period prescribed by the Tribunal.

2. In no event will a request for provisional measures or a prescription of provisional measures affect the time periods for the submission of pleadings or rendering of the awards under Article 8 above.

Article 12

1. a) The awards of the Tribunal shall state the reasons upon which they are based.

b) The awards of the Tribunal shall include the time period for their execution.

c) For each award of the Tribunal, each member of the Tribunal shall be entitled to attach an individual or dissenting opinion.

2. The Tribunal shall notify immediately to the Agents or Co-Agents its awards, signed by the President and the Registrar of the Tribunal, and any individual or dissenting opinion.

3. At the end of the second stage, the Tribunal shall make public both awards and any individual or dissenting opinions.

Article 13

1. The awards of the Tribunal shall be final and binding. The Parties commit themselves to abide by those awards, pursuant to Article 1, paragraph 2 of the Agreement on Principles. They shall consequently apply in good faith and immediately the awards of the Tribunal, at any rate within the time periods as provided for by the Tribunal pursuant to Article 12, paragraph 1(b), of this Arbitration Agreement.

2. The Tribunal is empowered to correct within three months of the rendering of its awards any material error relating to those awards such as arithmetical, mathematical, cartographical or typographical errors. Any such corrections shall in no event affect the timetables set out in Article 8 above.

3. Each Party may refer to the Tribunal any dispute with the other Party as to the meaning and the scope of the awards within thirty days of their rendering. The Tribunal shall render a decision regarding any such dispute within sixty days of the day on which the dispute is referred to the Tribunal. Pending this decision, the time periods for the submission of written pleadings set forth in Article 8 above may be suspended by the Tribunal.

Article 14

1. This Arbitration Agreement shall enter into force thirty days after the date of its signature by the two Parties.

2. The Tribunal shall apply the provisions of this Arbitration Agreement.

Article 15

1. Nothing in this Arbitration Agreement can be interpreted as being detrimental to the legal positions or to the rights of each Party with respect to the questions submitted to the Tribunal, nor can affect or prejudice the decision of the Arbitral Tribunal or the considerations and grounds on which those decisions are based.

2. In the event of any inconsistency between the Agreement on Principles and this Arbitration Agreement implementing the procedural aspects of that Agreement on Principles, this Arbitration Agreement shall control. Except with respect to such inconsistency, the Agreement on Principles shall continue in force.

Article 16

1. France shall deposit a copy of this Arbitration Agreement within thirty days of its entry into force with the Secretary-General of the United Nations, with the Secretary-General of the Organization of African Unity, and with the Secretary-General of the Arab League.

2. The President of the Tribunal shall deposit a copy of both awards as soon as possible after the rendering of the award on delimitation of maritime boundaries with the Secretary-General of the United Nations, with the Secretary-General of the Organization of African Unity, and with the Secretary-General of the Arab League.

IN WITNESS WHEREOF, the undersigned, being duly authorized by their respective Governments, have signed this Arbitration Agreement.

DONE AT PARIS, this third day of October, one thousand nine hundred and ninety-six, in three original copies, each one in the Arabic, English and French languages, the English text being authentic.

For the Government
of the Republic of Yemen

HUSSEIN ALI AL-HUBAISHI
Legal Advisor of the Government

For the Government
of the State of Eritrea

SALEH MEKY
Minister of Marine Resources

ANNEX 2
Questions Posed by the Tribunal and the Parties' Answers

Yemen's Answer to Judge Schwebel's Question Put to Yemen on Tuesday, 13 July 1999

On day 6 of the proceedings (Transcript, Day 6, 13 July 1999, pp. 99-100), Judge Schwebel put a question to Yemen's counsel as follows:

> "Ms. Malintoppi, during oral argument in the first round Yemen maintained that it was beyond the Tribunal's authority at that stage to consider matters of *res communis condominia* and the like, stating that to do so would prefigure topics which might be considered only at the second stage. An argument which was remarkable, since Eritrea had said nothing in such regards, nor had the Tribunal. Just now, you argue that it is too late for Eritrea to argue such matters indicating, if I understood correctly, that they were for the first stage. Are Yemen's pertinent arguments consistent?"

In Yemen's submission, Yemen's arguments are consistent. This can be seen from reviewing the context in which Yemen raised the matter in the first stage, the points raised by Ms. Malintoppi in her intervention relating to the second stage, and the terms of the Arbitration Agreement.

The matter first arose at paragraph 20 of Yemen's written submission on the relevance of the oil agreements and activities dated 8 June 1998. There, Yemen stated the following:

> "It is always attractive to seek to discover a basis for dividing a group of islands, not least in an arbitration. The attraction must be the greater when the task of the Tribunal extends to the process of maritime delimitation, and no doubt caution will be needed to avoid a prefiguring of equitable principles and concepts, which are in law only relevant in the second phase of these proceedings."

The point to which Yemen was referring concerned the applicable law. In the first stage, Yemen considered that the applicable law was derived from the principles of international law relating to territorial sovereignty and title to territory. It was Yemen's submission that equitable principles, *infra legem*, were primarily related to the law of maritime delimitation – a matter to be dealt with in the second stage – not to the law of territorial sovereignty *per se*. Yemen's view was thus that the concept of equitable principles was particularly relevant to the second stage of the proceedings, and that this issue should not be prefigured in the first stage. Yemen made no specific reference to concepts such as *res communis* or *condominia* when it raised the matter.

In the second stage of these proceedings, Yemen fully accepts that equitable principles form part of the applicable law of maritime delimitation. However, and this was the point discussed by Ms. Malintoppi, the application of equitable principles to maritime delimitation, when read in conjunction with the scope of the Tribunal's mandate as established in the Arbitration Agreement and the Agreement on Principles, does not encompass the creation or modalities of "joint resource zones" around Yemen's islands in the manner that Eritrea's Prayer for Relief requests.

It follows that Yemen does not maintain that Eritrea's arguments in favour of the creation of such zones are too late at this stage, but rather that the applicable law, together with the provisions of the Arbitration Agreement and the Agreement on Principles, does not provide a legal or jurisdictional basis for acceding to Eritrea's requests.

It should be noted, however, that the 1994 and 1998 Agreements between Yemen and Eritrea, particularly those sections related to fishing, clearly indicate that Yemen and Eritrea are currently involved in working together to administer the fish resources throughout the southern Red Sea region.

Yemen's Answer to the Tribunal's Question Put to Yemen on Friday, 16 July 1999

At the close of the oral hearings (Transcript, Day 8, 16 July 1999, page 45), the Tribunal put the following question to Yemen:

> "The Tribunal has noted that, in the arguments of Yemen, relatively little has been said about the traditional fishing regime which the Tribunal recalls is an essential part of the *Dispositif* of the Award of 9 October 1998. Would Yemen indicate how, if at all, the traditional fishing regime should be taken into account in the delimitation, particularly taking into consideration the agreements signed by the two Governments in 1994 and 1998?"

Yemen's answer was as follows:

Yemen recognises that, in deciding the issue of sovereignty over various Red Sea Islands in the first Award, the Tribunal stated in its *Dispositif* that the sovereignty found to lie with Yemen "entails the perpetuation of the traditional fishing regime in the region, including free access and enjoyment for the fishermen of both Eritrea and Yemen" (paragraph 527(vi) of the Award). This decision is final and binding between the Parties, as stipulated in Article 13(a) of the Arbitration Agreement. Yemen is fully committed to apply and implement the Award in all of its aspects, including with respect to the perpetuation of the traditional fishing regime for the fishermen of both Eritrea and Yemen.

As was clear from the Parties' presentations during the oral hearings, both Parties consider that the Tribunal's *Dispositif* must be read in conjunction with the reasoning that appears in the body of the Award. With respect to "the perpetuation of the traditional fishing regime in the region," Yemen has also taken note of the Tribunal's pronouncements in other parts of the Award which bear on the issue. For example, the first sentence of paragraph 526 provides:

> "In finding that the Parties each have sovereignty over various of the Islands the Tribunal stresses to them that such sovereignty is not inimical to, but rather entails, the perpetuation of the traditional fishing regime in the region."

The historical basis of this finding was further explained in paragraph 128 where the Tribunal stated:

> "This traditionally prevailing situation reflected deeply rooted cultural patterns leading to the existence of what could be characterized from a juridical point of view as *res communis* permitting the African as well as the Yemeni fishermen to operate with no limitation throughout the entire area and to sell their catch at the local markets on either side of the Red Sea. Equally, the persons sailing for fishing or trading purposes from one coast to the other used to take temporary refuge from the strong winds on any of the uninhabited islands scattered in that maritime zone without encountering difficulties of a political or administrative nature."

It is Yemen's view that the holdings of the Tribunal in the first Award with respect to the traditional fishing regime constitute *res judicata* without prejudice to the maritime boundary that the Tribunal decides on in the second stage of the proceedings. In other words, the traditional fishing regime that has existed for the benefit of the fishermen of both countries throughout the region is to be perpetuated notwithstanding the decision that the Tribunal reaches as to the delimitation of the maritime boundary between the two countries. Indeed, it is clear that both Parties understood this to be a mutual obligation which existed apart from the question of delimitation of their maritime boundary in that, as the November 1998 Agreement between the two Governments indicates, Yemen and Eritrea have been formulating a regime of cooperation with respect to fishing in the spirit of good neighbourliness and friendship which has prevailed since the Award in the first stage of this arbitration.

In Yemen's submission, the delimitation to be effectuated by the Tribunal in its second Award will have a different purpose than the preservation of the traditional fishing regime. For example, counsel for Eritrea admitted during its rebuttal presentation that issues such as mineral extraction were not included in the Tribunal's notion of the traditional fishing regime (Transcript, Day 8, 16 July 1999, page 27). Clearly, mineral extraction is related to the delimitation of the continental shelf, a matter which is relevant to the second stage.

Similarly, the delimitation of the column of water or Exclusive Economic Zone of the Parties, as well as of their respective territorial seas in the Central and Southern Sectors, involves matters which, pursuant to the 1982 Convention on the Law of the Sea, go beyond the preservation of the traditional fishing regime. It is in this connection that Yemen advanced the dependence of its coastal population on fishing and the incidence of Yemen's fishing practices in the region as relevant circumstances to be taken into account in the delimitation process.

In short, the perpetuation of the traditional fishing regime is not synonymous with the rights and obligations of the Parties that will be determined by a delimitation of a single maritime boundary throughout the relevant area. It is for these reasons that Yemen does not consider that the decision of the Tribunal on the traditional fishing regime should have any impact on the delimitation of the maritime boundaries between the two Parties in the second stage.

In this connection, it is appropriate to refer to the 1994 Agreement between Yemen and Eritrea to which specific reference is made in the Tribunal's question. As can be seen from its terms, the 1994 Agreement is entirely consistent with the preservation of the traditional fishing regime decided by the Tribunal in the first stage.

The Agreement was signed by the Minister of Fish Wealth on behalf of Yemen and the Minister of Marine Wealth on behalf of Eritrea. The latter, of course, also acts as Eritrea's Agent in the present arbitration.

It is significant that Paragraph 1 of the Agreement specifically provides for a fishing regime that is remarkably similar to that recognised in the Tribunal's first Award. That paragraph provides, *inter alia*, that:

> "Both the State of Eritrea and the Republic of Yemen shall permit fishermen who are citizens of the two States, without limiting their numbers, and who carry cards to engage in the occupation of fishing, to fish in the territorial waters of the two States, the contiguous zone and the Exclusive Economic Zone of the two countries in the Red Sea (with the exception of the internal waters), provided that the fishermen of the two countries be enumerated and that they be granted official licenses to engage in the occupation of fishing specifying the locations where they will be received and may market their products in Appendix No. 1."

Moreover, Paragraph 4 of the Agreement provides in relevant part that the persons included in Paragraph 1 shall be permitted to "market their fish products in the territory of the other State and in the locations specified in Appendix No. 1 of this Memorandum of Understanding." The Tribunal will note that these provisions are very similar to the Tribunal's findings set out in paragraph 128 of the Award in the first stage.

Unfortunately, the 1994 Agreement could not be fully implemented at the time due to the events of 1995. Nonetheless, the Agreement remains in effect, and Yemen remains fully committed to its implementation. As can be seen from its terms, the 1994 Agreement envisages a regulatory framework which is well suited to addressing the kinds of concern raised by Eritrea in its pleadings regarding traditional fishing in the region.

The Tribunal's question also makes reference to the Agreement signed between the two Parties in November 1998. In Yemen's view, this Agreement evidences the good faith of both Parties in pursuing mutual cooperation in a number of areas, including fishing. In particular, Article 1(d) of the Agreement provides for the formation of a Committee for Cooperation in the Area of Fish Wealth and Maritime Fishing. Pursuant to Article 3(4) of the Agreement, this committee would be expected to address the question of drafting a special agreement "in the area of fish wealth, maritime fishing and the protection of the maritime environment."

With respect to the relevance of the 1994 and 1998 Agreements to the perpetuation of the traditional fishing regime, it is appropriate to recall what counsel for Yemen had to say on this matter during the oral hearings:

> "Indeed, as Mr. Picard has shown, the Parties have already established a framework for addressing the modalities of their fishing activities in the Red Sea with their 1994 and 1998 agreements. These agreements could well represent a very important context within which any further questions between the Parties as to the preservation of the traditional fishing practices mentioned in paragraph 526 of the Award could be dealt with" (Transcript, Day 6, 13 July 1999, page 88).

Implementation of these two Agreements would also be consistent with the letter of the President of the Tribunal, dated 8 November 1998, which indicated that these issues "are a matter for the Parties themselves to resolve in good faith, bearing in mind what the Tribunal has found in Paragraph 526 of the Award."

In conclusion, Yemen considers that the Tribunal has already decided on the preservation of the traditional fishing regime between the Parties in its first Award. The Award as it stands is *res judicata*, and in view of the language of Article 13, paragraph 3 of the Arbitration Agreement, it is not appropriate to interpret the meaning and the scope of the Award in the first stage at this point in the proceedings. Therefore, and bearing in mind the framework that has been established by the 1994 and 1998 Agreements, Yemen does not believe that the traditional fishing regime needs to be further taken into account in the delimitation of the maritime boundary between the Parties at this stage of the proceedings.

Eritrea's Answer to Judge Schwebel's Question

[*letterhead: The State of Eritrea Zuqar-Hanish Archipelago Arbitration Office*]

Mrs. Phyllis Hamilton
Permanent Court of Arbitration
Peace Palace, the Hague
The Netherlands

August 12, 1999

By facsimile: 31-70-3024167

Re: Eritrea/Yemen Arbitration

Dear Mrs. Hamilton:

As you probably recall, during the July oral hearings on the maritime phase of the Eritrea/Yemen arbitration, the Tribunal requested that the State of Eritrea supply it with the coordinates for the historic median line which was referred to in Eritrea's written and oral pleadings. It was requested that these co-ordinates be supplied within four weeks of the close of the hearings (simultaneously with the filing of Yemen's response to the question that it was asked.)

I am attaching the co-ordinates to this letter. In fact, you will find attached to this letter two sets of co-ordinates, one for the historic median line and one for the western boundary of the shared resource zone described in Eritrea's written pleadings. The difference between the two is that the historic median line gives full effect to the Eritrean Mohabbaka and Haycock islands and to Southwest Rock. The western boundary of the shared resource zone does not, and thus runs to the west of the historic median line. The co-ordinates that have been chosen for drawing these two lines are either on land territory of Eritrea or on straight baselines drawn in accordance with the United Nations Convention on the Law of the Sea.

I hope that you will forward this information to the Tribunal, and also to Counsel for the Republic of Yemen (after Yemen submits its response to the question that was posed to them). At the point that you receive this, I will be in transit from Asmara to New Haven and so I hope that no problems arise concerning our submission. I will be reachable in New Haven by the end of the day on Friday, August 13 if any problems do arise, and I hope that you will be able to forward to me there the answer that Yemen submits to the question that the Tribunal has presented it with.

Many thanks again for your cordial assistance.

Sincerely yours,
/s/
Professor R. Lea Brilmayer
Co-Agent, the State of Eritrea

Basepoint Coordinates for Eritrea's Proposed Historic Median Line

	Longitude	Latitude
1	40.256123	16.261644
2	40.260834	16.088427
3	40.610901	15.894623
4	40.627377	15.881909
5	40.675121	15.845072
6	40.705509	15.821624
7	40.726833	15.800971
8	40.774303	15.754568
9	40.821114	15.722202
10	40.859592	15.697753
11	40.873196	15.684411
12	40.899334	15.658775
13	40.923637	15.634940
14	40.959450	15.599816
15	40.984978	15.574780
16	41.007191	15.552997
17	41.033173	15.527514
18	41.064766	15.496529
19	41.090080	15.471701
20	41.097931	15.464003
21	41.194546	14.617983
22	41.315613	14.490411
23	41.327480	14.467098
24	41.333321	14.454417
25	41.674259	14.101558
26	41.682278	14.093115
27	41.992912	13.888812
28	42.033104	13.856160
29	42.083229	13.815438
30	42.143177	13.766736
31	42.163944	13.749866
32	42.597202	13.634215
33	42.597584	13.634094
34	42.597961	13.633973
35	42.629669	13.539982
36	42.630470	13.539621
37	42.649868	13.350410
38	42.649937	13.349084
39	42.898411	13.022588
40	42.909142	13.015216
41	42.945763	12.990066

42	42.946693	12.989246
43	42.972328	12.966615
44	42.999687	12.942464
45	43.027813	12.909046
46	43.046738	12.879812

Basepoint Coordinates for Eritrea's Proposed Historic Median Line in Degrees and Minutes (Approximated)

	Longitude		Latitude	
	Degree	Minute	Degree	Minute
1	40	15	16	16
2	40	16	16	5
3	40	37	15	54
4	40	38	15	53
5	40	41	15	51
6	40	42	15	49
7	40	44	15	48
8	40	46	15	45
9	40	49	15	43
10	40	52	15	42
11	40	52	15	41
12	40	54	15	40
13	40	55	15	38
14	40	58	15	36
15	40	59	15	34
16	41	0	15	33
17	41	2	15	32
18	41	4	15	30
19	41	5	15	28
20	41	6	15	28
21	41	12	14	37
22	41	19	14	29
23	41	20	14	28
24	41	20	14	27
25	41	40	14	6
26	41	41	14	6
27	42	0	13	53
28	42	2	13	51
29	42	5	13	49
30	42	9	13	46
31	42	10	13	45

32	42	36	13	38
33	42	36	13	38
34	42	36	13	38
35	42	38	13	32
36	42	38	13	32
37	42	39	13	21
38	42	39	13	21
39	42	54	13	1
40	42	55	13	1
41	42	57	12	59
42	42	57	12	59
43	42	58	12	58
44	43	0	12	57
45	43	2	12	55
46	43	3	12	53

Basepoint Coordinates for the Western Edge of Eritrea's Proposed Delimitation

Western Basepoint Coordinates

	Longitude	Latitude
1	40.256123	16.261644
2	40.260834	16.088427
3	40.610901	15.894623
4	40.627377	15.881909
5	40.675121	15.845072
6	40.705509	15.821624
7	40.726833	15.800971
8	40.774303	15.754568
9	40.821114	15.722202
10	40.859592	15.697753
11	40.873196	15.684411
12	40.899334	15.658775
13	40.923637	15.634940
14	40.959450	15.599816
15	40.984978	15.574780
16	41.007191	15.552997
17	41.033173	15.527514
18	41.064766	15.496529
19	41.090080	15.471701
20	41.097931	15.464003
21	41.194546	14.617983
22	41.315613	14.490411
23	41.327480	14.467098

24	41.333321	14.454417
25	41.674259	14.101558
26	41.682278	14.093115
27	41.992912	13.888812
28	42.033104	13.856160
29	42.083229	13.815438
30	42.143177	13.766736
31	42.163944	13.749866
32	42.182957	13.719868
33	42.209858	13.677422
34	42.236946	13.629816
35	42.290718	13.558626
36	42.292160	13.556718
37	42.314285	13.507826
38	42.332073	13.468508
39	42.456223	13.322620
40	42.502346	13.277068
41	42.548088	13.231894
42	42.583633	13.196643
43	42.621857	13.158704
44	42.659718	13.121125
45	42.696766	13.084354
46	42.898411	13.022588
47	42.909142	13.015216
48	42.945763	12.990066
49	42.946693	12.989246
50	42.972328	12.966615
51	42.999687	12.942464
52	43.027813	12.909046
53	43.046738	12.879812

Eastern Basepoint Coordinates

54	41.725754	16.630884
55	41.734745	16.575695
56	41.738682	16.551414
57	41.749630	16.541800
58	41.775238	16.519312
59	41.812977	16.486170
60	41.839870	16.462553
61	41.863270	16.442003
62	41.890648	16.417961
63	41.961689	16.292364
64	42.269432	15.701784
65	42.266293	15.700562

66	42.274937	15.697087
67	42.276882	15.685533
68	42.366718	15.489594
69	42.401192	15.467257
70	42.512936	15.415102
71	42.530704	15.291346
72	42.594810	15.210606
73	42.603222	15.200403
74	42.690079	15.195890
75	42.612560	15.189135
76	42.749393	15.179667
77	42.621025	15.169647
78	42.638046	15.163574
79	42.972595	14.600204
80	42.983734	14.391216
81	42.983959	14.384205
82	43.016117	14.331829
83	43.034367	14.289636
84	43.052059	14.248733
85	43.085064	14.107971
86	43.096539	14.067361
87	43.103230	14.054599
88	43.122894	14.017092
89	43.141998	13.980651
90	43.158348	13.949471
91	43.189007	13.916190
92	43.229725	13.821691
93	43.252224	13.484743
94	43.248089	13.434113
95	43.242542	13.374463
96	43.228340	13.302191
97	43.224674	13.271644
98	43.208839	13.259463
99	43.207760	13.243280
100	43.225060	13.202319
101	43.225647	13.199706
102	43.236843	13.168642
103	43.253857	13.136574
104	43.288876	13.080974
105	43.303009	13.063622

Basepoint Coordinates for the Western Edge of Eritrea's Proposed Delimitation in Degrees and Minutes (Approximated)

Western Basepoint Coordinates

	Longitude		Latitude	
	Degree	Minute	Degree	Minute
1	40	15	16	16
2	40	16	16	5
3	40	37	15	54
4	40	38	15	53
5	40	41	15	51
6	40	42	15	49
7	40	44	15	48
8	40	46	15	45
9	40	49	15	43
10	40	52	15	42
11	40	52	15	41
12	40	54	15	40
13	40	55	15	38
14	40	58	15	36
15	40	59	15	34
16	41	0	15	33
17	41	2	15	32
18	41	4	15	30
19	41	5	15	28
20	41	6	15	28
21	41	12	14	37
22	41	19	14	29
23	41	20	14	28
24	41	20	14	27
25	41	40	14	6
26	41	41	14	6
27	42	0	13	53
28	42	2	13	51
29	42	5	13	49
30	42	9	13	46
31	42	10	13	45
32	42	11	13	43
33	42	13	13	41
34	42	14	13	38
35	42	17	13	34
36	42	18	13	33

37	42	19	13	30
38	42	20	13	28
39	42	27	13	19
40	42	30	13	17
41	42	33	13	14
42	42	35	13	12
43	42	37	13	10
44	42	40	13	7
45	42	42	13	5
46	42	54	13	1
47	42	55	13	1
48	42	57	12	59
49	42	57	12	59
50	42	58	12	58
51	43	0	12	57
52	43	2	12	55
53	43	3	12	53

Eastern Basepoint Coordinates

54	41	44	16	38
55	41	44	16	35
56	41	44	16	33
57	41	45	16	33
58	41	47	16	31
59	41	49	16	29
60	41	50	16	28
61	41	52	16	27
62	41	53	16	25
63	41	58	16	18
64	42	16	15	42
65	42	16	15	42
66	42	16	15	42
67	42	17	15	41
68	42	22	15	29
69	42	24	15	28
70	42	31	15	25
71	42	32	15	17
72	42	36	15	13
73	42	36	15	12

ANNEX 3

TRANSLATION

Memorandum of Understanding between the State of Eritrea
and the Republic of Yemen
For Cooperation in the Areas of Maritime Fishing, Trade,
Investment, and Transportation

Based on the spirit of friendship and cooperation and to translate into action the common objectives and interests between the two fraternal countries of the State of Eritrea and the Republic of Yemen and achieve the interests of the two fraternal peoples, the delegation of the Republic of Yemen headed by Dr. Abd al-Rahman Abd al-Qadir Ba-Fadhl, the Minister of Fish Wealth, visited the State of Eritrea and received a warm reception from Ali Sayyid Abdallah, the Interior Minister, on Friday, 11 November 1994. They held initial discussions at the Eritrean Interior Ministry in the capital, Asmara, followed by talks between the two parties in the city of Massawa. Dr. Salih Makki, the Minister of Marine Wealth for the State of Eritrea, chaired the Eritrean side, while Dr. Abd al-Rahman Abd al-Qadir Ba-Fadhl, the Minister of Fish Wealth for the Republic of Yemen, chaired the Yemeni side.

The talks between the two sides resulted in agreement on the following matters:

First: The Area of Fish Wealth

1. Both the State of Eritrea and the Republic of Yemen shall permit fishermen who are citizens of the two States, without limiting their numbers, and who carry cards to engage in the occupation of fishing, to fish in the territorial waters of the two States, the contiguous zone and the Exclusive Economic Zone of the two countries in the Red Sea (with the exception of the internal waters), provided that the fishermen of the two countries be enumerated and that they be granted official licenses to engage in the occupation of fishing specifying the locations where they will be received and may market their products in Appendix No. 1. Each fisherman must submit a fishing license application to the other party within three months from the date of the signing of this Memorandum of Understanding while complying with the following:

    a. The use of sound fishing methods, the non-use of explosives and not polluting the marine environment, as well as the non-use of poisons, chemicals or other means of extermination.

    b. Not to use methods and fishing equipment damaging the growth of marine organisms.

    c. Not to remove or cut marine plants or coral reefs of any kind.

    d. Confinement to the fishing seasons in both of the two countries.

e. Use of all means to ensure the protection of the environment and rationalization of fishing practices.

f. Adherence to all laws and regulations of the other country in the sea to the extent these laws and regulations are applicable and do not conflict with the above provisions.

2. For the purposes of Paragraphs 1.d and 1.f above, the concerned authorities in both States in the Red Sea must notify the concerned authorities in the other State of laws, regulations and rules or any agreements with a third party in the waters the other party is using. Each party shall undertake to issue directives for compliance with that information.

3. Each fisherman or worker on any fishing vessel located in the territorial waters of the other [S]tate must carry a fishing license and a card establishing his identity and nationality in accordance with the laws and regulations of his State, and he must fly the flag of his State over his vessel.

4. Persons included in the provisions of Paragraph (1) above shall be permitted to do the following:

   a. Market their fish products in the territory of the other State and in the locations specified in Appendix No. 1 of this Memorandum of Understanding.

   b. Obtain the appropriate facilities for maintenance of the vessels and obtain foodstuffs, fuels, and ice at the prevailing prices in the country where they are present and for the period during which they remain at sea.

5. If the authorities in either of the two States are compelled to detain any fishing vessel or fisherman or worker on board any vessel, the authorities of that State must notify immediately the authorities of the other State of the names of the detained individuals and the vessels and the property contain[ed] therein and specify the reasons for and date of the detention.

6. The two States shall cooperate in the area of fishery research, protection of the marine environment from pollution, and the exchange of technical expertise and training at specialized institutions in the two countries.

Second: The Area of Maritime Trade, Investment and Transportation

1. Study the possibility of creating joint fishing companies between the two States.

2. Study the conclusion of a maritime transportation agreement between the two States.

3. Study the conclusion of a trade agreement between the two States. Until such a[n] agreement can be concluded, the concerned authorities in each of the two countries

shall offer all facilities available to them according to their laws to facilitate the transporting of locally-produced goods in the two countries.

Third: The Area of Security

The two States shall work to implement the Protocol signed by the Interior Ministries of the two countries in Sanaa on 10 November 1993 to achieve the objectives provided for in the said Protocol.

Fourth: The Implementation of the Subjects of the Memorandum

1. The concerned authorities in each of the two States, following the signing of this Memorandum of Understanding, shall take all necessary measures including but not limited to the issuance of decrees, orders, licenses, or directives to implement the contents of this Memorandum of Understanding.

2. The concerned agencies in the two States shall organize patrols off their coasts in the Red Sea and establish communication networks between the major security centers of the two States in the Red Sea at a time and method to be agreed by them.

3. Special offices shall be established in the two States to monitor and execute the articles of this Memorandum[.] The headquarters for these offices shall be specified in Appendix No. 1 of this Memorandum.

4. Contacts between the two sides regarding the implementation of this Memorandum of Understanding shall take place through diplomatic channels while abiding by the contents of Paragraph (2) of Article (4) above.

5. The two Governments shall consult on matters tha[t] may arise from the implementation of this Memorandum of Understanding, anything related to amendment, deletion or addition, as well as amendment or addition to the Appendix.

Signed at Massawa on this day of Tuesday, 15 November 1994.

For the Republic of Yemen

Dr. Abd al-Rahman Abd al-Qadir Ba-Fadhl
Minister of Fish Wealth

For the State of Eritrea

Dr. Salih Makki
Minister of Marine Wealth

Appendix No. 1

A. Centers for Fishing Registration and Monitoring and Marketing in the Republic of Yemen:

1. Maydi
2. Khoba
3. Hodeidah
4. Khokha
5. Mocha

Centers for Fishing Registration and Monitoring and Marketing in the State of Eritrea:

1. Assab
2. Tio
3. Dahlak
4. Massawa

Appendix No. 2

Members of the State of Eritrea Delegation:

1. Dr. Salih Makki, Minister of Marine Wealth
2. Ramadhan Ouliay, Naval Forces Commander
3. Musa Rabi'a, Eritrean Police Chief
4. Muhammad Idris Amir, Middle East Bureau, Foreign Ministry

Members of the Republic of Yemen Delegation:

1. Dr. Abd al-Rahman Abd al-Qadir Ba-Fadhl, Minister of Fish Wealth
2. Col. Abd al-Karim Muharram, Chief of Staff, Naval Forces
3. Col. Muhammad Rizq al-Sarami, Undersecretary, Central Agency of Political Security
4. Ambassador Ahmad al-Basha, Ambassador of the Republic of Yemen to the State of Eritrea
5. Ambassador Muhammad al-Wazir, Chairman, African Bureau, Foreign Ministry
6. Dr. Rashad al-Ulaymi, Director-General, Legal Affairs, Interior Ministry
7. Najib Abd al-Qawi Hamim, Director-General, External Cooperation, Ministry of Supply & Commerce
8. Khalid Sa'id al-Dhubhani, Director, Fishing Administration, Ministry of Planning & Development
9. Ali al-Maqalih, Director, Office of the Minister of Fish Wealth

مذكرة تفاهم
بين دولة ارتريا والجمهورية اليمنية
للتعاون في مجالات الصيد البحري والتجارى
والاستثمار والنقل

انطلاقا من روح الصداقة والتعاون وترجمة للاهداف والمصالح المشتركة بين البلدين الشقيقين دولة ارتريا والجمهورية اليمنية وتحقيقاً لمصالح الشعبين الشقيقين زار دولة ارتريا وفد الجمهورية اليمنية برئاسة الاخ/ الدكتور عبدالرحمن عبدالقادر بافضل وزير الثروة السمكية وقد استقبل استقبالاً حاراً من الاخ/ علي سيد عبدالله وزير الداخلية يوم الجمعة الموافق ٩٤/١١/١١ م واجريت محادثات اولية في وزارة الداخلية الارترية في العاصمة اسمرا اعقبها محادثات بين الطرفين في مدينة مصوع رأس الجانب الارترى الدكتور صالح مكي وزير الثروة البحرية في دولة ارتريا ورأس الجانب اليمنى الدكتور عبدالرحمن عبدالقاد بافضل وزير الثروة السمكية في الجمهورية اليمنية .

وقد اسفرت المحادثات بين الجانبين الى الاتفاق حول الامور التالية :-

أولا : في مجال الثروة السمكية :-

١-تسمح كل من دولة ارتريا والجمهورية اليمنية للصيادين من مواطنى الدولتين دون تحديد أعدادهم والعاملين لبطائق مزاولة مهنة الاصطياد بالاصطياد في المياه الاقليمية للدولتين والمنطقة المتاخمة وكذا المنطقة الاقتصادية الخالصة للدولتين في البحر الاحمر (عدا المياه الداخلية) على أن يتم حصر الصيادين لكلا البلدين ومنحهم رخصاً رسمية لممارسة مهنة الصيد والمحدده اماكن استقبالهم وتسويق منتجاتهم في المرفق رقم (١) على أن يتقدم كل صياد بطلب الترخيص له بالاصطياد من الطرف الآخر وذلك خلال ثلاثة اشهر من تاريخ توقيع مذكرة التفاهم هذه مع مراعاة مايلى :-

أ - استخدام طرق الاصطياد السليمة وعدم استعمال المتفجرات وتلويث البيئة البحرية ، وكذا عدم استعمال السموم - والمواد الكيماشية وغير ذلك من طرق الابادة

ب - عدم استخدام وسائل ومعدات صيد تضر بنمو الاحياء المائية

ج - عدم نزع او قطع الاعشاب البحرية والشعب المرجانية على اختلاف انواعها

د - التقيد بمواسم الاصطياد في كلا البلدين .

ه - استخدام كل السبل الكفيلة بحماية البيئة وترشيد عملية الاصطياد .

و - التقيد بكافة قوانين وأنظمة البلد الآخر في البحر الى المدى الذى تسرى فيه هذه القوانين والانظمة ، وبما لايتعارض مع ماذكر أعلاه .

(٢)

٢- لأغراض الفقرتين (د) و (و) من (١) أعلاه ، على السلطات المعنية في كلا الدولتين في البحر الأحمر اعلام السلطات المعنية في الدولة الأخرى بالقوانين واللوائح والأنظمة أو أية اتفاقيات مع طرف ثالث في المياه التي يستخدمها الطرف الآخر ويتولى كل طرف اصدار التوجيهات بتلك المعلومات بالتقيد بها .

٣- يجب أن يحمل كل صياد او عامل على أي قارب صيد يتواجد في المياه الاقليمية للدولة الأخرى رخصة صيد ، وبطاقة تثبت شخصيته وجنسيته ، طبقاً لقوانين وأنظمة دولته ، ويجب أن يرفع علم دولته على قارب الصيد .

٤- يسمح للاشخاص المشمولين بأحكام البند (١) اعلاه بمايلي :-

أ - تسويق انتاجهم من الاسماك في إقليم الدولة الأخرى وفي الإماكن المحددة بالمرفق رقم (١) لمذكرة التفاهم هذه .

ب- الحصول على التسهيلات المناسبة لصيانة القوارب والحصول على المواد الغذائية والمحروقات والثلج بالاسعار السائدة في البلد الذي يتواجدون فيه ولفترة بقائهم في البحر .

٥- اذا اضطرت سلطات أي من الدولتين الى احتجاز قارب صيد أو صياد أو عامل على أي قارب فعلى سلطات تلك الدولة إشعار سلطات الدولة الأخرى فوراً بأسماء الاشخاص والقوارب المحتجزة وماتحتويه من ممتلكات وتحديد أسباب وتاريخ الاحتجاز .

٦- يتعاون الجانبان في مجال الابحاث السمكية وحماية البيئة البحرية من التلوث ، وتبادل الخبرات الفنية وتدريبها في المعاهد التخصصية القائمة في البلدين .

<u>ثانياً : في مجال التجارة والاستثمار والنقل البحري</u> :-

١- دراسة امكانية انشاء شركات صيد مشتركة بين البلدين .

٢- دراسة عقد اتفاقية للنقل البحري بين الدولتين .

٣- دراسة عقد اتفاقية تجارية بين الدولتين : وحتى يتم عقد تلك الاتفاقية تقدم الجهات المختصة في كلا البلدين كافة التسهيلات المتاحة لها بموجب قوانينها لتسهيل أمور انتقال البضائع ذات المنشأ المحلي في البلدين .

(٢)

ثالثا : فى مجال الأمن

تعمل الدولتان على تنفيذ البروتوكول الموقع بين وزارتى الداخلية فى البلدين فى العاصمة صنعاء بتاريخ ١٠ نوفمبر ٩٢م لما من شأنه تحقيق الاهداف المنصوص عليها فى البروتوكول المشار اليه أعلاه ...

رابعا : فى مجال تنفيذ مواضيع المذكرة

١- تتخذ السلطات المختصة فى كلا الدولتين بعد التوقيع على مذكرة التفاهم هذه كافة الاجراءات اللازمة شاملة دون حصر إصدار قرارات أو أوامر أو رخص اوتوجيهات لتنفيذ ماورد فى مذكرة التفاهم هذه .

٢- تسير الاجهزة المعنية فى الدولتين دوريات مقابل شواطئها فى البحر الاحمر وتنشأ شبكات اتصال بين المراكز الأمنية الرئيسية للدولتين فى البحر الأحمر فى الوقت والأسلوب الذى يتفق عليه بينهما .

٣- تنشأ مكاتب خاصة فى كلا البلدين لمراقبة وتنفيذ ماورد من بنود فى هذه المذكرة وتحدد مقار تلك المكاتب طبقا للمرفق رقم (١) من هذه المذكرة .

٤- يتم الاتصال بين الجانبين فى شأن تنفيذ مذكرة التفاهم هذه بالطرق الدبلوماسية مع مراعاة ماورد فى البند (٢) من رابعاً اعلاه .

٥- تتشاور الحكومتان حول ماقد ينشأ عن تنفيذ مذكرة التفاهم هذه او فيما يتعلق من تعديل او حذف او اضافة . وكذا تعديل او اضافة للمرفق .

وقع فى مصوع يوم الثلاثا الموافق ١٥ نوفمبر ١٩٩٤م .

عن الجمهورية اليمنية
د/ عبدالرحمن عبدالقادر بافضل
وزير الثروة السمكية

عن دولة ارتريا
د/ صالح مكى
وزير الثروة البحرية

المرفق رقم (١)

أ/ المراكز الخاصة بتسجيل ومراقبة الاصطياد والتسويق فى الجمهورية اليمنية :-

١- ميدى
٢- الخوبة
٣- الحديدة
٤- الخوخة
٥- المخا

المراكز الخاصة بتسجيل ومراقبة الاصطياد والتسويق فى دولة ارتريا :-

١- عصب
٢- طيعو
٣- دهلك
٤- مصوع

المرفق (٢)

اعضاء جانب دولة ارتريا :-

١- الدكتور صالح مكى	وزير الثروة البحرية
٢- رمضان اولياى	قائد القوات البحرية
٣- موسى رابعة	مدير الشرطة الارترية
٤- محمد ادريس عامر	دائرة الشرق الاوسط - بوازارة الخارجية

اعضاء جانب الجمهورية اليمنية :-

الدكتور عبدالرحمن عبدالقادر بافضل	وزير الثروة السمكية
٢- العقيد : كريم محرم	رئيس هيئة اركان القوات البحرية
٣- العقيد محمد رزق الصرمى	وكيل الجهاز المركزى للأمن السياسى
٤- السفير أحمد الباشا	سفير الجمهورية اليمنية لدى دولة ارتريا
٥- السفير محمد الوزير	رئيس دائرة افريقيا بوزارة الخارجية
٦- الدكتور رشاد العليمى	مدير عام للشؤون القانونية بوزارة الداخلية
٧- نجيب عبدالقوى حاميم	مدير عام التعاون الخارجى بوزارة التموين والتجارة
٨- خالد سعيد الذبحانى	مدير ادارة الاسماك بوزارة التخطيط والتنمية .
٩- علي المقالح	مدير مكتب وزير الثروة السمكية

Treaty Establishing the Joint Yemeni-Eritrean Committee for Bilateral Cooperation Between the Government of the Republic of Yemen And the Government of the State of Eritrea

Based on the progressive civilized example set by bilateral relations between the Republic of Yemen and the State of Eritrea, and

Affirming their shared desire to continue to strengthen and reinforce these relations in service to their common interests, and

Aware of the importance of strengthening and developing bilateral cooperation in all fields of mutual concern,

The two parties have agreed to the following:

Article One – The two parties shall form a Joint Committee for Bilateral Cooperation between them in all fields of mutual concern, containing representatives of each party, to be called the Joint Yemeni-Eritrean Committee for Bilateral Cooperation, hereinafter referred to as the "Joint Committee," with the two Ministers of Foreign Affairs presiding. The Ministry of Planning and Development from the Yemeni side and the Ministry of Foreign Affairs from the Eritrean side, with the presence of required assistants, shall have jurisdiction over the secretariat and monitor implementation of Joint Committee results.

Article Two – The Joint Committee shall assume the following tasks:

1. Studying programs and recommendations designed to expand bilateral cooperation between the two countries and signing agreements, protocols, and implementation programs in that regard.

2. Monitoring the implementation of agreements, protocols, memoranda of understanding and minutes signed between the two countries in the fields referenced in Paragraph 1 of this Article.

3. Discussing proposals submitted by either country with the purpose of strengthening and developing the horizons of cooperation between them in all various fields of mutual interest.

4. Encouraging the exchange of bilateral visits and meetings between officials of both countries, and exchanging information and documents relevant to joint cooperation relations.

Article Three

1. The Committee may form permanent and temporary subcommittees and work teams to carry out certain specific tasks in the framework of Joint Committee work.

2. The subcommittees and work teams referred to in Paragraph 1 of this Article shall submit their recommendations to the Joint Committee for approval.

Article Four – The draft agenda for each round of exchanging recommendations shall be prepared through diplomatic channels and shall be submitted sufficiently in advance of the convening of the round. The Joint Committee may assign a technical committee from both sides to prepare for its meetings.

Article Five – The Joint Committee shall convene its round annually, alternating between Sanaa and Asmara. Special minutes shall be prepared for each round, signed by the chairmen of both sides on the Joint Committee, and approved by the relevant authorities in both countries pursuant to the laws and regulations in effect in each country.

Article Six – This treaty shall come into force on the date the ratification instruments are exchanged in accordance with the constitutional procedures in effect in each country. It shall remain in force for five (5) years and shall be renewed automatically for identical periods, provided neither party informs the other party in writing of its desire to terminate the treaty six months prior to its expiration date. Any additions or amendments to the articles of this treaty shall only be made with the written approval of both parties thereto.

The treaty has been drawn up in Sanaa on Friday, 25 Jumada II 1419, equivalent to 16 October 1998, in two original copies in the Arabic language, both having equal legal weight.

For the Government of the State of Eritrea	For the Republic of Yemen
[Signed] Haile Woldense	[Signed] Abd al-Qadir Abd al-Rahman Ba-Jammal
Minister of Foreign Affairs	Deputy Prime Minister and Foreign Minister

اتفاقية

تأسيس اللجنة اليمنية – الإريترية المشتركة

للتعاون الثنائي

بين

حكومة الجمهورية اليمنية

وحكومة دولة إريتريا.

إنطلاقاً من النموذج الحضاري المتقدم الذي تجلى في العلاقات الثنائية بين الجمهورية اليمنية ودولة إريتريا.

وتأكيداً لرغبتهما المشتركة في مواصلة تقوية وتعزيز هذه العلاقات بما يخدم مصالحهما المشتركة.

وإدراكاً منهما بأهمية تعزيز وتطوير التعاون الثنائي في كافة المجالات ذات الاهتمام المشترك.

اتفقنا على ما يلي :-

المادة الأولى

يشكل الطرفان لجنة مشتركة للتعاون الثنائي بينهما في كافة المجالات ذات الاهتمام المشترك، تضم ممثلين عن كل منهما، تسمى "اللجنة اليمنية - الإريترية المشتركة للتعاون الثنائي" ويشار إليها فيما يلي :- "اللجنة المشتركة" ويرأسها وزيري خارجية البلدين، وتتولى سكرتارية اللجنة ومتابعة تنفيذ نتائجها وزارة التخطيط والتنمية عن الجانب اليمني ووزارة الشؤون الخارجية عن الجانب الإريتري بوجود المساعدين اللازمين للجانبين وذلك بحكم الاختصاص.

المادة الثانية

تضطلع اللجنة المشتركة بالمهام التالية :-

١- دراسة البرامج والمقترحات الهادفة إلى توسيع التعاون الثنائي بين البلدين، وتوقيع الاتفاقيات وبروتوكولات وبرامج تنفيذية بشأنها.

١

٢- متابعة تنفيذ الاتفاقيات والبروتوكولات ومذكرات التفاهم والمحاضر الموقعة بين البلدين في الحالات المشار إليها في الفقرة (١) من هذه المادة.

٣- مناقشة الاقتراحات التي يقدمها أي من البلدين والتي من شأنها العمل على تعزيز وتطوير آفاق التعاون بينهما في كافة المجالات المختلفة ذات الاهتمام المشترك.

٤- تشجيع تبادل الزيارات واللقاءات الثنائية بين المسؤولين من كلا البلدين وتبادل المعلومات والوثائق ذات الصلة بعلاقات التعاون المشترك.

المادة الثالثة

١- يمكن للجنة أن تشكل لجاناً فرعية وفرق عمل دائمة ومؤقتة لإنجاز بعض المهام المحددة في إطار عمل اللجنة المشتركة.

٢- تقوم اللجان الفرعية وفرق العمل المشار إليها في الفقرة (١) من هذه المادة برفع توصياتها إلى اللجنة المشتركة للمصادقة عليها.

المادة الرابعة

يتم إعداد مشروع جدول أعمال كل دورة بتبادل الاقتراحات عبر القنوات الدبلوماسية على أن يقدم قبل موعد انعقاد الدورة بوقت كاف ، ويجوز للجنة المشتركة تكليف لجنة فنية من الجانبين للإعداد لاجتماعاتها.

المادة الخامسة

تعقد اللجنة المشتركة دورتها سنوياً، وبالتناوب في كل من صنعاء وأسمرة ويعد لكل دورة من الدورات محضر خاص، يوقع عليه من قبل رئيسي الجانبين في اللجنة

٢

المشتركة ويصادق عليه من قبل السلطات المختصة في البلدين طبقاً للقوانين والأنظمة المعمول بها في كل منهما.

المادة السادسة

يبدأ العمل بهذه الاتفاقية اعتباراً من تاريخ تبادل وثائق التصديق عليها وفقاً للإجراءات الدستورية المعمول بها في كلا البلدين، وتظل سارية المفعول لمدة (٥) سنوات وتجدد تلقائياً لمدد مماثلة، ما لم يقم أحد الطرفين بإبلاغ الطرف الآخر كتابياً برغبته في إلغائها قبل انتهاء مدتها بـ(٦) أشهر وأية إضافات أو تعديلات في مواد هذه الاتفاقية لا تتم إلا بموافقة الطرفين الكتابية عليها.

حررت هذه الاتفاقية في صنعاء يوم الجمعة بتاريخ ٢٥ جمادى الآخر ١٤١٩هـ الموافق ١٦/١٠/١٩٩٨م من نسختين أصليتين باللغة العربية ولكل منهما نفس الحجة القانونية.

عن حكومة دولة إريتريا

هيلي ولدتنسائي

وزير الشؤون الخارجية

عن حكومة الجمهورية اليمنية

عبد القادر عبد الرحمن باجمال

نائب رئيس الوزراء

وزير الخارجية.

List of Abbreviations

EEZ	Exclusive Economic Zones
FAO	Food and Agricultural Organization of the United Nations
I.C.J. Reports	International Court of Justice – Reports of Judgments, Advisory Opinions and Orders
ICLQ	International and Comparative Law Quarterly
ILR	International Law Reports
UNDP	United Nations Development Program
WGS	World Geodetic System

FRENCH TRANSLATION

TRADUCTION FRANÇAISE

L'ARBITRAGE ERYTHREE-YEMEN

Son apport au droit international

par

Jean-Pierre QUENEUDEC*

Les deux sentences en date du 9 octobre 1998 et du 17 décembre 1999 entre l'Etat d'Erythrée et la République du Yémen ont été rendues en anglais, conformément à l'article 9 du compromis d'arbitrage signé à Paris le 3 octobre 1996. Aussi la communauté des juristes francophones saura-t-elle gré au Bureau international de la Cour permanente d'arbitrage d'avoir pris l'initiative d'en assurer la traduction et la publication en français; car il s'agit d'un des arbitrages internationaux les plus importants de la fin du 20ème siècle.

Cette importance tient en premier lieu à la qualité des personnes composant le Tribunal arbitral. En effet, parmi les cinq membres constituant l'organe d'arbitrage, on comptait notamment deux juges et un ancien juge de la Cour internationale de Justice, dont le Président en exercice et un ancien Président de la Cour, ce dernier assurant d'ailleurs la présidence du Tribunal. Nul ne peut douter que la présidence de Sir Robert Jennings a eu pour effet de renforcer le prestige des décisions prises. De plus, le fait que chacune des deux sentences a fait l'objet d'une décision unanime des cinq arbitres accroît encore leur autorité.

L'importance de cet arbitrage est due, d'autre part, au résultat atteint à travers lui. Il a certes mis un terme définitif au conflit qui avait éclaté en 1995 entre l'Erythrée et le Yémen, puisque les deux Etats ont signé ensuite à Asmara, le 18 avril 2001, un accord de coopération dans lequel, en plus de divers engagements spécifiques, ils ont repris solennellement les conclusions du Tribunal arbitral. Mais cet arbitrage a une portée plus grande qui dépasse le cadre de ce litige particulier. Il a aussi ouvert la voie d'une solution pacifique pour d'autres conflits dans la région de la Corne de l'Afrique, notamment entre l'Erythrée et l'Ethiopie.[1]

---

* Professeur émérite de l'Université de Paris I (Panthéon – Sorbonne); Président de la Société française pour le droit international.

[1] Le texte de l'Accord du 12 décembre 2000 entre l'Erythrée et l'Ethiopie est disponible sur le site internet de la Cour permanente d'arbitrage (http://www.pca-cpa.org, sous la rubrique Décisions récentes et affaires pendantes). Sur cet accord, voir Emmanuelle Jouannet, *Le règlement de paix entre l'Ethiopie et l'Erythrée: un succès majeur pour l'ensemble d'Afrique?*, 105(4) REVUE GÉNÉRALE DE DROIT INTERNATIONAL PUBLIC 849-896 (2001).

Il restera surtout dans l'histoire comme l'arbitrage par lequel a été réglé l'épineux problème de l'appartenance des îles du sud de la mer Rouge, et plus particulièrement des îles Hanish. Situées au milieu d'une des voies maritimes les plus fréquentées du monde, ces îles apparemment dépourvues d'attrait faisaient l'objet d'une controverse ancienne dont la solution était en suspens depuis la fin de la première guerre mondiale. A cet égard, d'aucuns regretteront peut-être qu'aucun nom particulier n'ait été donné à l'affaire soumise à l'arbitrage et qu'elle n'ait pas été officiellement désignée, par exemple, sous le nom d'"affaire des îles de la mer Rouge".

L'arbitrage Erythrée-Yémen est important encore à un autre titre, qui tient à la méthode arrêtée par les Parties et à la démarche suivie par les arbitres pour le traitement du différend.

Dans le compromis d'arbitrage, l'Erythrée et le Yémen avaient demandé au Tribunal de se prononcer en deux étapes, la première portant sur la souveraineté territoriale et la définition du champ du différend, la seconde portant exclusivement sur la délimitation maritime.[2] Cette façon de procéder offrait l'avantage de sérier les problèmes. Elle était non seulement logique mais aussi efficace, puisque le tracé des frontières maritimes entre les deux Etats dépendait en partie des réponses préalablement apportées aux questions de souveraineté sur les îles en litige. Après le prononcé de la première sentence, les Parties ont ainsi pu avancer en pleine connaissance de cause leurs prétentions et leurs arguments concernant la délimitation maritime, sans se préoccuper de présenter des positions alternatives et sans se fonder sur de pures conjectures.

De ce point de vue, la démarche adoptée pour l'arbitrage Erythrée-Yémen a certainement été préférable à celle suivie dans l'affaire assez semblable de la *Délimitation maritime et des questions territoriales entre Qatar et Bahreïn* qui était au même moment pendante devant la Cour internationale de Justice. Dans cette affaire, en effet, l'engagement des deux Etats de soumettre l'ensemble du différend à la Cour dans le cadre d'une seule et même instance[3] eut pour conséquence de placer chaque partie dans la situation inconfortable de devoir présenter la ligne de délimitation maritime qu'elle

---

2 L' Accord sur les principes en date du 21 mai 1996, que les deux Etats avaient signé à Paris à la suite d'une médiation du Gouvernement français, avait initialement prévu que le Tribunal se prononcerait dans une première étape sur la définition du champ du différend et qu'il statuerait dans une deuxième étape, d'une part, sur les questions de souveraineté territoriale et, d'autre part, sur les questions de délimitation des frontières maritimes. Le texte de cet accord et le texte du compromis d'arbitrage ont été publiés dans 100(4) REVUE GÉNÉRALE DE DROIT INTERNATIONAL PUBLIC, 1119-1137 (1996). Le compromis d'arbitrage est également reproduit à l'annexe 1 de la deuxième phase de la sentence, p. 503 de ce volume. Sur les conditions du recours à l'arbitrage, voir les observations du directeur-adjoint des affaires juridiques du ministère français des affaires étrangères, Jean-François Dobelle, qui présida les rencontres entre les représentants de l'Ethiopie et du Yémen, dans 42 ANNUAIRE FRANÇAIS DE DROIT INTERNATIONAL pp. 477-481 (1996).

3 Voir les arrêts du 1er juillet 1994, C.I.J. Recueil 1994, p. 112, et du 15 février 1995, C.I.J. Recueil 1995, p. 6, sur la compétence et la recevabilité.

défendait sans connaître le sort réservé à ses prétentions territoriales et donc en faisant comme si la Cour lui avait déjà donné gain de cause sur les questions de souveraineté territoriale.[4] Aussi peut-on souhaiter que l'arbitrage Erythrée-Yémen serve sur ce point de modèle pour l'avenir.

Dans les observations qui suivent, on voudrait en premier lieu attirer l'attention sur quelques-unes des particularités qui ressortent des décisions prises et qui ont marqué la procédure suivie et le rôle joué par le Tribunal. On verra ensuite que la sentence relative à la question de la souveraineté territoriale comporte une assez grande part d'originalité dans les raisons qui la sous-tendent, tandis que celle concernant le problème de la délimitation maritime fait application de règles et de méthodes désormais bien établies et s'intègre parfaitement dans le cadre de la jurisprudence internationale qui s'est progressivement affirmée en ce domaine.[5] Il n'est évidemment

---

[4] L'absence de deux phases distinctes ne présentait évidemment pas le même inconvénient pour la Cour. Dans son arrêt du 16 mars 2001, C.I.J. Recueil 2001, elle s'est logiquement prononcée d'abord sur les questions territoriales avant de statuer sur la délimitation maritime; et si elle a tranché le problème de souveraineté concernant une île minuscule (Qit'at Jaradah) et un haut-fond découvrant (Fasht ad Dibal) à l'occasion de l'examen de la question de délimitation maritime, c'est parce que, en raison des caractéristiques particulières de ces formations maritimes, les deux aspects étaient ici très étroitement liés (voir les paragraphes 191 à 209 de l'arrêt).

[5] Chacune des deux sentences a fait l'objet de nombreux commentaires dans différentes revues. Voir notamment Nuno Sérgio Marques Antunes, *The Eritrea-Yemen Arbitration: First Stage – the Law of Title to Territory Re-averred*, 48(2) INTERNATIONAL AND COMPARATIVE LAW QUARTERLY 362-386 (1999), et *The 1999 Eritrea-Yemen Maritime Delimitation Award and the Development of International Law*, 50(2) INTERNATIONAL AND COMPARATIVE LAW QUARTERLY 299-344 (2001); Gilles Despeux, *Das Schiedsurteil Jemen gegen Eritrea II vom 17. Dezember 1999: Entschiedung über die Seeabgrenzung*, 60(2) ZEITSCHRIFT FÜR AUSLÄNDISCHES ÖFFENTLICHES RECHT UND VÖLKERRECHT 447-487 (2000); Jean-François Dobelle & Jean-Michel Faure, *Le différend entre l'Erythrée et le Yémen: la sentence arbitrale du 9 octobre 1998 sur le champ du différend et la souveraineté territoriale*, 44 ANNUAIRE FRANÇAIS DE DROIT INTERNATIONAL 337-355 (1998), et *Le différend entre l'Erythrée et le Yémen: la sentence arbitrale du 17 décembre 1999 sur la délimitation des frontières maritimes*, 45 ANNUAIRE FRANÇAIS DE DROIT INTERNATIONAL 554-565 (1999); Giovanni Distefano, *La sentence arbitrale du 9 octobre 1998 dans l'affaire du différend insulaire entre le Yémen et l'Erythrée,* 103(4) REVUE GÉNÉRALE DE DROIT INTERNATIONAL PUBLIC 851-890 (1999), et *La sentence arbitrale du 17 décembre 1999 sur la délimitation des frontières maritimes entre l'Erythrée et le Yémen: quelques observations complémentaires,* 46 ANNUAIRE FRANÇAIS DE DROIT INTERNATIONAL 255-284 (2000); Barbara Kwiatkowska, *Red Sea: Award of the Arbitral Tribunal in the First Stage of the Eritrea/Yemen Proceedings,* 14(1) INTERNATIONAL JOURNAL OF MARINE AND COASTAL LAW 125-136 (1999), et *The Eritrea-Yemen Arbitration: Landmark Progress in the Acquisition of Territorial Sovereignty and Equitable Maritime Boundary Delimitation,* 32(1) OCEAN DEVELOPMENT AND INTERNATIONAL LAW 1-25 (2001); W. Michael Reisman, *The Government of the State of Eritrea and the Government of the Republic of Yemen: Award of the Arbitral Tribunal in the First Stage of the Proceedings (Territorial Sovereignty and Scope of the Dispute)*, 93(3) AMERICAN JOURNAL OF INTERNATIONAL LAW 668-682 (1999), et *Eritrea-Yemen Arbitration (Award, Phase II: Maritime Delimitation)*, 94(4) AMERICAN JOURNAL OF INTERNATIONAL LAW 721-735 (2000).

pas question d'entrer ici dans la voie d'une analyse approfondie ou d'un commentaire détaillé de ces décisions. Il ne s'agit que de quelques propos introductifs.

I

(1) Une première particularité concerne la manière dont le Tribunal a rendu sa décision relative à la définition de l'étendue géographique du différend.

Le compromis avait prévu que la première étape de l'arbitrage donnerait lieu à une sentence portant à la fois sur la souveraineté territoriale et la définition du champ du différend. Il précisait en outre, concernant cette dernière question : "Le Tribunal statue sur la définition du champ du différend sur la base des positions respectives des deux Parties" (article 2, paragraphe 2).

Or, la décision que le Tribunal a prise sur ce point n'est pas énoncée dans le dispositif de la sentence sur la souveraineté territoriale, c'est-à-dire dans la partie de la décision qui est en principe seule revêtue de l'autorité de la chose jugée. Elle est contenue dans la conclusion du chapitre II consacré à la présentation des positions des Parties concernant le champ du différend, c'est-à-dire qu'elle se trouve en réalité dans l'exposé des motifs de la sentence. Le Tribunal y a indiqué, en effet, qu'il "préf[érait] les vues défendues par l'Erythrée" et qu'il entendait donc rendre "une sentence sur la souveraineté intéressant la totalité des îles et des îlots au sujet desquels les Parties ont présenté des revendications opposées".[6] Mais il n'y a aucune mention formelle qu'il ait "statué" sur ce point. Sans doute les arbitres ont-ils pu valablement estimer qu'il était inutile de reprendre expressément dans le corps du dispositif l'énoncé de la décision qu'ils avaient prise à ce sujet, dans la mesure où celle-ci pouvait être réputée résulter implicitement des autres décisions qui y étaient mentionnées.

Ce qui paraît toutefois surprenant, c'est que le Tribunal a omis d'indiquer s'il avait tranché cette question à l'unanimité ou si sa décision avait été prise à la majorité. Cela semble d'autant plus étonnant que, sur les différents autres points tranchés dans sa sentence sur la souveraineté territoriale, il n'a pas été avare de ce genre d'indications. En effet, l'indication selon laquelle le Tribunal a décidé à l'unanimité sur ces autres points ne se trouve pas seulement dans le dispositif de la sentence, comme il est d'usage. Elle est en outre donnée, dans un chapitre de l'exposé des motifs intitulé "Conclusions", à propos de chacun des groupes d'îles sur lesquels le Tribunal s'est prononcé.[7]

---

6 L'arbitrage Erythrée-Yémen, Sentence de 1998, paragraphe 90.

7 Voir l'arbitrage Erythrée-Yémen, Sentence de 1998, paragraphes 475, 482, 484, 508 et 524 dans lesquels la formule utilisée est tantôt : "En conséquence le Tribunal estime à l'unanimité . . .", tantôt : "Le Tribunal décide donc à l'unanimité . . . ."

(2) Une autre particularité qui mérite également d'être relevée est apparue dans le déroulement même de la procédure.

Dans la première étape de l'arbitrage, aucune des deux Parties n'avait évoqué ni même mentionné les contrats pétroliers et les concessions pétrolières que l'une ou l'autre d'entre elles avait pu conclure et qui concernaient la mer Rouge et les îles en litige. Chacune d'elles se réservait apparemment d'évoquer cette question dans la deuxième étape sur la délimitation maritime. Ce fut le Tribunal qui les obligea à en faire état dès la première étape en leur posant des questions à l'issue de la procédure orale. Estimant toutefois insuffisantes les réponses apportées par les Parties, le Tribunal fut conduit non seulement à leur demander de nouvelles observations écrites, mais aussi à organiser une reprise de la procédure orale consacrée exclusivement aux accords pétroliers et aux activités pétrolières.

Si le compromis d'arbitrage autorisait bien le Tribunal, même après la clôture de la phase orale, à "demander aux Parties leur avis écrit sur toute question, nécessaire pour permettre au Tribunal d'élucider un aspect de l'affaire" (article 8, paragraphe 3.3), il ne contenait toutefois aucune indication concernant le pouvoir du Tribunal de provoquer une éventuelle réouverture des débats. On doit cependant considérer que, en l'absence de toute disposition contraire dans le compromis, il s'agit là d'un pouvoir inhérent à toute juridiction internationale,[8] étant entendu qu'une réouverture des débats peut seulement avoir pour objet de permettre aux Parties de présenter des observations orales strictement limitées à la question que le tribunal souhaite élucider.

Ce traitement obligé des contrats pétroliers *offshore* dans la première étape de l'arbitrage devait faire apparaître un paradoxe : si les conclusions susceptibles d'en être tirées en l'espèce n'étaient pas de nature à exercer une influence sur la décision relative à la souveraineté territoriale, la prise en compte de ces contrats pouvait toutefois jouer un rôle en matière de détermination de la ligne de délimitation maritime. Le Tribunal estima, en effet, dans sa première sentence, que ces contrats ne permettaient ni d'établir ni de conforter de manière significative les revendications de souveraineté de l'un ou l'autre des deux Etats sur les îles litigieuses, mais qu'ils "étay[aient] dans une certaine mesure le tracé d'une ligne médiane entre les côtes se faisant face de l'Erythrée et du Yémen".[9] C'est en se fondant notamment sur cet aspect du dossier que le Tribunal fut ensuite conduit, dans sa seconde sentence, à adopter comme principe de base de la

---

[8] En ce sens, voir notamment DURWARD V. SANDIFER, EVIDENCE BEFORE INTERNATIONAL TRIBUNALS 299 (1939). L'article 72 du Règlement de la Cour internationale de Justice prévoit expressément la possibilité d'une réouverture de la procédure orale, mais cette hypothèse ne s'est, semble-t-il, jamais présentée en fait devant la Cour. Voir GENEVIÈVE GUYOMAR, COMMENTAIRE DU RÈGLEMENT DE LA COUR INTERNATIONALE DE JUSTICE. INTERPRÉTATION ET PRATIQUE 467 (1983).

[9] L'arbitrage Erythrée-Yémen, Sentence de 1998, paragraphe 438.

délimitation maritime l'idée selon laquelle, entre côtes se faisant face, il convenait d'appliquer la méthode de la ligne médiane.[10]

(3) Enfin, on ne saurait oublier que, dans une procédure arbitrale internationale, le souci des arbitres n'est pas seulement de "dire le droit" et de régler le différend à eux soumis en faisant une stricte application des règles juridiques. Il est aussi d'apaiser les tensions et de favoriser le rétablissement et le développement d'une coopération durable entre les deux Etats en litige.[11] A cette fin, il ne paraît guère douteux qu'un tribunal d'arbitrage dispose du pouvoir de formuler des recommandations à l'intention des Parties à l'instance arbitrale, comme cela fut notamment rappelé par la sentence rendue dans l'affaire du *Rainbow Warrior* entre la Nouvelle Zélande et la France: "Le pouvoir d'un tribunal arbitral de faire des recommandations aux Parties en cause, en complément à des conclusions formelles et des décisions obligatoires, contenues dans la sentence, a été reconnu dans de précédentes décisions".[12]

Le Tribunal arbitral Erythrée-Yémen a fait usage de ce pouvoir à deux reprises, en situant toutefois l'exercice de ce pouvoir dans le contexte particulier des relations de voisinage entre les populations locales.

Se fondant sur le fait que "les idées occidentales de souveraineté territoriale sont étrangères à des populations élevées dans la tradition islamique" et invoquant la nécessité de respecter les "traditions juridiques propres à la région", il a ainsi recommandé le maintien et la perpétuation du régime de pêche traditionnel qui existait de longue date dans les parages des îles contestées au profit des pêcheurs des deux rives de la mer Rouge.[13] Il s'agit toutefois plus que d'une simple recommandation, car la forme sous laquelle elle est énoncée en fait une quasi-obligation et elle est en outre expressément incorporée dans le dispositif de la sentence sur la souveraineté territoriale.

De surcroît, dans la sentence sur la délimitation maritime, le Tribunal a tenu à apporter un certain nombre de précisions quant à la nature et à l'étendue de ce régime de pêche traditionnel. N'étant ni un titre détenu en commun ni un droit partagé sur les

---

[10] L'arbitrage Erythrée-Yémen, Sentence de 1999, paragraphe 83.

[11] La sentence arbitrale rendue le 22 janvier 1926 dans l'affaire des *Indiens Cayuga* (Etats-Unis/Grande-Bretagne) soulignait ainsi que "something more than the strict law must be used in the grounds of decision of arbitral tribunals in certain cases", VI NATIONS UNIES, RECUEIL DES SENTENCES ARBITRALES 175. Une illustration assez remarquable en fut donnée dans la 2ème décision rendue le 19 février 1968 dans l'affaire de la frontière indo-pakistanaise occidentale, ou affaire du *Rann de Kutch* (Inde/Pakistan), où le tribunal fit notamment appel à des considérations de paix et de sécurité dans la région, XVII NATIONS UNIES, RECUEIL DES SENTENCES ARBITRALES 5.

[12] Sentence arbitrale du 30 avril 1990, paragraphe 128. Texte dans 94(3) REVUE GÉNÉRALE DE DROIT INTERNATIONAL PUBLIC 838 (1990).

[13] L'arbitrage Erythrée-Yémen, Sentence de 1998, paragraphe 526.

ressources, ce régime autorise les pêcheurs des deux Etats à pratiquer librement la pêche artisanale dans l'ensemble des eaux autour des îles attribuées au Yémen, indépendamment du tracé de la frontière internationale. Il comporte en outre la jouissance de droits connexes, comme le libre accès aux îles et le droit de débarquer et de commercialiser les prises sans discrimination dans les ports de l'autre Etat. Il implique également le maintien du système traditionnel de règlement des litiges entre pêcheurs artisanaux.[14]

Ce faisant, le Tribunal a entendu consacrer l'existence d'un ordre juridique particulier de nature non territoriale, un ordre transnational de dimension inter-individuelle embrassant exclusivement les activités de pêche artisanale, une sorte de *lex pescatoria* dont la pérennité se trouve à présent garantie par le droit international en application des décisions du Tribunal arbitral.

De même, mais de façon nettement moins originale, concernant les gisements d'hydrocarbures liquides ou gazeux qui viendraient à être découverts et qui seraient à cheval sur la frontière maritime ou dans son voisinage immédiat, le Tribunal n'a pu que recommander aux deux Etats de s'engager dans la voie d'une exploitation commune ou conjointe de ces ressources. Il l'a fait en se fondant non seulement sur la pratique généralement suivie par les Etats en matière d'exploitation des ressources marines se trouvant à cheval sur des frontières maritimes, mais en faisant appel, ici aussi, à des considérations d'ordre local. Selon lui, cette recommandation pouvait se justifier en particulier au nom des liens historiques existant entre les peuples intéressés et eu égard aux relations amicales renouées entre les deux Etats depuis le prononcé de la sentence sur la souveraineté.[15]

II

En demandant aux arbitres de statuer "sur" la question de la souveraineté territoriale, le compromis d'arbitrage avait fixé la mission du Tribunal dans des termes que celui-ci considéra comme "inhabituels".[16] Cette disposition, qu'il qualifia même d'"insolite",[17] offrait, en effet, au Tribunal toute une gamme de possibilités puisqu'une telle formule, si elle lui permettait effectivement d'attribuer la souveraineté à l'un des deux Etats, l'autorisait aussi bien à dire que la souveraineté leur appartenait conjointement ou à se prononcer en faveur de toute autre forme de souveraineté partagée sur les îles. A la différence de l'affaire de *l'Ile de Palmas* où l'arbitre devait choisir entre deux titres imparfaits, l'un découlant d'un commencement d'occupation, l'autre dérivé de la découverte, le Tribunal arbitral Erythrée-Yémen n'était pas appelé à se prononcer en

---

[14] L'arbitrage Erythrée-Yémen, Sentence de 1999, paragraphes 103-107.

[15] L'arbitrage Erythrée-Yémen, Sentence de 1999, paragraphe 86.

[16] L'arbitrage Erythrée-Yémen, Sentence de 1998, paragraphe 455.

[17] L'arbitrage Erythrée-Yémen, Sentence de 1998, paragraphe 102.

se fondant sur la valeur relative des titres invoqués par chaque Partie, ni à se déterminer en fonction d'une différence marginale entre les éléments de preuve avancés.[18]

De plus, le Tribunal devait se prononcer sur la base notamment des titres historiques susceptibles d'être invoqués de part et d'autre. Aussi fut-il amené, face au volume du matériau documentaire dont il était saisi, à indiquer à cette occasion que, si l'expression "titre ancien" désignait généralement "un titre établi de si longue date par la commune renommée que celle-ci constitue en soi un titre suffisant", la notion de titre historique avait en droit international la signification plus précise de "titre qui a été créé ou consolidé par un processus de prescription, ou bien l'acquiescement, ou encore par une possession dont la durée est telle qu'elle finit, en droit, par être reconnue comme un titre".[19] Dans un cas comme dans l'autre, l'exigence de continuité et d'écoulement du temps était évidemment un élément essentiel. Or, les titres allégués par les Parties ne pouvaient satisfaire à cette double exigence, en raison des caractéristiques de la situation juridique des îles de la mer Rouge. Selon le Tribunal, celles-ci étaient devenues, après le Traité de Lausanne de 1923 avec la Turquie, des "orphelins internationaux laissés à l'abandon".[20]

L'article 16 du Traité de Lausanne disposait, en effet : "La Turquie déclare renoncer à tous droits et titres, de quelque nature que ce soit, sur ou concernant les territoires situés au-delà des frontières prévues par le présent Traité et sur les îles autres que celles sur lesquelles la souveraineté lui est reconnue par ledit Traité, le sort de ces territoires et îles étant réglé ou à régler par les intéressés."[21] Cette disposition , qui était applicable aux îles de la mer Rouge, entraînait pour celles-ci une double conséquence.

D'une part, en renonçant à sa souveraineté sur ces îles la Turquie se défaisait du titre territorial qu'elle détenait jusque là. Cette renonciation impliquait nécessairement qu'il ne pouvait pas exister d'autre titre territorial sur les îles en question et notamment que ne pouvait pas réapparaître un éventuel titre qui aurait existé antérieurement à l'exercice de la souveraineté ottomane. Il s'agissait là d'un corollaire logique que le Tribunal résuma en déclarant : "le fait que l'Empire ottoman renonce à sa souveraineté . . . porte logiquement et juridiquement atteinte à tout titre préexistant éventuel".[22] Il en résultait donc qu'il ne pouvait être question d'accueillir l'idée d'une quelconque réversion d'un titre ancien, comme le prétendait le Yémen; car admettre qu'un titre

---

[18] L'arbitrage Erythrée-Yémen, Sentence de 1998, paragraphe 454. Texte de la sentence de Max Huber du 4 avril 1928 dans II NATIONS UNIES, RECUEIL DES SENTENCES ARBITRALES 829; 39 REVUE GÉNÉRALE DE DROIT INTERNATIONAL PUBLIC 156-202 (1935).

[19] L'arbitrage Erythrée-Yémen, Sentence de 1998, paragraphe 106.

[20] L'arbitrage Erythrée-Yémen, Sentence de 1998, paragraphe 192.

[21] Texte dans LOUIS LE FUR ET GEORGES CHKLAVER, RECUEIL DE TEXTES DE DROIT INTERNATIONAL PUBLIC 752 (2ème édition, 1934).

[22] L'arbitrage Erythrée-Yémen, Sentence de 1998, paragraphe 124.

ancien serait resté en vigueur pendant la période ottomane revenait à rejeter la légalité du titre ottoman à la pleine souveraineté, alors qu'en vertu des principes du droit intertemporel cette souveraineté était légitime et comportait le droit de disposer des îles en question.[23]

D'autre part, l'abandon de la souveraineté turque n'avait pas eu pour effet de transformer les îles de la mer Rouge en *res nullius* et de les rendre susceptibles d'appropriation par le biais d'une prescription acquisitive. Le but poursuivi par les Puissances maritimes au moment du démembrement de l'Empire ottoman était de préserver la liberté de la navigation dans une région devenue importante pour la communauté internationale depuis l'ouverture du canal de Suez. A cette fin, elles imaginèrent une garantie consistant à subordonner l'acquisition éventuelle de la souveraineté sur ces îles à la preuve de la capacité d'assumer pleinement les responsabilités internationales qui leur étaient attachées, concernant en particulier l'entretien des phares installés sur lesdites îles. C'est pourquoi le Traité de Lausanne avait institué un gel des revendications territoriales sur les îles de la mer Rouge et créé pour elles "un statut juridique objectif d'indétermination jusqu'au moment où les parties intéressées se prononceraient à nouveau à leur sujet".[24]

Par la suite, l'accord international relatif à l'entretien de certains phares en mer Rouge, adopté par une conférence des principaux Etats utilisateurs du canal de Suez et ouvert à la signature à Londres le 20 février 1962, après avoir rappelé dans son préambule qu'aucun accord sur l'avenir de ces îles n'avait été conclu entre les intéressés, précisa en son article 8: "*Nothing in the present Agreement shall be regarded as constituting a settlement of the future of the Islands or territories referred to in Article 16 of the Treaty of Lausanne or as prejudicing the conclusion of any such settlement in the future*".[25] Aux yeux des Puissances maritimes intéressées, la situation juridique indéterminée des îles était donc inchangée depuis l'entrée en vigueur du Traité de Lausanne en 1926. Elle le demeura, même après le retrait des Britanniques de la région en 1967, jusqu'à l'extinction de l'accord de Londres le 31 mars 1990. Durant toute cette période, aucun titre territorial n'avait par conséquent pu être acquis sur les îles litigieuses, que ce soit de manière directe par occupation effective ou de façon indirecte par voie de succession comme le prétendait l'Erythrée.

---

[23] L'arbitrage Erythrée-Yémen, Sentence de 1998, paragraphe 444.

[24] L'arbitrage Erythrée-Yémen, Sentence de 1998, paragraphe 445.

[25] Texte dans NAGENDRA SINGH, I INTERNATIONAL MARITIME LAW CONVENTIONS 90 (1983). Outre les signataires originaires (Allemagne fédérale, Danemark, Etats-Unis, Grèce, Italie, Liberia, Norvège, Pakistan, Panama, Pays-Bas, République arabe unie, Royaume-Uni, Suède, URSS), cet accord fit l'objet d'une acceptation ultérieure de la part de la R.P. de Chine et du Portugal, mais l'Ethiopie et le Yémen n'y furent jamais parties. Voir John M. Gardner, *The Red Sea Lights Agreement: Another Instance of International Cost-Sharing*, 69(1) AMERICAN JOURNAL OF INTERNATIONAL LAW 129-134 (1975).

Les îles n'ont finalement été ouvertes à l'acquisition territoriale qu'après la fin du régime institué par le Traité de 1923 et, plus précisément, après la fin du régime internationalisé de gestion des phares, lorsque les Etats utilisateurs de la voie maritime se sont désengagés. Les "intéressés" sont alors devenus les Etats riverains de la mer Rouge qui se sont substitués aux usagers dans les responsabilités internationales relatives à la navigation dans ce secteur. Les préambules de l'accord sur les principes et du compromis d'arbitrage lui-même en portent d'ailleurs la trace : l'Erythrée et le Yémen s'y sont déclarés "conscients de leurs responsabilités à l'égard de la communauté internationale en matière de . . . sauvegarde de la liberté de navigation dans une région particulièrement sensible du monde."

Examinant l'attitude des Etats riverains successifs, le Tribunal constata que ni la Grande-Bretagne ou l'Italie, ni à leur suite le Yémen ou l'Ethiopie puis l'Erythrée n'avaient laissé transparaître un véritable *animus occupandi*, c'est-à-dire "une manifestation intentionnelle de pouvoir et d'autorité sur le territoire, par l'exercice continu et pacifique de la compétence et des attributs de la puissance publique".[26] De surcroît, s'inspirant de la jurisprudence de la Cour internationale de Justice qui avait considérer en 1953 que les activités liées à l'éclairage et au balisage d'îles ou d'îlots ne pouvaient pas être regardées "comme preuve suffisante de l'intention . . . de se comporter en souverain",[27] le Tribunal ne manqua pas de souligner: "assurer le fonctionnement ou l'entretien de phares et d'aides à la navigation est normalement lié à la sécurité de la navigation et n'est normalement pas considéré comme un critère de souveraineté".[28] Il était dès lors impossible de trouver des preuves convaincantes parmi toutes celles que l'Erythrée et le Yémen avaient produites au sujet de l'exercice des fonctions étatiques sur les îles qui faisaient l'objet du litige.

Dans ces conditions, la question de la souveraineté territoriale sur ces îles, telle qu'elle était posée au Tribunal, ne pouvait être tranchée ni sur la base d'un titre juridique, c'est-à-dire d'un droit clairement établi, ni en fonction d'effectivités véritablement déterminantes. Ce qui représentait une situation relativement inédite dans le contentieux territorial soumis à règlement juridictionnel à l'époque contemporaine. En effet, dans la jurisprudence internationale qui s'était développée dans les années précédant l'arbitrage Erythrée-Yémen, lorsque le recours au titre juridique n'était pas susceptible de fournir la base du règlement du conflit territorial, il était fait appel à

---

[26] L'arbitrage Erythrée-Yémen, Sentence de 1998, paragraphe 239.

[27] Affaire des Minquiers et des Ecréhous, arrêt du 17 novembre 1953, C.I.J. Recueil 1953, p. 71.

[28] L'arbitrage Erythrée-Yémen, Sentence de 1998, paragraphe 328. Dans l'affaire de la Délimitation maritime et des questions territoriales entre Qatar et Bahreïn, la C.I.J. a toutefois nuancé sa jurisprudence antérieure et a admis que, parmi les activités tendant à prouver l'intention d'agir à titre de souverain, " La construction d'aides à la navigation . . . peut être juridiquement pertinente dans le cas de très petites îles". Arrêt du 16 mars 2001, C.I.J. Recueil 2001, paragraphe 197.

l'effectivité pour établir une sorte de titre supplétif ou résiduel.[29] C'était ce qui ressortait en particulier des décisions de la Cour internationale de Justice dans les affaires du *Différend frontalier (Burkina Faso/Mali)*[30] et du *Différend frontalier terrestre, insulaire et maritime (El Salvador/Honduras; Nicaragua (intervenant)).*[31]

Le Tribunal a donc été contraint de recourir à des présomptions de fait et de se fonder sur des apparences qui pouvaient raisonnablement faire pencher la balance en faveur de l'une ou l'autre des Parties. Prenant en considération "la situation géographique de la majorité des îles, îlots et rochers en litige", qui forment un archipel occupant la totalité du bras de mer compris entre les côtes érythréennes et yéménites, le Tribunal y a vu un élément décisif, faute pour lui d'avoir été convaincu qu'il existait une autre source possible de titre à la souveraineté. Il en a tiré la présomption selon laquelle "toute île située au large d'une des côtes peut être considérée comme appartenant à cette côte en tant que dépendance sauf si l'Etat sur le territoire duquel se trouve la côte opposée a pu démontrer qu'il avait un titre manifestement meilleur".[32] Dans le cas particulier des îles Mohabbakahs au large de la côte érythréenne, il a en outre invoqué le "principe de la mer territoriale", en vertu duquel les îles situées dans la mer territoriale d'un Etat appartiennent nécessairement à ce dernier, en précisant toutefois que, si ce principe donnait naissance à une forte présomption, il ne s'agissait que d'une présomption *juris tantum*, comme le montrait en particulier l'exemple des îles anglo-normandes.[33]

L'appel à la notion de proximité géographique et le recours à la présomption d'appartenance des îles à la terre la plus proche n'ont cependant pas constitué une totale innovation, dans la mesure où l'idée de contiguïté avait déjà été conçue à deux reprises au moins dans le passé comme représentant une projection du principe de l'occupation effective, de nature à créer un titre imparfait ("*inchoate title*"). Cette idée avait, en effet, servi de base, d'une part, à la sentence rendue par la Reine d'Espagne le 30 juin 1865 dans l'affaire de l'*Ile d'Aves* entre les Pays-Bas et le Venezuela et, d'autre part, à la sentence du Président des Etats-Unis en date du 21 avril 1870 dans

---

29 Voir Giovanni Distefano, *La notion de titre juridique et les différends territoriaux dans l'ordre international*, 99(2) REVUE GÉNÉRALE DE DROIT INTERNATIONAL PUBLIC 335-366 (1995), et PHILIPPE WECKEL (DIR.), LE JUGE INTERNATIONAL ET L'AMÉNAGEMENT DE L'ESPACE : LA SPÉCIFICITÉ DU CONTENTIEUX TERRITORIAL (1998).

30 Arrêt du 22 décembre 1986, C.I.J. Recueil 1986, p. 554.

31 Arrêt du 11 septembre 1992, C.I.J. Recueil 1992, p. 351.

32 L'arbitrage Erythrée-Yémen, Sentence de 1998, paragraphe 458. Voir aussi le paragraphe 480, dans lequel le Tribunal a repris la même idée: "les arguments géographiques de la proximité par rapport à la côte . . . s'accordent bien avec l'opinion générale qui est que les îles situées au large d'une côte appartiennent à l'Etat côtier sauf s'il est possible de démontrer l'existence d'un autre titre qui serait supérieur."

33 L'arbitrage Erythrée-Yémen, Sentence de 1998, paragraphes 472 et 474.

l'affaire de l'*Ile de Bulama* entre la Grande-Bretagne et le Portugal.[34] Tout laisse à penser que l'influence du Président du Tribunal a pu être déterminante pour faire ici de la notion de proximité ou de contiguïté une sorte de substitut à l'occupation effective, si l'on veut bien se souvenir qu'il avait naguère affirmé, dans un écrit faisant autorité en la matière: "Contiguity is no more than evidence raising some sort of presumption of effective occupation".[35]

Le Tribunal s'est trouvé conforté dans cette démarche par le fait que le facteur de proximité sur lequel il se fondait avait exercé une influence dans l'histoire juridique des îles. En effet, à l'époque de la domination ottomane, "alors même que toute la région relevait d'une souveraineté unique, il a[vait] été jugé commode de partager la juridiction entre les deux autorités locales installées sur les deux côtes": [36] certaines îles relevaient de la juridiction du *khédive* d'Egypte pour le compte de l'Empire ottoman jusqu'en 1882, tandis que d'autres faisaient partie du *vilayet* ottoman du Yémen jusqu'à la dissolution de l'Empire à la suite de la 1ère guerre mondiale.[37] La référence ainsi faite à l'histoire juridique des îles présentait toutefois un caractère tout à fait surabondant dans le raisonnement des arbitres, car le Tribunal avait considéré par ailleurs que cette histoire n'était pas en elle-même concluante.

C'est la raison pour laquelle, afin de trancher la question de souveraineté sur le groupe des îles Hanish, le Tribunal a finalement été amené à prendre surtout en considération des éléments tout à fait récents et à "se fonder très largement sur ce qui paraît être avoir été la situation . . . pendant la période correspondant à peu près à la dernière décennie précédant le Compromis d'arbitrage".[38] A n'en pas douter, ce n'est pas là le moindre des paradoxes révélés par cette affaire. Appelé à se prononcer en se fondant sur des titres historiques et saisi par les Parties d'un volumineux dossier historique, le Tribunal a été conduit à écarter les titres anciens invoqués et à négliger les événements d'un passé lointain. Il s'est prononcé en se fondant en définitive sur des éléments issus de la partie la plus récente de l'histoire. Aussi a-t-il lui-même souligné ce point en faisant une comparaison avec l'attitude de la Cour internationale de Justice dans une affaire semblable: "comme . . . dans l'affaire des *Minquiers et Ecréhous* où s'opposaient aussi des arguments relatifs à des revendications de titres très anciens, c'est l'histoire relativement récente de l'utilisation et de la possession qui constitue en définitive un fondement essentiel des décisions du Tribunal."[39] On a

---

[34] Albert De Lapradelle & Nicolas Politis eds., II Recueil des arbitrages internationaux 413 et 613 (1905-1954).

[35] Robert Y. Jennings, The Acquisition of Territory in International Law 75 (1963).

[36] L'arbitrage Erythrée-Yémen, Sentence de 1998, paragraphe 458.

[37] L'arbitrage Erythrée-Yémen, Sentence de 1998, paragraphe 134.

[38] L'arbitrage Erythrée-Yémen, Sentence de 1998, paragraphe 503.

[39] L'arbitrage Erythrée-Yémen, Sentence de 1998, paragraphe 450.

d'ailleurs pu se demander s'il ne s'agissait pas là d'une tendance constante de la jurisprudence internationale en matière territoriale.[40]

III

Le compromis d'arbitrage avait défini la mission du Tribunal pour la délimitation des frontières maritimes en lui demandant de procéder à cette délimitation "de manière techniquement précise" et en indiquant qu'il devrait prendre en compte non seulement sa décision antérieure sur les questions de souveraineté territoriale – ce qui allait de soi, pour des raisons évidentes – mais aussi la convention des Nations Unies sur le droit de la mer, ainsi que "tout autre élément pertinent" (article 2, paragraphe 3).

La référence à la convention de 1982 était d'autant plus remarquable qu'il ne s'agissait pas d'un traité en vigueur entre les deux Etats litigants; seul le Yémen y était partie. En conséquence, en acceptant l'incorporation de cette référence dans le compromis, l'Erythrée avait par là même accepté l'application par le Tribunal des dispositions de la convention sur le droit de la mer qu'il jugerait pertinentes aux fins de la délimitation.

Comme on le sait, en dehors des règles relatives à la délimitation de la mer territoriale entre Etats voisins, les dispositions de la convention concernant la délimitation des autres zones maritimes nationales sont surtout caractérisées par le flou de leur formulation et l'incertitude de leur contenu exact. Ce que le Tribunal a lui-même noté en usant d'un euphémisme, lorsqu'il a fait remarquer, à propos des articles 74 (zone économique) et 83 (plateau continental) de la convention, qu'il fallait "admettre des différences d'opinion quant à l'interprétation d'articles qui, en un effort de dernière minute pour parvenir à un accord sur une question fort controversée, ont été volontairement conçus . . . de façon à trancher le moins possible".[41]

Les règles applicables en la matière sont essentiellement des règles coutumières. Or, le compromis ne faisait nullement mention du droit coutumier. Le Tribunal considéra cependant que cette absence de référence au droit coutumier de la mer était compensée par la circonstance que la convention de 1982 en reprenait de nombreux éléments pertinents.[42] Ce qui était une affirmation gratuite et représentait, de la part du Tribunal, une étrange pirouette dont il aurait pu fort bien se dispenser. Il lui aurait suffi pour cela de rappeler que le compromis d'arbitrage l'avait chargé "de se prononcer conformément au droit international, en deux étapes" (article 2, paragraphe 1) et que cette

---

[40] Voir Marcelo G. Kohen, *L'influence du temps sur les règlements territoriaux*, SOCIÉTÉ FRANÇAISE POUR LE DROIT INTERNATIONAL (COLLOQUE DE PARIS), LE DROIT INTERNATIONAL ET LE TEMPS 131-160 (2001).

[41] L'arbitrage Erythrée-Yémen, Sentence de 1999, paragraphe 116.

[42] L'arbitrage Erythrée-Yémen, Sentence de 1999, paragraphe 130.

formule générale l'habilitait à faire également application, dans la deuxième étape, des règles coutumières du droit de la mer.

Quant à la mention, dans le texte du compromis, de " tout autre élément pertinent", elle n'était pas d'une clarté évidente. Le Tribunal a paru éprouver une certaine gêne lorsqu'il a cherché à cerner le sens et la portée de cette expression. Il en a fait, par certains côtés, un synonyme de l'expression "circonstances pertinentes", mais en utilisant le mot "facteurs" pour désigner ces dernières, comme l'avait fait avant lui le Tribunal arbitral pour la *Délimitation de la frontière maritime Guinée/Guinée-Bissau* dans sa sentence du 14 février 1985.[43] On peut sans doute regretter qu'il n'ait pas saisi cette occasion pour tenter d'apporter un peu plus d'ordre et de rigueur dans l'emploi de termes ou d'expressions qui demeurent encore marqués par le caractère assez primitif et quelquefois sommaire du droit applicable aux délimitations maritimes. Il s'est donc contenté de noter que l'expression en cause "représente un concept très large et englobe sans nul doute divers facteurs dont il est généralement reconnu qu'ils influent sur l'opération de délimitation comme la proportionnalité, le principe de non-empiétement, la présence d'îles, et tout autre facteur de nature à affecter la recherche d'une solution équitable eu égard à la situation particulière".[44] Par là, il a donné l'impression que la notion en cause était une sorte de fourre-tout.

Si l'on peut ainsi formuler quelques regrets devant certains aspects de la sentence relative à la délimitation maritime, c'est en grande partie parce que le Tribunal aurait pu tiré davantage parti du fait que sa tâche était ici plus aisée que dans la première étape. Il s'en est acquitté en suivant scrupuleusement les prescriptions du compromis. Il convient toutefois de lui rendre aussi cette justice qu'il a apporté çà et là quelques précisions qui représentent une contribution non négligeable au développement du droit de la délimitation maritime.

Ainsi, le Tribunal a-t-il souligné qu'étant invité à délimiter des "frontières maritimes", il convenait de prendre le mot "frontière" dans son sens normal et ordinaire de frontière internationale entre les deux Etats parties à l'arbitrage. Il a fort opportunément saisi cette occasion pour bien marquer la différence entre une frontière maritime ainsi entendue et ce qu'on nomme habituellement une "limite" maritime, expression par laquelle on désigne généralement la limite extérieure d'un espace maritime national, comme la limite extérieure des eaux territoriales. Et il a tenu en outre à rappeler que, si la limite extérieure d'une zone maritime nationale pouvait par endroits coïncider avec la frontière maritime internationale, elle pouvait aussi se trouver modifiée par l'établissement de celle-ci.[45]

---

[43] Voir notamment le paragraphe 89 de la sentence. Texte dans 89(2) REVUE GÉNÉRALE DE DROIT INTERNATIONAL PUBLIC 484-537 (1985).

[44] L'arbitrage Erythrée-Yémen, Sentence de 1999, paragraphe 130.

[45] L'arbitrage Erythrée-Yémen, Sentence de 1999, paragraphe 129.

La précision ainsi apportée prend toute sa valeur si on la rapporte à certains prononcés de la Cour internationale de Justice concernant les expressions "frontière maritime" et "*maritime boundary*". Il suffit de rappeler que, dans l'affaire de la *Délimitation de la frontière maritime dans la région du golfe du Maine*, la Cour avait noté que les termes "frontière maritime" pouvaient paraître inadaptés en l'espèce, dans la mesure où ils "pourraient évoquer l'idée erronée d'une véritable frontière entre deux souverainetés", alors qu'était exclusivement en cause une délimitation entre des zones soumises à différentes formes de juridiction partielle.[46] Plus récemment, dans l'affaire de la *Délimitation maritime et des questions territoriales entre Qatar et Bahreïn*, la Cour a constamment usé de l'expression "limite maritime unique" dans le texte français faisant foi de son arrêt, là où la version anglaise utilise la formule "*single maritime boundary*"; de plus, faisant valoir que "le concept de "ligne maritime unique" peut revêtir plusieurs fonctions", elle a considéré qu'en l'espèce "la limite maritime unique procédera de la délimitation de diverses juridictions".[47]

Le Tribunal a, par ailleurs, repris et appliqué les principes et préceptes les mieux établis en matière de délimitation maritime, à savoir:

– la norme fondamentale du résultat équitable à laquelle est subordonnée toute opération de délimitation;[48]

– le principe selon lequel "entre des côtes se faisant face, c'est par une ligne médiane ou d'équidistance que s'obtient . . . une frontière équitable";[49]

– la règle en vertu de laquelle "cette ligne médiane devrait, dans toute la mesure du possible, être construite par rapport aux côtes continentales se faisant face";[50]

– la règle selon laquelle la côte à retenir pour la construction de la ligne médiane est celle qui est déterminée par la laisse de basse mer telle qu'elle figure sur les cartes marines officiellement reconnues par les Etats en litige;[51]

---

[46] Arrêt du 12 octobre 1984, C.I.J. Recueil 1984, p. 265, paragraphe 19.

[47] Arrêt du 16 mars 2001, C.I.J. Recueil 2001, paragraphe 169. La sentence Erythrée-Yémen reprend cette même idée en indiquant également que "la frontière internationale sera une frontière unique aussi valable à d'autres fins", l'arbitrage Erythrée-Yémen, Sentence de 1999, paragraphe 132.

[48] L'arbitrage Erythrée-Yémen, Sentence de 1999, paragraphes 116-117.

[49] L'arbitrage Erythrée-Yémen, Sentence de 1999, paragraphe 131.

[50] L'arbitrage Erythrée-Yémen, Sentence de 1999, paragraphe 132.

[51] L'arbitrage Erythrée-Yémen, Sentence de 1999, paragraphes 133 et 135.

- la nécessité de déterminer si et dans quelle mesure un effet peut ou doit être accordé aux îles situées dans la zone à délimiter, compte tenu de leur taille, de leur importance et d'autres aspects du contexte géographique général;[52]

- le principe de non-empiètement qui vise à éviter l'exercice, à proximité immédiate de la côte d'un des Etats, de droits qui mettraient en danger sa sécurité;[53]

- l'obligation de tracer la ligne de délimitation en évitant des zones où un Etat tiers pourrait faire valoir des revendications;[54]

- l'exigence de simplicité du tracé de la frontière internationale au voisinage immédiat d'une grande route maritime;[55]

- le principe de proportionnalité en tant que "test visant à apprécier le caractère équitable d'une délimitation", de façon à éviter toute disproportion dans le rapport entre les longueurs des côtes des deux Etats et le rapport entre les superficies des zones maritimes revenant à chacun d'eux.[56]

Sur ces différents points, le Tribunal s'est placé dans le droit fil d'une jurisprudence qui est désormais bien établie, même si subsistent encore certaines zones d'ombre qui nuisent parfois à la prévisibilité de la solution équitable que les Etats attendent du juge ou de l'arbitre international.

*

Au total, le travail accompli par le Tribunal entre l'Erythrée et le Yémen a été assez remarquable, non seulement pour les raisons exposées ci-dessus, mais aussi parce que, comme le montrent les deux sentences arbitrales reproduites ci-après, il s'est efforcé de remplir un rôle pédagogique auprès des deux Etats en prenant grand soin d'analyser scrupuleusement les thèses défendues par chacun d'eux et d'exposer franchement les motifs pour lesquels il estimait devoir les retenir ou, au contraire, les écarter. Le souci qu'il a manifesté d'être aussi explicatif que possible a incontestablement été couronné de succès.

---

52 L'arbitrage Erythrée-Yémen, Sentence de 1999, paragraphes 117 et 147. Eu égard au nombre relativement important d'îles et d'îlots existant dans la région, il est significatif que le Tribunal ait tenu à rappeler que "toute île, aussi petite soit-elle, y compris un rocher à condition que ce soit bien une île émergée à marée haute, est génératrice d'une mer territoriale pouvant atteindre 12 milles marins de large" (paragraphe 155).

53 L'arbitrage Erythrée-Yémen, Sentence de 1999, paragraphe 157.

54 L'arbitrage Erythrée-Yémen, Sentence de 1999, paragraphes 136 et 164.

55 L'arbitrage Erythrée-Yémen, Sentence de 1999, paragraphe 128.

56 L'arbitrage Erythrée-Yémen, Sentence de 1999, paragraphes 165-168.

ARBITRAGE FONDÉ
SUR UN COMPROMIS D'ARBITRAGE
EN DATE DU 3 OCTOBRE 1996

E N T R E :

LE GOUVERNEMENT DE L'ETAT D'ERYTHRÉE

-et-

LE GOUVERNEMENT DE LA RÉPUBLIQUE DU YÉMEN

SENTENCE RENDUE PAR LE TRIBUNAL ARBITRAL DANS LA PREMIÈRE ÉTAPE DE LA PROCÉDURE (SOUVERAINETÉ TERRITORIALE ET CHAMP DU DIFFÉREND)

Le Tribunal arbitral:

M. le Professeur Sir Robert Y. Jennings, Président
M. le Juge Stephen M. Schwebel
M. Ahmed Sadek El-Kosheri
M. Keith Highet
Mme le Juge Rosalyn Higgins

Représentants du Gouvernement de l'Etat d'Erythrée:

Son Excellence Haile Weldensae, agent
Mme le Professeur Lea Brilmayer et M. Gary B. Born, co-agents
M. le Professeur Gregory Fox, M. John Trenor et Mme Chiara Georgetti, conseils

Représentants du Gouvernement de la République du Yémen:

Son Excellence M. Abdulkarim Al-Eryani, agent
Son Excellence M. Abdullah Ahmad Ghanim, M. Hussein Al-Hubaishi,
M. Abdulwahid Al-Zandani et M. Rodman R. Bundy, co-agents
M. Ian Brownlie, Q.C., M. B. Donovan Picard, Mme Loretta Malintoppi et
M. Paul Luther, conseils

ARBITRAGE ERYTHRÉE-YÉMEN
PREMIÈRE ÉTAPE: SOUVERAINETÉ TERRITORIALE ET CHAMP DU DIFFÉREND

SENTENCE

TABLE DES MATIÈRES

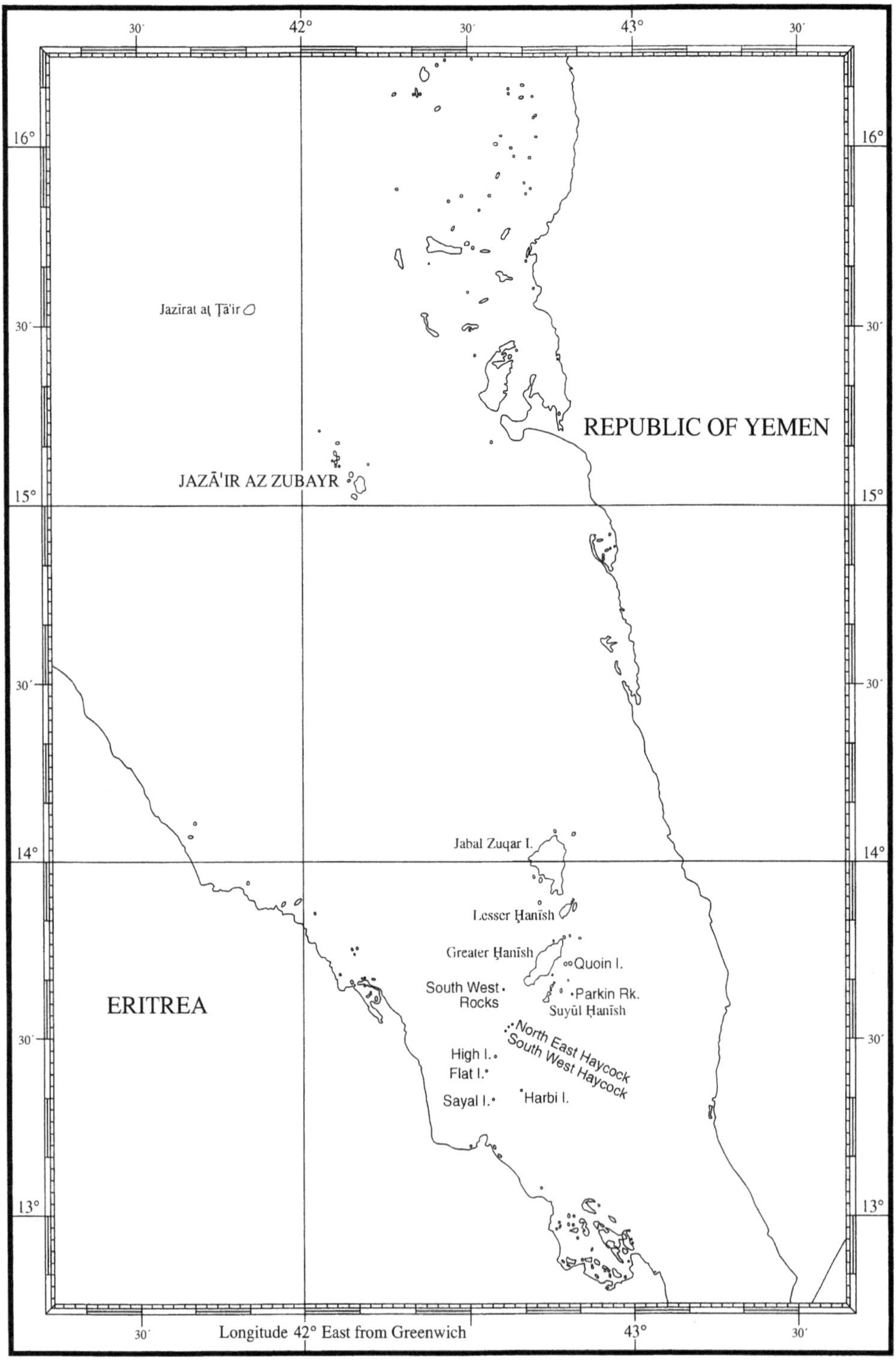
30´
42°
30´
43°
30´
16°
16°
Jazīrat aṭ Ṭā'ir
30´
30´
REPUBLIC OF YEMEN
JAZĀ'IR AZ ZUBAYR
15°
15°
30´
30´
Jabal Zuqar I.
14°
14°
Lesser Ḥanīsh
Greater Ḥanīsh
Quoin I.
South West Rocks
Parkin Rk.
Suyūl Ḥanīsh
ERITREA
30´
30´
North East Haycock
South West Haycock
High I.
Flat I.
Sayal I.
Harbi I.
13°
13°
30´
Longitude 42° East from Greenwich
43°
30´

ARBITRAGE FONDÉ SUR UN COMPROMIS D'ARBITRAGE EN DATE DU 3 OCTOBRE 1996

E N T R E :

LE GOUVERNEMENT DE L'ÉTAT D'ERYTHRÉE

-et-

LE GOUVERNEMENT DE LA RÉPUBLIQUE DU YÉMEN

SENTENCE RENDUE PAR LE TRIBUNAL ARBITRAL DANS LA PREMIÈRE ÉTAPE DE LA PROCÉDURE (SOUVERAINETÉ TERRITORIALE ET CHAMP DU DIFFÉREND)

CHAPITRE PREMIER – Organisation de l'arbitrage et argumention des Parties

Introduction

1. La présente sentence est rendue en vertu d'un compromis d'arbitrage en date du 3 octobre 1996 (le "Compromis d'arbitrage") conclu entre le Gouvernement de l'Etat d'Erythrée ("l'Erythrée") et le Gouvernement de la République du Yémen (le "Yémen") (ci-après dénommés "les Parties").

2. Le Compromis d'arbitrage a été précédé par la conclusion à Paris, le 21 mai 1996, d'un "Accord sur les principes" signé par l'Erythrée et le Yémen ainsi que par le Gouvernement de la République française, la République fédérale démocratique d'Ethiopie et la République arabe d'Egypte en qualité de témoins. Les Parties renonçaient à recourir à la force l'une contre l'autre et décidaient de "régler pacifiquement leur différend sur des questions de souveraineté territoriale et de délimitation des frontières maritimes." Elles ont à cette fin décidé d'établir un compromis portant constitution d'un tribunal arbitral. L'Accord sur les principes dispose en outre que

> . . . en ce qui concerne les questions de souveraineté territoriale, le tribunal statue conformément aux principes, aux règles et aux pratiques du droit international applicables en la matière, ainsi que sur la base notamment des titres historiques.

3. En même temps que cet Accord sur les principes, les Parties ont publié une brève déclaration commune pour manifester leur volonté de régler leur différend et de "favoriser le rétablissement et le développement d'une coopération fiable et durable entre les deux pays" qui puisse concourir à la stabilité et à la paix dans la région.

4. Conformément au paragraphe 1 de l'article premier du Compromis d'arbitrage, l'Erythrée a désigné comme arbitres M. le juge Stephen M. Schwebel et Mme le juge Rosalyn Higgins et le Yémen a de son côté désigné M. Ahmed Sadek El-Kosheri et M. Keith Highet. Par échange de lettres datées des 30 et 31 décembre 1996, les Parties ont convenu de recommander la désignation de sir Robert Y. Jennings à la présidence du Tribunal arbitral (ci-après le "Tribunal"). Les quatre arbitres se sont réunis à Londres le 14 janvier 1997 et ont nommé sir Robert Y. Jennings président du Tribunal.

5. Ainsi dûment constitué, le Tribunal a tenu sa première séance le 14 janvier 1997 à Essex Court Chambers, 24 Lincoln's Inn Fields, Londres WC1, Royaume-Uni. Le Tribunal a pris note de cette réunion des quatre arbitres et il a ratifié et approuvé les mesures autorisées et adoptées à ladite séance. Conformément au paragraphe 2 de l'article 7 du Compromis d'arbitrage, le Tribunal a désigné comme greffier M. P.J.H. Jonkman, secrétaire général de la Cour permanente d'arbitrage (la "CPA") à La Haye, a désigné comme secrétaire du Tribunal Mme Bette E. Shifman, premier secrétaire de la CPA et désigné pour greffe du Tribunal le Bureau international de la CPA.

6. Le Tribunal s'est ensuite réuni avec M. Gary Born, co-agent de l'Erythrée et M. Rodman Bundy, co-agent du Yémen, pour les informer de la constitution du Tribunal et s'entretenir avec eux de certaines questions concrètes intéressant la procédure d'arbitrage.

7. L'article 2 du Compromis d'arbitrage dispose:

> 1. Il est demandé au Tribunal de se prononcer conformément au droit international en deux étapes.
>
> 2. La première étape donne lieu à une sentence sur la souveraineté territoriale et la définition du champ du différend entre l'Erythrée et le Yémen. Le Tribunal statue sur la question de la souveraineté territoriale conformément aux principes, aux règles et aux pratiques du droit international applicables en la matière et sur la base notamment des titres historiques. Le Tribunal statue sur la définition du champ du différend sur la base des positions respectives des deux Parties.

3. La seconde étape donne lieu à une sentence sur la délimitation des frontières maritimes. Le Tribunal statue en prenant en compte l'opinion qu'il se sera faite sur les questions de souveraineté territoriale, la Convention des Nations Unies sur le droit de la mer et tout autre élément pertinent.

8. Conformément au calendrier indiqué dans le Compromis d'arbitrage pour les diverses phases de la procédure, les Parties ont soumis simultanément le 1er septembre 1997 leurs mémoires écrits concernant la souveraineté territoriale et le champ du différend et ont présenté le 1er décembre 1997 leur contre-mémoire. Conformément à la prescription énoncée au paragraphe 1 de l'article 7 du Compromis d'arbitrage, "le Tribunal siège à Londres", la procédure orale relative à la première étape de l'arbitrage s'est déroulée à Londres, dans la salle de conférences Durbar du Foreign and Commonwealth Office, du 26 janvier au 6 février 1998 compris, dans les délais fixés pour la procédure orale dans le Compromis d'arbitrage. L'ordre de présentation des exposés des Parties a été tiré au sort et l'Erythrée a été la première à s'exprimer.

9. A la fin de sa séance du 6 février 1998, conformément au paragraphe 3 de l'article 8 du Compromis d'arbitrage, le Tribunal a prononcé la clôture de la phase orale de la première étape de l'arbitrage Erythrée/Yémen. La clôture était subordonnée à l'engagement pris par les deux Parties de répondre par écrit le 23 février 1998 au plus tard à certaines questions posées par le Tribunal à la fin des audiences, notamment à une question sur l'existence d'accords de prospection et d'exploitation pétrolières. La clôture était également subordonnée à la disposition du paragraphe 3 de l'article 8 du Compromis d'arbitrage autorisant le Tribunal à demander aux Parties leur avis écrit sur toute question nécessaire pour lui permettre d'élucider un aspect quelconque de l'affaire.

10. Dans sa communication et ordonnance n° 3 du 10 mai 1998, le Tribunal a invoqué précisément cette disposition pour demander aux Parties de lui présenter le 8 juin 1998 au plus tard des observations écrites sur les considérations juridiques soulevées par leurs réponses aux précédentes questions du Tribunal concernant d'éventuelles concessions de prospection et exploitation pétrolières et en particulier sur la question de savoir si les accords pétroliers conclus et les activités pétrolières autorisées par les Parties pouvaient jouer un rôle aux fins de la sentence sur la souveraineté territoriale. Le Tribunal a en outre invité les Parties à accepter qu'une brève procédure orale soit consacrée à ces questions.

11. A la suite de l'échange des observations écrites des Parties, le Tribunal a tenu audience sur ces questions à Londres, au Foreign and Commonwealth Office, les 6, 7 et 8 juillet 1998. Les Parties avaient convenu que le Yémen s'exprimerait en premier. Au cours de ces audiences, le Tribunal a posé une série de questions sur l'interprétation à donner aux indications fournies sur les concessions pétrolières et les Parties ont été priées d'y répondre par écrit dans les sept jours suivant la fin des audiences. Le 17 juillet 1998, les deux Parties ont présenté par écrit leurs

réponses aux questions du Tribunal. L'Erythrée a fait savoir à ce moment-là qu'elle soumettrait avec un léger retard l'appendice documentaire destiné à accompagner ses réponses; cet appendice documentaire est parvenu le 22 juillet 1998 au Bureau international de la CPA. Le 30 juillet 1998, le Bureau international a reçu du Yémen un exposé intitulé "Yemen's Comments on the Documents Introduced by Eritrea after the Final Oral Argument" ["Observations du Yémen sur les documents présentés par l'Erythrée après les derniers exposés oraux"]. L'Erythrée a formulé des objections au sujet de ce dépôt tardif par le Yémen.

12. Au cours des audiences supplémentaires de juillet 1998, le Tribunal a fait savoir aux Parties qu'il avait l'intention de prendre contact avec le secrétaire général de la Ligue arabe pour savoir s'il existait des rapports officiels de la Ligue arabe sur d'éventuelles visites à l'une ou l'autre des îles en litige, notamment dans les années 1970, et pour en obtenir éventuellement copie. Une lettre a été adressée à cet effet le 20 juillet par télécopie au nom du Tribunal au secrétaire général de la Ligue arabe. La réponse de ce dernier en date du 28 juillet a été communiquée par le greffe aux co-agents et aux membres du Tribunal.

* - *

Les arguments des Parties sur la souveraineté territoriale

13. L'Erythrée revendique la souveraineté territoriale sur les "îles de la mer Rouge" (ci-après dénommées les "îles")[1] en se fondant sur une "chaîne du titre" longue de plus d'un siècle et sur les principes du droit international de l'"occupation effective". L'Erythrée affirme avoir hérité de son titre sur les îles en 1993, date à laquelle l'Etat d'Erythrée est devenu légalement indépendant de l'Etat d'Ethiopie. L'Ethiopie quant à elle tenait son titre de l'Italie, malgré une période d'occupation militaire britannique de l'ensemble de l'Erythrée au cours de la seconde guerre mondiale. Le titre italien serait passé alors à l'Etat d'Ethiopie en 1952-53, à la suite de la fédération de l'Erythrée avec l'Ethiopie, puis de l'annexion de l'Erythrée par l'Ethiopie.

14. L'Erythrée fait remonter cette chaîne du titre aux périodes historiques pertinentes, en commençant par la colonisation du territoire continental érythréen par l'Italie au cours de la seconde partie du 19ème siècle. Les Parties admettent toutes deux qu'avant cette colonisation italienne, l'Empire ottoman était le souverain

---

[1] L'identification des îles ou groupes d'îles en litige entre les Parties a été confiée au Tribunal par les dispositions de l'article 2 du Compromis d'arbitrage (voir paragraphe 7 ci-dessus), et il est procédé à cette identification dans la partie de la présente sentence qui porte sur la définition du champ du différend. La formule "les îles" dans la présente sentence vise les îles qui, pour le Tribunal, font l'objet de revendications opposées de la part des Parties. La région géographique dans laquelle lesdites îles sont situées est indiquée sur la carte figurant à la page 282.

incontesté qui régnait sur les deux côtes de la mer Rouge et sur les îles. En contournant les Ottomans et en traitant directement avec les chefs locaux, l'Italie mit en place des avant-postes pour faire triompher ses intérêts maritimes, coloniaux et commerciaux. En dépit des objections ottomanes, l'Italie s'est officiellement adjugé la colonie d'Erythrée en 1890. L'Erythrée soutient qu'en 1892 la Grande-Bretagne a reconnu à l'Italie un titre sur les îles Mohabbakah, c'est-à-dire un groupe d'îles situées à proximité de la côte érythréenne.

15. L'Erythrée affirme que, sans contester la souveraineté ottomane, l'Italie était également à la même époque activement présente sur d'autres îles du sud de la mer Rouge. Les navires italiens patrouillaient les eaux avoisinantes à la recherche de pirates, de marchands d'esclaves, de marchands d'armes de contrebande et l'administration coloniale aurait délivré des concessions d'exploitation commerciale sur les îles. D'après l'Erythrée, le Yémen ne revendiquait pas les îles à l'époque et n'y était pas présent non plus qu'aux alentours. L'imam Yahya, qui a finalement fondé le Yémen moderne, occupait en hauteur une région connue sous le nom de *Gebel* et, d'après l'Erythrée, reconnaissait ouvertement qu'il n'exerçait pas la souveraineté sur les basses terres côtières connues sous le nom de la *Tihama*. Cet arrangement territorial fut confirmé par le "traité de Da'an" de 1911, qui est une entente entre l'imam et l'Empire ottoman.

16. L'Erythrée dit que c'est l'affaiblissement de l'Empire ottoman au cours des années précédant immédiatement la première guerre mondiale qui a fortement incité à l'Italie à nourrir le projet d'occuper un groupe d'îles connues sous le nom des "îles Zuqar-Hanish". Ce projet a été déjoué par une brève période d'occupation militaire britannique en 1915, qui fut éphémère et, à en croire l'Erythrée, dépourvue de toutes conséquences juridiques. A la fin de la guerre, l'Italie aurait repris et développé ses activités commerciales et son contrôle en ce qui concerne ce que l'Erythrée appelle "les îles Zuqar-Hanish et les îles portant des phares". L'Erythrée cite ces activités parce qu'elles témoignent d'après elle de l'intention de l'Italie d'acquérir la souveraineté sur les îles.

17. La question de la souveraineté sur les îles a fait partie du processus de paix consécutif à la première guerre mondiale qui a abouti à la signature du traité de Lausanne en 1923. Si une partie de l'ancien territoire de l'Empire ottoman vaincu fut alors partagée entre des chefs locaux qui avaient apporté leur soutien aux alliés victorieux, l'Erythrée dit qu'aucun des dirigeants de la péninsule arabique qui avaient ainsi soutenu les alliés ne se trouvait suffisamment proche géographiquement des îles pour pouvoir être valablement considéré comme un détenteur de cette souveraineté. L'imam de Sanaa ne pouvait pas être considéré comme un possible détenteur pour deux raisons: il était allié aux Turcs ottomans et sa souveraineté ne s'étendait pas à la côte de la mer Rouge. L'Erythrée rappelle que la Grande-Bretagne a rejeté des revendications formulées par l'imam en 1917-1918 sur certaines parties de la région de la Tihama et dit aussi que, si l'imam signale que ces territoires avaient été "sous la domination de ses

prédécesseurs", cela veut dire que l'imam reconnaissait qu'à l'époque la possession et le contrôle de ces territoires lui échappaient.

18. L'Erythrée rappelle que la Grande-Bretagne n'est pas parvenue à convaincre les autres alliés de transférer les îles à des chefs arabes choisis par la Grande-Bretagne ou à la Grande-Bretagne elle-même et fait remonter cet échec au traité de Sèvres de 1920 qui ne sera pas ratifié et aux négociations aboutissant à la conclusion du traité de Lausanne en 1923. L'Erythrée impute aux articles 6 et 16 du traité de Lausanne l'ouverture des îles à l'occupation italienne. L'article 6 définit la règle générale qui, selon les termes mêmes du traité, est que "les frontières maritimes comprennent les îles et les îlots situés à moins de trois milles de la côte". L'Erythrée interprète cette disposition ainsi que la pratique ultérieure des Etats se conformant au traité de Lausanne comme soustrayant les îles en question à la souveraineté de *tous* les dirigeants de la péninsule arabique parce qu'aucune de ces îles n'est située à moins de trois milles de la côte arabique. L'Erythrée soutient en outre que l'article 6 a interdit d'attribuer les îles en litige à l'imam parce que le royaume de celui-ci n'était ni un "Etat" ni un territoire "côtier" à l'époque où le traité de Lausanne était signé.*

19. En vertu de l'article 16 du traité de Lausanne, la Turquie renonce expressément à tous droits et titres sur des territoires et des îles précédemment ottomans et il était prescrit que le sort de ces territoires et îles était à "régler par les intéressés". Pour l'Erythrée, puisque l'article 16 ne transférait les îles à aucun Etat particulier et ne prévoyait aucune procédure particulière pour transférer la propriété de ces îles, leur sort relevait en définitive des règles du droit international général de l'acquisition territoriale: la conquête, l'occupation effective et la situation géographique de l'île à l'intérieur de la mer territoriale. L'Erythrée prétend que sa thèse est confortée par la pratique ultérieure des Etats interprétant ledit article 16.

20. L'Erythrée affirme qu'à la fin des années 20, l'Italie avait acquis la souveraineté sur les îles en litige au moyen de l'occupation effective et que ni les entretiens de 1927 entre la Grande-Bretagne et l'Italie auxquels il a finalement été donné le nom de "conversations de Rome", ni la convention avortée de 1929 sur l'entretien des phares ne fournissent d'indications en sens contraire. Cette occupation effective a consisté notamment à construire en 1929 un phare sur l'île South West Haycock, ce qui, prétend l'Erythrée, a conduit la Grande-Bretagne à reconnaître à nouveau la souveraineté italienne sur les îles Mohabbakah, comme elle l'avait fait précédemment en 1892 et en 1917. L'Erythrée trouve un autre argument en faveur de cette occupation effective italienne pendant ladite période dans le fait qu'une expédition a été organisée sur les îles Zuqar-Hanish et qu'elles

* *NdT: Dans sa version anglaise, l'article 6 du Traité de Lausanne dispose littéralement: "Les frontières maritimes [de l'Etat côtier] comprennent les îles et les îlots situés à moins de trois milles de la côte."*

ont été ensuite occupées par des troupes italiennes. L'Erythrée affirme que pendant la période écoulée entre 1930 et 1940, l'Italie a exercé des droits souverains sur les îles par le truchement de son administration coloniale en Erythrée. A ce sujet, l'Erythrée cite notamment l'octroi de permis de pêche dans les eaux avoisinantes, l'octroi d'un permis de construction d'une conserverie de poisson sur la Grande Hanish ainsi que la remise en état et l'entretien d'un phare britannique abandonné sur l'île Centre Peak. Aux yeux de l'Erythrée, il s'agit là d'éléments constitutifs d'une occupation effective, le *corpus occupandi* de l'occupation effective et, ces éléments étant dûment accompagnés de la volonté d'exercer la souveraineté (*animus occupandi*), ils portent acquisition de la souveraineté par occupation effective.

21. L'Erythrée affirme en outre que le Yémen n'a pas protesté pendant cette époque contre les activités menées par l'Italie sur les îles et ne les a pas non plus mises en question. La Grande-Bretagne, toutefois, a voulu avoir l'assurance que ces activités de l'Italie ne constituaient pas une revendication de souveraineté. L'Italie a répondu que la question de la souveraineté était "en suspens" ou "en réserve" et l'Erythrée qualifie ces réponses de refus de donner des assurances dans le sens demandé. D'après l'Erythrée, cette formule a été interprétée tant par l'Italie que par la Grande-Bretagne comme préservant les droits de l'Italie tout en permettant à la Grande-Bretagne de s'abstenir de reconnaître diplomatiquement lesdits droits. Les tensions entre les deux Etats sur cette question parmi d'autres ont abouti à la conclusion de l'accord anglo-italien de 1938 qui, prétend l'Erythrée, donne la preuve de ce qu'étaient les vues italiennes et britanniques à l'époque. Cet accord montrerait notamment que, pour les parties signataires, les îles ne relevaient pas de la péninsule arabique et que l'Italie et la Grande-Bretagne étaient les deux seules puissances exerçant sur ces îles un intérêt valable du point de vue juridictionnel.

22. Cet accord anglo-italien de 1938 comprenait aussi un engagement exprès tant de l'Italie que de la Grande-Bretagne relatif aux anciennes îles ottomanes de la mer Rouge, selon lequel ni l'une ni l'autre n'"établirait sa souveraineté" sur lesdites îles ou y "érigerait des fortifications ou des moyens de défense". Selon l'Erythrée, cela ne revenait pas à renoncer à des droits existants, il s'agissait simplement d'un pacte concernant la conduite à adopter à l'avenir. L'Erythrée dit qu'à l'époque où a été signé cet accord anglo-italien, la souveraineté italienne sur les îles avait déjà été établie en droit et cet accord ne lui portait nullement atteinte. L'Erythrée affirme en outre qu'en décembre 1938, l'Italie a officiellement confirmé la souveraineté territoriale qu'elle exerçait sur les îles en promulguant un décret, portant le n° 1446 de 1938, confirmant très précisément que les îles avaient fait partie et faisaient toujours partie du territoire du *Commissariato* érythréen de Dankalia.

23. De l'occupation britannique de l'Erythrée qui a commencé en 1941 dans le sillage de la seconde guerre mondiale et va durer onze ans, l'Erythrée dit qu'elle

était conforme au droit de l'occupation en temps de guerre. Les frontières territoriales de l'Erythrée sont demeurées inchangées et le territoire de "toutes les colonies et dépendances italiennes" livré aux alliés lors de l'armistice de 1943, de l'avis de l'Erythrée, "comprenait incontestablement" les îles. Le traité de paix de 1947 prévoyait la liquidation des territoires africains de l'Italie par les puissances alliées, laquelle fut accomplie en 1952 par le transfert à l'Ethiopie, avec laquelle l'Erythrée était alors fédérée, de "toutes les anciennes possessions territoriales italiennes en Erythrée". Pour l'Erythrée, c'est alors que fut transmis à l'Ethiopie le titre de souveraineté sur les îles.

24. L'Erythrée dit aussi que l'historique de la rédaction de la Constitution érythréenne de 1952 confirme que les îles en litige entrent dans la définition du territoire érythréen. C'est là, d'après l'Erythrée, la seule interprétation plausible de la formule "Le territoire continental et insulaire de l'Erythrée" qui figure dans la définition du territoire de l'Erythrée et cette interprétation serait étayée par les avis donnés à l'Ethiopie à l'époque par son conseiller juridique, John Spencer. L'Erythrée soutient que cette interprétation est étayée en outre par la présence de la même formule dans des dispositions constitutionnelles et législatives ultérieures, en particulier le décret impérial de 1952 qui fédère l'Erythrée à l'Empire éthiopien et la Constitution éthiopienne de 1955.

25. L'Erythrée fonde également la souveraineté éthiopienne sur la situation des îles à l'intérieur de la mer territoriale éthiopienne. L'Erythrée s'appuie sur la règle du droit international coutumier et conventionnel suivant laquelle chaque île a droit à sa propre mer territoriale, mesurée conformément aux mêmes principes que ceux qui s'appliquent au territoire continental. De l'avis de l'Erythrée, une série d'îles qui se rattachent au territoire continental quand elles n'en sont pas distantes de plus de 12 milles relève intégralement de la mer territoriale de l'Etat côtier et par conséquent de sa souveraineté territoriale. Dans ces conditions, quand l'Ethiopie déclare officiellement en 1953 qu'elle est dotée d'une mer territoriale de 12 milles mesurée à partir des îles Mohabbakah dont l'Erythrée affirme qu'elles étaient incontestablement éthiopiennes, cette mer territoriale éthiopienne englobait les îles Zuqar-Hanish.

26. Pendant les 35 ans qui s'écoulent entre 1953 et l'indépendance de l'Erythrée en 1991, l'Ethiopie exerce très largement, aux dires de l'Erythrée, sa souveraineté sur les îles. Cet exercice aurait été notamment marqué par des patrouilles navales constantes, ne rencontrant aucune opposition, qui seraient devenues de plus en plus systématiques à mesure que le mouvement de libération de l'Erythrée acquérait de plus en plus de vigueur. En outre, à la suite du transfert en 1967 de la gestion des phares à Asmara par le Board of Trade, le ministère britannique du commerce et de l'industrie, l'Ethiopie aurait affermi davantage encore sa souveraineté en imposant aux travailleurs étrangers en poste sur les îles portant des phares de se munir d'un passeport et de documents analogues, en surveillant et réglementant l'expédition de toutes fournitures à destination de ces mêmes îles,

en intervenant dans l'adoption de toutes décisions relatives à l'emploi des travailleurs affectés aux phares, en autorisant toutes les missions d'inspection et de réparation dans les îles portant des phares et en exerçant un contrôle étroit sur les transmissions radio à destination et en provenance de ces îles. L'Erythrée a saisi le Tribunal d'autres manifestations alléguées de la souveraineté de l'Ethiopie, notamment de l'exercice de la compétence pénale sur des actes commis sur les îles, de la réglementation de la prospection pétrolière sur les îles et aux alentours, et d'une inspection opérée à l'époque par le président Mengistu et un groupe de hauts responsables éthiopiens de l'armée et de la marine à la fin des années 80, inspection dont l'Erythrée a versé au dossier un compte rendu vidéo.

27. L'Erythrée prétend que pendant toutes les années 70, les deux Etats yéménites et leurs alliés de la région ont reconnu dans leurs déclarations et dans leurs actions que l'Ethiopie exerçait son contrôle sur les îles. L'Erythrée allègue que jusqu'au début des années 70, ni le Yémen du Nord ni le Yémen du Sud n'avaient manifesté le moindre intérêt pour les îles. L'intérêt de la région à leur endroit aurait été éveillé par la diffusion de fausses nouvelles sur une présence israélienne dans les îles en 1973. D'après l'Erythrée, en présumant que l'Ethiopie avait loué les îles à Israël, le Yémen, les Etats limitrophes et les médias arabes reconnaissaient la souveraineté de l'Ethiopie sur lesdites îles. A l'appui de ces dires, l'Erythrée prétend que les Etats arabes non seulement ont condamné l'Ethiopie pour avoir mis des îles éthiopiennes à la disposition d'Israël, mais encore se sont finalement adressés à l'Ethiopie pour être autorisés à se rendre dans les îles afin d'enquêter sur les activités militaires israéliennes ainsi alléguées.

28. L'Erythrée soutient que les dernières années précédant immédiatement son indépendance ont été marquées par l'exercice d'une surveillance aérienne et de constantes patrouilles navales assurées par les forces éthiopiennes.

29. L'Erythrée dit qu'après avoir accédé à l'indépendance en 1991 elle a acquis le titre de souveraineté sur les îles et a exercé sur celles-ci son autorité souveraine. L'Erythrée affirme que, comme il en fut pour eux pendant toute l'histoire récente, les pêcheurs érythréens tirent des îles leurs moyens d'existence. La réglementation administrative de l'Erythrée contrôlerait très strictement la pêche autour des îles, prescrivant notamment l'octroi de permis pour tous ceux qui veulent pêcher dans les eaux avoisinantes. L'Erythrée soutient en outre que sa marine contrôle les bateaux de pêche étrangers dans les eaux territoriales érythréennes et organise des patrouilles régulières autour des îles pour assurer l'application de la réglementation de la pêche, et elle procède à la capture des bateaux de pêche en infraction. L'Erythrée dit que le Yémen n'assurait aucune présence officielle sur les îles et que ce n'est qu'en 1995 que des patrouilles navales érythréennes ont découvert sur la Grande Hanish un petit contingent civil et militaire yéménite prétendument occupé à installer une station touristique. D'où, en décembre 1995,

des hostilités qui ont pris fin avec l'occupation de la Grande Hanish par les forces érythréennes et l'occupation de Zuqar par les forces yéménites.

30. En ce qui concerne la souveraineté territoriale, l'Erythrée demande au Tribunal de dire dans sa sentence que l'Erythrée exerce la souveraineté territoriale sur chacune et chacun des îles, rochers et hauts-fonds découvrants indiqués par l'Erythrée dans ses écritures "sur lesquels le Yémen revendique la souveraineté".

* - *

31. Le Yémen, quant à lui, fonde sa revendication sur les îles sur "un titre yéménite originel, historique ou traditionnel". Le Yémen insiste tout particulièrement sur la disposition énoncée au paragraphe 2 de l'article 2 du Compromis d'arbitrage aux termes de laquelle "[l]e Tribunal statue sur la question de la souveraineté territoriale conformément aux principes, aux règles et aux pratiques du droit international applicables en la matière et sur la base, notamment, des titres historiques." Il est possible d'après le Yémen de faire remonter ce titre au *Bilad el-Yemen*, c'est-à-dire le royaume du Yémen, qui aurait existé dès le sixième siècle de notre ère. A l'appui de cette revendication, le Yémen présente des éléments de preuve cartographiques,[2] des déclarations de l'imam du Yémen et invoque ce qu'il appelle l'"attitude adoptée par des Etats tiers pendant une longue période".

32. Le Yémen soutient que son intégration à l'Empire ottoman entre 1538 et 1635 environ, puis à nouveau entre 1872 et la défaite ottomane de 1918, ne l'a pas privé de son titre historique sur son propre territoire. Le Yémen affirme que la création du *vilayet* ottoman du Yémen sous la forme d'une unité territoriale et administrative distincte correspondait à la reconnaissance par les Ottomans de l'identité distincte du Yémen. Et le Yémen s'appuie sur les travaux de cartographes des 17e, 18e et 19e siècles qui auraient représenté le Yémen sous la forme d'une entité territoriale distincte et identifiable. D'autres éléments de preuve cartographiques sont présentés pour conforter cette thèse yéménite suivant laquelle les îles font partie dudit territoire.

33. Pour conforter davantage encore ses affirmations quand il prétend avoir toujours conservé son titre historique sur les îles, le Yémen fait l'historique du traité conclu en 1934 avec la Grande-Bretagne en citant plusieurs échanges de correspondance à l'occasion desquels l'imam a fait valoir sous une forme ou sous une autre ses droits sur les "îles du Yémen". Le Yémen rappelle que la Grande-

---

[2] L'Erythrée a, elle aussi, présenté des éléments de preuve cartographiques montrant que les îles sont éthiopiennes, érythréennes ou, de toute façon, non yéménites, mais elle accorde relativement peu de poids aux éléments de preuve de ce type. Pour l'Erythrée, les cartes n'apportent pas la preuve directe de la souveraineté ni d'une "chaîne du titre" et elle ne leur accorde par conséquent qu'un rôle limité dans la solution des différends de ce type.

Bretagne a rejeté la proposition par laquelle l'imam voulait joindre au traité un appendice confidentiel concernant les îles en motivant son refus par le fait que le sort des îles, en tant qu'anciennes possessions ottomanes, devait être réglé conformément à l'article 16 du traité de Lausanne.

34. Le Yémen plaide que ce refus ne revenait pas à récuser le titre yéménite traditionnel et présente des documents qui, d'après lui, permettent de dire que, pendant la période allant de 1933 à 1937, les milieux officiels britanniques hésitaient à contester le titre yéménite. Le Yémen soutient en outre que le traité de Lausanne n'a eu aucun effet sur le titre yéménite parce que le Yémen n'était pas partie au traité et parce que la renonciation par la Turquie à ses droits ne pouvait pas préjuger les intérêts de tierces parties. Le Yémen est d'avis que l'article 16 a eu pour effet non pas de faire des îles une terre sans maître mais plutôt d'en faire un territoire "sur lequel le titre était indéterminé." Le Yémen soutient en outre que l'article 16 a de toute façon cessé d'avoir effet entre "les intéressés" en raison de l'attitude qu'ils ont adoptée et de celle d'Etats tiers pour ce qui est de reconnaître la souveraineté du Yémen sur les îles ou de s'abstenir de formuler des réserves à ce sujet.

35. Pour affirmer que son titre originel s'étend aux îles, le Yémen tire également argument du "principe de l'unité naturelle ou géographique." Le Yémen soutient que ladite doctrine est un corollaire de la notion de titre traditionnel et qu'elle s'applique pour accompagner des preuves de l'exercice d'actes de juridiction ou des manifestations de la souveraineté étatique. Le Yémen cite la jurisprudence de la Cour internationale de Justice ainsi que des décisions arbitrales pour soutenir qu'une fois que la souveraineté sur une entité ou une unité naturelle dans son ensemble a été démontrée, elle peut être, en l'absence de tout élément de preuve en sens contraire, réputée s'étendre à l'intégralité de ladite entité ou unité. D'après le Yémen, il y a "concordance chez les experts quant au caractère d'entité ou d'unité naturelle que présentent les îles", comme en témoignent notamment les cartes de l'amirauté britannique, le *Red Sea and Gulf of Aden Pilot*, publié par le Bureau hydrographique du Royaume-Uni et l'*Encyclopedia Britannica.*

36. Le Yémen s'appuie sur diverses catégories de preuve de la souveraineté, qui, selon lui, peuvent servir à confirmer et compléter les preuves du titre traditionnel ou historique en même temps qu'elles constituent des sources indépendantes du titre. Il s'agit en particulier des liens économiques et sociaux entre les îles et le territoire continental du Yémen, de l'exercice de la souveraineté sous la forme d'actes de juridiction, de la reconnaissance du titre yéménite par des Etats tiers et de la confirmation du titre yéménite par des témoignages d'experts.

37. Le Yémen invoque la jurisprudence et certains commentaires pour soutenir que, dans le cadre géographique approprié, l'activité privée de particuliers fournit des preuves pertinentes du titre historique exercé sur un territoire. Le Yémen analyse

les faits et les activités en question en commençant avec les appellations "Hanish" et "Zuqar", qui, d'après lui, ont une racine arabe. Le Yémen note aussi la présence sur la côte yéménite d'habitants dont le nom est tiré du terme "Hanish" et dont l'histoire familiale qui est celle de pêcheurs est intimement liée à celle des îles. Le Yémen fait observer qu'au cours des troubles de 1995, deux membres d'une telle famille ont été faits prisonniers par les forces érythréennes alors qu'ils pêchaient à proximité de la Grande Hanish. Le Yémen fait également état de l'existence de mouillages et de colonies sur les îles portant des noms arabes manifestement yéménites. Le Yémen prétend que depuis des générations les pêcheurs yéménites sont pratiquement les seuls à exploiter les îles et, par opposition aux pêcheurs érythréens, vont jusqu'à s'y installer à titre permanent et semi-permanent.

38. Le Yémen affirme aussi que les îles abritent un certain nombre de sites sacrés et d'autels yéménites, y compris les tombes de plusieurs saints vénérés. Il signale notamment la présence d'un tombeau saint que fréquentent principalement des pêcheurs qui ont pour tradition d'y laisser des vivres à l'intention des autres pêcheurs fréquentant la tombe.

39. Le Yémen signale de surcroît que les îles relèvent d'un régime traditionnel de règlement des différends entre pêcheurs dans le cadre duquel une sorte d'arbitre itinérant "se déplace dans la circonscription judiciaire" le long de la côte et parmi les îles pour permettre aux pêcheurs qui sont dans l'impossibilité de se déplacer d'accéder néanmoins à la justice.

40. Le Yémen accorde beaucoup d'importance aux liens économiques existant entre les îles et les pêcheurs yéménites auxquels lesdites îles et les eaux où elles baignent fournissent leurs moyens d'existence et qui vendent leurs prises à peu près exclusivement sur le territoire continental yéménite. Le Yémen oppose cette situation à celle des pêcheurs érythréens, faisant observer qu'en raison des difficultés éprouvées à assurer dans de bonnes conditions d'hygiène le transport de poisson dans l'intérieur de l'Erythrée (y compris dans la capitale Asmara), la consommation de poisson n'a rien de traditionnel en Erythrée. D'après le Yémen, la majorité des pêcheurs érythréens vendent plus facilement leurs prises sur la côte yéménite. Le Yémen affirme que pendant des siècles, l'exploitation ancienne, intensive et pratiquement exclusive des îles par les pêcheurs yéménites n'a jamais été gênée par d'autres Etats.

41. Le Yémen donne un aperçu historique des actes d'administration et de contrôle qu'il faudrait mettre à l'actif du Yémen et qui sont censés compléter et confirmer le titre historique du Yémen sur les îles en même temps qu'ils constitueraient des sources indépendantes du même titre se renforçant l'une l'autre. Le premier des actes en question serait une mission envoyée à Jabal Zuqar par le roi du Yémen en 1429 pour enquêter sur la contrebande et cet acte est antérieur à la domination ottomane. Pendant la période ottomane, le Yémen affirme que les îles étaient

censées faire partie du *vilayet* du Yémen et que l'administration ottomane s'occupait notamment des questions fiscales, des questions de sécurité et des questions maritimes concernant les îles. Le Yémen cite une concession accordée en 1881 par les autorités ottomanes à une société privée française en vue de la construction de phares dans tout l'empire, et ladite concession comprenait certaines des îles du *vilayet* du Yémen. Le Yémen cite également des cartes et des rapports annuels ottomans du 19e siècle qui situent les îles à l'intérieur du *vilayet* du Yémen.

42. Le Yémen souligne que, postérieurement à la période ottomane, la présence britannique sur les îles a été intermittente et que la Grande-Bretagne n'a jamais revendiqué la souveraineté sur elles. Après la création de la République arabe du Yémen en 1962, le Gouvernement yéménite aurait à deux reprises au moins exercé son pouvoir législatif sur les îles. Le Yémen prétend que sa marine a procédé à des manoeuvres sur les îles et tout autour et que ses forces armées ont joué un rôle central dans la confirmation de l'absence de soldats israéliens sur les îles en 1973. Quand le Yémen rend compte des événements entourant cet incident de 1973, les îles sont régulièrement qualifiées de yéménites et non d'éthiopiennes.

43. Le Yémen cite un certain nombre d'exemples d'octroi de permis à des entités étrangères désireuses de se livrer à des activités scientifiques, touristiques et commerciales sur les îles et aux alentours et d'exemples d'octroi de permis de mouillage. Le Yémen soumet également au Tribunal des éléments de preuve concernant l'autorisation accordée en 1995 à une entreprise allemande par le ministère yéménite de la culture et du tourisme et la direction yéménite des investissements pour la construction d'un hôtel de luxe et d'un centre de plongée sur la Grande Hanish. Le Yémen affirme en outre avoir exercé sa juridiction sur les îles pour la pêche, la protection de l'environnement, l'installation et l'entretien de stations géodésiques, la construction et la gestion de phares y compris la publication d'avis aux navigateurs. Le Yémen a aussi déposé à titre d'éléments de preuve des enquêtes chronologiques minutieuses portant sur diverses périodes qui recensent les prétendues activités yéménites "dans le groupe des îles Hanish et aux alentours".

44. Le Yémen soutient qu'entre 1887 et 1989, six Etats au moins ont confirmé par leur comportement ou d'une autre manière le titre yéménite sur les îles. Le Yémen signale par exemple qu'à la conclusion de l'accord anglo-italien de 1938, dont l'Erythrée dit qu'il définit exclusivement l'attitude à adopter ultérieurement, le Gouvernement italien a fait savoir à l'imam du Yémen qu'en vertu de cet accord l'Italie s'était engagée à ne pas étendre sa souveraineté sur le "groupe des îles Hanish" ni à fortifier ces îles et qu'elle avait, au cours des négociations, "gardé présents à l'esprit . . . avant tout les intérêts du Yémen." Le Yémen prétend trouver aussi confirmation de ses droits dans la pratique britannique et les "vues qui avaient cours dans les services" britanniques telles qu'en témoignent

des documents du Foreign Office et du Colonial Office des années 30 et 40. La reconnaissance par la France du titre yéménite serait, quant à elle, établie notamment par une demande d'autorisation en vue de manœuvres militaires organisées dans la région méridionale de la mer Rouge en 1975, et une demande visant par ailleurs à permettre à un navire océanographique français de se livrer à certaines activités à proximité des îles en 1976.

45. Le Yémen attribue une valeur probante du même ordre à l'attitude de l'Allemagne et à des publications allemandes ainsi qu'à des cartes officielles publiées par l'armée et par la Central Intelligence Agency des Etats-Unis à la date très récente de 1993. Le Yémen apporte aussi des indications sur ce qu'il appelle "une évolution révélatrice de la cartographie éthiopienne" pour étayer sa thèse qui est que l'Ethiopie n'a pas revendiqué de titre sur les îles. Le Yémen s'appuie tout particulièrement sur des cartes éthiopiennes de 1978, 1982, 1984 et 1985 sur lesquelles la couleur des îles semble les attribuer en totalité ou en partie au Yémen.

46. Le Yémen présente également un matériau cartographique dans lequel il voit la preuve du titre yéménite sur les îles apportée officiellement ou non par des experts. Pour le Yémen, ce matériau atteste de faits géographiques et de l'état des connaissances géographiques à un certain moment. Et le Yémen complète ce matériau cartographique par des publications d'historiens et autres professionnels.

47. Le Yémen retrace l'historique de tout ce matériau, en commençant par des cartes des 17e et 18e siècles qui représentent le *Bilad el-Yemen* indépendant. Le Yémen dit que si certaines cartes du 18e siècle ne représentent pas les îles avec précision, les plus exactes d'entre elles les attribuent au Yémen. Le Yémen accorde beaucoup de poids aux commentaires et aux cartes rendant compte des impressions de première main de Carsten Niebuhr, homme de science et explorateur danois qui s'est rendu sur la côte de la mer Rouge et y a séjourné de 1761 à 1764. Les travaux de Niebuhr donnent à penser qu'il existait une affiliation politique et d'autres liens aussi entre les îles et le territoire continental du Yémen.

48. Le Yémen fournit en outre à titre d'éléments de preuve un très grand nombre de cartes des 19e et 20e siècles, d'origines diverses, qui, d'après leur couleur, paraissent attribuer au Yémen la totalité des îles ou une partie d'entre elles. En même temps, le Yémen n'a pas nié que certaines cartes yéménites attribuent les îles à l'Ethiopie ou à l'Erythrée; en tout cas, qu'elles ne les attribuent pas au Yémen.

49. Sans se contenter d'apporter des éléments de preuve, cartographiques notamment, pour pouvoir affirmer détenir un titre historique sur les îles, le Yémen dit aussi que, jusqu'aux événements de décembre 1995, l'attitude de l'Ethiopie et de l'Erythrée était compatible avec la souveraineté yéménite. Le Yémen dit qu'à une date aussi récente que novembre 1995, l'Erythrée reconnaissait dans un

communiqué officiel adressé au président du Yémen que les îles étaient " . . . laissées de côté et abandonnées depuis de nombreuses années après l'époque coloniale, y compris pendant l'époque de Haile Selassie et de Mengistu et tout au long de la longue guerre de libération."

50. Le Yémen insiste sur le fait que, pendant la période ottomane, les îles ont été régulièrement administrées comme faisant partie du *vilayet* du Yémen et que le titre n'a jamais été transmis à l'Italie pendant la période où celle-ci a colonisé le territoire continental de l'Erythrée. Le Yémen cite plusieurs occasions dans lesquelles, à son avis, l'Italie a refusé de revendiquer la souveraineté. Il s'agit en particulier d'échanges entre le Gouvernement britannique et le Gouvernement italien à la fin des années 20 et 30, lesquels ont abouti à l'accord anglo-italien de 1938 qui, pour le Yémen, représente l'accord par lequel les deux parties s'engagent catégoriquement à ne pas établir leur souveraineté sur des îles sur lesquelles la Turquie avait renoncé à sa souveraineté dans l'article 16 du traité de Lausanne. Le Yémen interprète le décret italien n° 1446 du 20 décembre 1938 non pas comme la confirmation d'une souveraineté territoriale existante mais plutôt comme un simple "décret interne prescrivant que l'administration des îles doit être assurée par le département de l'Erythrée à Assab".

51. Le Yémen dit en outre que la formule "le territoire continental et insulaire de l'Erythrée" qui figure dans le texte de la Constitution érythréenne de 1952 mise au point par les services des Nations Unies ne vise pas les îles en litige parce que le rapport officiel de la Commission des Nations Unies pour l'Erythrée, établi en 1950, indique que le titre sur les îles est yéménite car elles ont la même couleur que le territoire continental du Yémen sur les cartes des Nations Unies accompagnant le rapport. Le Yémen conteste toutes les allégations de l'Erythrée concernant les actes de souveraineté ou d'administration accomplis par l'Ethiopie et affirme que le comportement de l'Ethiopie, tout particulièrement la publication de cartes officielles sur lesquelles les îles ont la même couleur que le territoire continental du Yémen, revenait à reconnaître la souveraineté yéménite sur les îles.

52. D'après le Yémen, si des pêcheurs yéménites ont toujours pêché aux alentours des îles et y ont toujours séjourné provisoirement, le Yémen a aussi exercé toute une vaste gamme d'activités étatiques sur les îles et aux alentours. Au nombre de ces activités auraient figuré, au cours des années 70, l'examen de demandes formulées par des étrangers désireux de se livrer à des recherches marines et scientifiques sur les îles, des visites périodiques de militaires yéménites en mission sur la Grande Hanish et Jabal Zuqar, et des patrouilles connexes sur ces îles et aux alentours. Le Yémen prétend également avoir protesté contre des vols militaires à basse altitude organisés par la France sur les îles Hanish, avoir protesté également contre l'arrestation par l'Ethiopie de pêcheurs yéménites dans le voisinage des îles et dit en outre avoir mené enquête sur un certain nombre

d'incidents marqués par la perte de bateaux étrangers ou des dommages subis par eux aux alentours de la Grande Hanish et de Jabal Zuqar.

53. Pendant les années 80 et 90, le Yémen dit avoir organisé diverses missions de reconnaissance exécutées par l'aviation et la marine yéménites dans l'espace situé au-dessus des îles et dans leurs parages. Le Yémen affirme également avoir accordé des permis autorisant des ressortissants d'Etats tiers à se rendre dans certaines îles à des fins scientifiques et touristiques et dit que certains de ces visiteurs étaient accompagnés par des représentants officiels yéménites. En 1988, le Yémen aurait mis en train un projet visant à aménager et construire une série de phares, accompagné de la publication d'avis périodiques aux navigateurs, intéressant l'île Centre Peak, Jabal al-Tayr, la Petite Hanish, l'île Abu Ali, Jabal Zuqar et la Grande Hanish. Le Yémen prétend également avoir érigé des stations géodésiques sur la Grande Hanish et Jabal Zuqar et autorisé la construction d'une piste d'atterrissage sur la Grande Hanish, piste qui a été fréquemment utilisée au début des années 90. Le Yémen dit aussi que pendant cette période, il a poursuivi ses patrouilles systématiques sur les îles, arrêtant des pêcheurs étrangers et saisissant des bateaux de pêche exerçant leur activité dans les eaux avoisinant les îles sans être munis d'un permis yéménite.

54. En ce qui concerne la souveraineté territoriale, le Yémen demande au Tribunal de déclarer dans sa sentence "que la République du Yémen exerce la souveraineté territoriale sur la totalité des îles qui constituent le groupe des îles Hanish . . . tel que défini dans les chapitres 2 et 5 du mémoire du Yémen."

* - *

Les arguments des Parties quant à la pertinence des accords et activités pétrolières

55. Pour répondre à certaines questions précises posées par le Tribunal, qui ont donné lieu à des écritures supplémentaires, à une reprise de la procédure orale en juillet 1998 et à des conclusions écrites à la suite des audiences, les Parties ont toutes deux présenté des éléments de preuve concernant des concessions pétrolières accordées dans la mer Rouge. Le Yémen dit que tout le dossier des concessions pétrolières offshore qu'il a accordées au cours des cinquante dernières années ne fait que renforcer et compléter un ensemble cohérent de preuves du titre yéménite sur les îles. Comme l'octroi de concessions pétrolières sert à confirmer et préserver un titre yéménite existant plutôt qu'à donner la preuve d'une occupation effective, il n'y a pas lieu, de l'avis du Yémen, d'étayer l'octroi de concessions par la preuve de revendications expresses. Cette position serait conforme à la thèse du titre historique que le Yémen défend.

56. Pour témoigner de ce qu'il appelle l'"administration ancienne et pacifique de ses ressources pétrolières" sur les îles et aux alentours, le Yémen a présenté des

accords et des cartes concernant les secteurs accordés ou proposés à titre de concessions pétrolières depuis 1974. L'un de ces secteurs (accordé à la société Tomen) englobe certaines des îles, en l'occurrence le "groupe des Hanish", tandis qu'un autre secteur (accordé à Adair) est limité par une ligne qui traverse la Grande Hanish. Le Yémen se fonde en outre sur une étude de 1991 sur les hydrocarbures dans les régions de la mer Rouge et du golfe d'Aden qui est due au Programme des Nations Unies pour le développement (PNUD) et à la Banque mondiale. Cette étude ayant bénéficié de la participation des gouvernements intéressés, en particulier le Gouvernement éthiopien et les gouvernements yéménites successifs, le Yémen y puise utilement un recensement des activités pétrolières entreprises par les deux Etats depuis le début des années 50.

57. Le Yémen s'appuie à la fois sur la jurisprudence (en particulier l'affaire du *Groënland oriental*[3]) et sur les travaux des publicistes pour étayer sa thèse qui est que l'octroi de permis de prospection et de concessions représente la preuve d'un titre, et il invoque les éléments dotés de force probante que sont l'attitude de l'Etat accordant le permis, l'octroi de la concession et la réglementation applicable à son fonctionnement, les activités ancillaires autorisées par l'Etat et l'attitude du concessionnaire et des institutions internationales. En outre, le Yémen déduit de l'absence de protestation la preuve de l'acquiescement donné par l'Ethiopie et par l'Erythrée.

58. Le Yémen fait valoir la présomption selon laquelle un Etat qui accorde une concession pétrolière détient un titre ou exerce des droits souverains sur les espaces concernés par la concession. Le fait de proposer et d'accorder des concessions sur des secteurs qui englobent ou avoisinent les îles constitue de l'avis du Yémen un exercice patent de la souveraineté yéménite sur lesdites îles. Le Yémen invoque en outre le fait que les accords correspondants réservent expressément le titre yéménite sur le secteur faisant l'objet de la concession. L'octroi de ces concessions économiques à des entreprises privées non seulement montre quelle est l'attitude du Yémen au sujet de ce titre mais constituerait la preuve de l'exercice de la souveraineté en ce qui concerne le territoire visé. Pour le Yémen, le contrôle qu'il exerce sur les activités des divers concessionnaires et la réglementation qu'il assure de ces activités ainsi que l'octroi par lui des permis voulus pour certaines activités ancillaires comme les sondages sismiques sont des preuves supplémentaires de l'exercice de la souveraineté du Yémen.

59. Le Yémen soutient en outre qu'une société ne négociera pas avec un Etat l'octroi d'une concession pour la mise en valeur des ressources pétrolières si elle n'est pas certaine que l'espace de la concession et les ressources de son sous-sol appartiennent en fait audit Etat. En outre, le fait que le titre yéménite soit réservé dans les accords de concession soumis au Tribunal par le Yémen constituerait de

---

[3] Statut juridique du Groënland oriental (Danemark c. Norvège), CPJI 1933 (Série A/B) n° 53.

la part des concessionnaires la reconnaissance expresse du titre yéménite sur les secteurs en question. Quant à l'étude PNUD/Banque mondiale, elle établit, de l'avis du Yémen, la reconnaissance du titre yéménite par les institutions internationales en question et représente un témoignage d'expert de même effet.

60. Le Yémen se réfère également à cette étude PNUD/Banque mondiale afin de prouver l'acquiescement de l'Ethiopie. Comme l'étude a été réalisée en collaboration avec tous les gouvernements intéressés et qu'elle a en définitive été diffusée auprès de la totalité de ces gouvernements, on peut être certain, estime le Yémen, que l'Ethiopie aura constaté l'existence et l'étendue des concessions yéménites mettant les îles en jeu et qu'elle n'a toutefois pas émis la moindre protestation. Le Yémen s'appuie également sur d'autres cartes et rapports publiés dans la documentation propre aux milieux pétroliers dont il affirme que l'Ethiopie et l'Erythrée doivent avoir eu connaissance.

61. En dernier lieu, le Yémen affirme que les activités pétrolières menées par l'Ethiopie et l'Erythrée n'englobaient pas les îles, n'étaient pas non plus exercées dans leur voisinage et ne peuvent donc pas étayer de revendication de souveraineté. Le Yémen dit n'en avoir pas moins protesté régulièrement en temps voulu dès que les concessions accordées par l'Ethiopie, de l'avis du Yémen, empiétaient, ne fût-ce qu'à peine, sur sa mer territoriale, son plateau continental et sa zone économique exclusive.

62. De son côté, l'Erythrée apporte des éléments donnant la preuve que des activités pétrolières au large ont été menées essentiellement par l'Ethiopie à une époque où, allègue-t-elle, "le titre de l'Ethiopie était d'ores et déjà établi." L'Erythrée dit que les activités liées à la prospection pétrolière "sur les îles" confirment la revendication de souveraineté préexistante de l'Ethiopie dont il n'est pas possible de se défaire à son avis sous l'effet de l'octroi unilatéral par le Yémen de concessions minières au large. L'Erythrée plaide également qu'en l'absence de la moindre manifestation physique de contrôle sur les îles ou dans leurs eaux territoriales, le simple fait pour le Yémen d'accorder des concessions ne suffirait pas à créer de titre par occupation effective, "même si les îles n'avaient eu au préalable aucun propriétaire."

63. D'après l'Erythrée, les moyens que le Yémen fait valoir en matière de concessions sont sans pertinence, parce que le Yémen cherche unilatéralement par là à se doter de droits permanents sur les fonds marins en violation du droit international coutumier et de la Convention des Nations Unies sur le droit de la mer (ci-après la "Convention sur le droit de la mer"). En outre, les accords de concession du Yémen seraient dénués de pertinence aussi parce qu'ils ont été conclus postérieurement à la naissance du présent différend, n'ont pas été suivis d'activités menées par le Gouvernement yéménite et n'intéressent pas le territoire en litige. L'Erythrée met également en doute l'exactitude factuelle des allégations du Yémen relatives à ces accords de concession, faisant observer que le Yémen

s'est abstenu de soumettre à titre d'élément de preuve la copie de certains de ces accords.

64. L'Erythrée rappelle que tant la Convention sur le droit de la mer que le droit international coutumier interdisent l'acquisition ou la perte des droits sur les minéraux des fonds marins par appropriation unilatérale de l'auteur de la demande agissant seul. Tant qu'il ne se serait pas entendu avec l'Etat côtier lui faisant face, le Yémen, de l'avis de l'Erythrée, n'avait le droit d'accorder de concessions qu'à titre provisoire. Si les concessions invoquées ne pouvaient pas conférer effectivement les droits sur les minéraux des fonds-marins qu'elles étaient censées avoir pour objet, elles ne pouvaient pas régler indirectement la question de la souveraineté sur les îles. D'après l'Erythrée, les concessions pétrolières n'ont de pertinence que là où elles établissent l'existence d'une ligne frontière de facto reconnue de part et d'autre. Or, en l'espèce, le Yémen n'avait nullement cherché à s'entendre avec l'Ethiopie ou l'Erythrée.

65. L'Erythrée dit que le caractère provisoire de toute concession accordée par le Yémen s'explique non seulement par le paragraphe 3 de l'article 83* de la Convention sur le droit de la mer qui autorise à accorder provisoirement des concessions à condition que ces arrangements provisoires soient sans préjudice de la délimitation finale, mais encore par la législation sur le plateau continental adoptée par le Yémen lui-même en 1977, laquelle dispose que "tant que le tracé des frontières marines ne sera pas établi par voie d'accord, les limites de la mer territoriale, de la zone contiguë, de la zone économique exclusive . . . ne doivent pas être situées au-delà de la ligne médiane ou de la ligne d'équidistance".

66. L'Erythrée affirme par ailleurs que les concessions accordées au large par le Yémen l'ont été postérieurement à 1973, alors que le Yémen savait parfaitement que l'Ethiopie revendiquait la souveraineté sur les îles. Cette prétention doit, pour l'Erythrée, non seulement avoir des incidences pour la délimitation des fonds-marins entourant les îles mais limiter également la valeur probante des moyens présentés par le Yémen en matière de concessions pour résoudre la question de la souveraineté.

67. L'Erythrée dit donc que l'octroi par le Yémen de concessions postérieurement à 1973 répond à la volonté de fabriquer artificiellement des liens avec les îles en litige. Cela est confirmé en outre, du point de vue de l'Erythrée, par l'absence de toute activité étatique connexe que le Yémen aurait consacrée précisément au territoire litigieux. D'après l'Erythrée, les concessions peuvent être appelées à jouer un rôle en matière d'acquisition territoriale de deux façons. Pour exemple du premier type d'intervention, l'Erythrée cite la concession de pêche en haute mer accordée par l'Italie à la société *Cannata* dans les années 30, qui sont

---

* *Note de l'éditeur: cette référence a été corrigée de la version anglaise originale.*

notamment à l'origine de la construction d'une station de pêche commerciale sur la Grande Hanish. D'après l'Erythrée, cette concession *Cannata* a conduit à faire directement appel à des fonctionnaires de l'Etat considéré, y compris à faire stationner des soldats italiens sur l'île.

68. Les concessions peuvent jouer un rôle dans l'acquisition territoriale d'une autre façon qui est celle dont on traite dans l'affaire du *Statut du Groënland oriental.* Suivant l'interprétation que l'Erythrée donne de cette affaire, le *Groënland oriental* n'impose pas nécessairement la présence physique de tel ou tel autre fonctionnaire de l'Etat, les activités requises sont menées par des particuliers qui, sans être eux-mêmes au service de l'Etat, agissent sous couleur de la loi dudit Etat. L'Erythrée invoque la doctrine à l'appui de sa position qui est qu'en matière de concessions, l'activité des particuliers n'a d'intérêt que si elle représente une véritable affirmation d'autorité, car "l'exercice ou la manifestation de l'autorité doit être authentique et ne pas être simplement qu'un chiffon de papier déguisé en acte de souveraineté." L'Erythrée dit que la portée que le Yémen et certains particuliers ont donnée à leur activité dans le domaine des concessions pétrolières "est loin d'avoir la qualité et l'importance du régime d'administration instauré depuis si longtemps par l'Ethiopie sur les îles en litige et tout autour." L'Erythrée affirme en outre que les quelques rares accords de concession réellement produits comme moyens de preuve par le Yémen n'ont finalement que peu de rapport avec les îles en litige, voire pas de rapport du tout.

69. En outre, pour l'Erythrée, une bonne partie de l'activité pétrolière du Yémen relève de la "recherche scientifique marine" et non de l'exploitation économique. Or, l'article 241 de la Convention sur le droit de la mer exclut que la recherche scientifique marine puisse constituer le fondement juridique d'aucune revendication sur une partie quelconque du milieu marin ou de ses ressources.

70. L'Erythrée soutient que l'absence de protestation contre les concessions accordées par le Yémen ne peut être considérée comme un acquiescement, d'autant plus qu'à cette époque, l'Ethiopie était en proie à un soulèvement militaire et politique. L'Erythrée a présenté des éléments de preuve tendant à montrer que l'étude PNUD/Banque mondiale de 1991 que le Yémen invoque comme portant les concessions à la connaissance de l'Ethiopie n'a peut-être jamais été reçu par l'Ethiopie qui s'occupait alors exclusivement de la chute du régime Mengistu et de la fin de la guerre civile. Et même si ce rapport était finalement parvenu à destination, l'Erythrée estime qu'en 1991, sachant qu'elle allait perdre à bref délai toute sa région côtière au bénéfice d'une Erythrée bientôt indépendante, l'Ethiopie n'aurait eu aucune raison de s'opposer aux concessions yéménites.

71. Même si elle avait été réellement mise au fait, en partie ou en totalité, des concessions accordées par le Yémen, l'Erythrée dit qu'elle était en droit de les

tenir pour provisoires en vertu du paragraphe 3 de l'article 83* de la Convention sur le droit de la mer et en vertu de la législation relative au plateau continental adoptée en 1977 par le Yémen lui-même.

72. En dernier lieu, lors des audiences qui ont eu lieu à Londres en juillet 1998, l'Erythrée a versé au dossier un accord de concession éthiopien datant de 1989 qui, à son avis, s'étendait à certaines îles au moins, notamment la Grande Hanish, dont elle tire la preuve d'activités connexes qui auraient eu lieu sur la Grande Hanish, notamment l'installation de balises. En outre, l'Erythrée a fait également état de la publication en 1985 d'une série de cartes, dont une intitulée "Petroleum Potential of Ethiopia" qui montrerait un secteur de prospection de la mer Rouge englobant les îles Hanish.

* - * - *

* *Note de l'éditeur: cette référence a été corrigée de la version anglaise originale.*

CHAPITRE II – Le champ du différend

73. Aux termes du Compromis d'arbitrage, le Tribunal doit rendre une sentence sur "la définition du champ du différend entre l'Erythrée et le Yémen." Le compromis donne également pour instruction au Tribunal de statuer sur la définition du champ du différend "sur la base des positions respectives des deux Parties."

74. Les Parties admettent l'une et l'autre que cette disposition figure dans le Compromis d'arbitrage parce qu'elles ont été dans l'impossibilité de s'entendre sur la définition du champ du différend. D'après l'Erythrée, à l'époque de la confrontation militaire de la fin de 1995 à la suite de laquelle l'Erythrée a militairement occupé la Grande Hanish et certaines des petites îles des alentours tandis que la République du Yémen occupait militairement Zuqar, l'Erythrée voulait soumettre toutes les revendications de l'Erythrée et du Yémen à la solution soit de l'arbitrage international soit du règlement judiciaire international. Le Yémen ne voulait pas s'engager dans cette voie tenant pour sa part, tel que l'Erythrée le rapporte, à limiter le champ du différend à l'occupation prétendument illégale de l'île Hanish par l'Erythrée. C'est parce que ni l'une ni l'autre des Parties ne voulait que ce désaccord sur la portée du différend empêche la conclusion de l'Accord sur les principes puis du Compromis d'arbitrage qu'elles ont convenu de confier au Tribunal la définition du champ du différend.

75. D'après l'interprétation que l'Erythrée donne du membre de phrase "[les] positions respectives des deux Parties", celles-ci ont l'une et l'autre la liberté de définir et préciser à n'importe quel stade de la procédure leur position concernant la portée du différend. L'Erythrée dit avoir adopté cette attitude en faisant figurer dans son mémoire, soumis le 1er septembre 1997, une liste non exhaustive d'"îles, rochers et hauts-fonds découvrants" sur lesquels elle affirme exercer la souveraineté territoriale et en demandant au Tribunal de décider que le champ du différend s'étend à chacun et chacune de ces "îles, rochers et hauts-fonds découvrants" ainsi énumérés. L'Erythrée fait valoir que, sa position au sujet du champ du différend n'ayant jamais varié, le moment auquel cette position a été définie est sans pertinence. Tout en indiquant qu'elle ne pensait pas que le Yémen revendiquerait les îles Mohabbakahs, l'Erythrée a exprimé l'intention de défendre sa revendication des Mohabbakahs, c'est-à-dire qu'elle veut faire entrer ces îles dans le champ du différend. L'Erythrée affirme en outre que le Yémen savait en fait que l'Erythrée revendique Jabal al-Tayr ainsi que le groupe de Zubayr.

76. Toutefois, le Yémen de son côté est d'avis que "[les] positions respectives des deux Parties" doivent être arrêtées à la date de l'Accord sur les principes (soit le 21 mai 1996). Le Yémen dit que "la tâche du Tribunal consiste à établir dans quelle mesure il y avait un différend entre les Parties au sujet de certaines îles de la mer Rouge et de leur limite maritime à cette date-là." Pour le Yémen, les

positions respectives des Parties à cette date faisaient apparaître que, pour l'une comme pour l'autre, il était entendu que Jabal al-Tayr et le groupe d'îles de Zubayr n'étaient pas censés entrer dans le champ du différend. Le Yémen définit ce champ du différend comme intéressant "le groupe des îles Hanish", lequel comprend à son avis l'île Abu Ali, Jabal Zuqar, la Grande et la Petite Hanish, Suyul Hanish, les divers petits îlots et rochers qui les entourent, les South West Rocks, les Haycocks et les Mohabbakahs. Le Yémen affirme que les "îles septentrionales" de Jabal al-Tayr et du groupe de Zubayr n'ont jamais été en litige entre les Parties et n'étaient pas prises en compte dans la "position" de l'Erythrée avant le 1er septembre 1997, c'est-à-dire la date du dépôt des mémoires des Parties, et qu'elles n'entraient par conséquent pas dans le champ du différend.

77. Les positions divergentes des Parties sur le fond du différend apparaissent dans un document daté du 29 février 1996, qui est intitulé "Mémorandum français à l'intention du Yémen et de l'Erythrée". Au lendemain des hostilités de décembre 1995, l'Erythrée et le Yémen avaient, sur le conseil du secrétaire général des Nations Unies, demandé au Gouvernement français de leur apporter son concours "dans la recherche d'un règlement pacifique du différend qui les sépare dans la mer Rouge." Ce mémorandum était le produit de trois missions diplomatiques envoyées dans la région, lesquelles avaient consisté en entretiens approfondis avec les représentants des deux gouvernements, et il a quant à lui abouti à la conclusion entre les Parties de l'Accord sur les principes en mai 1996 et à l'adoption du Compromis d'arbitrage en octobre 1997.

78. Tel qu'il est défini dans ce mémorandum français, "[l]e problème posé est le suivant: selon l'Erythrée, le différend porte actuellement non seulement sur l'île de la Grande Hanish qui a connu les événements que l'on sait à l'automne 1995, mais aussi sur l'ensemble des archipels Hanish-Zucur, en particulier l'île de Djebel Zucur, puisque le Yémen y a installé des troupes alors que ces archipels relèvent de la souveraineté érythréenne." Au sujet de la position du Yémen, le mémorandum français poursuit: "Selon le Yémen, le différend porte sur l'île de la Grande Hanish, où l'Erythrée a dépêché des troupes, mais ne peut concerner les archipels Hanish-Zucur dans leur ensemble, en particulier l'île Djebel Zucur, puisqu'ils relèvent de la souveraineté yéménite."

79. Le médiateur français a donc proposé de demander au Tribunal arbitral "de se prononcer sur les questions de souveraineté territoriale ainsi que de délimitation de frontières maritimes d'une zone définie par exemple par des coordonnées géographiques." Cette définition, d'après un projet français d'Accord sur les principes daté du 29 février 1996, tiendrait compte de "la souveraineté incontestée de chacune des Parties sur les îles et rochers tels que, par exemple, les îles Dahlak pour l'Erythrée ou les îles Zubayr pour le Yémen." Cette proposition a été rejetée par les Parties qui ont préféré s'en remettre au Tribunal arbitral pour la définition du champ du différend.

80. L'article premier de l'Accord sur les principes du 21 mai 1996 dispose:

> [. . .]
>
> 1.2 Les Parties] demandent au Tribunal de se prononcer conformément au droit international en deux étapes:
> a) dans une première étape, sur la définition du champ du différend entre l'Erythrée et le Yémen, sur la base des positions respectives des deux Parties;
> b) dans une seconde étape, et après s'être prononcé sur le point mentionné à la lettre a) ci-dessus, sur:
> i) les questions de souveraineté territoriale;
> ii) les questions de délimitation des frontières maritimes.
>
> 2. Elles s'engagent à respecter la sentence du Tribunal arbitral.

81. Toutefois, l'article 2 du Compromis d'arbitrage dispose:

> 1. Il est demandé au Tribunal de se prononcer conformément au droit international, en deux étapes.
> 2. La première étape donne lieu à une sentence sur la souveraineté territoriale et la définition du champ du différend entre l'Erythrée et le Yémen. Le Tribunal statue sur la question de la souveraineté territoriale conformément aux principes, aux règles et aux pratiques du droit international applicables en la matière et sur la base, notamment, des titres historiques. Le Tribunal statue sur la définition du champ du différend sur la base des positions respectives des deux Parties.
> 3. La seconde étape donne lieu à une sentence sur la délimitation des frontières maritimes. Le Tribunal statue en prenant en compte l'opinion qu'il se sera faite sur les questions de souveraineté territoriale, la Convention des Nations Unies sur le droit de la mer et tout autre élément pertinent.

82. L'article 15 du même Compromis d'arbitrage dispose en outre:

> 1. Nulle disposition du présent Compromis d'arbitrage ne peut être interprétée comme portant préjudice aux positions juridiques ou aux droits de chaque Partie concernant les questions soumises au Tribunal, ni ne peut affecter ou porter préjudice aux décisions du Tribunal arbitral ou aux considérations et motifs sur lesquels se fondent lesdites décisions.
> 2. En cas de contradiction entre l'Accord sur les principes et le présent Compromis d'arbitrage portant application des aspects de procédure dudit Accord sur les principes, c'est le Compromis d'arbitrage qui prévaut. Excepté le cas d'une telle contradiction, l'Accord sur les principes reste en vigueur.

83. Comme il y a effectivement en la matière une contradiction entre l'Accord sur les principes et le Compromis d'arbitrage, ce sont, conformément au paragraphe 2 de l'article 15 du Compromis d'arbitrage, les dispositions de ce dernier qui prévalent pour tout ce qui fait l'objet de la contradiction. Il faut donc que le Tribunal se prononce sur la question du champ du différend comme sur les questions de

souveraineté qui en découlent lors de la première étape de la procédure, c'est-à-dire la présente étape.

84. Cette décision relative au champ du différend doit être adoptée "sur la base des positions respectives des deux Parties", et, sur ce point, les dispositions des deux accords sont identiques. Il ressort toutefois des conclusions que les Parties ont formulées dans leurs écritures et dans leurs plaidoiries aux fins de la première étape de la procédure que les positions des deux Parties divergent quant à la portée de l'arbitrage. Pour l'Erythrée, l'arbitrage porte sur la totalité des îles de la chaîne des Zuqar-Hanish, les Haycocks et les Mohabbakahs, et aussi sur les îles septentrionales de Jabal al-Tayr et du groupe de Zubayr. Le Yémen toutefois, s'il revendique la totalité des îles de la chaîne des Zuqar-Hanish, y compris, de l'avis des Parties, les Haycocks et les Mohabbakahs, n'admet pas que les îles septentrionales soient en litige aux fins du présent arbitrage.

85. La thèse du Yémen, comme il est indiqué ci-dessus, est que les positions respectives des deux Parties à l'époque où fut conclu l'Accord sur les principes (le 21 mai 1996) étaient différentes de ce qu'elles sont devenues au moment où fut signé ensuite le Compromis d'arbitrage (le 3 octobre 1996). D'après le Yémen, à l'époque de l'Accord sur les principes, l'Erythrée ne cherchait apparemment pas à revendiquer les îles septentrionales ni à les faire entrer dans le champ de l'arbitrage, même si l'on peut noter qu'il existait d'ores et déjà un différend sur ces îles septentrionales.[4] Il paraît clair en outre que le Yémen, à l'époque de l'Accord sur les principes, ne revendiquait pas les Mohabbakahs.

86. Mais, d'après le Yémen, c'est la date de l'Accord sur les principes qui est "la date critique" aux fins de la définition par le Tribunal des "positions respectives des deux Parties" à partir desquelles il convient d'arrêter la portée de l'arbitrage, parce que ce fut la date à laquelle les Parties se sont définitivement entendues pour soumettre la question au présent arbitrage. Le Yémen tire de cette proposition la conclusion que les îles septentrionales n'entrent pas dans le champ du présent arbitrage.

87. De l'avis du Tribunal, cet argument assez technique de la "date critique" ne tient pas assez compte du changement crucial apporté par le Compromis d'arbitrage quand celui-ci indique que c'est au cours de la première étape de l'arbitrage que la question du champ du différend doit être déterminée par le Tribunal. En effet, alors que, selon l'Accord sur les principes, la première étape devait être

[4] Dans une lettre datée du 4 janvier 1996, le Yémen a officiellement protesté contre l'octroi par l'Erythrée d'une concession pétrolière à la compagnie Andarko, laquelle, d'après le Yémen, constituait "une violation flagrante de la souveraineté yéménite sur ses eaux territoriales dans la mesure où la concession s'étend aux eaux territoriales exclusives des îles yéménites Jabal al-Tayr et al-Zubayr en sus d'être une violation des droits de la République du Yémen dans sa zone économique exclusive."

intégralement consacrée à la délimitation du champ du différend, en vertu du Compromis d'arbitrage la première étape comprend et la question de la souveraineté et la question du champ du différend. C'est-à-dire que désormais, le Tribunal doit se prononcer sur le champ du différend "sur la base des positions respectives des deux Parties" uniquement après avoir entendu l'intégralité de l'argumentation des deux Parties sur la question de la souveraineté. Adoptée plus tard, cette disposition incite à douter que les Parties aient néanmoins considéré la date de l'Accord sur les principes comme étant la date critique aux fins de la détermination du champ du différend.

88. De surcroît, le Compromis d'arbitrage postérieur [à l'Accord sur les principes], au paragraphe 2 de son article 2, n'a pas du tout précisé comment devait être interprété le membre de phrase "sur la base des positions respectives des deux Parties." En l'absence de précision à ce sujet, le sens ordinaire à attribuer à ce membre de phrase dans son contexte et compte tenu de l'objet et de la finalité du Compromis d'arbitrage, consisterait, semble-t-il, à comprendre les "positions respectives des deux Parties" telles qu'établies à la date du Compromis d'arbitrage et non à une quelconque autre date.

89. En outre, et l'indication est implicitement conforme à cette analyse, le Yémen, tout en veillant de diverses façons à réserver sa position sur la portée du différend, a en fait présenté une argumentation complète à l'appui de sa prétention sur Jabal al-Tayr et le groupe de Zubayr, puis, lors des audiences supplémentaires de juillet 1998 relatives aux accords pétroliers, il a considérablement développé cette argumentation.

90. Le Tribunal par conséquent, sur la question de la portée du différend, préfère les vues défendues par l'Erythrée et rend donc une sentence sur la souveraineté intéressant la totalité des îles et des îlots au sujet desquels les Parties ont présenté des revendications opposées, y compris Jabal al-Tayr et le groupe de Zubayr ainsi que les Haycocks et les Mohabbakahs.

* - * - *

CHAPITRE III – Quelques particularités propres à l'affaire

D'un point de vue général

91. Il convient dès le départ de s'arrêter sur certaines particularités de la présente affaire. Il existe une opposition frappante entre les Parties elles-mêmes. Le Yémen peut faire remonter son existence à l'époque médiévale et même à une date antérieure à la création de l'Empire ottoman; l'Erythrée en revanche n'est devenue un Etat pleinement indépendant, distinct de l'Ethiopie, qu'au début des années 90 du vingtième siècle. L'Erythrée n'en fait pas moins remonter ce qu'elle considère comme son titre sur les îles contestées à une succession historique datant de la période coloniale italienne ainsi qu'à la période immédiatement postérieure à la seconde guerre mondiale où elle fut fédérée au très vieux pays d'Ethiopie. Le Tribunal a donc été saisi par les deux Parties d'un matériau extrêmement volumineux visant à prouver l'établissement d'un titre juridique au moyen d'une masse d'exemples d'allégations attestant la possession ou l'utilisation ou bien, s'agissant du Yémen, attestant la consolidation, la continuité et la confirmation d'un "titre ancien". Le Tribunal a dû trier, analyser tout ce matériau dont les éléments sont fort diversifiés et n'ont pas la même importance et il a dû en évaluer l'intérêt.

92. Comme une grande partie de ce matériau a trait aux actions, aux réactions ou au comportement des Parties ou de leurs prédécesseurs, il ne faut pas oublier que les deux Parties sont passées par des périodes où elles étaient absorbées par des guerres civiles se déroulant des deux côtés de la mer Rouge: ce fut le cas pour le Yémen entre 1962 et 1970 tandis que l'Ethiopie a été en proie à un grave et sanglant conflit avec les rebelles érythréens qui a abouti en 1993 à l'indépendance de l'Erythrée.

93. Les îles et les îlots contestés sont de petite taille et parfois minuscules, sont uniformément dépourvus du moindre attrait, sont également dépourvus d'eau et ne sont habitables qu'au prix de grandes difficultés. Mais le fait n'en est pas moins que ces îles sont situées au beau milieu de ce qui constitue, depuis l'ouverture du canal de Suez en 1869, l'une des voies navigables les plus importantes et les plus fréquentées du monde. Ces aspects contradictoires se retrouvent dans les éléments présentés au Tribunal. Au début de leur histoire, les îles paraissent souvent avoir à peine retenu l'attention des pays côtiers à part celle des pêcheurs locaux qui s'abritaient dans ces îles et mouillaient dans leurs eaux; mais elles ont été l'objet d'une attention considérable, qui est allée jusqu'à l'occupation provisoire, de la part de puissances coloniales rivales, notamment de la part de la Grande-Bretagne et de l'Italie. L'explication tient certainement au fait qu'après l'ouverture du canal, cette mer, qui devient plus étroite dans sa partie méridionale où sont précisément situées les îles, est devenue la voie principale à emprunter pour aller d'Europe en Inde, aux Indes orientales et en Extrême-Orient.

94. L'intérêt manifesté autrefois pour ces îles par la Grande-Bretagne, l'Italie et, dans une moindre mesure, par la France et par les Pays-Bas est un élément important du matériau historique présenté au Tribunal* par les Parties, d'autant que celles-ci ont eu accès aux archives de l'époque, notamment aux premiers documents des gouvernements britanniques de l'époque. Ce matériau est pour une bonne part intéressant et utile. Il convient toutefois de formuler une mise en garde d'un caractère général: certains des éléments se présentent sous la forme de notes de service puisées dans les archives du ministère des affaires étrangères, le Foreign Office britannique comme il s'appelait à l'époque, et aussi parfois dans les archives du ministère italien des affaires étrangères. Le Tribunal n'a pas oublié que des notes de service ne représentent pas nécessairement le point de vue ou la politique d'un gouvernement et peuvent n'être que le point de vue personnel qu'un fonctionnaire s'est senti obligé d'exprimer à un autre fonctionnaire à ce moment-là: il n'est pas toujours facile de démêler les éléments purement personnels dans ce qui ne constitue après tout que des notes internes, privées et confidentielles au moment où elles sont rédigées.

La date critique

95. Devant cette énorme masse d'éléments historiques, de caractère juridique et politique, le Tribunal a jugé bon de se demander si la notion de "date critique" ou de "période critique" l'aiderait peut-être à organiser ou à interpréter ce matériau volumineux. Mais il a constaté que les Parties elles-mêmes n'ont parlé de date critique qu'à propos de la question évoquée ci-dessus, qui est celle de savoir si, pour définir le champ de l'arbitrage, la date critique est celle de l'Accord sur les principes ou bien celle du Compromis d'arbitrage. Aucune des deux Parties n'a tenté de plaider l'argument de la date critique au sujet de l'une quelconque des questions intéressant le fond du différend. Dans ces conditions, le Tribunal a estimé que le mieux était de suivre l'exemple de la sentence rendue en 1966 dans l'arbitrage entre l'Argentine et le Chili qu'a présidé Lord McNair et a donc "examiné tous les éléments de preuve qui lui ont été soumis, indépendamment de la date des actes auxquels ces éléments ont trait."[5] [Traduction du Bureau international de la CPA.]

L'uti possidetis

96. Dans son contre-mémoire, le Yémen a invoqué la doctrine de l'*uti possidetis* pour expliquer quelle était, à son avis, la situation juridique des îles en cause après la dissolution de l'Empire ottoman à la suite de la première guerre mondiale. Cette situation aurait été, selon les termes même du Yémen, celle-ci: "[q]uand il y a

* *Note de l'éditeur: Ce mot a été modifié de la version anglaise originale.*

[5] Argentine c. Chili (9 décembre 1966), Nations Unies, Recueil des sentences arbitrales, vol. 16, p. 111, 115; ILR, vol. 38, p. 16, 20 (1969).

démembrement d'un empire tel que l'Empire ottoman, il est entendu par présomption, présomption de caractère à la fois juridique et politique, que les frontières des Etats indépendants qui remplacent l'empire correspondront aux frontières des unités administratives dont l'empire démembré était constitué." Le principe de l'uti possidetis donne vraisemblablement son aspect juridique à cette présomption qu'invoque le Yémen. L'Erythrée conteste fermement cet argument.

97. Les faits sur lesquels une présomption juridique d'*uti possidetis* serait censément fondée soulèvent toutefois une difficulté préalable. En effet, pour qu'une telle présomption juridique puisse être prise en considération, il faut savoir ce qu'étaient effectivement "les frontières des unités administratives dont l'empire démembré était constitué". On sait que par des *firmans* publiés en 1841, 1866 et 1873, la Sublime Porte a donné au khédive d'Egypte le droit d'exercer sa juridiction sur la côte africaine de la mer Rouge. On peut penser que ce droit à l'exercice de la juridiction sur la côte africaine aurait tout naturellement été étendu aux îles situées au voisinage de la côte qui, géographiquement tout au moins, semblaient appartenir à ladite côte. Mais la question de savoir jusqu'où cette juridiction s'étendait sur l'archipel qui constitue le principal élément du présent différend relève jusqu'à un certain point de la conjecture. Le *firman*, semble-t-il, et il ne faut guère s'en étonner, ne parlait pas de l'archipel. Les sources citées par les Parties au sujet de cette question sont avant tout des documents internes et des notes de service du Foreign Office britannique. Et les réponses que l'on y trouve s'inspiraient, comme on peut le déduire très clairement, de spéculations formulées à partir de connaissances fiables. On sait que, de temps à autre, de petites garnisons ottomanes se trouvaient sur Zuqar et sur Hanish, et il est donné à penser qu'elles venaient de la côte arabique et étaient probablement ravitaillées à partir de cette côte.

98. Il convient de citer en particulier le mémorandum de septembre 1880 dû à sir Edward Hertslet (auteur de la célèbre *Map of Africa by Treaty* qui faisait autorité, et bibliothécaire du Foreign Office), mémorandum établi au Foreign Office à l'intention du Board of Trade, qui était chargé d'entretenir des phares dans la mer Rouge et qui avait demandé au Foreign Office son concours sur la question de la juridiction exercée sur les îles portant des phares. Dans ce mémorandum, Hertslet a pris grand soin de faire la distinction entre la souveraineté revenant à l'Empire ottoman sur la totalité de ces possessions, d'une part, et, de l'autre, un droit à l'exercice de la juridiction sur le territoire africain, lequel avait été conféré au khédive. Hertslet a dressé trois longues listes répertoriant les îles de la mer Rouge. La première liste énumérait les îles qui à son avis pouvaient être dites situées "à proximité étroite" de la côte africaine, et la deuxième liste énumérait les îles situées à proximité étroite de la côte arabique. Dans la première liste figurent les Mohabbakahs et les Haycocks; dans la deuxième, figurent les îles du "groupe de Jabel Zukar", celles du "groupe de la Petite Harnish" et celles du "groupe de la Grande Harnish". Ce mémorandum a, semble-t-il, été accepté comme un document de travail à la fois par le Foreign Office et par le Board of

Trade, bien que l'on puisse contester l'idée que les îles du deuxième groupe soient "à proximité étroite" de la côte arabique d'un point de vue strictement géographique. Sur la troisième liste, relativement brève, figuraient les îles proches du "centre de la mer Rouge" dont Jabal al-Tayr et le groupe de Zubayr sur lesquelles la juridiction exercée était, pour Hertslet, "incertaine" bien que la souveraineté demeurât acquise à l'Empire ottoman.

99. On voit mal comment on pourrait véritablement fonder une présomption juridique inspirée du principe de l'*uti possidetis* sur ces spéculations émanant d'un ministère d'un gouvernement tiers qui est concerné mais non pas désintéressé; et la question est tout à fait indépendante des difficultés juridiques liées à la création d'une présomption qui serait très évidemment contraire à la disposition précise formulée au sujet de certaines de ces îles au moins à l'article 16 du traité de Lausanne de 1923.[6] Le Yémen plaide certes en l'occurrence la règle *res inter alios acta*. Mais la Turquie ayant été en mesure de refuser d'accepter le traité de Sèvres, la souveraineté sur ces îles est nécessairement demeurée acquise à la Turquie jusqu'à la signature du traité de Lausanne, et sans doute jusqu'à 1926, date de la ratification dudit traité. A ces difficultés s'ajoute la question du droit intertemporel et aussi la question de savoir si cette doctrine de l'uti possidetis, qui à l'époque semblait devoir s'appliquer essentiellement à l'Amérique latine, pourrait véritablement servir à interpréter une question juridique se posant au Proche-Orient peu de temps après la fin de la première guerre mondiale.

100. Il n'empêche que tout le matériau relatif à la situation des îles pendant la période de l'Empire ottoman et celle qui suit immédiatement l'empire demeure un élément instructif de l'historique juridique du différend. Il est tout particulièrement intéressant de constater que, même quand la région était tout entière soumise à la domination ottomane, il paraissait acquis que les pouvoirs de juridiction et d'administration sur les îles dussent être partagés entre les deux côtes opposées.

Article 15, paragraphe 1 du Compromis d'arbitrage

101. Ce paragraphe dispose:

> Nulle disposition du présent Compromis d'arbitrage ne peut être interprétée comme portant préjudice aux positions juridiques ou aux droits de chaque Partie concernant les questions soumises au Tribunal, ni ne peut affecter ou porter préjudice aux décisions du Tribunal arbitral ou aux considérations et motifs sur lesquels se fondent lesdites décisions.

---

[6] D'un bout à l'autre de la présente sentence, la date du Traité de Lausanne qui est citée est celle de sa signature, 1923, et non celle de son entrée en vigueur, 1924. *[Note de l'éditeur: cette référence a été modifée de la version anglaise originale.]*

Pour le Tribunal, cette disposition n'est pas parfaitement claire. Une question posée aux Parties à ce sujet a suscité des réponses différentes; mais l'effet général était chaque fois qu'il s'agissait d'une simple réserve, une clause qui évoque celles qui commencent par "sans préjudice", concernant les arguments et les points de vue que les Parties voudraient peut-être présenter au Tribunal. Comme les Parties ont l'une et l'autre plaidé intégralement leur cause sans avoir ni d'un côté ni de l'autre eu l'occasion d'invoquer cette disposition, le Tribunal estime qu'il est préférable d'en rester là.

La tâche incombant au Tribunal dans la première étape

102. Au paragraphe 2 de son article 2, le Compromis d'arbitrage dispose:

> 2. La première étape donne lieu à une sentence sur la souveraineté territoriale et la définition du champ du différend entre l'Erythrée et le Yémen. Le Tribunal statue sur la question de la souveraineté territoriale conformément aux principes, aux règles et aux pratiques du droit international applicables en la matière et sur la base, notamment, des titres historiques. Le Tribunal statue sur la définition du champ du différend sur la base des positions respectives des deux Parties.

Plusieurs des dispositions de ce paragraphe demandent qu'on s'y arrête. Il s'agit tout d'abord de la prescription suivant laquelle cette première étape "donne lieu à une sentence sur la souveraineté territoriale". C'est-à-dire que le compromis ne demande pas au Tribunal, comme c'est souvent le cas dans les compromis d'arbitrage, d'attribuer la souveraineté territoriale à l'une des Parties ou à l'autre. En outre, il est demandé une sentence "sur" la souveraineté territoriale, et non pas une sentence "de" souveraineté territoriale consistant à attribuer celle-ci. Le Tribunal aurait par conséquent compétence pour dire que la souveraineté est conjointe ou partagée. C'est ce qui découle de l'énoncé de la disposition, lequel a été librement choisi par les Parties. Il paraît justifié de faire observer que cette disposition insolite en matière d'arbitrage ouvrait un assez large éventail de possibilités. Et le Tribunal a effectivement examiné toutes ces possibilités.

103. Il faut ensuite s'arrêter sur la disposition par laquelle le Tribunal est prié de statuer "sur la question de la souveraineté territoriale conformément aux principes, aux règles et aux pratiques du droit international applicables en la matière et sur la base, notamment, des titres historiques."

104. Comme indiqué plus haut, les Parties s'appuient l'une et l'autre sur divers moyens de preuve de la possession et de l'utilisation comme génératrices du titre, ce qui, en soi, fait appel à un type de revendication historique bien connu. Comme l'a dit Max Huber dans l'affaire de l'*île de Palmas*: "Il est tout à fait

naturel que l'établissement de la souveraineté soit l'aboutissement d'une lente évolution, d'un développement progressif du contrôle étatique."[7]

105. Mais le Yémen se fonde aussi au premier chef sur ce qu'il appelle très précisément un "titre historique". D'où la nécessité de réfléchir au sens du terme "titre". Celui-ci vise non pas une revendication en train de prendre forme mais un droit clairement établi ou, pour citer Pollock, "le droit qui est dans l'absolu ou relativement le plus valable sur un objet qui peut être contesté."[8] Il s'agit là d'une question de droit et non de possession bien que ce terme dénote normalement un droit à la possession même si la possession de fait réside dans d'autres mains.

106. La notion de titre historique est bien connue en droit international, notamment en ce qui concerne les "baies historiques", qui sont régies par des règles dérogeant aux règles normales concernant les baies. Les baies historiques, elles aussi, font appel à une sorte de "titre ancien": un titre établi de si longue date par la commune renommée que celle-ci constitue en soi un titre suffisant. Mais un titre historique a aussi, en droit international, une signification différente, celle d'un titre qui a été créé ou consolidé par un processus de prescription, ou bien l'acquiescement, ou encore par une possession dont la durée est telle qu'elle finit, en droit, par être reconnue comme un titre. Ce sont là également des titres historiques en ce sens que la continuité et l'écoulement d'une certaine période de temps sont essentiels. L'Erythrée plaide diverses formes de cette sorte de titre, et le Yémen en fait autant qui voit dans cette dernière sorte de titre la "confirmation" de son "titre ancien".

107. L'instruction qui est donnée au Tribunal de s'appuyer "notamment" sur les titres historiques ne peut guère vouloir dire qu'il faut donner à ces titres historiques une sorte de priorité qu'ils ne possèderaient pas normalement; car s'il existe effectivement un titre établi – qui est le meilleur des droits à la possession –, il s'agit par définition d'un droit prioritaire. Dans ces conditions, l'adverbe "notamment" répond peut-être à un souci d'extrême prudence, parce que l'on craignait que le Tribunal, face à toute une série d'autres intérêts et d'autres utilisations, oublie qu'il peut exister une catégorie distincte de titre qui n'est pas tributaire de l'utilisation et de la possession mais qui est en soi un droit de posséder que la possession soit ou non exercée en fait. De toute façon, comme on le verra ci-après, le Tribunal n'a pas manqué, en examinant la présente affaire, d'étudier toutes les sortes de titres historiques.

---

[7] Ile de Palmas (Pays-Bas c. Etats-Unis d'Amérique), Nations Unies, Recueil des sentences arbitrales, vol. II, p. 829, à la p. 867 (4 avril 1928); trad. fcse de Ch. Rousseau, in Revue générale de droit international public, tome XLII, 1935, p. 198. Le professeur Max Huber qui était à l'époque président de la Cour permanente de Justice internationale, fut arbitre unique dans cet arbitrage qui s'est déroulé sous les auspices de la Cour permanente d'arbitrage, conformément à la Convention de 1907 pour le règlement pacifique des différends internationaux.

[8] SIR FREDERICK POLLOCK, A FIRST BOOK OF JURISPRUDENCE, p. 177 (6e éd., 1929).

108. Les Parties ont adopté des points de vue divergents sur les effets de la scission de l'arbitrage en deux étapes, la première étant consacrée à la souveraineté territoriale et la seconde aux frontières maritimes. C'est au cours de la procédure supplémentaire relative aux accords pétroliers conclu par les Parties que le Yémen s'est très fortement inquiété du risque de voir le Tribunal tenté de "préfigurer" (l'expression était bien choisie) l'issue de la deuxième étape concernant la délimitation maritime et de raisonner en conséquence au cours de la première étape. C'est ainsi qu'au paragraphe 20 des écritures du Yémen, dans la phase supplémentaire relative aux accords pétroliers, on lit ceci:

> Ce dernier élément [la préfiguration] préoccupe tout particulièrement le Gouvernement du Yémen. Il paraît toujours intéressant de rechercher le principe suivant lequel on partagera un groupe d'îles, surtout dans un arbitrage. L'intérêt est d'autant plus grand quand la tâche incombant au Tribunal s'étend à l'opération de la délimitation maritime, et il faut certainement faire attention à éviter de préfigurer des principes et des concepts équitables qui en droit ne sont pertinents que pour la seconde phase de la présente procédure.

Ce paragraphe fut répété mot pour mot par le Yémen lors de la phase orale supplémentaire de juillet 1998.

109. Le Yémen a présenté à un stade tardif de la procédure un argument d'un genre nouveau qui lui tenait manifestement beaucoup à cœur, concernant l'idée apparemment inacceptable qu'il était envisagé pour la première étape une solution équitable. L'argument était étonnant, ne serait-ce que parce que ce fut là, semble-t-il, la première et seule fois où l'une ou l'autre des Parties a fait mention de l'équité ou de principes équitables. En outre, aucun membre du Tribunal n'avait de son côté fait référence à l'équité ou aux principes équitables.

110. La question a surgi à nouveau sous une forme un peu différente dans les réponses que le Yémen a faites à quatre questions posées aux deux Parties à l'issue des plaidoiries du Yémen lors de la procédure supplémentaire, questions auxquelles les deux Parties ont répondu ensuite par écrit. Ces questions avaient pour objet de demander simplement aux deux Parties comment il se faisait que certains de leurs accords pétroliers, notamment ceux du Yémen, semblaient être conçus pour s'étendre à une sorte de ligne médiane côtière. En réponse, le Yémen s'est senti obligé d'"exprimer les réserves les plus fermes possibles contre la 'préfiguration' d'une ligne médiane".

111. L'Erythrée de son côté a répondu, et, pour le Tribunal, elle avait raison, qu'au paragraphe 2 de l'article 2 du Compromis d'arbitrage, le Tribunal était prié de "statu[er] sur la question de la souveraineté territoriale conformément aux principes, aux règles et aux pratiques du droit international applicables en la matière et sur la base, notamment, des titres historiques." La formule s'étend nécessairement à tout principe, règle ou pratique de droit international

effectivement applicable à ces questions de souveraineté, même si les principes, règles ou pratiques en question font partie du droit maritime. Certes, le Tribunal ne doit pas lors de cette première étape délimiter de frontière maritime quelconque ni préfigurer, le cas échéant, une telle délimitation. Mais cela n'a rien à voir avec le fait de faire appel à tout le droit international qui peut être pertinent aux fins de statuer sur la souveraineté, ce qui est du ressort de cette première étape.*

112. En règle générale, le Tribunal se voit dans l'impossibilité d'accepter la proposition suivant laquelle le droit international régissant l'espace terrestre et le droit international régissant les frontières maritimes sont non seulement différents mais également séparés et ne présentent aucune pertinence juridique l'un par rapport à l'autre. Cette théorie est d'ailleurs infirmée par le Yémen lui-même quand il demande au Gouvernement britannique l'autorisation d'assister à la conférence de 1989 sur les phares parce que les îles septentrionales sont situées dans la zone économique exclusive du Yémen.

113. Il est bon que le Tribunal donne son avis mûrement réfléchi sur ces questions dans les débuts de la présente sentence. En même temps, il y a également lieu de signaler que le Tribunal a dit comme le Yémen, et d'ailleurs aussi comme l'Erythrée, qu'il ne saurait être question, au cours de cette première étape de l'arbitrage, ne fût-ce que de "préfigurer", et encore bien moins de tracer une quelconque délimitation maritime, qu'il s'agisse de ligne médiane ou, du reste, d'une ligne répondant à des principes équitables.

* - * - *

* *Note de l'éditeur: cette phrase a été corrigée de la version anglaise originale.*

CHAPITRE IV – Les titres historiques et autres considérations historiques

114. Le Compromis d'arbitrage, à l'article 2, donne au Tribunal pour instruction de statuer sur la souveraineté territoriale conformément au droit international applicable "et sur la base, notamment, des titres historiques." Le Tribunal a donc accordé une attention particulière tant aux thèses relatives aux titres anciens et à leur réversion avancées par le Yémen qu'aux thèses relatives à l'attribution fort ancienne des Mohabbakahs à la colonie d'Erythrée et à l'établissement précoce de titres par l'Italie telles que l'Erythrée plaide ces thèses. Le Yémen accorde de l'importance au "titre historique" qu'il affirme détenir sur les îles, ce qui apparaît d'ailleurs dans l'énoncé même tant de l'Accord sur les principes que du Compromis d'arbitrage. Le Tribunal admet donc parfaitement que l'intention dont procède l'article 2 est qu'il faut, parmi tous les éléments pertinents du droit international, accorder une attention particulière à ces éléments-là. Indépendamment de l'analyse à laquelle il procède pour savoir comment les principes, règles et pratiques du droit international influent d'une manière générale sur la décision relative à la souveraineté territoriale qu'il doit rendre, le Tribunal a tenu on ne peut plus attentivement compte des titres historiques intéressant le présent litige.

115. De son côté, l'Erythrée n'invoque pas une souveraineté fondée sur un titre ancien, bien que le passé de l'Ethiopie remonte incontestablement fort loin. L'Erythrée choisit plutôt d'affirmer en partie qu'il y a eu consolidation historique d'un titre de la part de l'Italie pendant l'entre-deux-guerres qui a créé un titre sur les îles, lequel a été effectivement transmis à l'Ethiopie lors du règlement des questions territoriales après la défaite de l'Italie lors de la seconde guerre mondiale. Cet argument devra naturellement être traité dans les chapitres suivants consacrés à l'entre-deux-guerres, à l'armistice et aux événements connexes à la fin de la seconde guerre mondiale.

116. Le Yémen a quant à lui affirmé détenir un titre historique ou "titre ancien", remontant au Moyen-Age, en vertu duquel les îles auraient fait partie du *Bilad el-Yemen*. Le Yémen dit que ce titre ancien est antérieur aux diverses occupations de la région par l'Empire ottoman et est revenu au Yémen moderne après l'effondrement de l'Empire ottoman à la fin de la première guerre mondiale.

117. Le Yémen en l'occurrence est le seul à avoir soulevé d'importantes questions concernant un titre "historique" ou "ancien" qui aurait existé avant la seconde occupation ottomane du 19e siècle; le Tribunal va donc devoir à présent interroger l'histoire pour comprendre pourquoi le Yémen prétend détenir ce titre ancien. Le Tribunal examine dans le présent chapitre comment il convient de comprendre l'histoire globale de la péninsule arabique d'un point de vue juridique correspondant à l'époque considérée, avant de formuler sa conclusion définitive sur les questions juridiques relatives aux "titres historiques". En outre, le Tribunal examine aussi dans le présent chapitre la doctrine de la "réversion" avancée par

le Yémen, car elle est déterminante pour toute décision à adopter, quelle qu'elle soit, quant à l'effet juridique d'un "titre historique".

118. Le Yémen, quand il prétend détenir un titre historique et ancien, fait appel à plusieurs considérations historiques importantes. L'une de ces considérations a trait à l'identité du Yémen historique et au point de savoir si celui-ci s'étendait aux îles contestées. Une deuxième considération met en cause l'existence d'une doctrine de réversion reconnue par le droit international et une troisième considération a trait au rôle de la continuité dans le cadre d'une conception de la réversion d'un titre ancien. Les prétentions de l'Erythrée qui sont fondées à la fois sur l'histoire et sur le droit international sont traitées ailleurs. Dans le présent chapitre, le Tribunal traite en outre d'importantes questions historiques comme celle de la traditionnelle exploitation conjointe des eaux entourant les îles par des pêcheurs des deux rives de la mer Rouge, et l'attribution par les Ottomans d'une juridiction administrative s'exerçant entre les deux côtes.

119. La revendication yéménite est fondée essentiellement sur un titre "ancien" ou "historique" en vertu duquel la souveraineté intrinsèque et inaliénable de l'imam s'étendait à l'intégralité de ce que l'histoire connaît sous le nom de *Bilad el-Yemen*, lequel a existé pendant plusieurs siècles et, selon ce que dit le Yémen, aurait compris les îles de la mer Rouge méridionale. Le Yémen dit en outre que cette souveraineté serait demeurée intacte lors de l'annexion du Yémen par les Ottomans et aurait survécu à cette annexion, bien que la Sublime Porte eût déclaré que le Yémen était l'un des *vilayets* assujettis au maître ottoman.

120. Il convient d'apprécier les arguments avancés par le Yémen à cet égard dans le cadre historique et juridique propre à la période pertinente, laquelle va de la fin du 19ᵉ siècle à la dissolution de l'Empire ottoman.

121. Il faut tenir compte du caractère particulier de la relation entre l'Empire ottoman et le Yémen comme d'un élément historique important. En dépit du traité de Da'an conclu en 1911, qui accordait à l'imam du Yémen une plus large autonomie interne, l'imam est demeuré un suzerain relevant de la souveraineté ottomane jusqu'à la désintégration totale de l'Empire ottoman et la perte de toutes les possessions arabes de l'empire, y compris celle du *vilayet* du Yémen.[9] Ce n'est qu'en 1923, sous l'effet de l'article 16 du traité de Lausanne, que l'Empire ottoman non seulement a admis renoncer à tous ses droits souverains sur le Yémen, mais a expressément renoncé à son titre souverain sur les îles qui relevaient précédemment de la juridiction du *wali* ottoman résidant à Hodeidah.

---

[9] Voir en particulier, JOHN BALDRY, *One Hundred Years of Yemeni History: 1849-1948*, dans L'ARABIE DU SUD, VOL. II, p. 85 (pub. ss la dir. de J. CHELHOD ET AL. en 1984); ROGER JOINT DAGUENET, HISTOIRE DE LA MER ROUGE: DE LESSEPS À NOS JOURS, p. 113-116, p. 186-190, p. 240-241 (1997).

122. Du point de vue de l'étendue territoriale, il faut faire la distinction entre le Yémen de l'imam en tant qu'entité autonome et le *vilayet* ottoman du Yémen. Pendant toute la période qui va de la seconde moitié du 19e siècle à 1925, l'imam du Yémen n'avait ni souveraineté ni juridiction sur la Tihama ni sur les côtes de la mer Rouge. En vertu des accords qu'il avait passés avec le sultan ottoman, l'imam administrait exclusivement un territoire sans littoral, limité aux montagnes les plus élevées. C'est le *wali* ottoman qui a exercé jusqu'en 1917 une juridiction exclusive sur ces côtes. Puis, les côtes sont passées sous le contrôle de l'Idrisi, un chef tribal local soutenu d'abord par les Italiens, et plus tard par le Gouvernement britannique. La côte n'est passée sous le contrôle de l'imam qu'en 1926. Comme on le verra plus loin, ce fait a des incidences juridiques négatives pour la thèse de la "réversion" défendue par le Yémen, de même que pour l'application de certaines autres règles du droit international, y compris la notion de "titre historique" ancien entendue intégralement au sens classique.

123. Il ne fait pas de doute que la notion de titre historique a une résonance spéciale dans des situations qui peuvent exister même dans le monde contemporain, s'agissant par exemple de déterminer la souveraineté sur des terres utilisées par des nomades et occupées depuis des temps immémoriaux par certaines tribus qui font allégeance au souverain imposant son pouvoir sociopolitique sur cette région géographique. Il en va différemment en ce qui concerne des îles inhabitées dont on ne prétend pas qu'elles sont situées à l'intérieur des limites d'eaux historiques.

124. En la présente instance, ni l'une ni l'autre des Parties n'a formulé de prétention revenant à situer les îles en litige dans des eaux historiques. En outre, aucune des îles n'est habitée sauf à titre saisonnier ou temporaire, aucune ne présente même les conditions naturelles et matérielles qui autoriseraient une colonisation humaine permanente. Quels qu'aient pu être les liens entre les territoires côtiers et les îles en question, le fait que l'Empire ottoman renonce à sa souveraineté sur les îles sous l'effet de l'article 16 du traité de Lausanne de 1923 (examiné plus en détail au chapitre V) porte logiquement et juridiquement atteinte à tout titre préexistant éventuel.

125. Il a été reconnu au cours de la procédure orale que, sous l'effet de la loi en vigueur à l'époque, la souveraineté ottomane sur les régions en cause était licite. Le fait que le Yémen n'était pas partie au traité de Lausanne et qu'à ses yeux, tant les Britanniques que les Italiens avaient été des usurpateurs en mer Rouge, n'efface pas cette conséquence juridique. Par ailleurs, il n'a pas été établi à la satisfaction du Tribunal au cours de la procédure que la doctrine de la réversion fait partie du droit international. De toute façon, le Tribunal aboutit à la conclusion que, vu les faits en l'espèce, ladite doctrine ne s'applique pas. Il serait en effet impossible qu'il y ait "réversion", puisque la "chaîne des titres", c'est-à-dire la transmission de ces titres, a été nécessairement interrompue et qu'il ne serait guère possible d'invoquer à l'appui d'une telle revendication les éléments positifs qui ont éventuellement existé, quels qu'ils soient. Pendant plusieurs

décennies, le rôle prédominant a été exercé par les puissances navales occidentales en mer Rouge une fois que celle-ci fut ouverte au trafic maritime international par le canal de Suez, et qu'elle fut colonisée sur les deux côtes dans sa partie méridionale. Cette hégémonie a eu pour résultat important le maintien du statu quo imposé à la suite de la première guerre mondiale, lequel signifiait en particulier que la souveraineté sur les îles visée par l'article 16 du traité de Lausanne de 1923 restait indéterminée tout au moins tant que les puissances occidentales intéressées étaient toujours dans la région. Tant que régnait cette situation coloniale, ni l'Ethiopie ni le Yémen n'étaient en mesure de faire la preuve de l'existence d'un titre historique, de quelque type que ce fût, qui puisse servir à confirmer de façon satisfaisante la souveraineté sur l'une quelconque des îles contestées. Ce n'est qu'après le départ des puissances coloniales qu'il devenait possible de voir le statu quo modifié. Mais une modification du statu quo n'implique toutefois pas nécessairement réversion.

126. Il ne faut toutefois pas interpréter ces arguments comme ôtant aux considérations historiques toute importance juridique. Tout d'abord, la situation qui a existé pendant de nombreux siècles où il fut de tout temps possible d'exploiter les ressources marines de la mer Rouge méridionale et d'y pratiquer la pêche, d'y pratiquer aussi sans restriction la circulation d'une côte à l'autre, et où il fut aussi toujours possible aux populations des deux côtes d'utiliser conjointement les îles, présente par là d'importants éléments à même de créer certains "droits historiques" au bénéfice des deux Parties sous l'effet d'une consolidation historique constituant comme une sorte de "servitude internationale" beaucoup plus qu'une souveraineté territoriale.[10] De tels droits historiques fournissent un fondement juridique assez solide pour entretenir sous certains aspects une *res communis* qui existe depuis des siècles au profit des populations des deux côtes de la mer Rouge. En second lieu, la distinction qui existait sous l'Empire ottoman du point de vue de la juridiction entre les îles administrées depuis la côte africaine et les autres îles administrées depuis la côte arabique constitue un fait historique à prendre également en considération.

127. Les données qu'on puise des sources historiques et géographiques les plus fiables, tant anciennes que modernes, montrent bien que les populations des deux rives opposées du sud de la mer Rouge ont toujours été liées par la culture et ont toujours mené le même type d'activités socioéconomiques. De temps immémorial, outre qu'elles se livraient à des échanges de personnes ou de marchandises, elles pêchaient et naviguaient librement dans tout l'espace maritime en faisant étape dans les îles utilisées comme des îles relais et en y trouvant parfois refuge pour échapper aux forts vents du nord. Ces activités ont

---

[10] Voir à cet égard YEHUDA Z. BLUM, *Historic Rights*, dans ENCYCLOPEDIA OF PUBLIC INTERNATIONAL LAW, VOL. 7, p. 105 et seq.; et HISTORIC TITLES IN INTERNATIONAL LAW, p. 126-129 (1965).

été menées pendant des siècles sans qu'il soit nécessaire d'obtenir des autorisations des souverains aussi bien du côté asiatique que du côté africain de la mer Rouge et en l'absence de restrictions ou de réglementations imposées par les pouvoirs publics.

128. Cette situation qui a prévalu traditionnellement était le reflet d'habitudes culturelles profondément enracinées ayant débouché sur ce que l'on pourrait appeler d'un point de vue juridique une *res communis* permettant aux pêcheurs aussi bien africains que yéménites d'opérer sans aucune limitation dans la région tout entière et de vendre leurs prises sur les marchés locaux des deux rives de la mer Rouge. De même, les personnes naviguant d'une côte à l'autre pour pêcher ou commercer avaient coutume de s'abriter temporairement des vents violents sur l'une quelconque des îles inhabitées qui sont disséminées dans cette partie de la mer sans rencontrer d'obstacles d'ordre politique ni administratif.[11]

129. Ces faits historiques sont attestés par toute une gamme de sources présentées à titre de preuves au cours de la procédure arbitrale. L'étude détaillée de ces moyens qu'ont ainsi présentés les deux Parties fait apparaître des modes de comportement communs, profondément enracinés, ainsi que la poursuite, jusque pendant les dernières années, de relations croisées marquées parfois par le recours à des arbitres professionnels propres au milieu de la pêche (*aq'il*) s'occupant de régler les différends conformément au droit coutumier local. Cette interprétation est étayée par les déclarations attribuées à des pêcheurs originaires des deux rives de la mer Rouge, considérées dans leur ensemble, qui ont été présentées par les deux Parties.

130. Les schémas socioéconomiques et culturels décrits ci-dessus étaient en parfaite harmonie avec les concepts juridiques classiques du droit musulman, qui ignoraient pratiquement le principe de la "souveraineté territoriale" tel qu'il s'est constitué chez les puissances européennes et qu'il est devenu un élément fondamental du droit international occidental au 19e siècle.[12]

131. Il faut toutefois relever que l'Empire ottoman qui gouvernait directement ou par le truchement de ses suzerains la quasi-totalité des pays situés autour de la mer

---

[11] Voir en particulier CHARLES FORSTER, THE HISTORICAL GEOGRAPHY OF ARABIA, VOL. 1, p. 113, vol. II, p. 337 (1984) (la première édition date de 1844); JOSEPH CHELHOD ET AL., L'ARABIE DU SUD – HISTOIRE ET CIVILISATION, VOL. I, p. 63, p. 67-69, p. 252-255 (1984); ROGER JOINT DAGUENET, HISTORE DE LA MER ROUGE: DE MOÏSE À BONAPARTE, p. 20-24, p. 86-87 (1995); et YVES THORAVAL ET AL., LE YÉMEN ET LA MER ROUGE, p. 14-16, p. 17-20, p. 35-37, p. 43-47, p. 51-54 (1995).

[12] Voir en particulier A. SANHOURY, LE CALIFAT, p. 22, 37, 119, 163, 273, 320-321 (1926); MAJID KADOURI, *Islamic Law*, ENCYCLOPEDIA OF PUBLIC INTERNATIONAL LAW, VOL. 6, p. 227 *et seq.*; et AHMED S. EL KOSHERI, *History of Islamic Law*, ENCYCLOPEDIA OF PUBLIC INTERNATIONAL LAW, VOL. 7, p. 222 *et seq.*

Rouge au cours de la première moitié du 19e siècle, y compris le *Bilad El-Yemen* et ce qui fut connu ensuite sous le nom d'Erythrée, a commencé après la fin de la guerre de Crimée en 1856 à renoncer aux aspects communautaires du régime musulman de droit international pour adopter les règles modernes ayant désormais cours au sein du concert européen des nations auquel la Sublime Porte a adhéré pour s'y intégrer complètement au cours du Congrès de Berlin de 1875. Or, d'après le nouveau droit international moderne, la notion juridique de "souveraineté territoriale" devint une pierre angulaire pour la plupart des puissances de forme étatique et la situation existant dans la mer Rouge ne pouvait plus guère échapper aux conséquences juridiques de cette nouvelle réalité.

132. On peut donc comprendre facilement que les deux Parties admettent l'une et l'autre que les îles en litige aient toutes relevé au départ de la souveraineté territoriale de l'Empire ottoman. Et, dans le cadre de l'exercice de cette souveraineté ottomane sur ces îles, il convient de noter que la Sublime Porte a accordé au khédive d'Egypte le droit d'administrer les possessions ottomanes (*vilayet*) sur la côte africaine qui constituent actuellement "l'Etat d'Erythrée", et que cette délégation de pouvoir s'étendait à la juridiction à exercer sur les îles au large de la côte africaine, y compris les Dahlaks et finalement les Mohabbakahs.

133. La souveraineté de l'Empire ottoman sur les deux rives de la mer Rouge est incontestée jusqu'à 1880 et le resta aussi en ce qui concerne la côte orientale ou arabique jusqu'à la première guerre mondiale. Parmi les divers documents présentés à l'appui de ce fait historique, l'Erythrée a communiqué la version française d'un mémorandum daté du 6 décembre 1881, émanant du ministère khédival égyptien des affaires étrangères, lequel indique qu'en mai 1871, l'Italie a reconnu que le drapeau ottoman flottait depuis 1862 sur la côte africaine en un point situé au-delà du sud d'Assab. Ce mémorandum égyptien ajoutait que jusqu'en 1880, le Gouvernement égyptien a ajouté foi aux affirmations du Gouvernement italien selon lesquelles la présence italienne avait eu essentiellement un caractère privé et commercial. Par suite, toute la côte africaine et les îles au large de ladite côte sont demeurées jusqu'alors placées sous la juridiction du khédive. En même temps, toutes les autres îles étaient et continuaient d'être placées sous la juridiction du *wali* ottoman résidant à Hodeidah et nommé par la Sublime Porte.

134. Il faut donc faire clairement la distinction entre les îles de la mer Rouge placées sous la juridiction du khédive d'Egypte pour le compte de l'Empire ottoman jusqu'en 1882 et les autres îles de la mer Rouge qui ont fait partie du *vilayet* ottoman du Yémen jusqu'à la dissolution de l'empire à la suite de la première guerre mondiale.

135. Un mémorandum du Foreign Office britannique daté du 10 juin 1930, qui s'appuie expressément sur le mémorandum Hertslet de 1880, indique que le khédive d'Egypte exerçait alors sa juridiction au large de la côte africaine sur les

"îles Mohabakah, Harbi et Sayal". Pour ce qui est de l'autre catégorie, ce mémorandum britannique dit du "groupe de la Grande Hanish qu'il est situé au large de la côte arabique et relève donc de la souveraineté du sultan et de sa juridiction exclusive."

Le paragraphe 16 du même mémorandum souligne que:

> La Grande Hanish, Suyal Hanish, la Petite Hanish, Jebal Zukur, Abu Ail, étant situées plus près de la côte arabique, ont été considérées, semble-t-il, avant la guerre comme relevant à la fois de la juridiction et de la souveraineté de la Turquie.

136. En outre, l'Erythrée a présenté des documents du ministère italien des colonies, dont une note datée du 11 octobre 1916 qui est intitulée "Les îles de la mer Rouge" et qui rapporte les conclusions d'une enquête menée sur les îles elles-mêmes. La première partie de la note est consacrée à "Farsan", la deuxième à "Kameran", et la troisième porte sur "les autres îles", au nombre desquelles une rubrique intitulée "Gebel Zucur"; sous cet intitulé figurait non seulement le "groupe de 12 assez gros rochers", mais aussi "les deux îles Hanish, la grande et la petite". S'agissant de ces dernières îles, il était indiqué que "les autorités ottomanes y maintenaient une petite garnison de 40 hommes sous le commandement d'un mulazim pour contrôler les déplacements des navires chargés à destination de la côte yéménite en provenance de Gibut.", et en outre que, "face aux difficultés éprouvées à ravitailler en eau et en vivres la garnison faute de moyens suffisants, les autorités ottomanes l'ont retirée." A la suite du bombardement de Midi par les navires de guerre italiens, les autorités ottomanes auraient "rétabli la garnison en 1909 et porté à 100 le nombre des askaris."

137. Ces documents de l'époque coloniale italienne, qui confirment la souveraineté ottomane sur les îles Hanish-Zuqar et disent que celles-ci étaient toujours en 1916 administrées par le *vilayet* du Yémen, sont compatibles avec les vues exprimées dans un télégramme adressé au ministre italien des colonies par le gouverneur de la colonie d'Erythrée et communiqué le 18 octobre 1916 au ministre italien des affaires étrangères. Une note du ministère des affaires étrangères intitulée: "Les îles de la mer Rouge", qui remonte au 31 juillet 1901 est annexée à ce télégramme et porte l'indication "Appendice II". Cette note de 1901 répartit les îles en trois groupes:

> Les îles les plus septentrionales, qui n'ont qu'un rapport lointain, voire nul avec la colonie d'Erythrée en raison de la distance, les îles qui sont en face de Massaua et les îles les plus méridionales qui font face aux côtes érythréennes de Beilul et d'Assab. La quasi-totalité des îles sont situées sur la côte orientale de la mer Rouge, sauf les îles Dahalac, qui relèvent de nous, et quelques autres îles de beaucoup moins d'importance.

En ce qui concerne le deuxième de ces groupes, la note italienne indique:

> Mis à part l'archipel des îles Dahalac – qui est sous souveraineté italienne et qui comprend les îles les plus étendues de la mer Rouge – Cotuma, Diebel Tair et Camaran sont importantes dans ce deuxième groupe de l'archipel; toutes ces îles relèvent de la Turquie.

La note qualifie expressément de "turques": "Cotuma", "Djebel . . . appelée Gebel Sebair" et "Camaran".

Passant au troisième groupe, la note italienne de 1901 parle d'un:

> . . . groupe d'îles connues sous le nom de Hanish ou Harnish (turques). Ce groupe comprend l'île de Gebel Zucar, la Grande et la Petite Hanish ainsi que les autres petites îles d'Abu-ail, Syul-Hanish, Haycoc et Mohabbach, ainsi qu'un petit nombre d'îlots assimilables à de gros rochers.

138. Des documents britanniques contemporains procèdent également de l'idée que les îles en question, à l'exception des Mohabbakahs, faisaient partie du *vilayet* du Yémen, et paraissent rattacher le sort à leur réserver à l'avenir à ce lien historique avec la côte arabique.

139. Un mémorandum du Foreign Office en date du 15 janvier 1917 qui est intitulé "L'Italie et le partage de l'Empire turc" dit au paragraphe 38 ceci:

> Enfin, l'unanimité est semble-t-il réalisée sur le fait que les îles de la mer Rouge qui relevaient précédemment de la souveraineté turque vont normalement être transférées à l'Etat arabe, mais il faudra appliquer un régime spécial à l'île Kamaran en raison des déplacements de pèlerins.

140. Dans une lettre qu'il adresse le 13 mars 1919 à lord Curzon, lord Balfour a indiqué que la solution envisagée pour "Abu Ail, Zabayir et Jebel Teir" ainsi que pour "Kamaran, Zukur et les îles Hanish (soit le groupe de la Grande Hanish, la Petite Hanish et Suyul Hanish)" consistait soit "à les annexer" à l'Empire britannique soit à "plaider leur transfert à des souverains arabes indépendants du territoire continental qui ne soient pas l'imam de Sanaa ni l'Idrisi".

141. Dans une lettre qu'il adresse le 27 mai 1919 à lord Balfour, lord Curzon a de son côté lié la question d'un éventuel transfert à des souverains arabes à la question fondamentalement politique de l'avenir de la région: "toute la question de l'avenir des îles de la mer Rouge" devait être considérée comme "se rattachant finalement à celle du statut futur de l'Arabie." Lord Curzon disait par conséquent:

> [l]a politique du gouvernement de Sa Majesté devrait tout d'abord viser à faire reconnaître par les Hautes Parties contractantes le fait que les îles font partie du territoire continental et deviendront par conséquent la propriété des souverains arabes

intéressés; et que lesdits souverains doivent entretenir une relation particulière avec le gouvernement de Sa Majesté.

142. Comme on le verra plus amplement par la suite, l'attribution de pouvoirs d'administration sur les îles de la mer Rouge, que ce soit par l'Empire ottoman agissant comme une puissance souveraine sur les deux rives ou que ce soit sous l'effet de la juridiction exercée à partir de la côte arabique seule, représente un fait historique qu'il convient de prendre en considération et auquel il convient de donner un certain poids juridique.

143. Avant d'en terminer avec cette étude des considérations historiques, il faut aussi rappeler la question du titre yéménite ancien ou historique auquel le Yémen a accordé une importance cruciale dans ses exposés. Le Tribunal a expliqué dans le présent chapitre que l'argument soulève certains problèmes historiques. Il y a tout d'abord le fait historique que le Yémen médiéval était avant tout un pays montagneux qui n'exerçait guère son autorité sur les zones côtières, lesquelles servaient pour l'essentiel à entretenir le commerce maritime entre l'Inde ou les Indes orientales, d'une part, et, de l'autre, l'Egypte et les autres ports méditerranéens. Il convient de rappeler en second lieu que la notion de souveraineté territoriale était totalement étrangère à l'entité que représentait le Yémen médiéval. Du reste, la notion de souveraineté territoriale au sens du droit international moderne est parvenue tardivement jusqu'à l'Empire ottoman (ce ne fut pas avant le 19e siècle), cet Empire ottoman revendiquant alors la souveraineté territoriale sur la région tout entière et cette souveraineté lui a été reconnue.

144. Mais il se pose d'autres problèmes aussi au sujet de la revendication yéménite à un titre ancien, qui ont trait en particulier à l'effet de l'article 16 du traité de Lausanne et à la nécessité de faire valoir comme un principe de doctrine la continuité du titre ancien et sa réversion à la fin de l'Empire ottoman. Le Tribunal examine en détail cette question au chapitre suivant et donne au chapitre X ses vues définitives sur cette question du titre ancien.

--*

CHAPITRE V – L'histoire juridique et les principaux traités ainsi que les autres instruments juridiques en cause; questions de succession d'Etat

145. Il existe une série d'instruments de poids qui, sous la forme de diverses combinaisons, intéressent les usagers de la mer Rouge et qui constituent une importante toile de fond sur laquelle viennent s'inscrire les revendications des Parties au présent arbitrage. Savoir si ces instruments ont ou non un caractère obligatoire, si, juridiquement, ils jouent un rôle direct ou relèvent simplement d'une *res inter alios acta*, le sens qu'il faut donner à leurs dispositions, autant de questions qui ont retenu l'attention des Parties.

146. Ce qu'on appelle le traité de Da'an de 1911 fut en fait un instrument interne au moyen duquel l'imam du Yémen s'est assuré de plus grands pouvoirs d'autonomie interne à l'intérieur de l'Empire ottoman. Toutefois, la souveraineté sur la totalité des possessions ottomanes, y compris les îles en litige, est restée acquise à l'empire lui-même jusqu'à ce que celui-ci ait été juridiquement privé de ses possessions arabes à la suite de la première guerre mondiale.

147. Les principales puissances alliées (c'est-à-dire l'Empire britannique, la France, l'Italie et le Japon) ont conclu à Mudros un armistice avec la Turquie le 30 octobre 1918. Ce fut l'instrument par lequel il fut mis fin aux hostilités et qui permettait d'ailleurs l'occupation du terrain par les belligérants. Ce ne fut pas un instrument opérant un transfert de territoires. Il n'est pas contesté qu'immédiatement avant la signature de cet armistice de Mudros, le titre sur la totalité des îles était acquis aux Ottomans. Il était également entendu pour tous les participants à cette procédure que ce titre ottoman avait été garanti par une occupation militaire, ce qui était licite au regard du droit international de l'époque. L'un des éléments fondamentaux du titre souverain est le droit d'aliéner. Exactement comme l'Empire ottoman aurait eu la liberté de céder à un Etat tiers son titre sur les îles à n'importe quel moment au cours de la période allant de 1872 à 1918, l'empire avait encore juridiquement le droit de décider lui-même de la destination du titre après 1918. La liberté d'action de l'empire à cet égard était limitée non sous l'effet d'une doctrine de réversion qui entrerait en jeu dès que la Turquie se serait défaite d'un titre, mais par les vrais détenteurs du pouvoir à la fin de la guerre.

148. Il n'est donc pas possible que le titre ait été transmis en 1918 à l'imam. C'est pourquoi le Tribunal ne peut pas accepter que la souveraineté sur les îles en litige ait été rendue au Yémen.

149. Il était entendu de part et d'autre qu'un traité de paix énonçant comment devait être réglé le sort des territoires turcs en Europe et ailleurs serait conclu après l'armistice de Mudros de 1918. A cette fin, les principales puissances alliées (lesquelles formaient avec l'Arménie, la Belgique, la Grèce, le Hedjaz, la Pologne, le Portugal, la Roumanie, l'Etat serbo-croate slovène et la

Tchécoslovaquie les “puissances alliées”) d’une part, et, de l’autre, la Turquie ont signé un traité de paix à Sèvres le 10 août 1920. Parmi les dispositions longues et détaillées énoncées dans ce traité, il n’en figurait qu’une seule qui eût pu être applicable aux îles de la mer Rouge qui sont en litige en l’espèce. Il s’agit de l’article 132, qui disposait:

> A l’extérieur des frontières que lui fixe le présent traité, la Turquie renonce en faveur des principales puissances alliées à tous droits et titres qu’elle pourrait revendiquer pour quelque motif que ce soit sur tous les territoires situés en dehors de l’Europe ou concernant de tels territoires dont le sort n’est pas autrement réglé par le présent traité. La Turquie s’engage à admettre les mesures que pourraient prendre dès à présent ou à l’avenir les principales puissances alliées, en accord le cas échéant avec des puissances tierces, et à s’y conformer pour donner effet à la disposition ci-dessus. [Traduction du Bureau international de la CPA.]

150. Finalement, le traité de Sèvres n’a pas été ratifié par la Turquie et n’est pas entré en vigueur. Par conséquent, le titre sur les îles de la mer Rouge qui sont en litige est nécessairement resté aux mains de la Turquie – bien que celle-ci sût qu’elle serait le moment venu obligée de s’en défaire. D’ailleurs, la Grande-Bretagne occupait depuis 1915 certaines de ces îles pour prendre de vitesse l’Italie à cet égard et elle y arborait son drapeau sans toutefois revendiquer le titre.

151. La position initiale de la Grande-Bretagne lors des négociations de paix de Sèvres était que les îles situées à l’est des South West Rocks au large de la Grande Hanish devraient être placées sous la souveraineté des chefs indépendants de la péninsule arabique. Les Britanniques comprenaient bien que, pour des raisons historiques et géographiques, ces chefs de la péninsule arabique seraient des prétendants sérieux au moment où la Turquie abandonnerait finalement son titre et qu’il faudrait dire à qui la souveraineté revenait désormais, et ils estimaient d’ailleurs que la volonté, chez ces chefs arabes, d’empêcher toute puissance européenne de s’installer sur la côte orientale incitait à transmettre le titre à un “chef arabe considéré comme un ami”.[13] Mais cela ne correspond pas à une transmission automatique du titre par réversion entre la Turquie et le Yémen. Finalement, c’est une proposition différente qui a été acceptée et énoncée à l’article 132 du traité de Sèvres.

152. Le Yémen a fait grand cas du fait que, pendant toutes les années qui ont suivi, l’imam a protesté auprès de la Grande-Bretagne contre la non-restitution “[des]

[13] Voir, par comparaison, la politique envisagée par le Foreign Office pour les îles de Sheikh Saal, Kamaran et Farsan et pour Hodeidah, à savoir l’occupation. Finalement, un télégramme adressé en 1915 par le vice-roi des Indes fait savoir que le drapeau britannique a été hissé sur Jabal Zuqar et les îles Hanish. En l’occurrence, les faits ont été qualifiés, dans un message adressé au Foreign Office par le Résident britannique à Aden d’“annexion temporaire”. En 1926, la Grande-Bretagne ne considérait pas qu’elle détenait le titre de souverain sur les îles en question.

îles". Lesdites "îles" n'étaient pas précisées. Le phénomène peut effectivement étayer les allégations formulées au sujet de l'existence d'une prétention yéménite, mais rien ne prouve que ladite revendication était censée s'étendre aux îles en litige dans la présente affaire ni qu'elle fut interprétée en ce sens. En outre, les protestations qu'un Etat formule au sujet du refus opposé par des tiers de le laisser exercer un contrôle effectif sur un territoire qu'il estime lui appartenir ont peu d'importance en droit si l'Etat qui proteste ne détient en réalité pas le titre.* Le fait que la Turquie détenait incontestablement ce titre en 1918 et qu'elle ne s'en est pas défaite en 1920 est plus pertinent. L'instrument par lequel la Turquie s'est finalement défaite de ce titre fut le traité de Lausanne de 1923.

153. L'imam n'a pas été partie au traité de Lausanne et en ce sens technique, le traité fut donc pour le Yémen *res inter alios acta.* Si le titre avait été aux mains du Yémen à cette époque, les parties au traité de Lausanne n'auraient pas pu transférer le titre ailleurs sans le consentement du Yémen. Mais, comme indiqué ci-dessus, le titre était toujours aux mains de la Turquie. Les traités frontaliers et territoriaux conclus entre deux parties sont *res inter alios acta* pour toute tierce partie. Mais cette catégorie particulière de traités représente aussi une réalité juridique qui touche nécessairement les Etats tiers parce qu'ils ont effet *erga omnes*. Si l'Etat A détient le titre sur un certain territoire et le transfère à l'Etat B, il est alors juridiquement sans objet pour l'Etat C d'invoquer le principe *res inter alios acta* sauf si le titre détenu par lui est supérieur à celui de A (et non au titre de B). En l'absence d'un titre qui soit ainsi supérieur, il n'est d'aucune utilité sur le plan juridique d'invoquer le principe *res inter alios acta.*

154. Voilà les réalités juridiques qu'il faut garder présentes à l'esprit pour analyser le traité de Lausanne. Il y a encore deux autres éléments dont il faut tenir compte: le fait, que l'on vient d'évoquer, que l'imam avait formulé des revendications au cours de cette période sans toutefois préciser quelles étaient les îles qu'il visait ainsi et le fait que l'Italie, par le comportement qu'elle avait adopté, avait également manifesté l'envie de s'assurer la possession des îles. Le texte du traité de Lausanne a certainement été adopté par ses signataires alors que ces derniers connaissaient parfaitement et la position de l'imam et les ambitions de l'Italie.

155. La Grande-Bretagne (qui avait pendant un court moment en 1915 envoyé des soldats à Jabal Zuqar et dans les îles Hanish) aurait souhaité à un certain stade amender l'article 132 du traité de Sèvres pour ajouter à la disposition par laquelle la Turquie renonçait de façon assez générale à tous ses "droits et titres" une disposition plus précise visant les "îles situées dans la mer Rouge". Comme le premier paragraphe de cette proposition visait les droits et titres détenus sur la péninsule arabique, on peut présumer que, de l'avis de la Grande-Bretagne, les îles n'entraient pas dans le champ de cette disposition, et qu'il fallait ajouter une

* *Note de l'éditeur: cette phrase a été corrigée de la version anglaise originale.*

précision au texte si elles devaient être elles aussi soustraites à la souveraineté turque. Le traité de Lausanne, signé en 1923, fait donc mention des îles ainsi que des territoires encore qu'à ce moment-là, la précédente proposition dont s'inspirait le traité avorté de Sèvres fût abandonnée (ladite proposition étant que le titre turc soit transmis aux puissances alliées,[14] que ce soit sous la forme d'un condominium ou sous une autre forme quelconque).

156. Aux termes de l'article 6, en l'absence de dispositions contraires du traité, la frontière maritime comprend les îles et les îlots situés à moins de trois milles de la côte de l'Etat riverain. Certaines des îles Dahlaks et certaines des îles d'Assab étaient situées au-delà de cette limite des trois milles, mais elles étaient en général considérées comme se rattachant au littoral africain et comme appartenant par conséquent à l'Italie. Les Mohabbakahs (dont la plus proche est située à près de six milles de la côte) et les Haycocks ne rentraient pas dans ces dispositions encore que, comme on le verra plus loin, la *juridiction* italienne exercée sur ces îles eût été reconnue. Que les Mohabbakahs soient ou non des îlots plutôt que des îles et nonobstant le fait que l'article 6 fait mention des îlots tandis que l'article 16 n'en fait pas mention, les Mohabbakahs n'étaient pas des îlots transmis à l'Italie sous l'effet de l'article 6.

157. L'article 15 dispose que la Turquie renonce en faveur de l'Italie à certaines îles de la mer Egée qui sont précisées et nommées. Et l'article 16 dispose:

> La Turquie déclare renoncer à tous droits et titres, de quelque nature que ce soit, sur ou concernant les territoires situés au-delà des frontières prévues par le présent traité et sur les îles autres que celles sur lesquelles la souveraineté lui est reconnue par ledit traité, le sort de ces territoires et îles étant réglé ou à régler par les intéressés . . . .

158. Les "territoires" et les "îles" sont visés séparément mais le traitement prévu par l'article 16 est le même pour les uns comme pour les autres. Les formules employées visaient sans doute aussi les îlots sur lesquels la souveraineté n'était pas transférée sous l'effet de l'article 6. Les intentions des "intéressés" ne sont pas parfaitement claires, mais, comme les prétentions de l'imam étaient connues, de même que les ambitions de l'Italie, et en outre, comme la formule utilisée ailleurs dans le traité est celle des "Hautes Parties contractantes", il n'est pas déraisonnable d'en tirer la conclusion que ce qui était envisagé, c'était un règlement de la question à l'avenir par tous ceux qui feraient valoir des prétentions juridiques ou d'importants intérêts politiques sur les îles, qu'ils figurent ou non parmi les Hautes Parties contractantes du traité de Lausanne. Un document du Foreign Office britannique datant de 1923 reconnaît par exemple

---

[14] Le traité de Lausanne, entré en vigueur cinq ans après la fin des hostilités, utilise en fait la formule "les Hautes Parties contractantes" et ne dit pas "les puissances alliées". Les Hautes Parties contractantes sont en l'occurrence l'Empire britannique, la France, l'Italie, le Japon, la Grèce, la Roumanie et l'Etat serbe-croate-slovène, d'une part, et, de l'autre, la Turquie.

que la France, l'Italie et le Yémen figurent vraisemblablement parmi les "intéressés". Cette interprétation s'accorde bien avec les assurances que l'Italie a données à l'imam au moment de la signature de l'accord anglo-italien de 1938, d'après lesquelles les "intérêts" du Yémen "n'avaient pas été oubliés", et avec les hypothèses de travail du Board of Trade britannique au sujet du traité de Lausanne de 1923, qui étaient que "les chefs arabes locaux qui se trouvent sur le territoire continental pourraient peut-être prétendre faire partie des 'intéressés'".

159. Il n'est pas certain qu'en 1923 la Grande-Bretagne ou l'Italie auraient considéré que les Haycocks faisaient partie du groupe d'îles de la mer Rouge dont il était ainsi dit qu'elles relevaient de la Turquie. En effet, la juridiction italienne sur ces îles avait d'ores et déjà été reconnue. Jusqu'à la fin même du 19e siècle, les Ottomans traitaient les personnes résidant en Erythrée comme ayant la nationalité turque et comme étant soumises à la juridiction ottomane. Mais certains accommodements étaient intervenus. L'Italie avait conclu en 1883, 1887 et 1888 une série d'accords avec des dirigeants érythréens locaux. Le traité de 1888 conclu avec le roi de Shoa disposait à l'article VIII que "l'Italie protéger[ait] sur la côte maritime la sécurité du littoral Danakil" et à l'article IX que "l'Italie veiller[ait] à la sécurité de la mer et de la colonie". A l'article V, le sultan Mohamed Hanfari cédait à l'Italie "l'usage du territoire d'Ablis". En 1887 était signé un autre traité qui ne paraît pas présenter d'intérêt particulier pour les questions à examiner. En 1888, un traité d'amitié et de commerce conclu entre l'Italie et le chef des Danakils disposait que l'Italie garantirait la sécurité de la côte Danakil. En outre, "le sultan Mohamed Anfari reconnaî[trait] que la côte Danakil allant d'Afila à Ras Dumeira est intégralement possession italienne" (article 111). Comme un mémorandum du Foreign Office britannique de 1930 devait le dire par la suite: ". . . les droits de surveillance impartis à l'Italie ont peu à peu acquis la qualité de droits territoriaux sur le littoral" et la Grande-Bretagne n'ayant formulé aucune protestation, elle "ne pouvait pas revenir désormais aux dispositions de l'accord de mai 1887."

160. Etudiant la possibilité d'exploiter une nouvelle voie de navigation sur le flanc africain de la mer Rouge ainsi que la nécessité de l'éclairer, le Gouvernement britannique a écrit au Gouvernement italien en 1892 en signalant les sites envisagés: North East Quoin (ou bien, à défaut, Rahamet sur la côte), les South West Rocks, "l'une des Haycocks" et Harbi – et il donnait à entendre qu'en vertu de l'article 111 du traité de 1888, ces sites relevaient, semble-t-il, de la juridiction italienne (encore que l'on n'en fût pas certain dans les services en question en ce qui concerne les South West Rocks). Il paraît vraisemblable que cette interprétation de l'article 111 du traité de 1888 – dont la lecture n'est pas évidente au premier coup d'œil – était influencée par le mémorandum Hertslet de 1880 et la liste qui lui était jointe. Ce mémorandum parlait de la côte occidentale de la mer Rouge comme relevant de la juridiction du khédive d'Egypte et de la côte orientale comme relevant de la juridiction du sultan. Hertslet donnait à penser que "les diverses îles et récifs situés très près de la côte qui sont énumérés

dans la liste 1 seraient placés sous" la juridiction du khédive. Sur cette liste 1 figurent "Harbi", White Quoin Hill et "Mah-hab-bakah". Les groupes de "Jibbel Zukur", "la Petite Harnish" et de "la Grande Harnish" sont attribués à la côte orientale. "Haycock" est citée deux fois dans la liste d'îles se rattachant à la côte orientale et situées à proximité de celle-ci. Quant aux îles "situées à proximité du centre" (énumérées par Hertslet sous le nom de "Jibbel Teer" et du "groupe de Zebayar"), y compris une autre Haycock, Hertslet estimait en 1880: "... l'on ne sait pas bien, semble-t-il, qui exerce la juridiction sur elles ...; mais il ne fait pas de doute que la souveraineté sur ces îles appartient au sultan."

161. Il convient aussi de relever que d'autres diplomates des services britanniques accordaient moins d'importance à la proximité.[15] Quand elle fut priée de dire si elle revendiquait effectivement la juridiction sur les îles, l'Italie a confirmé que "les lieux cités" étaient soumis à sa juridiction. C'est de 1892 que date cette reconnaissance britannique de la juridiction italienne sur les Haycocks (et sans doute *a fortiori* sur les Mohabbakahs). En 1930, des notes de service britanniques parlent de la souveraineté italienne sur South West Haycock (ou parfois, tout simplement, sur "les Haycocks") comme ayant été acquise en juin 1892. Mais il était ajouté ceci: "l'Italie ne paraît pas revendiquer la souveraineté sur ces îles avec beaucoup de fermeté sauf à notre encontre" (souligné par nous).

162. Certaines indications ultérieures montrent que la Grande-Bretagne considérait que la question de la souveraineté n'était pas réglée, même si juridiction était reconnue à l'Italie. Par conséquent, tant les Mohabbakahs que les Haycocks devaient en 1923 être considérées par les parties au traité de Lausanne comme appartenant au territoire turc et relevant du point de vue de la souveraineté des dispositions de l'article 16, même si lesdites parties acceptaient de façon intermittente que ces îles fussent sous juridiction italienne.

163. La situation est plus claire en ce qui concerne Abu Ali, Jabal al-Tayr et le groupe de Zubayr. Ces îles étaient censées à l'époque avoir appartenu aux Ottomans (mais n'avoir jamais été revendiquées par l'imam). Ces trois îles tombaient sous le coup des dispositions de l'article 16 du traité de Lausanne.

164. L'article 16 met en jeu trois points essentiels. Le premier porte sur les incidences juridiques liées au fait que cet article est *res inter alios acta* pour le Yémen. La deuxième question est de savoir quelles îles en fait étaient visées par cette disposition, c'est-à-dire quelles îles relevaient toujours de la souveraineté ottomane à la date du traité. Le Tribunal a examiné ces deux questions ci-dessus (voir les paragraphes 153 à 159). Et la troisième question est de savoir si l'article 16 autorisait la prescription acquisitive par un même Etat de certaines de ces îles ou de leur ensemble et, dans la négative, si cette prescription acquisitive ne

[15] Voir REILLY, ADEN AND YEMEN, Colonial Office, 1960, p. 69-70.

pouvait pas avoir lieu et n'a pas eu néanmoins lieu (fût-ce en infraction à une obligation conventionnelle).

165. De l'avis du Tribunal, il faut analyser l'article 16 comme suit: en 1923, la Turquie a renoncé à son titre sur les îles sur lesquelles elle exerçait jusqu'alors la souveraineté. Lesdites îles ne sont pas pour autant devenues *res nullius* – c'est-à-dire susceptibles de faire l'objet d'une prescription acquisitive de la part d'un Etat quelconque, y compris l'une quelconque des Hautes Parties contractantes (dont l'Italie). Les îles ne sont pas non plus automatiquement revenues à l'imam (pour autant qu'elles lui aient jamais appartenu). Le titre souverain sur ces îles est donc resté indéterminé *pro tempore*. Pour sa part, la Grande-Bretagne estimait certainement possible que l'article 16 s'étendît à certaines îles non précisées qui "relevaient du Yémen". Cette situation d'indétermination pourrait être réglée par les "intéressés" à un moment ultérieur, – c'est à dire par les prétendants actuels (ou futurs) *inter se*. Le terme utilisé est incompatible avec l'idée qu'il était possible qu'une partie puisse à elle seule résoudre unilatéralement le problème au moyen de la prescription acquisitive.

166. Vu ce qu'était la politique des grandes puissances dans la région, il était inévitable que l'application de ces principes juridiques fût parfois assez peu claire. La Grande-Bretagne en fait s'est assuré la juridiction sur l'île Kamaran de cette manière; les archives montrent que les fonctionnaires et les ministres britanniques ont continué au fil des ans à entretenir l'idée que la Grande-Bretagne devait s'approprier certaines îles; mais la Grande-Bretagne s'employait néanmoins à garder à l'article 16 toute son efficacité à l'égard des mesures adoptées par l'Italie, en demandant fréquemment des informations au Gouvernement italien.

167. Les îles auxquelles la disposition de l'article 16 s'appliquait au départ étaient par conséquent les Mohabbakahs, les Haycocks, les South West Rocks, et certainement le groupe Zuqar-Hanish, Abu Ali, Jabal al-Tayr et le groupe de Zubayr.

168. Le traité de Lausanne, bien loin d'"ouvrir la voie" à la souveraineté italienne, comme l'Erythrée l'a donné à entendre, constituait un obstacle redoutable. On peut soutenir que l'Italie aurait néanmoins pu opérer une prescription acquisitive en dépit de ses obligations si les autres parties au traité de Lausanne l'avaient permis. L'Italie aurait essayé de s'assurer la position la plus favorable, tant sur le terrain que sur le plan de la diplomatie, pour la défendre le jour où il faudrait établir le titre. Du point de vue de l'aspiration politique, *l'animus occupandi* existait incontestablement. Mais il est fort douteux que des revendications de souveraineté aient été formulées et admises au point que certaines îles fussent hors d'atteinte de l'article 16 du traité de Lausanne. Et il est encore moins plausible de plaider que les Hautes Parties contractantes (et la Grande-Bretagne

en particulier) auraient autorisé une acquisition progressive de la souveraineté par l'Italie ou y auraient consenti.

Les conversations de Rome de 1927

169. L'histoire confirme cette conclusion par ce qui s'est passé à la suite de la conclusion du traité de Lausanne. En 1927, des entretiens eurent lieu à Rome entre le Gouvernement italien et le Gouvernement britannique au sujet des intérêts britanniques et italiens en Arabie méridionale et dans la mer Rouge (entretiens dénommés ci-après "les conversations de Rome"). Dans le compte rendu signé de ces entretiens, les deux pays ont convenu de coopérer pour chercher à pacifier Ibn Saud, l'imam Yahya et l'Idrisi d'Asir; et il fut indiqué que la Grande-Bretagne considérait comme "un intérêt impérial vital qu'aucune puissance européenne ne s'établisse sur la côte arabique de la mer Rouge et plus particulièrement sur les îles Kamaran ou Farsan et qu'aucune de ces îles . . . ne tombe entre les mains d'un chef arabe inamical." Cette disposition fut renouvelée, *pari passu*, pour la côte occidentale ainsi que pour l'île Kamaran et les îles Farsan.

170. Il n'a pas été formulé d'allusion aussi précise quant aux autres îles qui sont à présent en litige. Si les articles 4 et 6 visent Kamaran et Farsan, l'article 5, de l'avis du Tribunal, doit être interprété comme s'appliquant aux autres îles contestées. Cet article 5 dispose:

> La liberté économique et commerciale doit être assurée sur la côte arabique et les îles de la mer Rouge au bénéfice des citoyens et des sujets des deux pays et la protection sur laquelle lesdits citoyens et sujets peuvent légitimement compter de la part de leur gouvernement ne doit pas revêtir un caractère ni une coloration politique. [Traduction du Bureau international de la CPA.]

171. La seule signification qu'il soit possible d'attribuer à cet article est que les actes susceptibles d'être par ailleurs interprétés comme constitutifs d'une acquisition progressive de souveraineté ne devaient pas, conformément à la convention passée entre les parties, être interprétés en ce sens. Chercher à déterminer des actes "dotés d'un caractère souverain" perdait de cette façon toute justification juridique.

172. L'Erythrée a dit qu'il ne fallait attacher aucune force juridique à ces dispositions, tout d'abord parce que ce compte rendu ne fut pas enregistré conformément aux prescriptions de l'article 18 du Pacte de la Société des Nations et, ensuite, parce que le Yémen ne peut pas les invoquer, soit pour cette raison même soit à cause du principe *res inter alios acta*. Que ce compte rendu n'ait pas été enregistré s'explique incontestablement par le fait qu'il ne fut pas considéré comme un traité conclu entre Etats. Mais ce n'en était pas moins un compte rendu exact de ce dont étaient convenues les deux parties qui l'ont signé comme tel. Il faut y voir

simplement un témoignage supplémentaire des vues de l'époque – émanant cette fois des deux parties – plus ou moins identiques à la myriade d'autres éléments de preuve de caractère non conventionnel qui ont été présentés au Tribunal. Dans la mesure où le Yémen veut en faire état devant le Tribunal, il ne fait pas appel à un traité qui serait effectivement *res inter alios acta*, non plus d'ailleurs qu'il ne fonde sa propre revendication sur cet élément. Il s'agit d'un document diplomatique, comme tout document de ce type, qui présente toutefois sans aucun doute de l'intérêt parce qu'il est le reflet de ce que les deux parties ont consigné au sujet de ce dont elles étaient convenues.

173. Les dispositions de l'article 5 de ces conversations de Rome étaient, bien entendu, parfaitement compatibles avec celles de l'article 16 du traité de Lausanne, et d'ailleurs, renforçaient même ces dernières. L'article 5 des conversations ne remplaçait pas l'article 16 du traité de Lausanne mais mettait en place un mécanisme supplémentaire visant à garantir la possibilité de continuer à pratiquer la pêche, le commerce, les activités liées à la navigation sans compromettre le statut indéterminé des îles.

174. L'Italie et la Grande-Bretagne cherchaient désormais chacune de son côté à s'assurer que la souveraineté était effectivement réservée. Quand la Grande-Bretagne a proposé à la France certains arrangements relatifs à la gestion des vieux phares ottomans installés sur les îles Abu Ail, Jabal al-Tayr, Centre Peak et à Mocha, l'Italie a demandé qu'il soit reconnu que le dernier site appartenait au Yémen et que la souveraineté était bien réservée pour les trois premières îles. La Grande-Bretagne fut à même de lui donner cette assurance. Et quand Londres apprit que l'Italie était disposée à installer un phare sur South West Haycock (censée faire partie des Mohabbakahs), la Grande-Bretagne lui a demandé de lui donner l'assurance que les Haycocks ainsi que les îles Hanish étaient bien considérées par l'Italie comme relevant de l'article 5 des conversations de Rome. L'Italie a fait savoir en 1930 à la Grande-Bretagne qu'elle avait souveraineté sur South West Haycock, au sujet de laquelle elle formulait une réserve particulière, consistant à dire que cette île figurait parmi les Mohabbakahs, et qu'elle était disposée à ce que les South-West Haycocks et le reste des îles Hanish soient traitées conformément aux dispositions de l'article 5 des conversations de Rome. La réaction britannique fut de ne pas accepter l'offre de l'Italie qui souhaitait donc avoir des entretiens à ce sujet, de peur que l'Italie veuille ainsi faire "régler" la question de sa souveraineté sur South West Haycock au sens de l'article 16 du traité de Lausanne, et la Grande-Bretagne choisit d'accepter tacitement que toutes les solutions à concevoir le soient dans le cadre de l'article 5 des conversations de Rome.

175. En 1931, l'Italie a donné de nouvelles assurances concernant l'installation par elle de postes armés sur la Grande Hanish et Jabal Zuqar. L'Italie a assuré la Grande-Bretagne que ces postes visaient à assurer la protection de certains concessionnaires et que la souveraineté sur les îles Hanish était toujours en

suspens. Le statut juridique de ces îles était, disait l'Italie, exactement celui que les conversations de Rome de 1927 attribuaient à Farsan et à Kamaran. En outre, l'Italie rappelait qu'elle avait en 1926, lors de négociations menées aux fins de la convention de 1930 sur les phares qui sera finalement avortée, confirmé que la souveraineté sur Abu Ali, Zubayr et Jabal al-Tayr devait également demeurer en suspens, relevant aussi des dispositions de l'article 5 des conversations de Rome.

176. Ces assurances devaient également suffire à calmer les inquiétudes des autorités britanniques lors d'un incident qui eut lieu en 1933, lorsque le navire Penzance se rendit à Jabal Zuqar et aux Hanish, constatant notamment la présence de soldats italiens et du drapeau italien au faîte des mâts. Entre-temps, la Grande-Bretagne donnait à l'Italie des assurances comparables au sujet de Kamaran.

177. Un texte italien, le décret législatif royal n° 1019 du 1er juin 1936, a défini le dispositif adopté pour l'administration de l'Afrique orientale italienne. Ce texte disposait notamment à l'article 4 que le territoire de Dankalia était établi par rapport à une ligne tracée depuis les basses terres jusqu'à l'est du lac Ascianghi à la limite sud d'Aussa et faisait partie de l'Erythrée. Aucune île n'était désignée, mais les précisions concernant les lignes tracées qui ont joué le rôle de frontières administratives faisaient que le groupe des Hanish-Zuqar relevait du commissariat de Dankalia. Aucune des lignes tracées conformément au décret 1019 ne revenait à prendre en compte Abu Ali, Zubayr ou Jabal al-Tayr.

178. Et c'est là ce qu'affirma expressément le décret général du gouvernement n° 446 daté du 20 décembre 1938: "les îles Hanisc-Sucur sont censées être comprises dans les limites du commissariat du gouvernement de Dancalia et d'Aussa (Assab)." Aux yeux du Tribunal, ces arrangements administratifs ne peuvent pas, compte tenu des conversations de Rome et des assurances données ensuite, être considérés comme des revendications internationales de souveraineté plutôt que des revendications de juridiction. Et la Grande-Bretagne ne les aurait certainement pas considérés comme tels. Au reste, huit mois auparavant seulement, l'Italie avait assuré l'imam qu'elle s'était engagée avec la Grande-Bretagne à ne pas étendre sa souveraineté sur les îles Hanish (et qu'elle avait été en mesure d'envoyer un médecin italien à Kamaran grâce à cet engagement).

179. En même temps, l'Italie a demandé vainement à la Grande-Bretagne d'annuler son propre décret concernant Kamaran, qui, pour l'Italie, mettait à mal l'accord de statu quo conclu en 1927. La Grande-Bretagne n'en a pas moins continué à considérer que la souveraineté sur Kamaran demeurait réservée.

180. L'Italie, qui avait reconnu le Yémen indépendant en 1926, a conclu avec ce pays un traité d'amitié et de relations économiques en septembre 1937. L'Italie confirmait sans la moindre réserve qu'elle "reconnaissait l'indépendance totale et absolue, sans restrictions" du roi du Yémen et de son royaume, mais le

Tribunal ne voit là aucun éclaircissement concernant les problèmes qui lui sont soumis.

181. L'évolution de la situation au Yémen et en Arabie saoudite, y compris les relations entre ces deux pays, ont fait penser à l'Italie et au Royaume-Uni qu'ils avaient l'une et l'autre lieu de préciser le régime instauré. Après plusieurs mois de négociation, fut signé le 16 avril 1938 un accord assorti de protocoles qui est entré en vigueur le 16 novembre 1938. L'annexe 3 dudit accord énonçait des dispositions détaillées intéressant les îles de la mer Rouge:

> *Article premier*
> Aucune des deux Parties ne conclura le moindre accord ni n'adoptera la moindre mesure qui risque de porter atteinte sous quelque forme que ce soit à l'indépendance ou à l'intégrité de l'Arabie saoudite ou du Yémen.
>
> *Article 2*
> Aucune des deux Parties ne s'assurera ni ne cherchera à s'assurer une situation privilégiée de caractère politique dans aucun territoire, quel qu'il soit, qui appartient actuellement à l'Arabie saoudite ou au Yémen ou dans n'importe quel territoire, quel qu'il soit, que l'un ou l'autre desdits Etats pourra acquérir par la suite.
>
> *Article 3*
> Les deux Parties reconnaissent qu'en sus des obligations incombant à chacune d'elles en vertu des articles premier et 2 ci-dessus, il est de leur intérêt commun qu'aucune tierce puissance ne doive acquérir ni chercher à acquérir la souveraineté ni aucune situation privilégiée de caractère politique sur aucun territoire, quel qu'il soit, qui appartient actuellement à l'Arabie saoudite ou au Yémen ou que l'un ou l'autre desdits Etats pourra acquérir par la suite, y compris sur des îles quelconques de la mer Rouge appartenant à l'un ou l'autre desdits Etats, ou sur l'une quelconque des autres îles de la mer Rouge sur lesquelles la Turquie a renoncé à ses droits conformément à l'article 16 du traité de paix signé à Lausanne le 24 juillet 1923. En particulier, les deux Parties considèrent qu'il est d'un intérêt primordial pour chacune d'elles qu'aucune tierce puissance n'acquière la souveraineté ni aucune position privilégiée sur aucune partie quelconque de la côte de la mer Rouge qui appartient actuellement à l'Arabie saoudite ou au Yémen ni sur aucune des îles citées ci-dessus.
>
> *Article 4*
> 1) S'agissant des îles de la mer Rouge sur lesquelles la Turquie a renoncé à ses droits aux termes de l'article 16 du traité de paix signé à Lausanne le 24 juillet 1923, et qui ne sont pas comprises dans le territoire de l'Arabie saoudite ni du Yémen, aucune des deux Parties ne doit, sur une telle île, quelle qu'elle soit, ou en ce qui la concerne,
>   a) établir sa souveraineté, ni
>   b) ériger des fortifications ou des moyens de défense.
> 2) Les deux Parties sont convenues de ne s'opposer ni l'une ni l'autre
>   a) à la présence à Kamaran de fonctionnaires britanniques ayant pour mission d'assurer le service sanitaire du pèlerinage à la Mecque conformément aux dispositions de l'accord conclu à Paris le 19 juin 1926 entre les gouver-

nements de la Grande-Bretagne et d'Irlande du Nord et de l'Inde, d'une part, et, de l'autre, le Gouvernement des Pays-Bas; il est également entendu que le Gouvernement italien est habilité à désigner un médecin officiel italien qui séjournera à Kamaran dans les mêmes conditions que le médecin officiel néerlandais conformément audit accord;

b) à la présence sur la Grande Hanish, la Petite Hanish et Jebel Zukur de fonctionnaires italiens ayant pour mission de protéger les pêcheurs se rendant dans ces îles;

c) à la présence sur Abu Ail, Centre Peak et Jebel Teir de personnes chargées de l'entretien des phares installés sur lesdites îles. [Traduction du Bureau international de la CPA.]

182. Dans une note de service datée du 31 mars, le ministère italien des affaires étrangères avait clairement indiqué que la formule en cours de négociation confirmerait que les îles de la mer Rouge relevant précédemment de la souveraineté turque "n'appar[tenaient] ni à la Grande-Bretagne, ni à l'Italie, ni aux deux Etats arabes, et que la souveraineté sur ces îles demeu[rait] réservée." Une liste d'îles "dont la souveraineté [était] réservée" qui était jointe à la note indiquait que Kamaran, Abu Ali et Jabal al-Tayr étaient à l'époque sous occupation britannique, et indiquait aussi qu'étaient occupées par l'Italie: la Grande Hanish, Jabal Zuqar, Centre Peak, et la Petite Hanish. South-West Haycock ne figure pas sur cette liste de la note du ministère italien des affaires étrangères comme relevant de cet arrangement, malgré les assurances données à ce sujet en 1930 à la Grande-Bretagne au sujet de l'accord réalisé lors des conversations de Rome de 1927. Dans le traité 1938 on ne trouve pas là d'écho non plus d'une proposition interne britannique tendant à ce qu'il soit précisé que les engagements consacrés par les conversations de Rome de 1927 avaient pris fin.

183. Il semble que ce traité de 1938 ne doit pas être interprété comme remplaçant les engagements de 1927 (qui n'ont toujours pas autant de valeur qu'un traité officiel) mais qu'il faut considérer que ce traité complète et développe ces engagements de 1927 dont "le caractère politique et la complexité du dispositif ainsi mis en place ont été jugés peu satisfaisants." Le traité de Rome n'a jamais été enregistré auprès de la Société des Nations et, sous l'effet de l'article 18 du Pacte de la SDN, aucune des deux Parties ne pouvait l'invoquer contre l'autre. Mais il y a plus pertinent pour le Yémen: c'est le fait que celui-ci est une troisième partie au traité. Toutefois, rien n'indique que l'Italie ou le Royaume-Uni ait eu d'autre raison de ne pas enregistrer le traité que la menace de guerre qui se précisait à l'époque. Le texte du traité n'en présente pas moins de l'intérêt et le Tribunal peut à bon droit le prendre en compte comme exprimant l'accord des parties à l'automne de 1938 au sujet de la situation exacte des îles ainsi que de leurs intentions à l'époque quant à la façon dont il fallait continuer de les traiter. Pour l'essentiel, la situation demeurait rigoureusement inchangée: les revendications devaient rester en sommeil. Les îles n'étaient nullement *res nullius*, territoires sans maître à acquérir par l'Italie ou bien par la Grande-Bretagne.

184. Le libellé de l'article 3 de ce traité de 1938 n'est pas dépourvu d'ambiguïtés. Mais il montre en tout cas d'une part que certaines îles de la mer Rouge étaient bel et bien considérées en 1938 comme appartenant à l'Arabie saoudite et au Yémen. Ce texte montre aussi d'autre part que d'autres îles de la mer Rouge étaient considérées comme n'appartenant à aucun de ces deux Etats et que le titre sur ces îles était toujours indéterminé.

185. Comme l'article 4 du traité de 1938 dit très clairement et précisément que Kamaran, la Grande Hanish, la Petite Hanish, Jabal Zuqar, Abu Ali, Centre Peak et Jabal al-Tayr ne sont pas placées sous la souveraineté de l'Arabie saoudite ni du Yémen, on ne voit pas bien quelles îles étaient considérées comme "apparte[nant] actuellement au Yémen". De toute façon, l'Italie et le Royaume-Uni ne considéraient pas en 1938 que le titre sur l'une quelconque des îles nommément citées relevait du Yémen ou que la question de ce titre avait été réglée conformément aux dispositions de l'article 16 du traité de Lausanne; et l'Italie comme le Royaume-Uni s'engageaient l'une comme l'autre à ne pas établir leur souveraineté sur aucune de ces îles. Rien dans ce dossier ne prouve que le terme "établir" utilisé à l'article 4 revêtait une autre signification que la formule "acquérir" ou "chercher à acquérir" la souveraineté qui est utilisée à l'article 3, la souveraineté étant donc à acquérir au moyen des divers actes cités dans le traité, notamment l'érection de fortifications. On peut donc conclure que ce traité de 1938 n'apporte nulle preuve de la reconnaissance par l'Italie ou la Grande-Bretagne d'un titre yéménite quelconque sur les îles en litige. Mais en même temps, ce traité excluait expressément toute revendication italienne de souveraineté sur ces mêmes îles.

186. Cette série d'instruments et d'engagements internationaux eut pour conséquence que, de 1923 à 1938, l'Italie ne pouvait pas prétendre avoir d'ores et déjà un titre qu'il fallait reconnaître. La seule revendication précise de souveraineté de sa part visait South West Haycock – mais même cette prétention-là à un titre existant devait être considérée, à la suggestion de l'Italie elle-même, comme étant "en suspens" jusqu'à ce que la question du titre sur les îles en général soit réglée ultérieurement par les intéressés conformément à l'article 16 du traité de Lausanne.

* - *

187. Le Yémen pour sa part a formulé sporadiquement des revendications sur des îles de la mer Rouge au cours de cette période, sous une forme générale, sans apporter de précisions. La Grande-Bretagne avait bien assuré le Yémen que les mesures prises par l'Italie au sujet des phares ne préjugeaient pas la position du Yémen, mais ni la Grande-Bretagne ni l'Italie n'ont considéré jusqu'en 1938 que les îles étaient propriété yéménite. Comme les dispositions du traité de Lausanne avaient mis en place le mécanisme par lequel l'Empire ottoman cédait sa propriété sur ces îles, le fait n'est pas dénué de toute importance pour le Yémen,

qui, même quand il donne sa propre version de l'argument, doit prouver non seulement l'existence d'un droit de réversion mais encore prouver qu'un tel droit prend le pas sur la décision que le souverain précédent a été contraint d'adopter quant à l'avenir des îles.

188. En 1933, la Grande-Bretagne négociait en fait un traité avec l'imam. Certains, au Foreign Office, étaient d'avis que le Yémen avait juridiquement fait partie de l'Empire ottoman, que "les îles susceptibles de lui appartenir" se trouvaient "intégralement dans le champ de l'article 16 du traité de Lausanne et [que] leur sort devait par conséquent être réglé par voie d'accord international." Contrairement aux conclusions formulées par le Yémen, cela ne sous-entend pas clairement du tout que le titre revenait au Yémen – cela sous-entend que ce qui avait été souverain était désormais indéterminé, jusqu'au moment où le titre serait attribué par les "intéressés".

189. Les îles revendiquées par l'imam pendant la négociation avec le Royaume-Uni qui devait aboutir en 1934 à la conclusion du traité d'amitié et de collaboration de Sanaa n'ont pas été identifiées avec précision, mais les Britanniques ont clairement compris par la suite qu'il s'agissait de Kamaran et des diverses îles inhabitées dont les plus vastes sont Zuqar et la Grande Hanish. Il a été reconnu que la revendication était formulée mais cela n'apparaît pas dans le texte du traité et la position du Gouvernement britannique qui se refusait à aller plus loin a été clairement indiquée à l'imam.

* - *

190. Comme ni l'Italie ni le Yémen ne détenait de titre souverain lorsqu'a éclaté la seconde guerre mondiale, on peut poser par principe que les îles (à l'exception peut-être de South West Haycock et des Mohabbakahs) sont toutes tombées sous le coup des dispositions prononçant l'abandon officiel que l'Italie a été contrainte d'accepter. Cette conclusion est également confortée par l'étude des documents relatifs à la période 1941-1950.

191. La proclamation de 1941 instaurant la juridiction militaire britannique a rassemblé sous le commandement du lieutenant-général Platt "[t]ous les territoires d'Erythrée et d'Ethiopie." Pour le Tribunal, cet énoncé n'est ni "large" ni du reste "étroit", il est simplement général et ne donne aucune précision géographique ni juridique. L'armistice a bien parlé de "[l]ivrer immédiatement aux Alliés la Corse et la totalité du territoire italien, tant les îles que le territoire continental . . ." (par. 6). Mais on ne sait absolument pas de quelles îles il s'agit ici; l'explication fournie à l'article 41 des "conditions supplémentaires d'armistice" convenues avec l'Italie qui est que "la formule 'territoire italien' s'entend de toutes les colonies et dépendances italiennes . . . (mais sans préjudice de la question de souveraineté) . . ." n'éclaire pas davantage la situation. La formule continue d'éluder la question qui se pose et s'accompagne en outre d'une

mise en garde: les accords d'armistice sont des instruments qui visent à mettre un terme aux hostilités ou à les contenir, ils ne visent nullement à reconnaître ou nier l'existence d'un titre souverain.

192. En 1944, le ministère britannique des colonies (Colonial Office) a procédé à une étude interne du statut de Kamaran, du groupe de la Grande Hanish, du groupe de la Petite Hanish, du groupe de Jabal Zuqar (y compris Abu Ali), du groupe de Zubayr (y compris Centre Peak) et de Jabal al-Tayr. Dans une lettre de l'époque, l'histoire des îles est rappelée brièvement de même qu'il est rappelé qu'en vertu de l'article 16 du traité de Lausanne, "l'avenir de ces îles devait être réglé par les "intéressés". Mais leur sort n'a jamais été réglé. Il s'agit en fait d'orphelins internationaux laissés à l'abandon." Et la même lettre poursuivait: "Autrefois, les Italiens s'intéressaient à toutes ces îles." On pensait aussi à ce moment-là que les Néerlandais s'y intéressaient quelque peu désormais.[16] "Mis à part les Britanniques, toutefois, le prétendant le plus sérieux semble être le Yémen, car c'est au large de sa côte que toutes ces îles sont situées." Et la lettre rappelait les prétentions formulées par l'imam en 1934.

193. L'auteur de cette lettre (un fonctionnaire du Colonial Office) émettait l'idée que l'on pouvait laisser les choses en l'état ou bien les régler "de la même façon"; ou encore que le Royaume-Uni pouvait annexer les îles.

194. Mise à part l'indication qui est donnée sur la situation des îles qui seraient toutes "au large de la côte du Yémen" ou l'avis formulé, sans analyse juridique, comme étant acquis, suivant lequel ces îles se prêtaient désormais à annexion, la lettre témoigne d'une opinion apparemment très largement répandue au sein du Gouvernement britannique à l'époque qui est que la souveraineté sur ces îles n'était toujours pas réglée au sens de l'article 16 du traité de Lausanne.

195. Lorsqu'arrive l'année 1947, la question du titre a dû bien entendu se poser nettement dans le traité de paix avec l'Italie. Aux termes de l'article 23 dudit traité, l'Italie a renoncé alors "à tous droits et titres sur les possessions territoriales italiennes en Afrique, c'est-à-dire la Libye, l'Erythrée et la Somalie italienne." Le troisième paragraphe du même article dispose:

> Le sort définitif de ces possessions sera déterminé d'un commun accord par les Gouvernements des Etats-Unis d'Amérique, de la France, du Royaume-Uni et de l'Union soviétique dans un délai d'un an à partir de l'entrée en vigueur du présent traité . . .

---

[16] Les Néerlandais ne figuraient pas parmi les signataires du traité de Lausanne de 1923 et étaient en fait restés neutres au cours de la première guerre mondiale.

Que cette disposition n'intéresse nullement les îles aujourd'hui en litige ressort très clairement de l'article 43, qui dispose:

> L'Italie renonce à tous les droits et intérêts qu'elle peut avoir en vertu de l'article 16 du traité de Lausanne signé le 24 juillet 1923.

La place à laquelle cet article a été situé dans le traité (loin de l'article 2) et le fait même que l'on ait éprouvé le besoin de formuler une telle disposition montrent bien que les îles de la mer Rouge aujourd'hui en litige n'allaient pas voir leur sort réglé conformément au paragraphe 3 de l'article 23. Cette disposition de l'article 43 n'était pas censée porter révision ou renonciation par des parties autres que l'Italie de l'article 16 du traité de Lausanne.

196. Cet article 16 du traité de Lausanne au contraire demeurait intact. L'Italie était quant à elle contrainte désormais de renoncer "à tous les droits et intérêts" conférés par ledit article 16. Contrairement à ce qu'a soutenu le Yémen, cela ne vise pas simplement le droit de l'Italie de protester contre une prétendue acquisition par un tiers ou le droit d'être finalement partie à un règlement concernant le titre. Cela vise aussi la renonciation à toute revendication que l'Italie pourrait avoir formulée et à tous les intérêts juridiques qu'elle peut avoir fait valoir au sujet des îles.

197. Un document de travail des Nations Unies établi en décembre 1949 en rapport avec l'élaboration du projet de constitution érythréenne vient étayer l'idée que les îles Hanish, Zuqar et les îles les plus septentrionales ne figuraient pas parmi celles dont le sort devait être réglé (et dont il serait finalement dit qu'elles étaient transférées à l'Erythrée indépendante). Dans la partie du document consacrée à la géographie et à l'histoire de l'Erythrée, il est dit que la colonie italienne "comprend l'archipel des Dahlak au large de Massawa et les îles situées plus au sud au large de la côte du pays Danakil." Il s'agirait, semble-t-il, des Mohabbakahs à proximité d'Assab. Dans la partie qui rappelle les "essais de colonisation des hautes terres d'Erythrée", il n'est fait aucune allusion à une quelconque colonisation des îles.

198. Le ministère des affaires étrangères d'Ethiopie a quant à lui protesté quand il a formulé des observations sur le projet de constitution. Il a fait observer que l'énoncé de l'article 2 de ce projet de constitution "exclurait implicitement tous les archipels et toutes les îles au large de la côte. Cette exclusion n'a sûrement pas été voulue." *"Le territoire continental et insulaire de l'Erythrée est celui de l'ancienne colonie italienne d'Erythrée" – est demeuré intact dans la version*

*finale de la Constitution. Cette formulation ne précise pas si les îles auxquelles le texte fait réference exclue celles de l'archipel de Dahlak et les Mohabbakahs.**

199. Le Gouvernement italien avait également été invité à donner son avis sur l'avenir de l'Erythrée à la Commission des Nations Unies pour l'Erythrée. L'Italie a plaidé instamment pour l'indépendance de l'Erythrée, soulignant qu'en renonçant à tous ses titres elle ne faisait pas pour autant de l'Erythrée un territoire sans maître. Elle a évoqué les régions qui avaient été occupées par l'Italie pour créer l'Erythrée. Et elle a, à cette occasion, parlé des îles Dahlak. Toutefois, en plaidant pour le maintien de l'unité de l'Erythrée, elle n'a fait mention d'aucune des autres îles. Aucun des instruments adoptés ensuite assez rapidement – ni la proclamation de 1952 mettant fin aux pouvoirs de l'autorité militaire britannique, ni la Constitution révisée de l'Erythrée de 1955– n'ont modifié cette situation.

* - * - *

* *Le texte en italique représente le corrigendum adopté par le Tribunal arbitral en novembre 1998, suite au prononcé de la sentence aux parties.*

CHAPITRE VI – Les phares de la mer Rouge

200. Les phares de la mer Rouge entrent en jeu dans le présent arbitrage principalement à trois égards. Premièrement, chacune des parties a donné à différents moments à entendre qu'en installant ou entretenant des phares sur les diverses îles elle accomplissait des actes de souveraineté. Deuxièmement, la correspondance diplomatique concernant les phares donne peut-être des indications utiles sur les revendications sous-jacentes concernant les îles où ces phares sont situés, d'autant que les îles portant un phare étaient nécessairement nommées alors que le matériau soumis vise très souvent les îles sans autre précision. Troisièmement, le rapport entre les quelques conventions sur les phares à prendre en considération, d'une part, et, de l'autre, les dispositions de l'article 16 du traité de Lausanne a peut-être une certaine importance juridique.

201. Depuis la fin du 19e siècle, les phares de la mer Rouge ont une large place dans l'histoire dans cette région, bien que la découverte du radar l'ait aujourd'hui un peu entamée. Mais nombreux sont les pêcheurs fréquentant les îles Zuqar-Hanish qui ne disposent peut-être pas du radar. Les autorités ottomanes, et, par la suite, les divers Etats riverains, de même que les grandes compagnies de navigation usagères de la mer Rouge ont tous joué un rôle dans l'histoire des phares de la mer Rouge. En 1930, il a été établi un projet de régime conventionnel relatif à ces phares qui n'est jamais entré en vigueur. Mais entre 1962 et 1989, les phares ont bel et bien été assujettis à un régime conventionnel.

202. En 1881, l'Empire ottoman a accordé une concession de quarante ans à la *Société des phares de l'Empire ottoman*, dont les propriétaires étaient messieurs Michel et Collas, en vue de l'installation d'une série de phares en mer Rouge et dans le golfe Persique. Cette concession relative aux phares de la mer Rouge a été l'origine d'une série quasi ininterrompue de litiges.

203. Le Gouvernement britannique avait proposé à la Sublime Porte l'érection de quatre phares à Jabal al-Tayr, Abu Ail, Jabal Zubayr et à Mocha qui faciliteraient la navigation. Préoccupé par les difficultés rencontrées avec les concessionnaires, ce gouvernement a commencé en 1891 à envisager de nouveau, comme il l'avait déjà fait précédemment, la possibilité de créer dans la mer Rouge une voie de navigation occidentale. Comme l'itinéraire envisagé devait passer "à la hauteur des possessions italiennes à Assab", il a été demandé à l'Italie de faciliter la mission technique et d'autoriser un ravitaillement à Assab – et l'Italie a très facilement donné son agrément.

204. Quand le Board of Trade a recommandé l'adoption d'un itinéraire occidental, le Gouvernement britannique a dû s'intéresser à des questions de titre. Pour que l'on puisse suivre cet itinéraire dit des "Hanish occidentales", il fallait disposer de phares sur North East Quoin (ou bien à Rakmat), sur les South West Rocks, sur l'un des îlots des Haycocks et sur l'îlot Harbi. En 1891, le Board of Trade, se

fiant au mémorandum Hertslet de 1880, a dit qu'à son avis North East Quoin et Harbi relevaient de la juridiction de l'Egypte et les South West Rocks ainsi que les Haycocks, de la juridiction ottomane – la Sublime Porte revendiquant la souveraineté sur les quatre îles. Le marquis de Salisbury, écrivant en janvier 1892 à l'ambassadeur du Royaume-Uni à Rome, disait: "Les îles et les rochers recommandés par le Board of Trade . . ., à l'exception des South-west Rocks, semble [sic] relever en réalité de la juridiction italienne. Mais on ne voit pas bien qui exerce la juridiction sur les South-west Rocks." Entre 1881 et 1892, la correspondance internationale a été abondante sur cette question.

205. Le 3 février 1892 une note adressée au Gouvernement italien demandait des éclaircissements. Il était indiqué dans cette note que, "suivant l'article 3 du traité conclu entre l'Italie et le sultan Ahfari d'Aussa en date du 9 décembre 1888", l'exercice de la juridiction sur les nouveaux sites, "à l'exception peut-être des South-West Rocks, semble revenir à l'Italie". Il était demandé à l'Italie si elle assumait bien la juridiction sur ces sites, et, dans l'affirmative, si elle était disposée à ériger elle-même des phares sur ces sites ou bien si elle accepterait que la Grande-Bretagne s'en charge.

206. Le Gouvernement italien a répondu en juin de la même année que "le gouvernement de Sa Majesté le roi estime que lesdits sites sont un appendice maritime du territoire sur lequel il exerce sa souveraineté" mais il priait le Gouvernement britannique de bien vouloir ériger les phares en question, de les entretenir, et de fixer les modalités de remboursement.

207. Finalement, l'itinéraire occidental ne sera pas mis en place et les Ottomans ont pris les mesures voulues pour faire construire quatre phares, à Mocha sur la côte arabique, sur Jabal al-Tayr, sur Abu Ali et dans le groupe de Zubayr (sur Centre Peak). Ces phares seront entretenus par les concessionnaires français pour les Ottomans jusqu'en 1915. La Grande-Bretagne, en 1915, a occupé les trois îles ainsi dotées chacune d'un phare.

208. Quand il a été demandé à l'Empire ottoman de renoncer à ses possessions, il a été décidé en vertu de l'article 16 du traité de Lausanne que la question de la souveraineté sur les îles dotées d'un phare serait "à régler par les intéressés". S'agissant du phare situé à Mocha, la Grande-Bretagne a reconnu qu'il se trouvait sur le territoire dévolu par voie de succession à l'imam. La Grande-Bretagne avait parfois envisagé de chercher à acquérir la souveraineté sur les îles qu'elle occupait mais elle a en définitive estimé que lesdites îles ne présentaient pas assez d'intérêt stratégique. Il importe de constater que la Grande-Bretagne ne s'estimait pas empêchée de tenter d'acquérir cette souveraineté par les dispositions de l'article 16 du traité de Lausanne. Ce n'est qu'en 1927 que la Grande-Bretagne a déclaré officiellement (à la France) qu'elle avait définitivement renoncé à cette idée. Et, dans certains milieux, l'idée d'annexer Hanish

et Zuqar de même que Jabal al-Tayr et Abu Ali n'était pas encore totalement enterrée en 1944.

209. Il est également frappant de constater que, d'un bout à l'autre de la série de questions que la Grande-Bretagne allait poser à l'Italie après 1923 au sujet du statut de certaines autres îles, elle n'a jamais fait observer à l'Italie qu'une revendication de sa part serait contraire aux dispositions de l'article 16 du traité de Lausanne. La Grande-Bretagne s'est en fait contentée de s'assurer que l'Italie adoptait une position compatible avec l'accord bilatéral conclu lors des conversations de Rome de 1927.

210. Le Tribunal n'en a pas moins d'ores et déjà indiqué qu'à son avis, l'historique, le libellé lui-même et l'objet de l'article 16 militent contre l'acquisition unilatérale d'un titre sur les îles dont le statut a été déclaré comme indéterminé en 1923. Il n'est pas non plus indispensable d'examiner si l'Italie cherchait à établir un titre, contrairement à l'accord conclu et consigné dans le traité de Lausanne, car l'attitude adoptée par l'Italie fut en réalité beaucoup plus prudente.

211. En 1927, la Grande-Bretagne a négocié un accord avec la France pour faire assurer l'entretien des quatre phares par la société française et a pris contact avec les principaux usagers de la voie maritime concernée – l'Allemagne, les Pays-Bas, le Japon et l'Italie – en vue de réglementer la question au moyen d'une convention. L'Italie, qui a dit regretter de n'avoir pas été consultée plus tôt, a formulé deux observations. La première était que Mocha était revendiquée par l'imam et celui-ci devrait donc être partie à la convention en question. La seconde observation était que l'Italie voulait savoir si la souveraineté sur les îles allait être attribuée au pays côtier voisin ou bien si cette question de la souveraineté serait réservée. L'Italie ne formulait de revendication sur aucune des îles. Le Gouvernement britannique a admis que Mocha était bien soumise à la domination de l'imam et a affirmé que le statut des îles devait être réservé. Ces assurances ont abouti à la conclusion de la convention de 1930 relative à l'entretien de certains phares.

212. Cette convention n'est pas entrée en vigueur et il n'est donc pas possible de dire qu'elle lie les parties comme le ferait un traité, mais elle montre utilement ce que les parties pensaient à cette époque. Le préambule et l'annexe de la convention évoquent le fait que la Turquie a renoncé à la fois aux îles et à Mocha ainsi que l'occupation des îles par la Grande-Bretagne et la disposition de l'article 16 du traité de Lausanne suivant laquelle "le sort de ces territoires et îles [est] . . . à régler par les intéressés." L'annexe poursuivait: "e) . . . aucun accord sur cette question n'est intervenu entre les intéressés et il est utile, dans l'intérêt de la navigation, d'assurer l'entretien des phares installés sur lesdites îles." Il était ensuite indiqué dans cet exposé qu'une entreprise spécialisée prendrait possession des phares sur Abu Ali, Zubayr et Jabal al-Tayr et en assurerait

l'entretien. L'Italie était disposée à signer ce texte ainsi que l'article 13 qui confirmait nettement le maintien en vigueur de l'article 16 du traité de Lausanne:

> Article 13. Au cas où l'arrangement envisagé à l'article 16 du traité de Lausanne serait conclu entre les intéressés, les Hautes Parties contractantes devront se réunir en conférence pour décider s'il y a lieu de mettre fin à la présente convention ou d'en modifier les dispositions pour les rendre conformes à l'arrangement susmentionné. [Traduction du Bureau international de la CPA]

213. La convention de 1930 fut ratifée par l'Italie et les Pays-Bas mais elle n'est pas entrée en vigeur parce que le Gouvernement français et le Gouvernement britannique ne parvenaient pas à s'entendre sur le mode de calcul – à opérer ou non sur la base de l'étalon-or – de la rémunération à verser à la Société des phares Michel et Collas. La France refusa de ratifier la convention.

214. Entre-temps, la même année, l'Italie se préparait à ériger un phare sur South West Haycock. Il n'avait pas été fait expressément état des îles Haycocks lors des conversations de Rome de 1927 et les Britanniques tenaient beaucoup à ce que l'article 5 de l'accord conclu alors d'applique néanmoins, d'autant que "l'érection d'un phare . . . peut être considérée comme correspondant implicitement à une veéritable revendication de souveraineté." La Grande-Bretagne s'inquiétait de savoir si South West Haycock relevait bien, en fait, de ce qui fit l'objet des conversations de Rome – il existait des divergences dans les services intérieurs sur la question du titre – et elle notait que l'îlot n'était situé qu'à 20 milles de la côte "italienne". Il fut décidé de demander des assurances sur cette question, d'où un aide-mémoire établi le 18 février 1930, dans lequel les précédents échanges de 1927 étaient rappelés à l'Italie. Dans ce document, la Grande-Bretagne disait de South West Haycock qu'elle faisait partie "du groupe d'îles de Hanish".

215. Dans le mémorandum adressé en réponse le 11 avril 1930, l'Italie fit observer que le phare qu'elle projetait d'ériger visait à faciliter la navigation. Elle affirmait que South West Haycock ne faisait pas partie des îles Hanish, mais appartenait plutôt à l'archipel des Mohabbakah sur lequel, affirmait-elle, les Ottomans n'avaient jamais revendiqué la souveraineté.[17] L'Italie formulait donc "une réserve particulière concernant la souveraineté italienne sur cette île" et acceptait ensuite que "la question fût étudiée comme le serait celle de la souveraineté sur la totalité des îles du groupe des Hanish, dans l'esprit même des conversations de Rome de 1927."

216. On ne peut voir dans ce mémorandum qu'une revendication de souveraineté sur South West Haycock de la part de l'Italie (qui admettait en même temps que l'érection du phare devait être considérée comme une opération commerciale

---

[17] Le Tribunal note toutefois qu'avant l'occupation italienne, les îles situées au large de la côte africaine étaient administrées par le khédive d'Egypte pour le compte de l'Empire ottoman.

plutôt que comme un acte souverain) et on ne peut que constater aussi que l'Italie s'abstenait de toute revendication comparable quant au titre sur le groupe des Hanish. Les éléments de preuve issus des services internes montrent que c'était là une analyse que la Grande-Bretagne était à l'époque prête à accepter et dont elle était satisfaite; dans d'autres documents pourtant, la Grande-Bretagne considère que South West Haycock fait partie du groupe des Hanish et que l'île a été ottomane. Finalement, les îles seront toutes traitées comme le prescrivait l'article 16 du traité de Lausanne, qui fut renforcé par l'entente réalisée lors des conversations de Rome.

217. Le phare de South West Haycock a été éteint en 1940 et abandonné après 1945. Quand la convention de 1930 n'a pas pu entrer en vigueur, les autorités britanniques se sont retrouvées seules à supporter la charge financière des phares existants. Le Gouvernement britannique décida d'abandonner le phare de Centre Peak (dans le groupe de Zubayr) à partir de septembre 1932 et l'Italie (qui en avait été informée, tout comme la France) a remis en marche ce phare de Centre Peak en 1933.* Il fut décidé en Italie de faire savoir aux "puissances intéressées" que cette mesure répondait aux besoins de la navigation et que l'imam "qui revendique des droits sur les îles" devait être "informé du caractère provisoire de l'occupation et de l'utilité que revêtait pour lui la remise en marche du phare." Il fut apparemment prévu au départ de demander des contributions, mais finalement, cette décision-là ne fut pas prise.

218. Les autorités britanniques furent avisées par une note verbale datée du 4 octobre 1933 des inquiétudes qu'éprouvait le capitaine du port de Massawa quant à la sécurité de l'itinéraire Massawa-Hodeidah en l'absence du phare de Centre Peak, et de la décision prise par l'Italie de prendre possession du phare. Il était dit textuellement dans cette note verbale:

> . . . le ministère royal des affaires étrangères n'a guère besoin de préciser que la présence d'un personnel italien sur l'île de Zebair (Centre Peak), qui va assurer le fonctionnement du phare, n'entraîne aucune modification du statut juridique international de l'île elle-même, qui, avec les îles Abu Ail et Gebel Taiz [sic], a été étudiée par les Gouvernements italien et britannique en 1928 lors des négociations visant l'élaboration d'une convention sur les phares de la mer Rouge, et la conclusion a été formulée à cette date que la question de la souveraineté sur ces îles devait rester en suspens.

219. L'Italie avait par conséquent fait prévaloir dans les îles septentrionales aussi l'intérêt de la navigation en sa faveur mais elle affirmait que c'était sans incidence pour la souveraineté. Les Britanniques ont alors estimé qu'ils pouvaient se contenter de ne pas avoir à en débattre plus avant avec les Italiens.

---

* *Note de l'éditeur: cette phrase a été corrigée de la version anglaise originale.*

220. L'accord de 1938 n'a pratiquement rien changé à cette situation. A l'annexe 3, au paragraphe 2 de l'article 4, il était affirmé à nouveau que ni la Grande-Bretagne ni l'Italie n'instaurerait sa souveraineté sur les îles auxquelles la Turquie avait renoncé conformément à l'article 16 du traité de Lausanne et qu'il ne serait pas formulé d'objection contre la présence de personnel assurant l'entretien des phares.

221. On peut dire qu'au moment où la seconde guerre mondiale éclate, l'entretien des phares n'est pas considéré comme un acte de souveraineté et qu'il est convenu que le titre sous-jacent sur les îles en question est laissé en suspens – bien que l'Italie ait affirmé détenir le titre sur South West Haycock (même si elle choisissait de ne pas le faire valoir). Mais cette revendication de titre tenait au fait que South West Haycock passait pour faire partie des Mohabbakahs et non pas à l'idée qui n'avait jamais été formulée que l'érection d'un phare sur l'île favorisait l'instauration de la souveraineté. Au cours de la seconde guerre mondiale, les phares de South West Haycock et de Centre Peak furent éteints.

222. En juin 1948, l'autorité militaire britannique en Erythrée a demandé un avis juridique sur le point de savoir si elle était tenue par de quelconques conventions internationales à remettre en marche les divers phares entretenus précédemment par le Gouvernement italien. Au nombre de ces phares figuraient ceux de South West Haycock et de Centre Peak. L'avis sollicité (que rendit finalement le ministère des transports) fut qu'il n'existait à cet égard aucune obligation découlant d'une quelconque convention.

223. Si l'autorité militaire britannique décida ainsi qu'elle n'était pas responsable des phares de South West Haycock et de Centre Peak, ce ne fut pas parce qu'elle pensait que les îles en question n'étaient pas italiennes. On ne paraît pas s'être intéressé à cet aspect-là de la question. La décision a plutôt été que tant que le phare d'Abu Ali fonctionnait, il n'existait pas véritablement de danger pour la navigation. En outre, l'amirauté a fait savoir qu'aucun Etat n'était tenu d'éclairer ses côtes. Dans ces conditions, même si South West Haycock et Centre Peak avaient été italiennes (et ni l'une ni l'autre n'étaient qualifiées d'italiennes dans la correspondance de 1948, de même que rien ne vient prouver que les Britanniques aient jamais considéré Zubayr comme italienne), aucune obligation ne fut transmise à cet égard à l'autorité militaire britannique en sa qualité de puissance occupante.

224. Après la seconde guerre mondiale, les Britanniques ont continué de se charger des phares d'Abu Ali et de Jabal al-Tayr, et à partir de 1945 ils ont reçu un concours financier des Pays-Bas. L'arrangement a été officialisé en 1962 par un accord conclu entre le Danemark, les Etats-Unis, l'Italie, la Norvège, les Pays-Bas, la République fédérale d'Allemagne, le Royaume-Uni et la Suède, et il fut accepté officiellement aussi par le Pakistan, la République arabe unie et l'Union soviétique. Le Yémen n'était pas partie à cet accord non plus que l'Ethiopie. Pour

être invité à y adhérer, le critère déterminant était manifestement que la navigation joue pour le pays un rôle important et non pas que le pays possédât un titre sur les côtes ou les îles. Les considérants de cet accord de 1962 retracent l'historique des phares d'Abu Ail et Jabal al-Tayr, rappellent la convention avortée de 1930, évoquent l'article 16 du traité de Lausanne et ajoutent: "Il n'a jamais été conclu d'accord entre les intéressés sur l'avenir des îles sus-mentionnées."

225. En outre, l'article 8 de cet accord de 1962 devait indiquer on ne peut plus clairement que rien dans l'énoncé des dispositions suivantes ne devait être interprété comme réglant l'avenir des îles visées à l'article 16 du traité de Lausanne, "ni comme préjugeant la conclusion d'un tel règlement." Ledit article 8 reproduit les dispositions de l'article 15bis de la convention de 1930 sur les phares. Le Royaume-Uni était désigné comme le "gouvernement chargé de la gestion" des deux phares et habilité à désigner un agent à cette fin (article 2). L'article 6 prévoyait que le Royaume-Uni pouvait mettre fin à cette fonction à condition d'en aviser les autres parties, et indiquait les procédures à suivre au cas où l'éventualité se matérialiserait.

226. Comme en 1930, la fonction de gestion incombant au Royaume-Uni n'avait rien à voir avec la question du titre sur les îles; et cette fonction ne mettait même pas le Royaume-Uni dans une position favorable quand viendrait le moment où il faudrait résoudre la question du titre. Il y avait donc manifestement concordance avec l'entente réalisée à Rome (dans la mesure où les "conversations" visent la gestion des phares) et avec la convention avortée de 1930 – même si la convention de 1962 n'intéressait que deux phares.

227. Le Royaume-Uni a géré les phares de Jabal al-Tayr et Abu Ali à partir d'Aden, mais a compris qu'il faudrait songer à mettre en place un dispositif nouveau au moment où les Britanniques quitteraient Aden lorsque la République démocratique et populaire du Yémen accèderait à l'indépendance en 1967. L'entreprise Savon et Ries a donc été désignée, en vertu de l'article 2 de l'accord de 1962, comme l'agent chargé des fonctions de gestion. Il s'est trouvé que l'entreprise Savon et Ries avait installé ses bureaux à Massawa et que le personnel recruté pour l'entretien des phares à la demande du conseil d'administration était de plus en plus souvent originaire d'Ethiopie, mais, de l'avis du Tribunal, il faut y voir simplement un souci de commodité pratique. Le fait que l'Ethiopie ait dû autoriser des visites d'inspection ou de réparation dans les îles et exercer un contrôle sur les transmissions par radio n'avait aucune importance pour la souveraineté. En ce qui concernait le titre sur les îles, la situation est demeurée totalement inchangée – c'est-à-dire que l'article 8 de la convention de 1962 définissait toujours les règles applicables.

228. En 1971, le Gouvernement britannique a décidé de remplacer les phares par des feux automatiques et de se passer par conséquent des services des gardiens de

phare. Le Royaume-Uni a fait connaître au Yémen ses intentions, assurant le Gouvernement yéménite que "la mesure adoptée par le Board of Trade conformément à [la convention de 1962] n'empiète nullement sur des droits de souveraineté" et a demandé si le Yémen avait des objections à formuler. Le fait que cette communication fut adressée au Yémen, qui n'avait pas signé la convention de 1962, tendrait à montrer que, si les îles restaient non attribuées conformément aux dispositions du traité de 1962, le Royaume-Uni considérait le Yémen comme faisant partie des "intéressés" au sens de l'article 16 du traité de Lausanne et comme ayant sur Abu Ali et Jabal al-Tayr des prétentions dont il ne fallait pas préjuger l'issue. Il convient de noter aussi qu'à cette époque, l'Italie avait perdu ses possessions sur la côte de la mer Rouge et n'était par conséquent plus au nombre des "intéressés" au sens de l'article 16 du traité de Lausanne.[18]

229. Si, quelque temps auparavant, l'avis juridique qui avait cours au sein du Gouvernement britannique était que Abu Ali et Jabal al-Tayr (ainsi que Centre Peak) étaient des îles sans maître (*res nullius*) et si divers candidats avaient été présentés à divers moments comme faisant partie des "intéressés", il semble qu'au début des années 70, le Yémen était désormais considéré comme le premier des "intéressés" aux fins de l'article 16 du traité de Lausanne, tout au moins en ce qui concernait Abu Ali et Jabal al-Tayr.

230. En 1975, la gestion de ces deux phares a été transférée des bureaux de la société Savon et Ries en Ethiopie aux bureaux de la même société à Djibouti. Cinq ans plus tard, les autorités britanniques confièrent la charge de la gestion des phares à une nouvelle entreprise constituée par la précédente, la Red Sea Lights Company.

231. En 1987, le Yémen a rallumé le phare de Centre Peak, a publié des avis aux navigateurs et, en 1988, l'a réaménagé. Cela n'a suscité, semble-t-il, aucune protestation de la part de l'Ethiopie, qui ne pouvait pas avoir pensé que les mesures en question perdaient toute importance sous l'effet de l'article 16 du traité de Lausanne (auquel le Yémen n'était pas partie), sous l'effet des divers accords bilatéraux conclus entre l'Italie et le Royaume-Uni, ou encore sous l'effet de la convention de 1962 sur les phares – aucun de ces instruments n'étant opposable au Yémen.

232. Le 20 juin 1989, le Yémen a pris contact avec le Royaume-Uni au sujet de "la question des phares installés sur les îles Abu Ali (Ail) et Jabal al Tair qu'il est prévu d'examiner le mardi 20 juin 1989." Le Yémen disait officiellement ceci:

---

[18] Ni l'Italie ni du reste aucun autre Etat n'a affirmé estimer être au nombre des "intéressés" à cette fin. Le Tribunal en tire par conséquent la conclusion qu'en ce qui concerne les îles en litige, les "intéressés" sont aujourd'hui exclusivement les Parties au présent arbitrage.

1. Les deux îles citées sont situées dans la zone économique exclusive de la République arabe du Yémen.
2. Compte tenu de ce fait, la République arabe du Yémen est disposée à se charger de gérer les deux phares en question et d'en assurer le fonctionnement au profit de la navigation nationale et internationale. Comme vous le savez peut-être, la société des ports et des affaires de la mer assure déjà dans la République arabe du Yémen la direction et le fonctionnement de plusieurs phares dont certains sont situés dans la même zone que ces deux îles.

233. En l'absence de mesures visant expressément à proroger la convention de 1962, celle-ci devait expirer en mars 1990. En 1988 et 1989, on s'est clairement aperçu qu'un bon nombre des parties à ladite convention l'avaient dénoncée ou fait savoir qu'elles avaient l'intention de la dénoncer. Le Royaume-Uni, autorité de gestion des phares, était du nombre. L'Egypte proposa d'assumer désormais la fonction du Royaume-Uni, mais il apparaissait clairement qu'il n'y aurait pas assez de voix en faveur de la prorogation de la convention au-delà de 1990.

234. Une réunion des parties fut organisée à Londres en juin 1989. Après avoir fait valoir ses pouvoirs et ses intérêts, le Yémen fut invité en qualité d'observateur à cette conférence de 1989 visant à décider de l'avenir des deux phares septentrionaux, bien que, tout comme l'Ethiopie, il ne fût pas partie à l'accord de 1962. Dans le rapport qu'ils ont présenté au Gouvernement du Yémen, les techniciens yéménites ayant assisté à cette réunion de 1989 évoquent le fait que les Britanniques avaient confirmé que le Yémen avait installé de nouveaux phares sur Jabal Zubayr et Jabal Zuqar et en assurait le fonctionnement. La présence du Yémen semble avoir été motivée par l'intérêt manifesté par lui pour la question et aussi par un intérêt professionnel. L'Ethiopie ne fut pas invitée à cette conférence et ne l'avait pas demandé.

235. Lors de ladite conférence, le Yémen a appuyé une proposition égyptienne tendant à ce que le Yémen se charge de la gestion des phares situés sur Jabal al-Tayr et Abu Ali et n'a pas formulé de réserve concernant le titre sur ces îles. Les comptes rendus indiquent que le Yémen s'est également dit prêt à assurer le fonctionnement des phares sur les deux îles à ses propres frais avec effet quasi immédiat au cas où l'accord cesserait d'être en vigueur. On ne trouve dans les comptes rendus aucune allusion par le Yémen au fait que les îles sont situées dans sa zone économique exclusive – bien que le Yémen ait évoqué cette circonstance avant la conférence dans ses échanges avec le Royaume-Uni.

236. Le fait que le Yémen ait parlé de sa zone économique exclusive et non d'un titre sur les îles elles-mêmes ne paraît pas avoir été anodin. L'allusion figure deux fois à nouveau dans le rapport interne adressé après la conférence de 1989 au Gouvernement du Yémen par le directeur général yéménite des ports et des affaires de la mer. L'offre du Yémen – qui fut acceptée – fut formulée en d'autres termes qu'une revendication d'un droit à la souveraineté. Le Yémen n'a pas dit que le titre sur Abu Ali ou Jabal al-Tayr ni sur les îles situées à proximité lui

revenait et que donc le fonctionnement des phares lui incombait à lui seul. L'accord de 1962* n'avait pas la moindre chance de survie et l'offre de l'Egypte, quand celle-ci a proposé d'assurer la gestion des phares, ne pouvait pas constituer la solution à adopter. Le régime conventionnel international des phares de la mer Rouge parvenait à son terme.

237. La construction et l'entretien de phares en dehors de tous arrangements conventionnels et pour une durée indéterminée entraînaient certaines conséquences. L'acceptation de l'offre du Yémen ne valait pas reconnaissance de la souveraineté de celui-ci sur des îles. Mais elle valait acceptation du fait que le Yémen était le mieux placé pour se charger de l'établissement et de l'entretien de feux dans ce secteur de la mer Rouge et était disposé à le faire et que, lorsque viendrait finalement le moment de déterminer le statut de ces îles, le Yémen serait certainement au nombre des "intéressés". (Le Yémen n'était naturellement pas lié par l'article 8 de la convention de 1962 et ne semble d'ailleurs pas avoir été à l'époque au courant des arrangements pris en vertu de cette disposition.)

238. L'Erythrée dit que l'Ethiopie n'avait nul besoin de protester quand le Yémen a rallumé les phares sur Abu Ali et Jabal al-Tayr, car ses "activités ne faisaient que s'inscrire dans le prolongement des activités menées autrefois par la Grande-Bretagne sur Jabal A'Tair et Abu Ali." Mais le Yémen n'avait pas avec l'Ethiopie la même relation juridique concernant la question des phares que celle qu'avait eue la Grande-Bretagne et, si c'était là le raisonnement tendant à démontrer l'absence de réserve au sujet de la souveraineté revendiquée par l'Ethiopie, il était infondé.

* - * - *

---

* *Note de l'éditeur: cette référence a été corrigée de la version anglaise originale.*

CHAPITRE VII – Preuves de l'exercice des fonctions étatiques et de l'autorité de la puissance publique

Analyse des éléments de preuve

239. Les preuves concrètes d'"effectivités" présentées au Tribunal par les deux Parties sont fort nombreuses mais leur contenu utile est bien modeste. Cela s'explique sans doute par le caractère inhospitalier des îles elles-mêmes et la relative minceur de leur histoire humaine. Le droit international moderne de l'acquisition (ou de l'attribution) d'un territoire requiert de manière générale: une manifestation intentionnelle de pouvoir et d'autorité sur le territoire, par l'exercice continu et pacifique de la compétence et des attributs de la puissance publique. Ces deux derniers critères sont tempérés en fonction de la nature du territoire et de l'importance de sa population, s'il y en a une. Il faut apprécier les faits allégués par l'Erythrée et par le Yémen en la présente instance en fonction de ces critères, à la nuance suivante près: pendant très longtemps, ces îles ont été inhabitées et non administrées ou bien, pour autant qu'elles aient été administrées, elles l'ont été au sens le plus atténué du terme, mais en outre, les faits sur lesquels l'Erythrée se fonde sont des actes qui ont été commis par sa devancière, l'Ethiopie, lesquels n'étaient pas des actes "pacifiques", sauf s'il est possible ici d'appliquer le terme à des actes visant la poursuite d'une guerre civile. Il n'empêche que le Tribunal ne peut pas faire abstraction de ces faits en raison des circonstances singulières qui entourent la présente affaire.

240. Le Tribunal a jugé utile de classer les preuves concrètes très diverses citées par les Parties au sujet du thème du présent chapitre et va examiner chacune à leur tour les catégories de preuves ainsi recensées.

L'intention proclamée de revendiquer les îles

241. La preuve de l'intention de revendiquer les îles *à titre de souverain* [en français dans le texte] est un élément essentiel du processus de consolidation du titre. Cette intention peut être attestée par l'expression publique de la revendication d'un droit ou par une affirmation publique de souveraineté sur les îles, ainsi que par des actes législatifs visant ouvertement à y réglementer l'activité. Le Tribunal constate que les deux Parties abondent en affirmations de souveraineté et de juridiction mais que les preuves soumises par les Parties ne font pas la moindre allusion à la moindre île, quelle qu'elle soit et évoque de manière générale "les îles" sans autre précision.

Revendications publiques à la souveraineté sur les îles

242. L'Erythrée prétend que les îles en question ont été prises en compte comme faisant partie de "l'ancienne colonie italienne de l'Erythrée" par l'armistice militaire de 1943 conclu avec l'Italie, le traité de paix de 1947 et la Constitution

de 1952 mais les preuves présentées étayent fort mal cette prétention. Il est exact que l'Italie voulait revendiquer les îles et a effectivement établi une présence sur certaines d'entre elles; mais les faits en question ont toujours fait l'objet d'assurances constamment répétées confirmant que la situation juridique des îles était indéterminée conformément à l'article 16 du traité de Lausanne et à l'accord issu des conversations de Rome (voir chapitre V ci-dessus). La Constitution érythréenne de 1952 a défini le territoire de l'Erythrée comme étant un territoire continental "et insulaire" mais n'a pas défini de quelles îles il s'agissait. Et la même incertitude ressort de l'énoncé de l'article 2 de la résolution des Nations Unies portant approbation de la Constitution de 1952, de la Constitution de l'Ethiopie datant de 1955, de la révision de la Constitution éthiopienne datant de 1987, et de la Constitution du nouvel Etat indépendant d'Erythrée adoptée en 1997.

243. Les rares textes législatifs éthiopiens présentés à titre de preuves au Tribunal souffrent de la même incertitude que les dispositions constitutionnelles. Une proclamation fédérale éthiopienne sur la délinquance qui date de 1953 et une ordonnance maritime datant également de 1953, présentées l'une et l'autre par l'Erythrée à titre de preuves, ne sont guères explicites au sujet des îles. Le premier texte se contente simplement d'évoquer "toute île qui peut être considérée comme relevant de l'Ethiopie", et le second reprend simplement une fois de plus la formule "territoire continental et insulaire". Dans une proclamation maritime datant de 1953 figure simplement l'indication: "les côtes des îles éthiopiennes".

244. Dix-sept ans plus tard, en 1970, l'Ethiopie a promulgué une ordonnance instaurant l'état d'urgence. L'ordonnance ne visait pas expressément les îles, non plus que le règlement d'application promulgué par le ministre de la défense nationale. L'Erythrée a cité trois ordonnances opérationnelles de 1971 pour apporter la preuve que "les îles en litige relevaient bien de la compétence de l'Ethiopie". Dans ces ordonnances, la Grande Hanish et Jabal Zuqar sont qualifiées de "zones" devant faire l'objet de visites ou constituant des lieux de référence pour des itinéraires de patrouilles. En 1987, le ministère éthiopien de la défense nationale a été chargé "de la défense des eaux territoriales et des îles du pays" mais, là encore, lesdites "îles" sont restées non identifiées.

245. En 1973, le ministère des affaires étrangères de la République arabe du Yémen a fait savoir à l'ambassade impériale d'Ethiopie à Sanaa que le Yémen envisageait de procéder à un relevé aérien complet de son territoire qui couvrirait certaines "îles yéménites", lesquelles étaient identifiées; il s'agissait de "la Grande Hanish", de "la Petite Hanish", de "Jabal Zuqur", de "Jabal al Zair", de "Jabal Zal Tair", et de "Humar". La notification officielle était motivée, était-il indiqué, par le fait que les photographies, qui seraient prises à une altitude de 30.000 pieds [environ 10.000 mètres] montreraient peut-être des "parties de côtes éthiopiennes". L'Ethiopie réagit en faisant observer que "certaines des îles

énumérées dans la note susmentionnée n'ont pas pu être identifiées d'après la nomenclature utilisée, tandis que d'autres îles sont des îles éthiopiennes." Cet échange de correspondance est cité dans un mémorandum "ultrasecret" du ministère des affaires étrangères du gouvernement militaire provisoire de l'Ethiopie socialiste, datant de janvier 1977, lequel indique en détail les mesures que l'Ethiopie envisageait de prendre pour protéger ses intérêts. Le mémorandum évoque des îles situées dans la partie méridionale de la mer Rouge qui "n'ont eu aucun propriétaire reconnu comme tel", sur lesquelles l'Ethiopie "revendique la juridiction"[19] et sur lesquelles "tant le Yémen du Nord que le Yémen du Sud ont commencé à formuler des revendications." Ce mémorandum cite nommément les îles Hanish, Jabal Zuqar, Jabal al-Tayr et Jabal Zubayr, et signale que la réponse donnée en 1973 à la République arabe du Yémen avait délibérément revêtu un caractère vague, parce que l'on n'avait pas assez de temps pour réunir des éléments de preuve étayant la "revendication [éthiopienne] sur les îles" et que l'on craignait de provoquer une réaction militaire de la part du Yémen et de ses alliés arabes, qui s'inscrirait notamment dans le sillage de fausses nouvelles diffusées en 1973 au sujet d'une présence israélienne sur certaines îles de la mer Rouge. Le mémorandum incite instamment l'"Ethiopie . . . à prendre nettement position à cet égard pour protéger ses droits de propriété."

246. Le Yémen fait appel quant à lui à une revendication de titre historique, qui remonterait d'après lui à des temps immémoriaux. Le premier témoignage de ce titre daterait de 1429, date à laquelle le roi al-Zahir du Yémen a envoyé une mission sur l'île Jabal Zuqar pour enquêter sur deux navires pratiquant la contrebande qui se seraient échoués sur l'île. La pertinence de l'événement est fermement contestée par l'Erythrée pour divers motifs auxquels le Yémen n'a pas répondu au fond. Il s'agirait d'un incident unique en son genre et isolé. Le Tribunal n'estime pas l'événement important pour la détermination du titre sur Zuqar. Le seul intérêt que l'incident présenterait (lequel a du reste été sensiblement affaibli par l'opposition manifestée par l'Erythrée quant à sa pertinence, puisque le Yémen n'a pas répondu à ses objections) serait peut-être qu'il pourrait conforter une interprétation des ambitions de l'imam qui étendrait celles-ci au moins jusqu'à Jabal Zuqar, mais l'argument est lui aussi voué à l'échec car rien ne prouve qu'au moment où il a prétendu détenir des droits historiques, en 1918, l'imam était au courant de cette expédition de 1429. En outre, la source de l'information en question n'a été connue qu'en 1976, c'est-à-dire bien longtemps après que l'imam se soit prétendument mis à revendiquer des droits historiques.

247. On sait que, répondant à une proposition britannique tendant à la conclusion d'un traité d'amitié, l'imam a notamment demandé "2) l'établissement de son autorité,

---

19 L'Erythrée a présenté deux traductions [en anglais] de ce document, dont l'une parle de "juridiction" et l'autre de "souveraineté".

exercée en toute indépendance, sur la totalité du Yémen, c'est-à-dire sur la région qui était autrefois sous la souveraineté de ses prédécesseurs . . .". Cette revendication n'aurait pas pu avoir un caractère plus général. D'ailleurs, la formule utilisée "la région", qui est au singulier, ne paraît pas devoir normalement s'appliquer à des îles. Cette revendication de caractère général s'est apparemment manifestée à plusieurs reprises lors de conversations diplomatiques bilatérales pendant l'entre-deux-guerres, mais aucun acte constitutionnel ou législatif du Yémen ni du reste de l'imam lui-même n'a revendiqué avec précision l'une quelconque des îles ou ne l'a qualifiée avec précision de territoire yéménite.

248. Au cours de la procédure orale, le Yémen a affirmé qu'en 1933: " . . . certains représentants britanniques ont dit être étonnés que l'imam revendiquât avec autant de fermeté les îles d'Al-Yémen, y compris les îles du groupe des Hanish." Le ministre yéménite des affaires étrangères aurait fait clairement part de la "revendication de l'imam sur les îles Hanish à des fonctionnaires allemands en 1930, à la France en 1936 et, bien entendu, à l'Angleterre, en rapport avec le traité de 1934 et à beaucoup d'autres occasions aussi." Le Yémen a ajouté que "l'imam n'a cessé de formuler ses revendications historiques auprès des Britanniques, des Français et des Italiens chaque fois que ce fut concrètement possible", et des éléments de preuve contemporains semblent confirmer que tel fut bien le cas entre 1930 et 1936.

249. D'autres témoignages des communications échangées entre l'imam et les diplomates britanniques, notamment les comptes rendus de la mission Clayton de 1926 et les communications adressées par le colonel Reilly au Foreign Office, sont trop vagues pour prouver que l'imam revendiquait très précisément les îles à l'époque.

250. Le Yémen a bien affirmé au cours de la procédure orale qu'en réagissant à l'octroi d'une concession pétrolière par le Royaume-Uni dans la région de l'île Kamaran en 1956, le Yémen "renouvelait sa recommandation sur les îles de la mer Rouge", mais, d'après le texte même de la déclaration officielle, celle-ci disait simplement: "le Gouvernement yéménite estime que l'île Kamaran et les autres îles yéménites font indissociablement partie du Yémen." Il était dit aussi dans la déclaration: "le Gouvernement yéménite continue de faire valoir ses droits sur les îles yéménites et de réclamer leur libération." Il est permis de déduire de ce texte que les "îles" visées ne peuvent pas avoir été les îles en litige aujourd'hui puisqu'il ne s'agit pas d'îles dont il fallait réclamer la "libération".

251. En 1973, des journaux annoncent qu'Israël a occupé Jabal Zuqar avec l'autorisation de l'Ethiopie. Les deux parties à la présente procédure se sont beaucoup attachées à tenter de montrer que, de part et d'autre, les réactions à cette nouvelle présentaient de l'intérêt pour la question de la souveraineté sur les îles. Un communiqué de presse publié en 1973 par l'ambassade de la République

arabe du Yémen à Mogadiscio a fait savoir que les enquêtes menées par le Yémen avaient permis de constater que "la Petite Hanish, la Grande Hanish, Zuqar, Alzubair, Alswabe et plusieurs autres îles situées au large de la côte yéménite" étaient libres de toute infiltration étrangère et déclarait en outre que:

> [. . .]
>
> La République arabe du Yémen assure toujours le contrôle et maintient sa souveraineté sur ses îles de la mer Rouge, à l'exception des îles Gabal Abu Ali et Gabal Attair qui ont été cédées à l'Ethiopie par la Grande-Bretagne quand celle-ci a quitté Aden et remis le pouvoir à notre Yémen du Sud.

Cela permet de déduire que la formule "ses îles de la mer Rouge" visait les îles contestées; en outre, le même communiqué de presse soulignait que la République arabe du Yémen continuait de revendiquer la souveraineté sur les îles "cédées à l'Ethiopie par la Grande-Bretagne", et demandait instamment à l'Ethiopie de restituer ces îles.

252. La "revendication historique" du Yémen a d'abord été exprimée en des termes vagues et généraux après la fin de la première guerre mondiale et renouvelée dans les échanges diplomatiques bilatéraux pendant l'entre-deux-guerres. Après la seconde guerre mondiale, elle a été réaffirmée en 1956, mais de façon le plus souvent incertaine et indirecte. En 1973, toutefois, elle a été expressément reprise dans une déclaration publique (laquelle, tout en indiquant que Jabal al-Tayr et le groupe de Zubayr avaient été "cédés à l'Ethiopie", réaffirmait aussi "les droits et la possession" du Yémen sur lesdites îles et visait avec précision les autres îles "indiquées"). Cette déclaration ne permettait donc guère de douter que le Yémen maintenait ou renouvelait sa revendication sur toutes les îles les plus importantes, y compris les îles septentrionales – ou qu'il le faisait en tout cas à compter de 1973. Rien ne prouve que le Yémen ait ensuite abandonné cette revendication ou qu'il y ait renoncé. Les éléments de preuve disponibles donnent toutefois aussi à penser que le Yémen n'entretenait aucune présence à l'époque sur Jabal al-Tayr et le groupe de Zubayr et connaissait fort peu ces îles, et donnent en outre à penser qu'il supposait qu'elles étaient en la possession de l'Ethiopie. Le fait était que, depuis des années, les phares du nord étaient administrés à partir de l'Ethiopie par des salariés de la société chargée de l'entretien des phares.

* - *

Les actes législatifs visant à réglementer l'activité sur les îles

253. Dans les éléments de preuve que les Parties ont présentés, rien n'indique que la législation éthiopienne de l'après-guerre ait expressément cherché à réglementer l'activité sur les îles. Comme on l'a vu plus haut, aucun texte législatif éthiopien adopté entre 1953 et 1992 ne fut censé témoigner de l'exercice de la juridiction

et des fonctions étatiques sur les îles. Entre 1992 et le moment où le différend est né en 1995, aucune loi érythréenne n'a expressément traité les îles comme relevant de la juridiction et du contrôle de l'Erythrée.

254. La proclamation fédérale sur la délinquance et l'ordonnance de 1953 relative aux affaires maritimes, émanant l'une et l'autre de l'Ethiopie et citées à titre d'éléments de preuve par l'Erythrée, n'étaient guère explicites. Elles visaient "toute île qu'il est possible de considérer comme rattachée à l'Ethiopie" et "les îles". Une proclamation connexe de 1953 sur les affaires maritimes visait simplement "les côtes des îles éthiopiennes". Ces instruments étaient bien entendu applicables au groupe des Dahlak et aux îles de la baie d'Assab, mais ces îles ne sont pas en litige aujourd'hui.

255. Du côté du Yémen, les éléments de preuve constitués par des décrets administratifs et législatifs qui ont été présentés pour attester l'exercice de fonctions étatiques s'apparentent aux éléments émanant de l'Erythrée:* ces textes sont muets sur le point de savoir si les îles relèvent bien de l'application desdits décrets. La preuve n'existe pas que la législation yéménite ait manifestement cherché à réglementer l'activité sur les îles. Entre 1923 et la naissance du différend en 1995, la législation yéménite n'a jamais traité expressément les îles comme étant assujetties à la juridiction et au contrôle du Yémen.

256. En 1967, le président de la République arabe du Yémen a publié deux décrets concernant les eaux territoriales et le plateau continental. Mais ni l'un ni l'autre ne faisait nommément mention des îles. Le Yémen soutient par ailleurs que le fait d'avoir ultérieurement autorisé en 1987 un navire de recherche allemand, le *F.S. Meteor*, à exécuter un programme de recherche au large des îles, prouvait que ces textes étaient applicables à ces îles. Cette déduction n'est pas évidente, mais on peut soutenir que l'incident peut être considéré comme concrétisant la portée que le Yémen attribuait à ces textes législatifs de 1967.

257. En conclusion, les éléments de preuve présentés par les deux Parties correspondent à des actes législatifs et constitutionnels qui ne font pas nommément mention des îles. Il ne faut pas oublier que pendant la plupart des années ainsi évoquées, l'Ethiopie tout comme le Yémen étaient en proie à une guerre civile ou à des luttes intestines, et qu'il régnait donc une très forte instabilité sur le plan intérieur. Le Yémen ne s'est pas écarté des revendications générales et imprécises formulées avant la seconde guerre mondiale – lesquelles englobaient peut-être ou n'englobaient peut-être pas les îles en litige – mais il ne les a pas mises en œuvre ni définies avant 1973.

* - *

* *Note de l'éditeur: cette référence a été corrigée de la version anglaise originale.*

Les activités relatives à la mer

Les permis octroyés aux usagers des eaux au large des îles

258. Beaucoup d'éléments de preuve montrent que pendant de nombreuses années les unités navales éthiopiennes ont systématiquement surveillé la mer Rouge et en particulier les alentours de l'archipel Zuqar/Hanish. Comme nous le montrons plus loin, on ne voit pas bien si cette surveillance relevait d'un contrôle et d'une gestion de la pêche, si elle correspondait principalement à des mesures de sécurité ou si elle répondait à ce double objet, d'autant que les combattants de la liberté érythréens ont livré une lutte sans merci pendant les vingt ans qui ont précédé l'indépendance de l'Erythrée. De toute façon, on ne dispose guère d'éléments permettant de dire que cette activité de la part de l'Ethiopie procédait d'une réglementation ou d'une législation intéressant très précisément la pêche.

259. Pour ce qui concerne l'Erythrée, les éléments de preuve ne datent que depuis le début de 1992. En janvier de cette année-là, le gouvernement provisoire d'Erythrée a fait officiellement savoir qu'il interdisait en règle générale de pêcher sans permis dans "les eaux territoriales de l'Erythrée". Devant le Tribunal, l'Erythrée a dit que son ministère des ressources de la mer "réglemente la pêche dans les eaux érythréennes depuis peu de temps après l'indépendance de l'Erythrée." Le 1er avril 1995, ce ministère des ressources de la mer a publié un "manuel assorti de directives pour l'administration des permis à accorder aux navires étrangers et de leurs activités".

260. En septembre 1995, le ministère des ressources de la mer a édicté un premier règlement concernant les chalutiers. L'Erythrée dit que la notice annexée à ce règlement "étend l'application de cette dernière aux îles Zuqar-Hanish situées dans les zones n° 11 et 12 (Beilul et Bera'isole)".[20] Les zones sont séparées latéralement par des lignes en pointillé. Or, ces lignes ne s'étendent pas jusqu'à l'archipel Zuqar/Hanish ou n'entourent pas non plus cet archipel. (Si l'on compare avec les cartes 1 et 2, on constate que, quand la carte n° 2 définit l'archipel des Dahlak ("Dehalak"), il existe une frontière latérale soigneusement dessinée tout autour des Dahlak.)

261. S'agissant du Yémen, rien n'indique qu'un règlement ou qu'une ordonnance quelconque ait en tant que tel réglementé la pêche proprement dite dans les eaux yéménites. Le dossier ne contient rien qui puisse servir de fondement juridique officiel à la juridiction sur la pêche assumée par le Gouvernement yéménite dans les eaux entourant l'archipel Zuqar/Hanish. Un témoignage cité pour prouver que les vedettes du Gouvernement yéménite "veillent attentivement à réprimer la

---

[20] La carte n° 3 (datée de novembre 1993) montre la zone 10 ("Bera'isole") ainsi que la zone 11 ("Beilul"), mais la zone 12 est en fait celle de "Assab-Dumeira".

pêche illicite" précise simplement que le témoin (un capitaine de la marine) "a reçu pour mission de [sa] . . . hiérarchie d'arrêter les pêcheurs étrangers pirates . . . qui pillaient aveuglément, dans l'illégalité, les richesses de nos mers", mais il n'est pas donné d'autres détails.[21]

262. Le Yémen a pourtant affirmé avoir "strictement réglementé les activités de pêche sur les îles Hanish et aux alentours" et a affirmé que "le gouvernement a réprimé activement la pêche illicite". Il a été enregistré un nombre important de saisies de bateaux de pêche opérées par les autorités yéménites entre 1987 et 1990. Il convient toutefois de noter que ces saisies sont récentes et semblent viser principalement au cours des dernières années de gros bateaux de pêche industrielle de nationalité égyptienne.

263. Finalement, le Tribunal est d'avis que les activités menées par les Parties pour réglementer la pêche ne lui permettent pas d'en tirer de conclusion juridique claire. Les indications disponibles sur ces activités à l'époque de l'administration éthiopienne sont, comme on le verra ci-après, assez vagues. Depuis que l'Erythrée est indépendante, ces indications sont obscures. De son côté, le Yémen, depuis 1987, semble vouloir réglementer la pêche jusqu'à un certain point, en dirigeant principalement son action sur les navires de pêche les plus importants. Au total, ces éléments de preuve ne permettent de se prononcer ni dans un sens ni dans un autre.

Les saisies de bateaux de pêche

264. Le Tribunal constate d'après les éléments qui lui sont fournis que les saisies de bateaux de pêche coupables d'avoir violé la réglementation et les ordonnances promulguées de part et d'autre ont été assez nombreuses mais la période sur laquelle portent ces indications est courte. Il est donc difficile de qualifier ces mesures de "manifestation continue et pacifique de l'autorité étatique".

265. S'agissant de l'Ethiopie, les indications fournies au Tribunal sur la réglementation de la pêche ou les saisies opérées pour violation de ladite réglementation émanent quasiment toutes d'anciens officiers de la marine éthiopienne. Beaucoup de dépositions détaillées relatent le service accompli dans les unités de patrouille éthiopiennes pendant la guerre d'indépendance de l'Erythrée. Dans la plupart des cas, l'endroit où ont eu lieu certains incidents est indiqué de façon générale, mais il est souvent fait référence en particulier à des îles de l'archipel Zuqar/Hanish. Bien que les diverses saisies évoquées dans ces dépositions soient rarement datées, les actions signalées se situent majoritairement, semble-t-il, au cours des vingt années qui précèdent l'indépendance de l'Erythrée en 1991.

---

[21] L'échantillonnage de permis de pêche et de navigation fourni par le Yémen n'est guère utile; quand le permis précise la zone de pêche visée, il porte simplement la mention: "mer Rouge".

266. A bien lire ces dépositions, on constate que l'armée éthiopienne a pour objectif très largement prédominant au cours de cette période de lutter contre le Front populaire pour la libération de l'Erythrée (FPLE)* sur les îles et aux alentours et d'empêcher les forces rebelles de se servir des îles soit pour préparer des frappes sur la côte érythréenne de l'Ethiopie, soit comme des dépôts d'approvisionnement, soit comme des bases stratégiques. Les officiers de la marine éthiopienne concernés exerçaient aussi des pouvoirs de police qui les conduisaient à arraisonner et fouiller les bateaux de pêche.

267. L'exercice avait principalement pour objet de réprimer l'insurrection. Dans la plupart des cas cités, les témoins ont déclaré qu'il leur incombait notamment d'arraisonner tous les bateaux de pêche rencontrés pour vérifier leurs documents et leur cargaison. C'est ainsi que "les pêcheurs Dankali étaient soupçonnés de collaborer avec les rebelles et de faire passer en contrebande par la mer Rouge des armes, des munitions, entre autres fournitures." Mais ces patrouilles navales avaient également pour fonction d'empêcher les pêcheurs étrangers d'exercer leur activité dans ce que l'Ethiopie considérait comme ses eaux territoriales. Les bateaux qui n'étaient pas munis d'un permis de pêche ou qui n'étaient pas immatriculés en Ethiopie étaient arraisonnés ou recevaient l'ordre de partir.

268. Dans ses écritures, l'Erythrée dit que les éléments de preuve fournis montrent que les patrouilles ordinaires autour des îles avaient principalement pour objet d'inspecter les bateaux de pêche et/ou les navires de commerce." Or, la lutte qui se livrait pendant toutes les années en question dans cette zone et aux alentours ayant été acharnée, il n'est pas certain que ces patrouilles navales éthiopiennes aient eu principalement pour objet d'assurer la mise en œuvre de la réglementation relative à la pêche.

269. En même temps, toutefois, le Tribunal n'est pas disposé à écarter les moyens présentés par l'Erythrée parce que les actes invoqués n'étaient pas "pacifiques". L'action militaire menée dans le cadre d'une guerre civile n'est de toute façon pas considérée normalement comme une action belligérante dépourvue de toute pertinence juridique pour la question du titre. Par conséquent, le Tribunal, même s'il ne retient pas la thèse de l'Erythrée suivant laquelle cette activité navale visait principalement à réglementer la pêche, estime néanmoins que cette activité n'est pas dénuée de sens juridique.

270. En 1976, une patrouille navale éthiopienne a arrêté trois pêcheurs yéménites sur la Grande Hanish. Le Yémen s'est plaint auprès du Conseil de sécurité des Nations Unies de cet "acte flagrant d'agression et . . . cette violation manifeste de la souveraineté de la République arabe du Yémen." Dans une lettre adressée officiellement au président du Conseil de sécurité par son représentant permanent

* *Note de l'éditeur: cette phrase a été corrigée de la version anglaise originale.*

auprès des Nations Unies, l'Ethiopie a répondu que "les patrouilles navales éthiopiennes s'acquittaient de leurs responsabilités dans les limites de la juridiction éthiopienne." [Traduction du Bureau international de la CPA]

271. A la suite de l'indépendance, le dossier montre que l'on accorde désormais beaucoup d'attention au contrôle exercé sur la pêche érythréenne, ce qui se traduit notamment par un certain nombre d'arraisonnements, dont certains intéressent des pêcheurs yéménites. D'après bon nombre de dépositions, le ministère des ressources de la mer s'associe alors avec la marine érythréenne pour imposer son autorité et exercer sa surveillance, mais les éléments de preuve invoqués datent de l'époque de l'indépendance de l'Erythrée et quasiment tous les cas cités sont postérieurs à 1995. En l'absence d'indications précises sur les coordonnées des lieux et les distances, il est malheureusement difficile de voir si les activités et les arraisonnements évoqués se situaient dans les eaux entourant l'archipel Zuqar/Hanish ou bien Jabal al-Tayr et le groupe de Zubayr. Très souvent, les dépositions et les rapports n'indiquent pas avec précision à quelle distance rapprochée des îles en litige les incidents ont eu lieu.

272. De son côté, le Yémen a également fait état d'un certain nombre d'incidents enregistrés entre 1987 et 1995. Des documents font état de la saisie d'un chalutier égyptien en 1989, "à proximité de l'île de Zuqar . . . dans les eaux territoriales du Yémen." Un capitaine de la marine a dit aussi dans sa déposition qu'en mai 1995, il a reçu pour mission "d'arrêter les pêcheurs étrangers pirates" et qu'il a effectivement procédé à la saisie de "plusieurs canots automobiles", "dont le propriétaire était originaire du Golfe", dont l'équipage était égyptien, à la suite d'un échange de coups de feu, "dans les eaux territoriales yéménites", "dans une zone située entre al-Jah et Zuqar". Le Yémen a rapporté aussi qu'en 1990, quatre bateaux de pêche égyptiens ont été saisis "dans la zone du groupe des Hanish", et qu'il a été demandé à leurs propriétaires de verser une indemnité au Yémen et de s'engager à s'abstenir désormais de revenir dans les mêmes eaux, mais le document présenté à l'appui de ces indications ne précise pas le lieu des saisies.

273. Toutefois, un rapport datant de 1990, adressé au ministère yéménite de la défense, fait état de vingt incidents distincts ayant eu lieu entre 1987 et 1990, au cours desquels plus de soixante bateaux au total auraient été saisis, arraisonnés, "escortés" jusqu'à une base navale, ou bien "sommés de partir" et un bon nombre de ces incidents ont, semble-t-il, mis en cause des navires de pêche commerciale égyptiens. Certains de ces incidents auraient eu lieu, d'après le rapport, dans le voisinage de l'archipel Zuqar/Hanish ou de Jabal al-Tayr, Zubayr et Abu Ali, mais le rapport fait également état de "la zone de" telle île ou telles îles; une indication précise fait exception: deux chalutiers égyptiens auraient pêché sans permis "à Zuqar". Dans la plupart des cas, quand le navire a été sommé de partir, le rapport dit que la semonce précisait qu'il devait quitter "les eaux territoriales" ou bien "les eaux yéménites".

Octroi d'autres autorisations ou permis

274. La pêche mise à part, l'Erythrée n'a pas cherché à montrer qu'elle aurait systématiquement délivré des autorisations ou des permis en vue d'activités à mener dans les eaux situées au large des îles. De son côté, le Yémen dit avoir officiellement approuvé en 1993 le projet d'organisation d'une navette touristique par bateau entre al-Khawkha et la Grande Hanish. Le Yémen a également autorisé une entreprise allemande à construire un centre de plongée à l'extrémité septentrionale de la Grande Hanish en 1995. Comme on le verra ci-après, entre 1972 et 1993, le Gouvernement yéménite a enregistré huit demandes d'approbation d'activités revenant à utiliser les eaux entourant les îles, et il a à plusieurs reprises autorisé des expéditions de recherche et de plongée, etc.

* - *

Octroi d'autorisations en vue de croisières autour des îles ou d'escales sur les îles

275. Comme nous l'avons dit, le Tribunal est saisi de multiples éléments de preuve concernant les nombreuses activités menées par la marine éthiopienne pendant la période de 20 ans qui précède l'indépendance de l'Erythrée. Ces éléments montrent surtout que la marine éthiopienne a assumé un service intensif de patrouilles de surveillance dans les îles et tout autour pendant la guerre livrée par l'Ethiopie contre les rebelles érythréens. Ce rôle consistait pour les vedettes de la marine à arraisonner des bateaux de tous tonnages et des dhows circulant dans ces eaux, à leur faire préciser leur identité et à inspecter le matériel et la cargaison. Des navires transportant des touristes ancrés à proximité des îles Zuqar-Hanish étaient arraisonnés et conduits dans des ports éthiopiens aux fins d'enquête et les films saisis dans les caméras et appareils photo étaient détruits.

276. On sait d'après les indications fournies que des tiers ont parfois demandé officieusement aux patrouilles de la marine l'autorisation de faire de la navigation de plaisance, d'ancrer autour des îles ou d'y faire escale. Par exemple, une déposition de témoin indique que lorsqu'un bateau patrouilleur éthiopien était saisi par radio, de la part de "grands navires de commerce étrangers" (dont des navires de nationalité grecque, japonaise, yougoslave et italienne), d'une demande d'autorisation de mouillage "au large de la crique nord-ouest de Hanish", l'autorisation était octroyée pour différents motifs tels que: "réparations, abri, repos".

277. Du côté du Yémen, on sait par les éléments de preuve fournis qu'en 1978, trois chalutiers de pêche de nationalité koweïtienne ont demandé et obtenu l'autorisation de s'abriter d'une tempête à Jabal Zuqar et qu'à deux reprises en 1991, des navires battant pavillon étranger ont demandé et obtenu l'autorisation de mouiller à Zuqar et à Hanish pour procéder à des réparations.

278. En outre, entre 1972 et 1995, le Yémen a été sollicité officiellement à huit reprises au moins par des tiers, y compris un gouvernement étranger, pour qu'il les autorise à faire de la navigation de plaisance autour des îles, à y mouiller ou à y faire escale: en 1972, le Gouvernement de la République arabe du Yémen a refusé à une organisation italienne l'autorisation de mener des recherches sur Jabal Zuqar; en 1975, le Gouvernement français a demandé l'autorisation de procéder à des manœuvres navales dans le voisinage des îles Hanish; en 1983, une demande émanant d'une organisation française souhaitant tourner un film sur la vie sous-marine a été agréée; en 1987, l'Allemagne a demandé l'autorisation de procéder à des recherches scientifiques au moyen du navire *F.S. Meteor* autour des îles Hanish, l'autorisation a été accordée par décret gouvernemental officiel et le projet a été mené à terme sans incident; en fait, le *Meteor* a, semble-t-il, pris grand soin de rester en dehors des eaux territoriales tant de l'Ethiopie que du Yémen. En 1992, l'autorisation a été donnée à un yacht britannique, le *Lady Jenny V*, de faire une tournée de plongée autour des îles; en 1993, le Gouvernement yéménite a approuvé une expédition de recherche organisée avec la Royal Geographical Society dont la destination était très précisément l'archipel Zuqar/Hanish; en 1993 également, le Gouvernement yéménite a autorisé une expédition de recherche française organisée sur la Grande Hanish par la société Ardoukoba et a autorisé en outre une expédition allemande de plongée organisée sur le yacht *Cormoran*. Il semblerait aussi sans que cela soit prouvé qu'une demande polonaise d'autorisation de plongée dans la région ait été refusée à la fin de 1995.

279. Il faut toutefois noter que les îles visées ne sont pas indiquées dans la demande d'autorisation ni dans le rapport du voyage du *Meteor* bien qu'il soit fait mention des îles Hanish dans le rapport qui signale que "les valeurs maximales ont été enregistrées aux îles Hanish . . .". En outre, l'autorisation accordée précisait: "l'opération de recherche doit être menée en mer dans des eaux profondes de 100 mètres au moins", ce qui excluait par conséquent toute recherche à proximité étroite des îles.

280. La conclusion à tirer des indications ci-dessus est qu'en ce qui concerne l'autorisation de mener certaines activités autour des îles, le Yémen a été un peu plus actif que l'Ethiopie ou l'Erythrée pendant les périodes citées.

La publication d'avis aux navigateurs ou d'instructions de pilotage concernant les eaux entourant les îles

281. A part certains règlements sur la pêche, l'Erythrée n'a produit aucun élément de preuve relatif à la publication par l'Ethiopie ou par l'Erythrée d'informations générales concernant le pilotage ou la sécurité maritime.

282. De son côté, le Yémen, au cours des cinq années s'écoulant entre 1987 et 1991, a publié six avis aux navigateurs quand il a procédé à l'installation de nouveaux

phares sur les îles, s'agissant de Centre Peak (1987 et 1988) et de Jabal Zuqar (1989). A la suite de la conférence de Londres de 1989 sur les phares de la mer Rouge, le Yémen a publié un avis aux navigateurs concernant l'installation d'un nouveau phare solaire sur Jabal al-Tayr et un autre avis concernant l'installation d'un nouveau système sur Abu Ali. En 1991, la direction des ports du Yémen a construit un nouveau phare sur Low Island et un avis officiel a été adressé par télex à l'expert hydrographe de la Royal Navy à Taunton (dans lequel l'île est désignée sous le nom de "Hanish as Saghir"). En 1992, un télex analogue a fait savoir qu'il existait une "perche-balise" à "Jabal-at-Tair", un phare à "Sawabey" (al-Zubayr), un phare à Abu Ali, une balise à Zuqar et des balises à Hanish Sashir et Hanish Kabir.

283. Le Tribunal relève que ces avis accompagnent tout naturellement l'utilisation et l'entretien de phares, mais cette dernière fonction, dans les circonstances particulières propres à la mer Rouge, n'a généralement pas de sens juridique. La publication de ces avis toutefois, sans rien trancher quant au titre, suppose présence et connaissance parfaite du lieu. En outre, il faut bien voir qu'en ce qui concerne ces indications, il faut avant tout rechercher la précision dans l'identification de l'aide à la navigation dont il s'agit et de sa situation géographique et non pas tant chercher l'origine de l'information.

Opérations de recherche et de sauvetage

284. L'Erythrée a fourni des éléments prouvant qu'en 1974, le bâtiment *Star of Shaddia* s'est échoué au large de Zubayr. Il n'y a pas d'élément qui indique sa nationalité. Le bâtiment *HMS Ethiopia* a tenté un sauvetage mais n'a pas pu approcher du navire car la mer était trop grosse et il fallait parer en outre à des difficultés mécaniques, et le navire éthiopien a dû quitter les lieux sans pouvoir prêter son aide.

285. En 1990, la direction yéménite des ports a procédé au sauvetage d'un bateau iraquien, le *Basra Sun*, pris au piège de la côte rocheuse de Jabal Zuqar après que celui-ci ait appelé à l'aide.

286. Comme c'est une obligation pour tout individu ou bâtiment de prêter assistance à un vaisseau en détresse quand il est en mesure de le faire, on ne saurait par conséquent tirer la moindre conclusion juridique des cas cités ci-dessus.

Les patrouilles de la marine et du service des garde-côtes dans les eaux entourant les îles

287. L'Erythrée a présenté un grand nombre d'éléments de preuve sur les patrouilles systématiques de la marine autour des îles et sur les îles elles-mêmes. Les activités alléguées ne sont généralement pas consignées dans les documents présentés, elles figurent plutôt dans les dépositions sous serment recueillies par

écrit aux fins de la présente procédure. Le Tribunal relève toutefois que l'Erythrée signale qu'un très grand nombre de pièces d'archives de la marine éthiopienne ont été détruites au cours des hostilités.

288. **1953-1973:** Pour la première période de vingt ans (1953-1973), l'Erythrée a présenté des éléments de preuve de deux types: des livres de bord datant de la période 1959-1967 et des comptes rendus d'opérations de la marine datant principalement des années 70.

289. **Les livres de bord:** L'Erythrée dit dans son mémoire qu'"il est abondamment indiqué dans les informations disponibles que les îles étaient "visitées et/ou observées systématiquement" (mémoire de l'Erythrée, original anglais, p. 427), ce qui signifie implicitement que la plupart des livres de bord donnent cette indication. L'Erythrée dit aussi que ces renseignements "donnent avec des détails minutieux la preuve que l'Ethiopie était constamment présente sur les îles en litige" et qualifie ces indications de "comptes rendus de visites" aux îles.

290. Toutefois, les livres de bord concernant les années 1959, 1961, 1962, 1963 et 1967, par opposition aux rapports d'opérations, n'utilisent pas le terme "visite". En outre, le Tribunal ne voit pas très bien ce que ce terme recouvrait. Les "observations" figurent pour la plupart dans la colonne n° 13 du formulaire imprimé normalisé du livre de bord, laquelle est intitulée "Observations par sondages – relèvements de position", et une étude des entrées de ladite colonne montre qu'il s'agit quasiment toujours de "positions" de l'azimut relevé sur des points terrestres et des îles, à une distance parfois aussi éloignée que 15 milles au large.[22] En se fondant exclusivement sur ces livres de bord, le Tribunal ne peut donc guère tirer beaucoup de conclusions utiles sur l'exercice par l'Ethiopie de fonctions étatiques ayant trait aux îles.

291. **Rapports d'opérations et instructions:** L'Erythrée a présenté à titre d'éléments de preuve trois rapports d'opérations concernant deux croisières datant d'avril 1970 et une croisière datant de juillet 1971. Toutefois, les termes utilisés pour relater lesdites missions dans ces rapports sont trop vagues pour pouvoir servir à prouver l'exercice de fonctions étatiques en ce qui concerne les îles en l'occurrence: il est dit, par exemple, que l'on patrouille la "zone au sud" de la Grande Hanish et des Haycocks, que l'on va "jusqu'à la Grande Hanish et retour", et que l'on inspecte des bateaux "au sud de Zuqar" et "au voisinage de Jebel Attair". La seule précision pertinente qu'apportent les éléments de preuve en question se trouve dans le rapport d'opérations du HMS Ethiopia concernant

---

[22] Dans l'un des cas cités, il semble que l'officier de quart a obligeamment ajouté des distances calculées par radar, par exemple: "Ø Jabal at Tair 045° 6.0 par radar", et "Ø Haycock 106° 15 par radar", ce qui montre que, les deux fois, le navire opérant le relèvement (H.I.M.S. PC-12) était situé fort loin au large.

les 20 et 21 juillet ainsi que les 25 et 26 juillet, dates auxquelles le bateau "a mouillé à Zuqar" pour y passer la nuit et résoudre des problèmes mécaniques. Mais des épisodes de cette nature ne peuvent guère prêter à une revendication juridiquement valable d'occupation et d'exercice du contrôle.

292. De plus, même si l'Erythrée dans son mémoire indique, au sujet desdits rapports, que ceux-ci prouvent "la présence continue de la marine éthiopienne autour des îles en litige", pour la période de vingt ans considérée, ces rapports ne visent que deux voyages en avril 1970 et un seul en juillet 1971. Par suite, ces documents ne peuvent guère confirmer que la marine éthiopienne ait effectivement assuré une "présence continue" autour des îles pendant toute la période allant de 1953 à 1973.

293. Ont également été déposées quatre instructions en vue d'opérations de la marine éthiopienne datant de janvier, juillet, septembre et octobre 1971. Ces instructions visent l'établissement d'un "calendrier de visites des différentes zones", dont "Kebir Hanish" et "Zukar", ainsi que des patrouilles "autour des îles Hanish", "l'itinéraire étant: Dumeira is – Fatmah Lt. – Rs Darma – Kabir Hanish – Zuqar – Edd et Ras Darma", et visent aussi l'établissement d'un autre calendrier se rattachant à un itinéraire similaire. Ces instructions couvrent à peine une année sur les vingt ans recensés, mais cela s'explique peut-être par la destruction des dossiers de la marine éthiopienne au cours de la guerre civile, et cet argument a été présenté. Comme la guerre a duré plusieurs décennies, il ne paraît pas vraisemblable que l'Ethiopie n'ait manifesté la volonté de lutter contre l'insurrection que pendant une seule de ces années-là.

294. **1974-1980:** L'Erythrée a également soumis des pièces de caractère identique concernant les activités menées de 1974 jusqu'à la fin de 1980, mais les indications fournies sont tout aussi peu nombreuses que celles qui portent sur les vingt années précédentes. Il s'agit à nouveau de livres de bord et d'instructions de la marine qui présentent un intérêt particulier parce que ce sont des éléments contemporains, et il s'agit aussi d'échanges de correspondance. Les entrées des livres de bord, qui portent sur 1974, 1977 et 1980, témoignent de la même imprécision que celles des précédents livres de bord, puisque, par exemple, quand le livre est censé "enregistrer . . . [une] visite . . . à Hanish (le 16 août) [1977]", il est simplement indiqué "Hanish" dans la colonne 13, sous l'intitulé "Observations par sondages – relèvements de position", ce qui veut dire que Hanish a été vue par le bateau P-203 à 0400 le 16 août, avec un relèvement de 325° et à une *distance de 20 m.n.* Cela n'est pas la preuve d'une "visite", ni d'un transit par la mer territoriale de l'île en question.

295. Il a été présenté d'autres éléments qui décrivent la bataille que se sont livrée l'Ethiopie et l'Erythrée au large de l'île de Zuqar après la capture par le Front de

libération de l'Erythrée (FLE)* du navire de commerce *Salvatore* alors qu'il se rendait à Assab en juin 1979, mais on ne voit pas bien ce que cet incident apporte comme élément de preuve et quel intérêt on peut lui attribuer. En dernier lieu, le livre du patrouilleur P-203 indique en mai 1980 qu'il a été tiré des coups de semonce sur un bateau canadien et un bateau d'Allemagne de l'Ouest; l'endroit précis n'est pas indiqué dans le livre mais l'incident est enregistré dans une entrée qui commence par: "sortie pour patrouiller entre Hanish et Zuqar." La capture en 1980 de cinq bateaux en bois qui est évoquée dans les écritures n'est pas non plus située avec précision puisqu'il est simplement dit qu'elle a lieu "à proximité de la Petite Hanish". En avril 1980, quelques pêcheurs yéménites ont été faits prisonniers "près de l'île Zuqar", et d'autres ont été également faits prisonniers "au voisinage des îles Zuqar/Hanish". Le Yémen du Nord a en fait protesté contre cet incident.

296. Selon ce que dit l'Erythrée, "l'événement le plus important de 1980 pour la marine éthiopienne" fut l'"opération Julia"; cette opération s'est "traduite par une surveillance de 24 heures sur 24 et un blocus de toute la zone pendant l'intégralité de la période de trois mois qu'a duré l'opération." Quand on consulte la carte qui accompagne ces indications, on y voit ce qui semble être quatre secteurs de patrouille au large de la côte de l'Ethiopie/Erythrée: deux à proximité du rivage, un à mi-chemin entre la Grande Hanish et la côte et un approximativement à 3-4 m.n. à l'ouest de Near Island et de Shark Island sur la façade ouest de Jabal Zuqar, qui s'étend vers le sud en traversant Tongue Island pour aboutir juste au nord du rocher Marescaux. Le contexte dans lequel s'inscrit l'opération Julia montre très clairement qu'il s'est produit toute une série d'incidents graves en mer entre les forces navales éthiopiennes et les forces rebelles et que les forces navales éthiopiennes patrouillaient leurs propres rives ainsi que la mer principalement à l'ouest des îles faisant face à la côte érythréenne; l'opération avait principalement pour objet d'empêcher les rebelles "de s'infiltrer dans le district d'Assab."

297. **1973-1993:** Pour cette seconde tranche de vingt ans, l'Erythrée a également soumis au Tribunal beaucoup d'éléments de preuve, lesquels revêtent principalement la forme de sept dépositions de témoins recueillies spécialement auprès de sept anciens officiers de la marine éthiopienne et de deux autres dépositions émanant de deux anciens marins combattants du Front populaire pour la libération de l'Erythrée (FPLE). A une exception près, ces témoignages ne portent que sur des activités menées à partir de 1968. Résumés dans les écritures, les témoignages en question concernent en grande partie des activités menées en mer pendant d'assez longues périodes entre 1964 et 1991.

* *Note de l'éditeur: cette phrase a été corrigée de la version anglaise originale.*

298. Il n'est toutefois possible de faire fond sur ces témoignages que pour des indications extrêmement générales. Sur les trente incidents décrits par l'Erythrée, il y en a dix pour lesquels l'identité du navire éthiopien ou érythréen n'est pas donnée. La date de l'incident n'est donnée que dans neuf cas. Le lieu de l'incident n'est précisé que dans trois cas, mais, dans ces trois cas, le délai correspond à des périodes indéterminées de huit mois, de cinq ans et d'un mois respectivement. Pour toute la période allant de 1970 à 1995, il n'existe par conséquent aucun élément qui prouve que les forces navales éthiopiennes ou érythréennes ont procédé à un arraisonnement ou une saisie en donnant *à la fois* au sujet de l'incident un lieu précis et une date précise.

299. A lire attentivement les dépositions de témoins produites par l'Erythrée, on constate qu'il s'en dégage nettement trois autres points intéressants qui devraient permettre de mieux évaluer le contexte et la portée de ces éléments de preuve. Ces différents points n'ont pas été contredits pendant la procédure.

300. Le premier point à signaler est que sur les sept dépositions d'anciens officiers de la marine éthiopienne, il y en a trois qui ne font état d'aucun débarquement sur les îles. Les quatre autres sont imprécises soit quant à la date de ce qui est relaté soit quant au lieu. Et il y a deux dépositions de témoins qui signalent des débarquements plus systématiques qu'isolés pendant toute la période allant de 1973 à 1993.

301. Le deuxième des points à relever concerne la nature des patrouilles qui, outre qu'elles sont rapides, semblent avoir été organisées la nuit, et parfois les feux du navire éteints. Ces faits ont un lien avec l'absence de protestation de la part du Yémen.

302. Troisième point à relever: une partie des preuves fournies motivent bien "lesdites patrouilles par le souci primordial d'appréhender les bateaux transportant de la contrebande et d'empêcher les pêcheurs étrangers, qui étaient généralement originaires du Yémen, de pénétrer dans nos eaux territoriales", mais il n'est pas évident qu'une opération militaire majeure qui dure vingt ans et ne cesse de croître en intensité puisse être considérée comme étant principalement en rapport avec la pêche. Il est certainement vrai jusqu'à un certain point que l'inspection systématique des bateaux de pêche fasse essentiellement partie de la recherche d'insurgés et d'armes de contrebande. Tout comme il était indispensable d'inspecter les dhows du FLE pour vérifier qu'ils ne transportaient pas d'armes à feu et de munitions et mettre en échec les rebelles ("les dhows pouvaient transporter des centaines de moutons et de chèvres, et l'approvisionnement était caché sous les bêtes, là où il nous était impossible de fouiller"),* il fallait procéder à des vérifications auprès des pêcheurs (" . . . nous rencontrions souvent des

* *Note de l'éditeur: cette phrase a été corrigée de la version anglaise originale.*

pêcheurs Dankali plus à l'est, dans la région des îles . . . Nous inspections les papiers d'identité du bateau, du capitaine, de l'équipage et nous cherchions les marchandises de contrebande et les armes.") Toutefois, normalement, les opérations de surveillance de la pêche ne consistent pas à chercher des "marchandises de contrebande et des armes".

303. Il y a aussi, semble-t-il, dans ces témoignages, des contradictions dans les dépositions de témoins érythréens au sujet de la présence de pêcheurs yéménites. En effet, certains témoins disent: "Il n'était pratiquement jamais signalé de pêcheurs yéménites dans la région de Zuqar et de Hanish à cette époque" (c'est-à-dire à la fin des années 80) ou bien "Je n'ai jamais rencontré de pêcheurs yéménites dans les eaux autour de Zuqar et Hanish", tandis que d'autres témoins disent: "nous allions en patrouille à l'est des Dahlaks de même que jusqu'aux îles Hanish" et "parfois, nos patrouilles rencontraient des pêcheurs yéménites en train de pêcher en eau éthiopienne, y compris autour de Zuqar/Hanish."

304. **1983-1991:** Ces dépositions étaient également censées compléter les pièces fournies par l'Erythrée à titre de preuves concernant les activités menées entre 1983 et la fin de 1991, mais ces éléments de preuve sont très imprécis. Les formules utilisées sont presque toujours les suivantes: "autour de Hanish et Zuqar", "les environs de Hanish", "au voisinage de Jabal A'Tair", et, en outre, les opérations, les rapports et les ordres d'appareillage sont peu abondants du point de vue de la chronologie: mai 1983, octobre 1984, septembre 1984, mai 1986, juillet 1984 et août 1987. Et même si ces témoignages étaient précis quant au lieu et quant à leur rapport avec les îles, ils ne pourraient guère fournir vraiment la preuve d'une "présence continue de la marine éthiopienne autour des îles en litige" car ces témoignages ne couvrent que six mois sur quatre-vingt-seize et n'apportent aucun signe de cette présence continue de la marine pendant quatre ans sur la période totale considérée.

305. Vu leur ampleur et leur homogénéité, ces éléments de preuve n'en permettent pas moins de conclure que la marine éthiopienne, pendant la période en question, a bien en fait très largement mené des activités de surveillance et de reconnaissance militaire dans les eaux entourant les îles. Il n'est pas contesté que ces patrouilles étaient fréquentes et que leur intensité n'a cessé de croître pendant la guerre livrée par l'Ethiopie contre les mouvements de libération FLE et FPLE. Des bâtiments de la marine éthiopienne mouillaient fréquemment au large des îles, envoyaient à terre des détachements en mission de reconnaissance, et bombardaient même des installations sur les îles qui étaient soupçonnées d'appartenir aux rebelles.

306. A l'exception de l'incident de 1976 évoqué plus haut (qui a suscité des protestations adressées au Conseil de sécurité des Nations Unies), le Yémen du Nord (et, par la suite, la République du Yémen) n'a pas protesté contre ces activités de la marine éthiopienne. Cette absence de protestation correspondrait

normalement jusqu'à un certain point à l'acquiescement, mais le Tribunal doit, en examinant les éléments de preuve, peser quatre points: premièrement, la situation géographique des îles, le fait qu'elles n'étaient pas colonisées, et le fait qu'il n'existait pas de voie normale de communication à destination du territoire continental pour les personnes se trouvant sur les îles ou à proximité; deuxièmement, le fait que les patrouilles éthiopiennes ont souvent, semble-t-il, été menées la nuit tous feux éteints à bord; troisièmement, le fait que ces patrouilles étaient souvent menées à grande vitesse; et, enfin, le fait qu'il se livrait alors une guerre civile.

307. En même temps, l'absence de protestation du Yémen contre cette présence massive des forces navales éthiopiennes autour des îles et contre une présence sporadique sur les îles elles-mêmes pendant des années, peut être interprétée autrement. Si le Yémen n'était pas au courant de cette présence, l'assertion selon laquelle des pêcheurs yéménites s'étaient installés sur les îles et que le Yémen patrouillait les eaux des îles et allait même jusqu'à y entretenir des garnisons est fausse. Si, au contraire, le Yémen était au courant de la présence éthiopienne et si, comme l'indique le dossier, il n'a pas protesté à ce sujet, cela pourrait signifier que le Yémen ne se considérait pas comme ayant souveraineté sur les îles ou tout au moins qu'il reconnaissait ne pas exercer sur elles de contrôle effectif.

308. Le Yémen pourrait défendre l'idée que des actes de belligérance de la part de l'Ethiopie à l'encontre d'insurgés qui se servaient des îles ne participaient pas d'une occupation continue et pacifique de l'Ethiopie, ou bien que le fait pour l'Ethiopie d'assujettir à sa réglementation les bateaux de pêche yéménites trouvés dans les eaux des îles procédait de la situation de guerre propre à l'Ethiopie. Mais que ces actes soient ou non des actes de guerre, ils ne sont pas normalement compatibles avec la souveraineté du Yémen sur les îles. Dans ces conditions, si la présence de la marine éthiopienne dans les îles pendant des années n'aboutit pas à établir le titre de l'Ethiopie (et par conséquent celui de l'Erythrée), il est néanmoins possible de considérer que cette présence met en question le titre du Yémen.

309. Le Tribunal a estimé indispensable d'examiner assez longuement les éléments de preuve produits par l'Erythrée au sujet des patrouilles que la marine a donc pratiquées pendant une fort longue période. En même temps, il faut relever que le Yémen n'a pas donné à entendre au Tribunal qu'il met à son actif plus que quelques rares actions pendant toute cette période où la marine éthiopienne était ainsi présente dans la région. Le Yémen n'a pas expliqué pourquoi il s'est abstenu de protester.

310. Le Yémen se fonde essentiellement sur deux dépositions. Dans la première, le Yémen affirme que des patrouilles de surveillance des îles étaient "organisées périodiquement" – une fois par semaine en été et "une fois tous les mois ou tous les deux mois" en hiver, mais les dates ne sont pas précisées. Il est bien indiqué

une date, mais une date très récente, dans cette déposition qui évoque l'ordre "d'arrêter les pêcheurs étrangers pirates" (mai 1995). Cette déposition évoque aussi l'interception "dans ces îles" de navires de guerre étrangers (américains, français et russes) auxquels il a été demandé de partir, mais il n'est pas indiqué de date à ce sujet sauf pour un incident avec un bâtiment commercial russe "sur le flanc occidental de Zuqar au large de Shaykh Ghuthayyan aux environs de 1977-78." L'interception d'un dhow du FLE entre Zuqar et al-Jah est indiquée comme ayant eu lieu "aux environs de 1974-75".

311. Dans la seconde déposition, il est dit que "pendant la période allant de 1965 à 1977", la marine yéménite a systématiquement patrouillé autour des îles, et il est indiqué que "les bâtiments mouillaient toujours aux lieux de mouillage habituels des îles et patrouillaient tout autour" (les emplacements étant nommément cités), et que "nos soldats et nos officiers débarquaient sur ces îles." La même déposition ajoute sans donner de date précise: "très souvent nos officiers et nos recrues de la marine allaient à terre sur les îles en question (Zuqar, la Grande Hanish, la Petite Hanish, et al-Zubayr) en mission de reconnaissance à pied et aussi pour nager et se détendre." Il n'est pas donné de précision sur la période visée sauf pour l'indication générale: 1965-1977.

La protection de l'environnement

312. Le Yémen signale avoir enquêté sur un déversement de pétrole dû à un cargo russe à 10 milles environ de la Petite Hanish en 1990.

La pratique de la pêche par les particuliers

313. Les Parties ont abondamment discuté du point de savoir quelle est celle qui compte le plus grand nombre de pêcheurs et de savoir aussi quelle importance la pêche et le poisson revêtent dans l'économie de chacune d'elles. Pour le Tribunal, cette argumentation-là est sans pertinence, car, de toute façon, on peut s'attendre à ce que la démographie et les réalités économiques évoluent avec le temps. Ce qui peut être important aujourd'hui en matière de pêche peut ne pas l'être demain et la réciproque est également vraie.

314. L'Erythrée a soutenu qu': "Il existe plus de 2.500 pêcheurs érythréens, dont beaucoup sont des artisans pratiquant la pêche à petite échelle avec des méthodes et un matériel traditionnels" et aussi: "Les eaux qui entourent les îles Zuqar-Hanish fournissent une part importante des prises annuelles de l'Erythrée." De son côté, le Yémen a notamment dit ceci: "Les communautés de pêcheurs installées le long de la rive yéménite de la mer Rouge ont toujours été économiquement tributaires des îles voisines du groupe des Hanish."

315. Les deux Parties ont présenté de nombreuses dépositions de témoins pour prouver l'ancienneté et l'importance que revêt pour chacune d'elles la pratique de la

pêche ainsi que la vaste place que la pêche occupe dans le mode de vie de leur population. Certes, il est possible de voir dans les abondantes preuves de la pratique individuelle de la pêche qui sont ainsi versées au dossier une forme différente d'"effectivité" – c'est-à-dire l'expression de l'attitude et de la pratique généralement effectives d'individus qui sont des citoyens de l'Erythrée ou du Yémen – mais ce ne sont pas pour autant des preuves d'une activité étatique autorisant à revendiquer l'administration et le contrôle des îles. Ces éléments de preuve très divers et intéressants qui ont été produits de part et d'autre attestent éloquemment de l'attachement que manifestent apparemment depuis longtemps les populations de chaque rive pour la pêche pratiquée sur les îles et tout autour, en particulier autour des îles Zuqar-Hanish. Toutefois, cela ne constitue pas une preuve d'effectivité pour la simple raison qu'il ne s'agit dans aucun de ces cas d'actes accomplis à titre de souverain. Pour conclure à une activité étatique susceptible d'établir une revendication de souveraineté, le Tribunal doit pouvoir se fonder sur des activités de délivrance de permis et d'application d'une réglementation concernant les opérations de pêche décrites plus haut.

316. Le Yémen a fait état à titre d'éléments de preuve d'un grand nombre de saisies de bateaux de pêche commerciale opérées au cours des quelques dernières années dans les eaux entourant les îles. Ces saisies se sont accompagnées de procédures judiciaires, de l'expulsion des bâtiments en question et de lourdes amendes. Les bâtiments saisis étaient, semble-t-il, porteurs d'un pavillon étranger qui n'était ni éthiopien ni érythréen et était dans la plupart des cas égyptien. Ni l'Ethiopie ni l'Erythrée, d'après le dossier, n'a protesté contre les mesures ainsi prises par le Yémen. L'Erythrée a, elle aussi, produit un témoin qui a rapporté qu'"entre 1992 et 1993", alors qu'il était capitaine de la marine marchande naviguant dans les eaux des îles Zuqar-Hanish, il a signalé la présence d'une vingtaine de chalutiers égyptiens. "Certains de ces chalutiers ont été saisis . . .". Le même témoin a également indiqué que, dans l'exercice de ses fonctions actuelles au département des transports maritimes, il est chargé "de décider ce qu'il faut faire de ces chalutiers."

Autres actes juridictionnels concernant des incidents en mer

317. La perte d'un dhow a donné lieu à des recherches au large des îles et à une enquête menée par les autorités yéménites en 1976; une noyade en mer à la Grande Hanish a donné également lieu à enquête de la part des autorités yéménites en 1992.

-

Activités menées sur les îles

318. Pour étudier quels actes juridictionnels sont accomplis sur les îles, le Tribunal doit examiner les preuves fournies quant aux activités menées sur le territoire terrestre des îles et aussi sur les actes commis dans les eaux entourant les îles. Les

éléments de preuve qui ont été produits portent sur le débarquement de groupes sur les îles; la création de postes militaires sur les îles; la construction et l'entretien de certaines installations sur les îles; la délivrance de permis concernant certaines activités menées sur le territoire des îles; l'exercice de la juridiction pénale ou civile concernant des événements survenus sur les îles; la construction ou l'entretien de phares; l'octroi de concessions pétrolières; enfin, le caractère quasi-désertique et la colonisation restreinte de ces îles.

Les débarquements opérés sur les îles

319. D'après les éléments de preuve directs, aucune des deux Parties n'a vraiment pratiqué de débarquement systématique sur les îles.

320. D'après les preuves produites par l'Erythrée, au cours des vingt années de guerre civile, les bâtiments de la marine éthiopienne luttant contre les mouvements sécessionnistes ont déployé une intense activité sur les îles elles-mêmes et au large des îles. Il ressort clairement du dossier que les îles ont beaucoup servi aux forces rebelles pendant leur guerre d'indépendance. Comme on l'a vu plus haut, dans le cadre des opérations navales menées autour des îles, il a été signalé pour la période allant de 1970 à 1988, deux patrouilles importantes et un certain nombre de débarquements non précisés par des unités des forces militaires éthiopiennes.

321. De son côté, le Yémen a évoqué une visite officielle datant de 1973 dans les îles de Jabal Zuqar et Abu Ali qui faisait suite à la nouvelle annoncée par les médias d'une éventuelle présence israélienne sur ces îles. Le Tribunal ayant demandé des précisions, le secrétaire général de la Ligue arabe a écrit au président du Tribunal le 28 juillet 1998 pour lui faire savoir qu'il n'y avait jamais eu "de visite d'une délégation officielle de la Ligue des Etats arabes dirigée par son secrétaire général dans aucune des îles de la mer Rouge." La même lettre faisait savoir que le secrétaire général de la Ligue arabe et le ministre des affaires étrangères d'Ethiopie s'étaient rencontrés en 1973 pour parler de l'inquiétude éprouvée par les Etats arabes quand ils avaient entendu dire qu'Israël utilisait des îles Dahlak et d'autres îles de la baie d'Assab. Les Ethiopiens ont alors invité une délégation de la Ligue arabe à se rendre dans les îles pour qu'elle puisse constater qu'Israël n'y était nullement présent, "mais la visite n'a jamais eu lieu." En dernier lieu, la lettre de la Ligue arabe indique qu'"en 1971 et en 1973, des membres du comité militaire de la Ligue des Etats arabes, dont des officiers yéménites, se sont rendus dans les îles du groupe Hanish, dont Zuqar, ainsi que dans les îles de Zubayr avec la coopération et le concours exclusifs des gouvernements de la République démocratique et populaire du Yémen et de la République arabe du Yémen." D'après le secrétaire général il n'a été trouvé aucune trace de ces visites dans les archives de la Ligue arabe.

322. Pour témoigner de sa présence militaire sur les îles, le Yémen s'appuie par ailleurs très fortement sur une déposition de témoin qui fait état de débarquements non précisés opérés pendant toute une période dont les dates ne sont pas non plus précisées si ce n'est qu'il s'agit en général de la période allant de 1965 à 1977.

323. Le Yémen a également fait état de renseignements concernant des stages pratiques organisés en 1987 et 1990 pour les enseignants et les étudiants de l'école militaire. Ces stages n'ont, semble-t-il, duré que très peu de temps et n'ont pas laissé non plus de traces durables.

Installation de postes militaires sur les îles

324. Les éléments de preuve produits montrent qu'il n'y a pas de postes militaires permanents sur les îles avant 1995. L'Erythrée parle bien d'unités de débarquement, mais elle a expliqué qu'il n'avait pas été établi de garnison et que, du reste, la présence de garnisons n'était pas un argument pertinent. L'Erythrée a tenu à insister sur la pertinence qui s'attache plutôt à des actes souverains dûment adaptés au caractère du territoire en question, c'est-à-dire la surveillance militaire et la réglementation de la pêche.

325. Le Yémen, quant à lui, déclare dans ses écritures qu'"une garnison militaire temporaire" a été "établie . . . sur Jabal Zuqar à l'époque de la visite de 1973", et aussi que, "au cours des années 70, le Gouvernement yéménite a installé des postes de garde sur d'autres îles du groupe, dont la Grande Hanish", mais il n'a produit aucun élément de preuve pour étayer cette déclaration. Des photographies qui figurent au dossier de groupes de militaires posant debout sur l'île ne donnent pas l'impression de la permanence. Et l'on constate aussi qu'il ne figure aucune structure ni bâtiment sur ces photographies; s'il y avait eu la moindre construction ou bâtiment, on aurait pu s'attendre à les voir figurer sur la pellicule.

326. Le Tribunal en tire la conclusion qu'il ne lui est pas possible d'accepter qu'il ait été établi de garnison ou de poste militaire permanent sur les îles avant la naissance du litige en 1995.

Construction et entretien d'installations sur les îles

327. Rien ne prouve que l'Erythrée ait construit ou entretenu sur les îles des installations de quelque type que ce soit. L'Erythrée prétend néanmoins, pour que le Tribunal y voie le signe que l'Ethiopie "a consolidé son contrôle souverain sur les îles en litige", qu'à la suite du transfert d'Aden au Yémen en 1967, la gestion des phares installés à Abu Ali et Jabal al-Tayr a été confiée à une entreprise privée qui avait alors son siège à Asmara et que les opérations de gestion et d'entretien des phares effectuées par cette société étaient soumises à la réglementation éthiopienne. Pour le Tribunal, cet argument n'est pas convaincant.

328. Le Yémen a toutefois quant à lui construit certains phares et assuré l'entretien de certains autres phares. Mais assurer le fonctionnement ou l'entretien de phares et d'aides à la navigation est normalement lié à la sécurité de la navigation et n'est normalement pas considéré comme un critère de souveraineté. Le fait que des sociétés britanniques et italiennes ainsi que les autorités britanniques et italiennes aient assuré sur ces îles l'entretien de phares n'a pas suscité de revendications de souveraineté ni de conclusions en ce sens. Le Tribunal a étudié au chapitre VI quelle pertinence il faut attribuer à ces activités et à la présence du Yémen à la conférence de 1989 sur les phares de la mer Rouge.

329. Le Yémen fait aussi valoir comme exemples d'actes étatiques, la localisation et l'installation en 1992 de deux stations géodésiques par des sociétés françaises pour le compte du Gouvernement yéménite sur Jabal Zuqar et la Grande Hanish. L'Erythrée répond que ces repères ont été placés en secret et sont de toute façon modestes. Le Tribunal ne peut pas accorder trop de poids à d'aussi petites constructions de cette nature et doit aussi constater qu'en réalité, ces repères ont été installés avant l'échange de correspondance de 1995 entre les deux chefs d'Etat; le Tribunal constate aussi que ces repères existent; et qu'ils figurent sur la carte des stations géodésiques installées au Yémen.

330. L'entretien d'édifices religieux et de lieux saints dont le Yémen fait également état a, semble-t-il, un caractère privé; il n'est pas donné à penser qu'il y a là une activité étatique. Le Tribunal a été en outre saisi d'un témoignage non étayé, aux termes duquel: "Notre gouvernement a construit entre al-Shura et al-Habal [sur la Grande Hanish] un terrain d'atterrissage pour hélicoptères." Le Tribunal étudie au chapitre IX la question de la piste d'atterrissage construite par Total sur la Grande Hanish avec l'autorisation du Yémen dans le cadre de la concession octroyée en 1985 à Total, piste qui a été ensuite réservée aux séjours de repos et de loisir des salariés de Total.

331. Les éléments de preuve concernant les intentions imputables en mai 1995 à la Direction des investissements d'intérêt public du Yémen sont récents et ces indications visent exclusivement une action étatique dénuée d'objet précis, mais ils établissent néanmoins qu'à un niveau élevé, les instances gouvernementales du Yémen envisageaient sérieusement d'encourager les investissements à vocation touristique sur la Grande Hanish, la Petite Hanish, Abu Ali, Jabal al-Tayr et al-Zubayr; c'est-à-dire qu'à cette époque, la politique officielle de l'Etat yéménite tablait implicitement sur la souveraineté du Yémen sur lesdites îles.

La délivrance de permis autorisant à mener certaines activités sur le territoire terrestre des îles

332. L'Erythrée a donné à entendre que si la société privée Savon et Ries a eu besoin d'une autorisation pour faire transporter par la voie maritime des émetteurs radio sur Abu Ali et Jabal al-Tayr, c'est-à-dire les îles sur lesquelles cette entreprise

entretenait des phares, il y avait là une manifestation de l'exercice d'un contrôle étatique. Toutefois, le fait de réglementer l'usage d'un matériel électronique par une entreprise privée dont les agents sont en poste dans une zone où il est par ailleurs mené des opérations militaires ne peut pas être considéré comme une manifestation de l'exercice de la souveraineté en ce qui concerne le territoire terrestre des îles en question.

333. L'Erythrée a produit la preuve de l'octroi d'un permis d'exploitation d'une station émettrice de radio sur la Grande Hanish dans le cadre d'activités de prospection pétrolière à mener dans le voisinage.

334. Pour ce qui concerne le Yémen, le Tribunal examine ci-après les travaux de construction et d'entretien de phares qu'il a assumés sur les îles. Comme la plus grande partie de l'activité économique utile et de l'intérêt manifesté pour les îles s'explique par leur situation géographique, au milieu de la mer Rouge, et par leurs liens avec les eaux qui les entourent (qu'il s'agisse de contrebande, de pêche, ou de tourisme), la délivrance de permis a quasiment toujours porté sur des activités se rapportant à la mer. L'expédition de recherche scientifique amphibie que la société Ardoukoba a récemment effectuée sur la Grande Hanish avec l'autorisation du Yémen a constitué une brève mais non insignifiante utilisation du territoire terrestre des îles.

Exercice de la juridiction pénale ou civile en ce qui concerne des événements survenus sur les îles

335. En 1976, un tribunal militaire constitué par le Gouvernement éthiopien a traduit en justice des salariés de Savon et Ries, l'entreprise d'entretien de phares s'occupant des feux situés sur Abu Ali et Jabal al-Tayr, lesdits salariés étant accusés de diriger et de former sur les îles les membres d'un groupe subversif. A l'issue de ce procès, l'exécution de l'agent chargé du service des finances ainsi que l'expulsion ou l'incarcération d'un gardien-chef de phare et de certains autres inculpés ont incité la société en cause à déménager à Djibouti ses bureaux d'Asmara.

336. Pour citer en écho des exemples de l'exercice, à la même époque, de la juridiction pénale par les autorités yéménites au sujet d'événements survenus dans les îles, il convient d'évoquer l'enquête menée en 1976 sur un dhow porté disparu et, en 1992, l'enquête menée sur la disparition en mer d'un pêcheur au large de la Grande Hanish.

337. En outre, le Yémen affirme que, depuis des années, les pêcheurs locaux utilisent un système d'arbitrage pour le règlement des différends locaux, fondé sur le droit coutumier, sous l'autorité d'un *aq'il* – "personne connue pour sa sagesse et son intelligence". Il existe dans ce système un arbitre en chef, "*Aq'il* de la mer", dont le plus célèbre aurait "résidé une partie de l'année sur le continent yéménite et

une partie de l'année dans ses locaux ('Izbat al-Sayyid'Ali) sur la Grande Hanish." Le chef suprême qui a un rang supérieur aux *aq 'ils* de village ou à celui de l'*Aq'il* de la mer est l'"*Aq'il* des pêcheurs", qui est un dignitaire reconnu officiellement par le Gouvernement du Yémen.

338. Les *aq'ils* appliquent ce que le Yémen dit être "un ensemble de règles de droit coutumier propres au Yémen qui sont bien établies, connu sous le nom d'*urf*", afin de résoudre les différends entre pêcheurs. Des éléments présentés au Tribunal montrent que les jugements ou les décisions des *aq'ils* ont force obligatoire.[23] D'ailleurs, dans l'affaire relative à une disparition en mer évoquée ci-dessus, l'élément produit devant le Tribunal est que "le patron du bateau et son équipage ont l'un et l'autre informé le représentant de l'autorité sur place, connu sous le nom d'*Aq'il* Sheikh des pêcheurs, et l'*Aq'il* a avisé le département."

339. L'Erythrée ne paraît pas contester l'existence de ce système d'arbitrage des petits différends qui est fondé sur le droit coutumier. D'après certains éléments, il semble que ce système de l'*urf* et de l'*aq'il* soit applicable aux Yéménites comme aux non-Yéménites sur le territoire yéménite et qu'il soit systématiquement appliqué à la solution de problèmes se posant sur les îles.

340. Le Tribunal croit comprendre que les règles appliquées dans le système de l'*aq'il* ne trouvent pas leur origine dans le droit yéménite mais constituent des éléments d'une justice privée empruntés à l'activité de la pêche et applicables à celle-ci. Il s'agit d'une *lex pescatoria* appliquée à l'échelle régionale par ceux qui pratiquent la pêche. Cette situation traduit aussi la réalité qui est que le marché principal du poisson est à Hodeidah, sur la rive yéménite, et que, dans la région des îles, la pêche se pratique depuis fort longtemps sans la moindre discrimination, sur une échelle régionale, par des pêcheurs originaires de chacune des deux rives de la mer Rouge. Le fait que ce système bénéficie de la reconnaissance ou de l'appui du Yémen n'entame pas son caractère essentiellement privé.

La construction ou l'entretien de phares

341. La question des phares a déjà été examinée ci-dessus, au chapitre VI. Nous ne l'étudions dans la présente section qu'aux fins du présent chapitre qui est consacré aux effectivités. Les phares installés sur Abu Ali et Jabal al-Tayr étaient gérés par l'entreprise Savon et Ries spécialisée dans l'entretien des phares. Cette société a eu son siège à Asmara jusqu'en 1976, date à laquelle elle a déménagé en Somalie parce que le Gouvernement éthiopien traduisait en justice certains de ses employés accusés d'activités subversives (voir le paragraphe 335 ci-dessus).

---

[23] D'après une déposition de témoin présentée par le Yémen, " . . . toute personne partie à un différend qui cherche à se soustraire à une décision défavorable du Conseil risque des poursuites de la part de l'Etat, la sanction allant dans certains cas jusqu'à la prison."

Il n'y a pas de fondement juridique permettant de conclure que l'installation, dans un certain Etat, des bureaux d'une entreprise privée assurant aux termes d'un contrat de gestion l'entretien de phares érigés sur des îles constitue de la part dudit Etat une manifestation intentionnelle de son pouvoir et de son autorité.

342. De son côté, le Yémen, à partir de 1987, a entrepris un programme d'installation dans les îles de nouveaux phares, en commençant avec Centre Peak en 1987 et 1988 et Jabal Zuqar en 1989.

343. A la suite de la conférence sur les phares de la mer Rouge qui s'est tenue à Londres en 1989, le Yémen a installé de nouveaux phares solaires sur Jabal al-Tayr et Quoin (îles Abu Ali). En 1991, un nouveau phare a été construit sur Low Island. Enfin, un phare a été également érigé sur la Grande Hanish en 1991.

344. Les autorités gouvernementales yéménites ont fait connaître au public la construction et les caractéristiques de chacun de ces phares grâce à la publication d'avis à la population ou d'avis aux navigateurs, comme il est indiqué plus en détail au paragraphe 282 ci-dessus.

345. La question de l'effet juridique à accorder à la construction et à l'entretien de phares dans la présente affaire a été examinée ci-dessus au chapitre VI.

L'octroi de concessions pétrolières

346. Comme il a été accordé dans des écritures et une procédure orale supplémentaires une large place aux incidences juridiques des accords pétroliers ainsi que des activités de prospection pétrolière, ce sujet est traité à part au chapitre IX.

Les îles sont quasi-désertes

347. Il ressort aussi des éléments de preuve qui ont été produits que certains pêcheurs yéménites ont installé des "habitations" sur la Grande Hanish, la Petite Hanish, et Zuqar, et qu'ils ont habituellement entretenu longtemps ces constructions; ou bien qu'ils se sont "installés" sur la Grande Hanish pour l'été, ou bien sur les îlots d'Addar Ail ou la Petite Hanish pour l'été également.

348. L'Erythrée a produit quelques éléments tendant à prouver que des pêcheurs érythréens séjournaient pour de courtes périodes sur les îles pendant la saison de la pêche, mais les affirmations d'"installation" ne prennent pas autant de place dans ces éléments de preuve que dans ceux qui ont été produits par le Yémen. Il y a toutefois un pêcheur qui dit: "à ma connaissance, la personne qui a séjourné le plus longtemps sur les îles y aura passé de sept à huit mois."

349. Dans les écritures, le Yémen dit que "certaines familles de pêcheurs yéménites assurent depuis des générations une présence permanente dans le groupe des

Hanish", et il évoque les "familles de pêcheurs résidant dans le groupe des Hanish" quand il parle des "habitations temporaires" et autres lieux de résidence provisoire occupés par des pêcheurs. Il n'a pas été produit d'élément de preuve précis au sujet de familles vivant sur les îles.

350. D'après une déposition de témoin yéménite, les unités débarquées par la marine "rencontraient beaucoup de pêcheurs yéménites . . . qui s'étaient installés sur certaines de ces îles, s'occupaient à saler et sécher le poisson, et y séjournaient pendant plusieurs mois."

351. Pendant les saisons de pêche, on pouvait s'attendre à ce que les pêcheurs de chacune des Parties pêchent sans discontinuer pendant plusieurs jours et nuits sur les îles et tout autour, puisque rentrer au port, que ce soit en Ethiopie/en Erythrée ou bien au Yémen, leur coûtait une pleine journée de voyage même s'ils avaient les vents pour eux. D'après les éléments produits par l'Erythrée, les pêcheurs yéménites "ne restaient autour des îles que trois ou quatre jours, puis rentraient chez eux." D'après un autre vieux pêcheur érythréen, "nous nous rendions dans les îles deux fois par an, chaque fois pour trois mois. Certains d'entre nous préféraient dormir sur les îles, d'autres dormaient dans le bateau. Comme les îles étaient inhabitées, personne ne nous a dit que nous ne pouvions pas y dormir."

352. Un témoin yéménite a déposé comme suit: "Arrivé à la Grande Hanish, je m'installais au mouillage de al-Shura . . . Il y avait des arbres sous lesquels nous cherchions l'ombre. Nous n'avions pas à construire d'habitations." La déposition décrit ensuite les mouillages trouvés sur la Grande Hanish: "à proximité du mouillage de Jafir, on trouve l'habitation du capitaine Ibrahim Salim et de son équipage . . . A l'autre extrémité de l'île, ils sont nombreux à s'être installés, il y a par exemple le mouillage où je suis à al-Shura, puis l'habitation d'al-Habal, et après, le mouillage d'Ibn'Alwan. En été, ils sont nombreux à mouiller à Ibn'Alwan. Ne serait-ce que depuis al-Qataba, il y a plus de 40 *huris* [petits bateaux]."

353. La première conclusion doit être que les îles n'ont pas vraiment été colonisées, mais qu'elles donnent lieu à une occupation épisodique ou saisonnière qui semble être pratiquée depuis de très nombreuses années. L'Erythrée affirme que ses pêcheurs sont les plus nombreux et le Yémen affirme le contraire. Il n'y a pour le Tribunal aucune façon évidente de trancher dans un sens ou dans l'autre sur la base des éléments de preuve peu nombreux et contradictoires qui lui ont été fournis. Vraisemblablement, aucune des deux nationalités ne l'a emporté au point que l'autre soit absente; au contraire, elles ont dû être toutes les deux présentes sur les îles dans des proportions variables suivant l'époque et tout calcul précis de l'exploitation des îles par les uns et par les autres permettrait avec le temps de parler d'une exploitation authentiquement commune des eaux et de leurs ressources.

354. La deuxième conclusion semble être que le mode de vie sur les îles ne permet pas davantage de faire la moindre distinction: certains pêcheurs restent sur leur bateau; d'autres dorment sur la plage; certains construisent de petits abris; d'autres de grands abris; certains appellent leurs constructions des "établissements". La seule chose qui ressorte clairement du dossier est qu'il n'y a aucun édifice important et permanent servant d'habitation ni d'ailleurs aucun édifice important et permanent de n'importe quel autre type qui ait été construit et qui ait été utilisé comme habitation.

355. La troisième conclusion est que, même s'il est fait de temps à autre mention de "familles" séjournant sur les îles, les éléments de preuve disponibles ne permettent pas vraiment de savoir si la vie de famille y existait bien en fait. Dès lors que les îles ne peuvent être occupées que de façon saisonnière, cela paraît *a priori* incompatible avec une vie de famille quand on définit cette dernière par l'existence de cellules familiales qui se déplacent vers un endroit où les activités normales de la collectivité se poursuivent, comme c'est le cas, par exemple, pour les nomades qui élèvent du bétail.

356. La dernière conclusion ne peut être que celle-ci: la vie sur les îles, pour autant qu'elle existe, consiste exclusivement pour des pêcheurs à y trouver un abri saisonnier et temporaire. D'après les éléments fournis, les pêcheurs, qui sont à la fois érythréens et yéménites, sont nombreux, semble-t-il, à séjourner sur les îles pendant la saison de la pêche et pour sécher et saler leur poisson mais ces séjours, bien que saisonniers et réguliers, sont également temporaires et non permanents.

357. Pour l'instant toutefois, il ne fait guère de doute que cette sorte d'activité de la part d'individus qui ont la nationalité tant du Yémen que de l'Erythrée (et de l'Ethiopie) est une activité qui, comme la Cour internationale de Justice l'a dit en 1951 dans l'affaire des *Pêcheries anglo-norvégiennes*, impose "de faire place à une considération dont la portée dépasse les données purement géographiques: celle de certains intérêts économiques propres à une région, lorsque leur réalité et leur importance se trouvent clairement attestées par un long usage."[24]

Activités de caractère général

358. En dernier lieu, les Parties ont présenté au Tribunal des éléments attestant d'activités de caractère plus général. Ces éléments portent notamment sur l'attitude adoptée au sujet du survol et au sujet d'activités diverses.

[24] Affaire des pêcheries (Royaume-Uni c. Norvège), CIJ Recueil 1951, p. 116 (18 décembre), à la p. 133.

Le survol

359. Le fait de survoler un groupe d'îles qui sont très largement désertes n'est guère propre à constituer de façon vraiment convaincante une manifestation délibérée de l'exercice du pouvoir et de l'autorité sur lesdites îles. Il convient toutefois de relever que dans la pièce n° 2 jointe à la réponse donnée par le Yémen à la question 18 ("Chronologie de certains actes du Yémen manifestant l'exercice de la souveraineté . . ."), il est indiqué une série de survols qui commencent en avril 1982 et vont jusqu'à la fin de 1988. Ces survols furent incontestablement un bon moyen de suivre le déroulement de la lutte de libération de l'Erythrée pendant cette décennie, mais le Tribunal ne peut de toute façon pas accorder vraiment beaucoup d'importance à ces activités.

Activités diverses

360. Le Yémen a énuméré une vaste gamme d'actions et d'actes dans un document de seize pages qu'il joint à la réponse donnée à la question 18 du Tribunal. Diverses actions relevant d'un grand nombre de catégories différentes ont été présentées à l'appui des thèses respectives des Parties qui tendent à prouver comment s'est consolidé le titre sur les îles. Le Tribunal a déjà pris note dans ses précédentes analyses des actes et des prises de position qui ont le plus d'importance du point de vue juridique.

361. L'Erythrée a toutefois accordé une place considérable à une tournée d'inspection menée par le président Mengistu et ses collaborateurs en 1988. Il a également été fourni au Tribunal une cassette vidéo de cette tournée des îles. Le Tribunal est toutefois dans l'impossibilité de tirer la moindre conclusion de cet épisode car le président et son groupe sont passés par les îles très rapidement et assez loin au large, sans s'arrêter ni descendre à terre. Il ne saurait être question de voir dans une telle tournée une manifestation intentionnelle de l'exercice du pouvoir et de l'autorité sur un territoire.

--*

CHAPITRE VIII – Les cartes

362. Il convient en dernier lieu d'examiner les cartes. Le Tribunal a l'impression que les Parties se servent de cartes à différents moments à des fins différentes et que les cartes présentent de l'intérêt pour le différend de plusieurs façons.

Comment les Parties utilisent les cartes

363. Des cartes anciennes, datant du 18e et du début du 19e siècles sont produites par le Yémen afin d'étayer la thèse selon laquelle les îles ont appartenu autrefois au Yémen et que ce dernier détient par conséquent un titre ancien en vertu duquel la souveraineté sur les îles devrait lui revenir au moment où la mise en suspens décrétée par l'article 16 du traité de Lausanne prendra fin. De même, le Yémen se fonde sur des cartes postérieures à 1872 et antérieures à 1918 pour montrer que les îles ont été assujetties à la souveraineté ottomane pendant la période en question et intégrées au *vilayet* du Yémen. De son côté, l'Erythrée affirme que des cartes datant du début du 20e siècle et jusqu'à la fin des années 30 montrent que l'Italie prétendait exercer ou était tenue pour exercer la souveraineté sur les îles.

364. L'Erythrée et le Yémen ont aussi l'une et l'autre présenté des cartes établies par des tiers pour montrer que les milieux bien informés reconnaissaient que les îles faisaient respectivement partie de l'Ethiopie ou du Yémen pendant la période allant du début des années 50 au début des années 90.

365. Le Yémen a produit des cartes datant du début des années 50 pour prouver que l'Organisation des Nations Unies estimait que les îles ne faisaient pas partie de la province d'Erythrée (intégrée à l'Ethiopie). Les Parties ont toutes deux fourni des cartes datant des années 60 et postérieures à cette date dont les sources sont diverses et qui indiquent que le Yémen traitait les îles comme si elles étaient non yéménites et que l'Ethiopie les traitait comme si elles étaient non éthiopiennes – tandis que, pour des tierces parties et certaines sources faisant autorité, ces îles relevaient soit de l'une soit de l'autre.

366. En dernier lieu, le Yémen produit des éléments indiquant que l'Ethiopie, le mouvement de libération de l'Erythrée avant l'indépendance et le Gouvernement érythréen après l'indépendance de l'Erythrée ont considéré que les îles n'étaient ni éthiopiennes ni érythréennes mais plutôt yéménites. De son côté, l'Erythrée produit des éléments de preuve pour montrer que le Yémen a attribué les îles à l'Ethiopie ou à l'Erythrée. Chacune des Parties accuse également l'autre de livrer systématiquement une campagne de "cartes" – depuis le début des années 70 de la part du Yémen jusqu'au début des années 90 de la part de l'Erythrée – pour changer les appellations, les étiquettes et les couleurs sur les cartes afin de pouvoir "revendiquer" les îles comme faisant partie du territoire de la partie adverse.

367. En général toutefois, les Parties ont finalement des positions globalement opposées quant à l'utilité qu'elles attribuent aux cartes. Même lorsqu'elle cherche à fournir des indications dans le sens évoqué ci-dessus, l'Erythrée adopte essentiellement pour position que le témoignage des cartes en général (et notamment en l'espèce) est contradictoire, peu fiable, et ne peut pas servir à établir valablement une position juridique.

368. Le Yémen adopte une attitude diamétralement opposée: il justifie quant à lui le recours aux cartes par quatre raisons au moins: c'est "une preuve importante de la connaissance générale ou de la commune renommée" (selon les termes mêmes de sir Gerald Fitzmaurice, cité lors de la procédure orale); c'est la preuve de la position adoptée par les gouvernements; les cartes révèlent aussi l'intention des Parties quant à l'adoption de mesures propres à l'autorité étatique; et elles prouvent l'acquiescement ou l'aveu, c'est-à-dire l'admission de la thèse adverse.

L'objet imputé aux cartes en l'espèce

Avant 1872

369. Le Yémen a donc produit des cartes anciennes datant du 18e et du début du 19e siècles à l'appui de sa thèse selon laquelle il détient un titre fort ancien ou un titre historique. La plupart de ces cartes montrent nettement que le groupe des îles Zuqar-Hanish et les îles septentrionales s'identifient à la côte arabique plutôt qu'à la côte africaine de la mer Rouge. Le Tribunal n'est pas en mesure d'apprécier l'étendue précise du territoire du royaume du Yémen (*Bilad el-Yemen*). En outre, dans ces cartes anciennes, le territoire des îles n'est pas attribué au Yémen en tant que tel.

370. Il ne serait pas déraisonnable de déduire des cartes ainsi versées au dossier que les chefs locaux d'Arabie méridionale (y compris en particulier l'imam du Yémen) avaient probablement avant la conquête ottomane de 1872 le sentiment que les îles faisaient partie du territoire qu'ils revendiquaient parce qu'elles faisaient partie du Yémen ou de la côte arabique. Mais il convient de nuancer cette impression parce qu'il n'est pas possible d'apprécier la *couleur* des cartes établies à une époque où il fallait appliquer la couleur à la main sur les cartes quand celles-ci étaient déjà établies. Ces éléments ne sont donc pas déterminants face au problème d'un titre historique qui serait susceptible de réversion. En outre, rien ne prouve que les chefs locaux d'Arabie méridionale eux-mêmes aient jamais vu ou autorisé lesdites cartes. Ce matériau n'autorise guère à en tirer des conclusions solides.

La période 1872-1918

371. De même, le Yémen produit des cartes postérieures à 1872 et antérieures à 1918 pour montrer que les îles relevaient de la souveraineté ottomane pendant la

période en question, faisaient partie du *vilayet* du Yémen et étaient administrées comme partie intégrante dudit *vilayet*. Les cartes produites semblent confirmer le fait que l'Empire ottoman exerçait bien la souveraineté sur les îles, et, sur ce fait, les Parties s'ont d'accord.

Entre 1924 et 1939

372. Le Yémen a produit un certain nombre de cartes qui prouvent, semble-t-il, que, pendant l'entre-deux-guerres, l'Italie ne s'est pas officiellement considérée comme investie de la souveraineté sur les îles. Les cartes en question ont été publiées par le ministère des colonies en 1933, 1935 et 1937 et par le ministère de l'Afrique italienne en 1939, et elles montrent que les autorités coloniales italiennes n'estimaient pas à l'époque que les îles faisaient partie de la colonie italienne de l'Erythrée. Le Yémen a également présenté au Tribunal d'autres cartes italiennes officielles du ministère des colonies (datant de 1925 et 1933 environ) et aussi du ministère de l'Afrique italienne (1939), dont les deux premières attribuent manifestement les îles au *Yémen* par opposition à la province d'Erythrée, tandis que la troisième omet simplement de les inclure dans le territoire de l'Afrique orientale italienne.

373. De son côté, l'Erythrée a présenté une carte italienne officielle des années 20 pour prouver le contraire. Cette carte est toutefois difficile à déchiffrer et semble avoir été faite à la main. Comparée aux cartes italiennes officielles de la période produites par le Yémen, cette nouvelle carte n'est pas aussi claire que celles du ministère des colonies de 1933 et de 1935. Sa date n'est pas non plus précisée.

374. Dans la mesure où ces cartes pourraient être considérées, de la part de sources italiennes officielles, comme des aveux consistant à admettre la thèse adverse et que ces aveux ne sont pas contredits par les éléments de preuve produits par l'Erythrée, ces cartes jouent un rôle quand on entend l'Erythrée prétendre que l'Italie estimait exercer elle-même la souveraineté sur les îles au moment où éclate la seconde guerre mondiale. L'interprétation la plus valable de ces éléments est, semble-t-il, que la cartographie italienne officielle ne tenait pas à indiquer formellement que les îles relevaient de la souveraineté italienne pendant l'entre-deux-guerres – et qu'elle allait même jusqu'à attribuer les îles au Yémen. Finalement, ces moyens de preuve établissent, semble-t-il, que l'Italie, pendant l'entre-deux-guerres, n'estimait pas que les îles fussent sous souveraineté italienne ou tout au moins n'établissent pas que l'Italie, pendant cette période, considérait bien que les îles relevaient de la souveraineté italienne.

375. Toutefois, comme le Tribunal est parvenu à formuler ses conclusions juridiques sur le statut des îles en s'appuyant sur le dossier diplomatique et les accords conclus entre 1923 et 1939, les cartes produites à titre de preuves – bien qu'elles étayent les conclusions formulées et soient compatibles avec elles – ne sont pas

en soi déterminantes. S'il n'existait pas d'autres éléments de preuve concernant l'attitude ou les intentions de l'Italie, ces cartes revêtiraient plus d'importance.

La carte utilisée aux Nations Unies en 1950

376. Le Yémen a produit des cartes datant du début des années 50 pour prouver que l'Organisation des Nations Unies estimait que les îles ne faisaient pas partie de la province d'Erythrée (intégrée à l'Ethiopie). L'élément crucial ici est une carte des Nations Unies de 1950. L'Erythrée s'est fermement élevée contre la précision de ladite carte, contre ses origines, son authenticité et contre ses effets, affirmant: "Aucune carte officielle n'a été adoptée par les Nations Unies."

377. Or, il est largement tenu pour acquis que, dans la pratique des Nations Unies, le fait pour l'Organisation de publier une carte ne vaut nullement reconnaissance par les Nations Unies d'un titre souverain sur le territoire en question.

378. Il est, semble-t-il, inutile d'établir si la carte était jointe au rapport de la Commission des Nations Unies pour l'Erythrée à titre de carte officielle de ladite commission, ou bien à titre de compromis – voire simplement à titre d'illustration. Ce dont cette carte témoigne, c'est qu'elle a été utilisée, qu'elle a été diffusée et qu'elle n'a suscité aucune objection. Aucune protestation n'a été enregistrée en 1950 ni jamais par la suite, et l'Ethiopie a voté elle-même pour l'adoption du rapport tout en connaissant parfaitement l'existence de la carte.

379. Cette carte toutefois ne peut pas prouver positivement que les îles étaient yéménites, même si les îles ont sur cette carte la même couleur que le Yémen. En l'occurrence, les Nations Unies ne s'occupaient pas du Yémen, la carte ne concernait pas en fait le Yémen en tant que tel. Ce qu'indique la carte, c'est que les Nations Unies, quand l'Organisation a pris des mesures concernant l'avenir de l'Ethiopie et de l'Erythrée, *n'ont pas* considéré que les îles fussent éthiopiennes ou érythréennes. Le Tribunal l'a déjà indiqué au sujet des cartes italiennes datant des années 20 et 30 qui ont été produites comme éléments de preuve: ayant abouti à la conclusion que l'Italie en 1940 n'avait pas acquis la souveraineté sur les îles, le Tribunal ne peut pas non plus conclure que l'Ethiopie (et par conséquent l'Erythrée à la suite de l'Ethiopie) a pu acquérir le titre dix ans plus tard en l'héritant de l'Italie.

L'avis des milieux informés

380. L'Erythrée et le Yémen ont tous les deux produit un certain nombre de cartes établies par des tiers (par exemple, des services cartographiques indépendants ou commerciaux, ou bien les services du renseignement, de cartographie et de la navigation d'Etats tiers), pour prouver que les milieux bien informés ont reconnu que les îles faisaient respectivement partie intégrante soit de l'Ethiopie soit du Yémen pendant la période allant du début des années 50 au début des années 90.

381. Le Tribunal doit se méfier de ces éléments de preuve dans la mesure où ceux-ci ne peuvent pas être révélateurs du titre juridique, mais il s'agit néanmoins d'"éléments de preuve importants de reconnaissance générale ou de commune renommée", comme le soutient le Yémen. Si les cartes présentées sont très nombreuses à confirmer en général, semble-t-il, l'impression que les îles, à partir de 1952 et jusqu'à aujourd'hui, sont principalement attribuées au Yémen et non pas à l'Ethiopie ni à l'Erythrée, on constate néanmoins à cet égard des exceptions.

382. L'Erythrée, quant à elle, a fourni des preuves cartographiques indépendantes qui sont fort respectables, mais ces éléments sont contrebalancés, semble-t-il, par les éléments de preuve en sens contraire produits par la partie adverse. Il arrive parfois que le Tribunal ne puisse pas accepter la qualification des cartes due à la Partie qui les produit. De plus, en l'absence d'indications précises émanant de la carte elle-même, le Tribunal se refuse à attribuer un sens quelconque à des lignes en pointillé plutôt qu'à des couleurs ou des dénominations. Le Tribunal n'accepte pas les conclusions que l'Erythrée tire d'un certain nombre des cartes qu'elle présente en se fondant sur ce type d'argument.

383. Le Yémen a présenté en outre des cartes établies par la Central Intelligence Agency (CIA) des Etats-Unis et des dénominations qui les corroborent sont utilisées sur les cartes marines établies en 1994 par le service cartographique du ministère de la défense des Etats-Unis.

Des "aveux": certaines cartes plaident pour la partie adverse

384. En 1967, le département d'Etat des Etats-Unis a fait distribuer un dossier de presse à l'occasion du voyage officiel de l'empereur Haile Selassie à Washington, et ce dossier était accompagné d'un document d'information dans lequel figurait une carte: celle-ci montrait très clairement que les îles n'étaient pas éthiopiennes. Elles sont nettement indiquées en noir, tout comme le sont les îles Kamaran et Farasan; les Dahlaks sont également indiquées nettement en blanc, comme faisant partie de l'Ethiopie.

385. De son côté, le Yémen a produit des éléments indiquant que l'Ethiopie, le mouvement de libération de l'Erythrée avant l'indépendance et le Gouvernement érythréen après l'indépendance n'ont pas jugé que les îles fussent éthiopiennes ni érythréennes, mais les ont plutôt considérées comme yéménites. L'Erythrée a également invoqué des éléments de preuve pour montrer que le Yémen a attribué lui-même les îles à l'Ethiopie ou à l'Erythrée. Le Tribunal est quant à lui d'avis que la plupart de ces éléments de preuve tendent à s'annuler les uns les autres, sauf peut-être les cartes érythréennes publiées postérieurement à 1992.

386. Le Yémen a soutenu en outre qu'une certaine carte, dont l'Erythrée a affirmé qu'elle avait été établie par une entreprise privée à l'intention du ministère

érythréen du tourisme et qu'elle contenait un certain nombre d'inexactitudes, avait en fait été diffusée auprès des missions étrangères, y compris celles du Yémen et des Etats-Unis d'Amérique, et le Yémen a soutenu aussi que cette carte est également "affichée dans les bureaux du Gouvernement érythréen à Asmara". Cette déclaration n'a pas été contredite. Le Tribunal relève qu'une carte établie par l'Erythrée peu de temps après son accession à l'indépendance n'attribuait pas à l'Erythrée la totalité des îles qu'elle revendique aujourd'hui.

387. De son côté, l'Erythrée affirme également que le Yémen a autorisé la publication de cartes qu'il est possible d'interpréter comme plaidant contre lui, y compris une carte publiée en 1975 qui semble manifestement attribuer les îles à l'Ethiopie.

Conclusions concernant les cartes

388. Sur cette question, le Tribunal a finalement abouti aux conclusions suivantes:

Pour la période antérieure à 1872

Le Yémen a bien prouvé qu'en général les cartes les plus anciennes et celles du 19e siècle attribuaient les îles à la sphère d'influence arabique plutôt qu'à la côte africaine, mais il n'a pas été démontré que les îles étaient très précisément attribuées au "Yémen".

Pour la période 1872-1918

Les cartes produites par chacune des Parties prouvent sans difficulté que les îles étaient soumises à la domination ottomane au cours des dernières années de l'empire. Aucun élément de preuve n'a été versé au dossier, de même qu'aucune discussion n'a eu lieu sur la question de l'effet que cette large reconnaissance peut avoir sur la validité *vel non* de la prétention du Yémen au bénéfice de la réversion du titre.

Pour la période de l'entre-deux-guerres

Les cartes produites comme éléments de preuve sont contradictoires jusqu'à un certain point mais, dans l'ensemble, les cartes italiennes officielles de l'époque prouvent que même si l'Italie éprouvait le désir d'annexer les îles après le traité de Lausanne, elle ne l'a certainement pas exprimé par la moindre manifestation extérieure d'autorité étatique dans sa cartographie officielle.

Pour la période de l'après-guerre

Il n'est pas possible de tirer de l'historique des cartes établies en 1950 par les Nations Unies la conclusion que l'Ethiopie a acquis après la seconde guerre mondiale les îles qui lui auraient été transmises par l'Italie ou autrement.

Pour la période allant de 1950 à 1992

Pour cette période, les éléments de preuve fournis sont entachés de contradictions et d'incertitudes. Chacune des Parties a fait la preuve du manque de cohérence dont souffrent ses cartes officielles. Il faut toutefois constater que les cartes produites par le Yémen sont d'une portée et d'un volume supérieurs à ceux des cartes produites par l'Erythrée. Toutefois, le poids que l'on peut accorder aux cartes en faveur de l'une des Parties est contrebalancé par le fait que chacune des Parties a publié des cartes qui vont, semble-t-il, à l'encontre de ce qu'elle affirme en la présente instance.

Pour la période allant de 1992 à 1995

En dernier lieu, il figure au dossier des cartes officielles et semi-officielles publiées par l'Erythrée peu de temps après son accession à l'indépendance qui ont reçu beaucoup de publicité et qui montrent que, si elles ne sont pas yéménites, les îles ne sont pas érythréennes. Comme toujours quand il s'agit de cartes, il faut traiter ces éléments de preuve avec beaucoup de prudence.

* - * - *

CHAPITRE IX – Accords pétroliers et prospection pétrolière

389. La présente instance a ceci d'étonnant qu'aucune des Parties n'a de sa propre initiative invoqué ni même mentionné les contrats pétroliers et concessions pétrolières relatifs à la mer Rouge et aux îles en litige. Il a fallu, pour que les Parties en fassent état dans leurs écritures, qu'elles aient à répondre à des questions posées par un membre du Tribunal à l'issue de la procédure orale en février 1998; sans ces questions, il semble que ces exposés des Parties n'auraient pas été présentés pendant cette phase-ci de la procédure.

390. En réponse aux questions qui leur ont donc été posées, les Parties ont toutes deux fourni une masse de renseignements et d'arguments mais ceux-ci, de l'avis du Tribunal, ont cependant laissé certaines des questions sans réponse. Le Tribunal a donc organisé une reprise de la procédure orale consacrée exclusivement aux contrats pétroliers et aux concessions pétrolières de la mer Rouge. Ces nouvelles audiences ont eu lieu à Londres du 6 au 8 juillet, et ont permis d'examiner de nouveaux exposés écrits et oraux fort substantiels. Au cours de ces audiences tout comme à leur suite, de nouveaux éléments été produits. Au cours de ces audiences, l'Erythrée a principalement affirmé que ces contrats et ces concessions n'apportaient pas grand-chose de probant aux fins des questions à trancher par le Tribunal, tandis que le Yémen a au contraire soutenu que ces contrats et concessions confortaient considérablement sa position. Le Yémen a soutenu que les caractéristiques des concessions en mer qu'il a octroyées sans soulever de protestations de la part de l'Ethiopie ni de l'Erythrée, ainsi que les caractéristiques des concessions éthiopiennes, confirmaient les prétentions du Yémen à la souveraineté sur les îles en litige, l'acceptation de cette souveraineté et la décision d'investir sur une telle base par les compagnies pétrolières et l'assentiment de l'Ethiopie comme de l'Erythrée. Le Yémen a indiqué que c'était le manque de temps qui l'avait empêché de faire de sa propre initiative appel dans ses plaidoiries à ces contrats et à ces concessions.

Les dispositions des contrats et concessions pertinents

391. Le Yémen tout comme l'Erythrée ont conclu des contrats et des accords de concession visant la prospection pétrolière, la mise en valeur, la production et la vente commerciale du pétrole issu des gisements qui pourraient être trouvés dans le sous-sol de la mer Rouge. S'il n'a pas été trouvé jusqu'à présent de quantités de pétrole se prêtant à cette exploitation commerciale, ces contrats et concessions méritent néanmoins que le Tribunal les examine pour voir ce qu'ils montrent et ce qu'ils ne montrent pas. Pour les questions que le Tribunal doit trancher, les effectivités auxquelles ces contrats et concessions donnent naissance ou qui pourraient leur être liées revêtent une importance particulière.

Les contrats et accords de concession signés par le Yémen

392. Sur les contrats et accords de concession concernant la mer Rouge, le Yémen a fourni les informations ci-après.

Campagne de sondages sismiques, 1972

393. Le Yémen déclare qu'en 1972, sa devancière, la République arabe du Yémen, a conclu un contrat avec la Shell International Petroleum Company en vue d'une "grande campagne de reconnaissance géophysique en mer Rouge". Ladite campagne, réalisée pour le compte de Shell par la Western Geophysical Company of America en mars 1972, a notamment consisté à procéder à des sondages de reconnaissance sismique dans une zone de la mer Rouge qui comprenait les îles du groupe de Zuqar-Hanish, le groupe de Zubayr ainsi que Jabal al-Tayr et le Yémen se fonde sur ce fait pour soutenir que cette campagne de sondages confirme que le Yémen a souveraineté sur ces îles. Le Yémen fait savoir qu'à la suite de cette campagne, Shell a décidé que le tiers méridional de la zone recensée, soit un secteur assez important englobant le groupe des Zuqar-Hanish, n'était pas intéressant, mais qu'elle était prête à signer un accord de concession portant sur un secteur situé plus au nord qui comprenait l'île Zubayr.

394. Le Yémen n'a pas été en mesure de communiquer le texte du contrat de la campagne de sondages sismiques, dont l'Erythrée met en doute l'existence. Mais il communique néanmoins un rapport de la Shell International Petroleum Maatschappij N.V. qui date de janvier 1977 et fait état d'une campagne de repérages en mer dont les résultats ont servi à choisir la zone faisant l'objet de l'accord examiné ci-dessous. Le Yémen a également soumis au cours des audiences, le 7 juillet 1998, un rapport définitif sur cette campagne de sondages sismiques intitulé *Final Operations Report, Marine Seismic Survey, Offshore Yemen (Red Sea)*, établi par la Western Geophysical Company en mars 1972. Ce dernier rapport dit que la campagne en question avait pour objet de procéder à une étude sismique préliminaire de la "zone de la concession" (alors qu'à ce stade il n'y avait pas de concession), et indique que le bureau local et la base d'opérations en vue de cette campagne de sondages sismiques se trouvaient à Massawa, en Ethiopie. Il est annexé à ce rapport une carte indiquant "la zone approximative faisant l'objet du programme sismique" (planche I), sur laquelle la zone visée va jusqu'à la côte éthiopienne.

395. Ladite carte montre que la zone faisant l'objet de la campagne sismique est sans pertinence pour les questions de titre; le Yémen n'est guère en train de revendiquer la juridiction sur les eaux territoriales de l'Erythrée et ne peut pas avoir eu cette ambition sous couvert de l'autorisation ou de la réalisation de cette campagne sismique. Par suite, le fait que la zone de cette campagne englobait les îles en litige n'a pas de force probante.

L'accord pétrolier de Shell, 1974

396. La République arabe du Yémen et la Deutsche Shell Aktiengesellschaft ont conclu le 16 janvier 1974 un accord pétrolier. La zone visée dans le contrat y était définie comme correspondant à la zone indiquée ainsi que son sous-sol et les fonds marins “relevant de la juridiction de la République arabe du Yémen”. La zone comprenait un secteur de mer Rouge situé au nord des îles Zuqar et Hanish, îles qui sont nommées sans être englobées dans ledit secteur. Celui-ci n'englobe pas Jabal al-Tayr, qui est située à l'ouest de la zone définie dans le contrat, et qui n'est pas non plus nommée. Le contrat ne désigne nommément aucune des îles situées à l'intérieur du secteur visé. Le groupe de Zubayr figure parmi les îles non nommées situées à l'intérieur de la zone visée dans le contrat.

397. La société Shell a contracté pour une campagne de reconnaissance afin de recueillir des données sismiques, des renseignements sur la gravité et des données magnétiques dans la zone visée dans le contrat; le rapport de campagne ne dit pas que l'étude a été exécutée dans les eaux territoriales du groupe de Zubayr. La société Shell a foré un puits en un lieu situé loin des îles en litige; il n'y a pas été trouvé un volume de pétrole se prêtant à une exploitation commerciale et il a été mis fin à l'accord.

398. Dans un rapport définitif intitulé *Final Report on the Exploration Venture of Yemen Shell Explorations GMBH Yemen Arab Republic* qui date de mai 1981, il est dit ceci: “La zone de concession octroyée à la Deutsche Shell . . . conformément aux dispositions de l'accord pétrolier du 16 janvier 1974 s'étendait . . . du territoire continental du Yémen à l'est jusqu'aux environs de la ligne médiane de la mer Rouge à l'ouest.”

399. Compte tenu de l'indication ci-dessus et aussi du fait que le contrat de concession parle d'une zone, de son sous-sol et de ses fonds marins relevant non pas de la souveraineté mais de la juridiction du Yémen, le Tribunal conclut que la concession accordée à Shell en 1974 a été octroyée et mise en application dans l'exercice par le Yémen non de la souveraineté revendiquée sur les îles situées dans la zone du contrat et dans leurs eaux mais dans l'exercice de ses droits sur le plateau continental tels qu'ils existaient alors. Le Tribunal est en outre d'avis, compte tenu des éléments ci-dessus, que, puisque le contrat ne nomme pas le groupe de Zubayr et puisque Shell n'a pas mené d'activités sur les îles du groupe de Zubayr ni dans leurs eaux territoriales, l'accord pétrolier de 1974 conclu avec Shell l'a été sans qu'il soit tenu compte en particulier du groupe de Zubayr. Les îles en question sont, semble-t-il, comprises dans la zone visée dans le contrat parce que le groupe de Zubayr se trouvait du côté yéménite de la ligne médiane, au-dessus d'un plateau continental sur lequel le Yémen pouvait exercer sa juridiction.

400. En même temps, l'accord pétrolier conclu entre le Yémen et Shell a été porté à la connaissance du milieu professionnel, il a été publié, et l'Ethiopie pouvait être au courant de son existence et même de ses dispositions, pour peu qu'elle ait consulté les publications pertinentes (comme le recueil de Barrow intitulé *Basic Oil Laws and Concession Contracts*). On peut soutenir que l'Ethiopie a été avisée, du moins implicitement, de l'existence de cet accord et de ses dispositions. L'Ethiopie n'a pas protesté contre l'accord, bien que la zone octroyée comprenne le groupe de Zubayr que l'Erythrée revendique aujourd'hui. L'Erythrée soutient que l'Ethiopie ignorait en fait les dispositions de l'accord; qu'il ne peut être reproché à l'Ethiopie, pays pauvre alors en proie à une guerre civile, de ne pas avoir eu connaissance de l'accord et que, de toute façon, la conclusion et la publication d'un contrat de concession n'étant pas des actes générateurs de titre, il n'y avait absolument pas lieu pour elle de protester, notamment en l'absence d'activités concrètes et visibles de la société Shell ou du Gouvernement yéménite sur le groupe de Zubayr. Cette absence de protestation de la part de l'Ethiopie et plus tard de la part de l'Erythrée est à relever pour toutes les concessions accordées par le Yémen en mer Rouge et le Tribunal appréciera ci-après cet élément du dossier.

401. La zone visée dans l'accord pétrolier de 1974 conclu entre le Yémen et Shell est en outre reproduite sur une carte datée de décembre 1976. Cette carte a été établie par Shell et se trouve dans un rapport de Shell datant de janvier 1977 qui porte l'indication "confidentiel". Il n'est pas dit que cette carte a été publiée ou bien pouvait ou encore aurait dû être connue de l'Ethiopie. La carte montre la zone visée dans l'accord ainsi que les parties de la zone faisant l'objet d'un recensement approfondi (lesquelles ne sont pas situées à proximité du groupe de Zubayr). A l'ouest de la zone visée dans l'accord, il est tracé une ligne qualifiée de "frontière internationale approximative provisoire". Ladite frontière passe à l'ouest du groupe de Zubayr et à l'ouest également des îles Zuqar et Hanish. Il n'a pas été fourni d'élément de preuve au sujet des considérations que l'auteur de la ligne a prises en compte pour la tracer, et l'Erythrée n'a pas non plus formulé spécialement d'observations sur ladite ligne. Dans les *Observations du Yémen sur les documents présentés par l'Erythrée après la dernière des audiences, 29 juillet 1998*, les cartes 5 et 6 établies par le Yémen reproduisent ladite ligne d'après les indications fournies.

402. Pour le Tribunal, l'auteur de la carte de la société Shell était d'avis qu'il fallait tracer la "frontière internationale approximative provisoire" compte tenu de la souveraineté exercée par le Yémen sur la plupart des îles en litige et sur la totalité des plus importantes d'entre elles. Et cette impression du Tribunal n'est pas simplement étayée par le fait que ladite "frontière internationale approximative provisoire" passe à l'ouest desdites îles. Elle est renforcée par le fait que l'auteur de la carte a accordé un certain poids aux grandes îles en litige, notamment Zuqar et les îles Hanish, aux fins du tracé de la limite qu'il a retenu.

Le permis de sondages sismiques accordé à Tomen et Santa Fe, 1974

403. Un accord portant octroi d'un permis de sondages sismiques a été conclu en 1974 entre la République arabe du Yémen et la Toyo Menka Kaisha Ltd ("Tomen") et a été étendu à la société Santa Fe International Corp. L'accord a d'abord été qualifié par le Yémen au cours de la procédure de "concession", ce que l'Erythrée a contesté; quand le texte de l'accord a été versé par la suite au dossier, le Tribunal a constaté qu'il était intitulé "Permis de sondages sismiques", et autorisait Tomen à mener une campagne de sondages sismiques en mer dans la zone prévue dans le contrat. Il est précisé dans le contrat que la zone visée est indiquée sur la "pièce A"; or, le Yémen n'a pas versé au dossier cette "pièce A" et n'a pas non plus expliqué pourquoi cette pièce ne figure pas dans le texte du contrat correspondant qui a par ailleurs été communiqué intégralement. Le contrat lui-même donne les coordonnées de la zone visée et le Yémen a versé au dossier des cartes dont il dit qu'elles ont été établies aux fins de la présente instance à partir desdites coordonnées.

404. Le Yémen affirme en s'appuyant sur lesdites coordonnées et cartes que la zone visée dans le contrat comprenait la totalité des îles Zuqar et Hanish. Pourtant, dans une carte donnant "l'historique de la prospection" établie par le Programme des Nations Unies pour le développement (PNUD) et la Banque mondiale, laquelle n'est pas datée mais remonterait apparemment à la fin de 1991, et dont le Yémen n'a cessé de faire valoir la force probante, la ligne tracée à l'ouest n'est pas la même. Cette ligne occidentale semble passer à travers l'extrémité méridionale de la Grande Hanish et non la contourner (la légende explicative de la carte dit: "Tomen & Santa Fe, campagne sismique commencée en 1974, terminée en 1975, 2150 km"). Il est possible que la ligne tracée sur la carte du PNUD passe à travers la Grande Hanish en suivant une ligne médiane, comme semblent le faire deux autres concessions, l'une conclue par le Yémen et l'autre par l'Erythrée.

405. L'accord autorisant Tomen et Santa Fe à procéder à une campagne sismique dispose que le Yémen a "le pouvoir exclusif de prospection pétrolière dans l'intégralité" de la zone visée dans le contrat et que ladite zone "correspond à la zone située au large dans les limites du territoire du Yémen où l'extraction minière est légale" telle qu'elle est décrite dans le permis. La durée du contrat est de six mois (et semble avoir été portée à un an). Le contrat précise: "L'exécution du programme de travail ne doit pas entrer en conflit avec les obligations que le droit international impose au Gouvernement du Yémen." L'accord stipule que l'entrepreneur a le droit d'entrer dans la zone du contrat et les zones adjacentes ainsi que de sortir des mêmes zones. L'accord prévoit en outre que Tomen a pendant la durée du contrat le droit de demander un permis d'exploitation pétrolière concernant tout ou partie de la zone du contrat aux fins de prospection, mise en valeur et production de pétrole, dont les dispositions seront à arrêter d'un

commun accord sur le modèle des dispositions figurant dans des permis analogues en vigueur dans les pays de l'OPEP.

406. L'accord portant octroi du permis de sondages sismiques, sans être un accord de concession, est donc un contrat se rattachant à la prospection pétrolière qui prévoit la conclusion d'un accord de concession dans certaines conditions. Affirmer comme le Yémen le fait qu'il a le pouvoir exclusif d'exploiter les gisements de pétrole dans la zone établie par le contrat et faire mention du territoire du Yémen où l'exploitation minière est légale est compatible avec la conclusion d'un contrat visant l'exercice par le Yémen de ses droits sur son plateau continental. Le décret n° 16 concernant le plateau continental de la République arabe du Yémen en date du 30 avril 1967, en proclamant que le Yémen exerce des droits souverains sur les fonds marins et le sous-sol de son plateau continental et sur le plateau continental de ses îles, affirme que le Yémen a le droit exclusif de prospection en ce qui concerne les ressources minières naturelles du plateau. Il est également intéressant que le contrat fasse état des obligations imposées au Yémen par le droit international, ce qui peut être une allusion à une limitation des droits exercés sur le plateau continental. De l'avis du Tribunal, l'accord relatif au permis de sondages sismiques ne constitue pas en soi une revendication par le Yémen à la souveraineté sur les îles situées dans la zone du contrat, et l'absence de protestation contre ledit accord de la part de l'Erythrée n'indique pas non plus que celle-ci ait toléré pareille revendication. L'accord présuppose toutefois jusqu'à un certain point la détention dans une certaine mesure d'un titre sur les îles, quelles qu'elles soient, situées dans la zone visée dans le contrat. Ladite zone comprenait le territoire terrestre et les eaux territoriales des îles situées dans ses limites; c'est-à-dire que la zone du contrat comprenait le territoire terrestre et aussi les eaux territoriales de tout ou partie de la Grande Hanish et de l'intégralité de Zuqar et de la Petite Hanish.

407. L'Erythrée soutient que, de toute façon, les campagnes de sondages sismiques ne révèlent pas l'existence de revendications de souveraineté. L'Erythrée se fonde à ce sujet sur la Convention sur le droit de la mer, dont la partie XIII est consacrée à la "Recherche scientifique marine". L'article 241 de la Convention dispose: "La recherche scientifique marine ne constitue le fondement d'aucune revendication sur une partie quelconque du milieu marin ou de ses ressources." Et l'article 246 dispose que les Etats côtiers réglementent la recherche scientifique marine dans la zone économique exclusive et sur le plateau continental; ladite recherche est menée avec le consentement de l'Etat côtier. Dans des circonstances normales, les Etats côtiers consentent à la réalisation de projets de recherche scientifique marine par d'autres Etats ou par des organisations internationales compétentes "en vue d'accroître les connaissances scientifiques sur le milieu marin dans l'intérêt de l'humanité tout entière." De l'avis du Tribunal, ces dispositions sont sans rapport avec les campagnes sismiques et autres modes de prospection pétrolière utilisés à des fins

commerciales par les titulaires d'un permis octroyé par les Parties dans les conditions propres à la présente instance.

408. Par conséquent, les activités menées au titre du permis de sondages sismiques accordé à Tomen et à Santa Fe et autres autorisations du même ordre par les titulaires de permis octroyés par les Parties revêtent une certaine importance et le Tribunal se doit d'apprécier celle-ci. Pendant la période écoulée entre le 23 juillet 1974, date à laquelle le navire portant le nom *Western Geophysical I* est parti de Hodeidah, et le 9 septembre 1974, date de la fin de l'expédition, soit une période de six semaines environ, "sur les 1500 milles marins initialement prévus au programme, il n'a été recensé que 1336 milles parce que . . . les hauts-fonds sont dangereux dans la région des îles." Cela donne à penser qu'il était difficile de travailler à proximité des îles; le rapport fait mention à plusieurs reprises de Zuqar et des îles Hanish, mais ne porte aucune indication révélatrice de la moindre activité sur les îles. Il n'est pas facile de déduire du texte et des cartes fournies des indications permettant de dire si des sondages sismiques ont été réalisés dans les eaux territoriales des îles. Il est indiqué une fois, par exemple, qu'il a été réalisé un levé aérien sur une superficie de 2 milles carrés "à l'est de la Petite Hanish". Mais il n'a pas été dit à quelle distance à l'est le levé a été réalisé – ni s'il a été réalisé à l'intérieur ou à l'extérieur des eaux territoriales de la Petite Hanish, et la question n'a pas été précisée non plus par le conseil du Yémen qui s'est borné à dire que les opérations ont été menées "très près" des îles. Dans le rapport de la société Santa Fe, la figure 1 intitulée "Carte des emplacements et carte géophysique", indique que, pour procéder à un recensement minutieux, on évitait les eaux entourant immédiatement les îles, mais la carte ne montre pas par elle-même à quelle distance proche des îles les sondages sismiques étaient opérés. Toutefois, si, par exemple, on reporte la situation géographique indiquée "Flanc occidental de l'île Zuqar; croisement sud-ouest des lignes de sondage 50 et 8" sur le quadrillage de la zone à étudier présenté sur la figure 1 – dans lequel chacun des secteurs les plus importants a une superficie de 10 kilomètres carrés – il semble que les opérations sismiques ont été menées jusque très avant dans les eaux territoriales de Zuqar. Pour autant qu'on puisse l'établir par l'étude de ce rapport, on n'est pas sûr de pouvoir en dire autant en ce qui concerne les eaux des îles Hanish.

409. Le même rapport Santa Fe dit également: "Pendant la campagne sismique, l'auteur a observé les îles Zuqar et Hanish depuis le bateau, et elles semblent être intégralement constituées de roches volcaniques . . . . Par la suite, M. Hazem Baker, géologue au service du gouvernement yéménite, est descendu à terre sur l'île Zuqar et a recueilli des échantillons . . . qui sont tous des échantillons de basalte." Il est, semble-t-il, raisonnable de présumer que, pour l'auteur du rapport, le géologue débarquait sur une île qui, à tout le moins, relevait de la juridiction du Yémen.

Accord de partage de production offshore avec la Hunt Oil Company, 1984

410. Le Yémen et la Offshore Yemen Hunt Oil Company (Hunt) ont conclu le 10 mars 1984 un accord de partage de production offshore. On trouve dans le préambule de l'accord les indications suivantes: "Attendu que, dans leur intégralité, les gisements de pétrole existant sous leur forme naturelle dans des couches situées à l'intérieur des frontières du YEMEN sont la propriété de l'ETAT; et attendu que l'ETAT tient à promouvoir la mise en valeur des ressources pétrolières potentielles de la région et que l'ENTREPRENEUR partie à l'accord tient à s'associer à l'Etat et l'aider à prospecter et mettre en valeur en vue de la production de pétrole les ressources pétrolières potentielles de la région . . ."; la société Hunt est nommée Entrepreneur "exclusivement pour mener des opérations pétrolières dans la zone décrite . . . . L'ETAT conserve le titre qu'il détient sur la zone faisant l'objet des opérations . . .". L'accord dispose que la législation du Yémen est applicable à l'Entrepreneur à condition d'être compatible avec l'accord et que les droits et obligations des parties sont régis par l'accord et ne peuvent être modifiés qu'avec leur consentement réciproque. L'accord fut approuvé par décret gouvernemental. Les coordonnées de la zone faisant l'objet de l'accord sont définies à l'annexe A, à laquelle est jointe une carte intitulée annexe B et indiquant lesdites coordonnées sans nommer ni montrer aucune des îles en litige. Le Yémen a établi et présenté au Tribunal une carte qui indique cette concession Hunt comme s'étendant à l'ouest très près du bord de Jabal al-Tayr mais sans l'englober et, à l'extrémité méridionale de la limite de la zone du contrat, elle englobe tout juste le groupe de Zubayr.

411. Pour s'acquitter des obligations lui incombant en matière de prospection en vertu dudit accord, la société Hunt a conclu un contrat avec l'entreprise Western Geophysical pour mener une campagne de sondages sismiques dans la zone de la concession. Ce contrat a été conclu en 1985, et il "prend en compte" les renseignements recueillis par la Shell dix ans auparavant. La campagne a englobé la région des îles Zubayr et, d'après les indications fournies, Jabal al-Tayr bien que celle-ci ne figurât pas dans la zone de la concession. Des sondages sismiques ont été opérés "autour des îles Zubayr et Jabal al-Tayr" mais il n'est pas dit ni montré que des opérations sismiques aient été menées dans leurs eaux territoriales. Il n'est pas allégué ni montré que des activités aient été menées sur les îles. Des levés aéromagnétiques ont été réalisés dans la zone du contrat par un aéronef décollant du Yémen et, par conséquent, il a été demandé et accordé une autorisation de vol dans l'espace aérien yéménite; ce fait n'apporte rien qui étaye ou discrédite les prétentions du Yémen quant au statut de la zone du contrat. Est également neutre le fait qu'en matière de forage, il ait été demandé l'autorisation "de pénétrer dans les eaux territoriales de la République arabe du Yémen et de procéder à des opérations de forage en mer", opérations qui n'étaient nullement menées à proximité des îles. Deux puits ont été en fait forés à bonne distance des îles; ni l'un ni l'autre n'a produit de quantités de pétrole qui fussent commercialement exploitables, et la concession a été abandonnée.

412. L'accord de partage de production ne formule pas expressément de revendication de souveraineté du Yémen sur la zone de la concession et, comme on l'a relevé, il ne prête aucune attention aux îles situées dans ladite zone, ni expressément dans ses dispositions ni dans la carte qui lui est annexée. L'accord peut être interprété comme une concession octroyée dans la zone délimitée par une ligne médiane dont le tracé correspond à l'exercice des droits du Yémen sur son plateau continental, concession qui englobe le groupe de Zubayr mais ne va pas vraiment jusqu'à englober totalement Jabal al-Tayr. On peut dire que si le Yémen avait l'intention en accordant cette concession d'affirmer sa souveraineté sur les îles en litige, la concession aurait englobé Jabal al-Tayr. Mais ce qui paraît plus vraisemblable, c'est que cette concession comme d'autres aussi a été "octroyée alors que l'on avait à l'esprit des considérations d'ordre commercial et sans que l'on prenne particulièrement en compte l'existence des îles. Le fait qu'il soit dit que l'Etat du Yémen conserve le titre sur la zone du contrat n'est pas déterminant; le Yémen est propriétaire des ressources qui se trouvent sur son plateau continental et dans le sous-sol de ce dernier; mais comme l'accord précise que le Yémen conserve le titre exercé "sur la zone visée", on peut l'interpréter de la part du Yémen comme une clause de réserve de propriété. L'allusion aux "frontières du Yémen" évoque également une revendication de souveraineté, encore que le terme "frontières" n'exclut pas qu'il s'agisse des frontières du plateau continental. Cet accord de partage de production conclu avec la société Hunt a été signalé dans la documentation spécialisée de la recherche pétrolière et n'a suscité aucune protestation de la part de l'Erythrée.

Accord de partage de production conclu avec British Petroleum, 1990

413. Le Yémen et British Petroleum (BP) ont conclu le 20 octobre 1990 un accord de partage de production dont les dispositions sont très proches de celles de l'accord ci-dessus avec la société Hunt et, à certains égards pertinents, identiques. L'accord couvre le même secteur Antufash au large du Yémen dans lequel la société Hunt avait précédemment mené ses opérations et il englobe donc les îles Zubayr mais non pas Jabal al-Tayr. Toutefois, et ce peut être dû à la politique appliquée par le Yémen au sujet des secteurs potentiels proposés par lui dans les années 90 en vue de la prospection pétrolière, l'accord conclu avec BP décrit avec plus de précision que l'accord conclu avec la société Hunt le secteur à prospecter: "Attendu que l'Etat tient à promouvoir la mise en valeur des ressources pétrolières potentielles existant dans le secteur 8 de la zone visée dans l'accord, As-Sakir, province de Shabwa, République du Yémen . . .". Le texte de cet accord a été publié dans le recueil spécialisé de *Barrow*. Il n'a suscité aucune protestation de la part de l'Erythrée.

414. BP a procédé à de minutieux levés aéromagnétiques de la zone de l'accord. D'où des vols à basse altitude, organisés avec l'autorisation du Gouvernement yéménite, sur toute la zone, y compris les îles Zubayr ainsi que Jabal al-Tayr bien que celle-ci ne fût pas comprise dans la zone. Un officier de l'armée yéménite

était à bord de l'aéronef lors de ces opérations. Les résultats de cette campagne ont été peu encourageants et BP a renoncé à ses droits sur la zone en 1993.

415. Le Tribunal n'attache pas beaucoup d'importance aux survols opérés par l'une ou l'autre des Parties sur les îles en litige. Dans les circonstances de l'espèce, on ne voit pas bien si le survol de ces îles qui ne sont pas habitées équivaut à une revendication de juridiction, moins encore à une revendication de souveraineté, sur les îles en question. Toutefois, le fait que l'accord dit du secteur Antufash comprend une province de la République du Yémen ou est situé dans une telle province est un élément important en faveur du Yémen; c'est le signe d'une revendication de souveraineté plutôt qu'une revendication de juridiction. En même temps, le fait que l'accord a été conclu en 1990 et publié à cette époque environ est digne d'intérêt. L'Ethiopie, en effet, était alors dans la dernière phase de sa guerre avec le mouvement de libération érythréen, le régime de Mengistu était proche de l'effondrement et il peut paraître déraisonnable de donner à entendre qu'il y a lieu aujourd'hui de reprocher à l'Erythrée le fait que l'Ethiopie à l'époque n'a pas pris connaissance des dispositions de cet accord et n'a pas émis de protestation à ce sujet.

Accord de partage de production conclu avec Total, 1985

416. Le Yémen et Total-Compagnie française des Pétroles ont conclu en 1985 un accord de partage de production auquel Texaco est ultérieurement devenu partie. Ses dispositions paraissent proches de celles de l'accord conclu l'année précédente avec la société Hunt et résumé ci-dessus quant à ses passages pertinents. Ce nouvel accord énonce toutefois: "Attendu que, dans leur intégralité, les gisements de pétrole existant sous leur forme naturelle dans les couches situées à l'intérieur des frontières du Yémen et dans les fonds marins soumis à sa juridiction sont la propriété de l'Etat; . . .". Comme la zone visée dans l'accord se situe en partie sur la terre ferme aussi bien qu'en mer, on pourrait y voir l'indication que la revendication en mer n'est qu'une revendication de juridiction et non pas une revendication de souveraineté, et aussi l'indication que le Yémen applique le même principe dans les autres accords pétroliers. L'accord dit que la zone visée est décrite à l'annexe A et indiquée sur la carte désignée comme étant l'annexe B, mais aucune de ces deux annexes n'est jointe au texte soumis par le Yémen au Tribunal. Toutefois, les deux Parties s'accordent à reconnaître que la limite occidentale de l'accord conclu avec Total passe à l'est de Zuqar et des îles Hanish. Il n'y a pas lieu de conclure que ce fait serait susceptible d'empêcher le Yémen de conclure des accords englobant les îles en litige. Cela permet une fois de plus de penser plutôt que les accords pétroliers conclus par le Yémen l'ont été sans que l'on tienne compte de l'existence des îles.

417. Comme la zone visée dans cet accord ne comprend aucune des îles en litige, l'accord ne présente que peu d'intérêt pour la présente instance, sauf quant aux

points ci-après: Total a fait procéder à des études sismiques, lesquelles ont principalement eu lieu entre la limite occidentale de la zone visée dans l'accord (limite qui restait en-deçà des îles Hanish) et la côte du Yémen. Le seul et unique puits qui fut foré – lequel fut improductif de sorte que l'accord a pris fin en 1989 – était éloigné des îles Hanish et situé vers la côte. Toutefois, des campagnes de sondages sismiques moins intenses ont été menées à l'ouest des îles Hanish, en dehors de la zone visée dans le contrat, et des opérations ont eu lieu dans les eaux territoriales de ces îles. Le Yémen s'est comporté comme s'il était en droit d'autoriser ces sondages dans les eaux territoriales des Hanish et l'agent de Total s'est comporté comme s'il était en droit d'opérer ces sondages dans lesdites eaux.

418. Ayant découvert les îles Hanish grâce à sa concession offshore, Total a décidé en 1993 de devenir l'un des parrains de la mission scientifique française Ardoukoba qui voulait se rendre dans les îles pour procéder à une étude de la vie sous-marine autour des récifs. Total a demandé au Gouvernement du Yémen l'autorisation, qu'il a reçue, d'installer une piste d'atterrissage sur la Grande Hanish de façon qu'un aéronef affrété par Total puisse y transporter du matériel. Il a également été dit au Tribunal que Total a demandé l'autorisation, qu'il a reçue, d'installer une station radio sur la Grande Hanish et d'autoriser les scientifiques de passage à utiliser sa fréquence; il n'a pas été apporté d'élément de preuve à l'appui de cette prétention. Mais il a été fourni des éléments montrant qu'il fallait être doté, pour accéder aux îles Hanish, dont Total dit qu'elles sont inhabitées, d'une autorisation accordée par le "Bureau central de l'armée". Une fois la mission Ardoukoba menée à terme, Total a publié un rapport évoquant "les îles Hanish en République du Yémen". Total a ensuite demandé l'autorisation officielle, qu'il a reçue, d'aménager la piste d'atterrissage et de transporter sur la Grande Hanish du personnel de Total pour des séjours de repos et de loisir. Pendant un certain temps, un aéronef de Total s'est rendu fréquemment sur la Grande Hanish, en y transportant à ces fins des passagers.

419. Ce sont là peut-être des éléments tout à fait accessoires de l'accord pétrolier conclu avec Total mais la construction et l'exploitation d'une piste d'atterrissage sur la Grande Hanish constituent aux yeux du Tribunal une effectivité matérielle. Ces éléments démontrent l'exercice par le Yémen de sa juridiction sur la Grande Hanish, la reconnaissance de cette juridiction par Total, et l'existence de signes visibles de ladite juridiction – une piste d'atterrissage activement exploitée – pendant une certaine période. L'Erythrée semble ne pas avoir eu connaissance de ces éléments et n'a de toute façon formulé aucune protestation. L'Erythrée a pourtant soumis des éléments de preuve montrant qu'un rapport d'activité d'une société française menant des opérations dans les eaux entourant la Grande Hanish a été reçu en mai 1986, c'est-à-dire au moment où Total menait effectivement des opérations dans cette région; l'Erythrée a montré qu'un bateau patrouilleur éthiopien a été envoyé sur les lieux pour enquêter et qu'il n'a rien trouvé. Ces éléments de preuve-là donnent à penser que, du point de vue de l'Erythrée, ils sont le signe de la souveraineté exercée sur la Grande Hanish.

L'accord de partage de production conclu avec Adair International, 1993

420. Le Yémen et Adair International ont conclu en 1993 un accord de partage de production. Le texte de cet accord n'a pas été versé au dossier et le Tribunal n'est donc pas en mesure de l'analyser. Cet accord n'a pas été ratifié par le Yémen et n'est pas entré en vigueur. Le Yémen a toutefois fourni des cartes de la zone visée dans cet accord qui montrent que la zone s'inscrivait dans le secteur 24 ou le secteur Al Kathib dans lequel s'inscrivait aussi la zone confiée aux sociétésTomen et Santa Fe. Le Yémen dit avoir proposé à l'époque un secteur de prospection en mer qui englobait la totalité des îles Hanish et que la société Adair a préféré retenir une superficie légèrement inférieure à celle du secteur Total. Les cartes de la zone attribuée à Adair que le Yémen a fournies montrent que la ligne de délimitation occidentale traverse la partie méridionale de la Grande Hanish en inscrivant la plus grande partie de l'île, mais non sa totalité, dans la zone de l'accord. Le Yémen explique que Adair a tracé cette ligne occidentale pour des raisons d'ordre commercial. Pour autant que le Tribunal puisse en juger, la délimitation occidentale propre à l'accord conclu avec Adair suit en gros le tracé d'une ligne médiane entre les côtes du Yémen et de l'Erythrée, et ce tracé ne tient pas compte de l'existence des îles en litige.

Les secteurs proposés par le Yémen

421. A partir de 1990, le Yémen n'a plus donné de réponse aux propositions émanant de concessionnaires désireux d'exploiter des zones tracées par eux-mêmes, mais a commencé de proposer des secteurs de concession après avoir subdivisé en secteurs la plus grande partie du Yémen et des eaux situées devant sa côte. Le Yémen dit que les secteurs englobent les îles Zubayr et les îles Hanish – sans expliquer pourquoi Jabal al-Tayr n'est pas comprise dans lesdits secteurs – et voit là un nouvel élément prouvant qu'il estime exercer la souveraineté sur les îles en litige.

422. L'importance que le Tribunal pourrait être disposé à accorder à cette thèse est nuancée par les limitations occidentales des secteurs situés en mer telles qu'elles sont tracées d'après les éléments de preuve fournis par le Yémen. Ce dernier n'a pas seulement donné sa propre description des secteurs proposés à la prospection. Le Yémen a également présenté et cité, comme exprimant "l'avis d'experts confirmant l'exercice par le Yémen de l'autorité de l'Etat sur les îles Hanish et d'autres îles", un certain nombre de cartes établies par la société Petroconsultants S.A. de Genève, qui font partie d'une collection de cartes que Petroconsultants consacre à la prospection à l'étranger et qui dressent le tableau de la situation actuelle. Les cartes datent de la période allant de 1989 à novembre 1997. Trois d'entre elles indiquent une limite occidentale du secteur pertinent du Yémen qui passe non pas à l'ouest de la Grande Hanish mais à travers l'île, comme le fait la limite de la zone de l'accord conclu avec Adair. La carte établie pour 1994 est

rattachée à cet accord conclu avec Adair mais les cartes établies pour 1996 et 1997 ne le sont pas.

Les accords pétroliers et la prospection pétrolière du côté de l'Ethiopie et de l'Erythrée

423. L'Ethiopie a, dans les années 70, conclu un certain nombre d'accords de concession offshore portant sur une zone n'allant pas jusqu'à englober le sillon profond qui parcourt la mer Rouge en son milieu. A cette époque, la technologie de la prospection pétrolière n'était pas à même de faciliter les forages dans une fosse aussi profonde. Le Yémen, pour sa part, dit que les accords en question – il convient de noter que c'est le Yémen plutôt que l'Erythrée qui a versé ces accords au dossier – montraient que l'Ethiopie et les sociétés intéressées reconnaissaient que l'Ethiopie n'était pas en droit d'octroyer des concessions englobant les îles en litige mais, de l'avis du Tribunal, ces accords tiennent simplement compte des réalités technologiques et commerciales de l'époque et n'ont aucune incidence sur les droits des Parties qui sont en cause dans la présente instance. Le Tribunal adopte d'autant plus fermement cette conclusion que les concessions accordées par l'Ethiopie contiennent classiquement une formule telle que celle qui suit (de même que, *mutatis mutandis*, les cartes jointes aux concessions octroyées par le Yémen): "Le tracé de la frontière orientale de la zone du contrat n'est PAS nécessairement conforme aux frontières internationales de l'Ethiopie et par conséquent aucune des indications ci-dessus ne doit être réputée porter atteinte aux droits du gouvernement ou préjuger d'aucune manière les droits du gouvernement s'agissant des droits souverains qu'il exerce sur l'une quelconque des îles ou les fonds marins ainsi que le sous-sol de la zone sous-marine située en haute mer et contiguë à ses eaux territoriales ou à des secteurs de sa zone économique." Le Tribunal ne tire pas non plus d'enseignements de deux contrats pétroliers de prospection en mer Rouge conclus par l'Erythrée à des dates tardives, 1995 et 1996, à l'encontre desquels le Yémen a rapidement protesté parce que la zone visée chevauchait ses propres eaux. Mais le contrat conclu par l'Ethiopie avec International Petroleum/Amoco est important.

Accord de partage de production conclu avec International Petroleum/Amoco, 1988

424. L'Ethiopie a conclu le 28 mai 1988 un accord de partage de production avec International Petroleum Ltd of Bermuda. La concession visait "la zone terrestre et marine portant le nom de Concession Danakil en République démocratique populaire d'Ethiopie". Il y est indiqué: "ATTENDU QUE le titre de propriété de tout le pétrole existant à l'état naturel sur le territoire de l'Ethiopie ou dans son sous-sol appartient à l'Etat et au peuple d'Ethiopie . . . et que le gouvernement tient à promouvoir la prospection et la mise en valeur aux fins de production de la zone du contrat ou de son sous-sol . . .", et l'accord dispose ensuite que le gouvernement accorde à l'Entrepreneur "le droit exclusif de prospecter et mettre

en valeur les gisements de pétrole ainsi que de produire du pétrole dans la zone du contrat . . .". Le 1er novembre 1989, 60% du contrat ont été confiés à la société Amoco Ethiopia Petroleum Company. Amoco assumait désormais la charge des opérations à mener.

425. La carte jointe à cet accord de partage de production de 1988 montre la "superficie de l'Ethiopie – de la mer Rouge" à prospecter, sur terre et en mer, et la délimitation orientale de la zone en mer passe à travers l'extrémité sud-ouest de la Grande Hanish. Suivant la description qui est donnée de la zone du contrat, celle-ci va "jusqu'au point 13 en mer qui est situé à l'intersection du 14°30' de latitude avec la ligne médiane internationale entre le Yémen du Nord et l'Ethiopie, pour suivre ensuite la ligne médiane en mer." L'accord contenait une clause relative aux situations de force majeure, c'est-à-dire notamment les guerres, insurrections, rebellions et actes terroristes, qui prévoyait que dans ces cas, le contrat ne cesserait pas d'être applicable. En raison apparemment des combats qui avaient lieu entre des unités éthiopiennes et des unités érythréennes, l'état de force majeure a été déclaré le 9 février 1990 et considéré comme toujours en vigueur en juin 1992.

426. L'ambiguïté règne toutefois au sujet de la superficie de la zone du contrat, tout au moins quand celle-ci est représentée sur des cartes. La société Amoco Ethiopia Petroleum Company a adressé quatre rapports annuels à la République démocratique populaire d'Ethiopie qui mettent le fait en évidence.

427. Le rapport annuel pour 1989 fait savoir que des recherches géologiques ont été entreprises en 1989, qu'il a été accordé à la Delft Geophysical Company un contrat pour qu'elle recueille des données sismiques, des renseignements relatifs à la gravité et des données magnétiques, et que la société Delft a mené à terme en décembre une tournée de reconnaissance. Les techniciens ont mis en train les premiers essais d'interprétation des renseignements sismiques et l'établissement de cartes. La carte jointe au rapport de 1989 montre que la Grande et la Petite Hanish sont pratiquement en totalité situées dans la zone contractuelle, qui revêt ainsi une superficie considérablement supérieure que celle qui lui est attribuée sur la carte jointe à l'accord de partage de production.

428. Le rapport annuel pour 1990 signale que les recherches ont été suspendues avec l'instauration de l'état de force majeure le 9 février 1990; à la fin de l'année 1990, la situation, sur le plan de la sécurité, était considérée dans la région de Danakil comme n'autorisant pas de recherches sismiques normales. Le rapport signale néanmoins de considérables recherches géologiques et géophysiques antérieures à l'état d'urgence et des dépenses effectuées au titre de l'accord qui représentent environ deux millions de dollars. La description de la zone du contrat correspond à celle qui est donnée dans le rapport de 1989, mais deux cartes sont jointes à ce rapport annuel de 1990. Sur la première, où figure la zone de contrat autour de Danakil, la délimitation orientale ne traverse pas les îles

Hanish mais est située plutôt à l'ouest des îles. Sur la seconde carte, la Grande et la Petite Hanish sont pratiquement en totalité situées à l'intérieur de la zone du contrat, ce qui correspond aux indications déjà portées sur la carte jointe au rapport annuel de 1989.

429. Dans le rapport annuel pour 1991, il est indiqué que l'instauration de l'état de force majeure a concrètement abouti à prolonger la durée initialement prévue du contrat. Il a été jugé peu sûr de poursuivre les opérations sismiques normales en 1991, mais les techniciens ont poursuivi un gros travail d'évaluation des renseignements déjà recueillis. La carte de la zone du contrat qui accompagne le rapport annuel de 1991 montre que les îles Hanish sont pratiquement toutes situées dans ladite zone, l'indication à cet égard étant celle que fournissaient déjà les cartes des rapports de 1989 et 1990.

430. D'après le rapport annuel pour 1992, les travaux de retraitement ont été limités au cours de cette année-là. Il est indiqué que des représentants d'Amoco et International Petroleum ont rencontré le 24 juin 1992* à Asmara des représentants officiels de l'Erythrée qui venait d'accéder à l'indépendance, et il leur a été donné l'assurance que l'accord de partage de production de Danakil serait reconnu par l'Erythrée. Il est joint un résumé du contrat intitulé "Le secteur érythréen de Danakil" d'après lequel la date d'expiration du contrat est le 9 février 1997 et "sera retardée pour des raisons de force majeure". Il est signalé que la législation applicable est désormais la législation érythréenne. La carte du secteur de Danakil jointe au rapport annuel pour 1993 montre que les îles Hanish sont pratiquement toutes situées à l'intérieur de la zone du contrat, et c'est aussi le cas d'après une "carte magnétique composite de la concession de Danakil".

431. Une carte établie par la société Petroconsultants, dont les cartes d'ailleurs ont été constamment invoquées par le Yémen, montre également que la zone du contrat d'Amoco comprend la plus grande partie de la Grande Hanish.

432. Le Yémen ne nie pas n'avoir jamais protesté contre les dispositions de l'accord de partage de production conclu avec International Petroleum et Amoco ni contre l'étendue géographique de la zone visée mais soutient qu'on ne peut pas lui en faire reproche. Le Yémen fait observer qu'un article paru dans le périodique intitulé *Petroleum Economist* d'octobre 1991 publie une carte montrant une concession accordée à Amoco qui n'englobe pas les îles Hanish (la carte du PNUD retraçant "l'historique de la prospection", ne nomme pas la concession accordée à Amoco). Le Yémen soutient également que le contrat d'Amoco n'a été applicable que pendant trois mois environ et qu'au moment où ce contrat aurait peut-être retenu son attention, l'état de force majeure avait été instauré, ce qui peut avoir incité le Yémen à s'abstenir d'agir.

---

* *Note de l'éditeur: cette référence a été corrigée de la version anglaise originale.*

433. Le Tribunal ne juge pas la position du Yémen parfaitement convaincante. Comme le prouvent les rapports annuels évoqués rapidement ci-dessus, le contrat conclu avec IPC/Amoco a eu une durée très supérieure à trois mois et est resté applicable après l'accession à l'indépendance de l'Erythrée; sa durée de validité est comparable à celle des contrats qu'invoque le Yémen lui-même. Si le Yémen s'était procuré pour les lire les rapports annuels d'Amoco – les rapports annuels des sociétés pétrolières américaines sont généralement disponibles pour le grand public: il suffit de les demander – et si le Yémen avait manifesté à ce sujet la vigilance dont il a témoigné au sujet des contrats accordés par l'Erythrée en 1995 et 1996, il aurait constaté que l'Ethiopie revendiquait le droit de conclure des contrat à des fins de prospection pétrolière, de mise en valeur et de production du pétrole dans une région faisant d'après elle partie de son territoire qui comprenait certaines des îles relevant de la Grande Hanish, voire pratiquement toutes les îles en question. La compagnie Amoco fait partie des grandes compagnies pétrolières internationales et est présente dans les environs immédiats; d'ailleurs, l'une des cartes versées au dossier par le Yémen montre la compagnie Amoco ainsi que BP présente dans le secteur Antufash et montre aussi que la concession Danakil octroyée à Amoco empiète même sur la zone accordée à Adair dans le secteur Al Kathib.

434. Le Yémen a accordé beaucoup d'importance au fait que, d'après ses allégations, ni l'Ethiopie ni l'Erythrée n'a accordé de contrat de concession englobant des îles aujourd'hui en litige et que ni l'une ni l'autre n'a protesté quand le Yémen a accordé des concessions qui englobaient, quant à elles, lesdites îles. Mais il a été prouvé que, dans l'accord de partage de production passé avec International Petroleum et Amoco, dont il a été fait état tardivement, l'Ethiopie a bien accordé une concession englobant la plus grande partie des îles Hanish sinon l'ensemble de ces îles, et que le Yémen n'a pas protesté contre cet accord. Il est en outre intéressant de constater que la carte jointe à l'accord de partage de production parle d'un tracé de frontière qui suivrait la ligne médiane internationale entre le Yémen et l'Ethiopie.

435. L'Erythrée s'attribue également certaines effectivités pertinentes. Elle a présenté la copie d'un permis éthiopien d'utilisation d'un émetteur radio accordé aux alentours de 1988-89 (la première des dates figurant sur le contrat est apparemment celle du calendrier éthiopien) à la Delft Geophysical Co. en vue de l'installation d'une station radio sur l'île de la Grande Hanish, en liaison vraisemblablement avec les opérations sismiques confiées contractuellement à Delft par Amoco. L'Erythrée a communiqué le texte d'une instruction détaillée adressée au haut commandement militaire chargeant ses officiers supérieurs de protéger une expédition de prospection pétrolière du ministère éthiopien des mines et de l'énergie qui allait se rendre en certains lieux “y compris l'île de la Grande Hanish”. L'Erythrée a fourni également un mémorandum éthiopien concernant la prospection pétrolière en mer Rouge qui porte la date éthiopienne du 13 avril 1982 (environ l'an 1989 de notre ère), dans laquelle il est indiqué que

l'Amoco-Ethiopia Petroleum Company "a installé des balises de navigation pour lui permettre de procéder à une étude sismique . . . y compris sur l'île de la Grande Hanish." Le mémorandum poursuit: "Une équipe technique d'entrepreneurs de la société Amoco sera disponible à partir de la troisième semaine de décembre pour procéder au choix des lieux d'installation, comme suit:

> Pendant deux semaines, l'installation de balises de navigation sur les huit lieux choisis; à la fin de cette quinzaine, il sera procédé aux sondages sismiques pendant six semaines . . ."

et il est donné pour instruction d'assurer la protection des entrepreneurs et de leur matériel pendant l'installation des balises et de protéger également les balises qui seront installées. Il est demandé en outre d'assurer la protection du navire de la société Delft Geophysical pendant qu'il procède aux sondages sismiques. Aux termes d'un autre mémorandum, une équipe d'entrepreneurs d'Amoco doit procéder à des patrouilles par hélicoptère pour sélectionner des lieux où il sera installé des balises de navigation, y compris des lieux situés "sur la Grande Hanish". On ne voit pas très clairement si lesdites activités ont été en fait menées à bien, encore que le rapport annuel d'Amoco pour 1989 corrobore effectivement le fait que la société Delft Geophysical a bien effectué une tournée de reconnaissance en décembre 1989 (voir le paragraphe 427 ci-dessus).

* - *

436. A la suite de cet historique complexe des concessions pétrolières, le Tribunal aboutit aux conclusions ci-après:

437. Les contrats pétroliers offshore conclus par le Yémen ainsi que par l'Ethiopie et l'Erythrée ne suffisent pas à établir ou à conforter de manière significative les prétentions de l'une ou l'autre Partie à la souveraineté sur les îles en litige.

438. Toutefois, ces contrats étayent dans une certaine mesure le tracé d'une ligne médiane entre les côtes se faisant face de l'Erythrée et du Yémen, opéré sans prendre en compte les îles, pour séparer les juridictions respectives des Parties.

439. Pendant la mise en application de ces contrats pétroliers, des actes significatifs ont été accomplis sous autorité étatique qui demandent à être mesurés et évalués plus avant par le Tribunal.

* - * - *

CHAPITRE X – Conclusions

440. Après avoir procédé à un examen et une analyse très approfondis du volumineux matériau et des multiples éléments de preuve présentés par les Parties,[25] le Tribunal peut à présent en tirer les conclusions qui s'imposent.

Un titre ancien

441. Il faut pour commencer traiter la question d'un "titre ancien" à laquelle le Yémen attache beaucoup d'importance; en outre, le Compromis d'arbitrage demande au Tribunal de statuer sur la question de la souveraineté "sur la base, notamment, des titres historiques". Le Yémen soutient qu'il exerce un titre ancien sur "les îles", titre qui existait avant que l'Empire ottoman ait conquis l'hégémonie et qui remonte d'ailleurs au Yémen médiéval. Le Yémen soutient en outre que ce titre subsistait encore en droit international à l'époque où les Turcs ont été vaincus à la fin de la première guerre mondiale et que, par conséquent, quand l'Empire ottoman a renoncé par le traité de Lausanne de 1923 à sa domination sur les îles, laquelle était généralement reconnue, le "droit de retour" a rendu au Yémen l'exercice par la possession du titre en question.

442. L'argumentation est intéressante et soulève un certain nombre de questions relatives au droit international régissant la souveraineté territoriale. Personne ne doute que, sous l'Empire ottoman – et certainement pendant la seconde période ottomane qui va de 1872 à 1918 – les Ottomans avaient la possession de la totalité des îles aujourd'hui en litige et exerçaient pleinement la souveraineté sur elles, et qu'il ne s'agissait donc pas seulement d'une possession factuelle mais qu'il existait là aussi un titre souverain de possession. Quand ce régime a pris fin en 1923, y a-t-il eu alors "réversion" d'un titre encore plus ancien qui a rempli le vide résultant de la situation?

443. L'Erythrée doute qu'une telle doctrine de réversion ait cours en droit international. Le doute paraît justifié puisque le Yémen n'a invoqué que très peu d'éléments à l'appui de cette doctrine et que le Tribunal n'a pas non plus connaissance de quelque fondement qu'il serait possible d'invoquer pour soutenir que la réversion est un principe ou une règle acceptée du droit international général. De plus, même si la doctrine était reconnue, elle ne pourrait pas s'appliquer en l'espèce parce qu'il n'y a pas de continuité. Le Yémen a soutenu

---

[25] Le Tribunal tient à prendre acte ne serait-ce que du volume des écritures et des éléments de preuve que les Parties lui ont soumis lors de cette première phase de la procédure arbitrale. Chacune des Parties a présenté plus de vingt tomes d'annexes documentaires ainsi que d'épais atlas. En outre, le Tribunal a examiné attentivement le compte rendu in extenso des plaidoiries qui représentent globalement un bon millier de pages. Le Tribunal constate en outre que la majorité des documents ont été présentés dans leur langue originale, et qu'il a dû se fier à des versions traduites fournies par les Parties.

qu'il n'y a pas lieu de prouver la continuité quand il s'agit d'un titre historique, mais le Tribunal ne voit pas sur quoi cet argument-là peut s'appuyer.

444. L'argument du Yémen est difficile à concilier avec des siècles de domination ottomane sur toute la région, domination qui n'a pris fin qu'avec le traité de Lausanne (voir le chapitre V ci-dessus). La difficulté est d'autant plus grande qu'en vertu du principe du droit intertemporel, la souveraineté ottomane était légitime et s'accompagnait du droit à disposer du territoire. Accepter l'argument du Yémen qui dit qu'un titre ancien pourrait être resté en vigueur pendant une longue période de souveraineté exercée par un tiers reviendrait à rejeter la légalité du titre ottoman à la pleine souveraineté.

445. Le traité de Lausanne ne prescrivait pas expressément, comme l'aurait fait le traité de Sèvres, que la Turquie renonçait à ses titres territoriaux en faveur des Puissances alliées; une disposition en ce sens aurait certainement exclu toute possibilité de voir entrer en jeu une doctrine de réversion. Le Yémen n'était pas partie au traité de Lausanne, qui était par conséquent *res inter alios acta*. Aucun publiciste de renom ne doute néanmoins que les îles anciennement turques fussent en 1923 à la disposition des parties au traité de Lausanne, tout comme elles avaient été intégralement à la disposition de l'Empire ottoman, lequel était, quant à lui, partie au traité et renonçait dans ledit traité à sa souveraineté sur lesdites îles. L'article 16 du traité créait pour les îles un statut juridique objectif d'indétermination jusqu'au moment où les parties intéressées se prononceraient à nouveau à leur sujet; et cette situation juridique fut globalement reconnue comme telle, comme le démontre amplement la volumineuse documentation que les Parties ont soumise au Tribunal. Dans ces conditions, il est difficile de voir ce qui aurait pu subsister d'un tel titre après les épisodes de souveraineté ottomane alors que celle-ci était généralement considérée comme une souveraineté absolue; et il est difficile de voir ce qui aurait pu en subsister une fois cette souveraineté remplacée par le régime de l'article 16 qui mettait les îles totalement à la disposition des "intéressés".

446. Il y a encore une difficulté supplémentaire. Le Yémen existait certainement avant que la région fût soumise à la domination des Ottomans. Mais on est appelé à se demander si l'imam, qui à cette époque habitait une forteresse montagneuse dont il était le maître, avait vraiment établi son emprise sur "les îles". Et le problème tient en outre à ce qu'il serait tout simplement anachronique de chercher à imputer à cette société médiévale, tribale et musulmane vivant en pays montagneux le concept occidental moderne d'un titre de souveraineté, surtout si ce titre devait s'appliquer à des îles inhabitées et inhospitalières que seuls utilisaient à l'occasion des pêcheurs locaux exerçant un métier traditionnel.

447. Conformément aux prescriptions du Compromis d'arbitrage, les deux Parties, et surtout le Yémen, ont "notamment" invoqué des titres historiques comme source de souveraineté territoriale. Mais les Parties ne sont toutefois pas parvenues à

convaincre le Tribunal que ces titres existent vraiment, particulièrement en ce qui concerne ces îles.

448. Les revendications de l'Erythrée aussi, dans la mesure où elles sont censées tirer leur origine par voie de succession de l'Italie, par l'intermédiaire de l'Ethiopie, si elles ne sont guère fondées sur un titre "ancien", se fondent manifestement sur l'affirmation d'un titre historique. Il ne fait pas de doute, comme on l'a vu aux chapitres V, VI et VII ci-dessus, que, pendant l'entre-deux-guerres, l'Italie a nourri de sérieuses ambitions territoriales sur les îles de la mer Rouge; et l'Italie a effectivement cherché à réaliser ces ambitions en prenant concrètement possession de certaines de ces îles à différents moments. Comme on l'a vu plus haut assez en détail, l'Erythrée se heurte pour faire valoir ces prétentions à une souveraineté obtenue par voie de succession, à des difficultés majeures qui tiennent d'abord à l'effet de l'article 16 du traité de Lausanne de 1923 et ensuite aux effets des dispositions du traité de paix avec l'Italie de 1947. Mais il y a aussi le fait que, pendant l'entre-deux-guerres, le Gouvernement italien a constamment et systématiquement donné au Gouvernement britannique l'assurance expresse qu'il acceptait et reconnaissait pleinement la situation juridique indéterminée de ces îles telle que celle-ci avait été définie par voie conventionnelle en 1923. L'Italie espérait certainement que sa politique d'expansionnisme actif aurait finalement pour effet que "les intéressés" seraient un jour convaincus d'accepter un fait accompli. Mais ce jour n'est jamais arrivé.

449. Ces versions du titre historique créent donc de considérables difficultés aux deux Parties. Mais le Tribunal n'en a pas moins procédé à des recherches minutieuses sur les deux types de revendications de titres historiques. Or, les difficultés tiennent pour une très grande part aux faits que l'histoire elle-même rappelle. En fin de compte, ni l'une ni l'autre Partie n'ont été à même de convaincre le Tribunal que l'histoire démontre en l'occurrence l'existence juridique d'un titre historique, ou de titres historiques, sur les îles, îlots et rochers en question qui soit établi depuis si longtemps et ait un caractère effectif tel que le Tribunal peut y trouver un fondement assez solide pour statuer. Et il convient de dire aussi que, vu la nature de ces îles, îlots et rochers qui sont dépourvus d'eau et inhabitables, vu en outre le caractère intermittent des situations et des intérêts politiques qui évoluent dans la région au rythme d'un kaléidoscope, il n'est guère étonnant d'aboutir à cette conclusion.

450. Les Parties toutefois font aussi valoir l'une et l'autre ce qui est une forme de revendication historique mais revêt un caractère assez différent; c'est-à-dire que les deux Parties font la preuve de l'utilisation, de la présence, de la manifestation de l'autorité étatique, et de certaines autres façons encore de témoigner d'une possession susceptible de se consolider progressivement en un titre; on a vu cette façon de procéder dans l'affaire du *Groënland oriental*, dans l'affaire de l'*Ile de Palmas* et un très grand nombre d'autres affaires connues. Or, à côté des titres historiques à strictement parler, le Tribunal est tenu par les dispositions du

Compromis d'arbitrage de statuer conformément aux "principes, . . . règles et . . . pratiques du droit international"; il est clair que cette rubrique s'étend à ce type d'argumentation évoquée très fréquemment dans le cadre des différends territoriaux. Les Parties ont manifestement prévu qu'il faudrait peut-être recourir précisément à ce type d'argument pour fonder la décision – bien qu'il faille constater que le Yémen invoque expressément ce type d'argument pour confirmer un titre ancien tandis que l'Erythrée invoque ce type d'argument pour confirmer un titre existant acquis par voie de succession – et les Parties ont donc apporté au Tribunal un matériau considérable et une masse d'éléments tendant à prouver l'utilisation et la possession, éléments qui ont été exposés et analysés au chapitre VII ci-dessus, comme le chapitre VIII a été consacré aux cartes présentées et le chapitre IX, à l'histoire des accords pétroliers. On peut dire d'emblée qu'après analyse, la situation, qui ne cesse d'évoluer, ainsi créée par l'activité de la puissance publique sous tous ces différents aspects, montre que – comme d'ailleurs dans l'affaire des *Minquiers et Ecréhous*[26] où s'opposaient aussi des arguments relatifs à des revendications de titres très anciens, c'est l'histoire relativement récente de l'utilisation et de la possession qui constitue en définitive un fondement essentiel des décisions du Tribunal. Le Tribunal en vient donc à présent à examiner ce matériau et ces arguments.

Les preuves de l'exercice des fonctions étatiques et de l'autorité de la puissance publique

451. Les Parties ont saisi le Tribunal de tout ce matériau avec l'intention de prouver la création de la souveraineté territoriale sur les îles au moyen, comme l'a dit le juge Huber dans l'affaire de l'*Ile de Palmas*[27] "de l'exercice continu et pacifique des fonctions étatiques dans une région donnée." Mais le type d'actes servant à donner la preuve de cet exercice a, comme c'était inévitable, pris une certaine ampleur pour montrer comment s'opérait ce que Charles de Visscher appelait une "consolidation" progressive du titre. Par conséquent, le Tribunal se trouve en l'espèce face à toute une gamme de facteurs et d'événements remontant à de nombreuses périodes différentes qui visent à faire la preuve non seulement d'une activité et d'un comportement concrets mais aussi de la renommée, de même que des opinions et des attitudes de gouvernements tiers (les différentes catégories de matériau sont exposées ci-dessus au chapitre VII).

452. On sait parfaitement qu'en ce qui concerne les preuves à présenter de l'exercice concret de la souveraineté, les normes peuvent avoir évolué quand il s'agit, comme en l'espèce, d'un territoire difficile d'accès ou inhospitalier. Comme l'a dit la Cour permanente de Justice internationale dans son arrêt sur le *Statut*

[26] Minquiers et Ecréhous (Royaume-Uni c. France), CIJ Recueil 1953, p. 47.

[27] Ile de Palmas (Etats-Unis c. Pays-Bas), Nations Unies, Recueil des sentences arbitrales, vol. II, p. 829 (1929) [Traduction Ch. Rousseau, Revue de droit international public, tome IX, 1935.]

juridique du Groënland oriental, “Il est impossible d’examiner les décisions rendues dans les affaires visant la souveraineté territoriale sans observer que, dans beaucoup de cas, le tribunal n’a pas exigé de nombreuses manifestations d’un exercice de droits souverains pourvu que l’autre Etat en cause ne pût faire valoir une prétention supérieure.”[28]

453. Cette indication soulève toutefois une nouvelle question de principe qui est importante. Il s’agit en l’occurrence de l’établissement de la souveraineté territoriale et ce n’est pas là une affaire mineure. Vu son importance, on pourrait supposer qu’il faut, pour prouver l’acquisition d’un tel droit, remplir une sorte de condition minimale absolue et qu’en principe ce ne devrait pas normalement être là une simple question relative.

454. On se rappellera que cette question de principe s’est effectivement posée dans l’affaire de l’*Ile de Palmas*, mais l’arbitre Max Huber a pu alors y répondre en faisant appel aux dispositions particulières du compromis qui, comme l’a dit alors Huber, “présuppos[e], pour l’affaire actuelle, que l’île de Palmas (ou Miangas) ne peut appartenir qu’aux Etats-Unis ou aux Pays-Bas et qu’elle doit faire partie dans sa totalité du territoire de l’une ou de l’autre de ces deux Puissances, parties en cause”, et “[l]a faculté donnée à l’arbitre de fonder sa décision sur la valeur relative des titres invoqués de part et d’autre doit avoir été envisagée par les parties au compromis”.

455. Le Compromis d’arbitrage en l’espèce, toutefois, est énoncé en des termes différents qui sont même inhabituels. Le Tribunal est simplement appelé à rendre “une sentence sur la souveraineté territoriale” et “statuer sur la question de la souveraineté”. On ne peut pas faire appel en l’espèce à la disposition compromissoire qui donnait à Max Huber la possibilité de se prononcer en s’appuyant exclusivement sur une différence marginale entre les éléments de preuve.

456. Le matériau, les éléments de preuve, les arguments ne font certes pas défaut en la présente instance. Au contraire, le matériau présenté est très volumineux, les équipes des deux Parties ayant fourni un travail de recherche considérable et leurs conseils ayant présenté des exposés excellents. Mais ce matériau et ces éléments ont en fait donné l’image d’une sorte de damier dont les pièces se déplacent souvent, sur lequel la fortune et les intérêts des Parties se meuvent constamment avec le temps. En outre, il ne faut pas oublier que ni l’Ethiopie ni le Yémen n’ont eu tellement l’occasion de manifester activement et ouvertement leurs ambitions quant à la souveraineté sur les îles ou d’y exercer des activités étatiques avant la période postérieure à 1967, date à laquelle les Britanniques ont quitté la région. En effet, comme on l’a vu plus haut, la Grande-Bretagne a constamment veillé à

[28] Statut juridique du Groënland oriental (Danemark c. Norvège), 1933, CPJI (Série A/B), n° 53.

préserver la situation engendrée par le traité de Lausanne qui était que le statut juridique des "îles" était indéterminé.

457. Lorsque, pour toutes les raisons que nous venons d'évoquer, les activités dont les parties tirent argument, bien que nombreuses, ne sont parfois pas totalement convaincantes, le Tribunal a certainement raison de chercher si, en l'espèce, d'autres facteurs peuvent éventuellement concourir à lever certaines de ces incertitudes. Il n'y a aucun avantage à "ne pas exiger de nombreuses manifestations" de souveraineté quand cette recherche d'autres facteurs éventuels a quelque chance de renforcer le fondement de la décision.

458. Il existe en la présente instance un facteur qui joue clairement un tel rôle: la situation géographique de la majorité des îles, îlots et rochers en litige, lesquels constituent un archipel qui prend toute la largeur du bras de mer relativement étroit séparant les deux côtes se faisant face. Il est donc jusqu'à un certain point possible de présumer que toute île située au large d'une des côtes peut être considérée comme appartenant à cette côte en tant que dépendance sauf si l'Etat sur le territoire duquel se trouve la côte opposée a pu démontrer qu'il avait un titre manifestement meilleur. Ce facteur supplémentaire éventuel est encore plus intéressant quand on constate qu'il a incontestablement exercé une réelle influence dans l'histoire juridique des îles en question; et cette influence remonte d'ailleurs à l'époque de la domination ottomane où, alors même que toute la région relevait d'une souveraineté unique, il a été jugé commode de partager la juridiction entre les deux autorités locales installées sur les deux côtes (voir les paragraphes 132 à 136 ci-dessus). En outre, en l'espèce, l'examen des activités exercées montre lui-même très clairement que l'ensemble de cet archipel Zuqar-Hanish n'a pas connu la même histoire juridique; certains des éléments de preuve soumis visent, et ce n'est guère étonnant, certaines îles ou certains sous-groupes d'îles.

459. Le Tribunal a donc jugé nécessaire, pour statuer sur la question de la souveraineté, d'étudier séparément les divers sous-groupes d'îles, ne serait-ce que parce que ces différents sous-groupes ont, dans une large mesure tout au moins, une histoire juridique distincte, comme il faut du reste s'y attendre s'agissant d'îles occupant tout l'espace situé entre les deux côtes se faisant face. On peut ne voir là qu'une évidence, mais le Yémen a tout particulièrement tenu à souligner l'importance qu'il attache à ce qu'il appelle le principe de l'unité naturelle des îles et il convient donc de s'arrêter un moment sur cette théorie.

L'unité naturelle et physique

460. Le Yémen insiste très fortement dans ses écritures sur ce qu'il appelle "le principe de l'unité naturelle ou géophysique" quand il parle du groupe des îles Hanish; le Yémen utilise l'appellation "groupe des Hanish" à la fois dans ses exposés et dans ses cartes pour désigner toute la chaîne d'îles, y compris les

Haycocks et les Mohabbakahs (ne sont naturellement pas visées ici les îles septentrionales de Jabal al-Tayr et du groupe de Zubayr, que nous traiterons séparément ultérieurement).

461. Ce "principe" est développé au chapitre 5 du mémoire du Yémen, qui cite à ce sujet une impressionnante série d'auteurs faisant autorité, notamment Fitzmaurice, Waldock et Charles de Visscher. L'existence de la notion en question ne fait évidemment pas de doute. Mais ce n'est pas un principe absolu. Tous les auteurs cités en référence en parlent comme d'une source de présomption. Et, dans l'extrait puisé chez lui, Fitzmaurice parle clairement d'une présomption tenant à la proximité, c'est-à-dire que, lorsqu'un Etat exerce ou manifeste sa souveraineté sur une certaine étendue de territoire, il est possible de se demander si, par présomption, ladite souveraineté ne s'étendra pas aussi au territoire extérieur où les manifestations concrètes de l'autorité du même Etat sont faibles, voire nulles. Le Tribunal n'a pas de mal à accepter des jugements empreints d'une telle autorité; mais il y a là nettement plus qu'un simple principe d'unité. Il y a lieu à ce propos de citer à nouveau Fitzmaurice:

> *Question de l''entité' ou de l''unité naturelle'*
> Cette question peut être lourde de conséquences. Non seulement peut-elle orienter avec beaucoup de force les probabilités et les présomptions, mais aussi, s'il peut être démontré que la zone contestée fait partie (que ce soit sous l'effet d'une authentique contiguïté ou de la proximité) d'une entité ou d'une unité sur l'ensemble de laquelle l'Etat demandeur exerce sa souveraineté, cela peut rendre inutile (dans certaines conditions et dans certaines limites) – ou atténuer en tout cas la nécessité – d'apporter des preuves précises de l'activité consacrée par l'Etat en question à la zone contestée en tant que telle – à condition que ladite activité, correspondant à une occupation et une possession effectives, puisse être démontrée suivant le principe établi par l'affaire de l'Ile de Palmas qui est que 'la souveraineté ne peut pas être exercée en fait à tout moment sur tout point du territoire.'[29]

462. C'est-à-dire que les publicistes ayant autorité parlent d'"entité" ou d'"unité naturelle" sous l'angle d'une présomption, ou d'une probabilité, et l'associent en outre à la proximité, la contiguïté, la continuité et autres notions de cet ordre, dont on sait très bien en droit international qu'elles n'engendrent pas elles-mêmes de titre, mais créent simplement une possibilité ou une présomption tendant à étendre à la zone visée un titre existant déjà établi comme tel dans une partie de la même "unité" qui est distincte, mais qui est située à proximité ou bien lui est contiguë.

463. Ces idées, toutefois, sont susceptibles dans la présente instance d'une double application. Elles peuvent effectivement, comme le voudrait le Yémen, s'appliquer de façon que la manifestation de l'autorité gouvernementale sur une

[29] BRITISH YEARBOOK OF INTERNATIONAL LAW, VOL. 32 (1955-1956), p. 73-74.

île déterminée d'un groupe puisse étendre son effet juridique à une autre île ou à d'autres îles du même groupe. Mais le même raisonnement conduit à se poser une question complémentaire consistant à chercher jusqu'où l'emprise de l'Etat établi sur l'une des côtes du territoire continental doit être considérée comme s'étendant à certaines îles ou îlots au large de ladite côte qui sont situés naturellement "à proximité" de ladite côte ou lui sont naturellement "rattachés". L'idée était si bien acquise au cours du dernier siècle qu'il lui a été donné le nom de "doctrine du portique" et que celle-ci fut reconnue "comme un moyen d'attribuer la souveraineté à des formations situées au large qui subissent l'attraction du territoire continental."[30] Il n'est pas difficile de voir la pertinence que ces notions de droit international revêtent pour l'histoire juridique propre à la présente espèce.

464. Dans ces conditions, le principe de l'unité naturelle et physique est à double tranchant, car s'il faut vraiment l'appliquer, il faut alors se poser la question de savoir laquelle des deux côtes est la source de l'unité. En outre, comme le montrent clairement les affaires tout comme les auteurs cités par le Yémen, ces notions d'unité, etc., ne sont jamais en soi génératrices de titre, elles sont simplement susceptibles dans certaines conditions d'autoriser une présomption quant à l'étendue et à la portée d'un titre établi par ailleurs.

465. En dépit des théories de l'unité, le fait est que les Parties ont toutes deux tacitement admis, en tout cas aux fins de leurs exposés écrits, qu'il soit possible de considérer que le grand groupe d'îles présente des sous-groupes. La nomenclature communément utilisée fait état de trois sous-groupes au moins: les Mohabbakahs; les Haycocks; et ce qu'il est commode, pour le moment tout au moins, d'appeler le groupe Zuqar-Hanish assorti de ses nombreuses îles, îlots et rochers satellites. On trouve tous ces noms dans la publication intitulée *British Pilot and Sailing Directions for the Southern Red Sea* (le Yémen a cité cette publication pour soutenir qu'il faut considérer toutes ces îles comme ne constituant qu'un seul groupe, mais quand on s'intéresse à ces îles comme étant des dangers ou des repères pour le navigateur qui parcourt la mer Rouge, il n'y a bien entendu pas d'autre façon de les considérer). Il faut également prendre en considération les deux îles septentrionales: Jabal al-Tayr et le groupe dont l'île la plus importante est Jabal Zubayr. Le Tribunal va à présent exposer ses conclusions en ce qui concerne chacun des trois sous-groupes, puis, pour terminer, en ce qui concerne les îles septentrionales.

466. Ainsi donc, pour statuer sur la souveraineté territoriale, le Tribunal, comme il ne faut guère s'en étonner, n'a pas trouvé d'autre solution que de s'écarter des conditions dans lesquelles les Parties ont toutes deux plaidé leur cause, qui ont consisté pour chacune d'elles à présenter une revendication sur chacune des îles

---

[30] D. O'Connell, The International Law of the Sea, p. 185 (1982).

en litige. L'histoire juridique ne conforte tout simplement pas cette revendication ni pour l'une ni pour l'autre Partie.[31] En effet, comme nous l'avons expliqué ci-dessus, nous constatons à l'examen qu'une bonne partie du matériau présenté s'applique soit à une île en particulier soit à un sous-groupe d'îles. Le Tribunal a par conséquent dû aboutir à une conclusion qu'aucune des deux Parties n'était disposée à envisager, à savoir qu'il faudrait peut-être partager les îles; ladite conclusion n'est d'ailleurs pas imposée par le Tribunal, elle est due à la valeur même des éléments de preuve et des arguments présentés par les Parties, dont le poids ne se répartit pas également sur l'ensemble des îles et qui produisent des résultats différents pour certains sous-groupes et pour certaines îles.

Les Mohabbakahs

467. Il s'agit de quatre îlots rocheux qui ne représentent guère plus que des dangers pour la navigation. Sayal Islet, îlot qui n'est pas situé à plus de six milles marins du point le plus proche de la côte continentale de l'Erythrée, ainsi que les îlots appelés Harbi Islet et Flat Islet sont tous les trois situés à moins de douze milles de la côte continentale. En dernier lieu, il y a l'îlot High Islet situé à moins d'un mille au-delà de la limite des douze milles de la côte continentale, et à cinq milles marins environ de l'île Haycock la plus proche, en l'occurrence South West Haycock.

468. L'Erythrée a cherché à montrer que l'Italie a acquis le titre sur les Mohabbakahs en même temps qu'elle concluait des accords avec les chefs locaux (voir le paragraphe 159 ci-dessus), ce qui lui a permis de s'assurer le titre sur la côte Danakil; cette acquisition de titre n'a pas suscité de protestation de la part de la Turquie et a finalement été reconnue par la Grande-Bretagne. L'histoire diplomatique présente un certain intérêt à ce sujet, notamment pour permettre de savoir si South West Haycock fait partie des Mohabbakahs ou d'un groupe distinct qui est celui des Haycocks, ou encore d'un groupe plus important qui est

[31] Il est intéressant à ce sujet de considérer ce que dit le mémorandum "ultrasecret" de 1977 émanant du ministère des affaires étrangères du Gouvernement militaire provisoire de l'Ethiopie socialiste qui a été évoqué au paragraphe 245 ci-dessus. Ce mémorandum évoque des îles situées dans la région méridionale de la mer Rouge qui "n'ont pas eu de propriétaire reconnu", à l'égard desquelles l'Ethiopie "revendique la juridiction" et que "tant le Yémen du Nord que le Yémen du Sud ont commencé à revendiquer." "La position du Yémen du Sud est que ces îles ont été illégalement remises à l'Ethiopie par les Britanniques quand la Grande-Bretagne a renoncé à ses droits sur le protectorat d'Aden." Le mémorandum ajoute: "Le Gouvernement du Yémen du Nord soulève à présent la question de la juridiction sur ces îles." Le Yémen du Nord recommande des négociations bilatérales qui semblent avoir été en fait engagées avant même la rédaction du mémorandum car celui-ci indique ensuite: "Les deux Etats . . . ont officieusement évoqué la possibilité de se partager les îles. La proposition consiste à se servir de la ligne médiane pour ligne de partage, car elle divise la mer Rouge en parts égales à partir des côtes des deux pays . . . . L'Ethiopie a rejeté cette proposition parce qu'elle la désavantageait."

le "groupe Zuqar-Hanish" (voir le paragraphe 215 ci-dessus pour la revendication de souveraineté sur South West Haycock formulée en 1930 par l'Italie).

469. L'Erythrée soutient donc que les Mohabbakahs faisaient partie de ce qui a été cédé à l'Ethiopie et donc à l'Erythrée à la suite de la seconde guerre mondiale et que la confirmation à cet égard réside dans l'article 2 du traité de paix de 1947 avec l'Italie qui vise les îles situées "au large de la côte" et dans les dispositions constitutionnelles.

470. Le Yémen soutient de son côté que les seules îles sur lesquelles l'Ethiopie a acquis le droit d'exercer sa juridiction par l'intermédiaire des chefs locaux ont été les îles de la baie d'Assab; cette situation s'expliquerait par le fait que les deux côtes de la mer Rouge étaient auparavant soumises à la domination ottomane et qu'après la fin de la première guerre mondiale, son "titre historique" est revenu au Yémen; la thèse du Yémen est aussi qu'il faut normalement considérer que les Mohabbakahs font avec les Haycocks et le groupe Zuqar-Hanish partie d'une même unité, et que le titre sur la totalité de ces îles revient au Yémen. Le Tribunal rejette cette argumentation.

471. Le Tribunal a déjà noté que rien ne prouve que les îles Mohabbakah relevaient d'un titre historique originaire exercé par le Yémen, à supposer même qu'un tel titre eût existé et fût revenu au Yémen à la suite de la première guerre mondiale. Et quand bien même il serait exact que seules les îles de la baie d'Assab ont été transmises à l'Erythrée par l'Italie en 1947, le Yémen n'a pas sérieusement revendiqué depuis cette date les Mohabbakahs avant les événements qui ont débouché sur le présent arbitrage.

472. Le Tribunal n'a toutefois pas besoin de décider si le titre de l'Italie sur les Mohabbakahs a survécu au traité de Lausanne pour être transmis ensuite à l'Ethiopie, puis à l'Erythrée. Il suffit au Tribunal de constater que toutes les Mohabbakahs à l'exception de l'îlot High Islet sont situées à moins de douze milles de la côte érythréenne. Quelle que soit leur histoire, en l'absence d'un titre dont le Yémen puisse manifestement se prévaloir, les Mohabbakahs doivent aujourd'hui, pour cette raison, être considérées comme érythréennes.[32] Or, le Yémen ne s'est pas prévalu valablement d'un autre titre sur les Mohabbakahs. On n'a du reste pas oublié que l'article 6 du traité de Lausanne de 1923 consacrait d'ores et déjà ce principe de la mer territoriale en stipulant expressément que les

---

32 Voir D. Bowett, The Legal Regime of Islands in International Law (1978), p. 48, où l'auteur dit des îles situées dans la mer territoriale d'un Etat: "On présume dans ce cas que l'île relève de la même souveraineté que le territoire continental proche"; l'auteur cite aussi, de façon intéressante, Lindley, The Acquisition and Government of Backward Territory in International Law (1926), p. 7, lequel écrit, il faut le relever, au milieu des années 1920: "Une île inhabitée située dans les eaux territoriales est soumise à la souveraineté du territoire continental qui la jouxte."

îles situées dans la mer territoriale d'un Etat appartenaient nécessairement à ce dernier. A l'époque, le droit international et la coutume limitaient généralement à trois milles la largeur de la mer territoriale, mais celle-ci a depuis longtemps été portée à douze milles et la largeur de la mer territoriale de l'Ethiopie a été étendue à douze milles dans un décret daté de 1953.

473. Parvenu à ce stade de ses constatations, le Tribunal a lieu de considérer la théorie ingénieuse présentée par l'Erythrée, laquelle s'inspire d'une règle incontestée qui est que la mer territoriale a une largeur de douze milles qui est mesurée non pas seulement à partir de la côte mais peut l'être aussi à partir d'une ligne de base tracée de façon à englober toutes îles territoriales situées dans une ceinture de mer territoriale large de douze milles. La ligne de base peut donc légalement être tracée de façon à comprendre toute une chaîne ou tout un groupe d'îles quand il n'existe pas entre les îles d'intervalle supérieur à douze milles; il s'agit alors de ce qu'on appelle "la méthode du saute-mouton" qui sert à établir la ligne de base de la mer territoriale. Comme nous l'avons déjà signalé, toute cette chaîne ou tout ce groupe d'îles est constitué d'îles, îlots ou rochers constamment émergés et correspondant par conséquent techniquement à des îles, qui ne sont jamais distants l'un de l'autre de plus de douze milles. Le seul intervalle supérieur à cette distance est celui qui sépare l'île située le plus à l'est (les îles Abu Ali) de la côte du territoire continental du Yémen.

474. La difficulté que suscite en l'espèce la méthode du saute-mouton est qu'elle anticipe la réponse à la question litigieuse précisément posée au Tribunal: auquel des deux Etats côtiers est-ce que ces îles appartiennent? Il existe une forte présomption en vertu de laquelle des îles situées à l'intérieur d'une zone de douze milles de la côte appartiennent à l'Etat côtier, à moins que la conclusion contraire ne soit parfaitement établie (comme, par exemple, dans le cas des îles anglo-normandes). Mais il n'existe pas de présomption analogue en dehors de la zone côtière, où la propriété des îles devient manifestement litigieuse. La propriété d'îles adjacentes crée incontestablement un droit à une mer territoriale correspondante, mais le fait d'étendre simplement la largeur de la mer territoriale au-delà de la zone côtière autorisée ne peut pas créer en soi le titre de souveraineté sur les îles ainsi englobées. Et quand bien même il existerait une présomption en faveur de la souveraineté de l'Etat côtier sur les îles situées dans la mer territoriale de douze milles d'une île située elle-même dans la zone côtière, ce ne serait là guère plus qu'une présomption susceptible d'être valablement combattue par la preuve de l'existence d'un titre supérieur.

--*-*

475. En conséquence, après avoir examiné toutes les considérations pertinentes d'ordre historique, factuel et juridique, le Tribunal estime à l'unanimité en la présente espèce que les îles, îlots, rochers et hauts-fonds découvrants qui constituent les îles Mohabbakah, lesquelles comprennent sans s'y limiter Sayal

Islet, Harbi Islet, Flat Islet et High Islet, relèvent de la souveraineté territoriale de l'Erythrée. Il est exact que High Islet est un îlot rocheux petit mais saillant situé à une distance à peine supérieure à douze milles (12,72 milles marins exactement) de la ligne de base de la mer territoriale. Mais ici, la théorie de l'unité joue peut-être un rôle modeste mais justifié, car les Mohabbakahs ont toujours été considérées comme ne constituant qu'un seul et même groupe, partageant le même destin juridique. High Islet se rattache sans aucun doute aussi à la côte africaine.

Les Haycocks

476. Il s'agit de trois petites îles situées le long d'une ligne orientée grossièrement du sud-ouest au nord-est. Il s'agit, quand on va du sud vers le nord, de South West Haycock, Middle Haycock et Northeast Haycock. L'île South West Haycock est située à six milles marins environ du point le plus proche de Suyul Hanish, bien qu'un très petit rocher appelé Three Foot Rock soit situé à peu près à mi-chemin entre ces deux îles.

477. Comme nous l'avons déjà dit plus haut, les Haycocks ont véritablement une histoire juridique particulière et c'est principalement pour cela qu'il faut ici les étudier à part. Cet historique juridique est étroitement lié à l'histoire des phares de la mer Rouge. Mais l'on peut commencer, quand on rappelle les points marquants de cet historique juridique, par évoquer les *firmans* du sultan ottoman datant de 1841, 1866 et 1873 (voir le paragraphe 97 ci-dessus) en vertu desquels la côte africaine de la mer Rouge ainsi que les îles situées au large de ladite côte ont été placées sous la juridiction et l'administration de l'Egypte, même si, bien entendu, cette région du monde relevait alors intégralement de la souveraineté de l'Empire ottoman. Il ne fait guère de doute, semble-t-il, que cette administration de la côte africaine s'étendait alors aux Mohabbakahs et aux Haycocks. A l'époque, la mer territoriale avait une largeur limitée à trois milles, et le régime des eaux territoriales était encore très incertain quant à sa nature et à sa portée. On avait néanmoins le sentiment, qui s'inspirait de considérations de sécurité comme de considérations de commodité, que les îles situées au large d'une certaine côte relevaient, en l'absence d'un titre parfaitement établi en sens contraire, de la juridiction de l'autorité côtière la plus proche. Comme nous l'avons dit, c'est ce qu'on appelait parfois la "doctrine du portique".

478. On franchit une nouvelle étape de cet historique juridique à la fin du 19e siècle, quand le Gouvernement britannique s'est intéressé à la possibilité de créer pour les marines occidentales une nouvelle voie de navigation à travers la mer Rouge, qu'il fallait éclairer pour pouvoir l'exploiter la nuit. On a alors cherché quelles îles se prêtaient à l'installation d'un phare (voir les paragraphes 203 et 204 ci-dessus), parmi lesquelles South West Haycock, qui finalement fut la candidate retenue. On a donc cherché aussi de quelle "juridiction" l'île allait relever, et le Board of Trade britannique a admis pour sa part que South West Haycock

relevait de la juridiction italienne et ne relevait en tout cas probablement pas de la juridiction ottomane.

479. En 1930, au moment où les Italiens construisaient donc un phare sur South West Haycock, il y eu un échange instructif de correspondance entre le Gouvernement italien et le Gouvernement britannique. Une note de service interne du Foreign Office montre que l'on estimait alors que "la création de la colonie italienne d'Erythrée n'autorise par conséquent guère à contester l'idée que les îles situées au large de la côte érythréenne doivent être considérées comme normalement annexées à ladite colonie".[33] C'était là la réaction officielle à une lettre du 11 avril dans laquelle le Gouvernement royal italien revendiquait South West Haycock, notamment parce que l'île était située dans le "voisinage immédiat" de la côte érythréenne de la mer Rouge.

480. L'Erythrée utilise ces arguments à l'appui de la revendication qu'elle formule sur les Haycocks mais elle revendique ces dernières à la suite d'une succession dont elle aurait bénéficié de la part de la colonie italienne d'Erythrée et qui, à travers la fédération ultérieure de l'Ethiopie et de l'Erythrée, lui aurait été transmise lors de l'indépendance de l'Erythrée en 1993. Cette théorie de la succession soulève de difficiles problèmes juridiques, qui tiennent surtout aux dispositions de l'armistice de 1943 avec l'Italie et du traité de paix de 1947, dispositions par lesquelles l'Italie s'est défaite de ses territoires coloniaux et les a mis à la disposition des Alliés et, à défaut d'accord entre les Alliés, à la disposition des Nations Unies, ce qui correspond évidemment au sort qu'a finalement connu l'Erythrée. Il n'empêche que les arguments géographiques de la proximité par rapport à la côte érythréenne demeurent convaincants et s'accordent bien avec l'opinion générale qui est que les îles situées au large d'une côte appartiennent à l'Etat côtier sauf s'il est possible de démontrer l'existence d'un autre titre qui serait supérieur. Or, le Yémen n'a pas en l'espèce pu démontrer qu'il possédait un titre supérieur.

481. La prétention érythréenne sur les Haycocks est également étayée jusqu'à un certain point par les éléments fournis par les deux Parties en vue de l'audience supplémentaire concernant les incidences des accords pétroliers. Aucun des accords signés par le Yémen ne porte sur un secteur qui s'étend aussi loin vers le sud-ouest que les Haycocks; le secteur visé dans l'accord signé en 1974 avec les compagnies Tomen et Santa Fe englobe, semble-t-il, le groupe des Hanish mais sa limite se situe juste avant les Haycocks. En revanche, les accords conclus par le Gouvernement érythréen et Shell, Amoco et BP, au sujet desquels la documentation fournie est complète, visent des secteurs qui couvrent totalement les Haycocks et, bien entendu, les Mohabbakahs. Ces accords n'ont suscité aucune protestation de la part du Yémen, alors que celui-ci a protesté quand un

[33] Note de service du Foreign Office portant la date du 10 juin 1930, établie par M. Orchard.

accord conclu avec Shell lui a paru empiéter sur l'espace qu'il revendique dans la région des îles septentrionales.

482. En conséquence, après avoir examiné toutes les considérations pertinentes d'ordre historique, factuel et juridique, le Tribunal estime à l'unanimité en la présente espèce que les îles, îlots, rochers et hauts-fonds découvrants qui constituent les îles Haycock, lesquelles comprennent notamment sans s'y limiter North East Haycock, Middle Haycock et South West Haycock, relèvent de la souveraineté territoriale de l'Erythrée. Il s'ensuit que la même décision s'applique, mis à part les autres motifs valables indiqués ci-dessus, à High Islet, la seule île du sous-groupe des Mohabbakah qui soit située à l'extérieur de la mer territoriale de l'Erythrée.

483. Se pose encore la question de savoir si les South West Rocks doivent aux fins qui nous occupent être considérés comme ayant le même statut que les Haycocks. Il ne fait pas de doute que les South West Rocks portent ce nom parce que ces rochers sont situés au sud-ouest de la Grande Hanish et qu'il ne se trouve aucune autre formation entre eux et ladite île. D'après certains éléments de preuve, les South West Rocks ont été à diverses époques considérés comme la limite orientale du domaine soumis à la juridiction de la côte africaine. Si la documentation du Foreign Office britannique que les deux Parties invoquent témoigne de vues divergentes à ce sujet (qualifiant une fois au moins de "douteuse" la juridiction de l'Italie sur les South West Rocks), les Parties admettent l'une et l'autre qu'au début des années 1890, l'Italie, quand la Grande-Bretagne l'a directement interrogée sur les sites à retenir éventuellement pour l'installation de phares, a réagi en affirmant exercer sa juridiction sur la totalité des sites envisagés, y compris les South West Rocks. En outre, l'Italie ne s'est pas opposée à la suggestion formulée ensuite par les Britanniques qui souhaitaient que la Sublime Porte fût informée de la position de l'Italie. Cette même façon de voir s'est manifestée à nouveau en 1914, avec la proposition initiale de la Grande-Bretagne tendant à opérer après la guerre une distribution des territoires ottomans dont la Turquie se retirait, distribution qui aurait placé tout ce qui se trouvait à l'est des South West Rocks sous la souveraineté des "chefs indépendants occupant le territoire continental de la péninsule arabique".

484. Compte tenu des indications ci-dessus, il semble raisonnable d'appliquer aux South West Rocks le traitement déjà retenu pour les autres îles administrées à partir de la côte africaine: les Mohabbakahs et les Haycocks. Le Tribunal décide donc à l'unanimité que les South West Rocks relèvent de la souveraineté territoriale de l'Erythrée.

Le groupe Zuqar-Hanish

485. Il reste à déterminer qui exerce la souveraineté sur Zuqar et sur les îles Hanish ainsi que sur leurs îlots et rochers satellites, dont l'île Abu Ali, située à l'est de

l'extrémité septentrionale de Zuqar, laquelle fut longtemps un site largement retenu pour l'installation d'un phare.

486. Ce groupe d'îles ne s'est pas prêté facilement à une décision, l'un des motifs expliquant la difficulté étant que, comme ces îles sont situées dans la partie centrale de la mer Rouge, le facteur du rattachement oriente relativement moins fermement la solution. Une ligne médiane tracée entre les côtes passerait en fait à travers l'île de la Grande Hanish, dont une partie légèrement plus étendue se trouverait du côté érythréen. Zuqar serait nettement du côté yéménite de cette ligne médiane.

487. Les Parties ont présenté au Tribunal de nombreux aspects de l'histoire juridique locale qui sont censés orienter la décision dans un sens ou dans l'autre. Tous ces aspects ont été étudiés en détail dans les chapitres précédents. Il ressort toutefois d'ores et déjà de cet examen qu'il ne faut pas compter tirer de cette histoire juridique ancienne une réponse claire et absolue. L'idée chère au Yémen de la réversion en sa faveur d'un titre très ancien a déjà été étudiée dans le présent chapitre et le Tribunal a constaté qu'elle n'apportait guère de solution en ce qui concerne ces îles. Il y a peut-être plus d'enseignements valables à tirer des éléments donnant à penser que, lorsque les Ottomans ont décidé à la fin du 19e siècle d'accorder à l'Egypte l'exercice de la juridiction sur la côte africaine, la décision s'étendait peut-être aux îles se rattachant à ladite côte et, d'après certaines sources dignes de respect, le rattachement à la côte ne s'appliquait pas à ce groupe central d'îles, car Zuqar et Hanish étaient toutes deux considérées comme relevant encore de la juridiction du *vilayet* du Yémen. Si telle était bien la situation, encore qu'il soit difficile de penser qu'elle est restée inchangée jusqu'à aujourd'hui malgré l'article 16 du traité de Lausanne, il s'agirait là d'un précédent historique impressionnant. Ce que Hertslet pensait de la façon dont il fallait répartir l'exercice de la juridiction sur les îles de la mer Rouge a manifestement impressionné le Foreign Office britannique, mais il s'agit de ce que Hertslet pensait, semble-t-il, au sujet de ce qu'il fallait faire des îles de la mer Rouge, ce n'était pas là des preuves de l'existence de véritables titres.

488. On trouve quelques échos de l'idée que le Yémen détient un titre au début du 20e siècle, par exemple, dans le compte rendu des négociations entre l'imam et un envoyé britannique, le colonel Reilly, entretiens au cours desquels l'imam aurait évoqué la nécessité de se voir restituer certaines îles yéménites. Mais il ne fait pas de doute que les doléances de l'imam portaient alors principalement sur l'île Kamaran et les îlots qui l'entourent, île qui était alors occupée par les Britanniques. L'imam revendiquait aussi ce qu'une note de service du Foreign Office appelle alors des "îles non précisées". Les fonctionnaires britanniques étaient tout à fait disposés quant à eux à imaginer que Zuqar et Hanish figuraient peut-être au nombre de ces îles, puisque Zuqar et Hanish avaient été temporairement occupées par les Britanniques en 1915. Mais il est finalement

difficile d'accorder une importance déterminante à une revendication dont l'objet ne peut pas être défini de façon fiable.

489. L'Erythrée cherche à s'adjuger un titre historique qu'elle tiendrait à la suite de l'Ethiopie par voie de succession de l'Italie. Il est incontestable que l'Italie nourrissait de sérieuses ambitions au sujet de ces îles centrales pendant les années 30 et qu'elle y a établi une présence. Mais comme on l'a vu plus haut, cette attitude était constamment neutralisée par les assurances données au Gouvernement britannique qui garantissaient que l'Italie acceptait sans réserve que le statut juridique des îles fût toujours régi par l'article 16 du traité de Lausanne. Et il est en outre difficile d'hériter un titre transmis par l'Italie étant donné la teneur des dispositions du traité de paix de 1947 avec l'Italie.

490. Et il faut aussi considérer les cartes. Ces îles sont assez grandes pour trouver place très souvent – mais certes pas toujours – sur des cartes de la région même quand celles-ci sont établies à une échelle relativement petite. On peut sans doute dire que, grâce aux efforts des conseils des Parties et surtout ceux du Yémen, le Tribunal aura vu plus de cartes de toutes les périodes et de toutes les sources imaginables qu'il n'en aura été rassemblé auparavant et ce fut certainement là un ensemble de cartes beaucoup plus important que celui qu'aucun des principaux acteurs de la scène de la mer Rouge aura jamais pu consulter à un moment quelconque. En fait, la difficulté ne tient pas tant à l'obligation d'interpréter une masse de cartes aussi diverses d'origines aussi variées qu'à l'absence du moindre élément de preuve permettant d'établir que les acteurs en question ont beaucoup prêté attention ou accordé beaucoup d'importance à l'une quelconque de ces cartes. Le Tribunal est d'avis que, d'un point de vue très général, la cause du Yémen est très légèrement favorisée par les cartes mises à jour qui, quand on les considère dans leur ensemble, permettent en effet de penser qu'une certaine renommée attribue ces îles au Yémen.

491. Sous ses autres aspects, l'histoire juridique de ce groupe d'îles central témoigne, comme c'est inévitable, du flux et reflux de l'intérêt manifesté par les deux Parties, ou de leur négligence, selon le cas, intérêt d'intensité variable et toujours nuancé par le caractère inhospitalier de ces îles, qu'atténue parfois une fonction de pure circonstance, comme l'installation de feux destinés à la navigation, ou l'importance stratégique qui leur est parfois imputée à tort ou à raison; car ces îles n'ont jamais été considérées comme "éloignées" au sens où l'a été le Groënland ou bien l'Ile de Palmas. En conséquence, de l'avis du Tribunal, même si certains de ces éléments historiques anciens sont importants et contribuent dans l'ensemble à faire comprendre les revendications des deux Parties, et sont même indispensables à cet égard, ni l'une ni l'autre des Parties n'a pu en se fondant sur ces seuls éléments historiques plaider sa cause de façon à engager fermement le Tribunal dans une voie plutôt que dans l'autre. C'est pourquoi le Tribunal a examiné ce qui s'est passé au cours de la dernière décennie précédant la conclusion du Compromis d'arbitrage pour y chercher un complément d'infor-

mations et d'éléments susceptible de parachever le tableau dressé par les deux Parties afin de pouvoir statuer solidement au sujet de ces deux îles et de leurs îlots et rochers satellites. Le Tribunal estime avoir d'autant plus raison d'adopter cette approche que les deux Parties ont prévu qu'il aurait besoin de ce complément d'information et ont fourni elles-mêmes des indications supplémentaires aux fins des audiences de juillet 1998. Il faut toutefois préciser que l'histoire juridique récente de ces îles montre qu'il existe à certains égards des différences entre Zuqar et Hanish. C'est pourquoi il y a lieu de les considérer séparément et le Tribunal va procéder de cette façon. Il serait erroné de tenir pour acquis que les îles doivent être attribuées ensemble à l'une des Parties ou à l'autre. A cet égard, le Tribunal rejette la thèse du Yémen qui plaide que toutes les îles du groupe doivent en principe, du point de vue de l'exercice de la souveraineté, partager un même destin.

492. En ce qui concerne l'histoire récente, le premier chapitre à étudier est peut-être celui des phares de la mer Rouge, lesquels occupent une place importante dans l'argumentation des deux Parties. Il ressort clairement de l'histoire de ces phares, qui est traitée en détail, comme nous l'avons déjà dit, au chapitre VI ci-dessus, que lorsqu'un gouvernement s'engageait à entretenir l'un de ces phares, la décision était généralement considérée comme neutre du point de vue de l'acquisition de la souveraineté territoriale, mais il faut aussi se rappeler qu'au moment où la Grande-Bretagne a voulu, en 1892, garantir la construction d'un phare en vue de la nouvelle voie de navigation occidentale qui était envisagée, le Gouvernement britannique a tenu à savoir quel gouvernement exerçait la "juridiction" sur le site retenu, c'est-à-dire South West Haycock, et l'Italie a non seulement revendiqué alors cette juridiction mais a fait reconnaître par le Gouvernement britannique cette prétention à la juridiction. Quatre phares ont été construits et semblent être entretenus par le Yémen dans la région que le Tribunal examine à présent (mais il convient d'ajouter qu'aucun personnel d'entretien n'est évidemment plus affecté aujourd'hui à ces phares). Les phares en question sont situés sur l'île Abu Ali, située à trois milles marins environ à l'ouest de l'extrémité septentrionale de Zuqar, sur l'extrémité sud-est de Zuqar elle-même; sur Low Island qui est située au large de l'extrémité nord-est de la Petite Hanish; et sur l'extrémité nord-est de la Grande Hanish. Ce dernier feu a été construit en juillet 1991 par le Yémen et il a été versé au dossier une photographie portant une inscription donnant à ce phare le nom de la République du Yémen. On ne peut guère nier que ces feux, dont l'installation devait manifestement avoir un caractère permanent, donnent la preuve convaincante d'une certaine présence du Yémen dans toutes ces îles.

493. De son côté, l'Erythrée attache beaucoup d'importance, dans l'histoire relativement récente, aux patrouilles navales éthiopiennes et aux livres de bord qui attestent des tournées de ces patrouilles, lesquelles concernaient en particulier les îles Zuqar et Hanish; et c'est là d'ailleurs un élément qui incite peut-être à considérer ces îles comme faisant partie d'un même groupe car les patrouilles

circulaient généralement dans les eaux en question sans se rendre dans telle île ou telle autre. Il ne fait pas de doute que ces patrouilles étaient organisées à grande échelle, le Tribunal a étudié la question en détail au chapitre VII ci-dessus, et l'on sait fort bien que les îles en question étaient utilisées par les rebelles, probablement surtout comme des étapes et des mouillages relativement sûrs pour des navires cherchant à ravitailler les armées rebelles combattant sur le territoire continental de l'Ethiopie, certains de ces navires venant peut-être du Yémen, dont on sait qu'il sympathisait avec les rebelles.

494. Au sujet de ces patrouilles navales, il faut relever un fait surprenant qui porte peut-être sur plusieurs années – bien que les éléments de preuve que l'Erythrée a pu effectivement fournir soient lacunaires en ce qui concerne plusieurs périodes – et qui tient à l'absence de protestation de la part du Yémen. Si l'Ethiopie a systématiquement effectué des patrouilles autour des îles en estimant ne pas sortir des limites de son propre territoire, alors cette absence de protestation de la part du Yémen est d'autant plus remarquable et appelle quelque explication que le Yémen n'a purement et simplement pas fournie. Certes, le Yémen a dû livrer sa propre guerre civile entre 1962 et 1970; et les patrouilles navales dont nous parlons ont dû avoir lieu pour une bonne part en haute mer plutôt que dans les eaux territoriales des îles. L'Erythrée dit que ces patrouilles navales éthiopiennes visaient aussi à assurer l'application de la réglementation relative à la pêche. L'argument paraît crédible car cela aurait fourni un motif légitime pour vérifier les documents des navires même en haute mer et les rebelles n'auraient sans doute pas limité leurs opérations de ravitaillement à des navires battant pavillon éthiopien.

495. Pourtant, les livres de bord qui relatent ces patrouilles navales rendent relativement peu souvent compte d'activités exercées sur les îles ni même à proximité des îles. Il est intéressant de prendre en considération dans ce contexte le communiqué de presse publié par l'ambassade du Yémen à Mogadiscio le 3 juillet 1973, dans lequel il est dit: "la République arabe du Yémen exerce toujours sa souveraineté sur ses îles de la mer Rouge, à l'exception des îles Gabal Abu Ali et Gabal Attair qui ont été cédées à l'Ethiopie par la Grande-Bretagne quand celle-ci a quitté Aden et renoncé à exercer le pouvoir dans notre Yémen du Sud." Cette conjecture était bien entendu erronée. Mais cela revient effectivement à dire que le Yémen à cette époque n'était présent dans aucune des deux îles citées et ne savait guère ce qui s'y passait. Mais c'était aussi l'époque où la presse arabe se faisait l'écho de rumeurs selon lesquelles l'Ethiopie aurait autorisé Israël à utiliser certaines îles de la mer Rouge. Le même communiqué de presse disait aussi que le Yémen avait, en la compagnie de journalistes et de correspondants de presse, procédé à une enquête sur "la Petite Hanish, la Grande Hanish, Zuqar, Alzubair' Alswabe', et plusieurs autres îles au large de la côte du Yémen." Il n'avait été constaté sur ces îles "aucune infiltration étrangère de quelque nature que ce soit." On peut penser qu'il s'agissait également de l'inspection opérée par le comité militaire de la Ligue arabe (voir le paragraphe

321 ci-dessus). Cette déclaration sonne vrai. Très probablement, à l'époque, sur ces îles, dont Zuqar et les deux îles Hanish, il n'y avait normalement personne et il ne s'exerçait aucune activité si ce n'est que de petits pêcheurs de la côte pratiquant leur métier de la façon artisanale habituelle faisaient parfois escale dans ces îles. Mais il convient de retenir que le Yémen a pu apparemment procéder à l'inspection ci-dessus avec le groupe dont il parle sans aucune répercussion de la part de l'Ethiopie.

496. Les informations fournies sur ces patrouilles navales sont souvent ambiguës et laissent beaucoup de choses inexpliquées des deux côtés. Au total, l'épisode semble au Tribunal pencher légèrement en faveur de la cause érythréenne. Mais là encore, le poids est très relatif. Rien n'oriente fermement la décision au profit de l'une ou de l'autre Partie. Et il est à nouveau extrêmement difficile de se fonder sur ce matériau et de lui accorder beaucoup de poids, s'agissant de revendications de territoire terrestre.

497. Les accords pétroliers signés par le Yémen et par l'Ethiopie (puis par l'Erythrée) à partir de 1972 apportent, ce qui est étonnant, très peu d'éléments de solution, car ces accords, dans la mesure où la superficie à prospecter s'étend au large, ne visaient pas vraiment du tout les îles mais intéressaient soit la limite extérieure du secteur de fonds marins alors exploitables soit la ligne médiane tracée entre les côtes, qui constituait la frontière provisoire effectivement envisagée aux fins de tels accords par la législation relative au plateau continental que le Yémen a adoptée en 1977. Comme en témoignent les questions posées aux Parties à la fin des audiences de juillet 1998, les accords considérés semblent laisser pratiquement de côté les îles; il ne faut pas s'en étonner, puisque le caractère volcanique propre à la géologie desdites îles signifie que celles-ci ne présentaient strictement aucun intérêt pour les compagnies pétrolières.

498. Comme il l'a déjà indiqué, le Tribunal n'accorde guère d'importance aux accords passés par les deux Parties avec Shell en vue d'études géologiques. La superficie de la zone du contrat traversait vraisemblablement les îles en question mais le Tribunal est à peu près certain que Shell était munie de l'autorisation des deux Parties et cherchait à se renseigner essentiellement dans son propre intérêt, afin de décider sur quels secteurs du plateau continental il y aurait lieu de faire porter des accords de production.

499. Quand on arrive aux accords d'exploitation proprement dits, qui prennent soit la forme d'accords de partage de la production intégrale de pétrole soit une forme moins généreuse, on constate que deux des accords conclus par le Yémen englobent totalement les îles Zuqar-Hanish (un accord passé avec Adair, qui n'a existé que très peu de temps et n'est jamais entré en application, et l'autre conclu avec les compagnies Tomen et Santa Fe), tandis que les accords conclus par l'Ethiopie (Ethiopie/Shell) s'abstiennent d'étendre le secteur visé jusqu'aux îles ou bien, s'agissant de l'accord de 1989 Ethiopie-IPC/Amoco, font passer la limite

du secteur par la Grande Hanish, et le tracé de la limite dépend apparemment de la précision avec laquelle est calculé le tracé de la ligne médiane entre les côtes.

500. Après un examen attentif des secteurs visés dans les accords pétroliers conclus par les deux Parties, les conclusions à tirer de ce matériau paraissent raisonnablement claires. L'Erythrée peut tirer argument, et elle le fait, de l'accord IPC/Amoco conclu avec l'Ethiopie qui porte sur un secteur dont la limite coupe l'île Hanish. Il existe de cet accord plusieurs versions. Dans certaines d'entre elles, quand on dessine la zone du contrat sur une carte, seule l'extrémité de Hanish est située du côté érythréen de la ligne; selon d'autres versions, la ligne semble attribuer la plus grande partie de l'île à l'Erythrée, n'en laissant qu'une fraction relativement petite au Yémen. Cela indique incontestablement que le secteur du contrat était simplement défini en des termes adaptés aux intérêts de la partie contractante, lesquels avaient un caractère essentiellement maritime, et que, conformément à la pratique normale, quand il n'existe pas de frontière maritime arrêtée d'un commun accord et définitivement établie, on a tracé à cette fin la ligne médiane entre les côtes sans tenir compte de l'effet éventuel des îles. C'est en effet la ligne médiane qui paraît avoir été convenue d'un commun accord et dessinée sur la carte illustrant le secteur du contrat sans qu'il soit du tout tenu compte des îles. Si l'Ethiopie avait pensé pouvoir se servir de l'accord à l'appui d'une revendication visant l'île Hanish, elle ne se serait certainement pas attribué exclusivement les deux tiers de l'île; elle aurait fait faire un détour à la ligne de délimitation pour que le secteur pétrolier englobe la totalité de l'île. Dans ces conditions, il paraît au Tribunal que les accords conclus par l'Ethiopie et l'Erythrée ont concrètement un caractère neutre du point de vue de la tâche actuellement confiée au Tribunal; et c'est d'ailleurs ce que l'Erythrée a plaidé. Cela ne veut pas dire que la revendication de l'Erythrée sur ces îles est infondée; mais cela veut dire que les accords pétroliers ne fournissent pas beaucoup d'arguments à l'appui de cette revendication, si ce n'est que l'accord IPC/Amoco tend à neutraliser l'argumentation du Yémen qui, de son côté, plaide que les accords pétroliers en tant que tels confirment la souveraineté.

501. Le Yémen a d'abord voulu donner à entendre sans être convaincant que la campagne de sondages sismiques opérée par la société Shell sur un vaste secteur s'étendant à peu près sur toute la largeur de la mer Rouge méridionale confirme en quelque sorte les revendications du Yémen sur les îles Zuqar et Hanish, puis, avec l'accord conclu en 1974-75 avec Tomen et Santa Fe, il a évoqué un contrat englobant apparemment à la fois Zuqar et Hanish ou bien la plus grande partie de la Grande Hanish. D'où, également, certaines activités menées par la compagnie pétrolière, dont la collecte d'une série d'échantillons sur Zuqar (voir le paragraphe 409 ci-dessus). Mais une fois encore, cela ne signifie pas que le Yémen a ainsi validé sa prétention à la souveraineté sur ces deux îles. Comme le Tribunal l'a déjà dit ci-dessus en conclusion, les accords pétroliers produits par les deux Parties ne fournissent pas la preuve de la souveraineté. Peut-être cela aide-t-il à situer ces accords pétroliers des années 70 dans la bonne perspective

que de se rappeler qu'en 1973, le Yémen a procédé à une inspection des îles avec des journalistes et des représentants du comité militaire de la Ligue arabe, et qu'il a été alors constaté que ces îles étaient toutes vides.

502. C'est par la suite que l'activité s'est intensifiée; il y eut notamment la construction en 1993 par la société pétrolière Total d'une piste d'atterrissage sur Hanish destinée aux voyages de tourisme des salariés de la société, cette construction étant une retombée de l'accord de concession conclu avec le Yémen. Mais le secteur visé dans ledit accord n'englobait ni Zuqar ni Hanish. Toutefois, ces vols de tourisme réguliers sont une preuve de l'autorité étatique et de son exercice. Ces vols n'ont apparemment pas non plus suscité de protestation d'aucune sorte de la part de l'Erythrée alors que, bien entendu, à cette date, la guerre civile avait pris fin et que l'Erythrée était un Etat indépendant.

503. Comme, de l'avis du Tribunal, aucune des deux Parties n'a fait valoir de façon convaincante sa prétention à la souveraineté sur ces îles en se fondant, dans le cas du Yémen, sur un titre très ancien ou, dans le cas de l'Erythrée, sur l'acquisition d'un titre par voie de succession, le Tribunal doit pour statuer sur la souveraineté se fonder très largement sur ce qui paraît être avoir été la situation à Zuqar et à Hanish ainsi que les îlots et rochers les entourant pendant la période correspondant à peu près à la dernière décennie précédant le Compromis d'arbitrage. Il ne faut guère s'attendre à trouver sur ces îles le moindre signe évocateur d'un semblant de colonisation, ou la manifestation continue de l'autorité étatique et de sa présence qui s'apparente à ce qu'on trouve parfois dans les affaires classiques même quand le territoire dont il s'agit est inhospitalier. Trop rares sont ceux qui voudraient se rendre dans ces îles volcaniques dépourvues d'eau sauf à être motivés par une raison particulière et très probablement limitée dans le temps. Il ressort pourtant clairement de la documentation évoquée plus haut dans la présente sentence que tant le Yémen que l'Ethiopie avaient formulé leur revendication sur les deux îles tout au moins à la fin des années 80 et avaient d'ailleurs, semble-t-il, négocié en secret au sujet de ces revendications; ces négociations, tout au moins d'après le rapport interne érythréen portant l'indication "ultrasecret" dont il a été question, avaient d'abord permis d'espérer une solution de compromis reposant sur le tracé d'une ligne médiane attribuant sans doute Zuqar et la Petite Hanish au Yémen et la Grande Hanish à l'Ethiopie. Mais ces négociations n'ont finalement pas abouti. Il faut donc à présent pour trouver la solution considérer les effectivités.

504. Le Yémen est parvenu à présenter au Tribunal une liste d'environ 48 événements ou incidents allégués concernant les "îles", imputés au Yémen, lesquels s'inscrivent dans la période allant du début de 1989 au milieu de 1991. Cette liste ne se limite pas au groupe d'îles central, car il y figure par exemple les décisions de la conférence de Londres de 1989 sur les phares, et la construction d'un phare sur al Tayr en juillet 1989. Il n'en est pas moins patent que Zuqar occupe une très large place sur cette liste. Et il est également patent que l'Erythrée de son côté n'a

présenté que très peu d'indications en sa faveur en ce qui concerne Zuqar. Pour le Tribunal, il ne fait pas de doute que l'île Zuqar relève de la souveraineté du Yémen.

505. En ce qui concerne Hanish, la situation n'est pas aussi claire. La revendication de l'Erythrée est bien fondée en tant que revendication et revêt manifestement beaucoup d'importance pour ce pays qui vient tout juste d'accéder à l'indépendance. Le refus opposé à une inspection aérienne des îles projetée par le Yémen et la revendication de souveraineté formulée en réponse par l'Ethiopie sur certaines d'entre elles sont à prendre en considération. Il en va de même pour l'arrestation de pêcheurs yéménites opérée sur la Grande Hanish par l'Ethiopie qui affirme, quand le Yémen proteste auprès du Conseil de sécurité, que ce secteur est sous juridiction éthiopienne.

506. L'Erythrée a accordé une place assez importante dans ses plaidoiries à un projet d'installation, sur Hanish, de balises devant aider la compagnie Amoco à procéder à ses sondages sismiques; il ne ressort pas clairement des éléments de preuve que ces balises aient effectivement été installées. Tout projet de ce genre visait plusieurs sites d'installation de balises, la Grande Hanish n'en était qu'un, et l'installation était prévue comme provisoire: les éléments de preuve fournis par l'Erythrée évoquent une installation de deux semaines, et prévoient que les balises doivent être ôtées quand les sondages sismiques prennent fin. En outre, les balises étaient, d'après ce projet, installées par la compagnie pétrolière, Amoco, le Gouvernement éthiopien ne jouant en l'occurrence qu'un rôle limité consistant à protéger le personnel de la compagnie et les balises provisoires elles-mêmes contre toute "présence dangereuse". En dernier lieu, il a été fourni la preuve qu'en 1980, l'Ethiopie a délivré à la Delft Geophysical Company un permis d'exploitation d'un émetteur radio autorisant cette entreprise à installer une station d'émission sur "la Grande Hanish, au voisinage du port d'Assab".

507. En ce qui concerne la présence et la manifestation de l'autorité étatique, le Yémen fournit des indications plus nombreuses. Mise à part l'installation du phare au nord de l'île, il y eut l'expédition Ardoukoba et la mise en place du campement qui a été réalisée sous l'égide du Gouvernement yéménite. Il y a aussi la piste d'atterrissage, et l'organisation de ce qui semble être un programme de vols réguliers fréquents, desserte consacrée sans doute principalement aux loisirs des salariés de la société Total; et il y a cette licence accordée en mai 1995 à une société yéménite (associée apparemment à certains ressortissants allemands dans le cadre d'une coentreprise) aux fins d'un projet touristique à exécuter sur la Grande Hanish (la plongée sportive étant apparemment susceptible d'attirer des touristes).

* - * - * - *

508. En conséquence, après avoir examiné toutes les considérations pertinentes d'ordre historique, factuel et juridique, le Tribunal estime en la présente espèce qu'au total, tout en éprouvant le plus grand respect pour la sincérité manifestée par les deux Parties et pour les arguments qu'elles font l'une et l'autre valoir, le poids des éléments de preuve présentés donne l'avantage au Yémen quand celui-ci affirme exercer dûment l'autorité étatique en ce qui concerne le groupe des îles Zuqar-Hanish. Le Tribunal se prononce d'autant plus fermement en faveur du Yémen qu'il constate d'après le dossier que lesdites îles relevaient de la juridiction de la côte arabique sous l'Empire ottoman; et que l'on s'est ensuite durablement attendu, comme le prouvent les documents du Foreign Office britannique versés au dossier par les Parties, à ce que lesdites îles soient finalement rendues au maître arabe. Le Tribunal décide par conséquent à l'unanimité que les îles, îlots, rochers et hauts-fonds découvrants du groupe des Zuqar-Hanish, lequel comprend sans toutefois s'y limiter Three Foot Rock, Parkin Rock, les Rocky Islets, Pin Rock, Suyul Hanish, Mid Islet, Double Peak Island, Round Island, North Round Island, Quoin Island (13°43'N, 42°48'E), Chor Rock, la Grande Hanish, Peaky Islet, Mushajirah, les Addar Ail Islets, l'île Haycock (13°47'N, 42°47'E; à ne pas confondre avec les îles Haycock situées au sud-ouest de la Grande Hanish), Low Island (13°52'N, 42°49'E) y compris les îlots et rochers sans nom situés à proximité au nord, à l'est et au sud, la Petite Hanish y compris les îlots et rochers sans nom situés à proximité au nord-est, Tongue Island et l'îlot sans nom situé à proximité au sud, Near Island et l'îlot sans nom situé à proximité au sud-est, Shark Island, Jabal Zuqar Island, High Island et les îles Abu Ali (y compris Quoin Island (14°05'N, 42°49'E) ainsi que Pile Island) relèvent de la souveraineté territoriale du Yémen.

Jabal al-Tayr et le groupe d'îles de Zubayr

509. Tant l'île isolée de Jabal al-Tayr que le groupe de Zubayr qui est composé d'îles et d'îlots demandent à être traités séparément car ces îles et îlots sont situés à une distance considérable des autres îles et sont aussi très éloignés l'un ou l'une de l'autre. Ces îles et îlots sont non seulement relativement isolés mais également situés, tant la première que le groupe, en pleine mer, et ne sont pas aussi proches d'aucune des côtes, même si la première île et le groupe sont légèrement plus proches des îles côtières du Yémen que de la côte et des îles côtières d'Erythrée. La première île comme le groupe se trouvent très à l'est d'une ligne médiane tracée entre les côtes. Ici encore, le Tribunal a dû apprécier les mérites relatifs des preuves apportées par les Parties, qui sont rares des deux côtés, en ce qui concerne l'exercice des fonctions étatiques et de la puissance publique.

510. L'importance qu'ont toujours revêtue la première île et le groupe tient à ce qu'il s'agit d'îles à phares (le feu de Zubayr était installé sur Centre Peak, l'îlot du groupe qui se trouve le plus au sud). L'histoire des phares de la mer Rouge (voir le chapitre VI ci-dessus) montre clairement que bien que les phares fussent très importants pour la navigation du 19e et du début du 20e siècles ou peut-être même

en raison de cette importance, il pouvait être demandé à un gouvernement de se charger de ces phares, voire de proposer de s'en charger sans nécessairement paraître revendiquer pour autant la souveraineté sur le site ni l'acquérir. Concrètement, la question qui se posait n'était pas celle de la propriété du site, elle était plutôt de savoir quel gouvernement était disposé à assumer cette responsabilité et parfois le coût du phare, sinon à titre permanent, du moins pour une saison, ou bien quel gouvernement pourrait être persuadé d'assumer cette responsabilité et peut-être cette dépense.

511. On se rappellera que Centre Peak, laquelle fait partie du groupe de Zubayr, était une île à laquelle l'Italie s'est beaucoup intéressée pendant les années 30, période de son expansion coloniale; le phare de Centre Peak fut abandonné par les Britanniques en 1932 mais rallumé par l'Italie l'année suivante. Les Britanniques ont alors demandé à l'Italie de leur garantir que l'île conservait le statut défini dans le traité de Lausanne (voir les paragraphes 216 à 218 ci-dessus) et ont obtenu ces assurances. Pendant un moment au moins, par conséquent, ce groupe d'îles a été soumis à la juridiction de l'autorité qui était au pouvoir sur la côte africaine.

512. Pourtant, au cours de la seconde guerre mondiale et ultérieurement, quand les Britanniques ont occupé l'Erythrée, il fut décidé que la Grande-Bretagne n'était nullement tenue d'entretenir le phare installé sur Centre Point ni d'ailleurs le feu de Haycock.

513. La conférence qui s'est tenue en 1989 à Londres sur les phares de la mer Rouge a marqué véritablement un tournant dans l'histoire des îles septentrionales de Jabal al-Tayr et du groupe de Zubayr. Cette conférence n'a guère ressemblé à celles qui l'avaient précédée. Ce devait être la dernière de la série, car elle avait principalement pour objet de mettre un terme aux anciens arrangements internationaux présidant à la gestion des phares et au partage des dépenses. Les arrangements définitifs adoptés au sujet de ces feux (qui revêtaient alors encore la plus haute importance pour la navigation) étaient par conséquent censés avoir un caractère permanent. Il ne fut pas envisagé d'organiser de nouvelle conférence.

514. On se rappelle que le Yémen fut invité à cette conférence en qualité d'observateur après avoir fait valoir auprès du Gouvernement britannique que les deux îles Abu Ali et Jabal al-Tayr sur lesquelles des phares étaient installés "sont situées dans la zone économique exclusive de la République arabe du Yémen", et que, de ce fait, le Yémen était disposé à se charger de la gestion et de l'entretien des feux. Il y avait aussi le fait que le Yémen avait d'ores et déjà installé de nouveaux phares sur ces deux sites. L'offre du Yémen fut acceptée avec reconnaissance par les participants à la conférence. Certains avaient espéré que l'Egypte se chargerait peut-être de la tâche, mais l'Egypte ne s'est pas montrée disposée à assumer cette responsabilité.

515. La question de la souveraineté ne figurait pas à l'ordre du jour de la conférence et n'a pas non plus été discutée. Quand il avait demandé à être invité, le Yémen avait fort sagement évité de soulever la question. En outre, on entendit évoquer à la conférence, comme d'habitude, la formule du traité de Lausanne sur le caractère indéterminé de ladite souveraineté.

516. Il n'empêche que la décision prise lors de la conférence d'accepter l'offre du Yémen relative aux phares témoigne de la confiance éprouvée par les gouvernements participant à cette conférence qui comptaient manifestement que le Yémen maintiendrait sa présence sur les îles en question pendant un avenir prévisible à tout le moins. La renommée constitue elle aussi un élément important de la consolidation du titre.

517. Sous un autre aspect aussi, le Yémen est en mesure de conforter sensiblement sa cause en ce qui concerne les îles septentrionales dont il est question ici: le Yémen conforte sa cause grâce aux informations en grande partie nouvelles relatives à des accords pétroliers qui ont été fournies au Tribunal lors des audiences supplémentaires qui ont eu lieu à cette fin en juillet 1998. Ce sont deux accords qui semblent ainsi être pertinents pour les îles actuellement à l'étude.

518. Il s'agit tout d'abord de l'accord conclu par le Gouvernement yéménite avec la société Shell le 20 novembre 1973. La frontière occidentale du secteur faisant l'objet du contrat est tracée de façon que le secteur englobe le groupe de Zubayr. Jabal al-Tayr n'est pas englobée mais la limite passe à une distance telle qu'elle pourrait englober la mer territoriale de cette île, en fonction de la largeur qui serait attribuée à cette mer territoriale aux fins d'une délimitation maritime.

519. Le second accord à prendre en compte est l'accord de partage de production de pétrole conclu avec la société Hunt et ratifié le 10 mars 1985. Dans cet accord, la frontière occidentale du secteur visé dans le contrat englobe à nouveau dans ledit secteur le groupe de Zubayr, mais elle semble aussi d'après la carte jointe frôler l'île Jabal al-Tayr et, bien entendu, elle englobe manifestement dans le secteur visé une partie de la mer territoriale de ladite île.

520. Ces accords n'ont pas suscité de protestation de la part de l'Ethiopie (mais il ne faut pas oublier que l'accord conclu avec la société Hunt l'a été à un moment où la guerre civile faisait encore rage en Ethiopie).

521. Ni l'Ethiopie ni l'Erythrée n'ont conclu d'accord pétrolier englobant ces îles. L'Erythrée, toutefois, a bien conclu des accords en 1995 et 1997 avec la société Anadarko Oil Company, dans lesquels le secteur visé s'étendait en direction de ces îles et vers ce qui paraît être une ligne médiane approximative tracée entre

deux côtes. Le Yémen a protesté le 4 janvier 1996* contre le tracé de cette ligne parce qu'il constituait une violation "flagrante" des eaux territoriales des deux groupes d'îles et des droits économiques du Yémen lui-même "dans la région". L'incident est évidemment un peu postérieur à la signature de l'Accord sur les principes et même du Compromis d'arbitrage préludant à la présente espèce.

522. L'histoire juridique de ces îles septentrionales et isolées est ambivalente et diversifiée. On a vu qu'à une date aussi tardive que 1989, on pensait qu'en ce qui concernait la souveraineté, leur statut était toujours indéterminé comme le prescrivait à leur endroit le traité de Lausanne, l'indétermination devant régner jusqu'au moment où ce statut serait modifié dans les conditions légales. Néanmoins, en 1995, on ne pensait pas qu'il serait possible de décider d'un commun accord de soumettre à notre Tribunal un différend qui s'élèverait au sujet de la revendication formulée par le Yémen sur lesdites îles. A un certain moment, l'Erythrée a même proposé une formule de compromis qui ne faisait pas mention desdites îles.

523. Pour le Tribunal, cette question particulière n'a pas été facile à résoudre. Des deux côtés, il existe fort peu d'éléments qui témoignent d'activités réelles ou durables sur ces îles et aux alentours. Mais vu leur isolement et leur nature peu hospitalière, il sera probablement possible de se contenter d'un petit nombre d'éléments.

524. En conséquence, après avoir examiné toutes les considérations pertinentes d'ordre historique, factuel et juridique, le Tribunal estime à l'unanimité en la présente espèce, en se fondant sur les indications qui précèdent, que les preuves fournies incitent à conclure que l'île de Jabal al-Tayr et les îles, îlots, rochers et hauts-fonds découvrants constituant le groupe de Zubayr, lequel comprend sans s'y limiter Quoin Island (15°12'N, 42°03'E), Haycock Island (15°10'N, 42°07'E; à ne pas confondre avec les îles Haycock situées au sud-ouest de la Grande Hanish), Rugged Island, Table Peak Island, Saddle Island et l'îlot sans nom situé à proximité au nord-ouest, Low Island (15°06'N, 42°06'E) et le rocher sans nom situé à proximité à l'est, Middle Reef, Saba Island, Connected Island, les East Rocks, Shoe Rock, l'île de Jabal Zubayr et Centre Peak Island relèvent de la souveraineté territoriale du Yémen.

Le régime de pêche traditionnel

525. En rendant la présente sentence sur la souveraineté, le Tribunal savait fort bien que les idées occidentales de souveraineté territoriale sont étrangères à des populations élevées dans la tradition islamique et habituées à des notions de territoire très différentes de celles qui sont reconnues dans le droit international

* *Note de l'éditeur: cette référence a été corrigée de la version anglaise originale.*

contemporain. En outre, il est indispensable de tenir compte des traditions juridiques propres à la région pour rendre une sentence qui, selon les termes mêmes de la déclaration commune signée par les Parties le 21 mai 1996, va "favoriser le rétablissement et le développement d'une coopération fiable et durable entre les deux pays."

526. En concluant que les Parties ont chacune souveraineté sur diverses îles, le Tribunal souligne à leur intention qu'une telle souveraineté n'exclut pas, mais implique plutôt, la perpétuation du régime de pêche traditionnel dans la région. Ce régime existant s'est appliqué, comme l'attestent amplement les éléments de preuve présentés au Tribunal autour des îles Hanish et Zuqar et des îles Jebal al-Tayr et du groupe de Zubayr. Dans l'exercice de sa souveraineté sur ces îles, le Yémen veillera à ce que le régime de pêche traditionnel assurant libre accès et libre jouissance aux pêcheurs du Yémen comme de l'Erythrée soit préservé afin de protéger l'existence et les moyens d'existence de cette catégorie pauvre et industrieuse de la population.

--*

CHAPITRE XI - Dispositif

527. En conséquence, **LE TRIBUNAL,**

vu les considérations et les motifs ci-dessus,

DECIDE A L'UNANIMITE EN LA PRESENTE INSTANCE QUE

i. les îles, îlots, rochers et hauts-fonds découvrants constituant les îles Mohabbakah, qui comprennent sans s'y limiter Sayal Islet, Harbi Islet, Flat Islet et High Islet, relèvent de la souveraineté territoriale de l'Erythrée;

ii. les îles, îlots, rochers et hauts-fonds découvrants constituant les îles Haycock, qui comprennent sans s'y limiter North East Haycock, Middle Haycock et South West Haycock, relèvent de la souveraineté territoriale de l'Erythrée;

iii. les South West Rocks relèvent de la souveraineté territoriale de l'Erythrée;

iv. les îles, îlots, rochers et hauts-fonds découvrants du groupe Zuqar-Hanish, qui comprend sans s'y limiter Three Foot Rock, Parkin Rock, les Rocky Islets, Pin Rock, Suyul Hanish, Mid Islet, Double Peak Island, Round Island, North Round Island, Quoin Island (13°43'N, 42°48'E), Chor Rock, la Grande Hanish, Peaky Islet, Mushajirah, les Addar Ail Islets, l'île Haycock (13°47'N, 42°47'E; à ne pas confondre avec les îles Haycock situées au sud-ouest de la Grande Hanish), Low Island (13°52'N, 42°49'E) y compris les îlots et rochers sans nom situés à proximité au nord, à l'est et au sud, la Petite Hanish y compris les îlots et rochers sans nom situés à proximité au nord-est, Tongue Island et l'îlot sans nom situé à proximité au sud, Near Island et l'îlot sans nom situé à proximité au sud-est, Shark Island, Jabal Zuqar Island, High Island et les îles Abu Ali (y compris Quoin Island (14°05'N, 42°49'E) ainsi que Pile Island) relèvent de la souveraineté territoriale du Yémen.

v. l'île de Jabal al-Tayr et les îles, îlots, rochers et hauts-fonds découvrants constituant le groupe de Zubayr, qui comprend sans s'y limiter Quoin Island (15°12'N, 42°03'E), Haycock Island (15°10'N, 42°07'E; à ne pas confondre avec les îles Haycock situées au sud-ouest de la Grande Hanish), Rugged Island, Table Peak Island, Saddle Island et l'îlot sans nom situé à proximité au nord-ouest, Low Island (15°06'N, 42°06'E) et le rocher sans nom situé à proximité à l'est, Middle Reef, Saba Island, Connected Island, les East Rocks, Shoe Rock, Jabal Zubayr Island et Centre Peak Island relèvent de la souveraineté territoriale du Yémen; et

vi. la souveraineté qui a été jugée revenir au Yémen implique la perpétuation du régime de pêche traditionnel dans la région, y compris libre accès et libre jouissance pour les pêcheurs de l'Erythrée comme du Yémen.

528. En outre, attendu qu'il est prévu à l'article 12, paragraphe 1b) du Compromis d'arbitrage, que les sentences du Tribunal précisent le délai de leur exécution, le Tribunal prescrit que la présente sentence doit être exécutée dans les quatre-vingt-dix jours à compter de la date indiquée ci-après.

* - * - * - *

Fait à Londres le 9 octobre 1998

Le président du Tribunal

(Signé) le professeur sir Robert Y. Jennings

Le Greffier

(Signé) P.J.H. Jonkman

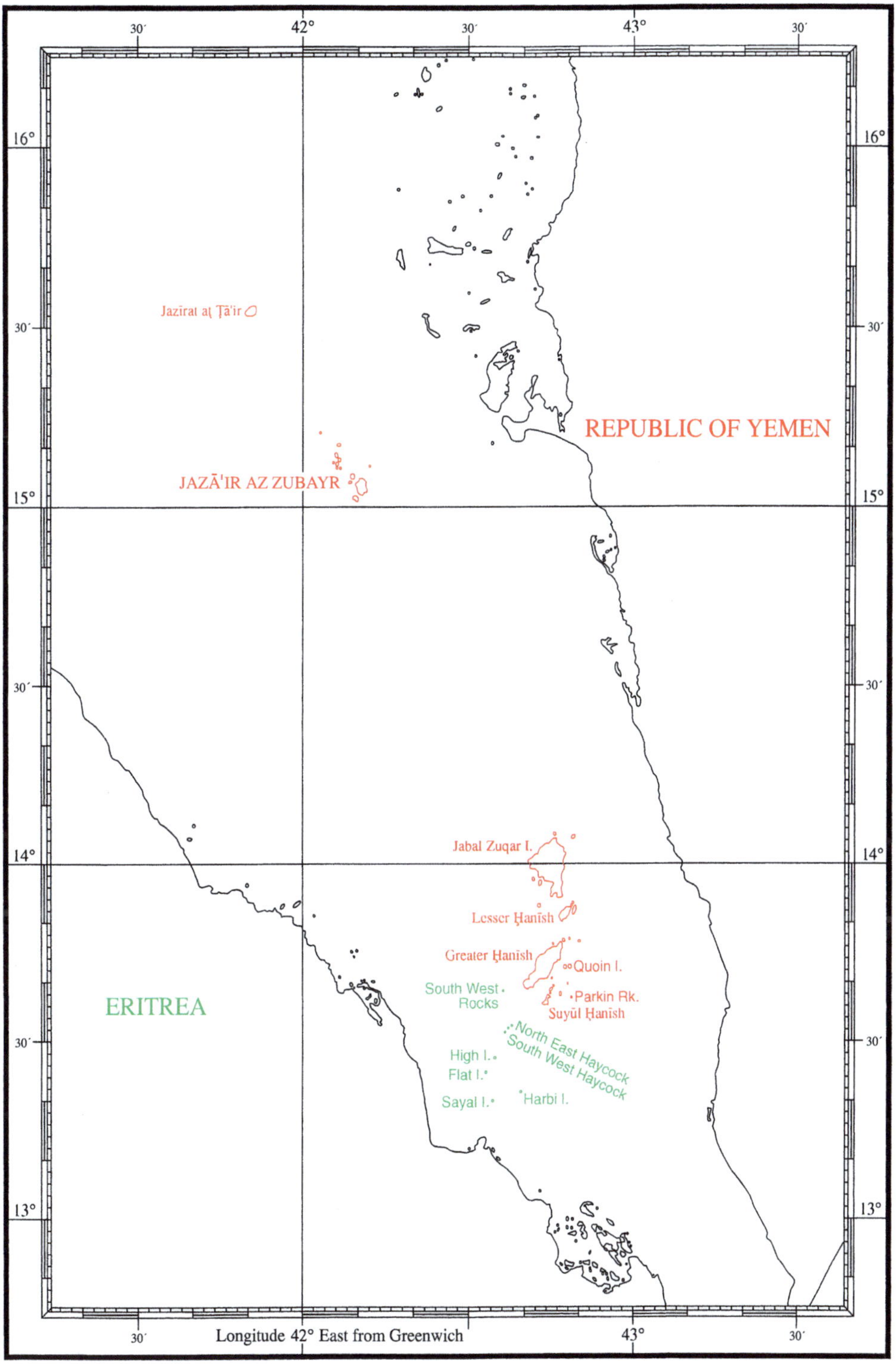

30′
42°
30′
43°
30′
16°
30′
15°
14°
13°
Jazirat at Ṭā'ir
REPUBLIC OF YEMEN
JAZĀ'IR AZ ZUBAYR
Jabal Zuqar I.
Lesser Ḥanīsh
Greater Ḥanīsh
Quoin I.
South West Rocks
Parkin Rk.
Suyūl Ḥanīsh
ERITREA
North East Haycock
South West Haycock
High I.
Flat I.
Sayal I.
Harbi I.
Longitude 42° East from Greenwich

ARBITRAGE FONDÉ SUR UN COMPROMIS D'ARBITRAGE EN DATE DU 3 OCTOBRE 1996

E N T R E :

LE GOUVERNEMENT DE L'ETAT D'ERYTHRÉE

-et-

LE GOUVERNEMENT DE LA RÉPUBLIQUE DU YÉMEN

SENTENCE RENDUE PAR LE TRIBUNAL ARBITRAL DANS LA DEUXIÈME ÉTAPE DE LA PROCÉDURE (DÉLIMITATION MARITIME)

Le Tribunal arbitral:

M. le Professeur Sir Robert Y. Jennings, Président
M. le Juge Stephen M. Schwebel
M. Ahmed Sadek El-Kosheri
M. Keith Highet
Mme le Juge Rosalyn Higgins

Représentants du Gouvernement de l'Etat d'Erythrée:

Son Excellence Haile Weldensae, agent
Son Excellence Haile Saleh Meky,
Mme le Professeur Lea Brilmayer et M. Jan Paulsson, co-agents
M. Robert Volterra et Mme Natalie Klein, conseils

Représentants du Gouvernement de la République du Yémen:

Son Excellence M. Abdulkarim Al-Eryani, agent
Son Excellence M. Abdullah Ahmad Ghanim, M. Hussein Al-Hubaishi,
M. Abdulwahid Al-Zandani et M. Rodman R. Bundy, co-agents
M. Ian Brownlie, Q.C., M. B. Donovan Picard, Mme Loretta Malintoppi et
M. Paul Luther, conseils

SENTENCE

TABLE DES MATIÈRES

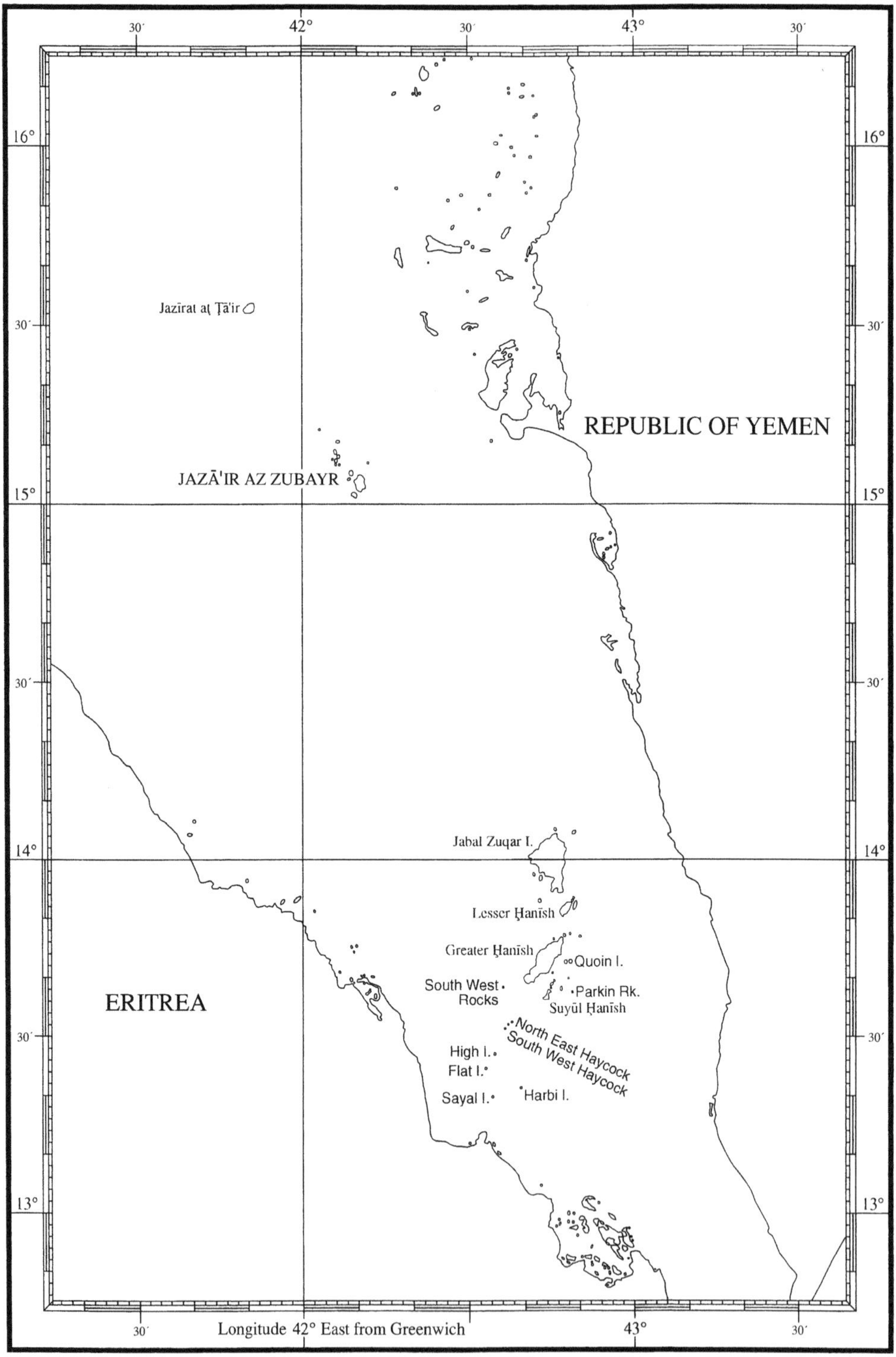

30′
42°
30′
43°
30′
16°
16°
Jazirat at Ṭā'ir
30′
30′
REPUBLIC OF YEMEN
JAZĀ'IR AZ ZUBAYR
15°
15°
30′
30′
Jabal Zuqar I.
14°
14°
Lesser Ḥanīsh
Greater Ḥanīsh
Quoin I.
South West Rocks
Parkin Rk.
Suyūl Ḥanīsh
ERITREA
North East Haycock
South West Haycock
30′
30′
High I.
Flat I.
Sayal I.
Harbi I.
13°
13°
30′
Longitude 42° East from Greenwich
43°
30′

INTRODUCTION – Procédure de l'étape de l'arbitrage relative à la délimitation maritime

1. La présente sentence concluant la seconde étape de l'arbitrage est rendue en vertu d'un compromis d'arbitrage en date du 3 octobre 1996 (le "Compromis d'arbitrage") entre le Gouvernement de l'Etat d'Erythrée ("l'Erythrée") et le Gouvernement de la République du Yémen ("le Yémen") (ci-après dénommés "les Parties").

2. Le Compromis d'arbitrage, dont le texte est reproduit à l'annexe 1, page *503*, a été précédé d'un "Accord sur les principes", signé à Paris le 21 mai 1996 par l'Erythrée et le Yémen en présence de représentants des Gouvernements de la République française, de la République fédérale démocratique d'Ethiopie et de la République arabe d'Egypte. Aux termes de l'Accord sur les principes, le Tribunal devait statuer sur des questions de souveraineté territoriale, et il a à cet effet rendu, à l'issue de la première étape, une sentence attribuant la souveraineté sur les îles de la mer Rouge en litige soit à l'Erythrée soit au Yémen (voir Sentence de la première étape, chapitre XI – Dispositif, paragraphes 527-528).

3. Dans une correspondance qui avait pour objet les pièces de procédure écrites pour la seconde étape, et contenait une demande de prorogation des délais prescrits, l'Erythrée a soulevé une question portant sur le régime de pêche traditionnel et la manière dont cet aspect pourrait être traité lors de la seconde étape de l'arbitrage. Le Président a donné la réponse suivante: "le Tribunal est d'avis qu'il appartient à l'Erythrée de décider elle-même du contenu de ses pièces écrites pour cette étape". Cet aspect est abordé au chapitre IV ci-après.

4. Conformément au calendrier établi dans le Compromis d'arbitrage, les Parties ont déposé chacune leur mémoire pour la seconde étape le 9 mars 1999 et leur contre-mémoire le 9 juin 1999. Le 25 mai 1999, M. Tjaco van den Hout, secrétaire général de la Cour permanente d'arbitrage, a succédé aux fonctions de greffier à M. Hans Jonkman, qui avait pris sa retraite. Conformément aux dispositions de l'article 7(2) du Compromis d'arbitrage, Mme Phyllis Pieper Hamilton, premier secrétaire de la Cour permanente d'arbitrage, a assuré les fonctions de secrétaire du Tribunal.

5. Avant les audiences de la seconde étape de l'arbitrage, et après avoir consulté les Parties, le Tribunal, ainsi qu'il était envisagé à l'article 7(4) du Compromis d'arbitrage, a souhaité prendre conseil pour les calculs relatifs aux frontières maritimes et l'établissement technique de la carte correspondante. Par ordonnance en date du 8 juillet 1999, en application de l'article 7(4), le Tribunal a informé les Parties qu'il désignait Mme Ieltje Anna Elema, ingénieur en géodésie, chef du Département de géodésie et des marées du Service hydrographique de la Marine royale des Pays-Bas, comme expert en géodésie.

6. L'article 2 du Compromis d'arbitrage dispose:

> 1. Il est demandé au Tribunal de se prononcer conformément au droit international, en deux étapes.
>
> 2. La première étape donne lieu à une sentence sur la souveraineté territoriale et la définition du champ du différend entre l'Erythrée et le Yémen. . . .
>
> 3. La seconde étape donne lieu à une sentence sur la délimitation des frontières maritimes. Le Tribunal statue en prenant en compte l'opinion qu'il se sera faite sur les questions de souveraineté territoriale, la Convention des Nations Unies sur le droit de la mer et tout autre élément pertinent.

7. Conformément au calendrier fixé dans le Compromis d'arbitrage pour les différentes étapes de l'arbitrage, et avec l'accord des Parties en ce qui concerne le lieu, les audiences pour la seconde étape de l'arbitrage se sont tenues du 5 au 16 juillet dans la Grande salle de Justice du Palais de la Paix à La Haye. Comme convenu entre les Parties, le Yémen s'est exprimé en premier.

8. L'excellente qualité des exposés oraux de l'une et l'autre Parties a grandement facilité la tâche du Tribunal.

9. Au cours des plaidoiries, et conformément aux dispositions de l'article 8(3) du Compromis d'arbitrage, qui autorisaient le Tribunal à demander aux Parties leur avis écrit sur toute question nécessaire pour permettre au Tribunal d'élucider un aspect de l'affaire, les conseils ont été priés de répondre à diverses questions. Le 13 août 1999, les Parties ont soumis leurs réponses écrites aux questions qui leur avaient été posées par le Tribunal les 13 et 16 juillet. Les questions du Tribunal et les réponses fournies par les Parties sont reproduites à l'annexe 2, page *513*.

CHAPITRE PREMIER – L'argumentation des Parties

Introduction

10. Le présent chapitre a pour objet de récapituler les principaux arguments des Parties tels que les comprend le Tribunal. Pour l'exposé des motifs ayant conduit le Tribunal à accepter, rejeter ou modifier ces arguments, il pourra être nécessaire de se reporter aux chapitres suivants. Dans ce chapitre décrivant les arguments des Parties, il conviendra en général de se conformer à l'ordre agréé par elles aux fins de leurs exposés oraux et de considérer en premier les arguments du Yémen avant d'examiner ceux de l'Erythrée.

11. Il y a lieu de noter d'emblée que les Parties ont toutes deux revendiqué une ligne de délimitation internationale de type médiane, encore que les lignes médianes revendiquées respectivement par l'une et par l'autre présentent des tracés fort différents et ne coïncident pas. Ces lignes suivent, néanmoins, des tracés similaires dans leur section la plus méridionale, correspondant à la partie resserrée de la mer. La ligne médiane de l'Erythrée est équidistante des côtes continentales, mais sa ligne médiane historique prend en compte les îles érythréennes (tout en faisant abstraction des îles yéménites situées au milieu de la mer); la ligne du Yémen est équidistante de la côte de l'Erythrée (y compris certains points sélectionnés sur les îles Dahlak) d'une part et des côtes de toutes les îles du Yémen d'autre part. Le Yémen avait indiqué les coordonnées, établies sur la base du Système géodésique mondial de 1984 (WGS 84), des points d'inflexion de la ligne tracée par lui; l'Erythrée ne l'avait pas fait, mais a cependant fourni les coordonnées des points de base en réponse à une question du Tribunal. Les lignes revendiquées rivales sont reproduites sur certaines des cartes regroupées à la fin du présent volume (cartes 3 et 7 de l'Erythrée et carte 12.1 du Yémen).

La ligne de délimitation proposée par le Yémen

12. La ligne revendiquée par le Yémen traversait successivement trois secteurs délimités par les parallèles suivants: 16° N, 14° 25'N et 13°20'N. On distinguait donc (i) un secteur nord où la ligne passait entre Jabal al-Tayr et le groupe de Jabal al-Zubayr du côté yéménite et les îles Dahlak du côté érythréen; (ii) un secteur central où elle s'établissait entre le groupe yéménite Zuqar-Hanish d'une part et la côte continentale de l'Erythrée faisant face à ces îles, les Mohabbakah, les Haycocks et les South West Rocks d'autre part; et (iii) un secteur sud où elle était commandée par les côtes continentales respectives du Yémen et de l'Erythrée au sud du groupe Zuqar-Hanish. Ces secteurs étaient définis en fonction de la latitude des points de base déterminant le tracé de la ligne du Yémen. C'est ainsi que 14°25'N correspondait à la latitude à partir de laquelle ces points de base cessaient de se situer sur l'îlot Centre Peak, dans le groupe de Zubayr, pour se situer sur la côte de Zuqar.

13. L'argumentation du Yémen prenait pour point de départ l'idée généralement admise, et entérinée par la Cour internationale de Justice dans les affaires du *Plateau continental de la mer du Nord*,[1] selon laquelle une ligne médiane produit en principe un résultat équitable lorsqu'elle est tracée entre des côtes se faisant face. Par conséquent, soutenait le Yémen, une importante tâche préliminaire du Tribunal consistait à décider quelles étaient les côtes qui serviraient de lignes de base.

14. Dans le secteur nord, la ligne proposée par le Yémen supposait qu'il fût reconnu que les Dahlak, groupe compact composé de quelque 350 îles et îlots, dont les plus vastes ont une forte population, faisaient partie de la côte continentale de l'Erythrée et que les eaux comprises entre ces îles étaient des eaux intérieures. Dès lors, les îlots les plus à l'est de ce groupe pouvaient servir de points de base pour construire la ligne médiane. Le Yémen utilisait la laisse de pleine mer comme ligne de base sur ces îles.

15. Le Yémen a proposé que, du côté est, les points de base soient choisis le long de la laisse de basse mer sur la côte orientale de l'île isolée Jabal al-Tayr, au milieu de la mer, et sur les côtes orientales du groupe de Jabal al-Zubayr, également au milieu de la mer. Selon le Yémen, ces îles devaient être utilisées comme points de base parce qu'elles étaient au moins aussi importantes que les toutes petites îles inhabitées situées à la lisière du groupe des Dahlak. De la sorte, il y aurait, selon le Yémen, "équilibre" dans le choix des points de base insulaires sur les côtes ouest et est, puisque dans ce secteur nord "chaque Partie possède des îles de taille comparable, d'où des façades côtières similaires situées à des distances similaires des territoires continentaux respectifs".

16. Dans le secteur central, la ligne revendiquée par le Yémen traversait ensuite la partie resserrée des eaux comprise entre le groupe des îles Hanish et la côte continentale de l'Erythrée. (Ce tronçon de la ligne de délimitation qualifié de "central" par le Yémen, a été parfois appelé secteur "sud" par l'Erythrée.) La ligne du Yémen était une ligne d'équidistance entre la laisse de pleine mer sur la côte continentale de l'Erythrée et la laisse de basse mer sur les côtes les plus occidentales du groupe yéménite des Hanish.

17. Le Yémen suggéra qu'il n'y avait pas lieu de retenir les "petits îlots érythréens compris entre" la côte continentale de l'Erythrée et les grandes îles yéménites aux fins de la délimitation. Aussi ne tint-il compte pour le calcul et le tracé de sa frontière ni des South West Rocks ni des trois Haycocks (que la Sentence sur la souveraineté avait attribués à l'Erythrée), considérant qu'il ne s'agissait là que de petits rochers dont la seule importance tenait au danger qu'ils représentaient pour

[1] CIJ Recueil 1969, p. 36, par. 57.

la navigation. Il reconnaissait toutefois la souveraineté de l'Erythrée sur ces îlots en les plaçant dans des enclaves limitées.

18. Dans le "secteur sud" postulé par le Yémen, la ligne pénétrait dans un étroit bras de mer ne comptant que peu d'îlots et pratiquement vide en son milieu d'îles ou d'îlots de nature à en compliquer le calcul, de sorte qu'elle devenait une simple médiane entre les côtes continentales se faisant face. En situant des points de base sur les îles Fatumas, Derchos et Ras Mukwar, le Yémen reconnaissait toutefois que la baie d'Assab faisait partie des eaux intérieures de l'Erythrée. Le Yémen ajouta la remarque suivante:

> Cette méthode de délimitation a été choisie de façon que les îles du secteur sud reçoivent le même traitement que les îles du secteur insulaire nord.

19. Résumant sa description des trois secteurs, le Yémen faisait observer que, conformément aux principes juridiques applicables, la délimitation appropriée serait obtenue en traçant une ligne médiane entre les côtes pertinentes. Rien ne justifiait un quelconque ajustement de cette ligne sur la base des principes équitables. Cette délimitation selon une ligne médiane entre côtes se faisant face était la seule solution équitable compatible avec les fins du présent arbitrage.

20. Le Yémen a également pris en considération d'autres facteurs pertinents. L'un d'eux avait trait à la proportionnalité, sur laquelle on va revenir dans la partie de l'examen des arguments de l'Erythrée qui lui est consacrée. Il s'est de même livré à une analyse de certaines "circonstances pertinentes de nature non géographique", la première étant la "dépendance des communautés de pêcheurs du Yémen à l'égard de la pêche dans la mer Rouge". C'est là un sujet sur lequel les deux Parties ont exprimé avec force des vues divergentes, qui seront décrites et analysées au chapitre II ci-après.

21. L'autre circonstance pertinente mise en avant par le Yémen était "l'aspect relatif à la sécurité de l'Etat côtier". Cette expression, a noté le Yémen, "ne désigne rien de plus excitant que le non-empiètement". C'est principalement dans la partie resserrée des eaux comprise entre le groupe des Hanish et la côte de l'Erythrée que se posait la question de la sécurité ou du non-empiètement. Aux yeux du Yémen, l'application du principe d'équidistance, visant à assurer l'égalité de traitement, fait automatiquement droit à cette préoccupation.

La ligne de délimitation proposée par l'Erythrée

22. L'Erythrée soutenait que l'argumentation avancée par le Yémen à l'appui de la ligne revendiquée par lui souffrait d'une faiblesse sur le plan juridique. Cette critique éclairait certains des postulats de base sur lesquels reposait sa propre ligne.

23. L'Erythrée soulignait avec quelque insistance ce qu'elle considérait comme une contradiction fondamentale dans l'argumentation du Yémen. Sur le tronçon nord de la ligne, où se posait la question de l'influence sur son tracé des îles septentrionales situées au milieu de la mer, la délimitation maritime était opérée entre les étendues de plateau continental et les zones économiques exclusives respectives. Ces deux types de délimitation, du plateau continental et de la zone économique exclusive, sont régis par les articles 74 et 83 de la Convention des Nations Unies sur le droit de la mer. Aucun des ces deux articles ne fait seulement mention de l'équidistance; il y est, toutefois, clairement dit qu'une délimitation de telles zones doit "aboutir à une solution équitable". Néanmoins, s'agissant précisément de ces zones, le Yémen revendiquait une ligne d'équidistance dont certains des points de base se situaient sur les côtes des petits îlots septentrionaux situés au milieu de la mer et relevant de sa souveraineté.

24. Pour sa part, l'Erythrée a fait valoir dans ses plaidoiries qu'il existe, dans la partie resserrée des eaux comprise entre l'archipel des Hanish et la côte continentale de l'Erythrée, une portion de mer où les distances sont inférieures à 24 milles[2] et qui est constituée par conséquent dans sa totalité d'eaux territoriales, auxquelles l'article 15 de la Convention "va s'appliquer de la manière la plus directe dans les parties situées tout au sud de la zone de délimitation en question, autour des îles Zuqar et Hanish. La raison en est, bien sûr, que les distances y sont plus courtes. Cela signifie que, autour des îles Zuqar et Hanish, la règle fondamentale est celle de l'équidistance."

25. Cela militerait en faveur d'une ligne médiane tenant pleinement compte des South West Rocks et des Haycocks, lesquels ont été jugés relever de l'Erythrée dans la sentence sur la souveraineté. De plus, en vertu de l'article 15, il ne saurait être question d'enclaves au sujet de ces îles.

26. L'Erythrée objecta aussi que les enclaves proposées par le Yémen auraient pour conséquence pratique de priver l'Erythrée de tout couloir d'accès dans la mer territoriale yéménite les entourant. Ainsi, tant les South West Rocks que les Haycocks, qui relevaient de l'Erythrée, se trouveraient "complètement isolés". L'Erythrée était opposée à la solution consistant à créer des enclaves parce que, faisait-elle valoir, ce serait placer le principal chenal navigable occidental, "entre l'île Haycock et les South West Rocks", dans la mer territoriale du Yémen, tandis que le principal chenal oriental, qui passe à l'est de Zuqar, se trouvait déjà dans une partie non contestée des eaux territoriales du Yémen. La proposition du Yémen aurait donc pour effet de "situer l'un et l'autre des deux principaux chenaux de navigation dans ce qui serait des eaux territoriales du Yémen si la délimitation proposée par ce dernier était acceptée".

---

2 Aux fins de la présente Sentence, le terme "mille" s'entend de milles nautiques.

27. La solution au problème de délimitation que proposait de son côté l'Erythrée comportait deux éléments. L'Erythrée proposait, d'une part, une frontière internationale et, d'autre part, un certain nombre de "périmètres" renfermant les îles situées au milieu de la mer, dont l'objet était de délimiter ce que l'Erythrée appelait des "zones de ressources conjointes". Cette délimitation des "zones maritimes partagées autour des îles" se présentait comme distincte de la reconnaissance "des eaux exclusives du Yémen, à l'est, et des eaux exclusives de l'Erythrée, à l'ouest". Ces propositions reflétaient la conception de l'Erythrée quant au sens qu'il convenait selon lui de donner aux dispositions de la première sentence subordonnant l'exercice de la souveraineté au respect du régime de pêche traditionnel, et quant aux mesures qu'il serait nécessaire de prendre pour donner plein effet à ce régime. Sur ce point l'Erythrée disait: "si ce régime doit être perpétué, il importe que les Parties sachent de manière techniquement précise en quoi il consiste et dans quelles circonstances il prévaut".

28. Il est à noter que les eaux "exclusives" de l'Erythrée à l'ouest n'incluaient pas seulement la mer territoriale, mais aussi la totalité des eaux s'étendant à l'ouest des îles en milieu de mer et à l'ouest de la ligne médiane historique. Ces deux propositions de l'Erythrée – ses deux versions de la ligne médiane et les périmètres délimitant les zones de ressources conjointes – étaient indissociables parce que constituant toutes deux des éléments essentiels de sa revendication globale. Par conséquent, sa "ligne médiane historique" était – hormis quelques variantes sur lesquelles on reviendra – une médiane tracée entre les côtes continentales en faisant abstraction des îles en milieu de mer relevant du Yémen, mais en tenant compte des îles relevant de l'Erythrée. (Ce type de délimitation trouve des précédents dans les accords pétroliers examinés au chapitre III). Le "système de zones de ressources" imaginé par l'Erythrée offrait les éléments essentiels d'une solution complexe au problème soulevé par ces îles. Les périmètres envisagés étaient de formes et de tailles diverses (voir cartes de l'Erythrée 4 et 7). L'Erythrée concevait, semble-t-il, ces propositions de "zones de ressources conjointes" comme une série de suggestions susceptibles d'ajustements. Son principal souci était celui, raisonnable, d'être en mesure d'indiquer aux pêcheurs érythréens à quels endroits précisément ils étaient en droit de pêcher.

29. Le couplage des deux questions – nature du régime de pêche traditionnel et délimitation de la frontière internationale – dans les écritures et plaidoiries de l'Erythrée contredit les arguments du Yémen. Le Yémen s'est dit d'avis que "le régime de pêche traditionnel ne devrait avoir aucune incidence sur la délimitation des frontières maritimes entre les deux Parties lors de la seconde étape". En réponse à une question du Tribunal, le Yémen a également exprimé l'opinion que "le paragraphe 3 de l'article 13 du Compromis d'arbitrage (voir annexe 1) et le cadre institué par les Accords de 1994 et 1998 rendaient inutile toute nouvelle prise en compte du régime de pêche traditionnel aux fins de la délimitation de la

frontière maritime". (Le texte des deux Accords de 1994 et 1998 est reproduit à l'annexe 3 à la présente Sentence).

30. L'Erythrée a répondu le 24 août à cette lettre du Yémen en ces termes:

> Les conclusions du Yémen donnent l'impression que les deux Etats ont conduit depuis octobre 1998 des discussions qui ont abouti à des arrangements concernant la mise en œuvre des droits traditionnels de l'Erythrée. Aucune discussion de la sorte n'a eu lieu sur ce sujet et aucun arrangement n'a été conclu à l'effet de protéger ou préserver les droits traditionnels de l'Erythrée dans les eaux entourant les îles situées au milieu de la mer.

Les arguments concernant les droits historiques et la souveraineté

31. La souveraineté sur les îles en litige a fait l'objet de la première étape du présent Arbitrage. L'Accord d'arbitrage enjoint le Tribunal de prendre en compte, lors de la présente seconde étape, "l'opinion qu'il se sera formée sur les questions de souveraineté territoriale". Il n'est donc pas surprenant que les deux Parties aient soulevé au cours de cette seconde étape un certain nombre de questions judicieuses sur la nature de la souveraineté et sa relation avec le problème de la délimitation et, point non moins important, avec celui du régime de pêche traditionnel.

32. L'Erythrée a ressenti la nécessité de revenir sur le passé historique des îles précédemment en litige, et en particulier sur la période marquée par l'influence et la présence italiennes. Ces considérations, et d'autres encore, ont donné corps à l'idée, suggérée avec force au Tribunal, que le fait que la souveraineté du Yémen sur ces îles avait été "récemment acquise" affaiblissait l'importance de celles-ci en tant que facteurs à prendre en considération aux fins de la délimitation. Cette conception a été exprimée en ces termes:

> L'Erythrée est aussi d'avis que les îles [situées au milieu de la mer] entrent dans la catégorie des petites îles inhabitées de souveraineté récemment acquise et proches de la ligne médiane que le Tribunal devrait reconnaître comme ne possédant que des zones maritimes restreintes.

33. L'Erythrée a poussé cette idée plus loin encore dans sa Demande, où il est dit à l'article 4 que:

> Les limites extérieures des zones maritimes des îles où existent de tels droits partagés sont définies comme s'étendant:
> A. du côté occidental de la mer Rouge, jusqu'à la ligne médiane tracée entre les deux côtes, lesquelles comprennent les îles qui étaient possessions historiques de l'un ou l'autre Etat dix ans avant le début de la procédure dans le présent arbitrage conformément à l'article 121 de la Convention des Nations Unies sur le droit de la mer; et

B. du côté oriental de la mer Rouge, aussi loin que la limite de douze milles de la mer territoriale du Yémen.

34. Poursuivant sur ce même thème, l'article 5 de la Demande dispose:

> 5. Les eaux qui s'étendent au delà de la zone partagée contenant les îles situées au milieu de la mer sont divisées selon une ligne médiane tracée entre les deux côtes, lesquelles comprennent les îles qui étaient possessions historiques de l'un ou l'autre Etat dix ans avant le début de la procédure dans le présent arbitrage conformément à l'article 121 de la Convention des Nations Unies sur le droit de la mer.

35. L'Erythrée s'est par conséquent estimée fondée à faire valoir que "l'Erythrée détient un titre historique sur toutes les eaux s'étendant à l'ouest de la ligne médiane historique, tracée par référence aux îles qui étaient possessions historiques". Cette conception, il y a lieu de le noter, aboutissait à une ligne médiane historique assez différente de la médiane construite entre les deux côtes continentales.

36. Le Yémen a répondu que son titre sur les îles précédemment en litige n'avait pas été créé par la décision le lui attribuant dans la sentence sur la souveraineté, mais que cette décision était plutôt venue confirmer un titre déjà existant; et que, "en matière d'arbitrage, la question du titre est déterminée à la fois pour ce qui concerne l'avenir et de façon rétroactive". Ces considérations ont amené à s'interroger sur l'effet d'une date critique.

37. Le Yémen s'inquiétait également de ce que la proposition de l'Erythrée concernant des zones de ressources conjointes présupposât que la souveraineté attribuée au Yémen lors de la première étape était une souveraineté "seulement limitée ou conditionnelle". C'est là semble-t-il en partie une querelle de mots. Toute souveraineté est "limitée" par le droit international. L'Erythrée ne peut guère vouloir suggérer que la souveraineté du Yémen sur les îles est "conditionnelle" au sens juridique où le non respect de la condition pourrait avoir pour effet d'y mettre fin.

38. Toutefois, l'Erythrée a répondu en citant le paragraphe 126 de la Sentence sur la souveraineté qui décrit le régime de pêche traditionnel comme ayant, par consolidation historique, établi des droits pour les deux Parties "comme une sorte de 'servitude internationale' beaucoup plus qu'une souveraineté territoriale". D'autres aspects de ces arguments sont examinés au chapitre IV ci-après.

La proportionnalité

39. L'une et l'autre Parties ont mis ce facteur en avant avec vigueur et ingéniosité. Toutes deux se sont appuyées sur la décision rendue dans les affaires de la *Mer du Nord* selon laquelle une délimitation doit prendre en compte "le rapport raisonnable qu'une délimitation opérée conformément à des principes équitables

devrait faire apparaître entre l'étendue des zones de plateau continental relevant de l'Etat riverain et la longueur de son littoral mesurée suivant la direction générale de celui-ci".[3] Toutes deux ont souscrit à la mise en garde formulée dans l'*arbitrage Royaume-Uni/République française*[4] qu'il s'agit là d'un test d'équité et non d'une méthode de délimitation, et ont convenu que ce qu'il fallait éviter, c'était une disproportion manifeste résultant de la ligne choisie. Par conséquent, les Parties différaient peu sur le principe, mais étaient en fort désaccord quant à la façon de mesurer la longueur de leurs côtes respectives et la signification de cette mesure une fois celle-ci opérée. La question de la mesure peut donner lieu à plusieurs interprétations du fait que la côte de l'Erythrée fait également face plus loin à l'Etat voisin du Yémen, le Royaume d'Arabie saoudite, avec lequel la frontière maritime n'est pas délimitée.

40. La position du Yémen était que la proportionnalité est un facteur à prendre en compte aux fins de vérifier le caractère équitable d'une délimitation déjà opérée par d'autres moyens. S'agissant en particulier du tracé de la ligne dans le secteur central, le Yémen a suggéré que les longueurs relatives totales des côtes étaient dénuées de signification parce que (i) dans la partie resserrée des eaux entre les îles yéménites et la côte érythréenne, toute modification de la ligne médiane ferait intervenir le principe de non-empiètement; (ii) en outre, dans le secteur central, la configuration générale des côtes est telle que seule une division par parts égales garantit un résultat équitable; (iii) le principe de non-empiètement étaye une division par parts égales; (iv) les côtes pertinentes aux fins de la présente délimitation sont la côte de l'Erythrée et les îles du Yémen; (v) la pratique des Etats conforte la ligne médiane; et (vi) la proportionnalité ne peut s'appliquer lorsqu'il y a chevauchement des mers territoriales.

41. A cela l'Erythrée répondit en se demandant si la ligne revendiquée par le Yémen dans le secteur central était bien conforme avec la ligne médiane envisagée à l'article 15 de la Convention; et de suggérer que non parce qu'elle ne comptait pas de points de base sur la laisse de basse mer des South West Rocks et des Haycocks, îlots érythréens.

42. Il n'est pas possible de décrire ici les multiples variations qui ont été avancées dans les écritures et plaidoiries quant à la méthode de mesure à utiliser, ni les analyses auxquelles ont donné lieu les ambiguïtés de l'expression "se faire face", bien que le Tribunal les ait toutes examinées. Qu'il suffise de dire que tandis que le Yémen avait calculé que la ligne revendiquée par lui divisait nettement les zones maritimes en parts presque égales qui, au vu des mesures de la longueur des côtes qu'il avait effectuées, constituaient le rapport correct, l'Erythrée avait estimé, à l'issue de son choix définitif parmi les différentes méthodes de calcul

[3] CIJ Recueil 1969, p. 57, par. 101.

[4] 18 ILM 60; 54 ILR 6.

envisagées, que sa propre ligne médiane historique entre les côtes continentales aboutirait à un découpage répartissant les zones respectives selon une proportion de 3 à 2 en sa faveur, qu'elle jugeait elle aussi refléter correctement le rapport entre les longueurs de côte mesurées selon sa méthode.

43. L'Erythrée, il convient de le mentionner, était particulièrement soucieuse qu'il ne soit pas tenu compte, dans le calcul des zones résultant de la délimitation, des eaux intérieures des Dahlak ou des baies échancrant ses côtes, y compris la baie d'Assab.

Les extrémités nord et sud de la ligne de délimitation

44. S'est également posée la question de savoir où arrêter le tracé de la frontière à ses extrémités nord et sud, étant donné qu'à ces endroits, elle risquait de préjuger le règlement d'autres différends frontaliers avec des pays limitrophes. De fait, le Royaume d'Arabie saoudite avait écrit au greffier du Tribunal le 31 août 1997 pour faire observer que ses frontières avec le Yémen étaient en litige, pour réserver sa position et pour suggérer que le Tribunal ne statue que sur des zones "qui ne s'étendent pas au delà de la latitude de l'extrême pointe nord de l'île de Jabal al-Tayr". Le Yémen a souhaité pour sa part que la frontière soit déterminée jusqu'au 16° de latitude nord, soit la limite de ce qu'il appelait le secteur nord. L'Erythrée a déclaré en revanche ne voir "aucune objection" à la proposition de l'Arabie saoudite.

45. Concernant l'extrémité sud, les Etats tiers concernés n'ont fait aucune déclaration au Tribunal, mais la question devra néanmoins être tranchée. L'Erythrée était tout particulièrement préoccupée à ce sujet par la flèche par laquelle le Yémen avait fait se terminer la ligne revendiquée par lui, car cette flèche, selon l'Erythrée, pointait dans une direction qui revenait à "couper" le principal chenal de navigation et à le situer dans les eaux territoriales yéménites. Le Yémen avait aussi utilisé une flèche pour marquer l'extrémité nord de sa ligne, et les deux Parties ont échangé un certain nombre de remarques sur le caractère opportun ou non de ces flèches.

46. A l'extrémité sud de la ligne, là où celle-ci se rapproche du détroit de Bab al-Mandab, apparaît une complication liée à l'effet possible de l'île de Perim sur son tracé. A cet égard, il pourrait manifestement être nécessaire de connaître les vues de Djibouti. Par conséquent, la ligne déterminée par le Tribunal ne doit pas se prolonger au-delà du point où toute incidence que pourrait avoir sur elle l'île de Périm commencerait à prendre effet. Le Tribunal a pris en considération ces diverses positions exprimées et est parvenu à ses propres conclusions, qui sont exposées de façon plus détaillée au chapitre V.

* – * – *

Les Conclusions du Yémen et la Demande de l'Erythrée sont reproduites ci-après.

Conclusions du Yémen

A la lumière des faits et des considérations juridiques présentés par le Yémen dans ses écritures et plaidoiries; et

Rejetant toutes conclusions contraires présentées par l'Erythrée dans sa "Demande"; et

Vu les dispositions de l'article 2(3) du Compromis d'arbitrage;

La République du Yémen prie respectueusement le Tribunal de dire et juger:

1. Que la délimitation maritime entre les Parties suit une ligne médiane, dont tous les points sont équidistants des points de base pertinents sur les côtes des Parties, tels que décrits aux chapitres 8 à 10 du mémoire du Yémen, compte dûment tenu des îlots et rochers qui comprennent les South West Rocks, les Haycocks et les Mohabbakah;

2. Que le tracé de la délimitation, y compris les coordonnées des points d'inflexion de la frontière établis sur la base du Système géodésique mondial de 1984 (WGS 84), est tel qu'il figure au chapitre 12 du mémoire du Yémen.

Demande de l'Erythrée

(Paragraphe 274 du Mémoire de l'Etat d'Erythrée)

Au paragraphe 3 de l'article 2 du Compromis d'arbitrage, il est demandé au Tribunal de prononcer une sentence délimitant les frontières maritimes entre les Parties de manière techniquement précise. Afin qu'une telle précision soit atteinte, l'Etat d'Erythrée prie respectueusement le Tribunal de rendre une sentence disposant ce qui suit:

1. L'utilisation historique par le peuple érythréen des ressources des îles situées au milieu de la mer comprend la pêche, le commerce, la pêche de coquillages et de perles, l'exploitation du guano et des minerais, et toutes les activités terrestres connexes, y compris le séchage du poisson, le puisage de l'eau, les pratiques religieuses et funéraires, et la construction et l'occupation d'abris pour la nuit et comme refuges;

2. Le droit à un tel usage, à partager avec la République du Yémen, s'étend à l'ensemble des parties terrestres et zones maritimes des îles situées au milieu de la mer;

3. Le droit à un tel usage sera préservé entier à perpétuité, tel qu'il a existé dans le passé, sans qu'y fasse obstacle l'imposition de nouvelles règles, contraintes, restrictions ou de toutes autres atteintes ou limitations de quelque nature que ce soit, à l'exception de celles dont seront convenus l'Erythrée et le Yémen aux termes d'un accord écrit entre eux;

4. Les limites extérieures des zones maritimes des îles où existent de tels droits partagés sont définies comme s'étendant:

A. du côté occidental de la mer Rouge, jusqu'à la ligne médiane tracée entre les deux côtes, lesquelles comprennent les îles qui étaient possessions historiques de l'un ou l'autre Etat dix ans avant le début de la procédure dans le présent arbitrage conformément à l'article 121 de la Convention des Nations Unies sur le droit de la mer; et

B. du côté oriental de la mer Rouge, aussi loin que la limite de douze milles de la mer territoriale du Yémen.

5. Les eaux qui s'étendent au-delà de la zone partagée contenant les îles situées au milieu de la mer sont divisées selon une ligne médiane tracée entre les deux côtes, lesquelles comprennent les îles qui étaient possessions historiques de l'un ou l'autre Etat dix ans avant le début de la procédure dans le présent arbitrage conformément à l'article 121 de la Convention des Nations Unies sur le droit de la mer.

6. Les deux Parties sont invitées à négocier les modalités d'un usage partagé des îles situées au milieu de la mer et de leurs eaux aux conditions suivantes:

A. Sitôt que le Tribunal aura rendu une sentence dans la seconde étape, les Parties engageront des négociations, de bonne foi, en vue de conclure un accord décrivant de quelles façons les ressortissants des deux Parties peuvent utiliser les ressources des îles situées au milieu de la mer et de leurs zones maritimes, telles que ces zones sont décrites dans la sentence du Tribunal, et de fixer les détails d'un mécanisme de résolution contraignante des différends aux fins de régler tout différend pouvant surgir au sujet de l'interprétation ou de l'application de l'accord;

B. Les Parties soumettront cet accord au Tribunal pour examen et approbation six mois au plus tard après la date à laquelle le Tribunal aura rendu sa sentence pour la deuxième étape;

C. Le Tribunal déterminera si l'accord est conforme à sa sentence pour la deuxième étape, et en particulier s'il préserve loyalement les droits traditionnels des deux Parties à faire usage des ressources des îles situées au milieu de la mer;

D. Si le Tribunal détermine que l'accord ne satisfait pas aux critères décrits au paragraphe précédent, ou si les Parties manquent à leur obligation de soumettre un accord, le Tribunal prononcera une sentence énonçant les modalités susvisées ou partageant les eaux de façon égale entre les deux Parties. Le Tribunal peut demander aux Parties de présenter leurs conclusions sur ce point.

E. Si le Tribunal estime que l'accord (ou un accord révisé) satisfait aux critères énoncés ci-dessus, il fera connaître son approbation aux Parties, entérinera l'accord comme sa propre décision et invitera en outre les Parties à lui donner effet sous la forme d'un traité ayant force obligatoire qui sera déposé auprès du secrétaire général de l'Organisation des Nations Unies;

7. Le Tribunal demeurera saisi du différend entre les Parties jusqu'au moment où l'accord relatif à l'usage partagé des îles situées au milieu de la mer aura été reçu en dépôt par le secrétaire général de l'Organisation des Nations Unies.

CHAPITRE II – La question générale de la pêche dans la mer Rouge

47. Le présent chapitre traitera en premier lieu des éléments de preuve et des arguments avancés par les Parties en ce qui concerne la question générale de la pêche dans la mer Rouge. Seront ensuite exposées les conclusions du Tribunal quant à ces arguments et à ces éléments de preuve.

Les éléments de preuve et les arguments des Parties

48. Chacune des deux Parties a fait grand cas de la pêche, tant du point de vue de l'histoire passée que de la situation actuelle, et en ce qui concerne non seulement ses propres ressortissants mais encore les pratiques des ressortissants de l'autre Partie. Les éléments de preuve et les arguments présentés par les Parties peuvent pour l'essentiel être regroupés sous cinq grandes rubriques: (1) la pêche en général; (2) l'emplacement des zones de pêche; (3) la dépendance économique des Parties à l'égard de la pêche; (4) la consommation de poisson au sein de la population des Parties; et (5) l'effet des pratiques de pêche sur les lignes de délimitation proposées par les Parties.

49. Les arguments de chaque Partie visaient essentiellement à démontrer que la ligne de délimitation proposée par elle ne modifierait pas la situation et les pratiques historiques existantes, qu'elle n'aurait pas d'effet catastrophique sur les pêcheurs locaux ou sur l'économie locale ou nationale de l'autre Partie, ni d'incidence négative sur l'alimentation de la population de l'autre Partie à l'échelon régional et que, à l'inverse, la ligne de délimitation proposée par l'autre Partie modifierait bel et bien la situation et les pratiques historiques existantes, qu'elle aurait un effet catastrophique ou du moins gravement préjudiciable pour le pêcheurs locaux ou pour sa propre économie régionale, ainsi que des conséquences négatives sur l'alimentation de sa population.

50. Les deux Parties se sont référées directement et indirectement au sujet de ces considérations aux critères généraux relatifs aux "effets catastrophiques" et au "long usage" énoncés pour la première fois dans l'*Affaire des pêcheries anglo-norvégiennes* de 1951 – et invoqués dans les dispositions, entre autres, du paragraphe 5 de l'article 7 de la Convention des Nations Unies de 1982 sur le droit de la mer.

51. Ces considérations trouvaient également un écho dans la "solution équitable" prescrite au paragraphe 1 des articles 74 et 83 de la Convention, étant entendu que ne saurait être équitable aucune "solution" qui serait incompatible avec un long usage, représenterait un danger manifeste et immédiat dont les effets seraient catastrophiques pour l'économie locale de l'une des Parties, ou qui ne tiendrait pas compte de la nécessité de réduire au minimum les incidences préjudiciables aux communautés de pêcheurs, et la désorganisation économique d'Etats dont les ressortissants ont l'habitude de pêcher dans la zone visée.

La pêche en général

52. La position de l'Erythrée était la suivante. Les documents historiques démontraient que l'industrie de la pêche érythréenne était une activité importante avant la guerre civile en Ethiopie et que l'Erythrée avait été la principale économie fondée sur la pêche dans la région, à la seule exception de l'Egypte. Depuis la fin de la guerre civile et l'indépendance, de sérieux efforts étaient faits pour relancer l'économie de la pêche en Erythrée. Il était, par conséquent erroné de considérer que – comme l'affirmait le Yémen – les pêcheries érythréennes étaient largement tributaires de la pêche en eau douce; en fait, celle-ci n'avait présenté aucune importance. En revanche, l'industrie de la pêche yéménite reposait en grande partie sur les pêcheries de l'océan Indien et ne dépendait pas de manière significative de la mer Rouge. Même si les activités de pêche du Yémen dans la mer Rouge sont beaucoup moins importantes que ne l'a affirmé le Yémen, elles n'en sont pas moins solidement établies et leur protection ne dépend en aucun cas de la ligne de délimitation particulière proposée par le Yémen.

53. Le Yémen a soutenu que les ressortissants yéménites dominaient de longue date les activités de pêche dans la mer Rouge; les activités traditionnelles de pêche yéménites – conduites à bord de petites embarcations, qu'il s'agisse de *sambouk* ou de *houri* – avaient revêtu dans le passé une importance bien plus grande que celles de l'Erythrée, qui étaient en grande partie axées sur la pêche côtière le long du littoral de l'Erythrée et dans et entre les Dahlak. De plus, Hodeidah au Yémen était le marché le plus actif pour les produits des pêcheurs tant érythréens que yéménites.

Dépendance économique à l'égard de la pêche

54. La position de l'Erythrée était que des efforts considérables avaient été déployés depuis la fin de la guerre pour réorganiser et renforcer l'industrie érythréenne de la pêche – y compris avec l'aide du PNUD et de la FAO – et que les perspectives d'un futur développement significatif des pêcheries érythréennes apparaissaient à la fois prometteuses et importantes. Même si elle n'a pas prétendu dépendre économiquement de la pêche en l'état actuel, l'Erythrée a fait néanmoins valoir que la délimitation décidée par le Tribunal ne devrait pas restreindre ou limiter les pratiques existantes de ses ressortissants en matière de pêcheries. S'agissant du Yémen, l'Erythrée affirmait non seulement que la présence des pêcheurs yéménites dans la mer Rouge était beaucoup moins importante que ne l'avait prétendu le Yémen, mais encore que la plus grande partie du poisson débarqué à Hodeidah l'était par des pêcheurs érythréens.

55. De son côté, le Yémen soutenait que ses pêcheurs avaient été de tout temps tributaires des pêcheries de la mer Rouge, qui constituaient leurs zones de pêche, et que cette activité représentait de longue date un élément important de

l'ensemble de l'économie nationale du Yémen et une composante majeure de l'économie régionale de la Tihama le long de la côte de la mer Rouge. Le Yémen prétendait que l'Erythrée n'était en rien fondée à invoquer une quelconque dépendance significative en matière de pêche, de pêcheries, de poisson ou de consommation du poisson, et que les préoccupations de l'Erythrée, telles qu'elles ressortaient des éléments de preuve documentaires soumis au Tribunal lors des deux étapes de l'arbitrage, avaient trait pour la plupart à des propositions et à des projets visant à développer à l'avenir des activités et des ressources halieutiques érythréennes encore inexistantes ou actuellement inexploitées.

Emplacement des zones de pêche

56. Les arguments de l'Erythrée se présentaient comme suit: pour l'heure, la pêche dans la mer Rouge était dans l'ensemble dominée par des pêcheurs artisanaux érythréens qui capturaient leurs prises autour des Dahlak, le long de la côte de l'Erythrée, autour des Mohabbakah, des Haycocks et des South West Rocks, et dans les eaux du groupe d'"îles situées au milieu de la mer" Zuqar-Hanish. (Ainsi qu'il a été noté plus haut, l'Erythrée a nié dépendre, pour une part quelconque de sa production halieutique, de pêcheries érythréennes situées à l'intérieur des terres telles que lacs et réservoirs.) Concernant le Yémen, l'Erythrée a soutenu que les pêcheurs yéménites n'avaient guère été, voire nullement été, tributaires des zones de pêche en eaux profondes s'étendant à l'ouest des îles situées au milieu de la mer et autour des Mohabbakah, des Haycocks et des South West Rocks; il n'existait guère d'éléments attestant une quelconque activité de ressortissants yéménites à l'ouest du groupe Zuqar-Hanish; et le Yémen n'avait pas réussi à prouver qu'un seul gramme de poisson consommé sur son territoire provenait de ces eaux.

57. Pour sa part, le Yémen a fait valoir que ses pêcheurs artisanaux et traditionnels pêchaient de longue date autour de Jabal al-Tayr et du groupe de Zubayr, dans les eaux entourant le groupe Zuqar-Hanish, et dans les grands fonds situés à l'ouest de la Grande Hanish et autour des Mohabbakah, des Haycocks et des South West Rocks. A l'appui de ces affirmations ont été produits à titre d'éléments de preuve lors de la première étape de l'arbitrage des dépositions de témoins dans lesquelles différents pêcheurs yéménites disaient pêcher depuis longtemps dans les eaux en question. S'agissant de la Partie adverse, le Yémen affirma là encore que les activités de pêche érythréennes étaient confinées dans les eaux de l'archipel des Dahlak et les eaux côtières le long du littoral de l'Erythrée et n'empiétaient d'aucune façon significative sur les eaux entourant les îles en cause lors de la première étape de l'arbitrage – y compris les grands fonds s'étendant à l'ouest de la Grande Hanish et autour des Mohabbakah, des Haycocks et des South West Rocks.

Consommation de poisson au sein de la population

58. L'Erythrée a soutenu que sa population côtière consommait beaucoup plus de poisson que ne le prétendait le Yémen et que, de surcroît, des efforts étaient faits pour développer la demande et l'offre de poisson frais dans l'ensemble de la population. Il a aussi affirmé que le Yémen avait grandement exagéré dans ses écritures et plaidoiries l'importance du poisson frais dans l'alimentation de la population yéménite, et que la population yéménite de la Tihama – et à plus forte raison celle du Yémen tout entier – ne dépendait dans aucune mesure significative de la consommation de poisson frais. Pour sa part, le Yémen a soutenu que sa population, en particulier dans les régions côtières telles que la Tihama, consommait d'importantes quantités de poisson et que – à l'inverse – la consommation de poisson était négligeable en Erythrée.

Effets sur les lignes de délimitation proposées par les Parties

59. La position de l'Erythrée était que le choix par le Tribunal d'une ligne de délimitation telle que la "ligne médiane historique" suggérée par l'Erythrée respecterait la pratique historique des Parties, n'aurait pas pour effet de déplacer ou de gêner les activités de pêche yéménites, et produirait un résultat équitable pour l'une et l'autre Parties. En revanche, aux yeux de l'Erythrée, la "ligne médiane" proposée par le Yémen priverait les pêcheurs érythréens de précieuses zones de pêche à l'est des îles situées au milieu de la mer, et attribuerait au Yémen des zones s'étendant à l'ouest de ces îles et autour des Mohabbakah, des Haycocks et des South West Rocks – où les pêcheurs érythréens exerçaient de longue date leur activité et où les ressortissants yéménites ne s'étaient jamais engagés dans une exploitation substantielle des pêcheries. Dans cette mesure, l'Erythrée faisait valoir que la ligne de délimitation proposée par le Yémen serait inéquitable et priverait les pêcheurs érythréens d'une ressource importante.

60. De son côté, le Yémen soutenait que la ligne médiane proposée par lui refléterait adéquatement les pratiques historiques, ne lui apporterait rien qu'il n'ait possédé auparavant, respecterait les droits existants, ne "pénaliserait" pas les activités de pêche érythréennes présentes ou passées et constituerait un résultat équitable. Quant à la "ligne médiane historique" proposée par l'Erythrée, elle empiéterait sans justification sur les zones de pêche traditionnelles du Yémen, priverait les pêcheurs yéménites des pêcheries en eaux profondes à l'ouest des îles situées au milieu de la mer et représenterait pour l'Erythrée une manne en conséquence.

* – * – *

Les conclusions du Tribunal concernant les éléments de preuve

61. Les arguments et éléments de preuve présentés par chaque Partie répondaient à plusieurs objectifs, mais visaient avant tout à établir que la délimitation proposée

par elle respecterait les pratiques historiques, n'aurait pas d'effet catastrophique pour les pêcheurs ou la population au niveau local, n'aurait pas d'incidence globalement négative sur l'économie (ou les plans futurs) de la Partie adverse, ni d'effet délétère sur l'alimentation et la santé de sa population. Dans le même temps, chaque Partie a affirmé ou laissé entendre que la ligne de délimitation proposée par l'autre aurait précisément les conséquences inverses. Les éléments de preuve mis en avant par les Parties ont été dans une très large mesure contradictoires et propres à créer la confusion.

A la lumière des arguments et éléments de preuve qui lui ont été présentés, le Tribunal aboutit aux conclusions ci-après.

Concernant la pêche en général

62. La pêche en général est une activité importante sur les deux rives de la mer Rouge. Cela a été reconnu par le Tribunal dans sa sentence sur la souveraineté. Il n'est pas nécessaire de tenter de déterminer le degré exact de cette importance à un quelconque moment particulier et cela risquerait probablement d'induire en erreur, mais il apparaît clairement de fait – comme le Tribunal l'a dit au paragraphe 526 de sa Sentence sur la souveraineté – que le "régime de pêche traditionnel dans la région . . . s'est appliqué, comme l'attestent amplement les éléments de preuve présentés au Tribunal, autour des îles Hanish et Zuqar et des îles de Jabal al-Tayr et du groupe de Zubayr".

63. De plus, la décision formulée par le Tribunal à l'alinéa vi du Dispositif de sa Sentence sur la souveraineté – que ce régime de pêche traditionnel soit perpétué de façon à assurer notamment "libre accès et libre jouissance pour les pêcheurs de l'Erythrée comme du Yémen" – revient tout entière à dire que le Tribunal a déjà jugé qu'une telle activité de pêche traditionnelle est importante pour l'une et l'autre des Parties et ses ressortissants des deux côtés de la mer Rouge. Il suffit donc de dire que la pêche, les pêcheurs et les pêcheries ont et conservent de l'importance pour chacune des Parties en la présente affaire. En raison précisément de la signification du paragraphe 526 de la Sentence sur la souveraineté et de l'alinéa vi de son Dispositif, les pratiques halieutiques des Parties au fil du temps sont sans rapport avec la tâche consistant à déterminer une ligne de délimitation.

Concernant la dépendance économique à l'égard de la pêche

64. Il n'est pas possible ou nécessaire pour le Tribunal de conclure que l'Erythrée ou le Yémen dépend sur le plan économique de la pêche dans une mesure telle que cela suggère une quelconque ligne de délimitation particulière. Les éléments de preuve présentés au Tribunal donnent à penser que l'activité halieutique et les revenus de la pêche constituent apparemment un aspect important de la vie économique du Yémen – en particulier dans la région de la Tihama – et que la

revitalisation et le développement de l'industrie érythréenne de la pêche sont un objectif prioritaire du Gouvernement de l'Erythrée qui leur a consacré une attention notable depuis l'indépendance de ce pays.

Concernant l'emplacement des zones de pêche

65. Durant les deux étapes de l'arbitrage ont été produits entre autres des éléments de preuve attestant que de nombreux pêcheurs de l'Erythrée étaient accoutumés à pêcher à l'intérieur et autour de l'archipel des Dahlak et dans les eaux côtières bordant le littoral de l'Erythrée, mais il apparaît aussi que certains pêcheurs érythréens exploitaient les eaux comprises à l'intérieur et autour des îles Hanish et Zuqar ainsi que les grands fonds s'étendant à l'ouest des îles situées au milieu de la mer et autour des Mohabbakah, des Haycocks et des South West Rocks. A ce constat a répondu par avance le souci du Tribunal de préserver le régime de pêche traditionnel "dans la région" dans son ensemble, "y compris libre accès et libre jouissance pour les pêcheurs de l'Erythrée comme du Yémen" (Sentence sur la souveraineté, Dispositif, paragraphe 527, alinéa vi).

66. Quantité de données historiques indiquent que les pêcheurs des deux rives, orientale et occidentale, de la mer Rouge poursuivaient librement leurs activités, y compris la pêche et la vente de son produit sur les marchés locaux, quels que soient leur appartenance politique à une nation ou leur lieu de résidence habituel.[5]

67. Ces informations sur les facteurs sociaux et économiques affectant l'existence des habitants des deux rives de la mer Rouge témoignent aussi des traditions sociales et juridiques profondément enracinées et communes qui ont prévalu durant des siècles au sein de ces populations, dont l'une et l'autre demeurèrent sous le contrôle direct ou indirect de l'Empire ottoman jusqu'à la deuxième moitié du 19e siècle.

68. Les éléments de preuve produits devant le Tribunal paraissent en outre établir qu'au fil des ans, les pêcheurs yéménites ont opéré aussi loin au nord que l'archipel des Dahlak et Jabal al-Tayr et le groupe de Zubayr, et aussi loin à l'ouest que les Mohabbakah, les Haycocks et les South West Rocks. Là encore, ce constat transparaît implicitement dans le souci du Tribunal de préserver le régime de pêche traditionnel "dans la *région*" dans son ensemble.

69. Sur un point qui n'est pas sans rapport avec les zones de pêche, il convient de noter que les éléments de preuve montrent assez clairement que les pêcheurs tant érythréens que yéménites jouissaient aussi d'un accès libre et ouvert à Hodeimah, le principal marché pour le poisson sur la rive yéménite de la mer Rouge, sans que

[5] Voir les notes 9 et 11 se rapportant aux paragraphes 121 et 128 respectivement de la Sentence sur la souveraineté.

leur nationalité constitue un obstacle. (Le Tribunal a également tenu compte de cet élément au paragraphe 527, alinéa vi, du Dispositif de sa Sentence sur la souveraineté.)

Concernant la consommation de poisson au sein de la population

70. Les éléments de preuve relatifs à la consommation de poisson avancés par chaque Partie visaient semble-t-il à établir que l'adoption par le Tribunal de la ligne de délimitation proposée par l'autre Partie constituerait une sérieuse menace pour l'alimentation ou la santé de sa propre population. Toutefois, ces éléments sont contradictoires et incertains. Il est difficile sinon impossible de dégager de quelconques conclusions générales de l'écheveau de faits allégués mis en avant par les Parties à cet égard.

71. Le Tribunal peut aisément conclure, sans avoir à peser des éléments de preuve intangibles et problématiques ou à se livrer à de subtils calculs sur la base de telle ou telle théorie de la nutrition, que le poisson revêt, en tant que ressource potentielle présente et future, de l'importance pour les populations nationales et locales de chaque Partie, sur chacune des deux rives de la mer Rouge. Le Tribunal peut aussi conclure, comme une chose tombant sous le sens et connue de tous, que l'intérêt pour le poisson et sa promotion en tant que source d'alimentation sont un objectif important et louable. A la lumière de ces deux conclusions, toutefois, le Tribunal ne voit aucune raison valable d'accepter – ou de rejeter – sur de telles bases les arguments de l'une ou l'autre Partie en ce qui concerne la *ligne de délimitation* proposée par elle ou par l'autre Partie.

Concernant l'effet sur les lignes de délimitation proposées par les Parties

72. Compte tenu de ce qui précède, le Tribunal ne trouve aucune raison valable d'accepter ou de rejeter sur toute autre base en rapport avec le poisson – qu'il s'agisse de la pratique historique en matière de pêche en général, de questions liées à la dépendance économique déclarée à l'égard de la pêche, de l'emplacement des zones de pêches ou des caractéristiques de la consommation de poisson au sein des populations – les arguments de l'une ou l'autre Partie au sujet de la ligne de délimitation proposée par elle ou par l'autre Partie. Aucune des deux Parties n'a réussi à démontrer que la ligne de délimitation proposée par la Partie adverse aurait un effet catastrophique ou inéquitable sur l'activité halieutique de ses ressortissants ou des conséquences néfastes pour les communautés de pêcheurs et l'organisation économique desdits ressortissants.[6]

---

[6] *Cf.* l'article 70, paragraphe 5, de la Convention des Nations Unies sur le droit de la mer: "Les Etats développés géographiquement désavantagés n'ont le droit de participer à l'exploitation des ressources biologiques, en vertu du présent article, que dans les zones économiques exclusives d'Etats côtiers développés de la même sous-région ou région, compte tenu de la mesure dans laquelle l'Etat côtier, en donnant accès aux ressources biologiques de sa zone économique exclusive

73. Pour ces raisons, le Tribunal est dans l'impossibilité d'accepter ou de rejeter la ligne de délimitation proposée par l'une ou l'autre Partie sur la base des pêcheries. Le Tribunal ne peut pas davantage conclure à un quelconque effet, sur les raisons juridiques motivant son propre choix d'une ligne de délimitation, de son examen des pratiques générales passées en matière de pêche de l'une ou l'autre Partie ou de la privation potentielle de zones de pêche ou d'accès à des ressources halieutiques, ou de considérations d'ordre nutritionnel ou autres.

* – * – *

74. Pour les raisons susmentionnées, les éléments de preuve et arguments avancés par les Parties en matière de pêche et de pêcheries ne sauraient avoir d'effets significatifs sur la détermination par le Tribunal de la délimitation à laquelle il conviendrait de procéder en vertu du droit international pour aboutir à une solution équitable pour les deux Parties.

à d'autres Etats, a pris en considération la nécessité de réduire à un minimum les effets préjudiciables aux communautés de pêcheurs ainsi que les perturbations économiques dans les Etats dont les ressortissants pratiquent habituellement la pêche dans la zone."

CHAPITRE III – Accords pétroliers et lignes médianes

75. S'agissant de la pertinence et de la force probante aux fins de la présente étape de la procédure des contrats et accords de concession pétroliers consentis par le Yémen et par l'Ethiopie ou l'Erythrée, les Parties ont semblé inverser leurs rôles.

76. Lors de la première étape, le Yémen a donné beaucoup de poids aux contrats et accords de concession pétroliers consentis par lui. Il a produit à titre d'éléments de preuve un certain nombre de ces contrats pétroliers et de cartes les illustrant, dont beaucoup avaient été dressées par la société Petroconsultants S.A. de Genève. Etant donné que quelques uns de ces arrangements donnaient corps à des frontières occidentales à l'est desquelles se situent certaines des îles en litige, le Yémen a voulu y voir la preuve que tant lui-même que les compagnies pétrolières signataires considéraient que le Yémen avait souveraineté sur ces îles en litige. Il a soutenu que, lorsqu'un Etat octroie une concession portant sur une zone donnée, il se présente comme exerçant sa souveraineté sur cette zone; et que, lorsqu'une compagnie pétrolière étrangère entreprend d'exploiter cette concession, et engage des ressources à telle fin, c'est qu'elle accepte la souveraineté de cet Etat et agit en se fondant sur elle. Le Yémen a souligné que non seulement certains des contrats pétroliers conclus par lui portaient sur une zone géographique englobant les îles en litige, mais que de surcroît, et de manière significative, ce n'était le cas, selon lui, d'aucun des contrats et accords de concession pétroliers conclus par l'Ethiopie ou l'Erythrée. Comme il est dit de façon résumée dans la Sentence sur la souveraineté, "Le Yémen a soutenu que les caractéristiques des concessions en mer octroyées par le Yémen, sans soulever de protestations de la part de l'Ethiopie ou de l'Erythrée, ainsi que les caractéristiques des concessions éthiopiennes, confirmaient les prétentions du Yémen à la souveraineté sur les îles en litige, l'acceptation de cette souveraineté et la décision d'investir sur une telle base par les compagnies pétrolières, et l'assentiment de l'Ethiopie et de l'Erythrée." (paragraphe 390.)

77. Lors de la première étape, l'Erythrée a fait au contraire valoir que le fait pour un Etat de conclure un contrat ou un accord de concession pétrolier n'était pas la preuve d'un titre mais, tout au plus, une simple revendication. De tels arrangements étaient dénués de force probante à moins que des activités n'aient été conduites en conséquence. Néanmoins, l'Erythrée opposa à l'argumentation du Yémen la preuve d'une concession octroyée par l'Ethiopie qui couvrait en partie ou en totalité la Grande et la Petite Hanish. Ni l'Erythrée ni le Yémen n'ont attaché de l'importance au fait qu'un certain nombre d'arrangements pétroliers conclus par le Yémen et par l'Ethiopie ou l'Erythrée portaient sur des zones s'étendant jusqu'à une ligne médiane tracée entre leurs littoraux respectifs.

78. Dans sa Sentence sur la souveraineté, le Tribunal est parvenu à la conclusion suivante:

> 437. Les contrats pétroliers offshore conclus par le Yémen, et par l'Ethiopie et l'Erythrée, ne suffisent pas à établir ou à conforter de manière significative les prétentions de l'une ou l'autre Partie à la souveraineté sur les îles en litige.
>
> 438. Toutefois, ces contrats étayent dans une certaine mesure le tracé d'une ligne médiane entre les côtes se faisant face de l'Erythrée et du Yémen, opéré sans prendre en compte les îles, pour séparer les juridictions respectives des Parties.

79. Au cours de la présente étape de la procédure, l'Erythrée a fait grand cas du paragraphe 438 et d'autres passages de la Sentence [sur la souveraineté], où il est dit que divers arrangements pétroliers indiquent des limites tracées selon une ligne médiane, et elle a soutenu que la sentence du Tribunal confortait la "ligne médiane historique" qu'elle a à présent proposé comme frontière maritime entre l'Erythrée et le Yémen. L'Erythrée a insisté sur le fait que, dans plusieurs contrats pétroliers conclus par le Yémen, la zone visée s'étendait de la côte continentale du Yémen à l'est jusqu'à la ligne médiane dans la mer Rouge, tracée sans prendre en compte des points de base sur les îles en litige. Elle a relevé qu'un contrat conclu par elle-même, et un autre conclu par le Yémen comportaient une ligne médiane traversant la Grande Hanish. Elle a fait observer que l'un des contrats de concession signés par le Yémen indique une ligne médiane, avec la mention "Ethiopie" à l'ouest et la mention "Yémen" à l'est. Elle a soutenu que le Yémen ne pouvait à présent écarter des cartes dressées par Petroconsultants, produites et invoquées par le Yémen lors de la première étape, et faisant apparaître des limites de concessions suivant une ligne médiane entre les côtes se faisant face du Yémen et de l'Erythrée, parce qu'il les avait produites à d'autres fins. L'Erythrée a reconnu que les contrats et la conduite du Yémen et de l'Ethiopie et de l'Erythrée n'équivalent pas à une acceptation mutuelle d'une frontière maritime suivant un tracé médian, ni même à un *modus vivendi* quant à une quelconque ligne. Mais elle a fait valoir qu'ils constituent néanmoins une base convaincante pour diviser les eaux de la mer Rouge selon une "ligne médiane historique", sur le tracé de laquelle les îles en litige "situées au milieu de la mer" n'auraient pas d'influence.

80. Le Yémen a soutenu pour sa part que, s'il avait produit des cartes de Petroconsultants comme preuves de sa souveraineté sur les îles en litige, il ne l'avait pas fait aux fins de faire apparaître des limites maritimes; que les cartes de Petroconsultants contiennent des "erreurs"; et que ces cartes et d'autres encore qui ont été produites lors de la première étape portent une note d'avertissement au sujet des lignes qui pourraient toucher ou porter atteinte aux droits souverains du gouvernement contractant. Le Yémen a souligné la conclusion du Tribunal selon laquelle les concessions avaient été "octroyées alors que l'on avait à l'esprit des considérations d'ordre commercial, et sans que l'on prenne particulièrement en compte l'existence des îles". (Sentence sur la souveraineté, paragraphe 412.)

81. Il y a lieu de noter que, au moment de statuer au sujet de la souveraineté sur les îles en litige, le Tribunal a jugé en effet que les contrats pétroliers "étayent dans

une certaine mesure le tracé d'une ligne médiane entre les côtes se faisant face de l'Erythrée et du Yémen, opéré sans prendre en compte les îles, pour séparer les juridictions respectives des Parties".

82. A ce stade, toutefois, le Tribunal agit à la lumière des dispositions du paragraphe 527 de sa Sentence. La question de savoir quelles sont les îles relevant de la souveraineté territoriale de l'Erythrée et quelles sont celles qui relèvent de la souveraineté territoriale du Yémen a été tranchée. Aux fins de délimiter les frontières maritimes des Parties, le Tribunal est prié en cette seconde étape de la procédure de prendre en compte, entre autres, l'opinion qu'il se sera faite sur les questions de souveraineté territoriale.

83. Ainsi qu'il est dit en d'autres endroits de la présente Sentence, le Tribunal a adopté comme base initiale, comme principe fondamental, l'idée que, entre côtes se faisant face, s'applique une ligne médiane. L'analyse des arrangements pétroliers qui figure dans la Sentence sur la souveraineté fait bien apparaître, comme on vient de le noter, des références répétées à une ligne médiane entre les côtes du Yémen et de l'Erythrée. Dans cette mesure, la position de l'Erythrée dans la présente étape est confortée par ces références. Mais ce n'est pas à dire que la frontière maritime qu'il s'agit à présent de tracer doit l'être sur toute sa longueur sans tenir compte des îles sur lesquelles la souveraineté a été déterminée; ni que cette frontière devrait suivre la "ligne médiane historique" revendiquée par l'Erythrée. Les lignes délimitant les concessions ont été tracées sans que l'on prenne en compte des îles volcaniques désertes sur lesquelles la souveraineté n'était pas déterminée. On peut difficilement les considérer comme s'appliquant encore dès lors que cette souveraineté a été déterminée. S'il convient dans un premier temps de prendre en considération les côtes continentales et les îles qui les bordent, il est ou pourrait être nécessaire d'accorder un certain poids aux îles, en ce qui concerne en tout cas leurs eaux territoriales. Quel poids, pour quelles raisons et de quelle manière – c'est ce que l'on va à présent examiner.

84. Au sujet des arrangements pétroliers et du tracé d'une frontière maritime entre les Parties dans la mer Rouge, le Tribunal rappelle la conclusion à laquelle est parvenue la Cour internationale de Justice dans son Arrêt dans les affaires du *Plateau continental de la mer du Nord*,[7] que la délimitation des zones de plateau continental de deux Etats peut conduire à "des chevauchements entre les zones relevant des Parties. La Cour considère qu'il faut accepter cette situation comme une donnée de fait et la résoudre soit par une division des zones de chevauchement effectuée par voie d'accord ou, à défaut, par parts égales, soit par des accords d'exploitation en commun, cette dernière solution paraissant particulièrement appropriée lorsqu'il s'agit de préserver l'unité d'un gisement." Dans son opinion individuelle en cette affaire, M. Jessup s'est référé à un article fécond de

[7] CIJ Recueil 1969, p. 52.

William T. Onorato[8] et a cité des exemples d'un telle coopération; et, au cours des trente dernières années, la pratique consistant pour des Etats à exploiter en coopération des ressources situées à cheval sur leurs frontières maritimes a connu un développement significatif. Les cas d'une telle pratique sont passés en revue et analysés dans les essais regroupés en un volume par le British Institute of International and Comparative Law,[9] ainsi que dans une étude plus récente de Masahiro Miyoshi, *The Joint Development of Offshore Oil and Gas in Relation to the Maritime Boundary Delimitations*, International Boundaries Research Unit, 1999.[10]

85. Cette pratique présente une pertinence particulière en l'espèce. La mer Rouge ne peut se comparer aux grands océans. L'Erythrée et le Yémen se font face de part et d'autre d'une étendue relativement étroite. Leurs peuples se sont longtemps mêlés et le plus souvent avec profit au cours du passé, un passé marqué non seulement par la liberté de mouvement des pêcheurs, mais encore par une activité commune plus vaste, et par l'adhésion à une même règle en même temps qu'à une même religion. Ces relations sont de beaucoup antérieures aux concepts relativement récents, d'origine européenne, de souveraineté exclusive. Si l'on n'a pas trouvé à ce jour de pétrole et de gaz en quantités commercialement exploitables sous les eaux de la mer Rouge, il est possible que l'une ou l'autre de ces ressources ou les deux le soient à l'avenir.

86. Au paragraphe 1 de sa Demande, l'Erythrée prie le Tribunal de déterminer que "L'utilisation historique par le peuple érythréen des ressources des îles situées au milieu de la mer comprend . . . l'exploitation . . . des minerais". Pour les raisons exposées au paragraphe 104 de sa Sentence, le Tribunal n'est pas à même d'accéder à cette requête. Toutefois, il est d'avis que, s'agissant de la frontière maritime établie par la présente Sentence, les Parties sont tenues de s'informer et de se consulter l'une l'autre au sujet de tout gisement de pétrole ou de gaz ou de toute autre ressource minière qui pourrait être découvert à cheval sur cette frontière maritime unique ou dans son voisinage immédiat. De plus, les liens historiques entre les peuples intéressés, et les relations amicales que les Parties ont renouées depuis que le Tribunal a rendu sa Sentence sur la souveraineté, de même que la pratique des Etats en matière d'exploitation de ressources marines se trouvant à cheval sur des frontières maritimes, exigent de l'Erythrée et du Yémen

---

[8] *Apportionment of an International Petroleum Deposit*, ICLQ, vol. 17, p. 85 (1958).

[9] Volume publié sous la direction de Hazel Fox sous le titre *Joint Development of Offshore Oil and Gas* (1990) avec des contributions de R.R. Churchill, Kamal Hossein, Isa Huneidi, Masahiro Miyoshi, Ian Townsend-Gault, Anastasia Strati, H. Burmester, Clive R. Symmons, Thomas H. Walde, Brenda Barrett, P. Birnie et A.D. Read.

[10] Voir aussi, I.F.I. Shihata et W.T. Onorato, *Joint Development of International Petroleum Resources in Undefined and Disputed Areas*, International Conference of the LAWASIA Energy Centre, Kuala Lumpur, 1992.

qu'ils étudient toutes les possibilités d'une exploitation partagée ou commune ou unifiée de telles ressources.

CHAPITRE IV – Le régime de pêche traditionnel

87. Au paragraphe 526 de sa Sentence sur la souveraineté territoriale et le champ du différend, le Tribunal a dit ce qui suit:

> En concluant que les Parties ont chacune souveraineté sur diverses îles, le Tribunal souligne à leur intention qu'une telle souveraineté n'exclut pas, mais implique plutôt, la perpétuation du régime de pêche traditionnel dans la région. Ce régime existant s'est appliqué, comme l'attestent amplement les éléments de preuve présentés au Tribunal, autour des îles Hanish et Zuqar et des îles de Jabal al-Tayr et du groupe de Zubayr. Dans l'exercice de sa souveraineté sur ces îles, le Yémen veillera à ce que le régime de pêche traditionnel assurant libre accès et libre jouissance aux pêcheurs du Yémen comme de l'Erythrée soit préservé afin de protéger l'existence et les moyens d'existence de cette catégorie pauvre et industrieuse de la population.

88. Aussitôt après, à l'alinéa vi de son Dispositif, le Tribunal a décidé que:

> la souveraineté qui a été jugée revenir au Yémen implique la perpétuation du régime de pêche traditionnel dans la région, y compris libre accès et libre jouissance pour les pêcheurs de l'Erythrée comme du Yémen.

89. L'Erythrée s'est dite d'avis que ces conclusions appellent l'établissement de zones de ressources conjointes, qu'il incomberait au Tribunal de délimiter dans sa Sentence de la deuxième étape. L'Erythrée, dans sa Demande, a pressé elle aussi le Tribunal d'enjoindre les Parties de négocier en vue de parvenir à certains résultats qu'elle estime requis par le paragraphe 527(vi) du Dispositif de la Sentence sur la souveraineté, et de prendre certaines autres dispositions connexes. Faute de quoi, a fait valoir l'Erythrée, le Tribunal statuerait *infra petita*. L'Erythrée a en outre soutenu que le dernier paragraphe de la lettre en date du 9 novembre 1998 adressée par le Président du Tribunal au conseil et co-agent de l'Erythrée laissait à l'Erythrée toute liberté de présenter des conclusions dans ce sens au cours de la présente étape de l'arbitrage. Dans ses plaidoiries, l'Erythrée n'est pas revenue sur certains des éléments contenus dans sa Demande, la principale requête qu'elle a alors formulée étant que le Tribunal dise avec précision ce qu'impliquaient ses conclusions concernant le régime de pêche traditionnel et où ce régime s'appliquait dans la mer Rouge. Toutefois, l'Erythrée a présenté sa Demande, non modifiée, comme représentant ses conclusions finales.

90. Le Yémen a estimé qu'il ressortait clairement du paragraphe 526 de la Sentence sur la souveraineté que c'était à lui, le Yémen, qu'il revenait, dans l'exercice de sa souveraineté, d'assurer la préservation du régime de pêche traditionnel; que, si les accords de 1994 et 1998 pouvaient se révéler d'utiles instruments aux fins de cet exercice de souveraineté, il n'était nullement question que cette souveraineté ait été rendue conditionnelle, de sorte qu'aucun accord avec l'Erythrée n'était nécessaire pour prendre les mesures administratives qui pouvaient se rapporter à ce régime; que le Tribunal n'avait nullement conclu qu'il

devrait y avoir des zones de ressources conjointes ou communes; que la décision du Tribunal selon laquelle la souveraineté du Yémen impliquait la perpétuation du régime de pêche traditionnel était une décision rendue en faveur des pêcheurs de l'Erythrée et du Yémen et non de l'Etat d'Erythrée; que l'article 3(1) de l'Accord sur les principes et l'article 2(3) du Compromis d'arbitrage signifiaient que le Tribunal outrepasserait ses pouvoirs s'il répondait favorablement à la Demande de l'Erythrée; et que, de fait, la lettre du Président en date du 9 novembre 1998 montrait que cette Demande était entachée d'irrégularité. En outre, le Yémen a fait valoir que les activités de pêche de l'Erythrée n'avaient jamais eu une ampleur significative au voisinage des îles.

91. Le contenu détaillé des positions adoptées par l'Erythrée et le Yémen est résumé plus haut aux paragraphes 48 à 60.

92. Le Tribunal rappelle que, s'agissant de cet aspect de sa Sentence sur la souveraineté, il s'est fondé sur le respect des traditions juridiques de la région. Il a pris note de l'abondante littérature consacrée aux réalités historiques qui ont marqué l'existence des populations des deux rives, orientale et occidentale, dans la note 9, se rapportant au paragraphe 121, et la note 11, se rapportant au paragraphe 128, de sa Sentence à l'issue de la première étape de la procédure. Cette situation factuelle bien établie fait apparaître des traditions juridiques communes profondément enracinées qui ont prévalu plusieurs siècles durant au sein des populations des deux rives de la mer Rouge, lesquelles sont demeurées jusqu'à la dernière partie du 19e siècle sous le contrôle direct ou indirect de l'Empire ottoman. Le concept fondamental de l'islam selon lequel tous les êtres humains sont les "intendants de Dieu" sur terre, jouissant du droit inhérent de pourvoir à leurs besoins alimentaires en pêchant de l'une à l'autre rive, libres de capturer le poisson des deux côtés et de faire commerce du surplus, est demeuré vivace dans la conscience collective des Dankhali comme des Yéménites.

93. Bien que les bénéficiaires immédiats de ce concept juridique aient été et soient les pêcheurs eux-mêmes, celui-ci s'applique également aux Etats dans leurs relations mutuelles. Comme l'a fait observer un éminent spécialiste: "L'islam n'est pas seulement une religion, mais aussi une communauté politique (*umma*) dotée d'un ensemble de lois conçues à la fois pour protéger l'intérêt collectif de ses sujets et pour réglementer leurs relations avec le monde extérieur".[11]

94. La souveraineté que le Tribunal a attribuée au Yémen sur Jabal al-Tayr, le groupe de Zubayr et le groupe Zuqar-Hanish n'est bien sûr pas une souveraineté "conditionnelle", mais une souveraineté qui néanmoins respecte et embrasse les concepts juridiques islamiques régionaux et leur est subordonnée. Comme il a été justement dit, "dans le monde moderne, il demeure vrai que les principes généraux

[11] Khadduri, *Encyclopedia of Public International Law*, volume 6, p. 227.

fondamentaux en matière d'éthique du *Quran* et de la *Sunna* peuvent être légitimement invoqués en vue de consolider et conforter les règles du droit international positif dans leur développement progressif vers la réalisation de l'objectif consistant à instaurer la justice et à promouvoir la dignité humaine pour l'ensemble de l'humanité".[12]

95. Dans sa Sentence sur la souveraineté le Tribunal ne s'est fondé sur aucune évaluation du volume, absolu ou relatif, des activités de pêche yéménites ou érythréennes dans la région des îles. Le fait pertinent était que les pêcheurs de l'une et l'autre de ces nations avaient, depuis des temps immémoriaux, utilisé ces îles pour la pêche et autres activités connexes. En outre, la décision concernant le régime de pêche traditionnel a été prise dans le cadre de la Sentence sur la souveraineté précisément parce que l'attribution d'une souveraineté territoriale au sens occidental classique aurait été comprise comme autorisant le pouvoir au sein de l'Etat souverain à exclure de ses eaux les pêcheurs d'une autre nationalité. Le Tribunal a constaté que, jusqu'à une date récente, le titre sur Jabal al-Tayr et le groupe de Zubayr et sur l'ensemble Zuqar-Hanish était demeuré indéterminé. De surcroît, ces îles se trouvent à une certaine distance des côtes continentales des Parties. En raison de leur situation, les pêcheurs en ont fait un usage particulier, comme escales et comme lieux où s'abriter, et non pas seulement, ni même principalement, comme zones de pêche. Ces facteurs particuliers sont à l'origine d'une tradition locale que la loi se doit de respecter et de protéger.

96. Il est clair que le Compromis d'arbitrage n'autorise pas le Tribunal à répondre par l'affirmative aux paragraphes 6 et 7 de la Demande de l'Erythrée. De fait, le Tribunal n'aurait pas davantage pu le faire quand bien même l'arbitrage aurait été conduit en une seule étape ou phase, comme envisagé initialement à l'article 3(1) de l'Accord sur les principes.

97. Toutefois, l'Erythrée est en droit de faire valoir devant le Tribunal que la décision de celui-ci quant au régime de pêche traditionnel a des incidences sur la délimitation des frontières maritimes lors de la seconde étape, et le Tribunal est libre de répondre à de telles conclusions.

98. De fait, il ne peut que le faire, faute de quoi il ne serait pas à même de se prononcer sur les conclusions présentées par le Yémen comme par l'Erythrée en cette seconde étape. Le fait que l'arbitrage soit rendu en deux étapes ne peut avoir pour effet que les Parties continuent de débattre de la question de savoir si le contenu de fond des conclusions du Tribunal sur le régime de pêche traditionnel est d'une quelconque pertinence aux fins de la délimitation, alors que le Tribunal serait tenu de garder le silence. La décision prise d'un commun accord par les

---

[12] *Encyclopedia of Public International Law*, volume 7, p. 229.

Parties de diviser l'arbitrage en deux étapes n'a jamais été dictée par un tel formalisme.

99. Bien entendu, en rendant sa Sentence sur la souveraineté, le Tribunal n'a pas "préfiguré" ni anticipé la délimitation maritime qu'il est à présent appelé à arrêter lors de la seconde étape, après avoir pleinement entendu les Parties. Au-delà, le Tribunal ne saurait être artificiellement bridé dans la réponse qu'il pourrait faire par les modalités de procédure convenues aux fins de l'arbitrage. Le mécanisme consistant à procéder en deux étapes ne doit pas être interprété comme interdisant aux Parties de présenter les arguments de leur choix, au moment de leur choix; ni comme limitant leur droit de chercher à protéger ce qu'ils perçoivent comme leurs droits substantiels.

100. L'article 15 du Compromis d'arbitrage (dont le sens n'est pas autrement aisément intelligible) vient conforter ce point de vue. Le paragraphe 2 décrit le Compromis d'arbitrage comme portant "application des aspects de procédure" de l'Accord sur les principes. Et le paragraphe 1 dispose ce qui suit:

> Nulle disposition du présent compromis d'arbitrage ne peut être interprétée comme portant préjudice aux positions juridiques ou aux droits de chaque Partie concernant les questions soumises au Tribunal, ni ne peut affecter ou porter préjudice aux décisions du Tribunal arbitral ou aux considérations et motifs sur lesquels se fondent lesdites décisions.

101. Comme le Tribunal l'a indiqué dans sa Sentence sur la souveraineté, le régime de pêche traditionnel autour des îles Hanish et Zuqar et des îles de Jabal al-Tayr et du groupe de Zubayr assure libre accès et libre jouissance aux pêcheurs de l'Erythrée comme du Yémen. Ce régime doit être préservé pour leur bénéfice. Cela ne signifie pas, toutefois, que l'Erythrée ne puisse agir au nom de ses ressortissants, que ce soit dans le cadre de contacts diplomatiques avec le Yémen ou en présentant ses conclusions au Tribunal. Rien ne justifie que l'on importe en mer Rouge cette fiction juridique occidentale – laquelle perd de toute manière de son importance – qui veut que tous les droits juridiquement protégés, alors même qu'ils sont en réalité détenus par des individus, soient réputés être ceux de l'Etat. Cette fiction juridique avait pour objet d'autoriser une représentation diplomatique (quand l'Etat représentant en décidait ainsi) dans un monde où les individus n'avaient aucune possibilité de faire valoir leurs propres droits. Il n'a jamais été entendu toutefois que, lorsqu'un droit était détenu par un individu, ni cet individu, ni l'Etat dont il était ressortissant n'auraient accès à un recours international.

102. En conséquence, le Tribunal répond à présent aux diverses conclusions qui ont été formulées en la présente étape par les Parties, en ce qui concerne tant les principes fondamentaux du régime de pêche traditionnel mentionné aux paragraphes 526 et 527(vi) de sa Sentence sur la souveraineté que toutes incidences que ceux-ci pourraient avoir sur sa tâche en l'étape actuelle. De fait, la réponse correcte est à

rechercher dans les pages de la Sentence elle-même. Il conviendrait en particulier d'appeler l'attention sur les paragraphes 102, 126-128, 340, 353-357 et 526.

103. Le régime de pêche traditionnel n'est pas un titre détenu en commun sur des ressources, ni un droit partagé sur elles. Bien plutôt, il autorise les pêcheurs tant érythréens que yéménites à pratiquer légitimement une pêche artisanale autour des îles que le Tribunal, dans sa Sentence sur la souveraineté, a attribuées au Yémen. Cela s'entend aussi de la collecte en plongée, effectuée avec des moyens artisanaux, de coquillages et de perles. De même, ces pêcheurs demeurent en droit de faire librement de ces îles les usages traditionnellement associés à une telle activité artisanale – pour faire sécher le poisson, faire escale, chercher temporairement refuge et pour procéder à des réparations.

104. Au paragraphe 1 de sa Demande, l'Erythrée prie le Tribunal de juger que: "L'utilisation historique par le peuple érythréen des ressources des îles situées au milieu de la mer comprend . . . l'exploitation du guano et des minerais . . . ". Dans ses plaidoiries devant le Tribunal, l'Erythrée s'est référée expressément à cet égard à des activités d'exploitation du guano qui avaient fait l'objet d'une licence délivrée par l'Italie. L'exploitation du guano ne doit pas être assimilée à l'exploitation de ressources minières de façon plus générale. De plus, il est clairement dit dans la Sentence sur la souveraineté que les droits présents de l'Erythrée ne découlent pas d'une continuité alléguée de droits autrefois détenus par l'Italie. Le régime de pêche traditionnel porte sur les droits que l'ensemble des pêcheurs ont exercés de façon continue au cours des âges. Le Tribunal n'a été saisi d'aucun élément prouvant que l'exploitation du guano, ou de façon plus générale l'exploitation minière, fait partie du régime de pêche traditionnel qui a existé et continue d'exister aujourd'hui.

105. Le Rapport sur le Projet de développement des infrastructures de pêche publié par la FAO en 1995 a trait à la pêche dans les eaux érythréennes. Néanmoins, ses conclusions concernant la pêche artisanale s'appliquent vraisemblablement à l'ensemble de la région. Le Rapport de 1995 indique clairement que les embarcations artisanales comme les engins qui les équipent se caractérisent par leur simplicité. Les embarcations sont habituellement des canots équipés de petits moteurs hors-bord, des barques de taille légèrement supérieure (9 à 12 m.) dotées de moteurs de 40 à 75 chevaux, ou des *sambuk* de pêche à moteur fixe. Sont également utilisés des pirogues et de petits radeaux (*rama*).[13] Il est fait usage de palangrottes, de filets maillants et de palangres. Dans son Rapport sur la pêche dans les eaux érythréennes, la FAO qualifie ce matériel de pêche artisanal, qui varie selon les embarcations et le poisson, de "simple et efficace".[14]

---

[13] FAO 24/95 ADB-ERI.4, 27 février 1995, paragraphes 2.19 et 3.44.

[14] *Ibid.*, paragraphe 2.20.

106. Toutefois, le terme "artisanal" ne doit pas être compris comme ne s'appliquant à l'avenir qu'à un certain type de pêche correspondant exactement à ce qui se pratique aujourd'hui. L'expression "pêche artisanale" est utilisée par opposition à "pêche industrielle". Elle n'exclut pas des améliorations dans la motorisation des petites embarcations, les techniques de navigation, les moyens de communication ou les techniques de pêche; mais le régime de pêche traditionnel ne s'étend pas à la pêche marchande ou industrielle à grande échelle, ni aux activités de pêche de ressortissants d'Etats tiers dans la mer Rouge, que celles-ci soient d'envergure modeste ou aient un caractère industriel.

107. Afin que les titres qu'il confère soient réels et non purement théoriques, le régime traditionnel a également consacré certains droits connexes. La circulation en direction et en provenance des îles visées doit être libre – y compris la traversée des eaux dans lesquelles le Yémen, en vertu de sa souveraineté sur les îles, est en droit d'exclure toutes parties tierces ou de subordonner la présence de celles-ci à l'octroi d'un permis, tout comme il peut le faire à l'égard de la pêche industrielle érythréenne. Ce libre passage accordé aux pêcheurs artisanaux a existé traditionnellement non seulement entre l'Erythrée et les îles, mais aussi entre les îles et le littoral du Yémen. Le droit de pénétrer dans les ports voulus, et d'y vendre et négocier le poisson, fait partie intégrante du régime traditionnel. Le Mémorandum d'accord de 1994 entre l'Etat d'Erythrée et la République du Yémen relatif à la coopération dans les domaines de la pêche, du commerce, de l'investissement et du transport maritimes précise utilement les centres de négoce du poisson sur chaque littoral. Les pêcheurs artisanaux érythréens pêchant autour des îles attribuées au Yémen ont eu librement accès à Maydi, Khoba, Hodeidah, Khokha et Mocha sur la côte du Yémen, tout comme les pêcheurs artisanaux yéménites pêchant autour de ces îles ont bénéficié d'un droit de passer sans entrave par Assab, Tio, Dahlak et Massawa sur la côte érythréenne et d'avoir accès à ces ports. Les ressortissants de chaque pays sont en droit de vendre leurs prises aux mêmes conditions et sans discrimination dans les ports de l'autre pays. Sur les marchés de pêche eux-mêmes, le principe traditionnel de non-discrimination – en ce qui concerne le nettoyage, le stockage et la commercialisation – doit être perpétué. Le recours traditionnel, par les pêcheurs artisanaux, au système de l'*acquil* pour résoudre leurs différends doit être lui aussi maintenu et préservé.

108. Le Yémen et l'Erythrée sont, il va de soi, libres de réglementer d'un commun accord la protection de ce régime de pêche traditionnel. Dans la mesure où des considérations écologiques pourrait nécessiter à l'avenir une réglementation, le Yémen ne prendra aucune mesure administrative ayant des incidences sur ces droits traditionnels sans l'accord de l'Erythrée et vice versa pour ce qui est de l'accès aux ports de l'Erythrée par les eaux érythréennes.

109. Le régime de pêche traditionnel ne s'applique pas aux seules eaux territoriales d'îles particulières; il ne peut pas davantage être limité selon des usages passés allégués en matière de pêche. C'est, comme le note le Yémen lui-même dans ses

réponses aux questions du Tribunal (voir annexe 2, page *515*), un régime "qui s'est appliqué pour le bénéfice des pêcheurs des deux pays dans toute la région". De par sa nature même, il n'est pas restreint par les zones marines spécifiées aux termes de la Convention des Nations Unies sur le droit de la mer, qui constitue par décision des Parties le droit applicable aux fins de la tâche présente du Tribunal en cette seconde étape de l'arbitrage. Le régime de pêche traditionnel s'applique dans la totalité de ces eaux au-delà des eaux territoriales de chacune des Parties, ainsi que dans leurs eaux territoriales et leurs ports, dans la mesure et de la manière indiquées au paragraphe 107 ci-dessus.

110. En conséquence, il ne dépend pas, du point de vue de son existence ou de sa protection, du tracé d'une frontière internationale par le présent Tribunal. De fait, le Yémen a tout au moins reconnu cela dans ses réponses aux questions du Tribunal lorsqu'il a fait observer que "les conclusions formulées par le Tribunal dans sa première Sentence au sujet du régime de pêche traditionnel ont l'autorité de la chose jugée sans préjudice de la frontière maritime sur laquelle le Tribunal statuera lors de la seconde étape de la procédure" (annexe 2, page *515*). Le Yémen a informé le Tribunal qu'il était "pleinement résolu à appliquer et mettre à effet la Sentence sous tous ses aspects, y compris en ce qui concerne la perpétuation du régime de pêche traditionnel au bénéfice des pêcheurs de l'Erythrée comme du Yémen". Le tracé de la frontière maritime n'est pas davantage subordonné à la décision rendue par le Tribunal, dans sa Sentence sur la souveraineté, quant à un tel régime.

111. Comme le Tribunal l'a expliqué plus haut, aucun nouvel accord conjoint n'est juridiquement nécessaire pour que soit perpétué un régime fondé sur la liberté réciproque et l'absence de conditions imposées unilatéralement. Toutefois, si l'Erythrée et le Yémen devaient décider que la coopération projetée, telle qu'illustrée par le Mémorandum d'accord de 1994 et l'Accord de 1998, peut utilement servir d'assise au régime traditionnel, ils pourraient choisir certaines des possibilités offertes par ces instruments. Par son objet, l'instrument de 1994 présente une pertinence particulière. (De surcroît, le Tribunal croit comprendre que les Parties n'entendaient pas conjointement priver des droits qui sont les leurs en vertu de ce régime traditionnel les pêcheurs qui n'auraient pas présenté un permis de pêche à l'autre Partie trois mois au plus tard après la date de la signature du Mémorandum d'accord.)

112. Le Tribunal a répondu aux demandes formulées par les deux Parties, comme elles en avaient le droit, en la présente phase de la procédure. Sa réponse indique comment il convient de comprendre sa Sentence sur la souveraineté en ce qui concerne les questions dont il a été à présent saisi par les Parties.

CHAPITRE V – La délimitation de la frontière internationale

Commentaires du présent Tribunal concernant les arguments des Parties

113. Du fait que, on le verra plus loin, le tracé de la frontière maritime internationale décidé par le Tribunal diffère à certains égards tant de celui qui a été revendiqué par le Yémen que de celui, ou ceux, qui a, ou ont, été revendiqué(s) par l'Erythrée, il convient d'expliquer tout d'abord brièvement en quels endroits et pourquoi les frontières revendiquées par les Parties ne sont pas confirmées dans la présente Sentence. C'est à quoi on va à présent s'attacher en examinant de manière générale en premier les revendications du Yémen, puis celle de l'Erythrée, puisque tel est l'ordre dans lequel les Parties sont convenues de plaider lors des audiences en cette seconde étape de l'arbitrage.

114. Le Yémen a revendiqué une frontière internationale unique. La ligne unique revendiquée par lui a été décrite comme une "ligne médiane" parce que le Yémen a considéré les côtes ouest de toutes ses îles comme des côtes pertinentes aux fins de la délimitation. S'agissant de la côte de l'Erythrée, le Yémen a situé ses points de base sur la côte continentale de l'Erythrée et n'a donc pas pris en compte les îles érythréennes présentes au milieu de la mer pour délimiter la frontière. Le Yémen a fait aussi valoir que cette ligne peut être proprement décrite comme une ligne médiane entre deux côtes. Selon lui, les côtes pertinentes comprenaient non seulement celles des îles sur lesquelles il s'était vu attribuer la souveraineté, mais encore celles de certaines des îles Dahlak; par conséquent, le Yémen, comme l'Erythrée, était prêt à considérer les Dahlak comme faisant partie de la côte érythréenne, et a donc situé des points de base sur les îlots constituant la frange extérieure de l'archipel. En revanche, lorsque l'Erythrée évoquait la "ligne médiane entre deux côtes", elle entendait par là la ligne médiane entre ce qui, à ses yeux, représentait les côtes *continentales* des deux Parties. Dans le même temps, l'Erythrée a revendiqué une ligne médiane historique pour laquelle seules ses propres îles offraient des points de base et qui ne prenait donc pas en compte les îles du Yémen. Ces diverses méthodes aboutissaient à différentes propositions de lignes médianes. Voir les cartes 3 et 7 de l'Erythrée et la carte 12.1 du Yémen. Voir aussi les cartes 1 et 2 faisant apparaître les points de base indiqués par l'Erythrée.

115. C'est dans ce que le Yémen a appelé le secteur nord de la ligne de délimitation que ces différences produisaient l'écart le plus grand, de plusieurs milles nautiques de fait, entre les lignes revendiquées par les Parties, par suite de leur divergence quant à l'appréciation de l'"effet" sur la ligne qu'il convenait d'attribuer aux îles yéménites septentrionales situées au milieu de la mer, à savoir la petite isolée Jabal al-Tayr et les groupes d'îles et d'îlots dénommés Zubayr. Le Yémen leur attribuait plein effet sur la ligne; l'Erythrée ne leur en accordait aucun.

116. Lorsque l'on considère cette nette divergence de vues, il est bon de se souvenir que, dans sa partie nord, la ligne de délimitation – y compris bien sûr les deux tracés rivaux qui en ont été revendiqués – est une frontière entre les étendues de plateau continental et les zones économiques exclusives du Yémen et de l'Erythrée; et qu'elle est par conséquent régie par les articles 74 et 83 de la Convention de 1982. En tout état de cause, il faut admettre des différences d'opinion quant à l'interprétation d'articles qui, en un effort de dernière minute pour parvenir à un accord sur une question fort controversée, ont été volontairement conçus lors de la troisième Conférence des Nations Unies sur le droit de la mer de façon à trancher le moins possible. Il est clair, toutefois, que les deux articles envisagent un résultat équitable.

117. Cette exigence de résultat équitable soulève directement la question de l'effet à accorder aux îles situées au milieu de la mer qui, en vertu de leur position centrale, et s'il leur est reconnu plein effet, peuvent manifestement produire un effet disproportionné – ou au demeurant un effet raisonnable et proportionné – selon leur taille, leur importance et autres aspects du contexte géographique général.

118. Le Yémen a très clairement perçu ce problème. Il a fait valoir que, bien que ces îles et îlots soient de petite taille et inhabitables (facteurs dont il a été fait grand cas lors de la première étape de l'Arbitrage), ces attributs étaient parfaitement contrebalancés ou "équilibrés" par la taille et l'importance tout aussi réduites des îlots à la lisière extérieure du groupe des Dahlak qui servaient de points de base à la frontière du côté érythréen. Toutefois, la situation de ces îlots diffère beaucoup de celle des îles situées au milieu de la mer. Les îlots à la lisière extérieure des Dahlak appartiennent à un groupe d'îles beaucoup plus vaste dont les deux Parties ont convenu qu'il faisait partie intégrante de la côte continentale de l'Erythrée. Par conséquent, les eaux comprises entre ces îlots et le continent sont des eaux intérieures érythréennes. Le Tribunal, on va le voir, a donc rejeté sans hésitation cet "équilibre" postulé par le Yémen, puisque mettant en balance des choses non comparables.

119. S'interrogeant sur le caractère équitable de l'"effet" à attribuer à ces îles et îlots septentrionaux, le Tribunal a décidé de ne pas accéder au voeu du Yémen que leur soit reconnu plein effet, ou du moins un certain effet, sur la ligne médiane. Cette décision s'est trouvée confirmée par le fait que, de toute façon, ces îles situées au milieu de la mer posséderaient une mer territoriale s'étendant jusqu'à la limite normale de 12 milles – y compris du côté occidental.

120. L'une des conséquences pratiques de l'équilibre postulé par le Yémen concernant les îles septentrionales situées au milieu de la mer fut qu'il n'envisagea pas comme autre solution possible des points de base sur les îles bordant la côte *continentale* de son territoire – lesquelles îles pouvaient de manière beaucoup plus convaincante être décrites comme faisant pendant aux Dahlak.

121. L'argumentation de l'Erythrée s'agissant de ce tronçon nord de la ligne était relativement simple: l'Erythrée contesta vigoureusement l'équilibre suggéré par le Yémen et postula dans ce secteur une ligne médiane entre les côtes continentales se faisant face. Dans un premier temps, les points de base utilisés par l'Erythrée n'apparurent pas clairement. Toutefois, en réponse à une question du Tribunal, l'Erythrée présenta dûment deux séries complètes de points de base sur la côte érythréenne, ainsi qu'une série sur la côte yéménite. (Voir les cartes 1 et 2.)

122. La limite représentée par le parallèle 14°25'N – qui sépare le secteur nord et le secteur central selon la terminologie du Yémen – résulte d'un autre facteur sur lequel les Parties diffèrent. Le Yémen n'a pas choisi cette latitude au hasard. Elle correspond au point où la ligne médiane revendiquée par le Yémen cesse d'avoir Zubayr comme point de base et est déterminée par le point nord-ouest sur l'île de Zuqar. Les lignes de l'Erythrée, puisqu'il y en a en effet deux, continuent vers le sud sans qu'il soit tenu compte de l'effet possible du groupe Zuqar-Hanish. Sa ligne médiane "historique" (carte 3) traverse Zuqar, tandis que la ligne médiane entre les côtes traverse l'île dite de la Grande Hanish (carte 7).

123. Le Tribunal a éprouvé quelque difficulté à résoudre cette divergence sur le plan de la méthode, mais a décidé pour finir de poursuivre son tracé comme celui d'une ligne construite entre les côtes continentales jusqu'au point où la présence de l'ensemble yéménite Zuqar-Hanish appelle à l'infléchir vers l'ouest. (Le tracé du Tribunal, comme il apparaîtra plus loin, ne coïncide ni avec la ligne du Yémen, ni non plus avec celle de l'Erythrée.)

124. A l'appui de sa solution consistant à définir des enclaves autour de certaines des îles de l'Erythrée, le Yémen entreprit d'évaluer la taille et l'importance relatives des îles érythréennes en général, comme s'il s'agissait d'îles dont il y a lieu d'apprécier l'influence sur la ligne de délimitation, non pas comme se trouvant éventuellement dans une zone de chevauchement des mers territoriales, mais comme devant être prises en compte uniquement par référence aux articles 74 et 83 de la Convention. Cette approche permit au Yémen de faire valoir que ces "dangers pour la navigation" érythréens étaient dénués d'importance, même comparés au groupe yéménite Zuqar-Hanish; et qu'en conséquence les South West Rocks et le Haycocks devraient constituer des enclaves et la ligne de délimitation passer entre eux et l'Erythrée, de sorte que les deux enclaves se trouveraient isolées du côté yéménite.

125. Le Tribunal, comme on le verra plus loin, n'a guère eu de difficulté à préférer les arguments de l'Erythrée, qui font intervenir l'article 15 de la Convention. Cette solution a aussi l'avantage d'éviter la nécessité de créer des enclaves peu pratiques à proximité d'une grande route maritime internationale.

126. Le “secteur sud” défini par le Yémen commençait au delà du parallèle 13°20'N. Là encore, le choix n’avait rien d’arbitraire. C’est à cette hauteur que la ligne médiane postulée par l’Erythrée, qui était jusque là commandée par Suyul Hanish, commençait à être déterminée par le point le plus proche sur la côte continentale du Yémen. Le tracé du Yémen demeurait ensuite dans tout le secteur sud celui d’une ligne médiane entre côtes se faisant face.

127. Dans la plus grande partie de ce secteur sud, les lignes postulées respectivement par le Yémen et l’Erythrée ne différaient par conséquent que sur des points de détail, du fait qu’aucune île située au milieu de la mer ne venait en compliquer la construction. La baie d’Assab et les îles qui la jouxtent créaient certes une importante complication, mais le Yémen considéra à juste titre que cette baie faisait partie intégrante de la côte de l’Erythrée et de ses eaux intérieures, et que les points de base déterminants devaient donc se situer sur la laisse de basse mer des îles côtières constituant sa lisière extérieure.

128. Une fois franchies les zones où les mers territoriales se chevauchent pour aborder le tronçon relativement simple entre côtes parallèles correspondant au secteur sud, la ligne proposée par le Yémen redevenait une ligne médiane déterminée par les îles yéménites d’une part et par la côte continentale de l’Erythrée d’autre part. Toutefois, la ligne qui aurait la préférence du Tribunal, compte tenu de la simplicité souhaitable au voisinage d’une grande route maritime, devrait marquer ce passage de façon directe et indépendamment des îles du Yémen et de l’Erythrée. Tracer la ligne médiane postulée par l’Erythrée dans ce secteur n’est pas chose aisée en raison de la complication que constituent les périmètres définis par lui autour des zones traditionnelles de pêche. De fait, la présente analyse des arguments des Parties et du point de vue du Tribunal ne rend pas vraiment justice au dispositif complexe et soigneusement étudié mis au point par l’Erythrée pour délimiter de la sorte ces zones de pêche, mais la question a été tranchée au chapitre IV.

Il s’agit à présent de décrire la ligne de délimitation déterminée par le Tribunal.

* – * – *

La ligne de délimitation déterminée par le Tribunal

129. La tâche du Tribunal en la présente étape de l’Arbitrage est définie à l’article 2 du Compromis d’arbitrage, aux termes duquel cette étape “donne lieu à une sentence sur la délimitation des frontières maritimes”. Le terme “frontières” est utilisé ici, peut-on raisonnablement supposer, au sens normal et ordinaire qui est le sien, à savoir comme désignant une frontière maritime internationale entre les deux Etats Parties à l’Arbitrage; et non pas au sens de ce que l’on appelle habituellement une “limite” maritime, telle que la limite extérieure d’une mer territoriale ou d’une

zone contiguë; encore qu'il puisse se faire que, par endroits, ces limites coïncident avec la frontière internationale ou se trouvent modifiées par elle.

130. L'article 2 dispose également que le Tribunal statue au sujet des frontières maritimes "en prenant en compte l'opinion qu'il se sera faite sur les questions de souveraineté territoriale, la Convention des Nations Unies sur le droit de la mer et tout autre élément pertinent". Les raisons pour lesquelles il importe de prendre en compte la Sentence sur la souveraineté sont tout à fait claires et les deux Parties ont convenu dans leurs écritures et plaidoiries qu'il ne pouvait être question, lors de cette seconde étape, de tenter de revenir sur les décisions arrêtées dans la première sentence. La disposition prescrivant de prendre en compte la Convention des Nations Unies sur le droit de la mer de 1982 est importante du fait que l'Erythrée n'est pas partie à cette Convention mais a accepté, dans ledit Compromis d'arbitrage, qu'en soient appliquées les dispositions qui seraient jugées pertinentes en la présente étape. Le Compromis d'arbitrage ne fait nulle mention du droit coutumier de la mer, mais la Convention en reprend dans ses dispositions de nombreux éléments pertinents. L'expression "tout autre élément pertinent" représente un concept très large et englobe sans nul doute divers facteurs dont il est généralement reconnu qu'ils influent sur l'opération de délimitation comme la proportionnalité, le principe de non-empiétement, la présence d'îles, et tout autre facteur de nature à affecter la recherche d'une solution équitable eu égard à la situation particulière.

131. Il est généralement admis, ainsi qu'en témoignent tant les écrits des publicistes que la jurisprudence, qu'entre des côtes se faisant face, c'est par une ligne médiane ou d'équidistance que s'obtient en principe une frontière équitable telle que prescrite dans la Convention, et en particulier dans ses articles 74 et 83, qui portent respectivement sur la délimitation équitable de la zone économique exclusive et du plateau continental entre Etats dont les côtes se font face ou sont adjacentes. De fait, l'une et l'autre Parties à la présente affaire ont revendiqué une frontière définie selon la méthode de l'équidistance, quoique sur des bases différentes et avec des résultats fort dissemblables.

132. Le Tribunal a décidé, après mûre considération de tous les arguments convaincants et judicieux qui lui ont été présentés par les deux Parties, que la frontière internationale sera une frontière unique aussi valable à d'autres fins suivant une ligne médiane et que cette ligne médiane devrait, dans toute la mesure du possible, être construite par rapport aux côtes continentales se faisant face. Non seulement cette solution est en accord avec la pratique et les précédents dans des cas similaires, mais elle est de surcroît déjà familière aux deux Parties. Comme le Tribunal a eu l'occasion de l'observer dans sa Sentence sur la souveraineté (paragraphe 438), les contrats pétroliers offshore conclus par le Yémen, et par l'Ethiopie et l'Erythrée, "étayent dans une certaine mesure le tracé d'une ligne médiane entre les côtes se faisant face de l'Erythrée et du Yémen, opéré sans prendre en compte les îles, pour séparer les juridictions respectives des Parties".

En la présente étape, le Tribunal est appelé à déterminer non pas seulement une limite aux fins de concessions et d'accords pétroliers, mais une frontière internationale unique aussi valable à d'autres fins. S'agissant d'une telle frontière, la présence d'îles exige que soit soigneusement pris en compte leur effet possible sur la ligne de délimitation; et c'est ce qui est fait dans l'analyse qui suit. Cela étant, on verra que la solution définitive est que la frontière maritime internationale demeure dans sa majeure partie une ligne médiane entre les côtes continentales des Parties.

133. Dans tous les cas, cette ligne médiane est, par définition, construite entre deux côtes puisqu'elle est définie comme une ligne "dont tous les points sont équidistants des points les plus proches des lignes de base à partir desquelles est mesurée la largeur de la mer territoriale de chacun des deux Etats" (article 15 de la Convention), définition qui, au demeurant, se retrouve à l'identique dans nombre de traités relatifs à une frontière maritime, ainsi que dans les écrits des spécialistes. La ligne de base "normale" de la mer territoriale, ainsi qu'il est précisé à l'article 5 de la Convention – ce qui est encore une fois conforme à la pratique établie de longue date ainsi qu'à la règle coutumière bien établie du droit de la mer – est "la laisse de basse mer le long de la côte, telle qu'elle est indiquée sur les cartes marines à grande échelle reconnues officiellement par l'Etat côtier". Cela soulève néanmoins un certain nombre de questions quant à ce qu'il faut entendre par "côte" à de telles fins, en particulier en présence d'îles; et ces questions, sur lesquelles les Parties divergent notablement, demandent à être tranchées par le Tribunal.

134. Tout d'abord, il est nécessaire d'examiner une complication qui surgit en la présente espèce en ce qui concerne la règle générale selon laquelle les mesures s'entendent à partir de la laisse de basse mer. Sur le plan de la législation nationale, le texte définissant la mer territoriale de l'Erythrée demeure la loi promulguée en 1953 par l'Ethiopie, aux termes de laquelle les eaux territoriales de l'Ethiopie étaient décrites comme "s'étendant à partir de l'extrémité du littoral à la marée maximale annuelle". Cette disposition a été prise bien qu'une loi sur les douanes adoptée par l'Ethiopie en 1952 ait défini une zone douanière mesurée à partir de "la laisse de basse mer moyenne aux marées de mortes eaux". Le Yémen soutenait que, compte tenu de cette législation de 1953, le Tribunal devrait calculer le tracé de la ligne médiane représentant la frontière à partir de la laisse de pleine mer plutôt que de la laisse de basse mer le long de la côte de l'Erythrée (comme l'a fait effectivement le Yémen pour calculer la ligne médiane proposée par lui).

135. En la matière, le Tribunal préfère l'argument avancé par l'Erythrée selon lequel l'utilisation de la laisse de basse mer est prescrite par une règle internationale générale à l'article 5 de la Convention, les deux Parties étant convenues que le Tribunal prendrait en compte les dispositions de la Convention au moment de statuer en la présente affaire. La ligne médiane représentant la frontière sera par

conséquent calculée à partir de la laisse de basse mer, telle qu'elle figure sur les cartes officiellement reconnues de l'Erythrée et du Yémen, conformément à la disposition de l'article 5 de la Convention. Les cartes officiellement reconnues auxquelles le Tribunal a eu recours sont les cartes de l'Amirauté britannique (BA Charts), dont le niveau de référence correspond approximativement à la marée astronomique minimale. Ces cartes figuraient parmi celles sur lesquelles se sont fondées les Parties en la présente étape de la procédure.

Extrémités nord et sud de la ligne de délimitation

136. Une autre difficulté a trait aux extrémités nord et sud de la frontière internationale. Aux termes du compromis d'arbitrage, le Tribunal a compétence et autorité pour décider de la frontière maritime entre les deux Parties. Mais il n'a ni compétence ni autorité pour décider d'une quelconque frontière entre l'une ou l'autre des deux Parties et les Etats limitrophes. Il sera donc nécessaire de fixer les deux points extrêmes de la ligne de délimitation de façon à éviter qu'elle n'empiète sur un territoire où d'autres revendications devraient être prises en compte. Il est clair toutefois qu'il convient d'examiner en premier lieu quels sont les points qui serviront de base à la construction de la ligne médiane, avant de se pencher sur la délicate question des points terminaux lorsque la ligne dont il faudra ainsi fixer les limites à ses extrémités nord et sud aura été définie.

137. Est à présent décrite la méthode de construction de la ligne représentant la frontière internationale unique arrêtée par le Tribunal, en procédant de façon générale du nord vers le sud.

Le tronçon nord de la ligne de délimitation

138. Sur ce tronçon, où les deux lignes revendiquées respectivement par l'Erythrée et le Yémen différaient si nettement dans leur tracé, se posaient trois problèmes principaux: que faire au sujet des îles Dahlak du côté érythréen; que faire au sujet de l'île isolée de Jabal al-Tayr et du groupe d'îles de Jabal al-Zubayr, au milieu de la mer; et que faire de l'ensemble d'îles et de rochers au large de la partie septentrionale du littoral yéménite. Ces trois questions sont à présent examinées dans cet ordre.

Les Dahlak

139. Ce groupe compact – ou "tapis", comme préférait le désigner l'Erythrée – d'îles et d'îlots, dont les plus vastes sont fortement peuplés, est l'exemple typique d'un groupe d'îles faisant partie intégrante de la configuration générale de la côte. Ce groupe semble avoir été toujours considéré comme tel dans la pratique, si bien que les eaux comprises au sein du système insulaire sont des eaux intérieures ou nationales et que la ligne de base de la mer territoriale se situe quelque part à la lisière extérieure de ce système.

140. Un problème surgit ici, toutefois, du fait que la lisière d'îles côtières du groupe des Dahlak se prête en outre à l'application non pas de la "ligne de base normale" de la mer territoriale, mais des "lignes de base droites" décrites à l'article 7 de la Convention (où elles sont traitées de façon distincte de la ligne de base "normale" décrite à l'article 5). Le système de lignes de base droites est décrit dans cet article comme "la méthode des lignes de base droites reliant des points appropriés". Le Yémen convient semble-t-il sans guère de difficultés que les Dahlak constituent un cas approprié pour l'établissement d'un ensemble de lignes de base droites.

141. L'Erythrée a soutenu pour sa part avoir déjà procédé à une telle opération. En réponse à une question du Tribunal, l'Erythrée a effectivement fourni les coordonnées des points de base du côté érythréen ayant servi à calculer les deux versions de la "ligne médiane" revendiquées par elle. Mais, dans la région des Dahlak, ces points de base apparaissent avoir été choisis sur une ligne passant par deux, ou peut-être trois, des îles situées à la lisière extérieure et le Negileh Rock (dont il sera question aux paragraphes 146-147 ci-après), puis continuant selon un tracé plus ou moins rectiligne vers le sud-est suivant la direction de la mer. Cette configuration fait probablement partie du système "quadrilatéral" de lignes de base droites auquel l'Erythrée a fait allusion dans son argumentation.

142. La réalité ou validité ou définition de ce système de lignes de base droites quelque peu inhabituel postulé dans les Dahlak n'est guère une question que le Tribunal est appelé à trancher. Il incombe cependant au Tribunal de décider des points de base qui détermineront le tracé de la frontière internationale. En traçant la ligne médiane revendiquée par lui, le Yémen a situé les points de base du côté occidental sur la laisse de pleine mer des petits îlots extérieurs de Segala, Dahret Segala, Zauber et Aucan. Ces îlots pourraient raisonnablement être inclus dans un système de lignes de base droites du type ordinaire et familier.

143. L'Erythrée, toutefois, a suggéré en particulier de prendre en compte une formation géographique baptisée "Negileh Rock" qui se situe plus en avant que ces îlots de plus grande taille mais néanmoins exigus et inhabités. Le Yémen a fait objection à l'utilisation de cette formation du fait que celle-ci est indiquée sur la carte 171 de l'Amirauté britannique comme étant un récif, qui de surcroît ne semble pas émerger à un quelconque moment de la marée. Il semble qu'il ne saurait être question d'utiliser comme point de base un récif qui ne soit pas en même temps un haut-fond découvrant, puisque l'article 6 de la Convention dispose (sous l'intitulé "Récifs"):

> Lorsqu'il s'agit de parties insulaires d'une formation atollienne ou d'îles bordées de récifs frangeants, la ligne de base à partir de laquelle est mesurée la largeur de la mer territoriale est la laisse de basse mer sur le récif, côté large, telle qu'elle est indiquée sur les cartes marines reconnues officiellement par l'Etat côtier.

144. Cette difficulté concernant le Negileh Rock se trouve accrue si les Dahlak donnent effectivement lieu à l'établissement d'un système de lignes de base droites, car le paragraphe 4 de l'article 7 dispose:

> Les lignes de base droites ne doivent pas être tirées vers ou depuis des hauts-fonds découvrants, à moins que des phares ou des installations similaires émergées en permanence n'y aient été construits ou que le tracé de telles lignes de base droites n'ait fait l'objet d'une reconnaissance internationale générale.

145. Bien que l'Erythrée ne soit pas partie à la Convention, elle a néanmoins consenti à son application en la présente espèce; et puisque l'Erythrée revendique l'existence d'un système de lignes de base droites, cette revendication semble exclure tout droit de se servir pour le tracé de la ligne de base d'une mer territoriale d'un récif qui n'émerge pas à marée basse.

146. Comme on le verra plus particulièrement ci-après, le Tribunal a décidé que les points de base à utiliser du côté ouest sur cette partie de la côte de l'Erythrée doivent se situer sur la laisse de basse mer de certains des îlots extérieurs des Dahlak, sur Mojeidi et sur un îlot sans nom à l'est de Dahret Segala.

* – * – *

Il convient ensuite de décider du traitement des îles situées au milieu de la mer, à savoir al-Tayr et Zubayr, car de cette décision dépend le point de savoir s'il sera nécessaire ou non de prendre en compte des points de base sur la côte du Yémen.

Jabal al-Tayr et le groupe de Zubayr

147. Le Yémen a utilisé à la fois la petite île isolée d'al-Tayr et le groupe d'îles appelé al-Zubayr comme points de base déterminants, de sorte que la ligne médiane revendiquée par lui n'est "médiane" que dans la partie de la mer s'étendant à l'ouest de ces îles. Celles-ci ne font pas partie de la côte continentale du Yémen. De plus, en raison de leur aridité et de leur caractère inhospitalier ainsi que de leur position très avancée dans la mer, déjà évoqués dans la Sentence sur la souveraineté, elles ne peuvent être prises en considération aux fins du calcul de la ligne de délimitation entre le Yémen et l'Erythrée.

148. Pour ces raisons, le Tribunal a décidé que ni l'île isolée d'al-Tayr ni le groupe d'îles d'al-Zubayr ne doivent avoir d'effet sur la ligne médiane représentant la frontière internationale.

* – * – *

Les points de base sur la côte du Yémen

149. Puisque Jabal al-Tayr et le groupe de Zubayr ne doivent avoir aucune influence sur le tracé de la ligne médiane représentant la frontière, il est nécessaire de décider des points de base qui seront utilisés sur cette partie de la côte du Yémen. Il s'agit là encore, si ce n'est d'un tapis, du moins d'un éparpillement considérable d'îles et d'îlots constituant l'amorce d'une vaste étendue d'îles et de récifs côtiers qui, plus loin au nord, se rattache pour finir à un important ensemble ou système insulaire au large du littoral de l'Arabie saoudite.

150. Le long de cette partie de la côte yéménite se trouve aussi l'île Kamaran, relativement vaste, habitée et importante. Avec le vaste promontoire que forme au sud le continent, cette île dessine une grande baie et l'on ne peut douter qu'il s'agisse là d'éléments faisant partie intégrante de la côte du Yémen et devant par conséquent influer sur le tracé de la ligne médiane. Un point de base déterminant se situe donc à l'extrémité occidentale de Kamaran. Il semble également raisonnable d'utiliser comme points de base les toutes petites îles situées immédiatement au sud de Kamaran et à l'ouest du promontoire susmentionné.

151. Il reste à examiner le cas des îles situées au nord de Kamaran. L'îlot relativement important de Tiqfash et les îles plus petites de Kutama et Uqban plus à l'ouest, paraissent tous appartenir à un système complexe d'îles, d'îlots et de récifs qui gardent cette partie de la côte. De fait, il s'agit là, aux yeux du Tribunal, d'un "système frangeant" du type envisagé à l'article 7 de la Convention, même si le Yémen n'apparaît pas l'avoir revendiqué comme tel. A la vérité, le Tribunal n'a pas bénéficié de quelconques vues du Yémen sur cette partie de la côte, celui-ci ayant choisi de déployer différemment son argumentation. Le Tribunal est néanmoins d'avis qu'il est juste d'utiliser comme points de base d'une ligne médiane non seulement Kamaran et les îlots l'entourant qui figurent sur la carte 12.1 du Yémen, mais encore les îlots au nord-ouest appelés Uqban et Kutama.

152. Les décisions ci-dessus étant prises, il est à présent possible de calculer et tracer la section nord de la frontière entre les points d'inflexion 1 et 13 (la liste des points d'inflexion accompagnés de leurs coordonnées est reproduite plus bas; voir aussi les cartes indicatives 3 et 4). Sur la totalité de cette section, la frontière devrait suivre une ligne médiane, ou ligne d'équidistance, entre côtes continentales.

153. A la hauteur du point d'inflexion numéro 13, toutefois, cette ligne médiane simple entre côtes continentales aborde un secteur où les îles du groupe Zuqar-Hanish peuvent influer sur son tracé, et cette situation appelle manifestement certaines décisions.

La section centrale de la ligne de délimitation

154. Pour d'évidentes raisons de commodité, il convient que le Tribunal se prononce d'abord sur la question de la frontière dans la partie resserrée des eaux comprise entre l'extrémité sud-ouest du groupe des Hanish d'une part et les îles érythréennes comprenant les Mohabbakah, High Island, les Haycocks et les South West Rocks de l'autre. Sur ce tronçon de la frontière s'ajoute au problème de la délimitation des zones de plateau continental et des zones économiques exclusives, celui de la délimitation d'une zone où les mers territoriales se chevauchent. Cela tient au fait que Zuqar et Hanish, sur lesquelles la souveraineté a été attribuée au Yémen, sont l'une et l'autre génératrices d'une mer territoriale chevauchant celle qu'engendrent les Haycocks et les South West Rocks, sur lesquels la souveraineté a été attribuée à l'Erythrée. Il semble au vu de la carte 12.1 du Yémen que celui-ci a estimé que l'Erythrée ne peut prétendre qu'à une mer territoriale d'une largeur strictement limitée à 12 milles à compter des points de base choisis par le Yémen le long de la laisse de pleine mer sur la côte érythréenne; il en résulterait, selon le Yémen, que les Haycocks et les South West Rocks demeureraient isolés à l'extérieur et au-delà de la mer territoriale proprement dite de l'Erythrée.

155. Cette proposition est discutable, en dehors même du fait qu'il serait à l'évidence irréaliste de créer des enclaves limitées autour d'îles et de récifs au voisinage immédiat d'une grande route maritime internationale. Il ne fait aucun doute que toute île, aussi petite soit-elle, y compris un rocher à condition que ce soit bien une île émergée à marée haute, est génératrice d'une mer territoriale pouvant atteindre 12 milles de large (article 121.2 de la Convention). Il s'ensuit qu'un chapelet d'îles distantes les unes des autres de moins de 24 milles peut générer une bande continue de mer territoriale. Tel est le cas des îles érythréennes jusques et y compris les South West Rocks.

156. Ce que le Yémen omet de prendre en compte dans sa suggestion est le fait que ce que l'on a appelé le "saute-mouton" pratiqué sur les îles et îlots érythréens présents dans cette zone a pour effet de prolonger la mer territoriale de la côte continentale au-delà de la limite des 12 milles mesurée à partir de cette côte. Aux termes de l'article 3 de la Convention, la largeur de la mer territoriale "ne dépasse pas 12 milles marins mesurés à partir de lignes de base établies conformément à la Convention". Un tel saut est acceptable parce que chaque île, si petite ou dénuée d'importance qu'elle soit, crée une nouvelle ligne de base sur sa laisse de basse mer à partir de laquelle doit être mesurée la mer territoriale attenante à la côte. Cet aspect a été invoqué avec force à l'appui des revendications de souveraineté de l'Erythrée. Ce raisonnement a été rejeté par le Tribunal dans sa Sentence sur la souveraineté, mais il est néanmoins pertinent dans le présent contexte.

157. S'il fallait encore une autre raison pour écarter la suggestion du Yémen tendant dans cette zone à enclaver les îles de l'Erythrée situées au-delà de la limite de 12 milles mesurée à partir de la laisse de pleine mer sur la côte continentale, on pourrait la trouver dans le principe de non-empiétement que le juge Lachs dans la sentence qu'il a rendu en l'affaire *Guinée/Guinée-Bissau*[15] a décrit en ces termes:

> Ainsi qu'il est dit dans la sentence, notre souci principal a été d'éviter, d'une façon ou d'une autre, que l'une des Parties se trouve confrontée à l'exercice, face à sa côte et au voisinage immédiat de celle-ci, de droits qui pourraient léser son droit au développement ou mettre en danger sa sécurité.

158. On verra que la frontière internationale doit donc passer quelque part dans un bras de mer dont la largeur n'excède pas quatre ou cinq milles. Une fois établie l'existence d'une mer territoriale attenante à la côte continentale de l'Erythrée, pouvant s'étendre au-delà du groupe d'îles que forment les South West Rocks et les Haycocks d'une part et chevauchant la mer territoriale engendrée par les îles yéménites du groupe des Hanish d'autre part, la situation appelle une frontière dont le tracé suit une ligne médiane. Aux termes de l'article 15 de la Convention, il est possible de s'écarter de la méthode normale pour construire une ligne médiane équidistante lorsque des raisons tenant à l'existence d'un titre historique ou d'autres circonstances spéciales indiquent de procéder autrement. Toutefois, le Tribunal a examiné ces raisons et circonstances et n'a pas estimé nécessaire de s'écarter de la règle.

159. Ayant en outre à l'esprit la délimitation qui constitue sa tâche globale, le Tribunal juge également que cette ligne est totalement équitable. Le Tribunal décide donc que la ligne médiane constitue la frontière internationale là où celle-ci traverse la zone de chevauchement des mers territoriales respectives des Parties.

* – * – *

Il reste toutefois à déterminer la section de la frontière destinée à relier la ligne médiane tracée entre les côtes continentales et la ligne délimitant les mers territoriales dans le secteur où elles se chevauchent. C'est à quoi il est à présent procédé.

La ligne de délimitation entre les points d'inflexion 13 et 15

160. Si la médiane entre côtes continentales se poursuivait au sud du point d'inflexion 13, elle couperait tout d'abord la mer territoriale de Zuqar, puis celle de Hanish et enfin le territoire terrestre de cette île. Elle doit donc dévier vers l'ouest en

---

[15] 25 ILM 251.

contournant le groupe Zuqar-Hanish, et en respectant également les mers territoriales de ces îles pour autant que celles-ci sont censées être génératrices de telles mers. Il semble raisonnable de considérer que ces îles possèdent une mer territoriale.

161. Le Tribunal a envisagé diverses hypothèses. S'il convient donc que la frontière internationale dévie après le point d'inflexion 13 où elle rencontre une mer territoriale s'étendant jusqu'à 12 milles de l'île de Zuqar, elle pourrait épouser les contours sinueux de la limite de cette mer territoriale jusqu'au point où il lui faut reprendre son cours vers le sud pour rejoindre la section de la frontière tracée conformément à l'article 15. Le Tribunal a décidé toutefois qu'il serait préférable que son tracé suive une ligne géodésique entre le point 13 et le point 14, moyennant le nécessaire infléchissement en direction du sud-ouest pour opérer la jonction avec la ligne médiane entre mers territoriales décrite plus haut. En outre, la tâche du Tribunal est, comme indiqué ci-dessus, de déterminer la frontière maritime; elle n'implique pas qu'il fixe aussi les limites des mers territoriales.

162. A partir du point 14, l'objectif étant là encore d'obtenir une ligne simple, l'infléchissement vers le sud de la frontière internationale prend la forme d'une ligne géodésique reliant ce point et le point 15, à partir duquel elle rejoint la médiane construite en vertu de l'article 15. Cette ligne tracée par le Tribunal entre les points d'inflexion 14 et 15 est également très proche de la limite supposée d'une mer territoriale yéménite dans ce secteur, mais constitue une frontière internationale plus nette et plus pratique.

La section sud de la frontière internationale

163. A partir du point d'inflexion 20, le plus au sud des points d'inflexion de la ligne médiane délimitant la zone où les mers territoriales se chevauchent, la frontière doit prendre la direction générale du sud-est pour rejoindre la ligne médiane entre côtes continentales. Elle le fait en suivant une ligne géodésique qui relie les points d'inflexion 20 et 21, le second correspondant à l'intersection du prolongement de la ligne médiane traversant la zone de chevauchement des mers territoriales et de la ligne médiane entre côtes continentales. Puis, la frontière internationale redevient une ligne médiane entre les deux côtes continentales. La baie d'Assab étant constituée d'eaux intérieures, les points de base déterminant le tracé de la frontière se situent à la limite de cette baie côté mer.

Les extrémités nord et sud de la ligne de délimitation

164. Mention a été faite plus haut de la nécessité de ne pas prolonger la frontière dans des zones où des parties tierces pourraient être concernées. Les points où le Tribunal a décidé de borner le tracé de la frontière sont, à l'extrémité nord, le point d'inflexion 1 et, à l'extrémité sud, le point 29. Le résultat apparaît bien sûr aussi sur les cartes indicatives 3 et 4 qui figurent au nombre des cartes jointes au

texte de la Sentence. Le Tribunal est d'avis que ces points terminaux sont bien en deçà des zones où un Etat tiers pourrait contester le tracé de la frontière.

* – * – *

Le test de proportionnalité

165. Le principe de proportionnalité a été décrit par la Cour internationale de Justice dans les affaires du *Plateau continental de la mer du Nord* comme "le rapport raisonnable qu'une délimitation opérée conformément à des principes équitables devrait faire apparaître entre l'étendue des zones de plateau continental relevant de l'Etat riverain et la longueur de son littoral mesurée suivant la direction générale de celui-ci, compte tenu à cette fin des effets actuels ou éventuels de toute autre délimitation du plateau continental entre Etats limitrophes dans la même région". Ce principe était également présenté comme l'un des "facteurs" à prendre en compte aux fins d'une délimitation.[*] Il ne s'agit pas d'un mode ou principe de délimitation indépendant, mais plutôt d'un test visant à apprécier le caractère équitable d'une délimitation opérée par quelque autre moyen.[**] Par conséquent, comme il est dit dans la Sentence rendue dans l'affaire de l'*Anglo-French Channel*, "c'est la disproportion plutôt qu'un principe général de proportionnalité qui constitue le critère ou facteur pertinent".[16]

166. Les Parties à la présente affaire se sont vigoureusement opposées dans leur argumentation sur ce point, non pas tant en ce qui concerne la signification du concept de "proportionnalité" qu'au sujet de la longueur de leurs côtes respectives à prendre en compte aux fins du calcul auquel il s'agissait de procéder. Il ne fait, de l'avis du Tribunal, aucun doute que l'expression "direction générale" du littoral signifie que le calcul de la longueur des côtes de l'Erythrée devrait être opéré en suivant le contour extérieur du groupe des Dahlak, même si l'Erythrée était plutôt encline à suivre le tracé de la côte continentale.

167. Un point fort débattu a été celui de savoir jusqu'où au nord il convenait de mesurer la côte de l'Erythrée. Cette dernière souhaitait prendre en compte dans le calcul de la proportionnalité la longueur totale de sa côte continentale jusqu'au parallèle de 16° de latitude nord; de fait, le Yémen a utilisé ce parallèle comme limite de ce qu'il a appelé le secteur nord dans la zone en question. Le Tribunal doute toutefois qu'il soit approprié d'utiliser la ligne horizontale d'un parallèle pour délimiter, aux fins du test de proportionnalité, les eaux de la mer Rouge qui

---

[*] CIJ Recueil 1969, p. 54.

[**] Voir CIJ Recueil 1985, par. 58 (affaire *Libye/Malte*). *[Note de l'éditeur: cette référence a été modifiée de la version anglaise originale.]*

[16] 18 ILM 60. Délimitation du plateau continental, décision du 30 juin 1977, La Documentation française, p. 105.

suivent un axe orienté selon un angle d'environ 45°. Il a donc pris en compte la partie pertinente de la côte érythréenne que l'on peut considérer comme "faisant face" au Yémen, qui s'arrête là où sa direction générale croise une ligne tirée, à partir de ce qui apparaît comme l'extrémité nord de la frontière terrestre du Yémen, à angle droit avec la direction générale de la côte du Yémen. De la même façon, le Tribunal a déterminé l'extrémité sud à prendre en compte pour calculer la longueur de la côte yéménite.

168. Le Tribunal, par les soins de son expert en géodésie, a calculé le rapport entre les longueurs des côtes en question, mesurées suivant la direction générale de celles-ci, et le rapport entre les superficies des eaux qu'il avait attribuées à l'une et l'autre Parties. Le premier rapport, entre longueurs de côte, est de 387026 mètres pour le Yémen contre 507110 mètres pour l'Erythrée, soit un rapport de *1 à 1,31*. Le second, entre superficies des eaux, y compris les mers territoriales, est de 25535 kilomètres carrés pour le Yémen contre 27944 kilomètres carrés pour l'Erythrée, soit un rapport de *1 à 1,09*. Le Tribunal est d'avis que la ligne de délimitation qu'il a adoptée ne produit aucune disproportion.

CHAPITRE VI – Dispositif

169. En conséquence, **LE TRIBUNAL,**
prenant en compte les considérations et motifs exposés ci-dessus,

DÉCIDE À L'UNANIMITÉ DANS LA PRÉSENTE AFFAIRE QUE

La frontière maritime internationale entre l'Erythrée et le Yémen est une série de lignes géodésiques joignant, dans l'ordre spécifié, les points suivants. Les points sont définis en degrés, minutes, secondes de la latitude et longitude géographique, basés sur le Système géodésique mondial de 1984 (WGS 84). La ligne et les indications chiffrées des points d'inflexion sont montrés à titre d'illustration seulement sur les cartes 3 et 4 dans la section des cartes de cette Sentence.

Point d'inflexion	Latitude	Longitude
1	15° 43' 10" N	41° 34' 06" E
2	15° 38' 58" N	41° 34' 05" E
3	15° 15' 10" N	41° 37' 31" E
4	15° 04' 00" N	41° 46' 43" E
5	15° 00' 12" N	41° 50' 42" E
6	14° 46' 06" N	41° 58' 47" E
7	14° 43' 30" N	42° 00' 42" E
8	14° 36' 05" N	42° 10' 02" E
9	14° 35' 14" N	42° 11' 35" E
10	14° 27' 16" N	42° 16' 54" E
11	14° 21' 11" N	42° 22' 04" E
12	14° 15' 23" N	42° 26' 09" E
13	14° 08' 39" N	42° 31' 33" E
14	14° 03' 39" N	42° 28' 39" E
15	13° 39' 30" N	42° 37' 39" E
16	13° 36' 13" N	42° 38' 30" E
17	13° 35' 51" N	42° 38' 14" E

18	13° 33' 38" N	42° 39' 37" E
19	13° 27' 28" N	42° 43' 25" E
20	13° 26' 39" N	42° 48' 21" E
21	13° 24' 01" N	42° 52' 47" E
22	13° 14' 23" N	42° 59' 47" E
23	13° 10' 54" N	43° 03' 03" E
24	13° 06' 57" N	43° 05' 21" E
25	13° 06' 08" N	43° 06' 06" E
26	13° 04' 05" N	43° 08' 42" E
27	13° 00' 27" N	43° 10' 54" E
28	12° 58' 10" N	43° 12' 45" E
29	12° 54' 23" N	43° 13' 58" E

Fait à Londres le 17 décembre 1999

Le président du Tribunal

(signé) Professeur Sir Robert Y. Jennings

Le greffier

(signé) Tjaco van den Hout

ANNEXE 1
Le compromis d'arbitrage

Le Gouvernement de l'Etat d'Erythrée et le Gouvernement de la République du Yémen (ci-après dénommés les Parties),

Animés par le désir de rétablir leurs relations pacifiques dans l'esprit de l'amitié traditionnelle entre leurs deux peuples,

Conscients de leurs responsabilités à l'égard de la communauté internationale en matière de maintien de la paix et de la sécurité internationales, et de sauvegarde de la liberté de navigation dans une région particulièrement sensible du monde,

Considérant l'" Accord sur les principes" entre l'Erythrée et le Yémen, signé à Paris le vingt et un mai 1996 (ci-après dénommé "l'Accord sur les principes"),

Conviennent de ce qui suit:

Article premier

1. Au plus tard le 31 décembre 1996, les Parties se communiquent mutuellement et communiquent à la France les noms et adresses des arbitres qu'elles ont désignés. Les quatre arbitres ainsi désignés se réunissent dans les deux semaines afin d'envisager le choix du Président du Tribunal.

2. Dans les deux semaines qui suivent, les quatre arbitres restreignent leur choix à une liste de cinq noms qu'ils transmettent aux Parties.

3. Les Parties disposent de deux semaines à compter de la date de transmission de la liste pour présenter leur avis sur cette liste.

4. Les quatre arbitres s'efforcent alors de se mettre d'accord sur le choix du Président. Lorsqu'ils se mettent d'accord, ils informent les Parties que le Tribunal a été constitué.

5. S'ils ne sont pas parvenus à un accord d'ici le 15 mars 1997, ils en informent le Président de la Cour internationale de Justice et lui demandent, conformément à l'Accord sur les principes, de choisir le Président du Tribunal. En transmettant cette demande, les quatre arbitres communiquent les avis exprimés par les Parties quant au choix du Président du Tribunal. Le Président de la Cour internationale de Justice effectue son choix dans les deux semaines et après consultation avec les arbitres désignés par les Parties. Au plus tard le 31 mars 1997, il informe les Parties, les quatre arbitres et la France que le Tribunal a été constitué et leur communique le nom du Président du Tribunal.

6. Le Tribunal se réunit au plus tard le 11 avril 1997.

7. Tous les membres du Tribunal s'engagent à exercer leurs pouvoirs de manière impartiale et en conscience.

8. La France transmet aux membres du Tribunal, dès qu'ils ont été choisis, une copie certifiée de l'Accord sur les principes et du présent compromis d'arbitrage.

Article 2

1. Il est demandé au Tribunal de se prononcer conformément au droit international, en deux étapes.

2. La première étape donne lieu à une sentence sur la souveraineté territoriale et la définition du champ du différend entre l'Erythrée et le Yémen. Le Tribunal statue sur la question de la souveraineté territoriale conformément aux principes, aux règles et aux pratiques du droit international applicables en la matière et sur la base, notamment, des titres historiques. Le Tribunal statue sur la définition du champ du différend sur la base des positions respectives des deux Parties.

3. La seconde étape donne lieu à une sentence sur la délimitation des frontières maritimes. Le Tribunal statue en prenant en compte l'opinion qu'il se sera faite sur les questions de souveraineté territoriale, la Convention des Nations Unies sur le droit de la mer et tout autre élément pertinent.

a) Le Tribunal procède à la délimitation de manière techniquement précise. A cette fin, la nature géométrique de tous les éléments de la délimitation est indiqée et la position de tous les points mentionnés est donnée par référence aux coordonnées du système géodésique mondial de 1984 (S.G.M. 84).

Le Tribunal fait également figurer la délimitation sur une carte, mais uniquement à titre indicatif.

b) Après consultation avec les Parties, le Tribunal désigne un expert technique pour l'aider à mener à bien ses fonctions énoncées à la lettre a) ci-dessus.

Article 3

1. La participation de tous les membres du Tribunal est requise pour les sentences. La présence de tous les membres est également requise pour toutes les procédures et décisions autres que les sentences, sauf si le Président estime que l'absence d'un seul membre pour une procédure ou une décision autre que les sentences est dûment justifiée.

2. a) Si un membre du Tribunal choisi par l'une des Parties ne peut pas ou ne veut pas agir et continuer à exercer ses fonctions, cette Partie désigne son remplaçant dans un délai d'un mois à compter de la date à laquelle le Tribunal déclaré la vacance.

b) Si le President du Tribunal ne peut pas ou ne veut pas agir et continuer à exercer ses fonctions, un remplaçant est choisi par les membres du Tribunal désignés par les Parties dans un délai de deux mois à compter de la date à laquelle le Tribunal a déclaré la vacance. S'ils ne parviennent pas à se mettre d'accord dans ce délai, le Président du Tribunal est choisi par le Président de la Cour internationale de Justice.

c) Lorsqu'une vacance a été pourvue après le début de la procédure, la procédure reprend là où elle s'était arrêtée au moment de la vacance.

3. Tous les membres du Tribunal sont réputés être présents aux fins du paragraphe 1 du présent article et nonobstant l'existence d'une vacance lorsque la seule question à l'ordre du jour est la déclaration d'une vacance aux fins du paragraphe 2 du présent article ou lorsque l'une des Parties a omis de pourvoir la vacance conformément au paragraphe 2 a) du présent article.

Article 4

1. Sous réserve du paragraphe 2 du présent article, les décisions du Tribunal sur des questions de fond ou de procédure, y compris les questions relatives à la compétence du Tribunal ou à l'interprétation du présent compromis d'arbitrage, sont prises à la majorité de ses membres, si elles ne peuvent l'être à l'unanimité.

2. En cas de partage égal des voix dans les conditions visées au paragraphe 3 de l'article 3 ci-dessus, la voix du Président est prépondérante.

Article 5

Sous réserve des dispositions du présent compromis d'arbitrage, le Tribunal arrête son règlement intérieur et statue sur toutes les questions relatives à la conduite de l'arbitrage.

Article 6

1. Chacune des Parties, dans les trente jours suivant la signature du présent compromis d'arbitrage, désigne un agent qui la représente et agit en son nom aux fins de l'arbitrage, et elle communique les nom et adresse de cet agent à l'autre Partie et, dès sa création, au Tribunal.

2. Chaque agent ainsi désigné est autorisé à choisir un ou plusieurs co-agents agissant en son nom lorsque cela est nécessaire. Les nom et adresse du ou des co-agents ainsi choisis sont communiqués à l'autre Partie et, dès sa création, au Tribunal.

Article 7

1. Le Tribunal siège à Londres.

2. Le Tribunal désigne un greffier après consultation avec les agents, dès que possible et au plus tard lors de sa première réunion. Le greffier exerce ses fonctions de manière impartiale et en conscience.

3. Après consultation avec les agents, le tribunal peut engager le personnel et procurer les services et équipements qu'il juge nécessaires.

4. Le Tribunal peut consulter les experts de son choix après notification aux Parties. Ces experts exercent leurs fonctions de manière impartiale et en conscience.

5. a) A tout moment durant la procédure d'arbitrage, le Tribunal peut demander à chacune des Parties de produire des documents ou tout autre élément de preuve se rapportant à la question, dans le délai qu'il aura fixé. Tous les documents et autres éléments de preuve ainsi produits sont également communiqués à l'autre Partie.

b) Si l'une des Parties omet de donner suite à une demande de documents ou d'autres éléments de preuve en vertu du paragraphe a), le Tribunal peut en tirer les conclusions qui s'imposent et rendre sa décision en se fondant sur les éléments de preuve dont il dispose.

c) A tout moment durant la procédure d'arbitrage, le Tribunal peut demander, si nécessaire, à une non-Partie au présent compromis d'arbitrage de lui fournir des documents ou d'autres éléments de preuve se rapportant à la question. Tous les documents et autres éléments de preuve ainsi produits sont communiqués simultanément aux deux Parties.

Article 8

1. La procédure devant le Tribunal est contradictoire.

2. Sans préjudice de toute question liée à la charge de la preuve, la procédure devant le Tribunal comporte les deux étapes suivantes.

3. La première étape concernant les questions de souveraineté territoriale et de définition du champ du différend, visées au paragraphe 2 de l'article 2 du présent compromis d'arbitrage, comprend deux phases, l'une écrite et l'autre orale.

3.1 Les conclusions écrites consistent en:

a) un mémoire que chacune des Parties doit soumettre au Tribunal et à l'autre Partie au plus tard le 31 août 1997;

b) un contre-mémoire que chacune des Parties doit soumettre au Tribunal et à l'autre Partie dans les trois mois suivant la communication des mémoires;

c) toute autre conclusion écrite que le Tribunal estime nécessaire, qui devra être soumis dans les deux mois suivant la communication des contre-mémoires.

3.2 Une phase orale fait suite à la phase écrite.

a) Elle se déroule au siège du Tribunal, aux lieu et dates fixés par lui après consultation des agents. Dans la mesure du possible, la phase orale débute au plus tard trois mois après la communication par les Parties des derniers documents écrits visés au paragraphe 3.1 de l'article 8 ci-dessus.

b) Chacune des Parties est représentée dans la phase orale de la procédure par son agent ou, selon le cas, par son co-agent, et par les avocats, conseillers experts qu'elle aura désignés.

3.3 A l'issue de la phase orale, le Tribunal déclare la fin de la première étape de la procédure. Nonobstant cette déclaration, le Tribunal peut demander aux Parties leur avis écrit sur toute question, nécessaire pour permettre au Tribunal d'élucider un aspect de l'affaire, jusqu'à ce que la sentence soit rendue sur les questions de souveraineté territoriale et de définition du champ du différend.

3.4 Le Tribunal rend sa sentence, qui est sans appel, sur les questions de souveraineté territoriale et de définition du champ du différend, dans la mesure du possible dans les trois mois qui suivent la fin de la procédure délarée conformément au paragraphe 3.3 de l'article 8 ci-dessus.

3.5 Le Tribunal communique cette sentence aux agents le jour où il la prononce. Le Tribunal et les Parties peuvent rendre cette sentence publique à compter du jour où elle est prononcée.

4. La seconde étape concernant la délimitation des frontières maritimes visée au paragraphe 3 de l'article 2 du présent compromis d'arbitrage débute immédiatement après qu'a été rendue la sentence qui termine la première étape. Elle comprend deux phases, l'une écrite et l'autre orale.

4.1 Les conclusions écrites consistent en:

a) un mémoire que chacune des Parties doit soumettre au Tribunal et à l'autre Partie dans les quatre mois suivant le prononcé de la sentence sur les questions de souveraineté territoriale et de définition du champ du différend;

b) un contre-mémoire que chacune des Parties doit soumettre au Tribunal et à l'autre Partie dans les deux mois suivant la communication des mémoires;

c) toute autre conclusion écrite que le Tribunal estime nécessaire, qui devra être soumise dans les deux mois suivant la communication des contre-mémoires.

4.2 La phase orale fait suite à la phase écrite.

a) Elle se déroule au siège du Tribunal, aux lieu et dates fixés par lui après consultation des agents. Dans la mesure du possible, la phase orale débute au plus tard trois mois après la communication par les Parties des derniers documents écrits visés au paragraphe 4.1 de l'article 8 ci-dessus.

b) Chacune des Parties est représentée dans la phase orale de la procédure par son agent ou, selon le cas, par son co-agent, et par les avocats, conseillers et experts qu'elle aura désignés.

4.3 A l'issue de la phase orale, le Tribunal déclare la fin de la seconde étape de la procédure. Nonobstant cette déclaration, le Tribunal peut demander aux Parties leur avis écrit sur toute question, nécessaire pour permettre au Tribunal d'élucider un aspect de l'affaire, jusqu'à ce que la sentence soit rendue sur les questions de délimitation des frontières maritimes.

4.4 Le Tribunal rend sa sentence sur les questions de délimitation des frontières maritimes, dans la mesure du possible dans les trois mois qui suivent la fin de la procédure devant lui déclarée conformément au paragraphe 4.3 de l'article 8 ci-dessus.

5. Le Tribunal a le pouvoir, uniquement pour des raisons dûment justifiées, de proroger les délais fixés dans le présent article de son propre chef ou à la demande de l'une des Parties. La durée totale cumulée des prorogations de délai accordées par le Tribunal à la demande de l'une des Parties au cours de la procédure conformément aux dispositions du présent alinéa ne peut excéder deux mois pour chaque Partie et pour chaque étape.

6. Le greffier communique aux Parties une adresse aux fins du dépôt de leurs pièces écrites ou de tout autre document. Le greffier transmet simultanément aux Parties des copies de toutes les pièces écrites et de tous les documents dès réception.

7. Si l'une des Parties omet, dans le délai fixé par le présent compromis d'arbitrage ou par le Tribunal, de comparaître à la date fixée ou de déposer ses conclusions écrites, le Tribunal poursuit malgré tout la procédure et rend une sentence sur la base des conclusions dont il dispose.

Article 9

1. La procédure écrite et orale devant le Tribunal s'effectue en anglais. Le Tribunal rend ses décisions en anglais.

Le Tribunal conserve une transcription intégrale de toutes les audiences.

Les transcriptions intégrales de la procédure orale sont communiquées aux agents dès que possible.

2. Toutes les pièces documentaires sont déposées par les Parties dans leur langue d'origine. Les Parties font effectuer les traductions qu'elles jugent nécessaires en ce qui les concerne pour la préparation de l'affaire.

Le Tribunal peut recourir à des services de traduction lorsqu'il le juge nécessaire.

Toutes les traductions ainsi effectuées sont communiquées aux Parties.

3. Toutes les conclusions écrites et les transcriptions intégrales de la procédure orale ainsi que toutes les délibérations du Tribunal sont confidentielles.

4. Le public n'a pas accès aux audiences.

Article 10

1. La rémunération des membres du Tribunal et du greffier est supportée pour moitié par chacune des Parties.

2. Les frais généraux de l'arbitrage sont supportés pour moitié par chacune des Parties. Le greffier tient un registre et rend compte de l'ensemble des frais exposés.

3. Chacune des Parties supporte les frais exposés par elle pour la préparation et le déroulement de l'affaire.

Article 11

1. Sans préjudice des dispositions de l'Accord sur les principes, le Tribunal peut, de son propre chef ou après avoir examiné la demande de l'une des Parties, prescrire toutes mesures provisoires qu'il juge appropriées compte tenu des circonstances pour prévenir un dommage ou un préjudice irréparable pour les ressources naturelles de la région ou pour préserver le *statu quo* du 21 mai 1996. Les Parties appliquent ces mesures dans le délai prescrit par le Tribunal.

2. La demande ou la prescription de mesures provisoires n'affecte en aucun cas les délais fixés pour la communication des conclusions ou le prononcé des décisions conformément à l'article 8 ci-dessus.

Article 12

1. a) Les sentences du Tribunal mentionnent les motifs qui les fondent.

b) Les sentences du Tribunal précisent le délai de leur exécution.

c) Pour chaque sentence du Tribunal, chaque membre du Tribunal peut y annexer une opinion individuelle ou dissidente.

2. Le Tribunal transmet immédiatement aux agents ou co-agents ses sentences signées par le Président et le greffier du Tribunal, ainsi que toute opinion individuelle ou dissidente.

3. A l'issue de la seconde étape, le Tribunal rend publiques les sentences et les opinions individuelles ou dissidentes.

Article 13

1. Les sentences du Tribunal sont définitives et sans appel. Les Parties s'engagent à respecter ces sentences conformément au paragraphe 2 de l'article premier de l'Accord sur les principes. Elles appliquent en conséquence les sentences du Tribunal de bonne foi et immédiatement, et dans tous les cas dans le délai prescrit par le Tribunal conformément au paragraphe 1 b) de l'article 12 du présent compromis d'arbitrage.

2. Le Tribunal a le pouvoir de corriger, dans les trois mois suivant le prononcé de ses sentences, toutes les erreurs matérielles se rapportant à ces sentences, telles que les erreurs arithmétiques, mathématiques, cartographiques ou typographiques. Ces corrections n'affectent en aucun cas les calendriers définis à l'article 8 ci-dessus.

3. Chaque Partie peut porter devant le Tribunal tout différend avec l'autre Partie relatif à la signification et au champ d'application des sentences dans un délai de trent jours après qu'elles ont été prononcées. Le Tribunal se prononce sur ce différend dans les soixante jours qui suivent la date à laquelle le différend a été porté devant lui. Dans l'attente de sa décision, le Tribunal peut suspendre les délais prévus à l'article 8 pour le dépôt des conclusions écrites.

Article 14

1. Le présent compromis d'arbitrage entrera en vigueur trente jours après la date de sa signature par les deux Parties.

2. Le Tribunal applique les dispositions du présent compromis d'arbitrage.

Article 15

1. Nulle disposition du présent compromis d'arbitrage ne peut être interprétée comme portant préjudice aux positions juridiques ou aux droits de chaque Partie concernant les questions soumises au Tribunal, ni ne peut affecter ou porter préjudice aux décisions du Tribunal arbitral ou aux considérations et motifs sur lesquels se fondent lesdites décisions.

2. En cas de contradiction entre l'Accord sur les principes et le présent compromis d'arbitrage portant application des aspects de procédure dudit Accord sur les principes, c'est le compromis d'arbitrage qui prévaut. Excepté le cas d'une telle contradiction, l'Accord sur les principes reste en vigueur.

Article 16

1. La France dépose une copie du présent compromis d'arbitrage auprès du Secrétaire général des Nations Unies, du Secrétaire général de l'Organisation de l'Unité africaine et du Secrétaire général de la Ligue arabe, dans les trente jours suivant son entrée en vigueur.

2. Le Président du Tribunal dépose une copie des deux sentences dès que possible après que la sentence sur la délimitation des frontières maritimes aura été rendue, auprès du Secrétaire général des Nations Unies, du Secrétaire général de l'Organisation de l'Unité africaine et du Secrétaire général de la Ligue arabe.

EN FOI DE QUOI les soussignés, dûment autorisés par leur Gouvernement respectif, ont signé le présent compromis d'arbitrage.

FAIT A PARIS, le trois octobre mil neuf cent quatre-vingt-seize, en trois exemplaires originaux, chacun en langues anglaise, arabe et française, le texte anglais faisant foi.

Pour le Gouvernement
de la République du Yémen

HUSSEIN ALI AL-HUBAISHI
Conseiller juridique du Gouvernement

Pour le Gouvernement
de l'Etat d'Erythrée

SALEH MEKY
Ministre des Ressources marines

ANNEXE 2
Les questions posées par le Tribunal et les réponses des Parties

Réponse du Yémen à la question qui lui a été posée par M. Schwebel
le mardi 13 juillet 1999

Le sixième jour des plaidoiries (Transcriptions, sixième journée, 13 juillet 1999, pages 99-100), M. Schwebel a posé au conseil du Yémen la question suivante:

> "Mme Malintoppi, au cours des plaidoiries de la première étape, le Yémen a soutenu qu'il n'entrait pas dans les attributions du Tribunal à ce stade d'examiner les questions de *res communis, condominia* et autres questions similaires, en déclarant que ce serait anticiper sur des points qui ne pourraient être considérés que lors de la seconde étape. Un argument remarquable puisque l'Erythrée n'avait dit mot à ce sujet, et le Tribunal pas davantage. Voici qu'à présent vous affirmez qu'il est trop tard pour que l'Erythrée invoque de telles questions, ce qui signifie, si j'ai bien compris, qu'il aurait fallu le faire lors de la première étape. Le Yémen est-il conséquent dans les arguments visés?"

De l'avis du Yémen, le Yémen est conséquent dans ses arguments. C'est ce qui apparaît lorsque l'on examine le contexte dans lequel le Yémen a soulevé cette question lors de la première étape, les points mis en avant par Mme Malintoppi dans son intervention se rapportant à la seconde étape, et les termes du Compromis d'arbitrage.

La question a été évoquée pour la première fois au paragraphe 20 de l'exposé écrit du Yémen sur la pertinence des accords et des activités dans le domaine pétrolier daté du 8 juin 1998. Dans ce paragraphe, le Yémen notait ce qui suit:

> "Il est toujours tentant de chercher à découvrir une base pour diviser un groupe d'îles, en particulier dans le cas d'un arbitrage. La chose est d'autant plus tentante lorsque la tâche du Tribunal comporte une délimitation maritime, et la prudence sera à n'en pas douter de mise si l'on veut éviter d'anticiper sur les principes et concepts équitables, qui ne sont pertinents en droit que dans la seconde phase d'une telle procédure."

Le point auquel se référait le Yémen portait sur le droit applicable. Lors de la première étape, le Yémen a considéré que le droit applicable découlait des principes du droit international relatif à la souveraineté territoriale et au titre à un territoire. Sa conclusion était que les principes équitables, *infra legem*, relevaient principalement du droit de la délimitation maritime – question qu'il convenait d'examiner lors de la seconde étape – et non du droit de la souveraineté territoriale en soi. Le Yémen était donc d'avis que le concept de principes équitables était particulièrement pertinent aux fins de la seconde étape de la procédure, et qu'il fallait se garder d'anticiper sur cette question au cours de la première étape. Le Yémen ne fit aucune allusion particulière à des concepts tels que ceux de *res communis* ou *condominia* lorsqu'il souleva cette question.

En cette seconde étape de la procédure, le Yémen admet sans réserve que les principes équitables font partie du droit applicable en matière de délimitation maritime. Toutefois, et c'est là le point qui fut soulevé par Mme Malintoppi, l'application de principes équitables à une délimitation maritime, considérée à la lumière du champ du mandat du Tribunal tel que défini dans le Compromis d'arbitrage et l'Accord sur les principes, n'englobe pas la création ou les modalités de création de "zones de ressources conjointes" autour des îles du Yémen de la manière dont l'Erythrée en fait la requête dans sa Demande.

Il s'ensuit que le Yémen ne soutient pas que les arguments de l'Erythrée en faveur de la création de telles zones viennent trop tard en la présente étape, mais plutôt que le droit applicable, ainsi que les dispositions du Compromis d'arbitrage et de l'Accord sur les principes, n'offrent aucune base juridique ou juridictionnelle pour accéder à la requête de l'Erythrée.

Il convient toutefois de noter que les Accords de 1994 et de 1998 entre le Yémen et l'Erythrée, en particulier les sections de ces instruments relatives à la pêche, montrent clairement que le Yémen et l'Erythrée s'emploient présentement à travailler de concert à la gestion des ressources halieutiques dans toute la partie méridionale de la mer Rouge.

Réponse du Yémen à la question qui lui a été posée le vendredi 16 juillet 1999

A l'issue des plaidoiries (Transcriptions, huitième journée, 16 juillet 1999, page 45), le Tribunal a posé au Yémen la question suivante:

> "Le Tribunal a noté que, dans son argumentation, le Yémen ne s'était guère exprimé au sujet du régime de pêche traditionnel qui, le Tribunal le rappelle, est un aspect essentiel du *Dispositif* de la Sentence du 9 octobre 1998. Le Yémen voudrait-il indiquer comment, le cas échéant, il conviendrait de prendre en compte le régime de pêche traditionnel aux fins de la délimitation, à la lumière en particulier des accords signés par les deux Gouvernements en 1994 et 1998?"

La réponse du Yémen était formulée comme suit:

Le Yémen reconnaît que, en tranchant la question de la souveraineté sur diverses îles de la mer Rouge, le Tribunal a indiqué dans le *Dispositif* de sa première Sentence que la souveraineté attribuée au Yémen "implique la perpétuation du régime de pêche traditionnel dans la région, y compris libre accès et libre jouissance pour les pêcheurs de l'Erythrée comme du Yémen" (paragraphe 527(vi) de la Sentence). Cette décision est définitive et contraignante pour les Parties, ainsi qu'il est stipulé à l'article 13(1) du Compromis d'arbitrage. Le Yémen est pleinement résolu à appliquer et mettre à effet la Sentence sous tous ses aspects, y compris en ce qui concerne la perpétuation du régime de pêche traditionnel au bénéfice des pêcheurs de l'Erythrée comme du Yémen.

Ainsi qu'il ressort clairement des exposés présentés par les Parties durant les audiences, l'une et l'autre d'entre elles considèrent qu'il convient de lire le *Dispositif* de la Sentence du Tribunal à la lumière du raisonnement qui apparaît dans le corps de ladite Sentence. S'agissant de "la perpétuation du régime de pêche traditionnel dans la région", le Yémen a également pris note des remarques formulées par le Tribunal en d'autres parties de la Sentence portant sur cette question. C'est ainsi que la première phrase du paragraphe 526 énonce ce qui suit:

> "En concluant que les Parties ont chacune souveraineté sur diverses îles, le Tribunal souligne à leur intention qu'une telle souveraineté n'exclut pas, mais implique plutôt, la perpétuation du régime de pêche traditionnel dans la région."

Les fondements historiques de cette conclusion ont été explicités plus avant au paragraphe 128, où le Tribunal déclare:

> "Cette situation qui a prévalu par le passé était le reflet d'habitudes culturelles profondément enracinées aboutissant à l'existence de ce que l'on pourrait appeler d'un point de vue juridique une *res communis* grâce à quoi les pêcheurs africains aussi bien que yéménites ont pu opérer sans limitation dans la région tout entière et vendre leurs prises sur les marchés locaux des deux rives de la mer Rouge. De même, les personnes naviguant d'une côte à l'autre pour pêcher ou commercer avaient coutume de s'abriter temporairement des vents violents sur l'une quelconque des îles inhabitées qui sont disséminées dans cette partie de la mer sans rencontrer d'obstacles d'ordre politique ou administratif."

Aux yeux du Yémen, les conclusions formulées par le Tribunal dans sa première Sentence au sujet du régime de pêche traditionnel ont l'autorité de la chose jugée sans préjudice de la frontière maritime sur laquelle le Tribunal statuera lors de la seconde étape de la procédure. En d'autres termes, le régime de pêche traditionnel qui s'est appliqué pour le bénéfice des pêcheurs des deux pays dans toute la région doit être perpétué quelle que soit la décision à laquelle parvient le Tribunal quant à la délimitation de la frontière maritime entre les deux pays. De fait, il est clair que les deux Parties ont compris que c'est là une obligation mutuelle qui existe indépendamment de la question de la délimitation de leur frontière maritime puisque, comme il est indiqué dans l'Accord conclu par les deux Gouvernements en novembre 1998, le Yémen et l'Erythrée ont établi un régime de coopération dans le domaine de la pêche dans l'esprit de bon voisinage et d'amitié qui a prévalu depuis la Sentence prononcée en la première étape du présent arbitrage.

De l'avis du Yémen, la délimitation à laquelle le Tribunal est appelé à procéder dans sa seconde Sentence servira une autre fin que la préservation du régime de pêche traditionnel. C'est ainsi que le conseil de l'Erythrée a admis dans sa réfutation que des aspects tels que l'exploitation minière ne faisaient pas partie du régime de pêche traditionnel tel que l'entendait le Tribunal (Transcriptions, huitième journée, 16 juillet 1999, page 2). A l'évidence, l'exploitation minière est liée à la délimitation du plateau continental, question qui est pertinente en cette seconde étape.

De même, la délimitation de la colonne d'eau ou de la zone économique exclusive des Parties, ainsi que de leurs mers territoriales respectives dans les secteurs central et sud, met en jeu des aspects qui, aux termes de la Convention sur le droit de la mer de 1982, se situent au-delà de la préservation du régime de pêche traditionnel. C'est dans ce contexte que le Yémen a suggéré que la dépendance de sa population côtière à l'égard de la pêche et l'incidence des pratiques de pêche yéménites dans la région constituaient des circonstances pertinentes qu'il convenait de prendre en compte aux fins de la délimitation.

En bref, la perpétuation du régime de pêche traditionnel ne se confond pas avec les droits et obligations des Parties qui seront déterminés par la délimitation d'une frontière maritime unique dans toute la zone pertinente. C'est pour ces raisons que le Yémen ne considère pas que la décision du Tribunal concernant le régime de pêche traditionnel doive avoir un quelconque effet sur la délimitation de frontières maritimes entre les deux Parties lors de la seconde étape.

A cet égard, il convient de se référer à l'Accord de 1994 entre le Yémen et l'Erythrée dont fait expressément mention la question posée par le Tribunal. Comme il ressort de ces termes, l'Accord de 1994 est pleinement compatible avec la préservation du régime de pêche traditionnel décidée par le Tribunal lors de la première étape.

L'Accord a été signé par le ministre des ressources halieutiques au nom du Yémen et par le ministre des ressources marines au nom de l'Erythrée. Ce dernier exerce aussi, bien sûr, les fonctions d'Agent de l'Erythrée dans le présent arbitrage.

Il est significatif qu'au paragraphe 1 de l'Accord, il soit fait spécifiquement mention d'un régime de pêche remarquablement similaire à celui qui est consacré dans la première Sentence du Tribunal. Ce paragraphe dispose, entre autres, que:

> "L'Etat d'Erythrée et la République du Yémen permettront tous deux aux pêcheurs qui sont citoyens de l'un ou l'autre Etat, sans limitation de leur nombre, et qui sont porteurs de cartes les autorisant à se livrer à des activités de pêche, de pêcher dans les eaux territoriales des deux Etats, dans la zone contiguë et la zone économique exclusive des deux pays dans la mer Rouge (à l'exception des eaux intérieures), sous réserve que les pêcheurs des deux pays soient dénombrés et aient obtenu des permis officiels de pratiquer la pêche, les endroits où ils auront accès et pourront vendre leurs produits étant spécifiés à l'Appendice No. 1."

De plus, le paragraphe 4 de l'Accord prévoit dans le passage pertinent que les personnes visées au paragraphe 1 sont autorisées à "commercialiser le produit de leur pêche sur le territoire de l'autre Etat et aux endroits spécifiés à l'Appendice No. 1 du présent Mémorandum d'accord". Le Tribunal notera que ces dispositions sont très proches des conclusions du Tribunal exposées au paragraphe 128 de la Sentence rendue en la première étape.

Malheureusement, l'Accord de 1994 n'a pu être pleinement appliqué à l'époque en raison des événements de 1995. Néanmoins, l'Accord reste en vigueur, et le Yémen demeure pleinement résolu à lui donner effet. Comme il ressort de ses termes, l'Accord de 1994 envisage la mise en place d'un cadre réglementaire bien propre à répondre aux préoccupations exprimées par l'Erythrée dans ses écritures et plaidoiries en ce qui concerne la pêche traditionnelle dans la région.

La question posée par le Tribunal mentionne également l'Accord signé par les deux Parties en novembre 1998. De l'avis du Yémen, cet Accord atteste la bonne foi des deux Parties dans la poursuite de leur coopération mutuelle dans un certain nombre de domaines, dont la pêche. En particulier, l'article 1(d) de l'Accord prévoit la création d'une Commission de coopération dans le domaine des ressources halieutiques et de la pêche maritime. Aux termes de l'article 3(4) de l'Accord, cette commission serait appelée à réfléchir à la rédaction d'un accord spécial "dans le domaine des ressources halieutiques, de la pêche maritime et de la protection de l'environnement marin".

En ce qui concerne la pertinence des Accords de 1994 et 1998 pour la perpétuation du régime de pêche traditionnel, il y a lieu de rappeler ce que le conseil du Yémen a eu à déclarer à ce sujet au cours des audiences:

> "De fait, comme l'a montré M. Picard, les Parties ont déjà établi par leurs accords de 1994 et 1998 un mécanisme en vue de définir les modalités de leurs activités de pêche dans la mer Rouge. Ces accords pourraient fort bien offrir un cadre substantiel à l'intérieur duquel il serait possible d'examiner toute nouvelle question surgissant entre les Parties en ce qui concerne la préservation des pratiques de pêche traditionnelles mentionnée au paragraphe 526 de la Sentence" (Transcriptions, sixième journée, 13 juillet 1999, page 88).

La mise en œuvre de ces deux accords irait également dans le sens de la lettre du Président du Tribunal en date du 8 novembre 1998 où celui-ci indiquait que ce sont là des questions "qu'il appartient aux Parties elles-mêmes de résoudre de bonne foi, en ayant à l'esprit les conclusions du Tribunal exposées au paragraphe 526 de la Sentence".

En conclusion, le Yémen considère que le Tribunal a déjà statué sur la préservation du régime de pêche traditionnel dans sa première Sentence. Cette Sentence, telle qu'elle est, a l'autorité de la chose jugée, et vu la formulation du paragraphe 3 de l'article 13 du Compromis d'arbitrage, il est inapproprié d'interpréter le sens et la portée de la Sentence rendue à l'issue de la première étape au stade actuel de la procédure. Par conséquent, et compte tenu du cadre qui a été établi par les Accords de 1994 et 1998, le Yémen ne pense qu'il soit besoin de prendre davantage en compte le régime de pêche traditionnel aux fins de la délimitation de la frontière maritime entre les Parties en la présente étape de la procédure.

ANNEXE 2

Réponse de l'Erythrée à la question de M. Schwebel

[*en-tête de la lettre: Office d'arbitrage de l'Etat d'Erythrée pour l'archipel des Zuqar-Hanish*]

Mme Phyllis Hamilton
Cour permanente d'arbitrage
Palais de la paix, La Haye
Pays-Bas

Le 12 août 1999

Par télécopie: 31-70-3024167

Objet: Arbitrage Erythrée/Yémen

Chère Madame,

Comme vous vous en souvenez probablement, au cours des audiences de juillet en l'étape de l'arbitrage entre l'Erythrée et le Yémen relative à la délimitation maritime, le Tribunal a demandé à l'État d'Erythrée de lui fournir les coordonnées de la ligne médiane historique à laquelle l'Erythrée s'est référée dans ses écritures et plaidoiries. Il a été demandé que ces coordonnées soient communiquées dans un délai de quatre semaines à compter de la clôture des audiences (en même temps que le dépôt de la réponse du Yémen à la question qui lui était posée).

Je joins les coordonnées à la présente. En fait, vous trouverez ci-joint deux séries de coordonnées, l'une correspondant à la ligne médiane historique et l'autre à la limite occidentale de la zone de ressources partagées décrite dans les pièces écrites de l'Erythrée. Les deux diffèrent en ce que la ligne médiane historique donne plein effet aux îles érythréennes de Mohabbaka et de Haycock et au Southwest Rock. Tel n'est pas le cas de la limite occidentale de la zone de ressources partagées, qui court par conséquent à l'ouest de la ligne médiane historique. Les coordonnées des points qui ont été retenus aux fins du tracé de ces deux lignes se trouvent soit sur le territoire terrestre de l'Erythrée ou sur des lignes de base droites tirées conformément à la Convention des Nations Unies sur le droit de la mer.

Je compte que vous ferez parvenir ces renseignements au Tribunal, ainsi qu'au Conseil de la République du Yémen (après que le Yémen aura soumis sa réponse à la question qui lui était posée). À l'heure où vous recevrez la présente, j'aurai quitté Asmara et serai en route pour New Haven, aussi j'espère qu'aucun problème ne se posera concernant le dépôt de notre réponse. Vous pourrez me joindre à New Haven en fin de journée le vendredi 13 août dans le cas où un problème se poserait effectivement, et j'espère que vous serez en mesure de m'y faire parvenir le texte de la réponse que le Yémen fera à la question qui lui a été posée.

Merci encore infiniment de votre cordiale assistance.

Je vous prie d'agréer, Chère Madame, . . .
(signé)
Professeur R. Lea Brilmayer
Co-agent de l'État d'Erythrée

Coordonnées des points de base de la proposition de l'Erythrée de ligne médiane historique

	Longitude	Latitude
1	40.256123	16.261644
2	40.260834	16.088427
3	40.610901	15.894623
4	40.627377	15.881909
5	40.675121	15.845072
6	40.705509	15.821624
7	40.726833	15.800971
8	40.774303	15.754568
9	40.821114	15.722202
10	40.859592	15.697753
11	40.873196	15.684411
12	40.899334	15.658775
13	40.923637	15.634940
14	40.959450	15.599816
15	40.984978	15.574780
16	41.007191	15.552997
17	41.033173	15.527514
18	41.064766	15.496529
19	41.090080	15.471701
20	41.097931	15.464003
21	41.194546	14.617983
22	41.315613	14.490411
23	41.327480	14.467098
24	41.333321	14.454417
25	41.674259	14.101558
26	41.682278	14.093115
27	41.992912	13.888812
28	42.033104	13.856160
29	42.083229	13.815438
30	42.143177	13.766736
31	42.163944	13.749866
32	42.597202	13.634215
33	42.597584	13.634094
34	42.597961	13.633973
35	42.629669	13.539982
36	42.630470	13.539621
37	42.649868	13.350410
38	42.649937	13.349084
39	42.898411	13.022588
40	42.909142	13.015216

41	42.945763	12.990066
42	42.946693	12.989246
43	42.972328	12.966615
44	42.999687	12.942464
45	43.027813	12.909046
46	43.046738	12.879812

Coordonnées des points de base de la proposition de l'Erythrée de ligne médiane historique en degrés, minutes (arrondis)

	Longitude		Latitude	
	Degrés	Minutes	Degrés	Minutes
1	40	15	16	16
2	40	16	16	5
3	40	37	15	54
4	40	38	15	53
5	40	41	15	51
6	40	42	15	49
7	40	44	15	48
8	40	46	15	45
9	40	49	15	43
10	40	52	15	42
11	40	52	15	41
12	40	54	15	40
13	40	55	15	38
14	40	58	15	36
15	40	59	15	34
16	41	0	15	33
17	41	2	15	32
18	41	4	15	30
19	41	5	15	28
20	41	6	15	28
21	41	12	14	37
22	41	19	14	29
23	41	20	14	28
24	41	20	14	27
25	41	40	14	6
26	41	41	14	6
27	42	0	13	53
28	42	2	13	51
29	42	5	13	49
30	42	9	13	46
31	42	10	13	45

32	42	36	13	38
33	42	36	13	38
34	42	36	13	38
35	42	38	13	32
36	42	38	13	32
37	42	39	13	21
38	42	39	13	21
39	42	54	13	1
40	42	55	13	1
41	42	57	12	59
42	42	57	12	59
43	42	58	12	58
44	43	0	12	57
45	43	2	12	55
46	43	3	12	53

Coordonnées des points de base pour la délimitation de la côte ouest proposée par l'Erythrée

Coordonnées des points de base ouest

	Longitude	Latitude
1	40.256123	16.261644
2	40.260834	16.088427
3	40.610901	15.894623
4	40.627377	15.881909
5	40.675121	15.845072
6	40.705509	15.821624
7	40.726833	15.800971
8	40.774303	15.754568
9	40.821114	15.722202
10	40.859592	15.697753
11	40.873196	15.684411
12	40.899334	15.658775
13	40.923637	15.634940
14	40.959450	15.599816
15	40.984978	15.574780
16	41.007191	15.552997
17	41.033173	15.527514
18	41.064766	15.496529
19	41.090080	15.471701
20	41.097931	15.464003
21	41.194546	14.617983
22	41.315613	14.490411

23	41.327480	14.467098
24	41.333321	14.454417
25	41.674259	14.101558
26	41.682278	14.093115
27	41.992912	13.888812
28	42.033104	13.856160
29	42.083229	13.815438
30	42.143177	13.766736
31	42.163944	13.749866
32	42.182957	13.719868
33	42.209858	13.677422
34	42.236946	13.629816
35	42.290718	13.558626
36	42.292160	13.556718
37	42.314285	13.507826
38	42.332073	13.468508
39	42.456223	13.322620
40	42.502346	13.277068
41	42.548088	13.231894
42	42.583633	13.196643
43	42.621857	13.158704
44	42.659718	13.121125
45	42.696766	13.084354
46	42.898411	13.022588
47	42.909142	13.015216
48	42.945763	12.990066
49	42.946693	12.989246
50	42.972328	12.966615
51	42.999687	12.942464
52	43.027813	12.909046
53	43.046738	12.879812

Coordonnées des points de base est

54	41.725754	16.630884
55	41.734745	16.575695
56	41.738682	16.551414
57	41.749630	16.541800
58	41.775238	16.519312
59	41.812977	16.486170
60	41.839870	16.462553
61	41.863270	16.442003
62	41.890648	16.417961
63	41.961689	16.292364
64	42.269432	15.701784

65	42.266293	15.700562
66	42.274937	15.697087
67	42.276882	15.685533
68	42.366718	15.489594
69	42.401192	15.467257
70	42.512936	15.415102
71	42.530704	15.291346
72	42.594810	15.210606
73	42.603222	15.200403
74	42.690079	15.195890
75	42.612560	15.189135
76	42.749393	15.179667
77	42.621025	15.169647
78	42.638046	15.163574
79	42.972595	14.600204
80	42.983734	14.391216
81	42.983959	14.384205
82	43.016117	14.331829
83	43.034367	14.289636
84	43.052059	14.248733
85	43.085064	14.107971
86	43.096539	14.067361
87	43.103230	14.054599
88	43.122894	14.017092
89	43.141998	13.980651
90	43.158348	13.949471
91	43.189007	13.916190
92	43.229725	13.821691
93	43.252224	13.484743
94	43.248089	13.434113
95	43.242542	13.374463
96	43.228340	13.302191
97	43.224674	13.271644
98	43.208839	13.259463
99	43.207760	13.243280
100	43.225060	13.202319
101	43.225647	13.199706
102	43.236843	13.168642
103	43.253857	13.136574
104	43.288876	13.080974
105	43.303009	13.063622

Coordonnées des points de base pour la délimitation de la côte ouest proposée par l'Erythrée en degrées, minutes (arrondis)

Coordonnées des points de base ouest

	Longitude		Latitude	
	Degrés	Minutes	Degrés	Minutes
1	40	15	16	16
2	40	16	16	5
3	40	37	15	54
4	40	38	15	53
5	40	41	15	51
6	40	42	15	49
7	40	44	15	48
8	40	46	15	45
9	40	49	15	43
10	40	52	15	42
11	40	52	15	41
12	40	54	15	40
13	40	55	15	38
14	40	58	15	36
15	40	59	15	34
16	41	0	15	33
17	41	2	15	32
18	41	4	15	30
19	41	5	15	28
20	41	6	15	28
21	41	12	14	37
22	41	19	14	29
23	41	20	14	28
24	41	20	14	27
25	41	40	14	6
26	41	41	14	6
27	42	0	13	53
28	42	2	13	51
29	42	5	13	49
30	42	9	13	46
31	42	10	13	45
32	42	11	13	43
33	42	13	13	41
34	42	14	13	38
35	42	17	13	34
36	42	18	13	33

37	42	19	13	30
38	42	20	13	28
39	42	27	13	19
40	42	30	13	17
41	42	33	13	14
42	42	35	13	12
43	42	37	13	10
44	42	40	13	7
45	42	42	13	5
46	42	54	13	1
47	42	55	13	1
48	42	57	12	59
49	42	57	12	59
50	42	58	12	58
51	43	0	12	57
52	43	2	12	55
53	43	3	12	53

Coordonnées des points de base est

54	41	44	16	38
55	41	44	16	35
56	41	44	16	33
57	41	45	16	33
58	41	47	16	31
59	41	49	16	29
60	41	50	16	28
61	41	52	16	27
62	41	53	16	25
63	41	58	16	18
64	42	16	15	42
65	42	16	15	42
66	42	16	15	42
67	42	17	15	41
68	42	22	15	29
69	42	24	15	28
70	42	31	15	25
71	42	32	15	17
72	42	36	15	13
73	42	36	15	12

ANNEXE 3

TRADUCTION

Mémorandum entre l'Etat d'Erythrée
et la République du Yémen
en matière de coopération dans les domaines de la pêche maritime,
du commerce, des investissements et du transport

Dans un esprit d'amitié et de coopération, et dans le but de mettre en œuvre les intérêts et les objectifs communs entre les deux pays frères que sont l'Etat d'Erythrée et la République du Yémen, la délégation de la République du Yémen dirigée par le docteur Abd al-Rahman Abd al-Qadir Ba-Fadhl, le ministre de la pêche, a rendu le vendredi 11 novembre 1994, une visite à l'Etat d'Erythrée et a reçu un accueil chaleureux de M. Ali Sayyid Abdallah, ministre de l'intérieur. Un première entrevue au sein du ministère de l'intérieur dans la capitale Asmara a été suivie de discussions entre les deux parties dans la ville de Massawa. Le docteur Salih Makki, le ministre de l'environnement marin de l'Etat d'Erythrée présidait du côté érythréen et le docteur Abd al-Rahman Abd al-Qadir Ba-Fadhl, le ministre de la pêche de la République du Yémen présidait du coté yéménite.

Les discussions entre les deux parties ont conduit à un accord portant sur les domaines suivant:

Premièrement : Le domaine de la pêche

1. Aussi bien l'Etat d'Erythrée que la République du Yémen permettent aux pêcheurs qui sont des nationaux d'un des deux états, sans limitation de nombre et détenant une carte professionnelle de pêcheur, de pêcher dans les eaux territoriales des deux Etats, la zone contiguë et la zone économique exclusive dans la mer Rouge des deux pays (excepté les eaux intérieures), à condition que les pêcheurs des deux pays soient comptabilisés et qu'ils disposent de permis officiels de pêche spécifiant les lieux dans lesquels ils se rendront et commercialiseront leurs produits tel que prévu dans l'appendice No. 1. Chaque pêcheur devra solliciter un permis de pêché de l'Etat dont il n'est pas ressortissant dans les trois mois suivant la date de signature de ce mémorandum et devra se conformer à ce qui suit :

   a. Recours à des méthodes de pêche par sondage, non utilisation d'explosifs et de moyens polluants l'environnement marin, de même que non recours aux poisons, produits chimiques ou moyens similaires d'extermination.

   b. Non-recours à des méthodes et à des équipements de pêche susceptibles de prévenir la croissance des organismes marins.

   c. Ne pas enlever ou couper des plantes marines ou des coraux de quelque nature que ce soit.

d. Respect des saisons de pêche de chacun des deux pays.

e. Recours à tout moyen afin d'assurer la protection de l'environnement et la rationalisation des pratiques de pêche.

f. Respect de toutes les lois et réglementations relatives à la mer d'un pays, dans la mesure où ces lois et réglementations sont applicables et ne sont pas contradictoires avec les prévisions ci-dessus.

2. En ce qui concerne les paragraphes 1.d et 1.f ci-dessus, les autorités concernées d'un des deux Etats, dans la mer Rouge, doivent notifier les autorités concernées de l'autre Etat, de toute loi, réglementation et règlement ou de tout accord mettant en cause une tierce partie dans les eaux que l'autre partie utilise. Chaque partie doit mettre en ouvre des directives afin que ce devoir d'information soit respecté.

3. Tout pêcheur ou travailleur sur un bateau de pêche situé dans les eaux territoriales de l'autre Etat doit être munis d'une autorisation de pêcher ainsi qu'une carte établissant sa nationalité et son identité conformément aux lois et réglementations de son pays. Tout bateau de pêche doit porter pavillon de son propre pays.

4. Les personnes évoquées dans les dispositions du paragraphe (1) ci-dessus doivent être autorisées à faire ce qui suit:

   a. Vendre leur produit de pêche dans le territoire de l'autre Etat dans les lieux spécifiés en appendice No. 1 de ce mémorandum.

   b. Bénéficier des facilités nécessaires pour la maintenance de leurs bateaux et obtenir de la nourriture, du fuel et de la glace aux prix en vigueur dans le pays dans lequel ils sont et ceci pour toute la période durant laquelle ils restent en mer.

5. Si les autorités de l'un des deux Etats sont conduits à arraisonner des bateaux de pêche, détenir des pêcheurs ou des travailleurs sur un bateau de pêche, les autorités de cet Etat doivent notifier immédiatement aux autorités de l'autre Etat, les noms des individus détenus, des bateaux ainsi que du contenu des bateaux et spécifier les motifs et la date du début de la détention.

6. Les deux Etats doivent coopérer dans le domaine de la recherche en matière de pêche, protection de l'environnement marin ainsi qu'échanger des connaissances techniques et organiser des formations dans des établissements spécialisés des deux pays.

Deuxièmement: les domaines du commerce maritime, des investissements et du transport

1. Etudier la possibilité de créer des sociétés de pêche communes entre les deux Etats.

2. Travailler sur la rédaction d'un accord de transport maritime entre les deux Etats.

3. Travailler sur la rédaction d'un accord commercial entre les deux Etats. Jusqu'à ce qu'un tel accord soit conclu, les autorités concernées de chacun des deux pays devront faciliter, conformément aux lois en vigueur, le transport des biens produits localement, dans les deux pays.

Troisièmement: Le domaine de la sécurité

Les deux Etats devront compléter le protocole signé par les ministres de l'intérieur des deux pays à Sanaa le 10 novembre 1993 afin de parvenir aux objectifs contenus dans ledit protocole.

Quatrièmement: la mise ne œuvre des points contenus dans le mémorandum

1. Les autorités concernées de chacun des deux Etats, dans la continuité de la signature de ce mémorandum, devront prendre les mesures nécessaires comprenant notamment la publication de décrets, ordres, permis ou directives dans le but de mettre en œuvre le contenu de ce mémorandum.

2. Les agences concernées dans les deux Etats devront organiser des patrouilles autour de leurs cotes dans la mer Rouge et établir des réseaux de communication entre les principaux centre de sécurité dans la mer Rouge des deux Etats, à une époque et selon une méthode qui sera établie entre elles.

3. Des bureaux spéciaux devront être installés dans les deux Etats afin de suivre et exécuter les termes de ce mémorandum. Les sièges de ces bureaux devront être spécifiés dans l'appendice No. 1 de ce mémorandum.

4. Les contacts entre les parties en ce qui concerne la mise en œuvre de ce mémorandum auront lieu par voie diplomatique nonobstant le paragraphe (2) de l'article 4 ci-dessus.

5. Les deux gouvernements devront se consulter pour toute question issue de la mise en œuvre de ce mémorandum, toute modification, suppression ou addition, de même que toute modification ou addition de l'appendice.

Signé à Massawa le mardi 15 novembre 1994.

Pour la République du Yémen	Pour l'Etat d'Erythrée
Le docteur Abd al-Rahman Abd-al Qadir Ba-Fadhl Ministre de la pêche	Le docteur Salih Makki Ministre de l'environnement marin

Appendice No. 1

A. Centres d'enregistrement, de contrôle et de vente des produits de la pêche en République du Yémen:

1. Maydi
2. Khoba
3. Hodeidah
4. Khokha
5. Mocha

Centres d'enregistrement, de contrôle et de vente des produits de la pêche dans l'Etat d'Erythrée:

1. Assab
2. Tio
3. Dahlak
4. Massawa

Appendice No. 2

Fonctionnaires de la délégation érythréenne:

1. Le docteyr Salih Makki, ministre de l'environnement marin
2. M. Ramadhan Ouliay, commandant des forces navales
3. M. Musa Rabi'a, chef de la Police érythréenne
4. M. Muhammad Idris Amir, Bureau du Moyen-Orient, ministère des affaires étrangères

Membres de la délégation de la République du Yémen :

1. Le docteur Abd al-Rahman Abd al-Qadir Ba-Fadhl, ministre de la pêche
2. Le colonel Abd al-Karim Muharram, chef des Forces navales
3. Le colonel Muhammad Rizq al-Sarami, sous-secrétaire, agence centrale de la sécurité politique
4. S. Exc. Ahmad al-Basha, ambassadeur de la République du Yémen en Erythrée
5. S. Exc. Muhammad al-Wazir, président du Bureau africain du ministère des affaires étrangères
6. Le docteur Rashad al-Ulaymi, directeur général, affaires juridiques du ministère de l'intérieur
7. M. Najib Abd al-Qawi Hamim, directeur général, coopération extérieure, ministère de l'approvisionnement et du commerce
8. M. Khalid Sa'id al-Dhubhani, directeur de l'administration des pêches, ministère de la planification et du développement
9. M. Ali al-Maqalih, directeur, bureau du ministère de la pêche

مذكرة تفاهم بين دولة ارتريا
والجمهورية اليمنية
للتعاون فى مجالات الصيد البحرى والتجارة
والاستثمار والنقل

مذكرة تفاهم
بين دولة ارتريا والجمهورية اليمنية
للتعاون فى مجالات الصيد البحرى والتجارى
والاستثمار والنقل

انطلاقا من روح الصداقة والتعاون وترجمة للاهداف والمصالح المشتركة بين البلدين الشقيقين دولة ارتريا والجمهورية اليمنية وتحقيقاً لمصالح الشعبين الشقيقين زار دولة ارتريا وفد الجمهورية اليمنية برئاسة الاخ/ الدكتور عبدالرحمن عبدالقادر بافضل وزير الثروة السمكية وقد استقبل استقبالاً حاراً من الاخ/ علي سيد عبدالله وزير الداخلية يوم الجمعة الموافق ١١/١١/٩٤ م واجريت محادثات اولية فى وزارة الداخلية الارترية فى العاصمة اسمرا اعقبها محادثات بين الطرفين فى مدينة مصوع رأس الجانب الارترى الدكتور صالح مكى وزير الثروة البحرية فى دولة ارتريا ورأس الجانب اليمنى الدكتور عبدالرحمن عبدالقاد بافضل وزير الثروة السمكية فى الجمهورية اليمنية .

وقد اسفرت المحادثات بين الجانبين الى الاتفاق حول الامور التالية :-

<u>أولا : فى مجال الثروة السمكية :-</u>

١-تسمح كل من دولة ارتريا والجمهورية اليمنية للصيادين من مواطنى الدولتين دون تحديد أعدادهم والحاملين لبطائق مزاولة مهنة الاصطياد بالاصطياد فى المياه الاقليمية للدولتين والمنطقة المتاخمة وكذا المنطقة الاقتصادية الخالصة للدولتين فى البحر الاحمر (عدا المياه الداخلية) على أن يتم حصر الصيادين لكلا البلدين ومنحهم رخصاً رسمية لممارسة مهنة الصيد والمحدده اماكن استقبالهم وتسويق منتجاتهم فى المرفق رقم (١) على أن يتقدم كل صياد بطلب الترخيص له بالاصطياد من الطرف الآخر وذلك خلال ثلاثة اشهر من تاريخ توقيع مذكرة التفاهم هذه مع مراعاة مايلى :-

أ - استخدام طرق الاصطياد السليمة وعدم استعمال المتفجرات وتلويث البيئة البحرية ، وكذا عدم استعمال السموم - والمواد الكيمائية وغير ذلك من طرق الابادة

ب - عدم استخدام وسائل ومعدات صيد تضر بنمو الاحياء المائية

ج - عدم نزع او قطع الاعشاب البحرية والشعب المرجانية على اختلاف انواعها

د - التقيد بمواسم الاصطياد فى كلا البلدين .

ه - استخدام كل السبل الكفيلة بحماية البيئة وترشيد عملية الاصطياد .

و - التقيد بكافة قوانين وانظمة البلد الآخر فى البحر الى المدى الذى تسرى فيه هذه القوانين والانظمة ، وبما لايتعارض مع ماذكر أعلاه .

(٢)

٢- لأغراض الفقرتين (د) و (و) من (١) أعلاه ، على السلطات المعنية في كلا الدولتين في البحر الأحمر اعلام السلطات المعنية في الدولة الأخرى بالقوانين واللوائح والأنظمة أو أية اتفاقيات مع طرف ثالث في المياه التي يستخدمها الطرف الآخر ويتولى كل طرف اصدار التوجيهات بتلك المعلومات بالتقيد بها .

٣- يجب أن يحمل كل صياد او عامل على أي قارب صيد يتواجد في المياه الاقليمية للدولة الأخرى رخصة صيد ، وبطاقة تثبت شخصيته وجنسيته ، طبقاً لقوانين وأنظمة دولته ، ويجب أن يرفع علم دولته على قارب الصيد .

٤- يسمح للاشخاص المشمولين بأحكام البند (١) اعلاه بمايلي :-
أ - تسويق انتاجهم من الاسماك في إقليم الدولة الأخرى وفي الاماكن المحددة بالمرفق رقم (١) لمذكرة التفاهم هذه .
ب- الحصول على التسهيلات المناسبة لصيانة القوارب والحصول على المواد الغذائية والمحروقات والثلج بالاسعار السائدة في البلد الذي يتواجدون فيه ولفترة بقائهم في البحر .

٥- اذا اضطرت سلطات أي من الدولتين الى احتجاز قارب صيد أو صياد أو عامل على أي قارب فعلى سلطات تلك الدولة إشعار سلطات الدولة الأخرى فوراً بأسماء الاشخاص والقوارب المحتجزة وماتحتويه من ممتلكات وتحديد أسباب وتاريخ الاحتجاز .
٦- يتعاون الجانبان في مجال الابحاث السمكية وحماية البيئة البحرية من التلوث ، وتبادل الخبرات الفنية وتدريبها في المعاهد التخصصية القائمة في البلدين .

<u>ثانياً : في مجال التجارة والاستثمار والنقل البحري</u> :-

١- دراسة امكانية انشاء شركات صيد مشتركة بين البلدين .
٢- دراسة عقد اتفاقية للنقل البحري بين الدولتين .
٣- دراسة عقد اتفاقية تجارية بين الدولتين : وحتى يتم عقد تلك الاتفاقية تقدم الجهات المختصة في كلا البلدين كافة التسهيلات المتاحة لها بموجب قوانينها لتسهيل أمور انتقال البضائع ذات المنشأ المحلي في البلدين .

(٢)

ثالثا : فى مجال الأمن

تعمل الدولتان على تنفيذ البروتوكول الموقع بين وزارتى الداخلية فى البلدين فى العاصمة صنعاء بتاريخ ١٠ نوفمبر ٩٢م لما من شأنه تحقيق الاهداف المنصوص عليها فى البروتوكول المشار اليه أعلاه ...

رابعا : فى مجال تنفيذ مواضيع المذكرة

١- تتخذ السلطات المختصة فى كلا الدولتين بعد التوقيع على مذكرة التفاهم هذه كافة الاجراءات اللازمة شاملة دون حصر إصدار قرارات أو أوامر أو رخص اوتوجيهات لتنفيذ ماورد فى مذكرة التفاهم هذه .

٢- تسير الاجهزة المعنية فى الدولتين دوريات مقابل شواطئها فى البحر الاحمر وتنشأ شبكات اتصال بين المراكز الأمنية الرئيسية للدولتين فى البحر الأحمر فى الوقت والأسلوب الذى يتفق عليه بينهما .

٣- تنشأ مكاتب خاصة فى كلا البلدين لمراقبة وتنفيذ ماورد من بنود فى هذه المذكرة وتحدد مقار تلك المكاتب طبقا للمرفق رقم (١) من هذه المذكرة .

٤- يتم الاتصال بين الجانبين فى شأن تنفيذ مذكرة التفاهم هذه بالطرق الدبلوماسية مع مراعاة ماورد فى البند (٢) من رابعاً اعلاه .

٥- تتشاور الحكومتان حول ماقد ينشأ عن تنفيذ مذكرة التفاهم هذه او فيما يتعلق من تعديل او حذف او اضافة . وكذا تعديل او اضافة للمرفق .

وقع فى مصوع يوم الثلاثا الموافق ١٥ نوفمبر ١٩٩٤م .

عن الجمهورية اليمنية	عن دولة ارتريا
د/ عبدالرحمن عبدالقادر بافضل	د/ صالح مكى
وزير الثروة السمكية	وزير الثروة البحرية

المرفق رقم (١)

أ/ المراكز الخاصة بتسجيل ومراقبة الاصطياد والتسويق فى الجمهورية اليمنية :-

١- ميدى
٢- الخوبة
٣- الحديدة
٤- الخوخة
٥- المخا

المراكز الخاصة بتسجيل ومراقبة الاصطياد والتسويق فى دولة ارتريا :-

١- عصب
٢- طيعو
٣- دهلك
٤- مصوع

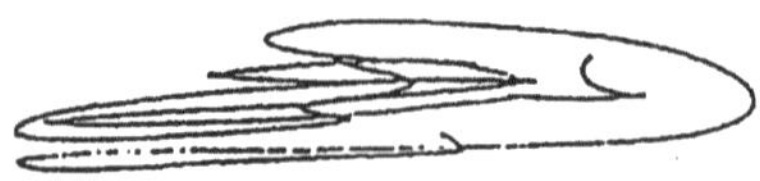

المرفق (٢)

اعضاء جانب دولة ارتريا :-

١- الدكتور صالح مكى	وزير الثروة البحرية
٢- رمضان اولياى	قائد القوات البحرية
٣- موسى رابعة	مدير الشرطة الارترية
٤- محمد ادريس عامر	دائرة الشرق الاوسط - بوازارة الخارجية

اعضاء جانب الجمهورية اليمنية :-

الدكتور عبدالرحمن عبدالقادر بافضل	وزير الثروة السمكية
٢- العقيد : كريم محرم	رئيس هيئة اركان القوات البحرية
٣- العقيد محمد رزق الصرمى	وكيل الجهاز المركزى للأمن السياسى
٤- السفير أحمد الباشا	سفير الجمهورية اليمنية لدى دولة ارتريا
٥- السفير محمد الوزير	رئيس دائرة افريقيا بوزارة الخارجية
٦- الدكتور رشاد العليمى	مدير عام للشؤون القانونية بوزارة الداخلية
٧- نجيب عبدالقوى حاميم	مدير عام التعاون الخارجى بوزارة التموين والتجارة
٨- خالد سعيد الذبحانى	مدير ادارة الاسماك بوزارة التخطيط والتنمية.
٩- علي المقالح	مدير مكتب وزير الثروة السمكية

Traité établissant la Commission mixte Yémen-Erythrée de coopération bilatérale entre le Gouvernement de la République du Yémen et le Gouvernement de l'État d'Erythrée

Inspirées par l'exemple de progrès et de civilisation que constituent les relations bilatérales entre la République du Yémen et l'Etat d'Erythrée, et

Affirmant leur souhait partagé de poursuivre, consolider et renforcer ces relations au service de leurs intérêts communs, et

Conscientes de l'importance de renforcer et développer la coopération bilatérale dans tous les domaines auxquels elles sont mutuellement attachées,

Les deux parties sont convenues de ce qui suit:

Article premier – Les deux parties établissent une Commission mixte chargée de la coopération bilatérale entre elles dans tous les domaines auxquels elles sont mutuellement attachées, qui portera le nom de Commission mixte Yémen-Erythrée de coopération bilatérale, ci-après dénommée "Commission mixte", et sera présidée par les deux ministres des affaires étrangères. Le ministère de la planification et du développement du côté yéménite et le ministère des affaires étrangères du côté érythréen, assistés des concours requis, exerceront leur juridiction sur son secrétariat et superviseront les résultats de la Commission mixte.

Article deux – La Commission mixte s'acquitte des tâches suivantes:

1. Étudier les programmes et recommandations conçus pour étendre la coopération bilatérale entre les deux pays et signer des accords, protocoles et programmes de mise en œuvre à cet effet.

2. Suivre en permanence l'application des accords, protocoles, mémorandums d'accord et procès-verbaux signés entre les deux pays dans les domaines visés au paragraphe 1 du présent article.

3. Examiner les propositions soumises par l'un ou l'autre pays en vue de renforcer et développer les perspectives de coopération entre eux dans tous les divers domaines d'intérêt mutuel.

4. Encourager l'échange de visites et de rencontres bilatérales entre fonctionnaires des deux pays, et échanger des informations et des documents intéressant les relations de coopération conjointes.

Article trois

1. La Commission est habilitée à former des sous-commissions et des groupes de travail permanents et temporaires chargés de mener à bien certaines tâches spécifiques dans le cadre des travaux de la Commission mixte.

2. Les sous-commissions et groupes de travail visés au paragraphe 1 du présent article soumettent leurs recommandations à la Commission mixte pour approbation.

Article quatre – Le projet d'ordre du jour de chaque cycle d'échange de recommandations est élaboré par les voies diplomatiques et soumis suffisamment tôt avant la convocation du cycle de réunions. La Commission mixte peut charger un comité technique composé de représentants des deux pays de préparer ses réunions.

Article cinq – La Commission mixte convoque son cycle de réunions une fois par an, alternativement à Sanaa et à Asmara. Des procès-verbaux spéciaux sont rédigés pour chaque cycle, signés par les deux présidents de la Commission mixte, et approuvés par les autorités compétentes des deux pays conformément aux dispositions législatives et réglementaires en vigueur dans chaque pays.

Article six – Le présent traité entrera en vigueur à la date de l'échange des instruments de ratification conformément aux procédures constitutionnelles applicables dans chaque pays. Il demeurera en vigueur durant une période de cinq (5) ans et sera tacitement reconduit pour des périodes de même durée, à moins que l'une quelconque des parties ne fasse savoir par écrit à l'autre partie qu'elle souhaite y mettre fin six mois avant la date d'expiration prévue. Toute addition ou modification aux articles du présent traité ne pourra leur être apportée qu'avec l'assentiment en forme écrite des deux parties.

Le présent traité a été établi à Sanaa le vendredi 25 Jumada II 1419, date équivalant au 16 octobre 1998, en deux exemplaires originaux en langue arabe, qui font tous deux également foi.

Pour le Gouvernement de l'État d'Erythrée	Pour la République du Yémen
[signé] Haile Woldense	[signé] Abd al-Qadir Abd al-Rahman Ba-Jammal
Ministre des Affaires étrangères	Vice-Premier Ministre et Ministre des Affaires étrangères

اتفاقية

تأسيس اللجنة اليمنية - الارترية المشتركة

للتعاون الثنائي

بين

حكومة الجمهورية اليمنية

وحكومة دولة إريتريا.

إنطلاقاً من النموذج الحضاري المتقدم الذي تجلى في العلاقات الثنائية بين الجمهورية اليمنية ودولة إريتريا.

وتأكيداً لرغبتهما المشتركة في مواصلة تقوية وتعزيز هذه العلاقات بما يخدم مصالحهما المشتركة.

وإدراكاً منهما بأهمية تعزيز وتطوير التعاون الثنائي في كافة المجالات ذات الاهتمام المشترك.

اتفقنا على ما يلي :-

المادة الأولى

يشكل الطرفان لجنة مشتركة للتعاون الثنائي بينهما في كافة المجالات ذات الاهتمام المشترك، تضم ممثلين عن كل منهما، تسمى "اللجنة اليمنية - الإريترية المشتركة للتعاون الثنائي " ويشار إليها فيما يلي :- "اللجنة المشتركة" ويرأسها وزيري خارجية البلدين، وتتولى سكرتارية اللجنة ومتابعة تنفيذ نتائجها وزارة التخطيط والتنمية عن الجانب اليمني ووزارة الشؤون الخارجية عن الجانب الإريتري بوجود المساعدين اللازمين للجانبين وذلك بحكم الاختصاص.

المادة الثانية

تضطلع اللجنة المشتركة بالمهام التالية :-

١- دراسة البرامج والمقترحات الهادفة إلى توسيع التعاون الثنائي بين البلدين، وتوقيع الاتفاقيات وبروتوكولات وبرامج تنفيذية بشأنها.

١

٢- متابعة تنفيذ الاتفاقيات والبروتوكولات ومذكرات التفاهم والمحاضر الموقعة بين البلدين في المجالات المشار إليها في الفقرة (١) من هذه المادة.

٣- مناقشة الاقتراحات التي يقدمها أي من البلدين والتي من شأنها العمل على تعزيز وتطوير آفاق التعاون بينهما في كافة المجالات المختلفة ذات الاهتمام المشترك.

٤- تشجيع تبادل الزيارات واللقاءات الثنائية بين المسئولين من كلا البلدين وتبادل المعلومات والوثائق ذات الصلة بعلاقات التعاون المشترك.

المادة الثالثة

١- يمكن للجنة أن تشكل لجاناً فرعية وفرق عمل دائمة ومؤقتة لإنجاز بعض المهام المحددة في إطار عمل اللجنة المشتركة.

٢- تقوم اللجان الفرعية وفرق العمل المشار إليها في الفقرة (١) من هذه المادة برفع توصياتها إلى اللجنة المشتركة للمصادقة عليها.

المادة الرابعة

يتم إعداد مشروع جدول أعمال كل دورة بتبادل الاقتراحات عبر القنوات الدبلوماسية على أن يقدم قبل موعد انعقاد الدورة بوقت كاف، ويجوز للجنة المشتركة تكليف لجنة فنية من الجانبين للإعداد لإجتماعاتها.

المادة الخامسة

تعقد اللجنة المشتركة دورتها سنوياً، وبالتناوب في كل من صنعاء وأسمره وبعد لكل دورة من الدورات محضر خاص، يوقع عليه من قبل رئيسي الجانبين في اللجنة

٢

المشتركة ويصادق عليه من قبل السلطات المختصة في البلدين طبقاً للقوانين والأنظمة المعمول بها في كل منهما.

المادة السادسة

يبدأ العمل بهذه الاتفاقية اعتباراً من تاريخ تبادل وثائق التصديق عليها وفقاً للإجراءات الدستورية المعمول بها في كلا البلدين، وتظل سارية المفعول لمدة (٥) سنوات وتجدد تلقائياً لمدد مماثلة، ما لم يقم أحد الطرفين بإبلاغ الطرف الآخر كتابياً برغبته في إنهائها قبل انتهاء مدتها بـ(٦) أشهر وأية إضافات أو تعديلات في مواد هذه الاتفاقية لا تتم إلا بموافقة الطرفين الكتابية عليها.

حررت هذه الاتفاقية في صنعاء يوم الجمعة بتاريخ ٢٥ جمادى الآخر ١٤١٩هـ الموافق ١٦/١٠/١٩٩٨م من نسختين أصليتين باللغة العربية ولكل منهما نفس الحجة القانونية.

عن حكومة دولة إريتريا

هيلي ولدتنسائي

وزير الشؤون الخارجية

عن حكومة الجمهورية اليمنية

عبد القادر عبد الرحمن باجمال

نائب رئيس الوزراء

وزير الخارجية.

Liste des abréviations

CIJ Recueil	Cour internationale de Justice, Recueil des arrêts, avis consultatifs et ordonnances
FAO	Organisation des Nations Unies pour l'alimentation et l'agriculture
ICLQ	International and Comparative Law Quarterly
ILR	International Law Reports
PNUD	Programme des Nations Unies pour le développement
WGS	Système géodésique mondial

Detailed Table of Contents

Table des matières détaillée

****

MAPS

CARTES

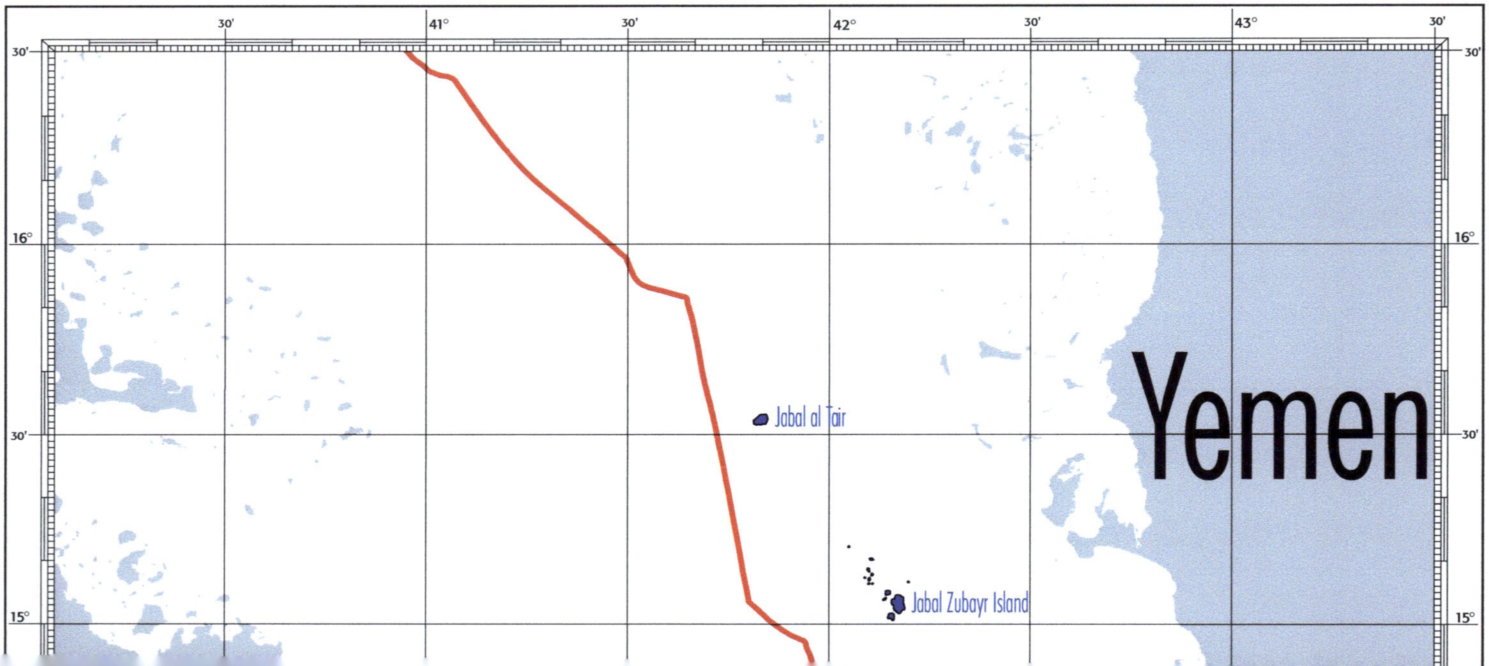
Yemen
Jabal al Tair
Jabal Zubayr Island
30'
41°
30'
42°
30'
43°
30'
16°
30'
15°

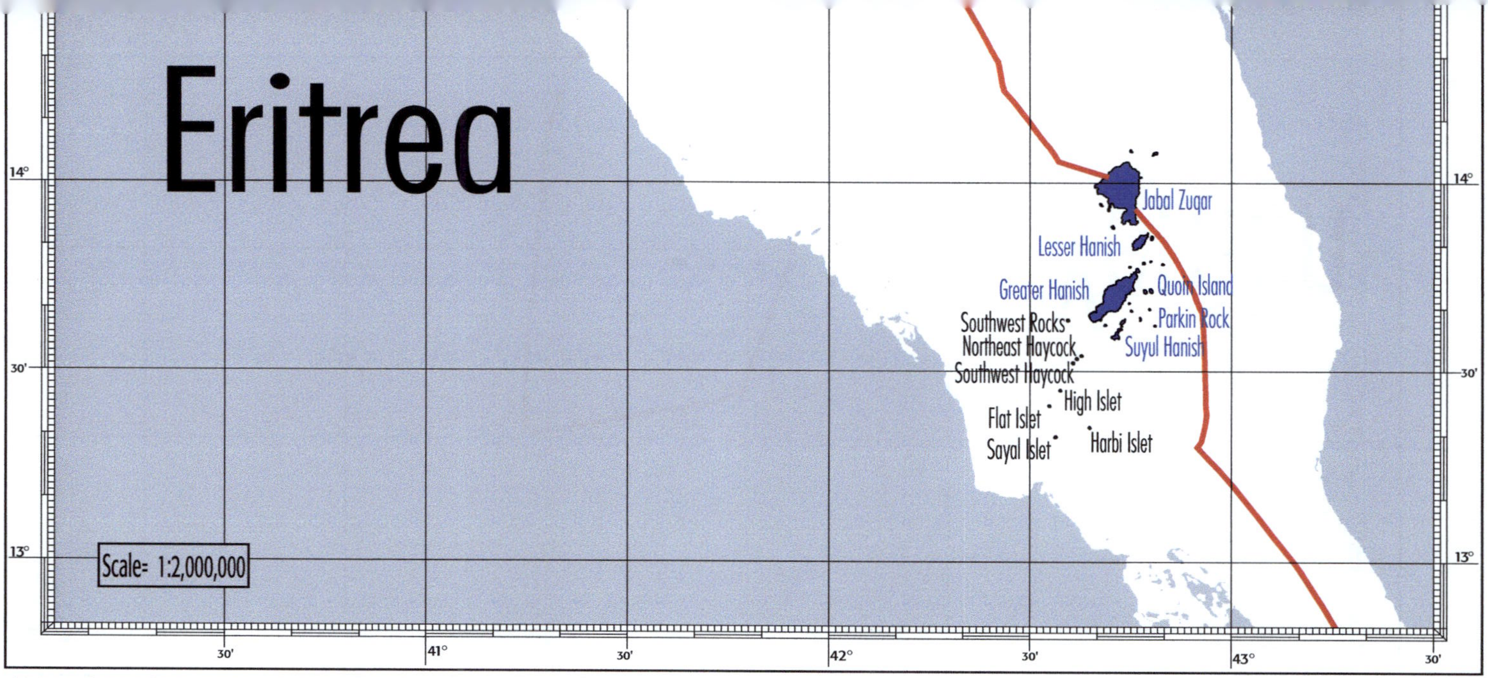

This is a re-formatted copy of the map as printed in the Award without any substantive change

MAP 3

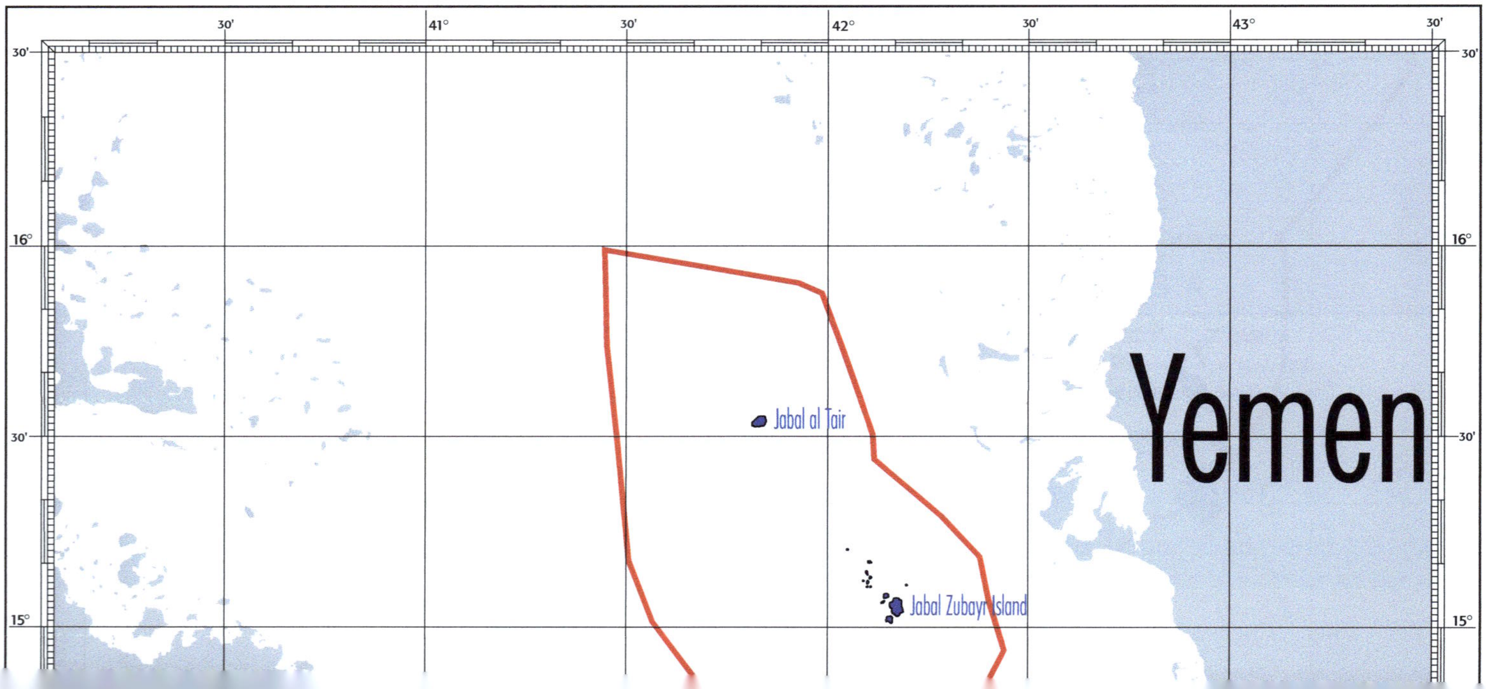
Yemen
Jabal al Tair
Jabal Zubayr Island
30'
41°
30'
42°
30'
43°
30'
30'
16°
30'
15°

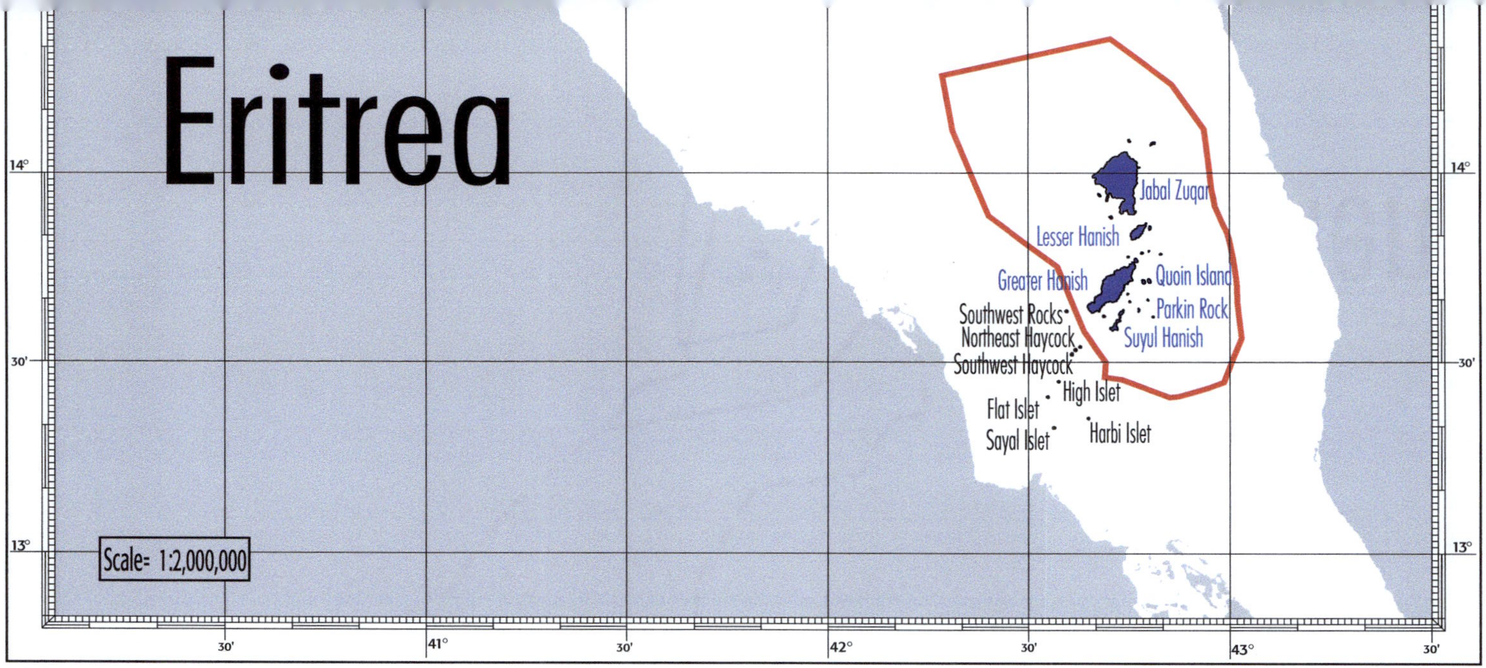

This is a re-formatted copy of the map as printed in the Award without any substantive change

MAP 4

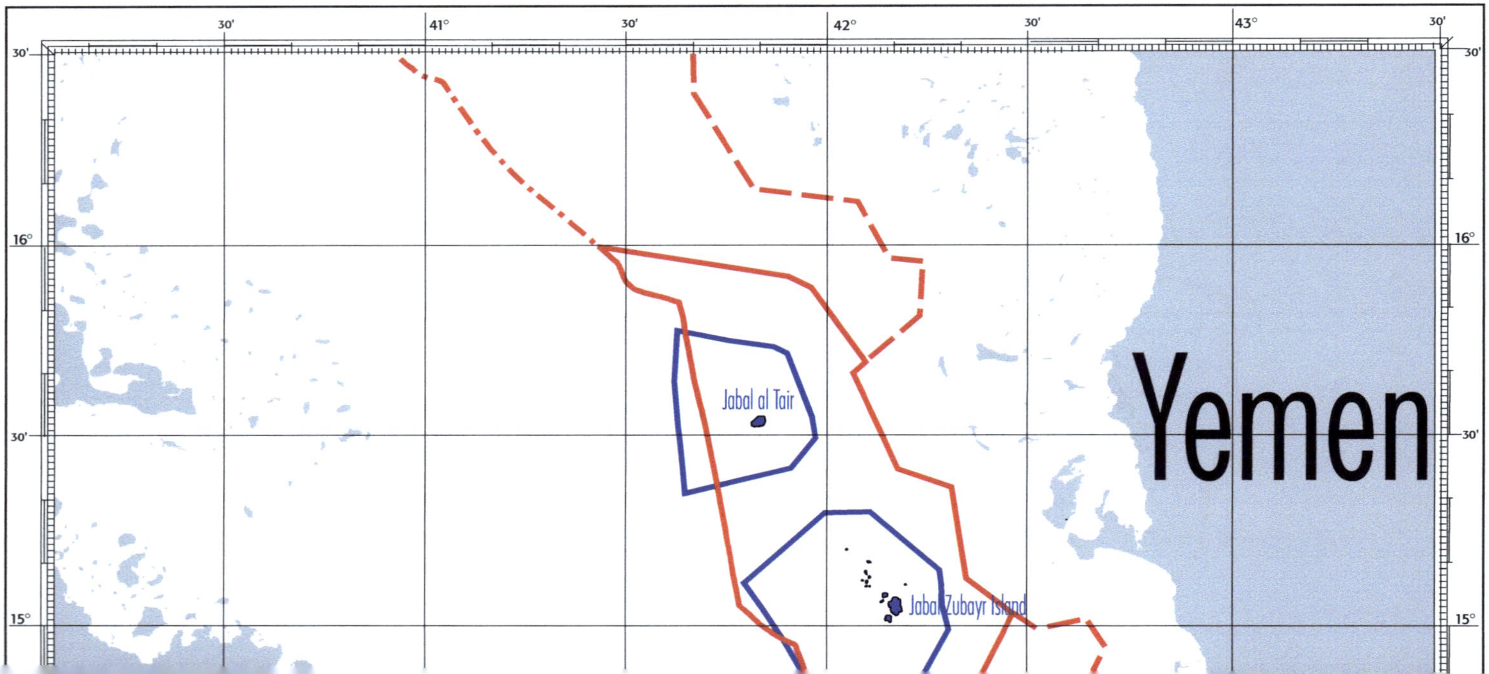
30'
41°
30'
42°
30'
43°
30'
30'
16°
30'
15°
Jabal al Tair
Jabal Zubayr Island
Yemen

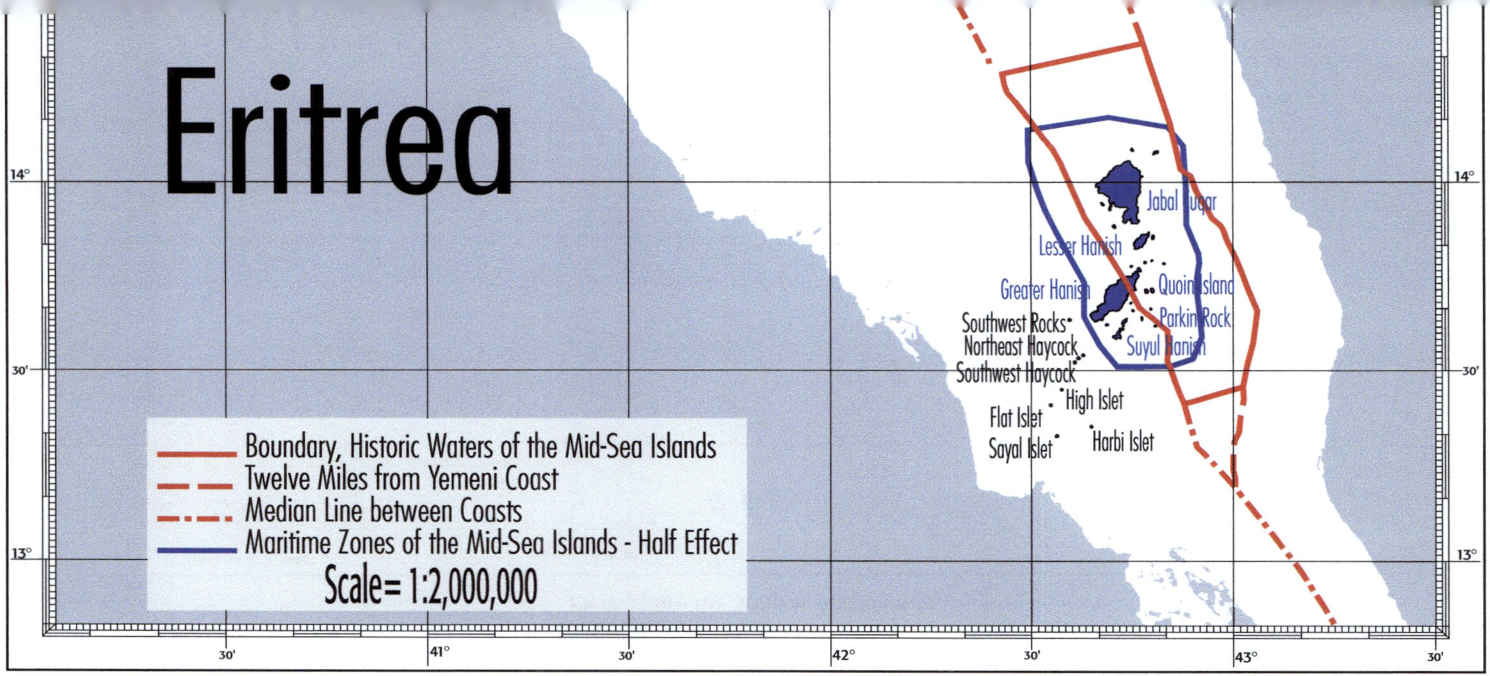

This is a re-formatted copy of the map as printed in the Award without any substantive change

MAP 7

Please note this map is not to scale.

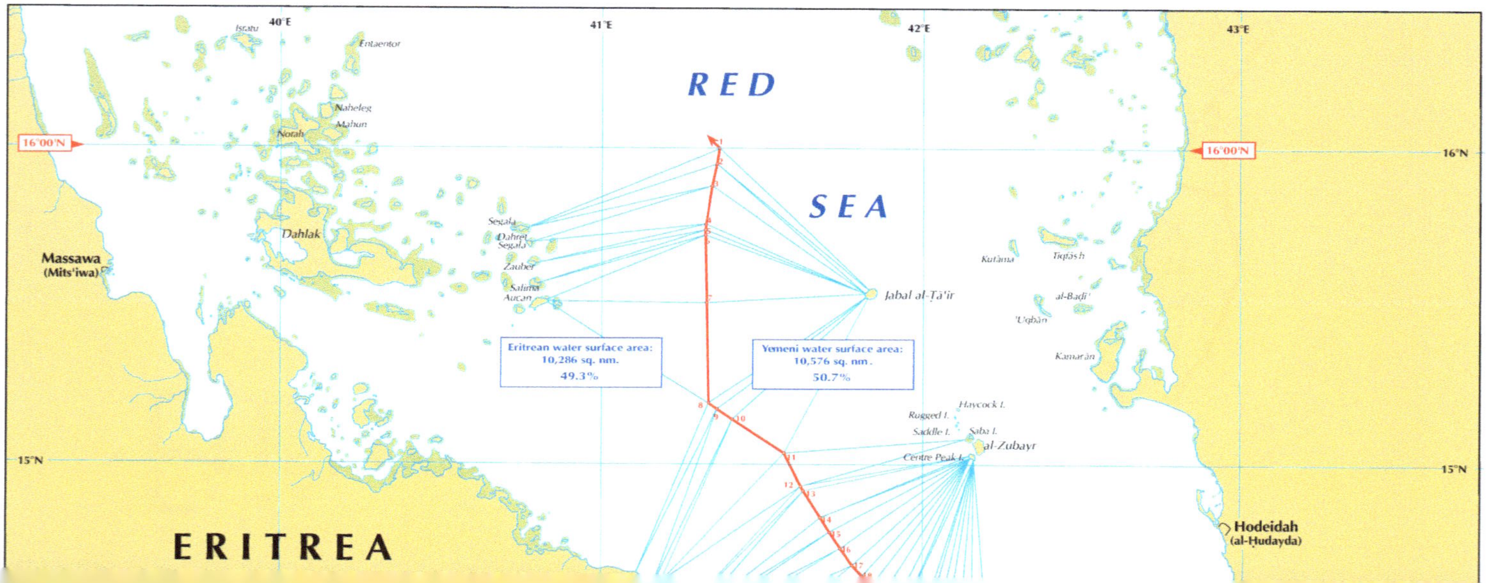

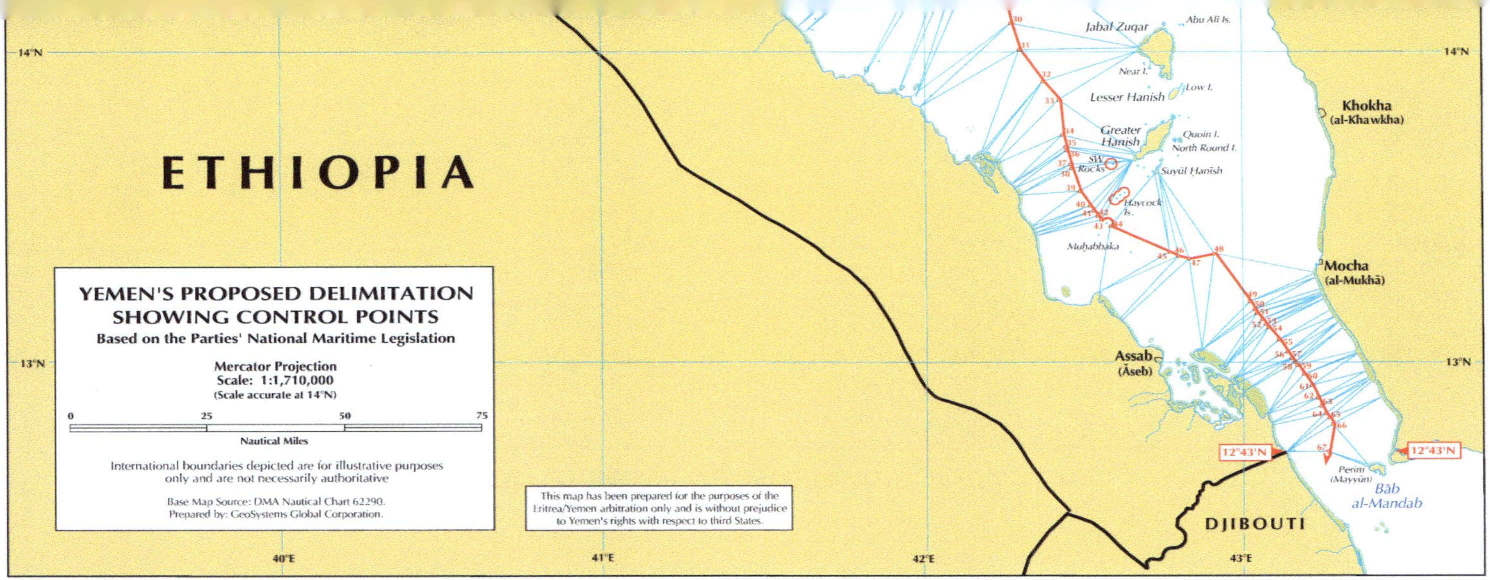

This is a re-formatted copy of the map as printed in the Award without any substantive change

Map 12.1

Basepoints for Eritrea's Proposed Historic Median Line

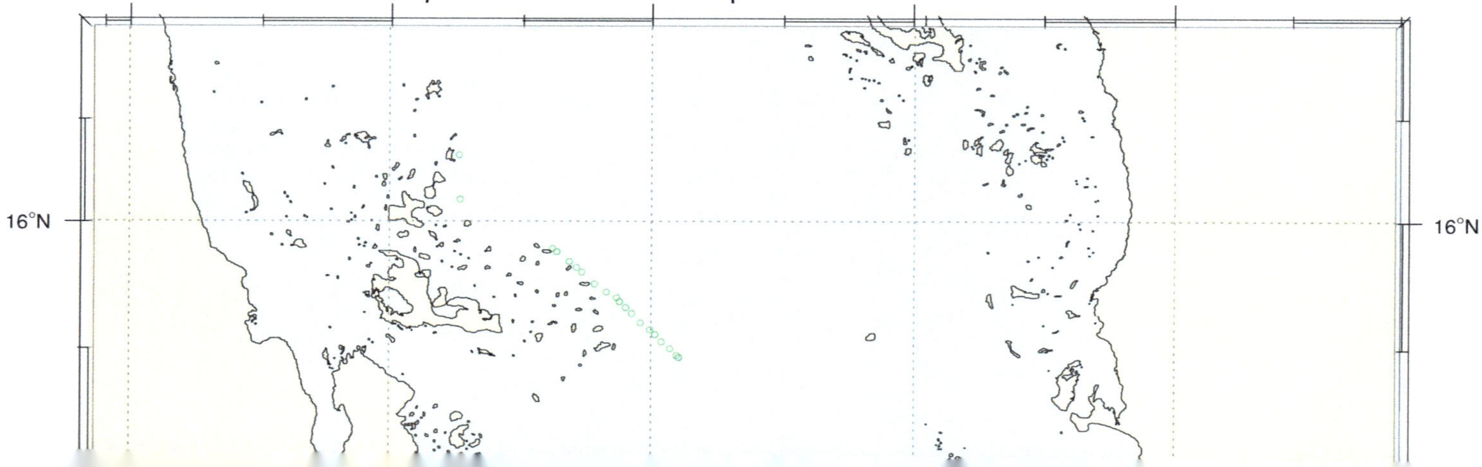

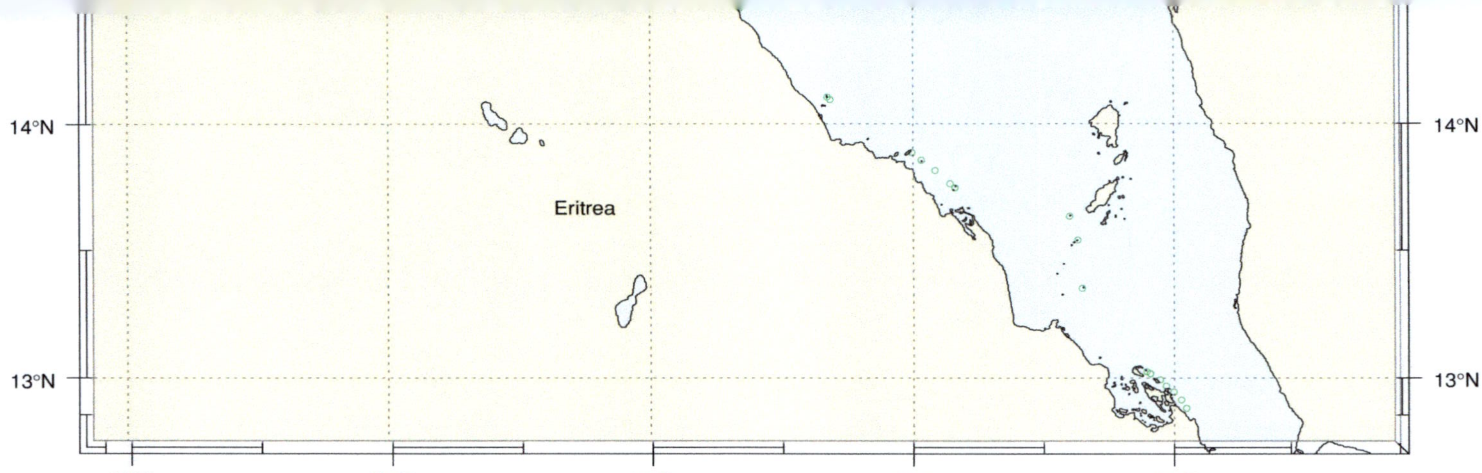

This is a re-formatted copy of the map as printed in the Award without any substantive change

Chart 1

Basepoints for the Western Edge of Eritrea's Proposed Delimitation

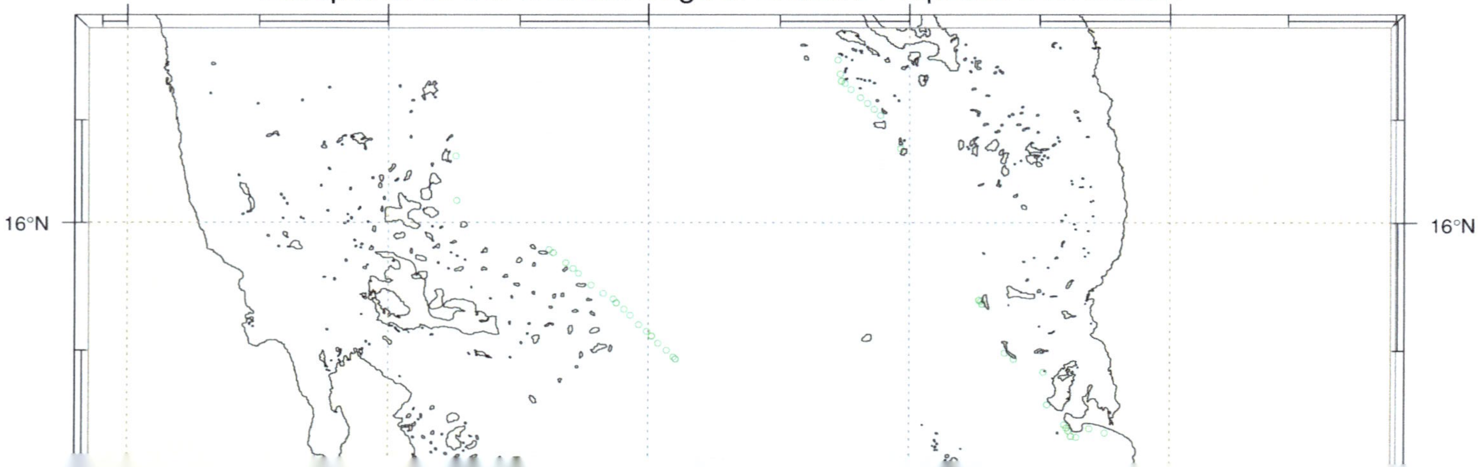

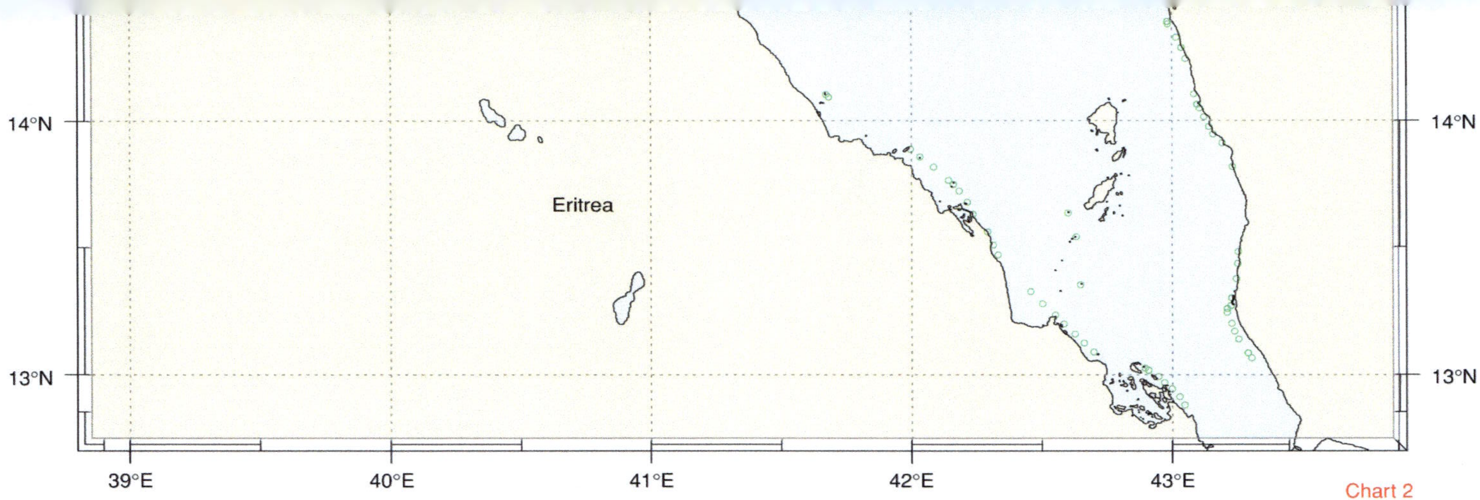

Chart 2

This is a re-formatted copy of the map as printed in the Award without any substantive change

The international maritime boundary line

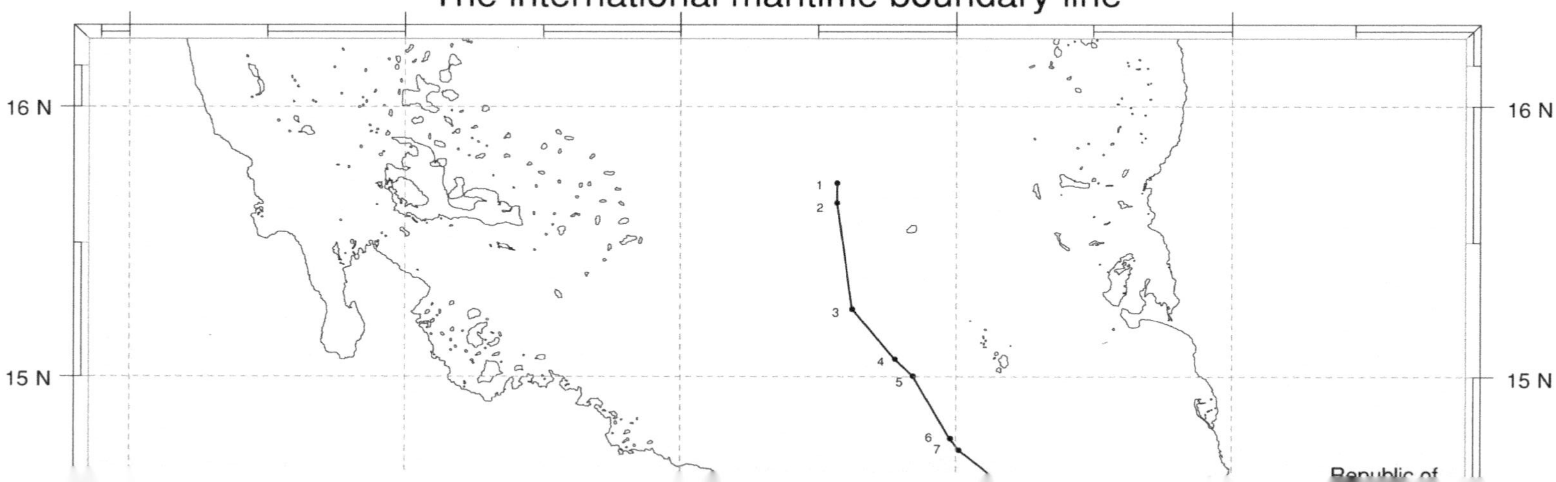

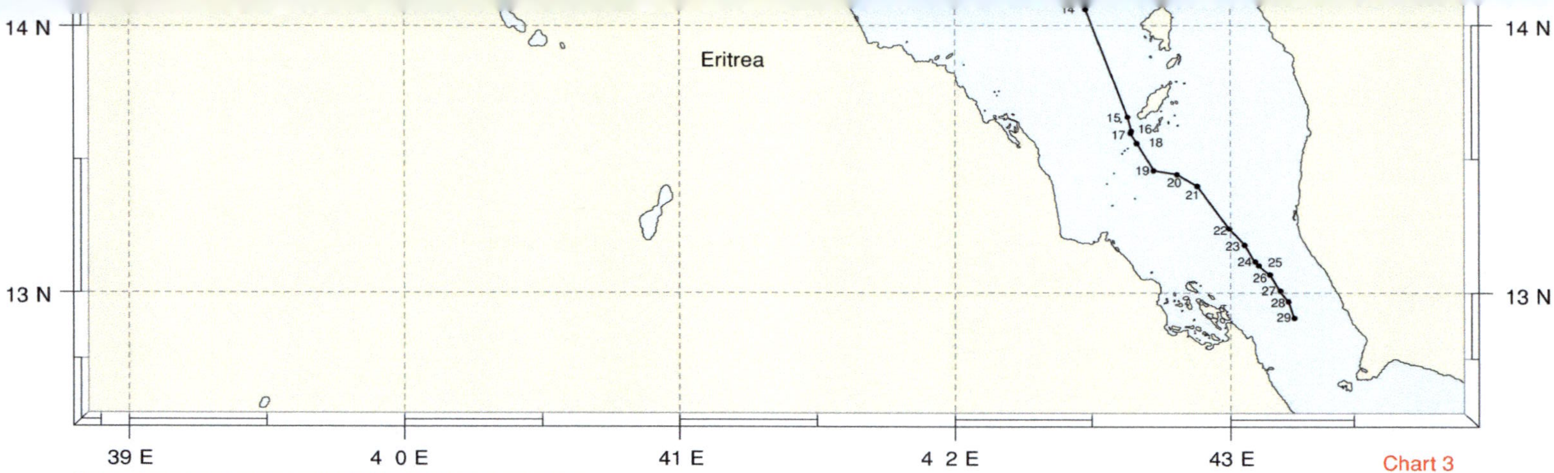

Chart 3

This is a re-formatted copy of the map as printed in the Award without any substantive change

The international maritime boundary line

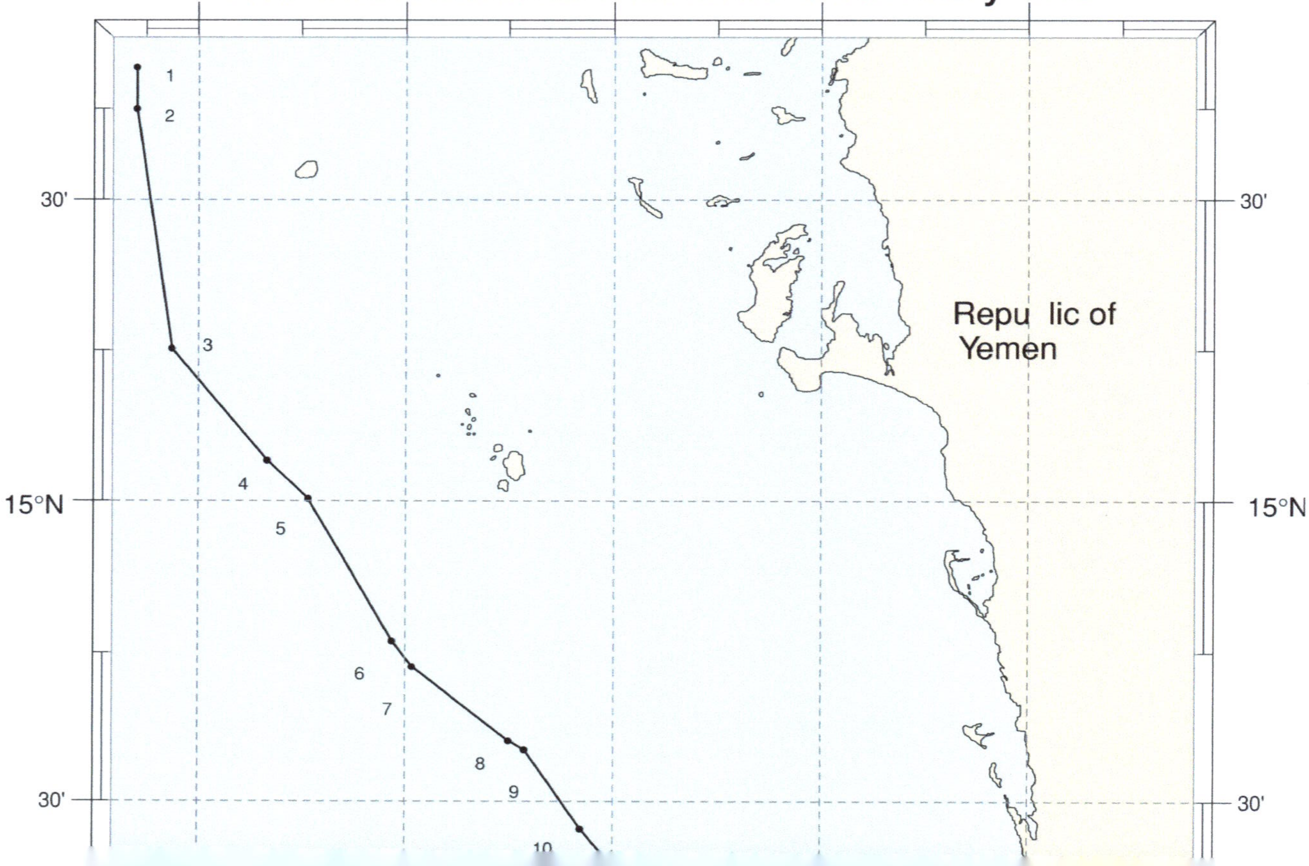

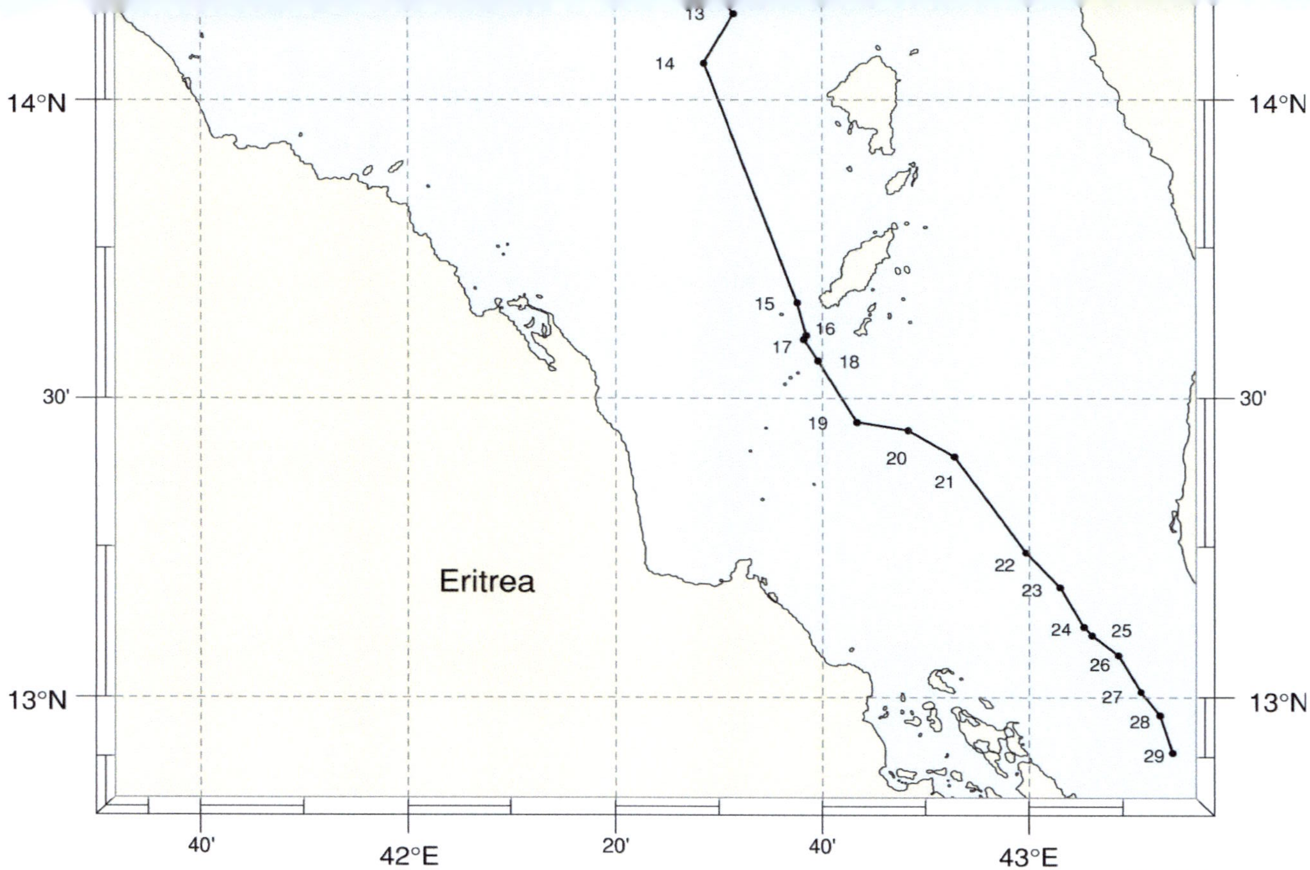

This is a re-formatted copy of the map as printed in the Award without any substantive change

Chart 4

MIX
Papier aus verantwortungsvollen Quellen
Paper from responsible sources
FSC® C105338

If you have any concerns about our products,
you can contact us on
ProductSafety@springernature.com

In case Publisher is established outside the EU,
the EU authorized representative is:
Springer Nature Customer Service Center GmbH
Europaplatz 3, 69115 Heidelberg, Germany

Printed by Libri Plureos GmbH
in Hamburg, Germany